Planning for Post-Disaster Recovery and Reconstruction

Jim Schwab, AICP
with
Kenneth C. Topping, AICP
Charles C. Eadie
Robert E. Deyle
and Richard A. Smith

By James L. Witt

Director, Federal Emergency Management Agency

Communities that undertake planning for post-disaster recovery and reconstruction must put into action the processes of hazard identification and risk assessment, public education, consensus and partnership building, visioning, and identification of risk-reducing activities. Community planning is essential to the creation of disaster-resistant communities. I am proud of the relationship built between the Federal Emergency Management Agency and the American Planning Association in the process of producing this Planning Advisory Service Report. I look forward to continued collaboration among emergency managers and community planners to reduce the effects of disasters in this country.

The United States cannot afford the continuing high costs of natural and technological disasters. We cannot afford the economic costs to the American taxpayer, nor can we afford the social costs inflicted on our communities and citizens. Good planning, with appropriately trained and educated planners, is one of the most effective means of reducing these costs.

But planning efforts do not have to wait until the post-disaster environment. Recognizing this, FEMA has responded to the escalating price tag of disaster recovery by initiating Project Impact/Building a Disaster Resistant Community, a full-scale, pre-disaster effort to help create more livable and disaster-resistant communities. Project Impact focuses on the same principles contained in this publication: increasing public awareness of hazards and loss reduction (mitigation) measures, reducing the risk of loss of life and property, and protecting our nation's communities, the environment, and the economy from all types of natural and technological hazards.

Successful recovery after disasters, or pre-disaster planning through activities like Project Impact, relies on partnership and collaboration among everyone involved in building disaster-resistant communities. FEMA can provide leadership and technical and financial support to our partners. We will do that with the help of federal, state, and local agencies, national and state legislative bodies, colleges and universities, professional organizations, private-sector organizations, volunteer organizations, and individuals. State and local government participation can forge and sustain relationships across public agencies, with private-sector organizations, and between their respective levels of government to create stronger, more resilient communities.

As planners, you have the opportunity to apply your training and education, as well as the legal and administrative tools and authorities available to you, working with all these stakeholders to create safe, livable, and sustainable communities. The report you are about to read contributes to this goal by providing a multidisciplinary approach to the identification and use of pre- and post-disaster emergency management resources to reduce the effects of natural disasters on communities. It is critical that you begin now to implement its guidance and information as part of your planning programs. Through wise planning approaches, we can make sure that everyone comes together to build a disaster-resistant America.

By Cecelia G. Rosenberg

Mitigation Directorate, Federal Emergency Management Agency

Natural hazards affect every jurisdiction in the United States. The key ingredients necessary to transform natural hazards into natural disasters are inappropriately placed or poorly constructed development—both of which are prevalent throughout this country. Yet, during the twentieth century, communities grew and developed in relative ignorance of the presence of natural hazards. Subdivisions, infrastructure, and economic systems were built on land exposed to riverine and coastal flooding, landslides, seismic disturbances, wildfire, and other hazards. As a result, natural disasters continue to injure and kill citizens, destroy the built environment, and disrupt the businesses of major metropolitan areas. Furthermore, the federal government continues to spend more and more tax dollars on disaster response and recovery, affecting all Americans, not just those in disaster-stricken areas. It is therefore critical that communities have a systematic way to ensure that post-disaster reconstruction, as well as new construction, is placed on safe ground and is built to withstand those forces of nature to which it is exposed.

The purpose of this document is to help community leaders and planners educate their constituents on how informed decisions and choices can affect the rebuilding process and yield a safer, more sustainable community. In the debates and deliberations within communities on post-disaster reconstruction policy, participants have many other interests to balance against concerns about natural hazards. These emotional debates pit the often overwhelming desire to perpetuate historic (and unsafe) development patterns and construction techniques against the desire to use disasters as opportunities to rethink these patterns and practices and to break away from the uninformed decisions of the past. Yet, balancing competing interests intelligently has always been at the core of planning. This document is thus designed to equip planners and all others involved in post-disaster reconstruction issues at all levels of government with the tools needed to create (or re-create) communities that will withstand most of what Mother Nature throws at them.

Planners typically are not taught about natural hazards and disasters in school—however, one could hardly think of a more suitable role for planners than influencing the reconstruction of their community (or parts of it). Planners spend years in academic settings studying the theories and practices of how to create desirable communities, from site planning techniques to large-scale community design approaches, incorporating a myriad of considerations, including affordable housing, efficient transportation, environmental quality, access to recreation and parks, historic preservation, and economic development opportunities. Planning is incomplete, however, without consideration of this intersection of communities' natural and built environments. As devastating as they are, disasters present planners with the opportunity to use their backgrounds to deal with both pre-existing and disaster-related social, economic, and physical issues. At the same time, planners must also seize the opportunity to influence reconstruction so that the rebuilt environment will be better able to withstand future natural hazard events. Unfortunately, there may be plenty of opportunities. From

1980 through 1998, there have been 455 presidentially declared flood, earthquake, and hurricane disasters. This does not include the untold number of local and state emergencies and declarations that did not require federal assistance.

Planners, by their training and education, possess many skills and abilities that serve as assets in dealing with post-disaster issues. Moreover, the authorities and tools that planners and planning departments use for routine short- and long-term planning and development activities can also be used to implement post-disaster reconstruction policies. Forward-thinking planners will take a proactive approach, using these tools and authorities to exploit opportunities presented in the post-disaster environment. By identifying the hazards and risks in the community now, by anticipating disaster-related issues, and by linking reconstruction policies with those already in the comprehensive plan, communities minimize the emotional conflicts inherent in the chaos of developing post-disaster recovery strategies. Communities that can identify and articulate their needs to state and federal officials quickly and precisely will move to the front of the line when post-disaster funding and technical assistance become available. These communities are better positioned to get the resources needed to accomplish recovery effectively.

This report introduces planners to their roles in post-disaster reconstruction and recovery, and provides guidance on how to plan for post-disaster reconstruction side by side with all the other players involved (city/county managers, business owners, and others). A key theme throughout this report, and one that should be equal in importance to community recovery, is the need to rebuild in such a way as to create a community that is more resistant to future disasters. This report is filled with references to technical resources that are available to assist in implementing planning and construction techniques that will minimize future risk to natural hazards in both the pre- and post-disaster time frames. Hazard mitigation is crucial to the long-term sustainability of communities, and therefore must be considered as important as other traditional planning considerations when making development decisions.

This report is essentially divided into two parts. How-to information is presented in the first, and background information, case studies, and appendices are in the second. Planners who are involved in disaster activity and need to quickly access guidance on the recovery planning process should concentrate on Chapters 1 through 6, and read Chapters 7 through 12 during that time when disasters do not preclude leisurely consideration of such information.

Chapter 1

The Role of Planners in Post-Disaster Reconstruction

Downtown Des Moines, Iowa, is ordinarily rather attractive in an understated, midwestern sort of way. Pedestrians can stand atop the bridges that cross the Des Moines River and watch the slow, steady flow of water far below while surveying the urban landscape. Just south of downtown lies the river's scenic confluence with its key local tributary, the Raccoon River. On a hot summer night, those lolling beneath the trees near City Hall may even hear the crack of a bat and the roar of a crowd at Sec Taylor Stadium, the home of the city's Iowa Cubs minor league baseball franchise. Up the hill on Locust Street, east of the river, rises the golden dome of the state capitol. For a medium-size city of 200,000 people, life in Des Moines can be serene and pleasant.

During the weekend of July 10-11, 1993, however, the central business district was a scene of chaos. No longer far beneath the bridges, the waters of both rivers were filling the underpasses and climbing their banks, not only downtown but in a half-dozen residential neighborhoods and industrial areas as well. Normally just 5.5 feet deep, with a previous record depth of 18.6 feet in 1944, the Des Moines River surged to a crest of 28.39 feet at the Grand Avenue Bridge downtown on Sunday, July 11 (Des Moines 1993a).

On Saturday night, members of the city's planning department staff, responding to the emergency, put aside their professional duties for the more immediate task of recruiting volunteers out of downtown bars and restaurants to help sandbag the riverbanks in a desperate bid to save the business district from inundation. Without such efforts, noted assistant planning director Gary Lozano, many downtown businesses would have been under two or three feet of water (Lozano 1993). The Des Moines River was flowing past the upstream Saylorville Dam at 40,000 cubic feet per second (cfs), some 20 times its normal rate. The Saylorville Reservoir exceeded its normal level by 56 feet.

Over the next few days, Chinook helicopters flown up from Texas airdropped sandbags to the volunteers, 70 at a time (Tackett 1993). Other parts of the Des Moines area, including the historic Valley Junction district of the adjoining suburb of West Des Moines, were similarly besieged. The rains seemed to pour down in biblical proportions, and no one knew when they would end. Des Moines was becoming the latest casualty of the rising waters that swamped nine states in the Midwest in the summer of 1993.

The crack of the bat and the roar of the crowd ceased. Lying in water at the triangle of land created by the river juncture, Sec Taylor Stadium remained unusable for the remainder of the season. Baseball was over; disaster cleanup was the new summer sport. The effective shutdown of the central business district affected some 60,000 jobs in Des Moines. Many of those were at the *Des Moines Register*, the state's leading newspaper, which was reduced to producing eight-page daily editions from another Gannett

The Des Moines River, flowing through downtown Des Moines, Iowa, set all-time record flood levels in the summer of 1993.

subsidiary in Iowa City after its downtown printing plant was flooded. In the dark of night, volunteers also struggled to move more than 10,000 books out of the basement of the main public library.

The planning department itself suffered serious damage. Operating out of a city building near the Des Moines River, the staff watched water flow over the nearby embankment and into the basement. The city was forced to commandeer the use of the gymnasium at East High School, located on higher, drier ground, as an emergency operations center. Thus, planners not only were pressed into chores well outside their job descriptions, but had to relocate their base of operations while doing them. Long hours and burnout were the order of the day, according to planning director James Grant (Grant 1993).

The bigger crisis for Des Moines arrived on Sunday morning. After midnight arrived, the Raccoon River began a rapidly dangerous rise, fueled not only by rainfall but by backwater from the overfilled Des Moines River. Some of that water was the result not only of overflow from the Saylorville Reservoir, but of backwater from the downstream Red Rock Reservoir (Des Moines City Manager 1993). Backwater conditions affecting smaller tributaries were, in fact, a major source of flooding in many midwestern locations in 1993, affecting numerous small towns like Chelsea, Iowa, where Otter Creek overflowed its banks in large part because of backwater from the Iowa River. The Raccoon, however, is much larger than many such creeks, and it flowed past the city's water treatment plant, the source of clean drinking water for more than 250,000 residents of the metropolitan area. The plant is protected by levees that rose well above previous record flood levels.

But this time, worried plant officials called the U.S. Army Corps of Engineers at Saylorville, the upstream dam that controls flooding on the Des Moines River, to get their prediction of the level at which the Raccoon was expected to crest. When, according to Lozano, they learned that the predicted level of 21 feet for July 13 was lower than the 22 feet they were already experiencing, the water department personnel realized that the time for panic had arrived, and they began a mad scramble to sandbag the levee for additional protection. It was all to no avail. Eventually, the Raccoon River, cresting at 26.7 feet at the Fleur Drive Bridge (Des Moines City Manager 1993), came crashing over the walls and into the plant, shutting it down, crippling its electrical connections, and contaminating the water supplies for the area's entire population. The entire city of Des Moines and its suburbs were suddenly awash in water, none of which was fit for human consumption. Residents were warned to boil any water they used and to rely on bottled water for drinking. A massive operation to supply bottled water began, with residents lined up day after day to get rationed supplies, provided by the U.S. Army Corps of Engineers, the designated agency for this function under the Federal Response Plan (FEMA 1998d, Emergency Support Function #3).

Emergency response was a massive operation involving National Guard troops, the Red Cross, and other charitable organizations, and long hours for city employees in numerous departments. Improvisation was the order of the day. With no running water, the fire department ordered that high-rise office buildings be evacuated until service could be restored to operate sprinkler systems. On Tuesday following the flood, the fire department coped with its first serious post-flood fire by trucking in 600,000 gallons of water from the duck pond at the Des Moines International Airport (Walsh and Berck 1993).

The first order of business was to restore clean running water to a quarter-million people, an operation that was promised within a month and accomplished within two weeks by L.D. McMullen, the chief of the water department. Extraordinary measures to achieve this included appeals to residents to report anonymously to an emergency hot line those who were violating city orders not to tap municipal water supplies. Where violators were found, valves were turned off. McMullen's calm television demeanor, orderly approach to the crisis, and heroics in managing the restoration of the water system made him something of an urban legend in Des Moines, some of whose residents bestowed on him the label of "Flood Stud." The *Des Moines Register* letters columns were filled with accolades and suggestions of high office for the previously unknown and unheralded administrator. The acclaim directed at McMullen, however, underscored the crucial importance of running water for the normal functioning of an urban area. McMullen's task literally involved making Des Moines livable again.

Restoring water was a first step. But even as that was happening, trucks were hauling to landfills a daily average of 2,300 tons of debris that volunteers and others were removing from flood-damaged homes and businesses. Des Moines by mid-July had a preliminary damage estimate in the city alone of $253 million, a figure that continued to grow with a second flood in August and a prolonged storm weather pattern that refused to allow Iowa to dry out until October. After the debris removal, residents in Des Moines and many other water-logged cities found that they faced a potentially health-threatening job of scrubbing away the mold, mildew, mud, and sewage the flood had left behind in basements and ground floors (Goering 1993).

Amid this cleanup, of course, residents and business owners were seeking information on how to apply for disaster aid or to pursue insurance claims, and city officials were busy providing it. A presidential disaster declaration was easily obtained in light of the widespread nature of the calamity, and announcements appeared in the state's media about the location of disaster applications centers.

Even as that recovery process began to take hold, secondary damage posed new threats. Exactly one week after the flood, city authorities ordered the evacuation of 700 homes in two neighborhoods southeast of downtown (Riverpoint and Columbus Park in Figure 1-1) after it was discovered that a dirt levee along the Des Moines River had suffered a 600-square-foot gouge as a result of flood pressures.

Figure 1-1. 1993 Flood Impact, Des Moines, Iowa

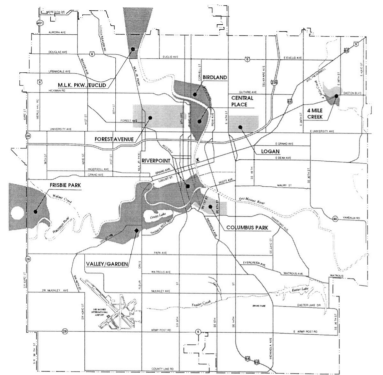

Amid the turmoil, the planning department was busy assessing damage and collecting the data needed to prepare the city's hazard mitigation grant application, which was completed by September and outlined projects for seven flood-impact areas (Figure 1-1), seeking $5,490,000 for the voluntary acquisition and relocation of 176 homes in the Valley/Garden, Frisbie Park, Central Place, and Birdland neighborhoods (Des Moines 1993a).

But, as if to underscore that nature allows no clear line in time between emergency response, recovery, and reconstruction functions, less than two weeks after this application was submitted, new storm clouds threatened to inundate the city with rain for a third time. As this author toured the city with assistant planning director Lozano on September 25, Lozano expressed apprehensions about this possibility toward the end of a thunderstorm that lasted nearly seven hours. The storm subsided, however, and Lozano breathed visible sighs of relief as the sky cleared.

Des Moines's experience illustrated that, in the aftermath of a natural disaster, planners and city administrators can expect everything to happen at once. There may be no clear announcement that the emergency is over and the time for recovery—or reconstruction—has begun. Often, different parts of the same community may be undergoing different phases of these humanly defined post-disaster processes at different times. The challenge is to gear up for mitigation of future hazards even as the current disaster is just beginning to fade away.

The focus of this PAS Report is on how to plan effectively before an event for post-disaster recovery and reconstruction. It is also useful for planners in a post-disaster situation who were not able either to read this document beforehand or to develop such a plan. The focus is strictly on natural, rather than human-induced, disasters and on how communities can apply the planning process and planning tools toward reducing future vulnerability to natural hazards. More specifically, it focuses on a way of thinking about natural disasters that emphasizes seizing opportunities for reducing such vulnerability that often exist only in the aftermath of a disaster. At the same time, it will emphasize ways in which planners and public decision makers can incorporate such thinking into the everyday routines of community planning.

THE PROCESS OF RECOVERY AND RECONSTRUCTION

In the aftermath of a natural disaster, property owners and local officials often make decisions to rebuild homes, businesses, and public facilities in the same style, place, and design as the originals. The pressures to do so vary with the type and intensity of disaster. They are, however, almost always a significant factor as short-term emergency response and recovery operations wind down and reconstruction begins to dominate post-disaster thoughts and activities. These early decisions can foreclose many opportunities to reshape the patterns of development in a community so as to make it better and safer by reducing vulnerability to future disasters. This can result in a cycle of damage and repair at intervals that also vary greatly depending on the types and frequencies of disasters for which the community is at risk, producing considerable and growing costs to all levels of government as well as greater human costs and displacement. Depending on the will and circumstances of the community, however, there can also be forces advocating changes in construction patterns over time to avoid future damages. If engaged properly, these forces can be significant allies for planners and public officials seeking to redirect the existing pattern of development to create a safer community. It is thus important to dissect and analyze the process that governs recovery and reconstruction in communities affected by major natural disasters in order to understand how planning can reduce these costs and improve public safety.

Perhaps the first important point is that the process of recovery and reconstruction is not really singular, but rather involves a series of ongoing and related processes all set in motion by the disaster event, all taking place more or less simultaneously, and lasting various lengths of time beyond the event. These include the process of financing reconstruction, of mapping where and under what conditions rebuilding will be allowed to occur, and facilitating or managing the reconstruction of public and private infrastructure damaged by the disaster. The nature and scope of these processes also vary with the scope of the disaster, the type of hazard involved, and the size and technical capacities of the jurisdictions affected. These differences will be explored carefully in later sections of this report. The intent here is to detail those features of the recovery and reconstruction process that are common to the vast majority of post-disaster situations.

Most of the research in this field is relatively recent, almost all of it having occurred since the late 1970s. In this regard, it is worth noting that even the federal government's interest in consolidating disaster-related programs and activities dates only to that same period, with the formation of the Federal Emergency Management Agency (FEMA) under the Carter administration in 1979. Thus, it was only in 1977 that a trio of researchers (Haas, Kates, and Bowden 1977) advanced the proposition that "disaster recovery is ordered, knowable, and predictable." A social reaction, even to a natural phenomenon, that is knowable and predictable is one that logically can be assumed to be at least somewhat manageable through various sorts of intervention, most notably, planning by public agencies. That assumption, considering all that is at stake in the redevelopment of disaster-stricken communities, has served to drive further research in this area, much of which has questioned, modified, or reframed many of the findings of not only Haas, Kates, and Bowden but other early researchers in this field as well. What follows is a summary of the progress of that research. The section that follows addresses its implications for planners and public officials dealing with recovery and reconstruction.

WHAT THE RESEARCH SAYS

As late as 1970, relatively little was known about the dynamics of post-disaster recovery, and most of that was summarized neatly in a single major work (Barton 1969). Even as research in this field grew in the 1970s, a good deal of it focused on individual case studies whose findings were often difficult to generalize to other case studies involving other disasters (Rubin

> In the aftermath of a natural disaster, property owners and local officials often make decisions to rebuild homes, businesses, and public facilities in the same style, place, and design as the originals. . . . These early decisions can foreclose many opportunities to reshape the patterns of development in a community so as to make it better and safer by reducing vulnerability to future disasters.

1985). In their own path-breaking comparative study of reconstruction processes following four major disasters, Haas, Kates, and Bowden (1977) noted the dearth of such comparative studies at the time. Rubin (1985) suggested, however, that the real need was not for findings that could be applied among other case studies but for theories that would advance the entire field of study. Many of those case studies did, however, offer significant early insights into features of the recovery process upon which other researchers have been able to build.

Haas, Kates, and Bowden (1977), however, made what was probably the most significant early contribution of this type. Three of their case studies involved earthquakes—San Francisco in 1906, Anchorage in 1964, and Managua in 1973—and one involved the Rapid City, South Dakota, flood of 1972. They argued that community decisions during the periods of recovery and reconstruction are based on value choices between the competing priorities of returning to normalcy, reducing future vulnerability to disasters, and seizing opportunities to improve efficiency, equity, or amenities in the city.

Haas, Kates, and Bowden divided disaster recovery into four overlapping periods.

1) The emergency period covered the initial hours or days following the disaster when the community was forced to cope with its losses in property, lives, and injuries, and when normal activities were disrupted.

2) The restoration period covered the time following the emergency period until major urban services and transportation returned, evacuees returned, and rubble was removed.

3) During the replacement reconstruction period, the city rebuilt its capital stock to pre-disaster levels and social and economic activities returned to their previous levels. Signs of its completion included the return to pre-disaster population levels and the replacement of homes, jobs, and urban activities.

4) Finally, in the commemorative, betterment, and developmental reconstruction period, major reconstruction activities took place, and future growth and development began to take hold.

One of the most interesting theories advanced by these authors was the notion that there was a logarithmic relationship between each of these periods in succession, so that, in effect, the second reconstruction period would last about 1,000 times longer than the initial emergency period. Within this broad framework, they also suggested that public policy could modify the length of each period, shortening the path to recovery and reconstruction, but only within fixed and knowable limits.

Rubin (1985), among others, has suggested that this model of the periods of the recovery and reconstruction process may be a little more neat and simplistic than the reality that she and others have studied. She found that many of these periods overlapped to a greater extent than the theory suggested and that, depending to a large degree on variations in access to resources and power, different portions of a community could be in different stages of recovery and reconstruction at the same time. In other words, a more affluent neighborhood with faster access to recovery assistance might well be further along on the road to reconstruction than a heavily damaged and largely forgotten lower-income district. Thus, any assumption of uniformity in the recovery process could serve to exacerbate these inequities by ignoring their existence.

Because definitions have been an ongoing problem in the field of post-disaster recovery, this thesis represented a major advance in disaster

---

Rubin (1985), among others, has suggested that this model of the periods of the recovery and reconstruction process may be a little more neat and simplistic than the reality that she and others have studied. She found that many of these periods overlapped to a greater extent than the theory suggested and that, depending to a large degree on variations in access to resources and power, different portions of a community could be in different stages of recovery and reconstruction at the same time.

recovery theory. Kates and Pijawka (in Chapter 1 of Haas, Kates, and Bowden (1977)) note the various labels that have been used for the various periods following a disaster—restoration, recovery, rehabilitation, redevelopment, and reconstruction, among others. Wide variations in the use of these terms, both among planners and between the various professions involved in disaster research, were uncovered in the course of the literature search for this report and posed significant complications in identifying literature appropriate to the goals of this study (Rubin 1985; South Florida RPC 1990; Godschalk, Brower, and Beatley 1989; Mader et al. 1989; Topping 1991a through 1994). Among those with an interest in disaster research, but who bring differing perspectives to the definitions and terminology they use, are emergency managers, civil engineers, geologists, urban planners, public administrators, social workers, psychologists, sociologists, and political scientists, to name just the most commonly involved professions. Definitions of the various post-disaster stages remain in flux and pose a continuing challenge to researchers seeking to compare findings from a variety of studies. In most instances, however, recovery and restoration seem to be used in a similar vein, although it has been noted that recovery is the post-disaster phase that has benefitted the least from investigation by researchers (Berke, Kartez, and Wenger 1994). For the purpose of consistency and clarity, this document offers a glossary in Appendix A. Because this document is about land-use planning, our use of terminology will emphasize a focus on the use of these terms in that context.

One of the most interesting early case studies examining the process of recovery and reconstruction studied the 1976 earthquake in the Friuli region of northern Italy (Geipel 1982). The author, using extensive statistical and chronological documentation, reported that cultural context has a critical influence on victims' perception of events. Friuli, a hilly area whose communes date in many cases to medieval times, might fairly be compared to Appalachia in its economic predicament, in that the region exports many of its young people, who emigrated to other parts of Europe and North America in search of better opportunities but provided a sort of long-distance support system for relatives who were affected by the disaster. Geipel also reported that a natural disaster produces differential impacts for its victims by heightening the existing inequalities of wealth and class. The merchants gained from post-disaster recovery opportunities while elderly residents suffered; differences in the quality and durability of temporary housing provided by outside relief agencies also produced problems and misunderstandings among residents.

But Geipel's most important statements echoed points made by Haas, Kates, and Bowden. First, the time required for reconstruction, he wrote, was a function of economic trends already in place before the earthquake happened; the earthquake served merely to accelerate those trends, either for redevelopment or for continued deterioration of the local economic base. Second, planners do not have unlimited time in which to develop grand schemes for the wholesale redesign of the city or region in question. They must remember in their deliberations that the citizens of the area have a post-disaster plan in mind even before the planners begin their work, and that this is the vision that is competing with any new scenario the planners are prepared to offer. That plan, according to Geipel, is the city as it was before the disaster. This final point of Geipel's work underscores as eloquently as any other work in the field the value of pre-event planning for presenting and implementing alternative redevelopment visions in the aftermath of a natural disaster.

> Planners must remember in their deliberations that the citizens of the area have a post-disaster plan in mind even before the planners begin their work, and that this is the vision that is competing with any new scenario the planners are prepared to offer. That plan, according to Geipel, is the city as it was before the disaster.

THE GROWING COST OF NATURAL DISASTERS

As with other research agendas, the growing interest in identifying better means to reduce community vulnerability during the post-disaster reconstruction process does not occur in a social or political vacuum. If American voters are sensitive to anything these days, it is the cost of operating their government. There is ample room for debate about the efficacy of various proposed cuts in governmental programs, but there is no doubt that public officials are under great pressure to find ways to reduce the cost and to increase the efficiency of government.

As a result, disaster relief programs, which used to enjoy relatively unquestioned support in large part on humanitarian grounds, are also undergoing intense scrutiny. The process of reassessment has been underway at least since the 1960s (May 1985). The impetus for reexamining these programs is coming not only from the Clinton administration and Congress, but from ordinary citizens and disaster experts as well. The recovery and reconstruction costs of major natural disasters have been rising steadily, and the last decade has witnessed a procession of the most expensive disasters in U.S. history (Figure 1-2). More importantly, on close examination, much of the property damage this nation suffers from natural disasters appears preventable. Critics have raised questions about the location and structural integrity of much of the damaged property and asked why development was allowed to happen in this way. Through the use of building codes, warning systems, and public education, the nation has steadily reduced the loss of lives in natural disasters in this century. Today the means also abound for reducing property damage.

Through the use of building codes, warning systems, and public education, the nation has steadily reduced the loss of lives in natural disasters in this century. Today the means also abound for reducing property damage.

Figure 1-2. Damage Estimates in Recent Disasters

1989

Hurricane Hugo
South Carolina
$9 Billion

Loma Prieta Earthquake
Northern California
$7 Billion

1994

Northridge Earthquake
Southern California
$28 Billion

1991

East Bay Hills Wildfire
Oakland/Berkeley,
California
$1.5 Billion

1993

Midwest Floods
Upper Mississippi Valley
$12-16 Billion

1992

Hurricane Andrew
Dade County, Florida, and
Southeastern Louisiana
Parishes
$30 Billion

Hurricane Iniki
Kaua'i Island, Hawaii
$1.8 Billion

Sources:

FEMA. 1997. *Multi-Hazard Identification and Risk Assessment: A Cornerstone of the National Mitigation Strategy.* Washington, D.C.: FEMA. (Hurricanes and earthquakes)

FEMA. 1997. *Report on Costs and Benefits of Natural Hazard Mitigation.* Washington, D.C.: FEMA. (1994 Northridge Earthquake)

Federal Insurance Administration. 1992. *Lessons from Hurricane Hugo: Implications for Public Policy.* Washington, D.C.: FEMA. (1989 Hurricane Hugo)

Interagency Floodplain Management Review Committee. 1994. *Sharing the Challenge: Floodplain Management into the 21st Century.* Washington, D.C.: Executive Office of the President. (1993 Midwest floods)

National Fire Protection Association (Grant EMW-90-G-3440). 1991. *The Loma Prieta Earthquake: Emergency Response and Stabilization Study.* Washington, D.C.: FEMA. (1989 Loma Prieta Earthquake)

U.S. Fire Administration. 1991. *The East Bay Hills Fire: Oakland-Berkeley, California.* Emmitsburg, Md.: FEMA. (1991 East Bay Hills Fire)

The reason for this heightened sensitivity extends beyond just the political climate. A large part of the cost of reconstruction following natural disasters is due to the simple fact that more development now stands in harm's way than ever before. Much of this situation can be attributed to large-scale population and migration trends. Using 1970 data, Petak and Atkisson (1982) calculated that 30.9 percent of Americans lived in areas subject to hurricane winds, 18.7 percent faced severe or substantial earthquake risks, and 21.7 percent lived in counties with high landslide risks. Since then, the percentage of Americans living near the seacoast or in seismically active regions clearly has grown. By 1990, half of all Americans lived within 50 miles of the coasts; while only those in Hawaii or Guam and along the Atlantic Ocean and the Gulf of Mexico were typically subject to tropical storms and hurricanes, the Pacific rim provides a host of seismic and volcanic threats combined with some possibilities for tsunami runup. The populations of hurricane-prone

A large part of the cost of reconstruction following natural disasters is due to the simple fact that more development now stands in harm's way than ever before.

Florida and Texas, and of earthquake-prone California, Washington, and Alaska, have grown dramatically in the second half of this century. (See Figure 1-3.) Moreover, 80 percent of Florida's population lives within 10 miles of the coast. And, in California, population growth pressures in the context of rapid suburbanization have increased development pressure on vulnerable hillsides. In addition to generating landslide disasters, development of these hillsides also places housing and other structures in direct contact with the sort of dry-weather vegetation that often fuels naturally occurring wildfires.

More recent demographic trends, significantly increasing the populations of states like Utah and North Carolina, continue to move people into other vulnerable areas of the country, the former facing seismic hazards and the latter famous for coastal hazards, particularly on its barrier islands.

Figure 1-3. Population Changes for Selected Hazard-Prone States, 1960-1990

STATE	1960	1970	1980	1990	PERCENT CHANGE, 1960-1990
Florida	4,951,560	6,791,560	9,746,961	12,937,926	161.3
California	15,717,204	19,971,069	23,667,764	29,760,021	89.3
Texas	9,579,677	11,198,655	14,225,513	16,986,510	77.3
Washington	2,853,214	3,413,244	4,132,353	4,866,692	70.6
U.S. Total	**179,323,175**	**203,302,031**	**226,542,203**	**248,709,873**	**38.7**

Source: U.S. Bureau of the Census

To assess the impact of these demographic changes, it is necessary to understand the distinction between a natural hazard and a natural disaster. Natural hazards exist with or without the presence of human populations and development. Hurricanes struck Florida with regularity long before recorded history, and the region's natural environment absorbed their impacts as part of its long-term ecological balance and evolution. The seismic disturbances that have rocked the entire Pacific Rim over thousands of years have left us with much of the majestic scenery that makes California and Puget Sound as attractive as they are. Natural disasters occur only when the built environment sits in harm's way and when human lives are affected.

A closer look at the development patterns along the Pacific Coast makes obvious that demographic trends have been moving more people closer to serious hazards. Four of the largest and fastest-growing metropolitan areas in those five coastal states—Los Angeles, the Bay Area, Seattle, and Anchorage—are directly affected by underlying active fault zones, and all have a history of recent seismic disturbances. Each of these areas has a large inventory of existing hazard-prone buildings already in place, a problem that Los Angeles has recognized for nearly two decades with an ordinance aimed at seismically retrofitting older structures. Moreover, local topography in both Southern California and the Bay Area add serious wildfire hazards to the mix, again with a history of costly recent disasters.

> Natural hazards exist with or without the presence of human populations and development. . . . Natural disasters occur only when the built environment sits in harm's way and when human lives are affected.

Figure 1-4 makes this point with greater specificity regarding coastal storm hazards. The ranking involves growth rates during the three decades from 1960-1990 when the nation's demographic shift to the Sun Belt was in full force. It includes only those counties with shorelines along the Gulf or Atlantic coasts, with the slight addition of those few noncoastal counties with shores along either Lake Pontchartrain in Louisiana or Lake Okeechobee in Florida. These have been added to the analysis here because the two lakes are large enough—and close enough to the coast—to extend the storm-surge impacts of hurricanes inland to those counties.

Ranking these counties according to their growth rates over the last generation allows us to perceive the magnitude of the changes that have occurred in some of the nation's most vulnerable locations. Several facts stand out. One is that some of the most densely populated metropolitan

Figure 1-4. 25 Largest Population Growth Rates in Counties along the Atlantic and Gulf Coasts, 1960-1990

(RANK) COUNTY, STATE	1960	1970	1980	1990	CHANGE, PERCENT 1960-1990
1) Citrus, Fla.	9,268	19,196	54,703	93,515	909.0
2) Collier, Fla.	15,753	38,040	85,971	152,099	865.5
3) Hernando, Fla.	11,205	17,004	44,469	101,115	802.4
4) Charlotte, Fla.	12,594	27,559	58,460	110,975	781.2
5) Pasco, Fla.	36,785	75,955	193,661	281,131	664.3
6) Flagler, Fla.	4,566	4,454	10,913	28,701	528.6
7) Lee, Fla.	54,539	105,216	205,266	335,113	514.4
8) Martin, Fla.	16,932	28,035	64,014	100,900	495.9
9) Virginia Beach, Va.	85,218	172,106	262,199	393,069	361.3
10) Okeechobee, Fla.	6,424	11,233	20,264	29,627	361.2
11) Ocean, N.J.	108,241	208,470	346,038	433,203	300.2
12) Dare, N.C.	5,935	6,995	13,377	22,746	283.3
13) St. Lucie, Fla.	39,294	50,836	87,182	150,171	282.2
14) Palm Beach, Fla.	228,106	348,993	576,754	863,518	278.6
15) Broward, Fla.	333,946	620,100	1,018,257	1,255,488	276.0
16) St. Tammany, La.	38,643	63,585	110,869	144,508	274.0
17) Liberty, Ga.	14,487	17,569	37,583	52,745	264.1
18) Sarasota, Fla.	76,895	120,413	202,251	277,776	261.2
19) Brevard, Fla.	111,435	230,006	272,959	398,978	258.0
20) Indian River, Fla.	25,309	35,992	59,896	90,208	256.4
21) Dorchester, S.C.	24,383	32,276	59,028	83,060	240.6
22) Berkeley, S.C.	38,196	56,199	94,745	128,776	237.1
23) Calvert, Md.	15,826	20,682	34,638	51,372	224.6
24) Hendry, Fla.	8,119	11,859	18,599	25,773	217.4
25) Camden, Ga.	9,975	11,334	13,371	30,167	202.4

The staggering, explosive growth of the fastest-growing counties raises an important issue. It is precisely those once sparsely populated counties experiencing explosive growth that are generally least prepared to manage and plan for such growth, often because they have lacked the personnel and in-house expertise to do so.

With so much at risk in their future, the federal government and states and local communities have a huge financial stake in ensuring that we "grow smart," that development will be sensitive to natural hazards, and that communities mitigate those hazards effectively.

growth corridors in the nation are missing from the top 25. Their growth, while remarkable, was simply less stunning than that of the counties listed. For example, in the 30-year period, Dade County, Florida, the scene of massive damage in the wake of Hurricane Andrew in 1992, grew by 107.2 percent. Harris County, Texas, which includes Houston, grew by 126.7 percent, and Jefferson Parish, Louisiana, containing most of the New Orleans suburbs, grew by 114.7 percent. All of these large and rapidly growing metropolitan areas are clearly subject to coastal storm hazards.

Second, counties are more likely to have attained this percentage ranking if they started with a smaller population, as it is obviously easier to double a small population than a large one. It is important to recognize a link between growth management and the quality of hazard mitigation efforts, for the former should surely include a sound basis for determining how to steer growth away from hazard-prone areas. In this vein, the staggering, explosive growth of the fastest-growing counties raises an important issue. It is precisely those once sparsely populated counties experiencing explosive growth that are generally least prepared to manage and plan for such growth, often because they have lacked the personnel and in-house expertise to do so. It is dangerous, of course, to apply this generalization to specific communities without further investigation. Even communities of the same size vary widely in the sophistication of their planning capabilities. But growth in triple-digit percentages within a single generation, in many cases within a single decade, poses a significant challenge for a community of any size even under the best of circumstances.

The third point is the preponderance of these counties in Florida, the state with the greatest exposure to hurricane hazards. Other states, such as Texas, have had their share of rapid growth, but nothing equals the huge percentage growth across the state of Florida, especially along the Gulf Coast. Outside Florida, which takes 9 of the first 10 slots in the ranking, the fastest-growing counties were Virginia Beach, Virginia, Ocean County, New Jersey, and Dare County, North Carolina. Relatively safer locations like New England do not even make the chart. The migration of tens of millions of Americans to rapidly developing Sun Belt and coastal states has also served to transplant them to more vulnerable locations. With so much at risk in their future, the federal government and states and local communities have a huge financial stake in ensuring that we "grow smart," that development will be sensitive to natural hazards, and that communities mitigate those hazards effectively.

At the same time, it is not the point here to suggest that these concerns should be limited in any way to high-hazard, high-growth communities. What is true, most especially in California and Florida, is that the experiences of these states and communities have tended to push them to the forefront of effective planning for post-disaster recovery and reconstruction. But, as the 1993 Midwest floods demonstrated, substantial devastation can still be wrought in small towns and older cities in regions with little or no growth, and the lessons of such planning can still be applied there to achieve significant public benefits. For that very reason, this document includes a series of case studies profiling a variety of disaster types in a variety of geographic settings. The lessons of such planning apply virtually anywhere.

THE IMPORTANCE OF MITIGATION IN POST-DISASTER RECONSTRUCTION

Walk down the street and ask a random sample of the people you meet whether they know what mitigation means. How many, if they are familiar with the term, will apply it to hazards as opposed to, say, "mitigating circumstances," a phrase they probably have heard repeatedly in television murder mysteries? Before planners can engage the public's attention for hazard mitigation, it may be necessary to clarify what we are talking about and to make crucial distinctions in our use of disaster-related terminology. Key terms used in disaster-related planning appear in Appendix B. Note that FEMA defines hazard mitigation as "any action taken to reduce or eliminate the long-term risk to human life and property from hazards" (FEMA 1996).

The most well-recognized mitigation techniques are those relating to flood hazards because floodplain mapping is fairly advanced and the areas expected to be damaged are clearly delineated, even as to matters of degree and probability over time. Flood hazard mitigation for pre-existing construction focuses heavily on two primary techniques: acquisition and removal of structures from the floodplain, and elevation or floodproofing of those that remain in the floodplain to levels of greater safety, most often with reference to 100-year flood levels (Holway and Burby 1993). Most other concepts in this field largely relate to refinements of these ideas and mitigation related to special flood circumstances, such as the problems involved in alluvial fans or mountainous areas subject to flash floods (FEMA 1987).

It should be noted that the 1993 Midwest floods added substantially to the drumbeat of calls for changes in floodplain management policy, with a noticeably greater emphasis on nonstructural solutions rooted in land-use planning (Interagency Floodplain Management Review Committee 1994). The most advanced thinking in the area of floodplain management moves public policy beyond a narrow mitigation focus on minimizing the danger to the built environment in or near the floodplain to a wider concern with watershed management. Included in this type of approach would be regulations designed to minimize stormwater runoff from upland areas. While these more sweeping initiatives may often spring from changes in public perception following a flood-related disaster, the planning involved to support these mitigation approaches, and those for all hazards, needs to be an ongoing activity based on the institutionalization of mitigation principles into the overall community planning process.

Mitigation efforts for other hazards naturally deal with the unique characteristics of each of those disaster types. For example, mitigation for coastal areas affected by hurricanes would generally seek to steer development away from storm surge zones (Long Island RPB 1984; Brower, Beatley, and Blatt 1987). For earthquake hazards, mitigation should account, through both structural and land-use regulations, for soil types, soil liquefaction dangers, and fault lines (Jaffe, Butler, and Thurow 1981). And, for urban/wildland interface areas subject to wildfires, mitigation should deal with setbacks, transportation access, water supply, and vegetation and fire resistance (NFPA; Operation Urban Wildfire 1992; Slaughter 1996). An emerging challenge for planners is the need to deal in many communities with the competing mitigation needs posed by vulnerability to multiple hazards, such as those areas of the Mississippi Valley that are now coming to terms with the need to mitigate both flood and earthquake hazards due to the New Madrid fault.

Mitigation plans are not the same as plans for post-disaster recovery and reconstruction. The primary purpose of mitigation planning is to identify community policies, actions, and tools for implementation over the long term that will result in a reduction in risk and potential for future losses communitywide. Hazard mitigation plans are continually applied to development decisions, and the action elements of a mitigation plan are implemented on an ongoing basis, as resources and politics allow. Post-disaster recovery and reconstruction planning identifies policies, operational strategies, and roles and responsibilities for implementation of hazard mitiga-

Seizing the Moment: Pattonsburg, Missouri

History is often rich with ironies. Take Pattonsburg, Missouri, for example. After Matthew Patton's mill was washed away in an 1844 flood, the town moved uphill a mile and a half away, and let the site return to farmland. But, when the Omaha and Chillicothe Railroad built on the cheaper lowlands near the Big Creek River in 1870, the town moved back to take advantage of the railroad, which profited handsomely from reselling the land. While the town grew to more than 1,000 people by the turn of the century, the old problem reasserted itself, and the town flooded repeatedly, slowly dying over the course of the century.

After the 1993 floods, however, people were ready to consider alternatives. Using a sustainable development design team assembled with help from the U.S. Department of Energy, residents considered a number of alternatives and chose to relocate to higher ground while adopting sustainable design principles to improve the local environment, conserve energy, and promote local economic growth. The town adopted a zoning code that it had lacked before and spurred the development of new enterprises, such as a landscaping firm which took advantage of newly acquired expertise in the use of indigenous plants. The design team arrived just in time, in early 1994, to provide the expertise community leaders needed to mobilize residents behind a new vision that would make the town more disaster-resistant at the same time that it gained a new lease on life (Skinner and Becker 1995).

tion elements within the process of recovery and reconstruction to enable the community to seize opportunities during the rebuilding process to fulfill previously identified goals. These goals would have been articulated through the comprehensive planning process as well as the mitigation planning process, with linkages among all documents. Post-disaster recovery and reconstruction plans could therefore be considered a subelement of the mitigation plan or comprehensive plan. (See Figure 1-5 for a diagram illustrating these relationships.) Often, however, communities in the post-disaster situation prepare recovery plans without having previously developed a mitigation plan.

Planning prior to a disaster for reconstruction afterwards is also very different from emergency preparedness and response. The latter is handled in an emergency operations plan, and FEMA (1996) has produced a guide for this process for state and local officials. The public officials involved in each process should be well aware of both plans, however, because they are bound to affect each other's eventual success. Emergency management personnel must, of necessity, focus their energy and attention on the immediate crisis period following a disaster, during which time a wide variety of complex infrastructure and human service needs can tax the abilities of both paid and volunteer help. (See Figure 1-6 for a sequential diagram of the disaster timeline. The timeline represents the average

> Planning prior to a disaster for reconstruction afterwards is also very different from [an] emergency preparedness and response [plan]. . . . The public officials involved in each process should be well aware of both plans, however, because they are bound to affect each other's eventual success.

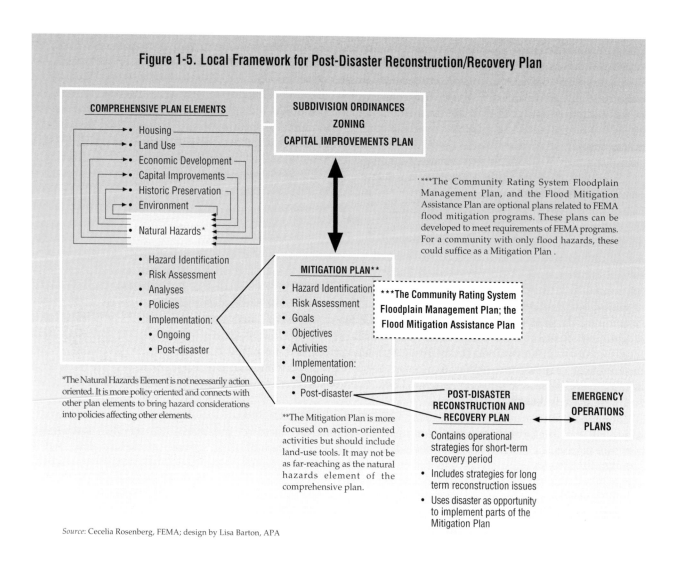

Figure 1-5. Local Framework for Post-Disaster Reconstruction/Recovery Plan

COMPREHENSIVE PLAN ELEMENTS
- Housing
- Land Use
- Economic Development
- Capital Improvements
- Historic Preservation
- Environment
- Natural Hazards*

  - Hazard Identification
  - Risk Assessment
  - Analyses
  - Policies
  - Implementation:
    - Ongoing
    - Post-disaster

*The Natural Hazards Element is not necessarily action oriented. It is more policy oriented and connects with other plan elements to bring hazard considerations into policies affecting other elements.

SUBDIVISION ORDINANCES ZONING CAPITAL IMPROVEMENTS PLAN

***The Community Rating System Floodplain Management Plan, and the Flood Mitigation Assistance Plan are optional plans related to FEMA flood mitigation programs. These plans can be developed to meet requirements of FEMA programs. For a community with only flood hazards, these could suffice as a Mitigation Plan.

MITIGATION PLAN**
- Hazard Identification
- Risk Assessment
- Goals
- Objectives
- Activities
- Implementation:
  - Ongoing
  - Post-disaster

****The Community Rating System Floodplain Management Plan; the Flood Mitigation Assistance Plan

**The Mitigation Plan is more focused on action-oriented activities but should include land-use tools. It may not be as far-reaching as the natural hazards element of the comprehensive plan.

POST-DISASTER RECONSTRUCTION AND RECOVERY PLAN
- Contains operational strategies for short-term recovery period
- Includes strategies for long term reconstruction issues
- Uses disaster as opportunity to implement parts of the Mitigation Plan

EMERGENCY OPERATIONS PLANS

Source: Cecelia Rosenberg, FEMA; design by Lisa Barton, APA

duration of the specific focus of post-disaster activity. It is based on experience with many different types of disasters.) The planner's focus in post-disaster reconstruction planning is not on managing emergency aid in this context but on the long-term process of recovery and redevelopment that must follow the emergency.

In practice, however, it is crucial to know that some decisions made during even the earliest hours of the emergency period can affect the viability of later options for reconfiguring the pattern of development in a community. For instance, a mayor who quickly commits his administration to rebuilding a particular neighborhood in the same place as it was prior to the disaster has already, at least in the public's mind, foreclosed a number of options that might otherwise have been available to planners and the community in general (Godschalk, Brower, and Beatley 1989). In addition, a number of researchers have observed that what seem like temporary measures, particularly with regard to housing, can often take on the character of permanence as disaster recovery proceeds (Haas, Kates, and Bowden 1979). In a more positive vein, however, the case study of Arnold, Missouri, illustrates that the pre-existence of a community plan for converting a floodplain into a greenway serves to obviate the need for hasty decisions that may limit future options. Those options will already have been chosen.

> In practice, it is crucial to know that some decisions made during even the earliest hours of the emergency period can affect the viability of later options for reconfiguring the pattern of development in a community. For instance, a mayor who quickly commits his administration to rebuilding a particular neighborhood in the same place as it was prior to the disaster has already, at least in the public's mind, foreclosed a number of options that might otherwise have been available to planners and the community in general

Figure 1-6. Chronology of Emergency Management Operational Phases and Planning for Reconstruction

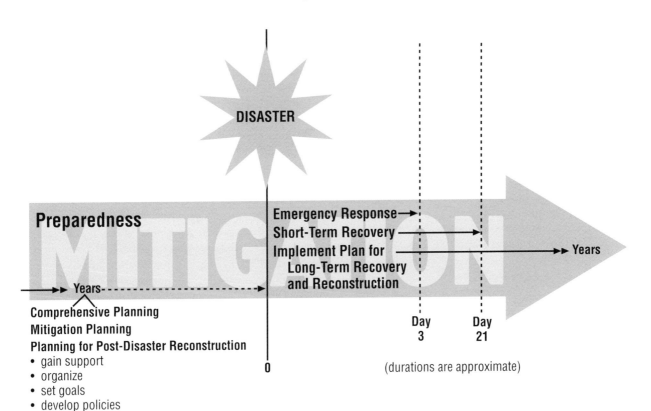

Source: Cecelia Rosenberg, FEMA; design by Lisa Barton, APA

Not Just for a Rainy Day

The worst thing that could happen to the knowledge any planner gains concerning planning for post-disaster recovery and reconstruction would be for that planner or the planning department or community to assume that it was relevant only in disaster situations. The tools and approaches involved are all relevant and applicable in everyday planning for hazard mitigation. As the case studies and other parts of this report will show, communities have gained the most from their post-disaster reconstruction plans when they have applied them to ongoing, routine planning activities long before a disaster strikes—for example, by monitoring the enforcement of hazard-related building code provisions, by preventing inappropriate types of development in hazard-prone areas, and by identifying targets of opportunity for hazard mitigation when funds become available. The community that makes hazard mitigation a routine part of planning will invariably find that it is better prepared for the task of post-disaster recovery and reconstruction than one that has ignored these questions.

A final but important point concerning planning for post-disaster reconstruction is that it serves to facilitate and optimize the process for deciding which mitigation techniques a community should use in each hazard-prone area. These decisions can have many significant consequences in building (or undermining) public confidence in planning. An invited comment by a city council member in the *Natural Hazards Observer* following the 1997 Grand Forks, North Dakota, flood highlights the perceptions of inequity that arise when some members of the community who had purchased flood insurance watched others get equal benefits after the community chose to buy the properties of the insured and uninsured alike (Glassheim 1997). When the guidelines for such decisions have been made clear in advance, rather than emerging ad hoc in the aftermath of disaster, planning is a winner.

THE ROLE OF PLANNERS IN HAZARD MITIGATION AND IN RECONSTRUCTION PLANNING

The foregoing discussion should make it obvious that there is an integral relationship between hazard mitigation and planning for post-disaster recovery and reconstruction. While mitigation is by no means the sole object of such planning, recovery and reconstruction that failed to accomplish any mitigation would defeat the purpose of post-disaster planning. The fundamental idea is to emerge from the process of long-term reconstruction with a safer community whose vulnerability to future disasters has been reduced significantly. At the same time, such planning should expedite the process of restoring normal residential life and economic activity as quickly as possible. One of the realities of post-disaster recovery is that public support for mitigation can dissolve easily if achieving it entails serious delays in restoring normal civic and economic activity.

The case studies included in this report and others published elsewhere have made abundantly clear how tempting it is for public officials, especially in the absence of any planned vision for reconstructing a community's future, to respond to exigencies and pressures of the moment by making promises or commitments that compromise opportunities to achieve a safer community through the process of reconstruction.

What is often less clear is that, in the relatively uncomplicated environment of "peacetime," constituencies can be mobilized behind an alternative vision of greater sustainability in the face of future disasters. Although planners should not necessarily act as community organizers, they can learn from veteran organizers like Saul Alinsky (1972), who once wrote that an organizer's role was to "rub raw" the sources of discontent in order to bring into focus recognizable targets for action. The real issue Alinsky was addressing was what motivates the desire for positive change. Discontent, of course, involves negative perceptions. As former Seattle planning director J. Gary Lawrence has pointed out (Schwab 1996b), planners need to borrow a page from modern marketing to offer an alternative vision that attracts people rather than merely discussing new regulations and requirements, which tends to make them lose interest. Environmentalists, business owners, insurance companies, tourist-oriented businesses, public safety advocates and officials, parks and recreation organizations, and even farmers, among others, all have some real or potential stake in helping to build consensus around plans for sustainable post-disaster reconstruction (FIFMTF 1995). In the floodplain management field, the concept of building coalitions of such multiple interests to support flood mitigation efforts has become known as multiobjective management (M-O-M).

It takes only a modest amount of imagination to see how M-O-M principles can be extended to pre-disaster mitigation planning for other hazards, particularly in communities facing potential scenarios involving multiple hazards. For instance, many of the interests cited could be persuaded to support an initiative to restore the natural landscape in fire-prone, mudslide-prone, forested hills and wilderness areas. The development of a mitigation-driven vision of what a community could become in the aftermath of a foreseeable natural disaster becomes the means of forestalling seat-of-the-pants decisions made under pressure in the immediate post-disaster period. Instead, public officials have a compelling vision already available to which they can point when asked, What do we do now?

The position of a mayor or other municipal executive in standing behind an existing plan is significantly enhanced when the state government has signaled its own willingness to promote or even require planning for hazard mitigation as part of post-disaster reconstruction. In a state where zoning must conform to a comprehensive plan, and the comprehensive plan must contain an element addressing hazard mitigation and post-disaster reconstruction issues, local government can use those mandates to undertake hazard mitigation both before and after a natural disaster occurs. The

Figure 1–7. Phases of Emergency Management: The Disaster Life Cycle

Source: Cecelia Rosenberg, FEMA; designed by Lisa Barton, APA

planning to do this is similar to the multiobjective management principle in that planning that enhances the community's resistance to natural hazards must be connected to other local goals and objectives through the comprehensive plan. Planners are critical to this process because of their role in balancing various community concerns and highlighting the relationships between them.

To date, however, only a handful of states have enacted mandates for natural hazards elements in local comprehensive plans. Using an approach that allows local governments to opt out of such a requirement only with proof that no natural hazards are present, APA has developed model legislation to address this issue. The language appears in its *Growing Smart Legislative Guidebook*, available online at the APA web site (www.planning.org). This report discusses the topic in greater detail at the beginning of Chapter 3. Even without such mandates, however, virtually any community can undertake voluntarily to include such elements in a comprehensive plan and use them to guide decisions affecting land-use patterns in the post-disaster recovery and reconstruction periods.

To date, only a handful of states have enacted mandates for natural hazards elements in local comprehensive plans. Using an approach that allows local governments to opt out of such a requirement only with proof that no natural hazards are present, APA has developed model legislation to address this issue.

The existence of a previously developed local mitigation plan makes the review process far more efficient and aids the community in meeting the state's application deadlines with a workable plan for post-disaster mitigation.

In any case, such local plans give communities a distinct advantage in the competition for Hazard Mitigation Grant Program (HMGP) funds. Authorized under Section 404 of the Robert T. Stafford Act Disaster Relief and Emergency Assistance Act (42 U.S.C. 5121, et. seq.), passed in 1988 and subsequently amended, HMGP provides up to 15 percent in additional funds atop the "estimated aggregate amount of grants to be made (less any associated administrative costs) with respect to" a presidentially declared disaster, for the purpose of reducing "the risk of future hardship, damage, loss, or suffering." The states, through state hazard mitigation officers (SHMOs), administer these grants in partnership with FEMA. Under Section 409 of the Stafford Act, states must prepare hazard mitigation administrative plans to outline their procedures for administering the program and to show that the money is being used in accordance with the regulations to institute safe land-use and construction practices in the area affected. Broader state-level hazard mitigation plans are also required in order to obtain any federal post-disaster assistance under the Stafford Act. These plans must contain:

- an evaluation of the natural hazards; a description of state and local policies, programs, and capabilities to mitigate those hazards;

- statements of goals, objectives, and proposed strategies or actions for mitigation; and

- descriptions of how the plan is to be implemented, monitored, evaluated, and updated (44 CFR Sec. 206.405).

These plans ideally should reflect any local mitigation plans developed. It stands to reason that SHMOs, in reviewing local applications for HMGP assistance, would set priorities that tend to favor communities with such plans already in place. The existence of a previously developed local mitigation plan makes the review process far more efficient and aids the community in meeting the state's application deadlines with a workable plan for post-disaster mitigation.

Florida and Rhode Island have recognized the value of local mitigation plan preparation by funding such efforts with the goal of making community participation in such planning statewide (Smith 1997). The difference in their approach may reflect the difference in scale between a very large and very small state. Florida largely seeks local participation in the program by providing the funds while allowing the community to decide the method of plan preparation. In Rhode Island, on the other hand, the University of Rhode Island's Coastal Resources Center (CRC) has been funded through a joint initiative of FEMA and Rhode Island Sea Grant to work with local communities to prepare plans. In either case, the trend is obvious: the community that refuses to plan for mitigation will be in a less advantageous position to make its case for receiving HMGP funds after a disaster compared to communities that have already planned and are ready to act on those plans. North Carolina has embarked on a statewide Mitigation Planning Initiative that features a local-level demonstration program, technical assistance and guidance to localities, as well as a focus on incorporating mitigation strategies into state planning agency policies and procedures.

Chapter 2

A Primer in Disaster Operations

n the tense days following Hurricane Andrew in 1992, Dade County Emergency Management Director Kate Hale issued a terse challenge to the federal government, "Where's the cavalry on this one?"

For many planners who have never worked in a disaster situation, the more immediate question may be, Who is the cavalry, anyway? Without knowing who should or will be doing which job in the response and short-term recovery phases of a disaster, planners will spend precious time just trying to learn the names and responsibilities of the most important players. This is a thoroughly preventable predicament because the structure of federal disaster response is spelled out clearly in the Robert T. Stafford Disaster Relief and Emergency Assistance Act (Stafford Act), in the Federal Response Plan (FRP) for major disasters or emergencies, and in other documents for emergency declarations, which are issued for lesser disasters involving the dispatch of federal assistance (see FEMA 1997a for a brief summary). States have their own legislation and emergency management protocols parallel to those at the federal level. These include arrangements for how state and local agencies will cooperate among themselves as well as with federal authorities in a presidentially declared disaster.

By law, a disaster declaration at the state or federal level activates temporary structures of governance that are overlaid atop normal operations at all levels. It is important that planners understand beforehand how they relate to these structures and to personnel from other agencies involved in post-disaster response, recovery, and short-term reconstruction in order to make best use of their opportunities. Knowing who is involved for what reasons also allows planners to include the most appropriate people in reconstruction committees or task forces, or to consult with them in a timely manner throughout the planning process.

With these considerations in mind, the purpose of this chapter is threefold:

- to describe the roles of various major municipal departments in the aftermath of a natural disaster;

- to describe the roles of state government;

- to describe the role of federal agencies and the functions of the FRP and their relationships to local and state post-disaster activities.

STATE AND LOCAL ROLES IN RESPONSE AND RECOVERY

As the Des Moines story in Chapter 1 helped to demonstrate, a disaster tends to force officials and workers of different community departments to work together in ways that they ordinarily would not. It also forces planners and many others out of ordinary daily work routines into a variety of unaccus-

Local emergency managers maintain plans for pre-event preparedness and for the immediate response to disaster—through evacuations, first aid, emergency shelter, food and water supplies, and other contingency arrangements. But they do not focus their energies on the task of long-term reconstruction.

tomed roles that they must master quickly even if they have never handled or been trained for such situations before. Local emergency managers maintain plans for pre-event preparedness and for the immediate response to disaster—through evacuations, first aid, emergency shelter, food and water supplies, and other contingency arrangements. But they do not focus their energies on the task of long-term reconstruction, which of necessity must fall to public works officials, land-use planners, engineers, redevelopment officials, and building officials. The amount of expertise this latter group can bring to the table varies widely, however, among different communities and different parts of the nation. These differences relate both to the frequency of occurrence of natural disasters and to differences in state legislation enabling or requiring such planning.

Regardless of the depth of local experience, however, there are state officials whose job it is to maintain plans for response to local emergencies

Figure 2-1. Overview of a Disaster Operation

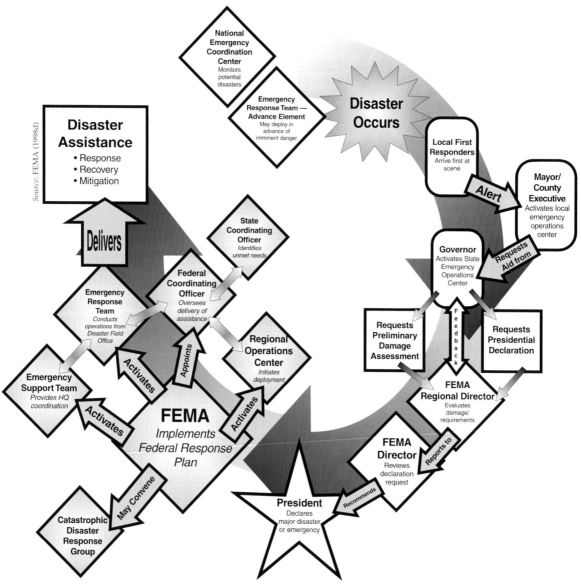

Source: FEMA (1998d)

that exceed local capability. At the federal level, the system of managing response to major disasters is contained in the FRP. Up to 26 federal agencies and the American Red Cross can be involved in the implementation of the FRP, which outlines the basic structure for interagency and intergovernmental coordination during the emergency response phase of a major disaster (FEMA 1998). For emergency declarations covering lesser disasters, the act and accompanying regulations spell out the types of aid available. In either case, the president appoints a federal coordinating officer (FCO), usually a FEMA official, to manage and oversee federal assistance.

Local Agencies and Their Roles

Figure 2-2 represents an attempt by FEMA, in its *Guide for All-Hazard Emergency Operations Planning*, to summarize the primary and support responsibilities of various typical agencies of local government in an emergency response situation. It is offered as a supplement to, but not parallel to, the discussion below, which goes beyond response activities to those involving short-term recovery. Hence, the reader will not find all the same agencies in both the text below and in the matrix, and the discussion below covers many short-term recovery activities not addressed in the matrix. It should also be remembered that the response period following a disaster will often blend quickly into or even overlap the short-term recovery period, sometimes in a matter of hours.

Police and fire. The idea that public safety personnel would be on the front lines in the aftermath of a natural disaster needs no explanation. People expect to see them there and would be distressed if they were not.

Primary among police functions at the onset of an emergency is the evacuation of a disaster-stricken area when that is necessary. Exactly when and how this happens will depend on the nature and severity of the disaster and depends heavily on the amount of warning the disaster provides. An order for mandatory evacuation requires authority from the chief executive of some unit of local government or the governor of the state, depending both on the extent of the emergency and the provisions in state and local law.

Both during evacuation procedures and after the disaster, police will also play a crucial role in coordinating the flow of traffic. A disaster-stricken community should expect major traffic arteries and facilities to be closed or at least partially disabled. People not yet aware of the proper detours will have to rely on police direction to assist them in finding alternate routes. Police may also have to guide local residents or business owners in and out of restricted areas so designated because of roadway impediments, flooding,

Figure 2-2. Organizational Responsibilities for Response Functions

	Chief Executive Official	Fire Department	Police Department	Health and Medical Coordinator	Public Works	Emergency Program Manager	EOC Manager	Communications Coordinator	Public Information Officer	Evacuation Coordinator	Mass Care Coordinator	Resource Manager	Education Department	Animal Care and Control Agency	Warning Coordinator	Comptroller/Chief Financial Officer	Volunteer Organizations	Other Organizations
Direction and Control	P	P/S	P/S	P/S	P/S	S	S	S	S	S	S	S	S	S	S	S	S	S
Communications	S	S	S	S	S	S	S	P	S	S	S	S	S	S	S	S	S	S
Warning	S	S	S	S	S	S	S	S	S	S	S	S	S	S	P	S	S	S
Emergency Public Information	S	S	S	S	S	S	S	S	P	S	S	S	S	S	S	S	S	S
Evacuation	S	S	S	S	S	S	S	S	S	P	S	S	S	S	S	S	S	S
Mass Care	S	S	S	S	S	S	S	S	S	S	P	S	S	S	S	S	S	S
Health and Medical	S	S	S	P	S	S	S	S	S	S	S	S	S	S	S	S	S	S
Resource Management	S	S	S	S	S	S	S	S	S	S	S	P	S	S	S	S	S	S

P .... Primary Responsibility
S .... Support Responsibility
P/S .... Depending on the nature and scope of the emergency, some jurisdictions will put one of these agencies in charge.

★ **Note:** *The above matrix is not all-inclusive, nor prescriptive; it is meant only to illustrate how responsibilities can be summarized.*

Source: FEMA (1996)

Governor's Emergency Powers

Under a state of emergency, the governor or a delegated surrogate usually has the power to:

- mobilize the National Guard and transfer and direct state agency personnel;

- require and direct evacuation of all or part of the population within a disaster area;

- prescribe routes, modes of transportation, and destinations for evacuation and prohibit certain conduct in the affected area;

- commandeer or use private property; and

- authorize emergency funds.

Source: Jim Solyst, *A Governor's Guide to Emergency Management* (Washington, D.C.: National Governors' Association, 1990).

structural damage, contamination, or other factors. At the direction of the local building department, police may also restrict access by contractors unless they can show a letter of authorization from the department, thus screening out less scrupulous operators and scavengers (BOAF 1994).

In addition, at a minimum after any storm or geological disturbance that disrupts electrical power, police will play an essential role in directing traffic wherever automated systems have ceased to function.

Fire departments do more than put out fires, although the need for doing so will certainly accompany all urban wildfires, many earthquakes, and thunderstorms that produce lightning strikes. They also provide paramedical and emergency rescue services that help to remove people trapped in debris, caught in flood waters, or who are otherwise desperate and helpless. Services include both on-site first aid and delivery by ambulances to area hospitals.

Planning for emergency operations can and should include the extensive use of all kinds of public safety personnel, including the state fire marshal's office, for public education campaigns to mitigate disaster damage to people and property through responsible individual actions. These efforts can take the form not only of written materials, but also electronic information posted on the Internet and publicly accessible electronic bulletin boards, broadcasted public information commercials, and the personal touch of direct contact with classrooms, civic groups, and other related means of delivering the message to public audiences. It is hard for public safety agencies, particularly those in highly hazard-prone communities, to oversaturate the public with this type of information. FEMA's U.S. Fire Administration has published guides to these programs that describe the diversity and effectiveness of such measures (USFA 1990; USFA 1993).

Emergency management. In the two generations since the aftermath of World War II, local emergency management has undergone a metamorphosis from early civil defense agencies focused on preparations for nuclear defense to the current emphasis on natural and technological disasters. The technical capacity and sophistication of local emergency management centers has grown considerably but still varies widely according to both the size of the jurisdiction and its willingness to commit resources to this purpose. The level of commitment tends to reflect the perception and extent of the hazards present. Also, the degree of emphasis on natural versus technological hazards tends to reflect the degree to which either category of threat predominates. The combination of local resources and technical expertise will in turn determine the point at which an emergency becomes a disaster beyond the scope of what the local government can handle (Drabek and Hoetmer 1991).

No matter what the specific hazards may be, the prime function of local emergency management is preparedness and response. Emergency managers are primarily responsible for organizing the immediate response to disaster, including the provision of emergency shelter, maintenance of vital services, access to essential provisions like food and drinking water, and the coordination of outside aid.

One special feature of emergency management that such agencies share with planning departments is a need to focus on planning for future and uncertain but plausible events that require the coordination of resources from a variety of other agencies that may not share the same vision or sense of urgency about the problem that the agency has defined (Kartez and Faupel 1994). Until a disaster strikes, the functions of the emergency manager may seem remote and hypothetical. In regions like Southern California, however, such emergencies occur frequently enough to erode that perception and replace it with a better understanding of the necessity of the job the office performs.

Planning. With an effective focus on mitigation strategies, planners can find common ground for cooperation with emergency management personnel. However, neither group of professionals has typically developed a high awareness of this shared forward-looking orientation. As a result, many local government bureaucracies have a long way to go in exploiting the potential for developing joint strategies for addressing threats posed by natural disasters despite the enormous potential for mutual support of agency agendas in this regard. This is essential because both types of agencies struggle with the need to promote a somewhat vague, comprehensive vision of the community's future and the need to coordinate and rationalize the roles and capabilities of other agencies in local government in pursuit of that vision (Kartez and Faupel 1994).

But the two can and should complement each other. Emergency management focuses on planning for the ability to respond rapidly and effectively to relieve or prevent suffering and to restore a community's vital functions quickly in the aftermath of a disaster. Planning departments typically have less of a direct role in the immediate aftermath of a disaster, but they can work to build consensus prior to an event around a vision of the post-disaster community that will guide long-term redevelopment. The crux of the relationship, then, lies in that pivotal point at which disaster response gives way to long-term recovery and reconstruction, so that both agencies are working toward a common goal of rebuilding a more disaster-resistant community. Effective mutual communication both in pre-disaster planning and in implementing those plans afterwards can reduce the potential for hasty decision making that will compromise the potential for achieving those goals. Planners, in this scenario, are both visionaries and salesmen prior to the disaster and, afterwards, watchdogs patiently waiting for their moment of opportunity to guide the community toward the implementation of its vision of itself.

In practical terms, what this means is that planners will have to move quickly after a disaster to identify the specific needs for rebuilding that will allow them to guide reconstruction down a more sustainable path. Where only minor damage is involved, it means acting quickly enough on applications for permits to rebuild to avoid the perception that planners are needlessly delaying the community's recovery. It means being able to identify and justify a set of priorities for mitigation efforts because the available money is almost never sufficient to complete a city's wish list of projects. Finally, it includes collecting and packaging the details needed for a convincing hazard mitigation grant application to be channeled through state and federal disaster authorities.

Downtown Coalinga, California, was cordoned off by public safety officials after a 1983 earthquake.

Hurricane Andrew destroyed this regional park in Homestead, Florida, in 1992, but it was rebuilt and finally reopened in 1995. With much community input, it was completely redesigned, and new facilities were added.

Bob Marshall Photography & Video

In short, for either group to do an excellent job, planners and emergency managers need each other and need a common ongoing, or pre-disaster, rapport with the other local and state agencies with which they must interact in the post-disaster period.

Redevelopment. Redevelopment agencies differ from planning departments in that they are focused on the physical redevelopment of all or particular areas of a community and most particularly in that their powers include the use of eminent domain to achieve that purpose. In essence, they are developers with a crucial role to play in post-disaster reconstruction. Within their designated redevelopment project areas, they also serve as land-use regulators exercising land-use control powers pursuant to their redevelopment plans.

The strength of a redevelopment agency in planning for post-disaster reconstruction lies in assisting the process of rebuilding in creative ways. . . . Sometimes this involves accelerating some economic changes and trends that were already in motion before the disaster.

While planners in planning and zoning agencies, depending on the nature of the hazard, may focus on such disaster-related land-use issues as preventing inappropriate development in hazard-prone areas, the primary purpose of a redevelopment agency is to stimulate economic activity or the physical improvement of an area. The strength of a redevelopment agency in planning for post-disaster reconstruction lies in assisting the process of rebuilding in creative ways. This may involve assembling viable parcels of land for projects that will advance the community's economic recovery, or it may involve the use of financial incentives and assistance to advance disaster-resistant rebuilding. Sometimes this involves accelerating some economic changes and trends that were already in motion before the disaster, such as buying land and/or buildings from businesses that are no longer tenable once reconstruction costs are factored into their operations in order to attract new ventures that are capable of rebuilding safely and making a long-term commitment to the community.

California's Seismic Safety Commission (1994a) offers a typical list of special authorities redevelopment agencies can use under the California Redevelopment Law, all of which are relevant to post-disaster recovery and reconstruction:

- buying real property, through eminent domain if necessary;
- developing property;

- selling real property without bidding;

- relocating persons (or businesses) with interests in property acquired by the agency;

- financing operations by borrowing from state or local governments or by selling bonds;

- imposing land-use and redevelopment controls pursuant to a comprehensive plan of redevelopment.

Although other states have variations in their laws authorizing the creation of municipal development agencies, most have powers similar to those in California. Variations deal more with procedures for creating local redevelopment agencies, for defining the boundaries of project areas, and in the details of financial management.

The breadth of these powers makes the redevelopment agency a key player, whether or not mitigation is a key factor in reconstruction. Two recent tornado recovery plans (Woodward-Clyde Associates 1997a and 1997b), for example, deal almost entirely with recovery and reconstruction issues that have little to do with mitigation simply because, for the most devastating tornado scenarios, there is very little mitigation possible that is cost-effective. On the other hand, earthquake recovery may necessitate the financing of extensive structural repairs of damaged buildings or even the demolition of hazardous structures, activities that can often be subsidized through redevelopment authorities. These agencies can use tools such as the establishment of tax-increment financing districts to provide funding for retrofits of public infrastructure, facilities, and buildings to increase their seismic resistance. For example, the City of Fullerton Redevelopment Agency in 1991 launched a program of no-interest loans to owners of commercial and family buildings to retrofit unreinforced masonry construction, a key problem in seismically threatened cities (Seismic Safety Commission 1994a). The case study in Chapter 12 offers two significant examples of the use of redevelopment powers in the aftermath of the Loma Prieta earthquake.

One interesting California statute is the Community Redevelopment Financial Assistance and Disaster Project Law (California Health and Safety Code Section 34000 et. seq.), enacted in 1964, which established an expedited process by which municipalities without an existing redevelopment agency may, in the aftermath of a disaster, create one and adopt a plan for redevelopment of a disaster-affected area. This law was used several times in the 1980s (Seismic Safety Commission 1994a). Alaska, also affected by severe earthquakes, has a specific code section (Alaska Statutes Sec. 19.55.932) devoted to urban renewal or redevelopment in disaster areas.

Building. Few agencies have a more sensitive job in the post-disaster environment than building code enforcement agencies. Their decisions determine which citizens may live in their homes or work in their businesses, sometimes for long periods of time after the event. As a result, those decisions about the habitability of damaged structures determine the extent of the community's need for emergency and longer-term shelter.

Moreover, building officials must respond effectively to at least two concerns that involve additional expertise beyond that of basic enforcement. One is familiarity with the National Flood Insurance Program (NFIP), whose requirements involve elevation or floodproofing of substantially damaged structures, which are defined as those determined to

Earthquake recovery may necessitate the financing of extensive structural repairs of damaged buildings or even the demolition of hazardous structures, activities that can often be subsidized through redevelopment authorities. These agencies can use tools such as the establishment of tax-increment financing districts to provide funding for retrofits of public infrastructure, facilities, and buildings to increase their seismic resistance.

Few agencies have a more sensitive job in the post-disaster environment than building code enforcement agencies. Their decisions determine which citizens may live in their homes or work in their businesses, sometimes for long periods of time after the event.

have suffered damage equaling or exceeding 50 percent of their pre-flood market value. This determination is usually made by the local building official. The second concern involves historic preservation and the determination, in cooperation with the state historic preservation official (SHPO), of those circumstances in which demolition of a historic building is warranted. This issue is one that, handled improperly or with inadequate communication, has produced serious conflict in post-disaster situations. For the most part, however, good communication and clear procedures can prevent such conflict.

A building inspector assesses damage in Hollywood, California, following the 1994 Northridge earthquake.

FEMA

Building officials' responsibilities fall into several categories, some of which are independent of other agencies' activities, and some of which interact importantly with the activities of planners. In the most drastic situations, those powers can include temporary condemning of damaged buildings that cannot be occupied in a safe and sanitary manner and buildings that cannot be rebuilt due to the extent of damage they have suffered. The latter situation can lead to emergency demolition powers over those buildings so badly damaged as to pose an immediate threat to public safety if left standing.

Building officials can use a placarding system to designate the condition of buildings and their suitability for occupancy. (Note that this is not always used. The ATC-20 standard has been adopted on an as-needed basis but is not required.) This is part of an assessment process that must begin as soon as possible after the disaster and often requires marshaling the energies of every available staff person, if not also borrowing needed staff from communities outside the affected area through intergovernmental mutual aid agreements. Depending on the extent of the damage from the disaster, a building permit moratorium may be a necessary initial step to allow officials to concentrate on the assessment process. The best means of conducting this assessment is by having a pre-existing plan for assigning teams, dispensing supplies, and for filling in gaps in managerial authority. It is entirely possible that key managers and even department heads may themselves be victims of the disaster or unable to assume their duties in a timely manner. For instance, Michael Gustafson, an official in the Pinellas Park, Florida, building division, notes that his superior was trapped under the rubble of his own home after a tornado damaged or destroyed some 1,000 residences in the city. He had to take over because no one else was qualified to do so (BOAF 1994).

The Building Officials Association of Florida (BOAF), one of the most experienced state associations in the nation in relation to disaster assessments, outlines the following essential building department tasks in the post-disaster period:

Building officials' responsibilities fall into several categories, some of which are independent of other agencies' activities, and some of which interact importantly with the activities of planners. In the most drastic situations, those powers can include temporary condemning of damaged buildings that cannot be occupied in a safe and sanitary manner and buildings that cannot be rebuilt due to the extent of damage they have suffered.

Figure 2-3. Habitability Assessment: Fieldwork Sheet

HABITABILITY ASSESSMENT — FIELD WORK SHEET　　Date_____

1. ADDRESS: _____

2. OWNERS NAME: _____

3. RENTERS NAME: _____

4. PERSON TO NOTIFY IN EMERGENCY: _____
   PHONE: (____) _____

5. TYPE OF STRUCTURE DAMAGED:　Residential ◯　　Frame ◯
   　　　　　　　　　　　　　　　Commercial ◯　　Metal ◯
   　　　　　　　　　　　　　　　Multi-Family ◯　Masonry ◯
   　　　　　　　　　　　　　　　　　　　　　　Mobile Home ◯

6. INSURANCE:　Owner Insured:　　Yes ◯　No ◯　　　　Unknown ◯
   　　　　　　Structure:　Fully Insured ◯　Under-insured ◯　Unknown ◯
   　　　　　　Renter Insured:　Yes ◯　No ◯　　　　Unknown ◯

7. IS THIS THEIR PRIMARY RESIDENCE?　Yes ◯　No ◯　　Unknown ◯

8. STRUCTURAL DAMAGE:

	5-25%	25-50%	50-100%
◯ FOUNDATION	◯	◯	◯
◯ ROOF/TRUSSES	◯	◯	◯
◯ EXTERIOR WALLS	◯	◯	◯
◯ INTERIOR WALLS	◯	◯	◯
◯ FLOORS/FLOORING	◯	◯	◯
◯ PLUMBING	◯	◯	◯
◯ ELECTRIC	◯	◯	◯
◯ A/C & HEAT	◯	◯	◯

9. DAMAGE CATEGORY:　◯ MINOR　　◯ MAJOR　　◯ DESTROYED
   　　　　　　　　(Damage Less than 25%)　(Damage From 25-50%)　(Damage Exceeds 50%)

10. STRUCTURAL INFORMATION:
    POWER, GAS, WATER should remain off?　Yes ◯　No ◯　Undetermined ◯
    Is ENGINEERING needed for Repair?　Yes ◯　No ◯　Undetermined ◯
    Is the Building LIVABLE?　Yes ◯　No ◯　Undetermined ◯
    Were PICTURES taken?　Yes ◯　No ◯　Team_____　Roll___ Frame___
    DEPTH OF WATER IN STRUCTURE: _____

11. TEAM MEMBERS:

    This assessment form was completed by _____ (Please Print)

Office Use Only:
Estimated Cost of Repairs
$_____

Put all comments on the back of this sheet.
City of Pinellas Park, Florida

- **Securing damaged areas.** As noted above, the police serve this function, but they take their instructions from the building code enforcement agency concerning the areas that need to be sealed off and who should be permitted entry.

- **Answering calls.** Residents are bound to have many questions about the safety of relatives and their own property. The department needs to be able to answer those questions as well and as quickly as possible.

- **Habitability assessment.** Teams of building inspectors are assigned to stricken areas to assess building damage. The data they collect are inventoried for use for disaster damage assessment purposes and by other city departments, such as planning. The information, organized by streets and areas, also becomes essential later for permitting of reconstruction and identification of potential hazard mitigation projects. (See Figure 2-3.) An important point concerning the habitability assessment is that it is guided by local health and safety concerns and thus differs in its criteria from those employed to determine substantial damage under NFIP, which affect the manner of rebuilding. It may be possible that a permit can be granted to rebuild, but it may not be possible to reoccupy the property immediately.

An important point concerning the habitability assessment is that it is guided by local health and safety concerns and thus differs in its criteria from those employed to determine substantial damage under NFIP, which affect the manner of rebuilding. It may be possible that a permit can be granted to rebuild, but it may not be possible to reoccupy the property immediately.

- **Inspections.** The quality of reconstruction can deteriorate if inspection standards are not maintained for all work done after a disaster. Again, additional help may be necessary.

- **Utilities.** Building code officials are the ones in a position to maintain coordination with the local electric and other utilities concerning restoration of service in affected areas. It is up to them to decide when it is appropriate to restore service to damaged buildings.

- **Permitting/NFIP Compliance.** Outside help in a major disaster is often necessary. Many areas already have mutual assistance agreements, such as the one BOAF uses to provide emergency permitting assistance in the aftermath of a disaster. In the context of NFIP, this process involves the necessary determinations of substantial damage discussed above, which then affect how structures located within the community's regulatory floodplain are allowed to be rebuilt. The issue of whether they are allowed to be rebuilt at all is significant if they are potential targets for buyouts.

Two key definitions and an explanation of their importance are worth introducing here, drawn from FEMA/NFIP regulations for post-flood guidance:

> **Substantial damage** means damage of any origin sustained by a structure whereby the cost of restoring the structure to its before-damage condition would equal or exceed 50 percent of the market value or replacement cost of the structure before the damage occurred. (Note: The cost of the repairs must include all costs necessary to fully repair the structure to its before-damage condition.)

Officials should keep in mind that enforcing floodplain management rules is required even in the aftermath of other types of disasters when damage to structures has occurred in a floodplain.

> **Substantial improvement** means any reconstruction, rehabilitation, addition, or other improvement of a structure, the cost of which equals or exceeds 50 percent of the market value of the structure before the "start of construction" of the improvement.

If a building is "substantially damaged" or "substantially improved," it must be brought into compliance with the community's flood damage prevention regulations, including elevating the building to or above the 100-year flood elevation.

The same document, in its Index 6 (Post-Flood Responsibilities of Floodplain Managers), does an excellent job of summarizing the measures officials must take to enforce regulatory compliance with NFIP. Officials should keep in mind, as the Plainfield, Illinois, case study in Chapter 9 illustrates, that enforcing floodplain management rules is required even in the aftermath of other types of disasters when damage to structures has occurred in a floodplain.

An additional consideration, as BOAF notes, is that opportunist contractors sometimes abound in the post-disaster environment. Building officials need to maintain control over the situation while expediting simple requests. In communities where a consumer protection office exists, that agency may need to play a supportive role in preventing additional victimization of those whose homes have been damaged.

- **Working with the media.** Building code officials must coordinate with the emergency manager, public information officer, and the news media to ensure that the public receives accurate information regarding access to property and time frames for permitting activities. Status and criteria for reconstruction activities are among the most important issues for victims.

Health. One reason disasters take a far smaller toll in human life than they used to is that public health measures for dealing with post-disaster conditions have improved remarkably in this century. Large displaced or homeless populations have always been breeding grounds for communicable diseases, especially when they are crowded together in temporary shelters. Local health departments have become well trained in mitigating and preventing such circumstances. In addition, these departments can oversee the provision of safe and uncontaminated food and drinking water for those dependent on emergency provisions. Health officials may also have to intervene in some housing decisions. In the aftermath of the prolonged 1993 Midwest floods, for instance, many homes were under water for as long as three months, more than enough time for a dangerous accumulation of microbial life and chemical contamination to take hold in waterlogged walls and basements. Such mold and mildew can pose a serious danger to contractors and homeowners (Berke et al. 1992).

In recent decades, growing attention has centered on the mental health needs of disaster survivors, and it is now common practice to provide mental health counseling to those who have suffered disaster-related stress. In addition to local mental health professionals and mental hospitals, the Red Cross and allied nonprofit disaster relief services now provide counseling for disaster victims (Drabek and Hoetmer 1991).

Transportation. The most drastic disruption of transportation infrastructure often occurs during severe earthquakes, but wind and water damage and inundation can also pose serious problems that local traffic and transportation officials must address. Wind damage from tornadoes, hurricanes, or even severe thunderstorms can disconnect or destroy power lines and electric traffic signals, knock down or disable street lights, or cause spills or leaks of hazardous materials that must be cleaned up under adverse circumstances. Floods can put airports, major roadways, and transit systems under water. In the 1993 Midwest floods, this problem assumed regional and interstate proportions by forcing the rerouting of railroad traffic away from inundated tracks at a cost of $51 million, in addition to $131 million in physical damage to facilities (Interagency Floodplain Management Review Committee 1994). Restoring these systems without undue delay is a major planning challenge for local and state transportation departments.

Planners normally interact with transportation officials in the pre-disaster period in the preparation of the transportation element of local comprehensive plans. At this stage, transportation officials can help planners identify alternatives to replacing damaged facilities such as roads or bridges. Following a disaster, facilities targeted for replacement can undergo merely temporary repairs while officials prepare for the construction of new facilities. In other cases, a retrofit may need to be considered to make a facility more disaster-proof than before. A good example is the elevation of two key bridges in Arnold, Missouri, following the 1993 floods (see case study in Chapter 8). The city's 1991 floodplain management plan had already identified such measures as a priority.

The Mitigation Assistance Corporation, Boulder, Colorado

After Hurricane Hugo knocked out power on Sullivans Island, South Carolina, in 1989, town officials decided to underground power and telephone lines at the two ends of the island that were most vulnerable to high winds.

Public works. Closely related to the problem of transportation in restoring normal community functions is that of public works. As Des Moines learned when the Raccoon River overpowered the levees surrounding the city's water treatment plant in 1993, water and sewage treatment systems can be vulnerable in a major disaster and contingency plans are required in the event of structural damage or disablement. The public works department thus takes on an essential role at the post-disaster planning table in assuming responsibility for restoring normal service to any public infrastructure under its control. It is particularly important that pubic works and planning departments collaborate in the pre-disaster time frame with regard to public policy on the extension and maintenance of any such infrastructure in hazard-prone areas, such as floodplains or coastal zones, and its restoration in the aftermath of a disaster. Utility service, after all, is an important prerequisite to development.

City manager or mayor. At the center of all these operations is the need for strong leadership and direction in setting policy and priorities and in focusing attention on the need for planning for post-disaster recovery and reconstruction. Executive leadership is a strong determinant of the kinds, quality, and quantity of human, physical, and financial resources devoted to both emergency management and long-term recovery activities. The mayor's or city manager's office should serve as the lead communicator, allowing the local government to speak with one effective voice rather than a babble of uncoordinated departmental messages. This means that the local chief executive's office must maintain effective communication internally with emergency management, departmental public information officers, and the emergency operations center.

> It is particularly important that pubic works and planning departments collaborate in the pre-disaster time frame with regard to public policy on the extension and maintenance of any such infrastructure in hazard-prone areas, such as floodplains or coastal zones, and its restoration in the aftermath of a disaster.

Exerting this leadership does not necessarily mean that the executive's office actually leads the post-disaster planning process during the pre-disaster period. It does mean, however, that the mayor's or city manger's office must assume responsibility for determining which department will do so. No other entity in local government is in a better decision to clarify the authority with which the lead department will then proceed or to emphasize that this matter is a priority.

The International City/County Management Association (ICMA) identifies the following key tasks for city managers in the aftermath of a disaster:

- information gathering and assessment
- organizational arrangements
- resource mobilization
- planning, administration, and budgeting
- regulation and approval
- coordination and interorganizational relations
- monitoring and evaluation (Ohlsen and Rubin 1993)

If there is a common element here, it is the clear need for someone to be in charge and to establish emergency response and planning for post-disaster recovery as governmental priorities. This is necessary not only for the emergency transfer of personnel among departments to places where they are needed, but also to coordinate the community's relationships with the outside world, including the state and federal government and relief agencies like the American Red Cross.

State Government Roles

State government is the crucial first link between overburdened local governments and the outside aid they need in the aftermath of a disaster.

Every state has some sort of emergency management agency designated to fulfill this function under gubernatorial leadership. Just as with local government capabilities at the municipal or county level, the size, personnel, and technical capacities of these agencies vary with the types of hazards the state faces and the commitment the state has made to dealing with them. Most observers would agree that the agencies in California and Florida are probably the most sophisticated, but that does not necessarily mean that the resources deployed in other states are less adequate for the tasks they face. California and Florida have been driven by a degree of necessity unfamiliar to many other parts of the nation.

States do not respond to natural disasters without a request for help from the local (usually county-level) jurisdiction. The structure for processing these requests largely parallels that at the federal level, with the request going to the state emergency management agency, which processes the request with a recommendation to the governor, who may then issue a state emergency declaration and, if the situation warrants, request a federal disaster declaration from the president through equivalent channels.

Although state disaster legislation varies, most states provide a means for the governor to delegate special powers to his state emergency management director or some similar departmental executive. These powers are primarily designed to allow the director to marshal resources from a variety of involved state agencies and to allocate and coordinate them as appropriate.

The governor's personal role is also that of primary communicator. Just as the city manager or mayor must control and direct the flow of information at a local level, so must the governor assume responsibility for keeping the news media informed. There may be many public information officers in all the state agencies involved, but in a disaster that requires the coordination of a wide array of state resources, it is important that such communication be channeled through and coordinated by the governor's press secretary. And, as with so many other facets of disaster management, the governor's functions will be better coordinated if a coherent plan and policy for handling the aftermath of natural disasters exist before the actual disaster. It is next to impossible for the governor's staff to make up such a plan as the crisis evolves.

The same function of executive leadership that is important at the local level is paramount at the state level. Only the governor can take effective responsibility for relationships with the federal government in the event of a presidentially declared disaster, and it is to the governor that local executives will look for the resolution of important policy decisions concerning state aid, the use of state emergency powers, and the coordination of governmental relationships within a broad affected area of the state.

Finally, there is the issue of reviewing the performance of state government after the crisis recedes. Was the state well enough prepared? What could have been done better? What mitigation and planning efforts could help to avert all or part of the type of disaster that occurred? What new information was gathered? What information is still needed? What new legislation may be warranted? These are just a few of the questions the governor and the state emergency management agency should be asking as a means of improving future performance (Solyst 1990).

THE ROAD TO A DISASTER DECLARATION

What constitutes a major disaster? Nature dispenses the impacts of its hazards along a wide spectrum of severity, from small tremors, inconsequential flooding, and merely brisk winds to major shifts in tectonic plates, miles of rampaging waters, and winds that wrench whole buildings from their foundations. Somewhere along that spectrum, a society decides that

Figure 2–4. The Presidential Disaster Declaration Process

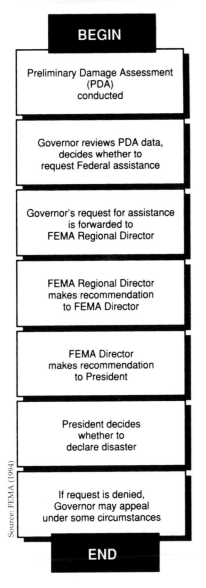

Source: FEMA (1994)

the impacts are great enough to justify outside assistance to the affected communities.

The decision as to when a community or state can no longer rely strictly on its own resources to respond to a crisis is inherently political. A nation may establish reasonable and consistent guidelines for making those decisions, but the very idea of providing outside aid to stricken communities emanates from some set of commonly held values.

Once a nation decides on a set of criteria for dispensing aid to disaster victims, it still must confront the logistical problems of implementing it. The difficulty of dispensing food to starving victims of prolonged drought in certain parts of Africa has demonstrated that the effectiveness of our generosity hinges also on the resources and infrastructure available for delivering aid. Temporary impediments can exist even in highly developed nations. In 1992, for instance, the severity of damage from Hurricane Andrew to local infrastructure in southern Dade County, Florida, delayed the arrival of outside help to many families by several days (Moore 1992).

In the United States, the policies that underlie the current process for determining the need for various types of disaster assistance have been evolving for nearly a half century. Congress first legislated a consistent policy on federal disaster assistance in 1950 (May 1985). That legislation, for the first time, empowered the president to issue a disaster declaration and release specific types of assistance without first obtaining congressional authorization. All previous disaster aid had depended on specific acts of Congress authorizing aid for victims of individual natural disasters.

While the process of obtaining a presidential disaster declaration is relatively straightforward (see Figure 2-4), it is worth understanding that the recovery and reconstruction process triggered by the disaster can be very complex. At the local, state, and even federal levels, a variety of agencies must respond and react to one another in ways that vary significantly from their ordinary relationships. For that reason, this chapter will not only outline the process of declaring a natural disaster but also discuss the roles of the many players involved, particularly at the local level.

It is often clear very early that an emergency is serious enough to warrant state or federal consideration for a disaster declaration. Within minutes after the Loma Prieta earthquake, for example, the damage was apparent and pervasive throughout the San Francisco Bay Area and near the epicenter further south near Monterey Bay. Well before Hurricanes Hugo and Andrew came ashore, weather officials knew that they were packing powerful winds, and Andrew already was being referred to as the Big One. In these cases, it is possible almost from the outset for state and local officials to enlist federal assistance in assessing the extent of the damage and determining the amount of outside help needed to effect recovery.

However, it is important for planners to know that the vast majority of emergencies stemming from events involving natural hazards do not lead to any sort of disaster declaration at all. Instead, they are handled adequately at a purely local level. Occasionally, they may require the implementation of various sorts of intergovernmental aid agreements among neighboring municipalities and state agencies. Presidential disaster declarations are the rarity, the result of unusually severe events that tax local and even state resources to the breaking point. Such declarations loom large in the public's mind, however, because they get the greatest news media attention.

One special part of the local response system that should be mentioned here, however, is the Incident Command System (ICS), which FEMA (1997a) describes as providing "a standardized means to command, control, and coordinate the use of resources and personnel at the scene of an emergency."

Major Federal Legislation Defining Disaster Policy

1950   Federal Disaster Relief Act (P.L. 81-875)

Until this time, Congress enacted separate laws providing relief for each specific disaster, doing so 128 times starting in 1803. This act for the first time established a process whereby a governor could request a presidential disaster declaration and authorized the president to provide supplementary federal assistance by making such a declaration.

1966   Disaster Relief Act of 1966 (P.L. 89-769)

Amendments to the 1950 act made rural communities eligible and extended funding for repairs to higher education facilities and public facilities under construction.

1968   National Flood Insurance Act (P.L. 90-448)

This act initiated the National Flood Insurance Program (NFIP), linking it to actions taken by local governments to reduce flooding risks in local hazard-prone areas. Subsequent amendments have refined and strengthened those links, but the basic NFIP structure remains intact.

1969   Disaster Relief Act of 1969 (P.L. 91-79)

Another extension of existing federal relief provisions authorized funding for debris removal from private property, revised loan programs of the Small Business Administration, Federal Housing Administration, and Veterans Administration, and authorized food coupons and unemployment compensation for disaster victims.

1970   Disaster Assistance Act of 1970 (P.L. 91-606)

New types of aid were added to existing federal relief, including individual assistance for temporary housing and relocation, legal services funding, and payments to communities to remunerate tax losses.

1973   Flood Disaster Protection Act (P.L. 93-234)

Congress amended the NFIP by linking the availability of federal and federally related financial assistance for buildings in Special Flood Hazard Areas to the purchase of a flood insurance policy on those buildings. This included mortgage loans and disaster assistance and introduced the concept of sharing the cost to those at risk.

1974   Disaster Relief Act of 1974 (P.L. 93-288)

Following Hurricane Agnes in 1972, Congress undertook a number of changes in federal disaster policy, including strengthening some provisions of NFIP. When tornadoes spun across 10 states on "Terrible Tuesday," April 3, 1974, Congress was spurred to consolidate many of these changes in permanent disaster policy. The act distinguished "major disasters" from "emergencies," thus providing some legal criteria for disaster declarations, and provided funding for local and state disaster planning.

1977   Earthquake Hazards Reduction Act (P.L. 95-124)

Under this act, spending was increased and a multiagency research effort on earthquake hazards was established, now headed by FEMA.

1979   Creation of Federal Emergency Management Agency (FEMA)

Prior to the Carter administration, federal disaster assistance functions were housed in a variety of agencies, being reorganized several times over the previous two decades. A series of presidential executive orders creating FEMA allowed the consolidation of a number of civil defense and natural disaster management functions under the roof of a single emergency-related agency.

1988   Robert T. Stafford Disaster Relief and Emergency Assistance Act (P.L. 93-288, as amended)

Current federal disaster relief policy and procedures largely stem from this landmark piece of legislation, which established cost-sharing requirements for public assistance programs, provides funds for states and local governments to manage such projects, and provides grants for hazard mitigation efforts and planning. The cost-sharing concept originated with the federal response to the volcanic eruption at Mt. St. Helen's in the state of Washington in 1980, in which the state provided 25 percent of the assistance costs. The Stafford Act is the cornerstone on which FEMA has built its growing emphasis on hazard mitigation.

1994   National Flood Insurance Reform Act (P.L. 103-325)

The 1993 Midwest floods triggered a great deal of federal and state soul searching on the focus and effectiveness of existing floodplain management policy. A major new feature (among nearly 40 changes) in this revision of the original flood insurance legislation established a flood mitigation fund, which provides flood planning and mitigation assistance grants to state and local governments replacing the previous forms of mitigation assistance under NFIP. It also provides new insurance coverage for the increased cost of compliance with NFIP mitigation requirements, such as building elevation.

Disaster Declarations: What Does FEMA Consider?

- How extensive is the damage?

- What is the nature of the damage?

- What is the impact of these losses on people, businesses, and government?

- What state, local, and non-profit resources are already available?

- What kind and amount of insurance will cover the losses?

- What federal assistance is available that does not require a declaration?

- What is the danger to health, life, and safety?

- What is the context in terms of other recent disasters in the state?

The designation of an incident commander varies with individual communities but allows someone to be in charge of personnel from the variety of agencies involved. Although this concept has its roots in the management of hazardous materials emergencies, it has become increasingly useful for natural hazards emergencies as well. More information on this is available not only in FEMA's *Guide for All-Hazard Emergency Operations Planning* but also in the International City/County Management Association's *Emergency Management: Principles and Practice for Local Government* (Drabek and Hoetmer 1991).

Although no one has a precise figure, FEMA estimates that approximately 3,500 disasters are handled locally each year without assistance. In contrast, from 1982 to 1991, FEMA received an average of 38 requests yearly for presidential disaster declarations, of which an average of 27, or 71 percent, were granted. In other words, less than one percent of a typical year's disasters are severe enough to warrant such aid (FEMA 1994). A larger number of less severe disasters resulted in state emergency declarations, usually made by a governor under that state's authorizing statutes, which vary considerably. These, in effect, release various forms of state aid without tapping those resources of the federal government whose release requires a presidential declaration.

For now, however, let us assume that the disaster is of major proportions. The first step for local and state officials is to declare an emergency, which then establishes their authority to take such measures as reallocating resources to handle the disaster, spend emergency allocations, and secure assistance from other jurisdictions and outside sources. (See the sidebar for definitions of "major disaster" and "emergency.") After various response activities are undertaken, such as search and rescue, reopening blocked roads and highways, and completing secondary evacuations, local and state officials, including the governor's office, can conduct a preliminary damage assessment (PDA), whose purpose is to document the need for federal assistance. If it is already assumed that the disaster may lead to such a declaration, the initiative for this effort—and an invitation to federal officials to participate in conducting the PDA—is likely to come from the governor's office. The request for a presidential declaration must come from a state's governor, who must review the PDA data in order to decide whether to request federal assistance. In an obvious major disaster like Hurricane Andrew, the PDA may be relatively quick and cursory because the need is already clear. In less obvious situations, a more detailed assessment may be necessary to make clear that the disaster really is of proportions that justify federal assistance.

Circumstances may dictate the way in which a PDA is conducted. Major natural disasters often complicate emergency access for damage assessment personnel. For example, where major highways are flooded or bridges have collapsed, officials may be forced to resort mostly to aerial surveys.

The information compiled in a PDA serves more purposes than simply justifying a presidential declaration. It is also extremely valuable for focusing assistance efforts with or without the declaration by documenting the nature, location, and extent of needs resulting from the disaster, both to the public sector (e.g., repairs to public facilities, fire and safety equipment) and to families and businesses (e.g., public health personnel, relocation assistance, temporary housing). PDA data invariably become essential front-line management guidance once disaster relief efforts get underway. Mitigation issues can also be identified in the PDA; it is becoming more commonplace to include mitigation staff on PDAs in larger disasters.

Once the governor has determined that the damage justifies a request for a presidential declaration, the request is forwarded to the director of the regional FEMA office. (See Appendix D.) With the help of regional staff, the regional director can then develop an appropriate recommendation for acceptance or denial and forward the request to the FEMA director. The FEMA director reviews the information and makes a final recommendation to the president, who must decide whether to grant the disaster declaration.

At both the state and federal level, a disaster declaration releases assistance to the stricken area in accordance with state and federal legislation authorizing disaster aid. The nature of that aid is discussed both in the last part of this chapter and in the model ordinance in Chapter 4. However, it is also important to know that some agencies at both levels are free to provide disaster assistance without a Stafford Act declaration because of other authorizing legislation, provided that the state, as a precursor to federal assistance, has already provided assistance under its own emergency declaration. For instance, the U.S. Department of Agriculture can provide aid through both its Emergency Conservation Program, which can aid farmers in replacing damaged fencing or in removing debris from cropland, and its Livestock Feed Program, which can help replace damaged livestock feed supplies following a disaster. The Small Business Administration has some similar programs whereby assistance can be provided through direct requests to the agency without a Stafford Act declaration (FEMA 1995a).

Federal Government Roles

As noted earlier, only about 1 percent of all natural disasters in any given year lead to a presidential disaster declaration. Disasters that warrant such a declaration, however, produce a vastly disproportionate and largely unpredictable share of the overall damage suffered in any given year. Because of the magnitude of the worst natural disasters, it became essential for the federal government to organize and rationalize its management of the wide-ranging resources it can tap to handle such crises. The recognition of that managerial need led to the development of the FRP under the authority of the Stafford Act (FEMA 1998). Under the FRP, FEMA is the designated lead agency in managing the response to a presidentially declared catastrophic disaster. The purpose of this section is to delineate the roles and responsibilities of the various federal agencies involved in disaster response and to summarize the workings of the FRP.

In discussing the use of federal disaster assistance, it is critical to understand two essential points:

- Federal assistance is strictly supplemental to state and local resources; and

- The needs for assistance engendered by the disaster must exceed the capacities of both state and local governments to address them.

The number of federal agencies and departments involved in disaster response in some way is too large to analyze all their responsibilities here. Only a few key agencies whose aid and functions are critical to post-disaster response and recovery will be discussed in detail in this section. But Figure 2–5, drawn from the FRP, serves to illustrate the range and diversity of agencies and tasks that can be mustered into action to support federal response to a major disaster. Readers who wish to gain a full understanding of the plan are advised to order a copy from FEMA. (See Appendix C.)

Major Disasters and Emergencies

Under the Robert T. Stafford Disaster Relief and Emergency Assistance Act, two categories of events may trigger the release of federal funds and assistance:

A *major disaster* is defined as "any natural catastrophe (including any hurricane, tornado, storm, high water, wind-driven water, tidal wave, tsunami, earthquake, volcanic eruption, landslide, mudslide, snowstorm, or drought), or, regardless of cause, any fire, flood, or explosion, in any part of the United States, which in the determination of the President causes damage of sufficient severity and magnitude to warrant major disaster assistance under this Act to supplement the efforts and available resources of States, local governments, and disaster relief organizations in alleviating damage, loss, hardship, or suffering caused thereby."

An *emergency* is defined as "any occasion or instance for which, in the determination of the President, Federal assistance is needed to supplement State and local efforts and capabilities to save lives and protect property and public health and safety, or to lessen or avert the threat of a catastrophe in any part of the United States."

Source: Robert T. Stafford Disaster Relief and Assistance Act (P.L. 93-288, as amended by P.L. 100-707), Sec. 102.

The summary descriptions that follow are drawn from the Emergency Support Function (ESF) annexes of the FRP. These annexes, which make up the bulk of the document, describe specific functions and designate the primary agency for managing each function as well as the supporting agencies working with them. Note from the chart, however, that for each lead agency below, many others are playing important supportive roles in helping them achieve their objectives.

Agencies Other Than FEMA

Department of Transportation (DOT). As noted in the discussion of local agencies, transportation systems are often severely disrupted in a major disaster. DOT's role is to ensure that relief agencies are able to deliver supplies and personnel where they are needed with whatever resources it can muster for the purpose. This includes both establishing effective communications concerning the condition of major access routes and the use of transport modes, such as helicopters, that can bypass obstructions.

National Communications System (NCS). Local communications infrastructure is often another prime casualty of storm or earthquake damage. The National Telecommunications Support Plan authorizes NCS to plan for and manage telecommunications support for federal agencies in such emergencies. With whatever emergency equipment is needed, the NCS's goal is to maintain the flow of accurate and timely information for the disaster relief agencies involved.

Department of Defense (DOD). The DOD has the lead role in handling public works and engineering needs through the U.S. Army Corps of Engineers. The task includes the clearing of debris along major access routes, the construction of emergency access routes, the restoration of essential services such as water delivery, and other kinds of technical assistance.

Department of Agriculture (USDA). Fighting wildfires is a long-time area of expertise for the USDA's Forest Service, and the agency coordinates this task when firefighting is needed in a major disaster. This function may not be limited explicitly to urban wildfires, however, for fires and explosions are a common byproduct of the disruptions caused by earthquakes. USDA is also responsible for the transportation of food assistance to disaster-stricken areas after identifying such needs. This includes authorizing, as necessary, disaster food stamp assistance.

American Red Cross. The Red Cross is chartered by an act of Congress dating to 1905 to assume responsibility for the mass care of disaster victims, and the FRP grants the organization lead agency responsibility in this area. Other private relief agencies assisting in disasters coordinate their efforts through the Red Cross, whose specific missions include provision of shelter, food, and emergency first aid for victims and operation of a Disaster Welfare Information System to "collect, report, and receive information" about victims and to aid family reunification. It is worth noting that the other private relief agencies belong to an umbrella organization called National Voluntary Organizations Active in Disasters (NVOAD), which maintains a liaison with FEMA and seeks to foster communication, coordination, and cooperation among its member groups. Because of its congressional charter and authorization under later legislation, most significantly the Disaster Relief Act of 1974 (P.L. 93-288), the Red Cross operates under a set of regulations governing disaster relief management.

General Services Administration (GSA). Logistical and resource support for other federal agencies is GSA's everyday function, but it takes on a special significance when time is precious and procurement must take place on an emergency basis. GSA has the authority to marshal the needed supplies for federal post-disaster functions and to allocate them where they are needed.

Figure 2-5. Federal Response Plan Emergency Support Functions (ESF)

ESF #1: TRANSPORTATION

Coordinate Federal transportation support to State and local governments, voluntary organizations, and Federal agencies performing disaster assistance missions.

Primary Agency: DOT

Support Agencies: USDA, DOD, DOS, Treasury, FEMA, GSA, TVA, USPS

ESF #2: COMMUNICATIONS

Provide Federal telecommunications support to response efforts and establish temporary telecommunications.

Primary Agency: NCS

Support Agencies: USDA, DOC, DOD, DOI, FCC, FEMA, GSA

ESF #3: PUBLIC WORKS AND ENGINEERING

Provide public works and engineering support to assist State(s) in lifesaving or property protection.

Primary Agency: DOD

Support Agencies: USDA, DOC, HHS, DOI, DOL, VA, EPA, TVA

ESF #4: FIREFIGHTING

Detect and suppress wildland, rural, and urban fire resulting from or occurring with a disaster or other event requiring Federal response.

Primary Agency: USDA

Support Agencies: DOC, DOD, DOI, EPA, FEMA

ESF #5: INFORMATION AND PLANNING

Collect, process, and disseminate critical information about a potential or actual disaster or emergency, to facilitate Federal response activities.

Primary Agency: FEMA

Support Agencies: USDA, DOC, DOD, DOEd, DOE, HHS, DOI, DOJ, DOT, Treasury, ARC, EPA, GSA, NASA, NCS, NRC, SBA

ESF #6: MASS CARE

Provide coordination for sheltering, feeding, and emergency first aid efforts; collect, receive, and report status of victims and assist family reunification; coordinate bulk distribution of relief supplies.

Primary Agency: ARC

Support Agencies: USDA, DOD, HHS, HUD, VA, FEMA, GSA, USPS

ESF #7: RESOURCE SUPPORT

Provide logistical and resource support to Federal entities.

Primary Agency: GSA

Support Agencies: USDA, DOC, DOD, DOE, DOL, DOT, Treasury, VA, FEMA, NASA, NCS, OPM

ESF #8: HEALTH AND MEDICAL SERVICES

Supplement State and local public health and medical care resources.

Primary Agency: HHS

Support Agencies: USDA, DOD, DOE, DOJ, DOT, VA, AID, ARC, EPA, FEMA, GSA, NCS

ESF #9: URBAN SEARCH AND RESCUE

Coordinate Federal resources to locate, extricate, and provide initial medical treatment to victims trapped in collapsed structures.

Primary Agency: FEMA

Support Agencies: USDA, DOD, HHS, DOJ, DOL, AID, NASA

ESF #10: HAZARDOUS MATERIALS

Provide Federal support in response to actual or potential releases of hazardous materials.

Primary Agency: EPA

Support Agencies: USDA, DOC, DOD, DOE, HHS, DOI, DOJ, DOL, DOS, DOT, NRC

ESF #12: ENERGY

Facilitate restoration of the Nation's energy systems.

Primary Agency: DOE

Support Agencies: USDA, DOD, DOI, DOS, DOT, NCS, NRC, TVA

ESF #11: FOOD

Identify food assistance needs; obtain and transfer food supplies.

Primary Agency: USDA

Support Agencies: DOD, HHS, ARC, EPA, FEMA, GSA

ABBREVIATIONS:

USDA	U.S. Department of Agriculture	**AID**	Agency for International Development
DOC	U.S. Department of Commerce	**ARC**	American Red Cross
DOD	U.S. Department of Defense	**EPA**	U.S. Environmental Protection Agency
DOEd	U.S. Department of Education	**FCC**	Federal Communications Commission
DOE	U.S. Department of Energy	**FEMA**	Federal Emergency Management Agency
HHS	U.S. Department of Health and Human Services	**GSA**	General Services Administration
HUD	U.S. Department of Housing and Urban Development	**NASA**	National Aeronautics and Space Administration
DOI	U.S. Department of the Interior	**NCS**	National Communications System
DOJ	U.S. Department of Justice	**NRC**	Nuclear Regulatory Commission
DOL	U.S. Department of Labor	**OPM**	Office of Planning and Management
DOS	U.S. Department of State	**SBA**	Small Business Administration
DOT	U.S. Department of Transportation	**TVA**	Tennessee Valley Authority
VA	U.S. Department of Veterans Affairs	**USPS**	U.S. Postal Service

Source: FEMA 1998d.

Essential Elements of Information

THE FEDERAL RESPONSE PLAN, EMERGENCY SUPPORT FOUNDATION (ESF) #5

a. Boundaries of the disaster area

b. Social/economic/political impacts

c. Jurisdictional boundaries

d. Status of transportation systems

e. Status of communications systems

f. Access points to the disaster area

g. Status of operating facilities

h. Hazard-specific information

i. Weather data affecting operations

j. Seismic or other geophysical information

k. Status of critical facilities

l. Status of aerial reconnaisance activities

m. Status of key personnel

n. Status of ESF activation

o. Status of emergency or disaster declaration

p. Major issues/activities of ESFs

q. Resource shortfalls

r. Overall priorities for response

s. Status of upcoming activities

t. Donations

u. Historical information

Department of Health and Human Services, U.S. Public Health Service. In a truly major disaster, it is all too possible for local and state medical resources to be overwhelmed by the number of disaster victims needing emergency or long-term assistance. When such federal aid is requested, the Public Health Service can take responsibility for any of 16 functional areas ranging from controlling the spread of disease-causing agents to patient evacuation to mortuary services. This being no small function, it should be no surprise that this ESF consumes more pages in the FRP than any other.

Environmental Protection Agency (EPA). Although not always necessary, the cleanup, removal, or deactivation of toxic and hazardous materials following a disaster is undoubtedly one of the touchiest and most dangerous tasks imaginable. EPA heads a National Response Team of 15 agencies involved in this task to manage environmental and public health responsibilities for oil and hazardous substance releases. As our society has come to depend on a growing number of exotic and hazardous chemicals for all sorts of routine business activities, such as dry cleaning, heavy industrial manufacturing, and transportation, releases of these materials as the result of terrorist acts, civil disturbances, and technological accidents, as well as natural disasters, are a source of increasing concern. This is also, however, an area where strict local regulations concerning storage and disposal can have a significant mitigating impact.

Department of Energy (DOE). Power and fuel are critical in a modern society, yet the delivery and storage systems on which people depend can be vulnerable to damage from a natural disaster regardless of the typical precautions taken to safeguard them. In the 1993 Midwest floods, for example, the Union Electric Company's Sioux electric power station in St. Charles County, Missouri, was surrounded by flood waters and came within one week of exhausting its stockpile of coal before the waters receded. DOE handles the assessment of damage and aids energy suppliers in meeting public needs through technical assistance and by recommending federal actions to conserve energy, and through a variety of public information and logistical functions.

FEMA and the Federal Response Plan

Emergency operations in a major disaster obviously involve a multitude of players and require a wide range of resources. What keeps all of this organized and operating with some semblance of efficiency? That is the purpose of the FRP, and it is also the reason that FEMA is the lead federal agency coordinating the management of the FRP. The purpose of the final section of this chapter is to describe the managerial structure of federal disaster operations.

Before summarizing the overall disaster management structure, it should be noted that FEMA has lead agency responsibility for two of the 12 ESFs. These are ESF #5, the information and planning annex, whose purpose is to "collect, process, and disseminate information about a potential or actual disaster or emergency to facilitate the overall activities of the federal government in providing response assistance to an affected state," and ESF #9, which involves managing national urban search and rescue response system resources. In the first role, FEMA specifically lists 21 essential elements of information commonly needed to facilitate response activities. These are listed in the accompanying sidebar. This ESF is important for planning purposes because it opens the door for creative interaction by state and local planners with FEMA on issues like the development of geographic information systems for mapping local hazard zones and tracking damage reports (Topping 1994).

The size and scope of any disaster operations depend, naturally, on the nature and scope of the disaster itself. When the full range of resources must be deployed, the operation can become quite complex, as illustrated in Figure 2–5, but this is fortunately not always the case. Nonetheless, it is important to close with this particular chart to show not only the relationships that can exist within the federal response to a major disaster but also the overall network of responsibilities that must be fulfilled. It is rather humbling to think about the number of people whose efforts may be necessary to help restore some semblance of normalcy after the initial hours of chaos.

Recognizing that disasters often do not produce the need for federal response resources, but do require federal and state recovery and mitigation programs and resources, the newest version of the FRP contains a Recovery Function Annex. This annex describes the structure and coordination activities to carry out federal disaster programs, and technical and financial support that assist state and local governments, individuals, and businesses. Appendix C, adapted from this annex, describes the array of federal resources available from various federal agencies for recovery purposes.

The Stafford Act designates FEMA to serve as a coordinator for the delivery of federal recovery resources. Note that this is different from managing or directing operations. In this role, FEMA ensures that the needs articulated by the state(s) are addressed appropriately, given each agency's statutory or legislative authorities. It should be noted that, in this section of the FRP, it is emphasized that it is the responsibility of state and local governments to identify and rank such recovery needs. It further states that ranking these needs should be done in close partnership with the federal government, with collaboration continuing through the implementation of program resources.

And that is only the beginning. If planners have done an adequate pre-disaster job of identifying the opportunities for reconstructing a better and safer community, it then becomes their role to implement their well-laid plans for doing so. If planners have established effective rapport and coordination with other local, state, and federal officials involved in disaster recovery, they will be more effective in pursuing that goal. Planning for that possibility is the subject of the next chapter.

> If planners have done an adequate pre-disaster job of identifying the opportunities for reconstructing a better and safer community, it then becomes their role to implement their well-laid plans for doing so. If planners have established effective rapport and coordination with other local, state, and federal officials involved in disaster recovery, they will be more effective in pursuing that goal.

Chapter 3

Policies for Guiding Planning for Post-Disaster Recovery and Reconstruction

Every plan has a purpose. Under the U.S. Constitution, land-use planning has been used to advance legitimate state purposes concerning public health, welfare, and safety. Beneath these broad categories are a number of more specific policy objectives that justify a wide range of plans, plan elements, and accompanying regulations. Chapter 6 of this report deals with the legal issues surrounding land-use planning concerning natural hazards. The focus of this chapter is on establishing the policy objectives that underlie the exercise of developing plans for post-disaster recovery and reconstruction.

Simply put, the driving factors behind such plans are public safety and economic recovery, the latter obviously being a specific aspect of the public welfare. Allowing unwise and inadequately protected development in locations known to involve serious dangers from natural hazards amounts to a failure of planning to serve one of its most vital public functions. If planners take great care in many communities to separate residential housing from noxious industrial fumes or vibrations, or to establish minimum distances of churches and schools from sexually oriented businesses, does it make less sense to keep homes and schools out of the path of floods and landslides? Even more to the point, if a post-disaster situation affords the opportunity to remedy some past land-use planning mistakes in this regard, does it make sense for the community to forego such opportunities simply because it failed to plan for them?

By the same token, if planners involved in economic development take great care to try to attract an effective mix of industrial and commercial uses that will enhance the local economy and make best use of its labor pool and other resources, is it wise to put all that at risk by failing to consider how the local economy can be protected from the impact of natural disasters? Both the business community and working residents have a major stake in plans that help to ensure a quick and efficient recovery from whatever economic devastation may occur in a natural disaster. A plan for post-disaster recovery and reconstruction that is well crafted to assist business recovery, ideally with the aid of a local redevelopment agency that has given serious thought to such contingencies, clearly is a major means of advancing the public welfare.

Nonetheless, only half the states, in their planning enabling statutes, mention natural hazards at all as a concern that should or may be addressed in comprehensive plans. Of those, only 11 mandate some sort of planning for natural hazards, either in the form of a distinct natural hazards element (sometimes referred to as a safety element, as in California and Nevada) or in the form of hazards-related content in another element (as in Maryland, where certain natural hazards must be addressed in a sensitive areas element). Of those 11, only Florida includes a requirement for a local plan for post-storm recovery, and the mandate applies only in coastal counties.

This information (see Figure 3-1) was gathered while preparing the model state planning legislation for APA's Growing Smart℠ *Legislative Guidebook*.

Figure 3–1. State Enabling Statutes with Natural Hazards Content

1 State	2 Local Plan Mandated	3 State Land Use Policy Basis	4 Strength of State Role	5 Internal Consistency Required	6 Hazard Statute Citation	7 Jurisdictions Covered	8 Hazards Element Mandatory?	9 Discrete Hazards Element	10 Geographic Coverage	11 Which Hazards Specified	12 Post-Disaster Recovery Element	13 State Technical Assistance
AZ	P(CT, T); M(C)	N	1	N	11-806.B.	C, CT	CT>50,000	Y	All	C (F), CT (H, G)	N	DOC-DMG; OES
CA	M(C, CT)	N	2	Y	65302(g); 65302(e)(7)	C, CT	Y	Y	All	G,T,S,F,W	N	
CO	P(C, CT)	N	1	N	30-28-106; 31-23-206	C, CT	N	N	All	F	N	
FL	M(C,CT)	Y	3	Y	163.3177 (6)(g) and (7)(h) and (l); 163.3178	C, CT	Y	Y	Coastal River corridors	C,W,F	Y	DCA
GA	M(C, MN)	Y	3	Y	12-2-8	C, MN	N	N	All	F*	N	
ID	M(C, CT)	N	2	N	67-6508(g)	All	Y	Y	All	G,S,F	N	
IN	P(C, CT)	N	1	N	36-7-4-503	All	N	N/Flood control & irrigation	All	F	N	
IA	O(CT)	N	1	N	281.4	?	N	N	All	F	N	
KY	M(C>300K); M(CT>300K); P(C)	N	2	Y	100.187 (5)	Same as column 3	N	Y	All	F	N	
LA	P(P, MN)	N	1	N	R.S. 33:107	P, MN	N	N/Growth areas implementation strategy	All	W,H	N	
ME	P(CT, T)	Y	3	Y	30-A 4326.A(1)(d)	MN	Y	N/Sensitive areas	All	F	N	
MD	P(C, MN)	Y	3	Y	3.05(a)(1)(viii)	C, MN	Y	N	All	F,S	N	DNR
MI	P(CT, V, TP, C)	N	1	N	125.36	All	N	N	All	F	N	
MT	P(CT, T, C)	N	1	N	76-1-601(2)(h)	C, T, CT	N	N	All	F	N	
NV	M(C, CT)	N	2	N	278.160.1(k) and (l)	All	Y	Y	Seismic-all; safety plan- C>400,000	G,F,W,S	N	CRC, EMC
NC	O(C, CT)	N	1	N	113A-110 ff.	C	Y	Y	Coastal	F,C	N	
OR	M(C, CT)	N	1	Y	197.175	C, CT	Y	Y	All	F,T,E?	N	LCDC

Figure 3–1. State Enabling Statutes with Natural Hazards Content (continued)

State	Local Plan Mandated	State Land Use Policy Basis	Strength of State Role	Internal Consistency Required	Hazard Statute Citation	Jurisdictions Covered	Hazards Element Mandatory?	Discrete Hazards Element	Geographic Coverage	Which Hazards Specified	Post-Disaster Recovery Element	State Technical Assistance
PA	P(C, CT, T, TP, B)	N	2	N	10301(2)	All	Y	N/Land use	All	F,H	N	
RI	M(CT, T)	Y	3	Y	45-22.2-6(E)	CT, T	Y	N/Natural and coastal resources	All	F	N	CRC
SC	P(C, CT, T)	N	2	N	6-7-510	C, CT, T	N	N	Coastal	F, H (under Beachfront Management Act)	Y (under Beachfront Management Act)	
UT	O(C, T, CT)	N	2	N	10-9-302(2)(c)	C, CT, T	N	N/Environment	All	F,F,S	N	
VT	P(T, CT, V, G)	Y	3	N	4382(a)(2)	All	N	N/Land use	All	F	N	
VA	P(C, T)	N	1	N	15.1-446.1.1	C,T	N	N/Land use	All	F	N	
WA	M(C, CT therein)	Y	3	Y	36.70.330 (1)	C, CT	N	N/Land use	Puget Sound watershed	F	N	
WV	P(C, CT, T, V)	N	2	N	8-24-17(a)(9)	All	N	Y	All	F	N	

Key to Figure 3–1

1. Only those states with statutes that mention natural hazards are listed. There are 25 such states.

2. This overview, which is based on more than one statute, indicates whether municipalities must have a natural hazards or similar element. (See column 7 for a list of specific jurisdictions covered by the state's natural hazards legislation.) The letters M, O, and P are used to indicate whether planning is Mandatory, Optional, or mandated if a Precondition is met (e.g., if a planning commission is created). The other symbols in this column are keyed to type of jurisdiction: B (borough); C (county); CT (city); G (gore); M (municipality); P (parish); T (town); TP (township); and V (village).

3. Indicates whether there is a state land-use policy regarding natural hazards.

4. The state role is classified as 1 = weak; 2 = significant; and 3 = substantial.

5. Indicates whether internal consistency between plans is required.

6. This column provides a citation to the provisions that reference natural hazards. In some cases, these references occur in more than one place (e.g., in enabling legislation covering municipalities and counties). In others, the provisions may be in a part of the state code governing natural resources or coastal zone management.

7. Natural hazards provisions or hazard mitigation planning provisions specifically apply to these types of jurisdictions. See note 2 for the key to jurisdiction types. More elaboration is provided in columns 10 and 11 about geographic coverage and which hazards are specifically covered.

8. Indicates whether a hazards element is mandatory in local planning and which jurisdictions are covered, along with population requirement, if any. See column 9 to see whether the mandate is for a discrete plan element focused on natural hazards or a mandate to include natural hazards in a related element (e.g., environment or land use). See also columns 10 and 11 for the specifics of the mandate.

9. Y indicates that a discrete natural hazards plan element is required. N indicates that the issue of natural hazards is covered in another element, which is named after the slash. For example, steep slopes and floodplains are mentioned in the mandatory sensitive areas element in the Maryland statutes.

10. A few states apply the natural hazards element mandate only to areas of the state; those areas are specified here.

11. Indicates which types of hazards are mentioned in the state legislation. The key is as follows: C (coastal storm); E (earthquake); F (floodplain); G (geologic hazards generally); H (all hazards generally); S (slope-related hazards, including hillside erosion, avalanches, and landslides); T (tsunami); V (volcano); and W (wildfire).

12. Only one state in this column has a post-disaster recovery element; we include this column to draw attention to this device as a distinct element from the natural hazards element. Such an element would not just identify hazards; it would identify how a community plans to rebuild so as to become less vulnerable to future disasters.

13. This column provides a shorthand for the agencies that provide assistance in the preparation of a natural hazards element. In California, these agencies are the Department of Conservation, Division of Mining and Geology (DOC-DMG) and the Office of Emergency Services (OES). In Florida, it is the Department of Community Affairs (DCA). In Maryland, it is the Department of Natural Resources (DNR). In North Carolina, it is the Coastal Resources Commission (CRC) and Environmental Management Commission (EMC). In Oregon, it is the Land Conservation and Development Commission (LCDC). And in Rhode Island, it is the Coastal Resources Center (CRC).

Model Post-Disaster Plan Language for a Natural Hazards Element

**(Chapter 7, Section 7-210, of the *Growing Smart*ˢᴹ *Legislative Guidebook)*

(5) The natural hazards element shall consist of:

. . .

(f) a plan for managing post-disaster recovery and reconstruction. Such a plan shall provide descriptions that include, but are not limited to, lines of authority, interagency and intergovernmental coordination measures, processes for expedited review, permitting, and inspection of repair and reconstruction of buildings and structures damaged by natural disasters. Reconstruction policies in this plan shall be congruent with mitigation policies in this element and in other elements of the local comprehensive plan as well as the legal, procedural, administrative, and operational components of post-disaster recovery and reconstruction.

For the complete text of the Natural Hazards Element, see Appendix E.

Chapter 7 of that guidebook includes legislation and commentary concerning local comprehensive plan elements. Specifically, the work involved drafting statutory language concerning the preparation of a natural hazards element in local comprehensive plans. This language included specific provisions concerning the preparation of a plan for post-disaster recovery and reconstruction.

Two factors should be noted about the general absence of planning enabling statutory provisions concerning natural hazards. First, most states have planning enabling legislation that remains based to varying degrees on the original model statutes promulgated by the U.S. Department of Commerce under Secretary Herbert Hoover in the late 1920s. At that time, research of any type about the pattern of natural disasters and the potential to ameliorate their impact through planning was virtually nonexistent. Consequently, statutes drafted in that era with only modest subsequent revision reflect that lack of awareness of the role that planning could play. Only as legislatures have taken note of the more recent research in this area, or have been prodded to some degree by federal programs, such as NFIP, has this changed in states that have not yet engaged in a wholesale redrafting of planning enabling legislation. However, in states like Florida, Oregon, and Maryland, where planning laws have been completely rewritten, specific provisions concerning natural hazards tend to be included. Even still, only Florida includes planning for post-disaster recovery as part of that process.

Second, while state mandates certainly push communities in the direction of planning for post-disaster recovery and reconstruction, that is not the only way in which such planning happens. Several communities outside the states with mandates have simply taken the initiative of doing such planning on their own and for their own benefit. Los Angeles, concerned about a range of hazards that most significantly includes earthquakes and wildfires, adopted such a plan in early 1994. Arnold, Missouri, highlighted in a case study in Chapter 8, is an example of a city that effectively used its floodplain management plan for this purpose. Part of Chapter 4 will discuss the means by which officials and interested citizens in these and other communities built public support behind the need to develop such a plan.

However the community arrives at the decision to develop its plan, four simple constant factors pervade the process: goals, strategy, priorities, and criteria. These factors apply equally well to hazard mitigation plans intended to be employed before the disaster strikes. First, having decided on the goals for the plan—say, reducing vulnerability to coastal storms by preserving the integrity of barrier islands and ecologically sensitive tidal wetlands—the community must then develop a strategy for achieving that goal. The choice of appropriate strategies will depend on technical data concerning the feasibility of specific strategies for coping with local hazards, political preferences for specific approaches to the problem, and cost implications. Creative planners employ the concept of multiobjective management, in which hazard mitigation objectives are made to coincide with the policy objectives of other stakeholders in the community. Such stakeholders may include parks and recreation advocates who see benefits in preserving a greenbelt and trail system along the riverbank, tourism promoters who may see great value in preserving undisturbed views of the mountainsides just outside the city, or even developers of multifamily housing who can gain a density bonus through a transfer of development rights from hazardous areas. Multiobjective strategies can help to expand the resource base available to accomplish mitigation objectives and thus widen the community's vision of what can be accomplished.

Implementing strategies requires the elaboration of priorities, and the establishment of priorities must be based on clear criteria. Criteria in a plan are the hands-on means for planners to make day-to-day decisions about what actions are more important than others. How does one rank preferences for action in acquiring flood-prone land, for instance? Given an inevitably limited pot of staff time, money, and other resources, decision makers may choose to rank possible acquisitions based on rated criteria, such as elevation, erosion potential, and the contiguity of the parcels being acquired, among other likely considerations. The choices of criteria will vary depending on local circumstances, values, and politics.

One final point in introducing the next section of this chapter deserves repetition throughout the entire discussion of planning for post-disaster recovery and reconstruction. It deals with timing. Hazard mitigation that occurs after a disaster is still hazard mitigation in preparation for another disaster further in the future. Natural disasters are cyclical occurrences. Communities must incorporate that expectation into their planning and their environmental consciousness. Only the interval between disasters will vary with circumstance.

Regardless of the specific natural hazards that must be identified and addressed, planning for post-disaster recovery shares some common elements. Disasters and their aftermaths tend to follow essentially the same sequence of events, with adjustments varying with the scope of the event. Much of this sequence will occur with or without planning, and much of the early research in this area examined communities that lacked plans for post-disaster recovery simply because very few–if any–communities had such plans. What we have gained from disaster recovery research is the knowledge of how to focus the efforts behind such plans to achieve meaningful, lasting results toward sustainability. Achieving sustainability, which, in a disaster-related context, means the ability to survive future natural disasters with minimum loss of life and property, is the overarching goal of planning for post-disaster reconstruction. Policy objectives are the measurable landmarks a community sets out for itself in seeking to achieve that goal. This section is about the process of defining those objectives.

LONG-TERM GOALS AND SHORT-TERM PITFALLS

The immediate post-disaster period is obviously one with immense potential for confusion, or at least for many of those involved to take actions that serve opposite or divergent purposes. Decisions must be made quickly, with little time for reconsideration before new problems urgently demand resolution. Thus, an essential purpose of the plan for post-disaster recovery and reconstruction is to provide some vision that serves as a beacon for decision makers and some framework within which decisions will be taken. However, it is the role of civic leadership to help maintain that focus when it really matters. The policy objective in this respect is to avoid situations in which short-term decisions adversely affect the community's potential for achieving long-term post-disaster goals.

Unexpected contingencies can always arise in the aftermath of a disaster, no matter how good the pre-disaster planning, in large part because no plan developed in the pre-disaster period can anticipate the precise nature of the next disaster. But the plan can provide decision makers with some general guidance as to the policy objectives their decisions must aim to achieve. This serves to minimize unintended consequences and to keep the maximum number of players working toward the same ultimate goals. Communities that develop plans for post-disaster recovery and reconstruction can highlight what they regard as their most essential objectives in what is sometimes called a vision statement in other types of plans. It is, essentially, the place where the community articulates its overall desires with regard to the focus of the plan in question. Because so much is at stake in planning for

Creative planners employ the concept of multiobjective management, in which hazard mitigation objectives are made to coincide with the policy objectives of other stakeholders in the community.

An essential purpose of the plan for post-disaster recovery and reconstruction is to provide some vision that serves as a beacon for decision makers and some framework within which decisions will be taken.

post-disaster recovery and reconstruction, the vision statement should be clear but broad in its view of the positive consequences for the community if the plan is properly implemented. It should provide an overall framework within which more specific policy objectives, discussed below, can fit.

Short-Term Recovery Issues that Affect Long-Term Reconstruction Goals

The vision statement can help provide overall motivation and inspiration for a community to achieve its objectives during post-disaster recovery and reconstruction. But attention to detail also counts for a great deal. Real success in long-term reconstruction stems from both effective plan guidance concerning the big picture and an acute awareness by planners and other local officials involved in post-disaster recovery of the short-term obstacles that often thwart the achievement of those larger goals. Here, we shall explore what those are.

National Weather Service

Winds from Hurricane Hugo in 1989 were powerful enough to blow down the Ben Sawyer Bridge, which connects Sullivans Island and Isle of Palms to the South Carolina mainland. That left island residents with only boat access to their homes and businesses.

One of the earliest messages to arise from modern disaster recovery research was that public decisions taken in the heat of the emergency period immediately following a disaster often compromise significant opportunities to rebuild a safer community for the future. The pressure exerted by residents and property owners to have their disaster-stricken community rebuilt to its pre-disaster form and condition as quickly as possible remains a powerful factor in local, state, and federal emergency management to this day.

There are ways to restrain such pressures and maintain mitigation and other post-disaster goals as high priorities during the process of long-term reconstruction even as the ashes, the rubble, and the water are receding or being cleared away. The secret lies in identifying in advance those decisions that will need to be made after a disaster that are most likely to have long-term repercussions for hazard mitigation. The case studies in the later chapters of this report are replete with examples of these decisions, but listing a few here will serve to illustrate the point:

- the location of temporary housing, which often becomes more permanent than was originally intended

- the siting of temporary business locations, which begin with the aim of allowing local businesses to continue to operate, but may become de facto long-term relocations

- the selection of sites for dumping disaster debris

- road closures and reopenings

- bridge closures and reopenings

- restoration of critical infrastructure that might otherwise have been suitable for relocation

- permitting the reoccupation of homes that have suffered substantial damage

Some tools for this process are already built into the emergency management system. For instance, emergency managers will already have a list of priorities for restoration of vital public facilities following a natural disaster. The local planning department, working with the emergency manager and other city departments responsible for infrastructure development and maintenance, can then review that list to determine areas of potential concern. Various types of damage assessments performed during the early recovery period provide opportunities to assess the effectiveness of previous mitigation efforts. The planning staff can establish a procedure for participating in the assessments themselves or for reviewing these damage assessments to glean any meaningful land-use lessons they may offer. Making effective use of those lessons often requires a planning department to buy time, which can be done through an ordinance establishing the authority for declaring a temporary building permit moratorium during an emergency. The ordinance should provide for necessary exemptions for building activities that are vital to public health and safety during the recovery period, which may include restoring essential public services or constructing an emergency shelter for those rendered homeless by the disaster, and should specify the duration of its effectiveness. More details on this particular planning tool appear in Chapter 5.

> Making effective use of those lessons often requires a planning department to buy time, which can be done through an ordinance establishing the authority for declaring a temporary building permit moratorium during an emergency.

The central element of good decision making in the short-term recovery period following a disaster is the community's designation of a recovery management team that is empowered to monitor the process and implement the community's post-disaster recovery policies. (This is a management team that is distinct in both function and form from the plan development task force that will be discussed at the beginning of Chapter 4.) Relatively few communities have done this to date, but the idea is making headway. Lee County, Florida, and the town of Nags Head, North Carolina, both can claim actual experience in implementing such a policy, and Los Angeles had just barely adopted such a scheme when the Northridge earthquake hit the city in 1994. Although some doubt has been expressed concerning the planning department's effectiveness in the Los Angeles scenario, its limitations following that disaster appear to be attributable to circumstances that include a mayor and city council concerned primarily about business recovery and a pervasive perception within city government that the earthquake did not warrant planning intervention. Nonetheless, prior training may well have internalized many of the mechanisms prescribed in the plan for line agencies performing recovery operations (Spangle Associates and Robert Olson Associates 1997).

The big question for any community establishing such a team is its composition. Figure 3-2 shows the structures used by some of the communities mentioned above. These are larger jurisdictions that have primarily chosen to use department heads representing major agencies that must act quickly during the post-disaster period or have major stakes in the outcome. Representatives of major private-sector agencies, such as the local business community (e.g., Chamber of Commerce) or social service agencies (e.g., United Way) are essential additions to such a task force. Involving private citizens, whether as individuals or as representatives of civic organizations such as block clubs or neighborhood organizations, is critical in enhancing the quality and breadth of input into decision making during this crucial period.

Figure 3-2. Recovery and Reconstruction Task Force Composition

The table below offers a comparison of the organizational composition established by three different Florida counties for task forces empowered to guide recovery and reconstruction following a disaster. In addition, the lead agencies are listed for Los Angeles as designated by its recovery and reconstruction plan, although they do not serve on a task force like those in the three Florida counties. The information is drawn from the *Post-Disaster Redevelopment Guide for Pinellas County*; Lee County Ordinance No. 95-14, adopted August 2, 1995; the *Palm Beach County Post-Disaster Redevelopment Plan*; and the Los Angeles Recovery and Reconstruction Plan.

One interesting point is that Lee County, in a 1990 ordinance, gave its recovery task force a role in pre-disaster mitigation planning, an idea that is worth copying elsewhere. However, it revised this initial structure with the 1995 ordinance, which established a two-tier arrangement in which a new Post-Disaster Recovery Task Force (RTF) is mobilized after a disaster while containing, as ex-officio members, the members of a separate Disaster Advisory Council (DAC), which officially replaced the former recovery task force. Thus, in the Lee County column below, positions are followed in parentheses by designations of either RTF, DAC, or both. The Lee County ordinance also specifies four positions, with specific listed duties, to be filled by recommendations from the task force. These are disaster recovery coordinator, economic recovery coordinator, hazard mitigation coordinator, and tourism recovery coordinator. Also, "other representatives" may be added by the county administrator in Pinellas County. The Palm Beach County plan seems to leave room for other representatives but does not make clear who would designate them.

Finally, because jurisdictions often use different titles to describe similar functions, the generic term is used in the Member column, but any unique label that a specific county applies to that function is used in that county's box in place of the "x" that otherwise designates that the director of that agency is part of the task force. Where someone else is officially designated to represent the agency, that is also noted in the box.

MEMBER	PINELLAS	LEE	PALM BEACH	LOS ANGELES
County Administrator/Mayor	X	RTF/DAC	X	Mayor
Legislative Liaison				Chief Legislative Analyst
Emergency Management				Emergency Operations Board
Clerk's Office				X
Public Safety	Civil Emergency Services	RTF/DAC	X	Police/Fire
Planning & Zoning	X	Local planning agency member (DAC)	Planning, Zoning and Building	City Planning
Public Works	X	RTF/DAC	County Engineer	X
Transportation		Transportation Director and Transit Director (both DAC)	Surface Transportation	X
Building	X		*see Planning and Zoning above	Building & Safety
Environment	Environmental Management		Environmental Resources Management	Environmental Affairs
Legal	X	DAC		X
Fire Chief		Representative of County Fire Chiefs Association (DAC)	X	
General Services	X	Admininistrative Services Director (DAC)		X

(continued)

Figure 3-2. Recovery and Reconstruction Task Force Composition (continued)

MEMBER	PINELLAS	LEE	PALM BEACH	LOS ANGELES
Utilities	X	DAC		Telecommunications/ Water and Power
Risk Management	X			
Social Services	X	Human Services (DAC)	X	
Management and Budget	X	Budget Services Director (DAC)	Financial Management and Budget	City Administrative Officer/Personnel/ Treasury
Public Information	Public Services and Information	DAC		Information Services
Animal Control	X			X
Redevelopment				Community Redevelopment Agency
Housing				X
Community Development	X	Community Services (DAC)	Community Services	X
Finance		DAC		
Tourism		Visitor & Convention Bureau (DAC)	Tourist Development Council	
Port Authority		DAC		
Equal Opportunity		DAC		
Health		Health Director and County Medical Examiner (DAC)		
Historic Preservation		H.P. Board member (DAC)		
Waste Management		Solid Waste Director (DAC)		
Parks & Recreation		DAC		X
Economic Development		DAC		
Facilities Planning, Design and Construction			X	
Cultural Affairs				X
Local Government Liaisons		Cities of Cape Coral, Fort Myers, Sanibel	Liaison to Municipal Governments	
Other Public Sector Liaisons		County Sheriff, County School District, SW Florida RPC	County Sheriff, County Solid Waste Authority, County School Board, South Florida Water Management District, Florida Department of Environmental Regulation, Department of Transportation	
Private Sector		Business community representatives	Private utilities	

While the examples above and in Figure 3-2 involve communities that established the makeup of a recovery task force in a plan developed during the pre-disaster period, other communities have established recovery task forces in the aftermath of natural disasters. Two examples materialized in the spring of 1997 with the tornadoes that struck parts of Arkansas. Arkadelphia, a community of about 10,000, within days of the March 1 event, established an open-ended recovery task force, inviting all residents, officials, and business owners to participate, forming several committees in the process. Later, a 15-member disaster recovery plan committee was appointed to work directly with Woodward-Clyde Associates, the contractor directed by FEMA to mobilize resources to develop and implement a recovery plan. Chaired by a foundation official, the committee included the mayor and city manager and various local citizens (Woodward-Clyde Associates 1997a). On the other hand, College Station posed a special problem because it is not a jurisdiction in its own right but a community that straddles the city of Little Rock and parts of unincorporated Pulaski County. There, constructing an eight-member disaster recovery plan committee, including officials of the community development corporation and credit union, a local civic group, and the Watershed Human Development Agency, required the cooperation of the city, the county, and the community itself (Woodward-Clyde Associates 1997b). A major theme that has emerged from such efforts is the need to include in some way all those who must be heard to ensure the plan's successful implementation.

Smaller communities may wish to pursue other approaches using simpler structures. Brower, Beatley, and Blatt (1987) also list three alternatives that emphasize greater involvement by elected officials. One is to create a group representing broadly based community interests, among which would be some agency heads who meet that criterion. This has the advantage of bringing a number of perspectives into play and ensuring a healthy variety of expertise. A second alternative would be to empower the local planning board or commission, which would ensure a familiarity with land-use planning but might often require some special training of citizen commissioners on disaster recovery issues. A final possibility is simply to devise a board wholly composed of local elected officials. This last option has a serious drawback in that the task force members might prove to be sorely overburdened in the aftermath of a serious disaster. In the end, however, each community must think through the issues connected with its own decision-making practices and circumstances and produce its own optimum solution. The model recovery ordinance that appears in Chapter 5 provides some options and language for communities seeking to craft a mechanism for guiding the post-disaster recovery process.

Nonconforming Uses

Planners everywhere become accustomed to problems involving nonconforming uses. These arise when zoning for a particular area is changed in a way that does not encompass some land uses already present in the affected zoning district. The standard procedure is to allow the continuation of the nonconforming use, but not to allow its expansion, its conversion to another nonconforming use, or its restoration in the event of its discontinuance or destruction. Thus, in the aftermath of a fire or flood that substantially damaged a nonconforming structure, the owner would not be allowed to rebuild that use at that location. The goal is to respect the vested rights of the owner of the nonconforming use while gradually or eventually eliminating such uses.

Under normal circumstances, issues involving the restoration or discontinuation of nonconforming uses arise one at a time, as a result of events such as fires, conveyance of the property to new owners, or the dissolution or relocation of existing businesses. As such, they pose mostly a routine burden for local zoning officials. Major disasters, however, can create hundreds, even thousands, of nonconforming uses virtually overnight, each of which adds to the workload of an already stressed planning department, as well as posing serious questions for the integrity of the entire redevelopment process. In such circumstances, it is both politically and practically unlikely that the community will want to take an uncompromising stand against allowing the repair and reconstruction of all nonconforming uses. Disasters may pose an opportunity to eliminate nonconforming uses, even to reshape existing patterns of development along lines deemed more desirable, but they also generate enormous pressures from property owners to allow the reestablishment of the existing development pattern, complete with nonconforming buildings and uses. Such pressures result in part from the difficulty of finding enough suitable locations in the proper zoning districts for the relocation of those uses not permitted to be rebuilt. Under such circumstances, the community may need to face the question of where and how to compromise and for what reasons.

> Major disasters can create hundreds, even thousands, of nonconforming uses virtually overnight, each of which adds to the workload of an already stressed planning department, as well as posing serious questions for the integrity of the entire redevelopment process.

The solution, or at least an amelioration of the problem, may lie in establishing criteria for allowing the reestablishment of nonconforming uses under disaster-related circumstances. Section 7.9 of the model ordinance in Chapter 5 attempts to prescribe such conditions.

ECONOMIC RECOVERY

Economic recovery is quite likely the most serious issue facing most communities in the post-disaster period, and almost certainly the central issue in every major disaster. The extent of the disruption of normal economic activity varies with the type of disaster, the size and economic makeup of the community, and other factors, but the disruption invariably adds to the property losses already suffered by shrinking incomes, profits, and productivity.

> Small businesses, in particular, are vulnerable, with some 30 percent not surviving when stricken by a natural disaster.

The Tampa Bay Regional Planning Council (1994) introduced its *Model Community Post-Disaster Economic Redevelopment Plan* by recounting the staggering economic losses suffered in Dade County, Florida, following Hurricane Andrew:

- 8,000 businesses and more than 100,000 jobs seriously affected

- disruption of a $500 million-per-year tourist industry for several years

- $1 billion in damage to agriculture with permanent income loss of $250 million

- daily lost output in storm-affected areas of $22 million

The potential duration of some business disruptions is considerable. In December 1997, the island of Kauai in Hawaii finally witnessed the reopening of the Sheraton Kauai resort on Poipu Beach, closed after the September 11, 1992, destruction of Hurricane Iniki. Despite that reopening, three of the island's five major hotels remained closed at that point (Cannon 1997). The disruptions can entail substantial costs, such as the $200 million in business disruptions suffered by Des Moines following the 1993 floods. Small businesses, in particular, are vulnerable, with some 30 percent not surviving when stricken by a natural disaster (Armstrong 1998). Other disaster-ravaged communities have their own statistics, all indicating that economic recovery needs to be at the top of the planning agenda for long-term recovery and reconstruction.

Establishing the Means to Facilitate Recovery

The first step in facilitating any type of recovery is anticipation of the consequences of a disaster as a means of identifying the strategies and resources needed to make it happen. While hazard identification per se is the topic of Chapter 7, the object here is to highlight the kinds of impact assessment needed in the pre-disaster period to allow planners to develop effective contingency plans to facilitate post-disaster economic recovery. In this respect, the Tampa Bay plan cited above offers a good model and a reasonably detailed example of a substantial compilation of that type of information, albeit on a regional basis. The report details estimated damages for various types of structures from hurricanes of varying strength, initial job losses, population displacement, and similar projections. Individual communities can certainly make their own detailed assessments. These projections can be delineated within a couple of major categories and several subcategories.

Inventory of potential structural damage. This is essentially what the Tampa Bay study does by positing potential hurricane paths and wind velocities in relation to the vulnerability of housing stock, industrial property, and commercial buildings. Also vital in this category of direct losses to structures is the estimated potential damage to public and private infrastructure.

Overall economic impact. These projections will estimate all possible indirect losses, such as the loss of economic activity suffered in Des Moines, Iowa, following the temporary closure of the water treatment plant. During the same Midwest floods, Iowa and other states suffered major disruption of railroad traffic, much of which had to be rerouted due to flooded tracks. Transportation-related economic losses can take other forms, such as the loss of major highway corridors, the collapse of the Oakland Bay Bridge during the Loma Prieta Earthquake, or the closing of local airports. As noted above, the loss of tourism, even in the short term, poses a major economic threat to many disaster-affected communities, particularly in the Sun Belt. All of these problems entail direct or indirect consequences that include job losses and the closure of previously viable businesses. Moreover, in communities with severely damaged residential neighborhoods, employee dislocation can result in the inability of much of the work force to continue its normal work patterns, at least temporarily complicating economic activity for businesses that might otherwise be unaffected.

In fact, that last issue is so potent in its impacts that the Tampa Bay model plan lists as its first goal, "Restore and enhance residential communities." Not only is this a matter of restoring normal life for the local work force in order to minimize productivity losses, but it is also a matter, as the plan notes, of reestablishing the residential market base for local retailers. Goal 2 in the plan is the restoration and enhancement of employment opportunities; Goal 3 the provision of public and nonprofit infrastructure and support services.

A related issue that good comprehensive planning should address in this regard is the differential impact of disasters on different communities or sectors within communities. Some low-income communities may, for instance, suffer disproportionate damage due to the relative age of housing stock and the limited financial capacity of many residents to undertake (or, in the case of tenants, even influence) effective mitigation measures or post-disaster repairs. Recovery thus becomes relatively more difficult and prolonged than might be the case in a more affluent neighborhood, and neighborhood businesses may also suffer accordingly.

Another important point that should be addressed by planners in facilitating economic recovery as a prime policy objective is the fact that disasters

Some low-income communities may suffer disproportionate damage due to the relative age of housing stock and the limited financial capacity of many residents to undertake (or, in the case of tenants, even influence) effective mitigation measures or post-disaster repairs.

produce an inevitable roller-coaster impact on subsequent economic activity. Economic activity takes a rough ride in which there is, first, a rapid downhill cycle in the immediate post-disaster period, during which the consequences detailed above are sustained. As recovery progresses, the local economy experiences an accelerated rate of growth, nurtured in large part by infusions of outside aid and the need for rapid restoration of local buildings and structures. During this period, the shape of local economic

activity will also shift dramatically, emphasizing construction and services. As this physical restoration of the community comes to a close, economic activity flattens out to a more normal pace, and the structure of the local economy begins to regain its pre-disaster balance. The objective of the plan for post-disaster recovery and reconstruction is to take advantage of this process to build a community that is both economically stronger than it might otherwise have been and less vulnerable to future disruptions from natural disasters.

Downtown Grand Forks, North Dakota, was completely awash in water during the 1997 winter floods. The business district suffered severe economic setbacks and required substantial aid.

Building a Disaster-Resistant (Sustainable) Economy
The plan for post-disaster recovery and reconstruction should have, as part of its policy objectives concerning economic recovery, not just the objective of restoring normal economic activity but that of making it more resistant to such disruptions should nature strike again. In essence, this means seizing the opportunity, where it is deemed appropriate, to move the community's most vital businesses out of harm's way. In other cases, such as waterfront or water-related activities that must remain along the coast or shoreline or in a floodplain, the objective may instead be to make them less vulnerable to damage through floodproofing, elevation, or other structural mitigation approaches.

The most dramatic examples of building a disaster-resistant economy have come from small towns that have either completely relocated or at least moved their central business district from the path of disaster. Soldiers Grove, Wisconsin, set a notable example by relocating its entire downtown away from the Kickapoo River floodplain in the early 1980s, thus forever eliminating what had been a repetitive problem (Becker 1994a). With assistance from the U.S. Department of Energy, Pattonsburg, Missouri, relocated to higher ground and likewise buffered its future business activity from flooding after the 1993 Midwest floods, as did Valmeyer, Illinois (Becker 1994b; Skinner and Becker 1995).

These small towns provide particularly clear examples of using post-disaster opportunities to build a more disaster-resistant economic base mostly because wholesale relocation on a small scale makes the results more obvious than is the case with measures taken to protect business districts in small parts of much larger communities. The same principles apply, none-

Bill Becker

Valmeyer, Illinois, a town along the Mississippi River that relocated to higher ground after the 1993 floods, has incorporated solar heating into many of its new buildings, including the community center.

theless, to the need to make industrial and commercial areas of larger communities more disaster resistant as a means of reducing the economic impact of future disasters. Most communities will face situations involving at most only partial relocations. Determining exactly which measures are appropriate and effective in accomplishing this mission is an essential function of the local planning process, much as the specific measures for mitigating all other structural and building damage must be chosen in light of the local hazard context. On a small scale, these measures include the relocation of vulnerable businesses from floodplains or the seismic retrofitting of older commercial and industrial facilities. On a larger scale, however, they may involve contingency plans for wholesale planned redevelopment of devastated central business districts, such as occurred in Fillmore, California, following the Northridge Earthquake (McSweeney 1997).

The Soldiers Grove and Pattonsburg examples, however, highlight more than just the issue of relocation of vulnerable businesses from the path of known natural hazards. Both communities have also seized the opportunity to make their local businesses and residential sector more environmentally and economically sound by institutionalizing energy efficiency in the rebuilding process. For instance, the Soldiers Grove building code requires that all new structures receive at least half their energy from renewable sources. Valmeyer's new civic buildings employ solar heating principles. These communities are, in effect, insulating themselves not only from future natural disasters but from economic shocks as well, by reducing energy costs and thus retaining in the local economy the additional dollars saved, presumably generating new jobs as money recirculates locally instead of leaving the community. Of course, many of these measures can be taken at times other than following a disaster. However, few events besides disasters result in the need to rebuild so much of the community so quickly and hence pose the same opportunity to reshape the local economy so dramatically. The significant benefits of integrating principles of sustainable development into the process of post-disaster redevelopment have resulted in a modest but growing collaborative effort among federal agencies, such as DOE, FEMA, and HUD, and various state, local, and private-sector entities to facilitate this integration. (A particularly good source of examples can be found by clicking "Operation Fresh Start" within DOE's sustainable development Web site at http://www.sustainable.doe.gov.)

One final pair of points can be made here. The process of planning for post-disaster recovery and reconstruction affords the opportunity to think about building a disaster-resistant economy not only in a structural and locational sense, but in terms of the kinds of businesses that are more likely to recover quickly from disasters. For instance, a town totally dependent on tourism will probably face a more dire predicament following a disaster than one with a more diversified economy, some of which consists of industries more capable of withstanding the impact of a local disaster. The second point, closely related and intuitively obvious, is that making the local business sector more resistant to disasters in these and other ways discussed above provides fiscal insurance to the local government by making the local tax base itself more disaster resistant. When it comes to disasters, what is good for the local business sector is also good for the municipal budget.

MITIGATION

Local government engages in hazard mitigation whenever it undertakes activities that are designed either to prevent future disasters (by keeping development out of harm's way) or to minimize or reduce their deleterious effects on property and infrastructure. Many activities that local government may not be able to mandate for private property owners may nonetheless be worth encouraging through means like public education campaigns and financial or other incentives. Also, while the damage from natural disasters is typically structural, the solutions need not be. Much of the most effective mitigation consists of nonstructural measures directing land use away from hazardous areas or even seeking simply to influence human behavior. The all-time classic example of the latter type of nonstructural mitigation is the U.S. Forest Service's Smoky the Bear advertising campaign, designed to reduce the risk of wildfires. For decades, most of the public was completely unaware of any positive role for fire in the natural environment. The fact that many wildfire experts now consider that campaign, in retrospect, almost too effective in shaping these exclusively negative public perceptions of wildfires serves to underscore the very power of the technique.

While little empirical research to date has been done relating plan quality to actual results in reducing damages from natural disasters, French et al. (1996) found in a study of the Northridge earthquake that a regression analysis of variables influencing damage showed the influence of public awareness policies in local plans to be a significant factor, along with the age of the buildings (correlated, obviously, to the building codes and land-use measures then in effect) and programmatic policies (affecting existing development). More research along these lines may serve to strengthen the hand of land-use planners urging greater emphasis in these areas.

The precise details of local hazard mitigation policies should grow out of the data amassed through hazard identification and risk assessment at the

The process of planning for post-disaster recovery and reconstruction affords the opportunity to think about building a disaster-resistant economy not only in a structural and locational sense, but in terms of the kinds of businesses that are more likely to recover quickly from disasters.

The Benefits of Implementing Hazard Mitigation

Pinellas County, Florida, in its redevelopment guide, provides an excellent summary list of the local benefits of implementing hazard mitigation.

- Saving lives and reducing injuries

- Preventing or reducing property damage

- Reducing economic losses

- Minimizing social dislocation and stress

- Minimizing agricultural losses

- Maintaining critical facilities in functional order

- Protecting infrastructure from damage

- Protecting mental health

- Limiting legal liability of government and public officials

- Providing positive political consequences for government action

outset of the planning process, coupled with the development of community consensus concerning the means for mitigating those hazards and the extent of the effort directed toward that goal. McElyea, Brower, and Godschalk (1982) list six generic questions as key issues in a hazard mitigation planning process. The Florida Department of Community Affairs, in a model plan developed by the Tampa Bay Regional Planning Council and the Hillsborough County Planning and Development Management Department (1995), also uses those and details others for specific hazards, such as high winds, flooding, wave action, and severe erosion. Other Florida jurisdictions like Pinellas County (1994) have used them as well. More recently, the Florida DCA (1997) developed statewide guidance in two documents addressing mitigation planning. Jurisdictions outside Florida, of course, will need to develop their own hazard-specific issues for other hazard categories more relevant to local circumstances. A few model and actual hazard mitigation plans and guides from around the country that planners can tap for examples relevant to their own communities are listed in the sidebar. Many of these necessarily deal also with long-term reconstruction and redevelopment issues because the two goals so often are pursued concurrently. Six basic questions can be asked about the policies and regulations in effect. Do the policies and regulations:

1. recognize the existence of different hazard areas that are subject to different forces?;

2. cover all types of structures (single-family, multifamily, commercial, etc.)?;

3. apply to public facilities as well as private?;

4. encourage higher-density uses to locate outside the most hazardous areas?;

5. result in nonconforming uses and structures being brought into conformity after they are damaged?; and

6. relate the level of development in the community to the capacity of existing evacuation routes and the time it would take to evacuate those areas?

Having listed these questions, it is worth noting that, as with many issues in the field of planning, there will always be exceptions concerning their validity in certain circumstances. For instance, higher densities in some areas, such as earthquake zones with liquefaction potential, may actually better support the cost of structural mitigation measures. Also, as was discussed above, it is not always possible or desirable to seek the complete elimination of nonconforming uses.

Florida is one of a mere handful of states with a specific mandate requiring communities to include particular kinds of natural hazards mitigation elements in their comprehensive plans. In view of research by Burby and Dalton (1993) finding stronger plan quality where state mandates with sanctions drive a process of development and implementation of hazard mitigation elements, it may be unfortunate that so few states have gone this route as yet.

As discussed elsewhere in this report, NFIP also provides some guidance on mitigation specific to flood hazards, and the Coastal Zone Management Act and Coastal Barrier Resources Act provide some reinforcement in coastal areas. The 1994 National Flood Insurance Reform Act (Public Law 103-325) created the Flood Mitigation Assistance (FMA) program to assist local governments with funding for mitigation planning and projects.

Under its Hazard Mitigation Grant Program and Public Assistance program, FEMA has also sought to facilitate local cost-benefit analysis by developing a worksheet to determine funding levels. Local planning agencies can adopt or adapt it to their own needs.

The main impetus for most state and local mitigation planning, however, is contained in Section 409 of the Stafford Act (Public Law 93-288, as amended), which requires state and local governments to develop a hazard mitigation plan as a condition of receiving federal disaster aid. The state or local government must agree to evaluate natural hazards in the areas where the loans or grants are used and to take appropriate action to mitigate them. The rules for implementing these requirements are in the Code of Federal Regulations (44 CFR, Part 206, Subpart M), but a FEMA (1990) handbook, *Post-Disaster Hazard Mitigation Planning Guidance for State and Local Governments*, can serve as an effective guide to the process of planning and plan review (see sidebar on page 60). More recently, however, FEMA has been reshaping its relationship with state emergency management and mitigation agencies through clarifying its own expectations of state and local mitigation efforts, which emphasize the implementation of ongoing mitigation planning programs.

Structural approaches to hazard mitigation can include the building of seawalls and revetments, levees, seismic retrofitting, landslide barriers, and other measures designed to make the built environment more resistant to the onslaught of natural forces. There is a temptation for decision makers to rely on such approaches and to avoid the more difficult options of restricting development in hazardous areas, but such a one-sided attack on the problem suffers from two major deficiencies: first, that catastrophic damage can

Model and Actual Plans and Guides for Local Hazard Mitigation

For full citation information, see Appendix A. Also note that each state has a state-level mitigation plan that all local planners in that state can request from their state emergency management office.

• California Department of Forestry and Fire Protection, *California's I-Zone: Urban/Wildland Fire Prevention & Mitigation*

• California Seismic Safety Commission, *California at Risk: Steps to Earthquake Safety for Local Governments*

• Federal Emergency Management Agency, *Post-Disaster Hazard Mitigation Planning Guidance for State and Local Governments*

• Florida Department of Community Affairs, *The Local Mitigation Strategy: A Guidebook for Florida Cities and Counties; Workbook in Local Mitigation Strategy Development; Model Local Government Disaster Mitigation and Redevelopment Plan and Model Local Redevelopment Regulations*

• Hilton Head Island, South Carolina, *Post-Disaster Recovery and Mitigation Plan*

• Long Island Regional Planning Board, *Hurricane Damage Mitigation Plan for the South Shore—Nassau and Suffolk Counties, N.Y.*

• Massachusetts Department of Environmental Management, *Flood Hazard Mitigation Planning: A Community Guide*

• Nags Head, North Carolina, *Hurricane and Storm Mitigation and Reconstruction Plan*

• Pinellas County, Florida, *Post-Disaster Redevelopment Guide for Pinellas County*

• South Florida Regional Planning Council, *Post-Disaster Redevelopment Planning: Model Plan for Three Florida Scenarios*

• Tampa Bay Regional Planning Council, *Tampa Bay Region Hurricane Recovery Planning Project, Volume I—Phases I and II Regional Recovery Planning Guide*

exceed the design capabilities of cost-effective engineering solutions (Petak and Atkisson 1982), causing additional damage; second, that the avoidance of more difficult land-use decisions produces a false sense of security that allows more development in hazardous areas than might otherwise have occurred (Burby and French et al. 1985). Nonstructural approaches may include stricter building codes and improved enforcement, the acquisition of vulnerable properties, zoning and subdivision regulations aimed at minimizing or prohibiting undesirable land uses, setbacks, floodplain regulations, and relocation programs.

Implementation of the chosen strategies must then depend on the priorities established in the mitigation plan. Where do limited funds get spent first? Regulatory solutions (e.g., zoning) are obviously less costly than alternatives that involve direct public expenditures, but, with the exception of nonconforming uses substantially damaged by a disaster, do not affect existing development. Retrofitting costs money, but a community can become more adept at identifying funding sources to assist in these objectives and in developing incentives for property owners so that they are more palatable politically. Because most mitigation money is available after a declared disaster, communities must also build into their mitigation plans targets of opportunity, in effect shifting their priorities to fit the resources available at any given time. That is so commonly the circumstance that planners would be well advised to assume that such opportunism is a necessary element of a good mitigation plan. Part of the essence of good post-disaster planning is preparation to seize the moment. The best way to marshal the resources to do so is to have a ready set of priorities.

Finally, planners should develop criteria for implementing those priorities. Risk assessment is a critical factor in establishing those criteria because considerations related to protection of population (including density) and critical facilities will inevitably drive these priorities. Criteria are the workhorses of day-to-day plan implementation. At some point, for example, planners and other local officials must decide, with limited resources, which flooded house is bought and/or relocated from a willing seller, and which one must wait. These criteria may include a variety of very detailed factors, such as repetitive loss history, elevation within the floodplain, the condition of the property, the percentage of the surrounding subdivision or neighborhood that either has been relocated or remains intact, and the cost of the transaction. Many communities have developed scoring systems for rating the relative priority of various properties for acquisition or other mitigation strategies. In an area vulnerable to high-wind damage, for instance, which utilities should be undergrounded first, and how soon? Which local roads and bridges should be elevated or seismically retrofitted, and how soon? Which culverts most need to be expanded to facilitate the flow of flood waters? The answers to these questions are as varied as the communities themselves and involve as many possibilities as the items listed in Chapter 5.

From this discussion, it should be apparent that hazard mitigation is an implicit function of all other objectives of the plan for post-disaster recovery and reconstruction. Nonetheless, mitigation needs to be highlighted in its own right in the plan in order to achieve the visibility and priority it deserves. As a policy objective, mitigation should be seen as posing two distinct sets of opportunities that deserve distinct treatment—those pursued during the pre-disaster period and programmed into local government activities and budgets on an ongoing basis, and those created as an immediate result of a natural disaster and which must be acted upon in a timely manner during the recovery and long-term reconstruction periods. There are two essential reasons why these sets of opportunities are different. First,

Primary Steps for Hazard Mitigation Planning

Implementing regulations for Stafford Act mitigation planning list four primary components of a state hazard mitigation plan that are also outlined in Section 409 of the Stafford Act:

• An evaluation of the natural hazards in the designated area

• A description and analysis of the state and local hazard management policies, programs, and capabilities to mitigate the hazards in the area

• Hazard mitigation goals and objectives and proposed strategies, programs, and actions to reduce or avoid long-term vulnerability to hazards

• A method of implementing, monitoring, evaluating, and updating the mitigation plan. Such evaluation is to occur at least on an annual basis to ensure that implementation occurs as planned, and to ensure that the plan remains current.

Source: 44 CFR Part 206, Subpart M

the post-disaster period, especially if the local government has planned effectively for this eventuality, is one in which additional outside resources become available that would not otherwise exist. Second, the damage caused by the disaster and the consequent need to rebuild produce an atmosphere of heightened urgency in decisions concerning when, where, and how to rebuild. In other words, there is no substitute for a good plan in these circumstances.

Pre-disaster Mitigation

Despite the emphasis placed in this report on preparing to seize opportunities for hazard mitigation that arise in the aftermath of a disaster, nothing could make less sense in the context of post-disaster planning than to wait for such opportunities before doing anything. Hazard mitigation works best as a policy objective of local planning when it is so completely integrated into the comprehensive plan that it becomes a normal assumption behind all daily planning activities. There is far more political and institutional momentum in the post-disaster period behind a policy objective that is already in place and being actively pursued than in one that is suddenly activated from scratch, no matter how well the community planned for its contingency.

Any doubts on that point ought to be resolved by the case study of Arnold, Missouri, which appears in Chapter 8. That city's existing plans, part of its 1991 floodplain management plan, called for the establishment of a greenway along the Mississippi and Meramec rivers through a program of gradual buyouts of floodplain properties. When the 1993 floods arrived unexpectedly soon and with unexpected intensity, the city's pre-existing commitment to this objective made it easier to accelerate the whole process. This maxim need not be limited to land acquisitions; the same principle applies to other mitigation measures like elevation, floodproofing, seismic retrofitting, and various wildfire mitigation techniques.

An excellent example of an ongoing commitment to a major hazard mitigation challenge is the Los Angeles program for seismic retrofitting of a large stock of unreinforced masonry buildings (URMs), based on the earthquake hazard reduction ordinance the city passed in 1981. When it began, Los Angeles required almost 8,000 URM owners over several years either to improve their buildings, vacate them, or face demolition. Despite the massive damage of the 1994 Northridge earthquake, matters could have been much worse. By 1996, one-third of the URMs were vacated or demolished, and 95 percent of those remaining were in compliance (FEMA 1997c).

Stricter building and zoning codes for future development, whether stemming from a planning process related to natural hazards and post-disaster recovery or not, also play a role in achieving the policy objective of pre-disaster hazard mitigation. The severe housing damage following Hurricane Andrew that stemmed from admittedly uneven compliance with the Southern Florida Building Code served, if anything, to highlight the value of the code where it had been observed. It is sometimes easy to lose perspective on just how much we have learned about effective hazard mitigation techniques regardless of the specific disasters involved. No American city, for example, is even remotely likely today to suffer the same type of massive housing and infrastructure damage that occurred in San Francisco in the 1907 earthquake. The reason is simply that so much has been done to secure newer buildings and structures over time even though the city and region have grown significantly since then.

The objective of a pre-disaster mitigation program is to identify vulnerable buildings and infrastructure and to program the needed improvements into governmental budget priorities, as well as to persuade private property

Hazard mitigation works best as a policy objective of local planning when it is so completely integrated into the comprehensive plan that it becomes a normal assumption behind all daily planning activities.

This home in Lewes, Delaware, was elevated to raise it above the base flood level in a coastal high hazard area.

owners to undertake such commitments themselves to the extent possible. To return to the Arnold, Missouri, example, it is far easier to convince outside funding sources to assist with such efforts if it is clear that the local government, and ideally its business sector and citizens as well, already are taking the issue seriously.

Seizing Post-Disaster Opportunities

It should be obvious by now that pre-disaster and post-disaster mitigation should be two parts of a seamless whole in a sound plan for post-disaster recovery and reconstruction. The only difference, although it is often a major difference, is one of scale, of accelerating the pace with which existing mitigation plans are implemented, as a result of the influx of outside assistance. What is important about planning for post-disaster hazard mitigation is that the additional resources that facilitate local hazard mitigation in the aftermath of a disaster do not materialize by accident. Local governments manage to secure such resources in large part because they have planned to do so.

That does not mean that they know when those plans will be put into effect. Arnold took advantage of the post-disaster elements of its 1991 floodplain management plan far earlier than anyone had expected, and on a grander scale than it had expected. Los Angeles was forced to activate its plan for post-disaster recovery and reconstruction during the Northridge earthquake almost as fast as it had adopted it. Disaster could strike even in the midst of the planning process. One never knows, but initiating the process now usually ensures more success than waiting.

Planners and city officials also find themselves in a position to accelerate mitigation in the post-disaster period because a disaster captures people's attention for such matters like nothing else. This attention span can be very short, however, unless local officials are able to focus it quickly and point to existing plans to address the problem because there is little time in the recovery period for developing plans from scratch. Many property owners are facing the need to rebuild or to repair damaged buildings, and while this

- drafting
- adopting
- impleme

By 1994,
reform was
Insurance I
voluntary,
flood insur
mended ac
provided f
structures
provide gra
activities to
program re
FEMA, who
409 of the S
erty owner

- direct th
  that the
  tion ma
  lender w
  was in a
- require 1
- require 1
  also esc
  homeow
  receivin
- require
  covered
  a second

These m
a voluntary
aid is seen 1
intergover

CONNECTIN
Although a
ceived and
a commun
all other el
so many as
of a city's
section is 1
objective is
considerat

Linkages w
Consider 1
Northridg
governme
of a local c

circumstance generally leads to pressure to allow them to rebuild the same structures in the same places, this need not always be the outcome—certainly not where the local government is prepared with some alternatives and has identified in advance some resources with which to implement them. Specific details of the issue of using disaster assistance effectively is addressed later in this chapter.

One noticeable result, for example, of the 1993 Midwest floods was a growing public willingness to consider such alternatives, leading to the complete relocation of towns like Valmeyer, Illinois, and Pattonsburg, Missouri, and significant alterations to local development patterns in many others. The targets of opportunity are not just those physical structures that are most vulnerable to natural hazards, but the public attitudes toward those opportunities and the prospect of mobilizing public opinion behind the idea of implementing a new vision. Ideally, that new vision will have been considered in the process of developing a plan for post-disaster recovery and reconstruction, but even where that is not the case, it may still be possible to act quickly. Neither Valmeyer nor Pattonsburg had such a plan prior to the 1993 floods, but, with outside assistance, their civic leaders, particularly their mayors, were able to rally local public opinion. Their job may have been made easier by the small scale of their communities. In larger communities, the pre-disaster preparation of a plan for post-disaster recovery may be more essential to success.

Because only very small communities will likely ever undertake wholesale relocation, planners need to focus on those less drastic but nonetheless significant opportunities that are more likely to present themselves. These opportunities may include rezoning hazard-prone areas to lower densities, designating areas where acquisition of property would be most effective and establishing priorities to guide those purchases, designating target areas for various kinds of retrofitting, and revisiting subdivision controls for hazard-prone areas (Morris 1997). In the aftermath of disaster, planners may also discover unique opportunities to reassess the effectiveness, extent, and policy basis of existing hazard mitigation programs.

The National Flood Insurance Program (NFIP)
By far the most significant and far-reaching federal legislation affecting local land-use planning is NFIP. It remains the one program deliberately designed to have some direct federal policy-making impact on local land-use planning related to disasters. It thus merits some special discussion related to local hazard mitigation policy objectives because of its unavoidable influence on local decisions concerning those objectives.

Put simply, NFIP has steadily become more specific in encouraging the type of local planning and land-use regulation that will yield results. That is not always readily apparent because so much of the program has relied from the beginning on incentives rather than direct mandates, although there are more than a few of the latter once a community is in the program. Participation in the program is voluntary; otherwise, its effectiveness relies on the willingness and desire of property owners to buy the insurance, whose availability depends on the compliance of their local government with the terms of the program. Those terms include the adoption and enforcement of a floodplain management ordinance, which necessarily imposes requirements for construction and post-disaster reconstruction within the regulatory floodplain.

Beyond the actual requirements of NFIP, FEMA encourages communities to undertake floodplain management programs that consider a number of factors that, it is hoped, will provide for a more comprehensive approach than the simple adoption of mandatory regulations. These are delineated in

The targets of opportunity are not just those physical structures that are most vulnerable to natural hazards, but the public attitudes toward those opportunities and the prospect of mobilizing public opinion behind the idea of implementing a new vision.

- Telecommunications were disrupted where telephone lines were down.

- Transportation was disrupted by damaged bridges, fallen trees, and other obstacles.

- Utility service was unavailable where power lines were down.

- Education was interrupted at all levels not only because of the above problems but also because school buildings were damaged, roofs had collapsed, and schools were used as temporary shelters.

- Economic development agencies had suddenly inherited the huge job of helping businesses reestablish themselves in the face of a weakened economy, structural damage, loss of customer access, cleanup priorities, inability of employees to commute to work, and related nightmares.

- Thousands of residents needed emergency housing, and others faced the task of arranging for costly repairs.

- Environmental damage was substantial, particularly where fragile ecosystems were harmed or spills of hazardous waste occurred.

Clearly, the list of local comprehensive plan elements called into question can be even longer. Land-use elements, dealing with the community's plans for zoning changes and subdivision regulations, among other issues, are an obvious additional point of linkage for post-disaster considerations because many communities may find a need to revisit such regulations based on lessons learned from the disaster. (See Figure 3-3.) Public safety, capital improvements, and other elements may also be examined for their potential role in addressing mitigation and disaster planning.

Particularly important are the linkages between a natural hazards and post-disaster element and the implementation element of a comprehensive plan. Pre-disaster mitigation plans need clear goals and a time frame to be achieved and in order to avoid gathering dust on a shelf. It is all too easy for mitigation objectives to remain unfunded for years. Although post-disaster recovery and reconstruction plans may seem to be self-activating once disaster strikes, experience indicates that the unpredictable timing of disasters can allow them to be forgotten by the time the event occurs. It is essential that oversight and agency responsibilities be clearly assigned. The designation of a post-disaster recovery task force, as discussed above, is one obvious way to accomplish this purpose.

The principal point is simply that post-disaster issues must be considered as these other plan elements are prepared, and cross-references within them to the post-disaster element can then make the plan an effective instrument for taking cognizance of both the problems and opportunities for improvement that the disaster itself may engender. Des Moines, for instance, was forced in the aftermath of the 1993 floods to reconsider the vulnerability of its single water treatment plant in the downtown area and take steps to plan for some alternatives. Although no one anticipated the duration or extent of those floods, prior consideration of this issue might have given rise to other options much earlier.

Linkages with Other Plans

The comprehensive plan, while clearly the most important set of linkages and the ideal repository for the plan for post-disaster recovery and reconstruction itself (as an element), is not the only linkage that matters. The opportunities for integrating disaster planning awareness into local plans

---

Sidebar:

Particularly important are the linkages between a natural hazards and post-disaster element and the implementation element of a comprehensive plan. Pre-disaster mitigation plans need clear goals and a time frame to be achieved and in order to avoid gathering dust on a shelf. It is all too easy for mitigation objectives to remain unfunded for years.

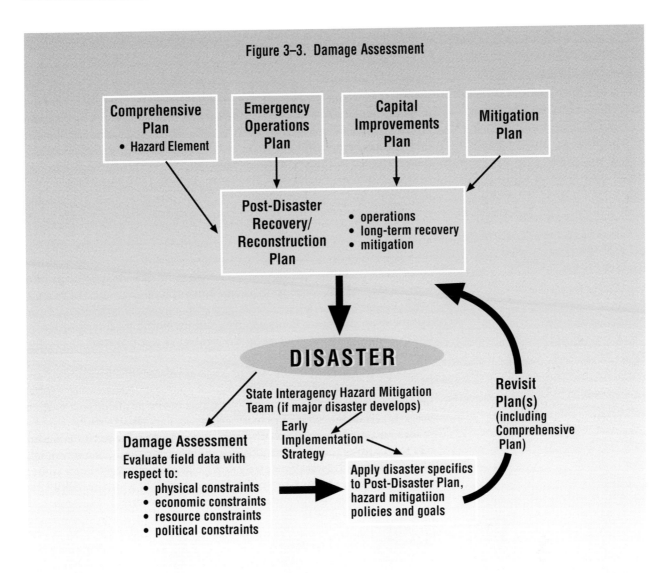

Figure 3–3. Damage Assessment

Source: Cecelia Rosenberg, FEMA; designed by Lisa Barton, APA

and their implementation extends much further. Many special plans developed by local governments also deserve such attention.

Neighborhood plans, for instance, allow an ideal opportunity to sharpen the focus of post-disaster planning. Neighborhoods in hazard-prone areas, especially if they are developed with a high level of citizen participation, can serve well to raise citizen awareness of the need for preparedness and mitigation and of possibilities for more sustainable methods of rebuilding (such as improved energy efficiency in more disaster-resistant structures) in the aftermath of a disaster. Could better stormwater detention systems that resulted in the construction of swales or that took better advantage of natural runoff patterns ease a neighborhood flooding problem? Might fire-resistant landscaping requirements for a subdivision or homeowners association help avert disaster? What access patterns could be changed to benefit residents and improve public safety? Under what conditions should treasured but vulnerable historic buildings and homes be demolished? Linking the post-disaster element with the development of neighborhood plans presents an opportunity to nail down details of post-disaster reconstruction and mitigation that might otherwise escape notice in the larger scheme of things.

Linking the post-disaster element with the development of neighborhood plans presents an opportunity to nail down details of post-disaster reconstruction and mitigation that might otherwise escape notice in the larger scheme of things.

Area and corridor plans likewise present special opportunities to examine specific issues, the latter particularly in the area of transportation. Downtown or business district plans for areas with significant natural hazards can address the questions of how business activity will be restored in the aftermath of a disaster, what sort of economic redevelopment may be necessary, and which resources will be available to make it all happen. Narrowly focused infrastructure considerations, such as planning for the undergrounding of utility lines in a waterfront business district, can undergo detailed scrutiny in such plans.

One special area that absolutely needs linkage consideration is capital improvements programming. Because such programming involves the scheduling of public improvements over a multiyear period (typically five years), it presents a recurring opportunity to consider and include those improvements needed to make the community more disaster resistant. The list of potential improvements that fall into this category includes nearly every item of public expenditure mentioned in this report, from road resurfacing and the retrofitting of vital infrastructure for wind or seismic resistance, to the creation of emergency management shelters and the seismic retrofitting of schools and community buildings. As important as the improvements themselves is the provision for financing them, the subject of later chapters in this report.

> Resources that may not be available on a routine basis for certain improvements may become available from various disaster relief sources, particularly where careful planning has allowed the community to identify certain needs in advance, saving critical time in the aftermath of the disaster.

Because of the unpredictability of disaster-related reconstruction costs, however, it is also important to recognize the wish-list aspect of capital improvements planning. Resources that may not be available on a routine basis for certain improvements may become available from various disaster relief sources, particularly where careful planning has allowed the community to identify certain needs in advance, saving critical time in the aftermath of the disaster. This is particularly true with regard to assistance under Section 406 of the Stafford Act (42 U.S.C., Section 5172), which deals with the federal cost share for the repair, restoration, or replacement of damaged facilities. The act permits some flexibility by allowing a local government to receive 90 percent of the federal cost share if it chooses not to repair or replace a damaged facility but to channel that money into mitigation for other facilities instead. Incorporating mitigation-related concerns into capital improvements planning thus eases the path to quickly identifying the community's unmet needs when it counts.

> Finally, there is the most important link of all to a plan independent of the local comprehensive plan, in no small part because it brings together two groups of professionals who need to collaborate more than has traditionally been the case: planners and emergency managers. The latter develop their own emergency operations plans, which are in the vast majority of cases focused almost exclusively on immediate response and recovery functions following a disaster.

Finally, there is the most important link of all to a plan independent of the local comprehensive plan, in no small part because it brings together two groups of professionals who need to collaborate more than has traditionally been the case: planners and emergency managers. The latter develop their own emergency operations plans, which are in the vast majority of cases focused almost exclusively on immediate response and recovery functions following a disaster. These are, of course, extremely important, but the opportunity has generally been missed for discovering the synergies involved in linking long-term post-disaster recovery and reconstruction planning with emergency management concerns. The two professional communities have much to say to each other, for there is no clean division in time between the response period that begins with the onset of disaster and the initiation of long-term recovery and rebuilding functions.

To cite one example, planners and emergency managers at the same table might agree that a new subdivision of any type with no basements—whether because it consisted of manufactured housing or because, as is often the case along the Gulf Coast, the climate does not permit such construction—might be better off with a required storm shelter to prevent deaths and injuries from tornadoes, hurricanes, and other violent weather. In the absence of collaboration, however, such concerns may never be voiced during the development process, and the concept of a later retrofit seldom acquires much urgency. In the end, a form of mitigation that might have been incorporated into the site plan at only modest additional expense never happens. After disaster strikes, the inevitable question is Why?

Similar examples of the value of cross-breeding emergency management and comprehensive planning can be found with regard to virtually every disaster scenario imaginable. Many of these have to do with public safety functions during the emergency period that nonetheless have some repercussions for the long-term rebuilding process, such as the reopening of blocked roads in flooded areas or emergency access to fire-prone hillside developments.

Moreover, the discussion between these two groups, particularly if augmented by environmental and sustainable development perspectives, could open up new opportunities and approaches for post-disaster redevelopment. For instance, to the extent that centralized power sources are vulnerable to certain kinds of disruption, creative efforts to introduce renewable power sources that can be generated on site might open the door to further explorations of new possibilities in local energy planning. In a severe northern ice storm, for example, buildings with their own solar power and heating sources can maintain operations where those dependent on downed power lines cannot. Might this not be a potential consideration relative to shelter sites? Once in place, might it not serve as a provocative example for the rest of the community? Collaborative thinking by planners and emergency managers concerning these eventualities can open the door to some exciting new ideas for rebuilding more disaster-resistant communities.

Linkage with Land-Use Regulations

State laws vary widely concerning the required degree of consistency, if any, between local land-use regulations, particularly zoning, and the comprehensive plan (Dennison 1996). Some state courts require strict consistency and view the comprehensive plan as the controlling document to which the local zoning ordinance must adhere. In others, zoning may occur with no comprehensive plan whatsoever, and sometimes in the view of state courts serves as the master plan itself. In the absence of any consistency in state rules regarding consistency, it is impossible here to discuss in depth the legal relationship of the plan or element for post-disaster recovery and reconstruction to land-use regulations.

As a practical matter, however, a community clearly advances its agenda for post-disaster recovery and reconstruction by using the development of such a plan to review the logic of its existing land-use regulations and to revise them in accordance with its own stated goals as a byproduct of that planning process. These are inevitably very hazard-specific. For instance, coastal erosion is a recurring concern in communities facing hurricane hazards. Nags Head, North Carolina, used its plan to address this problem by requiring future subdivisions to have ocean-to-road linear orientations, an approach of little relevance to most other types of hazards. On the other hand, vegetation, slope ratios, and soil stability would be relevant regulatory considerations in wildfire and landslide hazard areas.

APA recently published a PAS Report (Morris 1997) dealing with subdivision controls in flood-hazard areas. Various earlier PAS Reports have dealt with land-use regulatory and design issues concerning other types of hazard-prone areas, such as steep slopes and earthquake fault zones. Mostly, however, these deal with the design and zoning for new subdivisions and other developments rather than those affected by disaster and needing to undergo reconstruction. The reconstruction situation can be

Moreover, the discussion between planners and emergency managers, particularly if augmented by environmental and sustainable development perspectives, could open up new opportunities and approaches for post-disaster redevelopment.

State laws vary widely concerning the required degree of consistency, if any, between local land-use regulations, particularly zoning, and the comprehensive plan (Dennison 1996). Some state courts require strict consistency and view the comprehensive plan as the controlling document to which the local zoning ordinance must adhere.

considerably more daunting because of existing lot lines and, far more often than not, a crazy-quilt pattern of damaged and undamaged structures within the same area. For these areas, rezoning considerations, especially with regard to lot size and configuration, or floor-area ratios and impervious surface coverage, can be a treacherous enterprise, but it is certainly made easier by some forethought about potential alternatives in a plan devised prior to the emergency.

USING DISASTER ASSISTANCE EFFECTIVELY

The first step in effectively using disaster assistance, says consultant Clancy Philipsborn (1997), principal of the Mitigation Assistance Corporation of Boulder, Colorado, is to learn not to focus on the disaster alone. A community's narrow focus on simply gaining access to the limited pools of disaster assistance money available from FEMA leads to a cramped vision of the its options and keeps it from getting a handle on the bigger picture. In other words, planning for post-disaster recovery and reconstruction needs to be well integrated into the community's comprehensive plan and stitched into its larger vision of its own future. Not only does this open up much larger options for attracting outside resources to aid in post-disaster recovery and reconstruction, but it also helps the community itself to identify more creative solutions to a range of problems exposed by the damage wrought by a disaster. Furthermore, it provides an opportunity to identify a range of resources to assist in dealing with ongoing or pre-disaster mitigation issues. For instance, many small Midwest communities had long-running economic difficulties that may have been exacerbated, but certainly were not caused by, the 1993 floods. For those communities that latched onto a multiobjective approach, recognizing those larger problems and seizing opportunities to address them through the rebuilding process was the key to creative planning for economic renewal.

Among the examples that emerged from the Midwest floods is that of Valmeyer, Illinois. Although the total relocation of a town is an exceptionally rare outcome, Mayor Dennis Knobloch showed unexpected opportunistic zeal when, after initial skepticism, he sought the help of an outside design team organized by DOE to bring sustainable design principles to the relocation process. Knobloch acquired his enthusiasm while attending a conference on sustainable redevelopment underwritten by DOE, with support from the Johnson Foundation, at the Wingspread Conference Center in Racine, Wisconsin, in January 1994. The regional planning agency had already laid out the new town site, and time did not allow for reconsideration of its conventional suburban-style street layout. Valmeyer, however, still derived substantial benefits in other ways, particularly by incorporating superior energy efficiency into its new buildings, using incentives provided by the Illinois Department of Energy and Natural Resources.

Pattonsburg, Missouri, because it did not yet have a new town site platted by the time it connected with DOE's design team, was able to use such help more extensively in pursuing a more neotraditional design and opening more questions to public discussion in its citizen participation process. Mayor David Warford latched onto the idea of sustainable redevelopment by attending a workshop in Valmeyer. Pattonsburg was then able to marshal resources from the Division of Energy in the Missouri Department of Natural Resources, in addition to FEMA, DOE, and the Economic Development Administration (Skinner and Becker 1995).

A number of other communities, including Darlington, Wisconsin, and Arnold, Missouri, were able to act on their own dreams of connecting their river corridors to larger existing greenways and trails, using money from the special $130 million supplemental appropriation for the buyout pro-

A community's narrow focus on simply gaining access to the limited pools of disaster assistance money available from FEMA leads to a cramped vision of the its options and keeps it from getting a handle on the bigger picture.

gram designated by Congress for use in the Midwest (Design Center for American Urban Landscape 1994).

Homestead, Florida, which was forced by Hurricane Andrew to undertake extensive rehabilitation of its downtown and nearby residential areas, constructed a package of improvements under a newly created community redevelopment agency called Homestead Economic and Rebuilding Organization (HERO). Its five-year plan reveals heavy reliance on a combination of state and federal resources including various grant programs of the

City of Homestead, Florida

federal Economic Development Administration and grants for road improvements from the Florida Department of Transportation, in addition to the use of Community Development Block Grants (CDBG) and Housing Opportunities Made Equal (HOME) funds from the U.S. Department of Housing and Urban Development for residential redevelopment (Enterprise/Homestead Planning/Action Team and City of Homestead 1993).

FEMA is simply not the only game in town when it comes to applying for disaster assistance. Many agencies and institutions that may have no direct connection to disaster management may be viable sources of funding for communities that can tie other development objectives to their plans for post-disaster recovery and reconstruction. (Appendix C provides a directory of federal programs providing various types of disaster assistance.) This allows a community to assemble a better array of funding to achieve its own longstanding objectives. Moreover, a more substantial local effort, including the extra effort that goes into identifying and pursuing such funds, will go a long way in impressing FEMA

Code enforcement and crime had been problems in this Homestead, Florida, neighborhood (below, right). After Hurricane Andrew flattened the area, the Homestead Economic Redevelopment Organization acquired and cleared the property and constructed 18 single-family houses (above), which were sold to first-time buyers.

officials with the level and quality of the local contribution to the post-disaster effort, potentially bumping the creative community up the priority list in the competition for disaster funds. The Nags Head, North Carolina, *Hurricane and Storm Mitigation and Reconstruction Plan* (1988) contains a provision for retaining an assistance facilitator-consultant who would be responsible for:

- determining the types of assistance available to the town and the type of assistance most needed;

- assisting in the coordination of federal disaster recovery effort;

- coordinating federal and state programs of assistance;

- informing the community of types of assistance programs available; and

- recommending to the recovery task force and board of commissioners programs that are available to the town and then to act as facilitator in securing those programs.

It is important to consider the community's contribution of staff time and energy in addition to any specific budgetary allocation it makes to match federal and state grants. Many communities, Philipsborn says, fail to account for this "soft match" of resources for disaster assistance. For some projects, that staff time may be quite substantial.

Boone: A Case Study

Boone, North Carolina, a town with recurrent flood problems, provides an example of a community with a particularly thoughtful and flexible plan for using disaster-related assistance to achieve several outcomes and to use a "soft match" to generate more resources. Part of the town's mitigation program entails a three-phase project within one neighborhood. Phase One of the project is the acquisition and relocation of 15 houses on 17 lots, all of which are located within the floodway and 12 feet below the base flood elevation. The town conducted appraisals and offered the building owners fair-market value. For those owners who wanted to retain their structures, relocation assistance was envisioned in lieu of purchase—but only if the cost of relocation was less expensive than outright purchase. To accomplish this effort, the town assembled a package of funding consisting of FEMA Hazard Mitigation Grant Program (HMGP) funds, state division of emergency management funding, HUD-state CDBG funds, and town resources.

In many communities, that might have been the whole story. Boone, however, is planning to eliminate the demolition and removal costs by bringing other priorities into play. It turned out to be more manageable for the town to plan to relocate the majority of acquired structures to a new low- and moderate-income housing development elsewhere within Boone (rather than allow the few interested owners to relocate the structures themselves). Owners who wanted to reoccupy their homes and meet the income eligibility requirements will be provided the highest priority to purchase within the development. In addition, several structures are being donated to Habitat for Humanity and to a women's domestic violence organization. The organizations taking possession of the structures will be responsible for their relocation, but the town has lined up additional low-interest funding that is available to help defray the costs should the organizations be interested. Finally, if a structure remains unmoved, it will be donated to the town fire department and burned for training purposes. Thus, a variety of housing and other community goals are being served by identifying stakeholders with an interest in the physical property.

Phase Two, which also was funded, involved the acquisition and relocation of 15 additional structures. The only difference is that these structures are in the floodplain, rather than the floodway. According to project manager Jim Byrne (1998), by December 1998, 24 of the total of 30 units acquired had been relocated and were to be rehabilitated to create low- and moderate-income housing. Philipsborn added that a "reuse plan has been developed for the area vacated by both Phase I and Phase II that incorporates open space, bicycle and pedestrian trails, and an open-air amphitheater."

Phase Three of this project is for the relocation of a 104-bed residential health care facility. Funding of this phase exceeds that of Phases One and Two together and required a different strategy. An HMGP application for Phase Three was submitted to the state in December 1997 and is pending approval when funds become available. The primary focus initially was to assist the health care facility to relocate its business to a flood-free location and to promote the reuse of the structure as a nonresidential daytime use. This would be considerably safer than the current use, which is a 24-hour residential care facility for individuals with disabilities. To date, the town has successfully supported the facility's application for an increase in the state-controlled number of beds. This provides the means for the business to operate profitably in a new location. Second, the town waived current policy by agreeing to extend water and sewer services to the proposed new site, which is beyond the town's current limits. Then, the town approved a request for rezoning of the existing building's site to improve the ability to attract a suitable nonresidential day use. According to Byrne, however, in the end, the nursing home operator was unable to make the move without selling the old building, so the application ultimately involved purchasing and demolishing the facility.

The options for preserving the newly created floodplain open space are equally diverse and the result of the emergence of other local priorities and interested parties. Of course, the final results will be contingent on many factors, not the least of which is 100 percent voluntary participation of the building owners to sell their properties and vacate the floodplain. Among the parties interested in the reuse of the floodplain property is the state department of transportation. They "owe" several acres of reconstructive wetlands to replace those destroyed elsewhere within the county during a construction project. This site meets their criteria, thus creating a situation where environmental regulatory priorities may enhance the funding sources for a hazard mitigation project. The state also has funding for a greenways program, and consideration is being given to using some of the land to fill a missing link of the town's existing trail system. Clearly, the greenway and wetlands project could be linked together. In addition, Appalachian State University is located in Boone, and it has an interest in obtaining more open space for use as recreation and/or parking. And, of course, both the town and the county are interested in using the space for similar purposes themselves.

A key element in the Boone story concerns the local match for federal disaster assistance, which can provide up to 75 percent of the cost of a project. Finding a variety of other funding sources can make the community's grant application look more attractive by reducing that federal match. In Boone's case, that federal percentage fell to just 63 percent, a very attractive proposition for agencies dispensing limited funds to competing local governments. Even more importantly, this is an attractive proposition for the state, which must prioritize and select projects to stretch the available money and provide matching funds.

The Essential Lesson

The essential lesson is that a community's ability to marshal disaster assistance and use it effectively does not depend solely on its ability to make a case for the need to rebuild the community. It depends instead on the community's ability to relate those reconstruction goals to larger plans it has developed for the community's overall future. Fitting disaster assistance aims into those larger aims allows officials to be more creative in thinking about the kinds of funds that may be appropriate to the situation. Those can include a variety of possibilities: rural economic development, housing, transportation, environmental protection, parks and recreation, urban redevelopment, and even health and sanitation.

Chapter 4

The Planning Process

Capter 3 reviewed the underlying public purposes of planning for post-disaster recovery and reconstruction. This chapter will move beyond that discussion to examine the steps a community should follow in preparing such a plan, based in large part on the experiences of a number of communities that have already done such planning. (See the sidebar on the next page for an overview of these steps.)

In the United States, the centerpiece of planning efforts has long been the comprehensive plan. The individual elements included in local comprehensive plans have varied significantly in response to both community needs and state planning mandates, although certain staples, such as transportation, community facilities, and land use, are nearly universal. In addition, various kinds of jurisdictions have evolved specialized plans to address particular needs, such as inner-city redevelopment, the cleanup of environmentally contaminated areas, or the expansion of public parks and recreation facilities. The previous chapter covered the need for strategic linkages between the plan for post-disaster recovery and reconstruction and these other plans or plan elements. In some communities, post-disaster plans themselves have been devised as independent, or stand-alone, special plans. In either case, plans or comprehensive plan elements addressing the need for post-disaster recovery and reconstruction represent one more way for planners to help their communities cope with a defined problem and to shape a vision of how the community can improve its situation and take advantage of opportunities for positive change (Berke, Kartez, and Wenger 1994).

Importantly, this section will not consider those issues that are largely addressed by emergency managers in their own operational plans for disaster response. Rather, it will be limited to those that affect the long-term reconstruction of the community. The more operational emergency management issues may well find a place in an actual post-disaster plan, but that integration needs to be developed through local cooperation between planners and emergency management officials. Where the latter set of issues intersects both categories, the emphasis will be on their implications for long-term reconstruction.

FORMING A TASK FORCE

The plan for post-disaster recovery and reconstruction must tap a uniquely broad combination of resources and expertise in order to reflect the complex realities that must be addressed. An interdisciplinary reconstruction planning task force is the best way to guide the process of constructing the plan. This allows the interagency task force that must implement the plan to have a hand in guiding its creation. In relatively small communities, however, the staff may be able to develop the plan with less formalized public and

Steps in the Planning Process

Below is a simple chronological outline of the steps described in this chapter for initiating and completing the process of preparing a plan for post-disaster recovery and reconstruction:

1. **Make the decision to plan** for post-disaster recovery and reconstruction

2. **Form a task force** to develop the plan

3. **Put someone (some agency) in charge** of the process

4. **Document the hazards and risks** for your community

5. **Present your findings** to the community and get feedback
   a. Develop clear, effective educational materials
   b. Hold public forums to discuss the problem

6. **Build public consensus** around the need to develop and implement a plan

7. **Develop the plan**
   a. Prepare plan elements as needed
   b. Link the plan to other plans
   c. Link the plan to land-use regulations

8. **Present the plan for adoption**
   a. Hold public hearings
   b. Get the legislative body and chief executive to adopt the plan

9. **Implement the plan**
   a. Set pre-disaster elements in motion
   b. When disaster strikes, be ready to act

10. **Review and amend plan as appropriate**
    a. On periodic basis
    b. When planning laws change
    c. After disasters

interagency input, but citizen participation in the plan's development will remain essential for building public consensus. The sidebar on page 78 lists the composition of the post-disaster planning task force proposed in a Key West, Florida, ordinance that was awaiting city council action as this document was being completed, as well as an existing intergovernmental task force in Escambia County, Florida.

These task forces have taken different names and forms depending on the nature of the hazards being addressed. In many communities, for instance, a floodplain management plan task force would suffice. In Los Angeles, on the other hand, the multiplicity of natural hazards present necessitates a multihazard perspective that accounts for wildfires, mudslides, floods, and earthquakes. Regardless of the specific circumstances, the plan is more likely to succeed if a broad range of stakeholders has worked on its development. This is particularly true when hazard mitigation can serve some additional planning objectives in the bargain.

Organizing appropriate representation on the task force is as important in this case as with any other interdisciplinary planning effort. The sidebar on page 80 suggests a number of the key players from local government sectors whose representation is likely to be at least essential if not mandatory for success. Two considerations enter into the process: whose participation is essential in guaranteeing technical accuracy and thoroughness for the plan?, and whose participation and support will enhance its political acceptability? With regard to the first question, the input involves issues of both hazard mitigation and emergency management. Those involved in mitigation activities will bring to the process their professional knowledge of both the structural and land-use implications of attempting to minimize or eliminate dangers to life and property from natural hazards. These players include planners and zoning administrators, environmental specialists, and building inspectors. Emergency management perspectives will come from a combination of both emergency managers themselves and allied public safety forces, such as fire and police departments, who can help identify issues like the feasibility of evacuation and shelter plans. Beyond these players, various other local government personnel whose functions either aid or are affected by the post-disaster plan should be involved as is locally appropriate. Common candidates would be transportation and economic development personnel.

In soliciting public input and building public support for the plan, the topics of the next section of this chapter, it is wise to involve some nongovernmental representatives in the task force. Nonprofit service delivery agencies often have a major stake in the plan, considering the resources they often are called upon to deploy in the aftermath of a disaster. Neighborhood and civic organizations representing the most hazard-prone areas of the community may be better able to sell components of the plan affecting those areas to their members if they have been part of the process and learned along the way what stakes are involved in ensuring the plan's success. The chamber of commerce and other business organizations can play a major role not only in selling the plan to the local business community but in providing important perspectives on the challenges involved in facilitating economic recovery. Religious institutions often provide volunteers, shelter, and food in disaster situations and probably deserve a role in helping devise the means of reducing the severity of the crisis beforehand. Environmental organizations can lend support for the multiobjective benefits of sound floodplain management. All of these constituents of the community have played a role in some task force somewhere, but the right mixture for any one community will depend on its history, local politics, the nature and extent of its natural hazards, and the resources needed.

Launching the Post-Disaster Planning Process: Three Case Studies

What launches the process of planning for post-disaster recovery and reconstruction in a community? Much like death, which they sometimes bring in their wake, natural disasters are a subject people often don't want to discuss. It is human nature to try to deny the inevitable, even when we know better. Preparing for the consequences of natural disasters thus becomes a subject shunted into a corner where a handful of professionals, such as emergency managers and fire chiefs, can tend to such nasty business.

The reality, however, is that disasters are everyone's business, a fact that becomes abundantly clear when they strike. Like other less threatening aspects of city planning, they should therefore be the subject of considerable public scrutiny and of a planning process that involves a wide cross-section of the public. Soliciting public input in public hearings on the plan is one way to accomplish that, but it is just as important to construct a process that involves a variety of public and private-sector representatives from the outset in order to guarantee adequate consideration of all the relevant issues. The result will be a plan in which the vast majority of the community, whether or not people are comfortable with peering into the mouth of the beast, feel a sense of ownership of the decisions that resulted. It is vitally important that the plan enjoy wide enough support to ensure its implementation.

Case studies presented on pages 84, 87, and 88 describe how three jurisdictions of widely varying sizes handled the problem of initiating the planning process and of managing public involvement to produce positive results. All three have had their post-disaster plan in place for several years, allowing some perspective concerning their achievements. The case studies are based on both the documentary materials and the plans themselves, as well as telephone interviews with local planners.

Gaining an effective mix of representation can be a prelude to some creative cross-breeding of perspectives in the planning process over the long term. This is important because the disaster recovery plan, once created, will need to evolve over time and respond to new circumstances. In this respect, Lee County, Florida, offers a worthy example of a jurisdiction where, over nearly two decades, emergency management concerns have been steadily integrated into the development approval process. For instance, David Saniter (1998), the county's emergency programs manager, reported that effective intervention by his department helped induce a change in design for a planned hockey stadium to make it possible to use the facility for an emergency public shelter, should the need arise. Such advocacy within the planning process has raised local awareness of the problem, he says, to a level where developers and their attorneys now call him regularly to find out what sorts of shelter space are needed and to discuss what they can offer.

In a sense, Saniter is unusual in that he brought three years of planning experience to his emergency management job when he arrived 17 years ago. But it is not necessary to have people who combine both types of professional experience. Planners can play a significant role in introducing land-use planning concerns to the thinking of local emergency managers, just as Saniter has introduced emergency management concerns into land-use planning. This type of awareness and cooperation in planning for post-disaster recovery does not come easily. The first step on the long road to such a cultural change in resident and developer perspectives on planning for post-disaster reconstruction is to ensure that, at a minimum, planners and emergency managers are exchanging their concerns on the plan development task force, preferably with other vital players involved from the start as well.

> The first step on the long road to such a cultural change in resident and developer perspectives on planning for post-disaster reconstruction is to ensure that, at a minimum, planners and emergency managers are exchanging their concerns on the plan development task force, preferably with other vital players involved from the start as well.

Task Force Composition in Escambia County and Key West, Florida

As is stressed elsewhere in this chapter, no one formula for constructing a post-disaster planning task force is ideal for all communities and jurisdictions. The suggestions offered in this report are all generic in nature, subject to adaptation to local politics and circumstances. That said, examples never hurt.

The first example below is a description of the composition of the Intergovernmental Recovery Task Force prescribed in the *Post-Disaster Redevelopment Plan* of Escambia County, Florida (1995). It should be considered in light of the fact that Escambia County has just one major city: Pensacola. The remainder of the county is unincorporated. The plan envisions a simple structure in which the task force is "created to provide opportunities for cooperation between local governments during pre-disaster planning and post-disaster mitigation analysis and redevelopment." In other words, it serves double duty as a plan development task force and in managing post-disaster redevelopment, although the latter duties must wait upon activation by the board of county commissioners asking the governor to declare the county a disaster area. The designated chairperson is the county administrator.

The following text is from the plan:

COMPOSITION OF RECOVERY TASK FORCE

The Recovery Task Force will be composed of the individuals (or their designees) that reflect a broad-based representation of community interests and shall be appointed annually by the Board of County Commissioners. The Recovery Task Force shall consist of, but not be limited to, the following individuals:

1. County Administrator
2. County Special Projects Director
3. County Attorney
4. County Emergency Preparedness Director
5. County Solid Waste Director
6. County Neighborhood Services Director
7. County Public Works Director
8. County Medical Director
9. County Utilities Authority Director
10. County Neighborhood Improvement Chief
11. County Budget and Finance Chief
12. County Building Safety Chief
13. County Growth Management Director
14. County Planning and Zoning Chief
15. Santa Rosa Island Authority General Manager

Ex officios:

1. Representatives of the business community (appointed by the Chamber of Commerce)
2. City of Pensacola Liaison
3. City of Gulf Breeze Liaison
4. Santa Rosa County Liaison
5. County Sheriff Liaison
6. County School District Liaison
7. Northwest Florida Regional Planning Commission Liaison
8. Santa Rosa Island Authority Liaison
9. Other representatives as appointed by the Board of County Commissioners or the Recovery Task Force (i.e., Home Builders Association, League of Women Voters, etc.)

The county followed the major provisions of the plan in the aftermath of Hurricane Georges, which hit the Gulf Coast on September 28, 1998. These provisions include dealing with operational issues like debris cleanup, damage assessment, and reconstruction policy. At this writing, the activation of the local interagency task force had not occurred.

Task Force Composition in Escambia County and Key West, Florida (continued)

Key West, unlike Escambia County, is a single municipal jurisdiction in Monroe County, an archipelago jutting into the Caribbean that comprises the southernmost part of the state. In August 1997, the consulting firm of Solin and Associates drafted a post-disaster recovery and redevelopment ordinance that will be revised prior to sending it to the city council for adoption. It provided for a redevelopment task force that would meet within 90 days of adoption to "establish a regular schedule of meetings to determine a management framework for resolving issues confronted in times of disaster." Its proposed duties are typical of those discussed elsewhere in this chapter, and its composition would be as follows:

a. City Manager

b. City Attorney

c. City Planner

d. City Emergency Operations Coordinator

e. Chief Building Official

f. Fire Chief

g. Chief of Police

h. Director of Public Works

i. Director of City Electric System

j. Director of Transportation

k. Finance Director

l. Director of Florida Keys Aqueduct Authority

m. Monroe County Liaison

n. School Board Liaison

o. Tourism Office Liaison

p. Red Cross Representative

q. Liaisons to Private Utilities (Telephone, Cable, and Natural Gas)

In this draft ordinance, the city manager would be the designated chairperson of the task force, and the city planner would serve as the vice-chairperson. As a result of following the operational aspects of the recovery ordinance, the city will be reviewing portions of it. The size of the redevelopment task force and the need for a planner to actually go out on damage assessments (with the chief building official and director of public works) are two particular concerns.

Leading the Charge

Who organizes the task force and ultimately takes responsibility for driving the process is a question central to the success of the entire enterprise. Ideally, this role should fall to the community's chief executive, whether that be a mayor, city or town manager, or county executive or board president. However, it is not uncommon for this executive official to delegate lead agency responsibility to some other official, such as the planning director. When this happens, it remains important that the chief executive has initiated or at least actively blessed the process and that this surrogate retains the active support of the chief executive. In many cases, particularly in larger jurisdictions, a post-disaster planning effort will bring together representatives of agencies or departments that have not worked together in years. In smaller communities, it is more likely that a good deal of informal interpersonal contact takes place on a regular basis, but it is still vitally important that the lead agency or official in the planning process has the clear support of the mayor or town manager in order to ensure the full cooperation and support of the other participants.

The need for such support may seem less apparent in communities where a state mandate drives the necessity for preparing a post-disaster plan, but that would be an unfortunate perception. Even in Florida, with the strongest mandate in this area and the clearest guidance, plan quality varies widely

In many cases, particularly in larger jurisdictions, a post-disaster planning effort will bring together representatives of agencies or departments that have not worked together in years.

Getting the Right People: Task Force Representation

As suggested in this chapter, two essential participants of a task force would come from agencies involved either hazard mitigation or emergency management activities. The list below suggests specific types of officials who should be involved in post-disaster planning at either a state or local level as well as some typical private-sector participants who have a major stake in the policies and objectives of the plan. Those with a more direct stake in the process are italicized.

1. HAZARD MITIGATION

Local:

- *Environmental officer*
- *Floodplain manager*
- *Building official*
- *Planner/planning director*
- *Zoning administrator*
- *Public works director/city engineer*
- *Parks and recreation (where acquisition is a viable option)*
- *Stormwater management official*
- *Economic development director*
- Finance officer
- Transportation official
- Housing department

Special Districts:

- *Regional planning organization*
- *Regional flood control organization*

State:

- *State hazard mitigation officer*
- *State NFIP coordinator*
- *State planning agency*
- *State insurance commission*
- *State housing/building code agency*
- *Natural resources department*
- *State environmental protection agency*
- *Tourism and economic development agency*
- Transportation department

2. EMERGENCY MANAGEMENT

Local

- *Emergency manager*
- Police chief
- Fire and rescue official

State:

- Emergency management agency
- State police

3. GENERAL

Local

- Public information officer
- GIS specialist

State:

- Public information officer

4. PRIVATE SECTOR

- Chamber of commerce
- Utility companies
- Neighborhood organizations
- Homeowners associations
- Local religious or charitable organizations
- Social service agencies
- Red Cross representative (quasi-governmental)
- Environmental organizations
- Private development agencies

and executive support for interagency cooperation can make a significant difference in the results achieved. This is also true whether the plan is simply an element of the comprehensive plan, which almost invariably is prepared under the leadership of the planning department, or is a stand-alone plan, sometimes prepared under leadership from emergency management. Because of the extensive interagency cooperation needed to effect successful post-disaster reconstruction, executive leadership remains essential in all circumstances.

Choosing the right leadership for the task force itself will vary with the circumstances and may depend heavily on personal characteristics of potential candidates for this role. French and Associates (1995) suggests a resident as leader—at least for the flood-related planning efforts that the firm's guidebook addresses—and that the "planner or other staff member" provide administrative support. This is probably wise, but more important is the qualification that this person have an "ability to get people to work together and get things done." This should include an ability to pace the work so that neither members' expectations nor the schedule become unrealistic.

When the Clock Is Ticking

It is generally best that a community initiate the process of developing a disaster recovery and reconstruction plan when no disaster is looming on the horizon and there is ample time to consider the welter of complex issues and interrelationships involved in implementing effective post-disaster reconstruction and mitigation. There are times, however, when it is either apparent that the clock is ticking down to a major disaster or when the disaster strikes in the midst of the planning process. Much less ideally, but frequently, a community is spurred by the aftermath of a disaster to construct a plan virtually overnight. An example of the first instance might involve a northerly or mountainous community that becomes aware that heavy snowmelt and, perhaps, looming ice jams portend a flooding crisis within weeks or months. In heavily forested areas, a prolonged drought often signals the potential for wildfire disaster. The other two possibilities are obvious enough from historical experience. In these cases, executive leadership is essential in determining which steps are most essential in preparing a minimal post-disaster plan with details that will attend to the most important issues at hand, while shortcutting most others. Planners and emergency managers are likely to play some of the most decisive roles in helping to determine what those suitable shortcuts might be.

One shortcut candidate is hazard identification, simply because there may be no time for careful work in this area and much existing information can be marshaled into service in choosing appropriate short-term targets for mitigation efforts. Conversely, it would seem that much immediate emphasis in such circumstances ought to be placed on developing an inventory of funding sources for post-disaster activities that can be tapped efficiently and quickly during the post-disaster period, so that the maximum amount of outside resources can be brought to bear on the problems the jurisdiction has chosen to address.

Despite the necessity of such decisions when these occasions warrant, planners ought not to miss the opportunity to muster support in the disaster aftermath for more substantial planning efforts in the future. Post-disaster crises have nurtured a fair amount of invention in the realm of emergency public participation, notably through the increasingly frequent use of charettes, which typically involve residents, a team of design experts from outside the community, FEMA, and the state emergency management agency in intense efforts to solve problems within a highly compressed time frame. Within 30 days of the March 1, 1997, tornado that devastated Arkadelphia, Arkansas, a four-day recovery planning charette was conducted by a project team composed of planners, urban designers, economists, and engineers. Within another 30 days, the project team and the Disaster Recovery Committee developed a reconstruction strategy that provided a framework for the community's long-term recovery (Woodward-Clyde 1997a; Schwab 1998). The primary advantage in the post-disaster setting is that the limited time allowed forces everyone involved to focus on essential issues in practical but, hopefully, creative ways. Charettes have played a major role in communities facing either total relocation or massive redevelopment.

This sketch for a rebuilt marketplace was developed during an Urban Land Institute charette held in Watsonville, California, following the 1989 Loma Prieta Earthquake.

French and Associates (1995) suggests five points to consider when dealing with time constraints for preparing a post-flood mitigation plan after the disaster "in order to take advantage of the window of opportunity that the flood has presented and to settle any uncertainties residents may have about their future." It is noted here that these same points could easily apply to most other post-disaster scenarios.

• Dedicate a person to work on it full time

• Have frequent (e.g., twice per week) planning committee meetings that involve residents

• Do not delay the planning effort in order to obtain detailed data; an adequate plan can be based on generalized information

• Enact a temporary moratorium on reconstruction in areas most likely to be acquired

• Design the plan to address overall issues and make general recommendations (e.g., recommend that additional studies be conducted before finalizing some projects)

As has been said elsewhere in this report, natural disasters are almost invariably cyclical and will happen again. As the Hilton Head Island story (see the sidebar on page 87) suggests, even a near-miss can become the impetus for a more serious public commitment to planning for post-disaster recovery and reconstruction.

Setting the Stage

The goal of this chapter is to review the steps involved in pursuing the development of a plan for post-disaster recovery and reconstruction, including an overview of the process of rallying support behind the very idea of building a more disaster-resistant and sustainable community.

In order to make hazard mitigation and post-disaster recovery and reconstruction a focus of political action, planners must seize strategic opportunities to raise and maintain the profile of natural hazards as a public issue. A major point of this document is that there are specific times in the cycle of natural disasters when people become more receptive to messages concerning change. Once the issue has gained that profile, a crucial component of the planning process is to propose and organize a multiagency task force that will involve all key players in local government in soliciting public input and molding it into a plan of action. (See Chapter 5 for a model ordinance establishing a task force to guide this process.) No group of professionals is likely to be better than planners at orchestrating that process and maintaining its focus on the big picture, so long as elected officials support that orchestration and allow planners the necessary time and resources to do that work.

DEVELOPING COMMUNITY CONSENSUS AND VISION

Requiring implementation in the midst of crisis, a plan for post-disaster recovery and reconstruction is an unusually fragile instrument of public policy. It is unlikely to succeed unless it enjoys broad and knowledgeable support both from the public and within local government. The question is how to build and maintain that support so that it is available to undergird difficult decisions at crucial moments in the aftermath of a disaster.

As a general proposition, the need to build consensus around a vision for the community's future in order to make a plan successful is not a new subject for planners. Since the late 1960s, urban planning literature has contained a profusion of writings concerning techniques and strategies for encouraging citizen participation, enhancing public education about the goals and benefits of planning, and shaping the resulting awareness into agreement on basic public values and objectives (for example, Smith 1979; De Sario and Langton 1987; Moore 1995). Federal, state, regional, and local government agencies have published a host of manuals, studies, and guidelines concerning public participation in planning processes.

The central theme of many of these writings concerns the need to build public awareness that a specific problem exists and that there is a need to solve it through some type of public action. In the view of Innes (1996), the development of these tools for fostering meaningful participation, through what some have called "communicative rationality," has gone far enough to put to rest old criticisms like those of Altshuler (1965) that planners lacked the kind of broad-ranging knowledge needed to prepare a comprehensive plan that retained any validity for decision makers. Instead, they can tap the resources, ideas, and expertise of diverse participants in the planning process, producing a plan that reflects the informed wisdom of the community as a whole.

The process of building consensus has two stages. The first involves building consensus around the very need for a plan in the first place. While this may often be taken for granted in developing comprehensive plans for communities long accustomed to the idea of planning and zoning, it may yet be a necessary step for communities with no historical context for land-use planning. The mere fact that a community is accustomed to zoning does not guarantee that residents will accept new land-use restrictions based on concerns related to hazard mitigation. Planners will likely find a need to build public acceptance of the value of planning for post-disaster recon-

A major point of this document is that there are specific times in the cycle of natural disasters when people become more receptive to messages concerning change. Once the issue has gained that profile, a crucial component of the planning process is to propose and organize a multiagency task force that will involve all key players in local government in soliciting public input and molding it into a plan of action.

Launching the Post-Disaster Planning Process: Nags Head, North Carolina

Nags Head is a small town (pop. 1,838) on a barrier island, making it highly vulnerable not only to hurricanes, which strike occasionally, but to steady coastal erosion from northeastern storms every winter and spring. Erosion rates, according to town planner Bruce Bortz, vary from two to 10 feet per year, but are not consistent. A mild winter can slow that rate for a while, but a severe hurricane can escalate the damage dramatically. Morover, depending on the weather patterns, any given location may receive as much new sand in deposition as another loses to erosion.

In such an environment, it did not take a major disaster to spur Nags Head at least to study the situation. In 1984, the town hired David Brower, a professor of urban planning at the University of North Carolina, as a consultant to prepare a study that examined the value of structures close to the oceanfront and the policies that would be needed to protect such real estate. The study, prepared every five years as part of the town's participation in the federal Coastal Zone Management Program, determined that 40 percent of the town's real estate value was within 300 feet of the ocean.

"Our town council is very proactive about protecting the tax base," Bortz says, "so this study evolved into pretty strong policies on a land-use plan to protect that value and our citizens and structures." Those policies evolved into a post-disaster and mitigation plan, adopted in 1988, that looks at a number of issues ranging from ordinance amendments to development policies. One example that Bortz cites concerns the fate of private roads that wash away in a storm. "We won't expend public funds to replace them," Bortz says, "and we don't allow private roads anymore." The plan has undergone some minor changes since its adoption, and the town is now completing, with Brower, a follow-up study looking at the same property value issues but "with much greater accuracy using GIS." It will examine by value the property directly adjacent to and in floodplains using a series of criteria, with the help of two planning grants to support updating the town's mitigation plan.

One aspect of the development of the plan probably reflects Nags Head's nature as a small town. There was no special task force set up to develop the plan, which was handled by the town's staff in cooperation with the town council and planning board. That does not mean the public had no say in the plan. "One overriding goal that helped in this plan," Bortz says, "was the strong feeling that we wanted to retain the town's family beach atmosphere. That means single-family, low-density, no high-rise hotels. And that helped sell the plan."

It has also been accepted well by the construction community. "It provides a scenario for getting the town back on its feet," he adds. "There are several things that must happen [after a disaster] before a builder can get a building permit, but there is some certainty in the process for builders."

Given the town's early start, it is unsurprising that Bortz sees Nags Head as having driven the development of state requirements under North Carolina's Coastal Area Management Act (CAMA), which requires mitigation plans in 20 coastal counties and their municipalities. "Communities have to develop strong mitigation policies we already addressed in 1985," he notes. CAMA, passed in 1985, "was weak on hurricane mitigation," he says. But new policies, distributed to municipalities in 1990 and 1995 by the Department of the Environment and Natural Resources' Division of Coastal Management, strengthen the original requirements concerning land-use plans. Bortz says they contain a number of ideas that appear to have been borrowed from the Nags Head plan.

struction, particularly where the risk is perceived as distant or infrequent. Gaining acceptance of the need to address natural hazards serves as the prelude to the second stage, that of developing a plan and building consensus around its goals and policies. At this point, the planning process is accepted, and the debate is over the specific goals that will emerge and the means of realizing them. Public involvement should permeate this process, and the best modern tools, such as the Internet and cable television, should be used in combination with direct public contact to maintain and promote an intelligent dialogue on the natural hazards problems the community is addressing. Keeping the editorial boards of local newspapers apprised of the planning process also helps gain support.

Probably the closest analogy to the type of consensus building involved in planning for natural hazards reduction is the experience of environmental regulators, who often must raise the public awareness of complex scientific and technological questions in order to build support for new policies (Ozawa 1991). Many of the environmental threats that environmental agencies must address are somewhat abstract or confusing to the average citizen, yet the nation as a whole has forged a remarkable consensus behind the need for strong environmental protection. This consensus has held firm despite a wide array of attacks on specific programs and regulations.

Planners will often encounter a certain amount of fatalism in public perceptions of natural hazards. The occasional observation that no place is without its hazards, for instance, is true enough if one cares nothing about probabilities. Here we have the link between the debate over natural hazards policy and that over environmental policy, for in both areas critics repeatedly have noted a need for public education concerning assessments of comparative risk. Despite the technical jargon that surrounds much discussion of risk, planners are in an ideal position to help elevate public awareness of natural hazards. Especially at the local level, they are in a position to mobilize and redirect public concern both before and after natural disasters and to mold it into a lasting base of support for new land-use policies.

The key to success seems partly to involve timing because the essential task in mustering support for a change in policy is that of winning sustained public attention. Historically, advocates of natural hazard risk reduction have not always been noticeably effective. Concerning the growing potential for disaster as a result of new residential development in fire-prone areas of California, for instance, Coleman (1996) notes that an "entire series of reports have been written over the last 35 years, all of which contain essentially the same kinds of concerns and even have amazingly similar recommendations." While some state legislation resulted, the results in terms of adoption and implementation of those recommendations at the local level were far from universal.

How do planners sustain public attention for reducing risk from natural hazards? The experience of cities like Tulsa in developing effective and comprehensive floodplain management strategies suggests that it can be a prolonged process based on nurturing public dissatisfaction with the disastrous results of existing policies and land-use practices (Schwab 1996a). Planners need to accept a crucial but demonstrable paradox. The immediate aftermath of a disaster may not be the ideal time to start constructing a plan for long-term reconstruction because people are anxious to restore normalcy to their lives. However, in most disasters, there is about a 30-day window of opportunity to incorporate a planning framework into the disaster recovery effort. It is also an ideal time to raise awareness that a process needs to be undertaken to reexamine land-use patterns and to plan for the aftermath of future disasters. In the absence of any existing plan for post-disaster recovery and reconstruction then, the immediate aftermath of a disaster is a time for planners to do what they can to mitigate future hazards, to also accept the limits of what they can do under the circumstances, and to look toward fostering an ongoing and probing discussion of how the community will address its vulnerabilities in the future. It is precisely this sense of timing and opportunity that FEMA has been encouraging in local communities as it has strengthened its emphasis on planning for hazard mitigation (FEMA 1990).

As a result, planners should not rule out the possibility of initiating a public discussion of natural hazards in the aftermath of an event. The real point is that the damage from natural disasters is cyclical and will likely spiral upwards with subsequent events as long as the issue remains unaddressed. Thus, it is possible in a city with a floodplain to make clear that even minor, frequent events, such as 10- or 20-year floods, augur much larger disasters unless changes are made.

Some infrequent events, however, provide little in the way of warning. The New Madrid earthquake fault is a classic example of a low-probability, high-risk hazard. It would be folly to wait for this estimated 200-year event before raising public awareness of the need for action. Planners and emergency managers in Missouri, Arkansas, Kentucky, Indiana, Illinois, Alabama, and Tennessee must do what they can to arouse public concern and support for whatever mitigation measures can be developed before a highly uncertain but potentially devastating event ultimately occurs. These steps can serve to minimize the confusion and controversy that will inevitably follow such an event (CUSEC 1993).

Communities that plan for long-term reconstruction have no way of knowing when their plans will be implemented. They can only rest assured that, when that time comes, they will be better prepared than most to make effective use of the available state and federal assistance to emerge from the disaster with a safer, more disaster-resistant community. Without wishing for the worst, their civic leaders at least can know that they will be in an advantageous position to extract a silver lining from future disasters when they occur.

The next section of this chapter will outline the initial task of identifying the hazards that must be the subject of public discussion in this planning process.

HAZARD IDENTIFICATION AND RISK ASSESSMENT

Meaningful local land-use policy cannot address hazards in the abstract. The starting point of the planning process must be an identification of the hazards facing the community and the risks they pose to life and property. FEMA's *National Mitigation Strategy* (1995c) describes hazard identification and risk assessment as "the cornerstones of mitigation," establishing "both a common point of departure and the bounds within which plans and alternatives can be formulated, debated, and decided on." Moreover, empirical research by French et al. (1996) indicates that "high-quality information (hazard data, mapping, interpretation, etc.) would translate reasonably into less damage from earthquakes," and, by extension, for other well-researched hazards as well. An abundance of good information serves to guide the local development market as well as drive local plans and their implementation. A 1997 FEMA document, *Multi-Hazard Identification and Risk Assessment*, is a good initial source for information about the identification of natural and technological hazards and the risks they pose to life and property. Chapter 7 will go into more detail on hazard identification and risk assessment for each of the major natural hazards dealt with in this document.

Three key terms defined in the glossary in Appendix B are worth differentiating here before discussing the process. These are, in the order in which they should be addressed in the planning process, hazard identification, vulnerability assessment, and risk assessment. FEMA (1997b) describes hazard identification as a process of "defining and describing a hazard, including its physical characteristics, magnitude and severity, probability and frequency, causative factors, and locations/areas affected." Assessing vulnerability means taking stock of the degree to which human life and property are exposed to damage from that hazard; in other words, how much damage and loss of life could the

> Communities that plan for long-term reconstruction have no way of knowing when their plans will be implemented. They can only rest assured that, when that time comes, they will be better prepared than most to make effective use of the available state and federal assistance to emerge from the disaster with a safer, more disaster-resistant community.

Launching the Post-Disaster Planning Process: Hilton Head Island, South Carolina

Like Nags Head, Hilton Head Island (pop. 24,000) occupies a barrier island along the Atlantic coast, but with a much larger real estate base and population at stake. Compliance with South Carolina's Beachfront Management Act required Hilton Head to develop a plan for post-disaster recovery. However, Hilton Head Island also had a close call that further motivated its planning. When she arrived in 1988, says long-range planner Jill Foster, the town council had budgeted money to draft a post-disaster and mitigation plan, but had never actually done it. But within a month after Hurricane Hugo hit, narrowly missing the town, the council budgeted money to hire The Mitigation Assistance Corporation (TMAC) of Boulder, Colorado, to prepare a plan.

TMAC president Clancy Philipsborn stationed one of his staff members on the island for three months to solicit citizens' input into the plan. The town recruited a planning committee with more than 20 members representing a diverse cross-section of public and private organizations including utility companies, property owner associations, emergency medical crews, the fire department, and the chamber of commerce, among others. The 140-page plan (not counting its extensive appendices) touches on an impressive range of practical post-disaster issues, including troublesome areas like immediate reentry into disaster-affected zones, and entailed coordination with Beaufort County emergency management officials and other public entities and jurisdictions throughout the area. Philipsborn's team and the committee also "went directly to several organizations" for their comments. In all, Foster estimates, about 100 people were directly involved in the plan development process.

Like its neighbor to the north, South Carolina also has special planning legislation affecting coastal areas, in this case its Beachfront Management Act, passed in 1990, which contains a mandate for coastal communities to prepare post-disaster plans. Like the Hilton Head Island plan, the act was largely motivated by the fallout from Hurricane Hugo. But Foster says the Hilton Head Island plan did not result from the act because "the intent to plan preceded the act," although the plan does state that it was prepared under the act's authority. If the Hilton Head Island plan proves anything, it is that good fortune with respect to what could have happened can be as effective in motivating post-disaster planning as being hit by the real thing.

community conceivably suffer? This is differentiated from risk assessment, which focuses on probabilities and is described by FEMA (1997b) as a process for "evaluating risk associated with a specific hazard and defined in terms of probability and frequency of occurrence, magnitude and severity, exposure, and consequences."

Step 1. Identify and Map the Community's Natural Hazards

The first step in hazard identification and risk assessment involves mapping the known natural hazards, a procedure that will vary with the nature of the disaster. By now, every planner in a municipality with a floodplain should know that FEMA for years has developed maps of local flood hazard zones as part of NFIP. These are probably among the most precise guides to the contours of any local natural hazard. However, seismic mapping also exists for earthquakes and volcanic hazards, and storm surge zones have been identified for coastal areas. Tornadoes are by far the most problematic threat because they can occur virtually anywhere given the right atmospheric circumstances. Regardless of these variances, the first step is to document all of them and identify as accurately as possible the areas potentially affected by them.

Step 2. Document and Quantify What's at Risk

The second step in hazard identification and risk assessment is to develop an inventory, to the extent possible, of the built environment that potentially

Launching the Post-Disaster Planning Process: Lee County, Florida

Lee County (pop. 335,000), unlike the towns in the two previous case studies, qualifies as a truly large—and rapidly growing—jurisdiction. Nonetheless, like Hilton Head Island, says David J. Saniter, the county's emergency programs manager, the county used the experience of Hurricane Hugo to motivate the development of its post-disaster ordinance. Although Florida specifically requires a post-coastal storm recovery plan for communities in coastal counties, Saniter also concedes that the quality of and commitment to such planning can vary significantly from one jurisdiction to another (a situation noted by Robert Deyle and Richard Smith in their case study of Hurricane Opal in Chapter 10). Thus, it is not unimportant that he observes that Lee County "expanded upon that plan after Hurricane Andrew," which "put a scare into people about what could happen in Lee County."

Lee County is quite possibly the nation's leading example of creative initiatives to inject emergency management concerns into the development approval process as a result of an unrelenting emphasis by Saniter's office on implementation. "We have to fight and fight and fight," Saniter says of such efforts, "but we started getting things into the comprehensive plan. And at least we discharged our responsibility. We told the county board what would be impacted." This intervention is unusual, Saniter concedes, noting that in other counties, "my colleagues are scared of planning" and hesitate to intervene in the process to express their concerns. Saniter, however, brought three years of planning experience into his emergency management job when he was hired 17 years ago.

One truly unique implementation device that Saniter doubts can be found anywhere else in the country is the county's All Hazards Protection District, which uses a property tax levy to generate about $900,000 yearly to fund mitigation measures and emergency public shelters, all with the blessing of the board of county commissioners.

Saniter emphasizes that successful post-disaster planning requires a long-term commitment to the process, but adds that this "learning and educating process" has resulted in support from the development community and its attorneys.

would be affected by these hazards. This inventory not only will indicate the extent of possible damage from the hazard but will also serve as a rough indicator of the threat to human life because people tend to be where transportation or buildings are, and the total or partial collapse of structures or parts of structures is a primary cause of death and injury in a disaster. This potential damage to life and property is what constitutes vulnerability, and the likelihood of that damage–quantifying the probabilities—is what constitutes risk. A flood in an unpopulated and unbuilt area, for example, poses little or no risk. On the other hand, the risk posed by even a modest earthquake in downtown Los Angeles can be quite high. The potential damage from an eruption of Mt. Rainier, located as it is within view of Washington's major metropolitan areas, could easily be catastrophic (Krakauer 1996).

Because predicting the future is strictly a matter of probabilities, the only certain data come from past experience. Thus, planners documenting risk must include in their reports the history of previous natural hazards events, their magnitudes, and an inventory of the human and property damages that occurred. Those magnitudes should be expressed numerically, in a statistical or other mathematical measure, such as the Richter scale (earthquakes), Saffir-Simpson scale (hurricanes), Fujita scale (tornadoes), or flood probabilities (for example, an x-year flood). More detailed explanations of such documentation appear in Chapter 7.

The age of housing stock and other structures can vary significantly within a community. It is no accident that, when a natural disaster strikes, some parts of town suffer disproportionate losses, including some types of historic properties, older housing that often serves lower-income residents, and older commercial districts that may often lie just outside the central business district. It is important to build into the process, preferably with the use of computerized databases and GIS, a pre-disaster inventory of vulnerable structures and to use this information to evaluate building performance on a geographic basis. This is not just a building department function, though building officials are necessarily involved, because it can also reveal much to planners about needed changes in development patterns for the future.

It is important to realize generally that advances in information management technology are making the automation of these tasks possible at an increasingly rapid rate. A good deal of technical sophistication is now available far less expensively today than ever before, and progress will continue at an exponential rate. In addition, coordination of hazard-related databases and GIS technology can occur at a statewide level through state emergency management agencies. Probably the most promising venture in this regard is underway through the Governor's Office of Emergency Services (OES) in California, which faces possibly the most daunting array of natural hazards anywhere in the nation. Topping (1994) has prepared the agency's GIS strategic plan as a first step in guiding the development of a system that gained considerable value following the Northridge earthquake. A valuable part of the plan discusses strategies for funding this cooperative effort.

Planning agencies often need technical assistance from scientific experts and from state and federal officials in doing a complete hazard inventory and risk analysis for their local plans. Many communities hire outside consultants for this purpose. Chapter 7, which examines hazard identification in greater detail, discusses for each hazard the available resources to which communities can turn for information and advice.

ELEMENTS OF THE POST-DISASTER PLAN

As discussed in the previous chapter, the aftermath of a natural disaster can be an extremely trying period for public officials seeking to restore normalcy to the community and to rebuild. A well-organized plan rooted in good factual detail can make the process manageable and give an appreciative public the sense that someone is in charge and had the foresight to think through the issues and contingencies the community might face during the long process of reconstruction.

Focusing on the details of implementation is at the heart of preparing the elements of the plan for long-term post-disaster reconstruction. Everything matters. The point of this section is to outline briefly the issues that ought to be addressed. Figure 4-1 is a matrix that outlines the various long-term reconstruction policy issues covered in this section and the types of local agencies that would usually be designated with responsibility for that function in a local ordinance, which implements the plan itself. It should be noted that an actual plan will detail many specific implementation measures with agency assignments on a more detailed level than this matrix suggests. Consulting existing plans from other communities is a good way to adapt this level of detail to the precise needs of a particular local government. As these plans usually tend to involve numerous players (depending on the size of the jurisdiction), the watchword in post-disaster planning is cooperation. Planners, however, are in a good position, if supported in this role by the local chief executive, to orchestrate or coordinate the process and to ensure that the plan is a meaningful reference point for all the actors involved.

Focusing on the details of implementation is at the heart of preparing the elements of the plan for long-term post-disaster reconstruction. Everything matters.

As these plans usually tend to involve numerous players (depending on the size of the jurisdiction), the watchword in post-disaster planning is cooperation.

Figure 4-1. Agency Assignments for Post-disaster Recovery and Reconstruction Functions

The chart on the opposite page is intended as a suggestive indication of the local government agencies likely to be assigned to specific action tasks in a municipal post-disaster plan. Agency assignments at a county level obviously would be somewhat different. The list of functions mirrors those in the section of Chapter 4, "Elements of the Post-Disaster Plan," but is not intended to be exhaustive. Agency designations are intended to be relatively generic, and the overall pattern is distilled from a variety of local plans submitted to APA for this project and does not reflect the experience of any particular jurisdiction. Moreover, in typical plans, the functions listed would often be broken down into specific actions assigned to individual lead agencies; no attempt is made here to be so specific, hence multiple agencies may be listed for single functions.

To clarify the typical roles of planners, five columns have been left with a white background to highlight these functions: building, community development, historic preservation, planning, and redevelopment. Although planners can be found in a wide variety of agencies in local government, these agencies employ the vast majority of planners and are the ones where planners are likely to have some role in the process of preparing and implementing the post-disaster plan. In smaller communities, in particular, planners are most likely to find themselves in combined planning and building departments that handle both building and zoning code enforcement.

It should also be noted that this chart includes an additional category of functions beyond those listed in this chapter. Response/Early Recovery deals with functions that are implemented immediately during or after the disaster and are addressed in detail largely in the community's emergency operations plan, a document developed through the local emergency management office. They are listed here to round out the inventory but are not discussed in the text because they are not part of planners' direct involvement in post-disaster recovery. The exception would primarily be any role planners would play prior to a disaster in identifying appropriate sites for emergency shelters and emergency operations centers.

Key to agency abbreviations in chart:

BF	Budget and finance	HP	Historic preservation commission
BG	Building		
CA	City attorney	PL	Planning and zoning
CD	Community development	PR	Parks and recreation
CM	City manager or mayor	PS	Public safety (police/fire/ emergency medical crews)
ED	Economic development		
EM	Emergency management	PW	Public works (including publicly owned utilities)
EN	Environment	RD	Redevelopment agency
HE	Health	SW	Solid waste/sanitation
HO	Housing	TR	Traffic/transportation

FUNCTION	BF	BG	CA	CD	CM	ED	EM	EN	HE	HO	HP	PL	PR	PS	PW	RD	SW	TR
RESPONSE/EARLY RECOVERY																		
Evacuation							X							X				
Urban search and rescue														X				
Emergency shelter provisions							X					X	X					
Mass care (food, water, medicine)							X		X					X				
ORGANIZATION AND AUTHORITY																		
Empower recovery task force			X		X													
Designate lead agency					X													
Operations policy					X													
Set up disaster accounting systems	X				X													
Coordinate with emergency manager					X		X					X						
Public participation and hearings												X				X		
REHABILITATIVE																		
Temporary housing		X		X						X		X				X		
Refuse disposal																	X	
Damage assessment		X			X							X					X	X
Restoration of utility services														X				
Establish reconstruction priorities					X		X					X		X		X		
Reoccupancy permits		X							X			X	X	X				
Emergency demolition		X	X		X													
Emergency permitting		X			X							X						
Loan processing	X			X		X				X						X		
Toxic cleanup								X	X					X			X	
LAND USE																		
Identify sites for emergency operations												X		X				
Identify new lessons		X					X					X		X				
Compliance with regs. from lessons							X					X			X			
Replanning of stricken areas		X		X			X		X			X	X	X	X			X
Reexamine street patterns for access					X							X	X	X	X			X
Feasibility of emergency evacuation							X					X	X	X				X
Historic preservation		X								X	X				X			
Implement area building moratoria		X	X		X							X						
Reevaluation and update of plan		X		X	X	X	X			X		X			X			
REGIONAL COORDINATION																		
Coordination with relief agencies							X											
Temporary housing				X						X	X							
Financial assistance channels	X			X	X	X				X					X			
Transportation repairs/restoration														X			X	X
Emergency legislation			X		X													
Media contact					X													
Mutual aid agreements		X			X								X	X			X	X

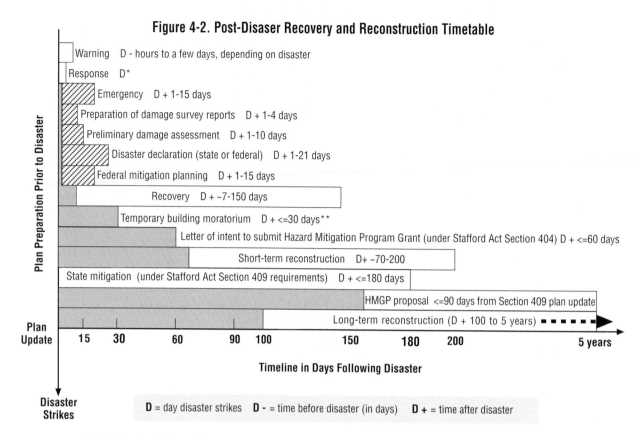

Figure 4-2. Post-Disaser Recovery and Reconstruction Timetable

The timeline above is derived from a number of sources, some pertaining to specific types of disasters or jurisdictions. It is intended to be suggestive but not precise, except where statutory requirements apply.

*Response generally refers to those activities undertaken to deal with the immediate crisis as soon after the disaster as it is possible for relief efforts to be mobilized. Often, these may last only a day or two. But in situations where a disaster occurs more than once, as with continuing earthquake aftershocks or prolonged flooding (as occurred in the Midwest in 1993), this response can be stretched to several weeks. Please see Appendix B for definitions of response, recovery, reconstruction, and related terms as used in this document.

**The duration of moratoria generally ought not to be more than 30 days. Often communities will distinguish between very short-term moratoria for permits involving minor repairs (for example, 10 days in Lee County, Florida) and a longer moratorium for more serious repairs or reconstruction of totally destroyed buildings.

> Who is in charge? Who reports what to whom? Waiting for a disaster is no way to find out.

Implementation also inevitably involves time lines and sequences. Figure 4-2 delineates the time periods during which various certain essential tasks must or likely will be performed, focusing to some extent on external deadlines that drive the process. The matrix in Figure 4-3 suggests the likely period, using the definitions in the glossary (Appendix B), during which a community would expect to implement the elements of its post-disaster plan.

Organization and Authority

Who is in charge? Who reports what to whom? Waiting for a disaster is no way to find out. As discussed in Chapter 2, the emergency period immediately following a disaster is largely the responsibility of the local and state emergency management agencies and, in a presidentially declared disaster, of FEMA and its partners in the *Federal Response Plan*. Most people are still accustomed to thinking that the story ends there. As this chapter has tried to demonstrate, it is only the beginning of a long period of recovery and

Figure 4-3. Timeline for Post-Disaster Plan Elements

The table below uses the same post-disaster plan elements as those in Figure 4–1 and in the final section of Chapter 3. The intent here, however, is to illustrate roughly the time periods during which the various functions would come into play, allowing for the fact, discussed earlier, that these periods are not fixed in time or even in absolute sequence. Different parts of a community or region may enter more advanced periods earlier than others. Nonetheless, this table may help to give some sense of work flow for communities developing their own plans.

Note: Unshaded boxes with comments are intended to define limited amounts of preparatory work, or, in the case of mutual aid agreements, to indicate a need simply to make operational agreements worked out during the pre-disaster period.

FUNCTION	PREDISASTER	EMERGENCY PERIOD	SHORT-TERM RECOVERY	LONG-TERM RECONSTRUCTION
ORGANIZATION AND AUTHORITY				
Select recovery task force	▓▓▓			
Empower recovery task force		▓▓▓		
Designate lead agency	▓▓▓			
Operations policy	▓▓▓			
Set up accounting systems for disaster assistance	▓▓▓			
Coordinate with emergency manager	▓▓▓			
Public participation and hearings	▓▓▓			
REHABILITATIVE				
Temporary housing	Identify sites	▓▓▓	▓▓▓	
Refuse disposal	Identify sites	▓▓▓	▓▓▓	
Damage assessment	Train teams, set MOUs	▓▓▓	▓▓▓	
Restore utility services		▓▓▓	▓▓▓	
Establish reconstruction priorities	▓▓▓	▓▓▓		
Reoccupancy permits	Set policies		▓▓▓	
Emergency demolition	Set policies	▓▓▓	▓▓▓	
Emergency permitting	Set policies			
LAND USE				
Identify new lessons from damage assessments	Review case studies	▓▓▓	▓▓▓	▓▓▓
Compliance of rebuilding with regulations from new lessons				▓▓▓
Replanning of stricken areas	Identify nonconforming uses, pre-FIRM bldgs.		▓▓▓	▓▓▓
Identify sites for emergency operations	▓▓▓			
Reexamine street patterns	Plan		▓▓▓	▓▓▓
Feasibility of emergency evacuation plans	Identify shelters, road capacity, vulnerability		▓▓▓	▓▓▓
Historic preservation	Identify vulnerable structures	▓▓▓	▓▓▓	
Implement building moratoria	Adopt policies	▓▓▓	▓▓▓	▓▓▓
Reevaluate and update plan				
REGIONAL COORDINATION				
Coordinate with relief agencies	Predisaster planning	▓▓▓	▓▓▓	
Temporary housing	Identify sites	▓▓▓	▓▓▓	
Financial assistance channels	Prepare inventory	▓▓▓	▓▓▓	
Transportation	Plan			▓▓▓
Emergency legislation	▓▓▓			▓▓▓
Media contact	Predisaster education			▓▓▓
Mutual aid agreements	▓▓▓	Put into effect		

reconstruction. The question few communities have addressed directly is who will manage long-term reconstruction in accordance with a post-disaster plan. Establishing both the authority and the organizational structure for managing reconstruction is the primary objective of the model ordinance in Chapter 5. The objective here is to outline the rationale and the method.

Designated lead agency. Who will coordinate the process and oversee compliance with the intent of the post-disaster plan? There is no single answer to this question, but there are several possibilities that have worked or can work, depending on local traditions, local government structure, and other factors that may influence this decision, such as the nature of the jurisdiction (e.g., city, county, jurisdiction size). Three likely candidates are the mayor's or city manager's office, the planning or community development department, or a local redevelopment agency. Where a post-disaster plan and local ordinance establish a recovery and reconstruction task force, a designated representative of the lead agency, presumably its director, will then serve as the task force chairperson.

The real issue is not so much which entity is put in the lead role but whether, if it is someone other the city manager or mayor, that entity and its director enjoy the full support of the local chief executive and legislative body in that role. Because a disaster often involves a good deal of reliance on outside assistance, a clear choice of leadership for managing long-term recovery and reconstruction also provides a central point of contact, information, and accountability for the outside world. This, in turn, increases the community's ability to marshal the external resources it needs.

Empowerment of a reconstruction planning task force. The plan should set out the circumstances and guidelines for empowering a task force specifically to deal with overseeing the process of planning for long-term reconstruction following the disaster. The point of this element should be to incorporate the intent of the discussion in Chapter 3, under "Long-Term Goals and Short-Term Pitfalls," dealing with task force composition. This element of the post-disaster plan should establish the composition of the task force in advance of a disaster, so that the actors can anticipate and train for their roles. This group is distinct from the broader body overseeing plan development, mentioned at the beginning of this chapter, and is focused on implementing the reconstruction process itself. The Los Angeles plan (1994) describes this as a "proactive rather than reactive approach. . .through post-event formation of a long-term reconstruction task force and preparation of a strategic plan for reconstruction."

Operations policy. Once the lead agency has been chosen, it is important to establish the line of reporting and responsibility for implementing recovery and reconstruction. If this report in its entirety has established anything, it is that this process is complex and often represents a struggle by the entire community to reassert its viability. That struggle will proceed much more smoothly if a post-disaster plan already has established the mechanisms and timelines for various municipal officials to perform their assigned tasks and to report to the lead agency in order to keep the recovery process well-coordinated.

In an analysis of the effectiveness of the Los Angeles plan after the Northridge earthquake, Spangle Associates and Robert Olson Associates (1997) found that prior training and rehearsal of these responsibilities tends to allow many types of urban officials (primarily in line agencies) to internalize their operational responsibilities to a point where they can follow the plan without even consulting it during the recovery period. For the lead agency, and even for other staff agencies, consultation is more likely to be necessary, but, for many other local officials, the time constraints involved

The real issue is not so much which entity is put in the lead role but whether, if it is someone other the city manager or mayor, that entity and its director enjoy the full support of the local chief executive and legislative body in that role.

Prior training and rehearsal of these responsibilities tends to allow many types of urban officials (primarily in line agencies) to internalize their operational responsibilities to a point where they can follow the plan without even consulting it during the recovery period.

in post-disaster responsibilities may make internalization through training a more efficient option. The point is to establish this in the plan and train people accordingly, and, then, after the plan has been tested, to reevaluate how well it has worked and to update the plan on the basis of experience.

Just as there is a lead agency for overseeing the recovery and reconstruction process, post-disaster plans spell out specific actions to implement their stated policies and designate lead agencies and participating agencies for those actions.

Operations policy should also address the probable need for interdepartmental assignment of personnel with special skills needed in an emergency and beyond. For instance, employees with bilingual skills may be vital for certain recovery operations in agencies other than those that hired them and can be lent to others that need such services.

Coordination with emergency manager. This topic was covered in Chapter 2, so it should be sufficient to note here that a point repeatedly made in current disaster literature is that there are no clear lines between the emergency period, short-term recovery period, and long-term reconstruction. Certain aspects of all three of these processes may be occurring within different parts of a community and its local government at the same time. In many of the communities studied for this report, including those examined by Robert Deyle and Richard Smith for the Hurricane Opal case study in Chapter 10, it is apparent that planners and emergency managers too seldom communicate with each other. The result is that planners do not have an effective sense of the challenges facing the community in managing emergency response and post-disaster recovery and a lack of understanding among emergency managers of the important role planning can play in moving the community beyond short-term recovery and in incorporating hazard mitigation into everyday (i.e., pre-disaster) planning activities.

Public participation and hearings. The first section of this chapter discussed the need to build community consensus behind a vision for how the community will rebuild after a disaster in accordance with the goals it has already laid out in its comprehensive plan. The plan itself should contain reasonably extensive and effective opportunities for public input and comment before it is adopted, and those opportunities should allow for meaningful public education in the bargain. Because economic recovery is so central to the success of any post-disaster recovery effort, special attention needs to be paid to involving the business community and soliciting its expertise on issues that will facilitate business revitalization. Because the plan will need both to be updated periodically and to undergo revisions in the aftermath of actual disasters, it helps if the plan includes provisions for ensuring continued public education and input on the plan's goals and purposes. The resources on citizen participation mentioned in that section, as well as others available from organizations like APA and the International City/County Management Association, should be sufficient to allow any community planning agency to craft an effective system for involving the public and winning its cooperation in implementing a post-disaster plan.

Rehabilitative Functions

No matter how brilliant a community's vision for long-term reconstruction may be, in the aftermath of a disaster few residents will show much patience with that vision unless the local government is prepared to respond quickly and effectively in restoring fundamental needs like housing and basic services like trash disposal. Unfortunately, as various examples throughout this document illustrate, trash disposal—including the disposition of toxic materials spilled or released during the disaster—takes on gargantuan proportions compared to normal circumstances. In the absence of some clear procedures, the city may not

The plan itself should contain reasonably extensive and effective opportunities for public input and comment before it is adopted, and those opportunities should allow for meaningful public education in the bargain. Because economic recovery is so central to the success of any post-disaster recovery effort, special attention needs to be paid to involving the business community and soliciting its expertise on issues that will facilitate business revitalization.

only find itself hard-pressed to make emergency arrangements for such services, but it may also be paying private contractors premium prices in a seller's market. The rehabilitative functions necessary to buy time to handle long-term issues include all aspects of cleaning up and assessing damaged sites, and of processing those assessments and repair permits so as to facilitate the return to habitable structures of the maximum number of local residents in the shortest possible time frame.

This rehabilitation occurs simultaneously in both the public and private sector, with the former overseeing the latter through regulation. For the sake of sorting out operational from regulatory responsibilities in the plan, the following discussion divides rehabilitative functions into those involving primarily public or private responsibilities. It should be noted that building departments, not planners, are principally involved in the latter group of responsibilities, but that these elements address issues about which planners may wish to express some concerns during the plan development process.

Public-Sector Responsibilities

Temporary shelter. Providing the temporary shelter people need is a function for emergency managers, but planners should play a vital role by identifying appropriate sites in advance. Emergency shelter sites generally revert to their original uses, such as schools and community centers, after the recovery period, but other forms of temporary housing, including manufactured housing, can and often do become more permanent than may have originally been envisioned. Planners can help to ensure during the pre-disaster period that, if this happens, the sites identified for such housing are zoned appropriately.

Refuse disposal sites. Planners are normally involved in solid waste management only to the extent that facilities to accomplish this mission must be sited somewhere. Certainly, the process of contracting for collection and disposal is most likely to be handled by a public works or sanitation department to whatever extent the local government is not performing this

This debris was moved to the side of the streets in southern Florida after Hurricane Andrew in 1992. Clearance and removal require planning and coordination to avoid creating extra work.

FEMA

function itself. However, the post-disaster plan can make provisions for gaining a quick estimate of the scope of the problem, as in the plan for Hilton Head Island (1993), which incorporates this into the damage assessment process described below. Debris clearance is often traffic clearance as well, to the extent that roadways are blocked by felled trees or flood muck and thus impede other recovery functions. Lee County, Florida, (Ordinance 95-14) establishes road clearance as its first priority in this area, followed by area medical, fire, law enforcement, and emergency response facilities, recognizing, in effect, that the overriding priority is access.

The volume of debris amassed for collection and disposal following a major disaster can easily escalate overnight by orders of magnitude (U.S. EPA 1995); in the aftermath of Hurricane Andrew, in fact, the area had to dispose of a volume of debris equal to what it normally manages over a five-year period. Rush-hour traffic jams in parts of southern Dade County, Florida, in the fall of 1992 sometimes consisted of nothing but long lines of trucks carrying their daily load of construction debris to designated area landfills. That situation was an extreme but speaks to the crisis planners must anticipate: Where will the debris go? Designating appropriate temporary and permanent disposal sites as part of the post-disaster plan allows this question to be incorporated into an area's long-term land-use plans for the siting and eventual closure of landfills. The issue, however, does not stop there, for a great deal of construction debris is potentially recyclable. Planners can help to designate appropriate sites and procedures for managing the process of sorting recyclable materials from nonrecyclables and thereby aid in conserving landfill space for the longer term. Ensuring the smooth functioning of this service also speeds the clearance of debris-ridden sites so that properties may be repaired and rebuilt, and enhances the prospects for economic recovery by eliminating potential eyesores.

Assessment of building conditions and overall damages. This process was described at the beginning of Chapter 2 in the description of the preliminary damage assessment (PDA). The PDA is used to determine whether a presidential disaster declaration is justified. However, damage assessment is an ongoing task that may take different forms at different stages of response and recovery, starting with a minimal windshield survey, involving observations from passing vehicles by fire, police, and emergency management personnel, to more detailed and in-person surveys by building inspectors. The function of damage assessment should be included and addressed as an element in a post-disaster plan regardless of the magnitude of the disaster as a matter of clarifying lines of responsibility. For instance, the Florida Department of Community Affairs model (TBRPC/Hillsborough County 1995) provides for the designation of a local damage assessment team responsible for conducting the assessment.

The town of Hilton Head Island (1993) spells out three levels of damage assessment, which ends with a damage survey report. Doing so provides local officials with a quick general survey early on that anchors progressively detailed assessments as needed within the days following the initial event. These types of assessments are, in order:

- the windshield survey, usually done within 24 hours to assess overall impact and conducted from a moving vehicle;

- the initial assessment, more detailed and done within three to four days and conducted with town and county, and if necessary, state officials; and

- the preliminary damage assessment, or PDA, to warrant federal assistance.

Restoration of utility services. Few of the effects of a disaster make people feel more helpless and isolated than the loss of heat, power, and telephone service. Although various modern technological innovations in solar heating, photovoltaic cells, and cellular telephone service are making some people increasingly independent of highly centralized service delivery systems, the fact remains that most people rely on grid-based utility services most of the time. Moreover, even these decentralized utility technologies are vulnerable to interruption under certain circumstances. Restoring utility services is an essential prerequisite for beginning economic recovery and for restoring some measure of comfort to those whose routines have been disrupted. It is a matter of public safety, as well, for local firefighting ability is at stake when electrically operated water pumps no longer work. It can also be a matter of life and death for home-bound elderly people, the disabled, and others, or for families stranded without power in cold climates, such as happened in January 1998 in Quebec and upstate New York.

> Restoring utility services is an essential prerequisite for beginning economic recovery and for restoring some measure of comfort to those whose routines have been disrupted.

Unless a publicly owned electric utility is involved, most of the problem of restoring utility services will typically fall to the private sector. However, utility services that typically are in the public sector, such as sewer and water lines, are necessarily affected by electric power outages. Also, the nature of the service disruption will vary with the nature and extent of the disaster. Floods, for instance, are far less likely to disrupt electric service (with the exception of ground-level transformers) than are disasters involving high winds or seismic shaking. But the 1993 Midwest floods did disable water service for the entire Des Moines metropolitan area by overflowing the levees protecting the water treatment plant.

It is thus essential that the post-disaster plan address the need for restoration of all utilities and outline priorities for accomplishing this mission. This is often linked closely with the restoration of critical public facilities. For instance, the Hilton Head Island plan (1993) establishes three top priorities each for restoration of electrical and telephone service. (See Figure 4–4.)

Where private utilities have their own plans for emergency restoration of services, it is sufficient to refer to that plan and simply make clear who the responsible parties are in each instance. For instance, the Hilton Head Island plan lists both public service districts and private companies and the specific services and locations for which they are responsible. However, the local government's indication of desired public priorities can assist and direct the privately owned utility in its operations. It may also be necessary to detail any required cooperative efforts between units of government where public service districts serve more than one jurisdiction or municipality or where regional entities are involved. This may involve making arrangements with other utilities for mutual support. Incorporating mitigation techniques into the reestablishment of utilities may also affect timelines and procedures, as well as requiring mutual assistance from an outside utility.

Establishment of reconstruction priorities. Public facilities often suffer as much damage as private property in a disaster. Civic buildings, fire and police stations, hospitals, and schools have all suffered damage or destruction in major disasters. One critical function of a post-disaster plan is to establish the community's priorities concerning reconstruction of these facilities, given the obvious fact that limited resources and personnel may not allow simultaneous rebuilding of everything.

In many plans for post-disaster recovery and reconstruction examined for this report, a single element dealing with restoration of public facilities addresses both the restoration of public utilities and the reconstruction of public buildings and facilities. While these issues clearly are interrelated,

Figure 4-4. Priorities for Utility Restoration, Hilton Head, South Carolina

Electrical Restoration Priority

1. Hilton Head Hospital

2. Fire Stations and Emergency Medical Service Bases

3. Hilton Head Federal Emergency Operations Center

Telephone Restoration Priority

1. Hilton Head Hospital

2. Hilton Head Dispatch

3. Hilton Head Federal Emergency Operations Center

they can be quite different in an operational sense, and so we recommend that these issues not be confused or conflated. There are many variables that may enter into the selection of priorities for rebuilding public facilities, including the likelihood that the damage will cripple essential public services whose operation depends on the condition of the facility, and the urgency of the need for the services provided. In this sense, hospitals and public safety facilities almost always rise to the top of the list, as do any facilities that serve as emergency operations centers or shelters. (However, other elements listed in this chapter ought to address siting of the latter two functions with an eye to making them as immune to danger as possible.) On the other hand, the restoration of public recreational facilities, while important in the long term, would not seem as urgent in the immediate post-disaster environment.

Dealing with demand for building permits. This issue is tightly tied to the implementation of mutual aid agreements, another element discussed below under regional cooperation. It deserves attention here, however, because one of the most predictable consequences of the damage and destruction resulting from a disaster is a surge in permit applications. While this is not a problem with which planners will deal directly (except when they assist in performing paperwork functions to fill in for building officials out in the field), it is an issue the plan itself should address because of the serious problems that a growing backlog of applications can cause, including poor oversight in the permitting process, inadequate and hurried inspections, and public disgruntlement at the slow pace of the recovery.

FEMA provides limited assistance to states and communities to perform building department functions, such as inspections and substantial damage determinations under NFIP, and planning functions, such as plan review, but the requested assistance must have been addressed in the post-disaster FEMA-state agreement. There are two parts to this assistance. First, the community can get help in evaluating local codes and the building department's existing capacity. Second, as a result of the evaluation, the community may be eligible for assistance for extraordinary costs involved in the plan review and in the permitting of reconstruction. In addition, for the short term, under the public assistance program in Section 406 of the Stafford Act, FEMA can help local departments with health and safety inspections related to determining the habitability of buildings.

Financial assistance channels. Knowing where to access financial assistance both for restoration of business activity and for residential reconstruction allows for a more smoothly functioning process of recovery and reconstruction. This is the primary reason why the effective use of disaster assistance was identified as a policy objective of the plan in Chapter 3. People are deeply concerned about money in the recovery period following a disaster. Local officials can point people in the right direction and even help find sources of money they might otherwise never have known existed.

Private-Sector Responsibilities

Reoccupancy standards and permitting. Post-disaster conditions can pose a bewildering variety of threats to public health and safety, many of them lurking in residential buildings and in workplaces. The safety of residential buildings is particularly crucial because of their round-the-clock occupancy. When and under what conditions may people reoccupy partially damaged structures? Clearly, the goal is to rehouse people as soon as this can be done safely. The plan needs to establish how the work involved in performing this task can be done expeditiously and the standards that will be applied for interim reoccupancy of damaged structures. These policies need to be established in the pre-disaster period, though the implementation will flow out of the information generated through the damage assessment process.

One specific set of criteria that must play a role in this element relative to buildings in floodplains pertains to NFIP minimum regulations governing the determination of substantial damage, which refers to damage where the cost of restoring the building to its preflood condition would equal or exceed 50 percent of its preflood market value. Any community participating in NFIP must enforce provisions of its floodplain management ordinance dealing with measures to reduce future flood damage.

Emergency building demolition procedures. Disasters result in irreparably damaged buildings, many of which may constitute an imminent danger to public health and safety. There is no question that the city may use its police powers to remove these dangers in a timely fashion, but it still must follow due process. Moreover, having the capability in place to do so requires some planning because the work load can escalate dramatically, particularly following a significant earthquake or wind-driven event like a tornado or hurricane. While most of the implementation usually will fall to the building department, the plan should spell out the criteria and procedures that apply in an emergency.

As an example, the Los Angeles plan (1994) makes it the city's policy that demolition "be done as expeditiously as possible." It then calls for:

- establishing criteria for contractual agreements (and the contracts themselves) with the private sector;

- due processes and procedures for demolition;

- clarifying roles and prerogatives concerning historic buildings and reconciling legitimate hazard mitigation and historic preservation interests;

- doing the same concerning design review decisions connected with post-disaster repair and rebuilding of public structures; and

- including historic preservation and design review representatives in the investigations to minimize potential controversy.

Emergency permitting of building repairs. As with demolition proceedings, the work load for processing permits for building repairs will escalate dramatically after a disaster. A community without special procedures, including mutual aid agreements to borrow building permit personnel from other communities or private contractors, will find its residents growing surly as bureaucratic delays prevent necessary repairs, or even worse, residents may bypass the permitting process entirely, thus derailing post-disaster mitigation efforts.

In addition to importing permit-processing personnel as needed, an issue covered under the subsection below on regional coordination, the community can establish in its post-disaster plan and by ordinance criteria and procedures for streamlining and expediting permit review. In some cases, as in Oakland following the East Bay Hills fire (see case study in Chapter 11), this can be accomplished in part with the use of a special one-stop permit processing and disaster assistance center near the scene of the disaster.

The ordinance should spell out the length of time during which this system will apply. It may also make special provisions for deferring the payment of required fees to allow people a chance to recover first. Of course, permitting must still take place with an eye to mitigation, for example, by requiring elevation or similar measures in a floodplain, in accordance with local ordinances implementing NFIP. Local departments will want to avoid permitting that is at cross purposes with the substantial damage requirements of NFIP, particularly where the need arises to delay rebuilding to facilitate acquisition of substantially damaged properties.

Land Use

Of the various categories of elements in the post-disaster plan, this section is the most crucial. The overall intent is to provide for the means of learning valuable new land-use lessons from the disaster, to enable the city to incorporate them consistently into its mitigation plans and to amend its post-disaster plan as needed, and thus to minimize future risk by fostering a culture of adaptation to new information. This is, in other words, the primary feedback loop. More specifically, the appropriate amendments would tend to focus on updating priorities for changes in land uses or properties for acquisition or various forms of hazard mitigation, as well as planning changes in capital improvements planning, street width and design, and other issues affecting overall urban design.

Identifying new lessons. It is important for planners to remember that the first day of the post-disaster period is also the first day of the pre-disaster planning period that should precede the next event. When that lesson permeates the community's thinking, the identification of new lessons can serve as a powerful driver for all other land-use elements in the post-disaster plan, most particularly including the process of reevaluating and updating the plan after each disaster and modifying appropriate linkages with the local comprehensive plan as well. Thus, the progression from identifying new lessons to their incorporation into an amended plan should be seen not as a sequence of planning steps, but instead as a closed loop that leads to steady improvements in shaping a more disaster-resistant community. The most explicit way to remind the entire community of the need for reassessment is to include in the plan itself a discussion of planners' intent to revisit the hazard identification section of the plan after any disaster in order to incorporate new lessons.

What is the relationship of newly discovered or known hazards coming out of recent hazard events to existing or planned land-use patterns? Are these hazards serious or probable enough in future events to justify new land-use efforts to mitigate their effects? Earthquakes remain a key area where these

Local departments will want to avoid permitting that is at cross purposes with the substantial damage requirements of NFIP, particularly where the need arises to delay rebuilding to facilitate acquisition of substantially damaged properties.

It is important for planners to remember that the first day of the post-disaster period is also the first day of the pre-disaster planning period that should precede the next event.

Thus, the progression from identifying new lessons to their incorporation into an amended plan should be seen not as a sequence of planning steps, but instead as a closed loop that leads to steady improvements in shaping a more disaster-resistant community.

lessons are continuing to materialize because of the difficulty of adequately identifying subterranean faults. The fault slippage that caused the Northridge earthquake, for instance, was approximately 11 miles below the surface and had not previously been identified. Once these new lessons have been identified, land-use planning can provide a mechanism for associating them with appropriate new policy responses. These responses can extend to implications for infrastructure extension or replacement, for access routes and the feasibility of future evacuations, and for the zoning of various types of buildings and building construction techniques. State agencies can play a role in this process by facilitating the transfer of geologic and other data that local planners can use as a tool to reduce local hazards (for example, see the recommendations in Seismic Safety Commission 1994b).

Compliance of rebuilding with regulations developed from new lessons.

It does little good to learn valuable new lessons about natural hazards affecting the community if none of them are put to use. It is essential to prepare in the post-disaster plan a means for incorporating those lessons as rapidly as possible into the development regulations that will guide the reconstruction process. This may be, however, one of the most challenging elements of the entire plan precisely because it takes time to study, identify, and analyze new hazards information from a disaster, and even more time to craft regulations in response to them. It is often not possible for all rebuilding to await such analysis. But the plan should contain policy statements indicating clearly, before the disaster occurs, that the most hazardous areas will not necessarily be rebuilt.

Nonetheless, the entire process of rebuilding often takes years. In the initial stages, a temporary rebuilding moratorium of reasonable duration can buy some time where land use, rather than construction standards for rebuilding, is the central issue. Many of the plans and ordinances examined for this report anticipate a moratorium of up to 30 days, but what is allowable in any given jurisdiction may depend on state planning laws and existing local ordinances. (For a summary of applicable state laws concerning building moratoria, see Ziegler (1997), Section 11.03 [2], dealing with express statutory authority.) The model ordinance in Chapter 5 provides advance authority for a designated director of the local recovery organization to establish a moratorium for up to 90 days, subject to review by the city council within that time. The actual time needed will depend to a considerable degree on the type of hazard involved and the history and extent of knowledge of its occurrence locally. In other words, some cases are fairly obvious and require little additional study, but others are more complex and demanding, particularly where new hydrologic or geologic studies are required.

While it is likely to be impossible to apply these lessons to all post-disaster reconstruction, it is better to apply it where possible than not at all. Providing for some process of review and revision that will allow this to happen is an astute move for any local government.

Siting of emergency operations centers. If a local government is going to function effectively during a crisis, it must at least secure its own facilities for continual operation. More than one city hall found itself below decks in the Midwest floods of 1993, a situation that forces the staff to pay primary attention to salvaging and relocating valuable documents and equipment when they should be focused on recovery and reconstruction. During a 1996 flood, the same thing happened to the village of Plainfield, Illinois, whose 1990 tornado is the subject of the case study in Chapter 9.

While the security aspects of emergency operations are the responsibility of local emergency managers, planners can play a role in the pre-disaster

It does little good to learn valuable new lessons about natural hazards affecting the community if none of them are put to use. It is essential to prepare in the post-disaster plan a means for incorporating those lessons as rapidly as possible into the development regulations that will guide the reconstruction process.

The plan should contain policy statements indicating clearly, before the disaster occurs, that the most hazardous areas will not necessarily be rebuilt.

period by identifying alternate sites for continued governmental operations during disasters. If there is any danger that existing city offices will be affected by predictable types of disasters, planners can find suitable office locations outside known or probable hazard-prone areas that would allow government to resume its essential functions in the post-disaster period.

Replanning of stricken areas. Replanning uses the new lessons about local hazards to reshape the community's long-term vision for particularly hard-hit parts of the city. This function ought to be addressed in two stages: pre-disaster and post-disaster. The pre-disaster portion of this element would entail the identification of areas that may not be rebuilt after a disaster, accompanied by options for how those areas may be treated during the post-disaster period. The post-disaster aspect would consist of a review and analysis of these same areas to determine the most appropriate resolution of the planning problems they present.

If an area has proven more vulnerable than previously thought, perhaps reducing density or even considering acquisitions or easements for open space should become an option. The Los Angeles plan (1994) incorporates this function into its process of long-term reconstruction with both a restrictive and an opportunistic action program:

If an area has proven more vulnerable than previously thought, perhaps reducing density or even considering acquisitions or easements for open space should become an option.

Pre-event

D.5.1 Identify the relationship of identified natural and man-made hazards and unique economic, housing, growth management, and urban design opportunities to Safety Element and community plan land-use and hazard mitigation policies.

D.5.2 Revise community plans to acknowledge areas with identified natural and man-made hazards and, where appropriate, adjust land-use and other designations with the involvement of community planning advisory councils and the city planning commission.

D.5.3. Conduct studies leading to adoption of specific plans and special overlay zones in areas with identified natural and man-made hazards, providing for appropriate mitigation based on specific circumstances.

Post-event, long term

D.5.4. Modify community plan land-use designations in response to newly discovered hazard conditions which cannot be mitigated other than through change of use or reduction of planned land-use densities.

D.5.5. Modify community plan land-use, circulation, and other designations (elements) to reflect economic development, housing, growth management, or urban design opportunities generated by the disaster.

Reexamination of street patterns for emergency access. The Oakland fire case study in Chapter 11 illustrates the significance of this element all too well. The issue applies to other hazards as well. For example, Topping and Sorensen (1996) describe the use of GIS in a new town plan formulated for Kobe, Japan, following its 1995 earthquake. The plan provides multiple road crossings across a fault zone to and from the community so as to preserve access if one or more is blocked. Reexamination of street patterns is also a potent consideration in coastal and riverine floodplains, particularly in areas of active erosion (see the Nags Head case study in Chapter 4 on page 84). In floodplains, roads should approach buildings from the direction opposite the floodplain and avoid disrupting the natural drainage pattern (Morris 1997).

Disaster Threats and Planning Solutions for Historic Buildings

"Haste makes waste" is an adage that has special poignancy with regard to historic properties in the aftermath of a disaster. Hasty decisions are particularly devastating when they are made without any guidance from a post-disaster plan developed beforehand. Local planning departments and historic preservation commissions can play an important role in preparing owners and building officials to make informed decisions during a period when time is often critical. It is important that they understand the obstacles to survival that historic properties may face in the aftermath of a disaster. Carl L. Nelson (1991), in *Preserving the Past from Natural Disasters*, lists the "unthinking or seemingly uncontrollable actions" that may hasten the destruction of damaged historic resources in the aftermath of a natural disaster.

WHAT COULD GO WRONG

1. Restorable buildings are torn down.

2. Architectural elements are carted away with the debris.

3. Trees are tossed out rather than replanted.

4. Property owners make hasty and inappropriate repairs.

5. Archeological resources are disturbed by heavy equipment.

6. Government agencies—such as building permit offices and landmarks commissions—may operate with conflicting goals.

7. Normal design review procedures for changes to historic properties may be suspended.

8. A crush of construction applications may overburden officials.

9. Inspections of historic structures may be carried out by persons with minimal or no qualifications, including volunteer structural engineers and other experts from outside the area.

Preplanning for these problems can make a big difference. The following are some options to consider in preparing the historic preservation element of a post-disaster plan, which should be clearly linked to the historic preservation element of the local comprehensive plan.

WHAT COULD GO RIGHT

1. Provide local public safety officials with maps and floor plans for major historic facilities, such as museums, private libraries, etc. Having these may help to prevent damage from some of the emergency operations such officials must perform following a disaster.

2. Establish lines of communication in advance between local planning and building officials and a designated disaster coordinator for such facilities.

3. Use a thorough inventory of local historic resources and their vulnerabilities to establish priorities for post-disaster preservation efforts. Not everything may be saved, but it is important to know what is most likely to be restorable and why.

4. The historic preservation community can be mobilized by plan to muster second opinions about buildings that might otherwise be deemed appropriate for demolition. Maintaining efficient and effective review procedures for such buildings may identify alternatives that save such buildings from the wrecking ball. Evaluating historic buildings for structural repairs often requires special expertise beyond that of a structural engineer or building inspector.

5. Work with the state historic preservation officer (SHPO) and others to provide or identify for the owners of historic buildings training resources and opportunities pertinent to protecting their buildings from the impacts of disasters.

6. Identify, create, and promote the use of financial and technical assistance resources for hazard mitigation and retrofitting for historic resources and, where possible, incorporate suitable historic properties into local hazard mitigation plans.

Feasibility of emergency evacuation plans. The logic of addressing this point, and of reassessing it in the disaster aftermath, flows naturally from the point above. However, in addition to public safety officials, emergency managers should be involved in the preparation of this element.

In some highly vulnerable locations, such as coastal barrier islands, evacuation issues may be deemed to pose larger questions concerning long-term development patterns. For instance, in its section addressing post-disaster mitigation opportunities, Hilton Head Island (1993) explores the merits of an evacuation-based growth cap. The idea was to conduct a study of what would constitute an acceptable growth limit given the fact that the town has only a single bridge and causeway for access to the mainland. In a separate section (pages 134-136), the plan discusses the constitutionality of such a cap, noting decisions from Florida (*City of Hollywood v. Hollywood, Inc.*, 432 So.2d 1332, 1983; *Healy Co. v. Town of Highland Beach*, 355 So.2d 813, 1978) that suggested that an annual growth cap based on sound planning would pass muster. Such a cap has been in effect in Sanibel, Florida, for some years without any apparent legal challenge. However, it is important to note that Sanibel is nearly built out. A community cannot use a growth cap to escape its responsibilities to build adequate infrastructure for the growth it has already permitted, including that necessary to facilitate evacuation.

One important caveat noted in the Hilton Head Island plan's legal discussion is that a town's refusal to invest in the expansion of evacuation infrastructure might undercut the justification for growth controls. A second that has continued to vex the town since the plan was prepared is its inability to win effective cooperation from mainland communities and the state in coordinating evacuation traffic in hurricane situations. Long-range planner Jill Foster (1997) reports that this lack of cooperation results, as in Hurricane Fran, in traffic congestion immediately after residents reach mainland routes. During Hurricane Hugo, she says, the mere lack of a highway patrolman at a rural intersection three counties away from Hilton Head Island resulted in a 55-mile-long backup that delayed traffic for three hours. Nonetheless, Hilton Head Island plans to revisit the issue as it develops new plans in the future including a combination flood and hurricane hazards mitigation plan.

Historic preservation. Built in another era, engineered to earlier standards, many historic buildings are no longer deemed seismically safe or capable of standing up to other natural hazards, such as wind and flood damage. Reconciling the preservation of the historic structure with public safety needs in view of modern engineering standards poses one of the more vexing dilemmas in disaster planning. As noted previously, involving representatives of the historic preservation community in the necessary decisions and task forces can aid in reducing the level of tensions. Nelson (1991) describes how Mayor Joseph P. Riley of Charleston, South Carolina, succeeded in saving much of that city's heritage following Hurricane Hugo with a timely invitation to historic preservation leaders to assist in the reconstruction process. Nelson also discusses the role California preservationists played in slowing the demolition of damaged historic structures with a second opinion campaign directed at saving those that needed only minor surgery to remain usable. The accompanying sidebar highlights both the obstacles to successful post-disaster historic preservation and the planning solutions that can minimize the losses that might otherwise result.

Turner (n.d.), in one of a series of handbooks produced for the U.S. Geological Survey, outlines the essential measures that can be taken to ensure adequate attention to historic preservation during post-earthquake

Reconciling the preservation of the historic structure with public safety needs in view of modern engineering standards poses one of the more vexing dilemmas in disaster planning.

The point is that a moratorium should be anything but indiscriminate, as different parts of a community, especially a larger city, are often affected in very different ways.

recovery and reconstruction. Despite problems in this area following the Loma Prieta earthquake (described in a case study in Chapter 12), he notes that California shortly thereafter enacted California Public Resources Code, Section 5028, which requires a local government to obtain permission from the State Office of Historic Preservation before demolishing any disaster-damaged building. This forces the local government to document the extent of damage. Turner suggests that such mechanisms could well be adapted in other states and that Ohio set a midwestern precedent by including in its state disaster plan provisions for including state historic preservation office (SHPO) personnel on damage assessment and damage survey teams regarding public historical sites. Since the 1993 Midwest floods, representatives from SHPOs are often included on hazard mitigation teams.

Plans for hazard mitigation of historic properties in the post-disaster plan should take account of the funding assistance provided by FEMA under the Hazard Mitigation Grant Program created under the Stafford Act, as discussed previously, and the technical assistance available for preparing the required state hazard mitigation plan, which certainly can include guidance on the treatment of historic buildings. In addition, public assistance money may reimburse the costs of demolition for unsafe historic buildings after the proper determinations are reached in cooperation with a SHPO. Other sources of monetary and technical assistance outside FEMA that the plan can incorporate include the National Endowment for the Arts, the National Park Service, and the American Institute of Architects.

In addition to Nelson (1991) and the USGS guidebook, FEMA Region I (n.d.) and the National Trust for Historic Preservation (1993) have produced helpful short guides for safeguarding, or restoring, historic properties from the effects of natural hazards.

Implementation of area-specific building moratoria. A building moratorium is a typical post-disaster plan device, designed to buy time for local officials to gain control of the recovery and reconstruction process before irrevocable decisions compromise opportunities for mitigation. It also provides building officials with the time they need to complete damage assessments and establish priorities, often in triage fashion, for the use of limited local public resources. Although the formulas vary, plans spell out levels of damage that will trigger the imposition of a building moratorium for a specific area of the community. The point is that a moratorium should be anything but indiscriminate, as different parts of a community, especially a larger city, are often affected in very different ways. Where little or no damage has occurred, there is little or no rationale for restraining development. Hilton Head Island provides for three damage classes depending on levels of damage. For more commentary on this point, see the model ordinance in Chapter 5. Although placing this issue within other land-use elements in the post-disaster plan is an option, addressing it in a separate element would ensure that the plan establishes a clear rationale for putting a building permit moratorium into effect.

Nature on the rampage shows little respect for humanly designed political boundaries, and the vast proliferation of suburban, township, and small town governmental structures that dot the American landscape has made the need for interjurisdictional cooperation ever more apparent.

Regional Coordination

Rare indeed is the disaster of any consequence that affects just one local jurisdiction and whose impacts stop at the city limits. Nature on the rampage shows little respect for humanly designed political boundaries, and the vast proliferation of suburban, township, and small town governmental structures that dot the American landscape has made the need for interjurisdictional cooperation ever more apparent. The need for coordination is accentuated when a disaster reaches the level of a state or presidential declaration because mechanisms of state and federal disaster relief come into play. As if that were not enough, a host of nonprofit services stand ready to respond but need effective points of contact in local communities so that their efforts are not duplicated and wasteful. Natural disasters spur marvelously the generosity of the American people, but effectively distributing donated relief supplies requires some planning and coordination lest their arrival merely add to the chaos or frustration. (Although it is a more extreme example, Underhill (1956) comments in her wonderful book on the Navajo Nation on the tribal president's bewildered reaction when he examined boxes of totally inappropriate donations sent in the early 1950s to help suffering Navajos cope with a crippling winter blizzard in the Arizona mountains.)

Santa Cruz Sentinel

The essential point is that no post-disaster plan can be regarded as complete without some component detailing the nature of the community's relationships with:

This civic auditorium served as an emergency shelter in Santa Cruz, California, in the aftermath of the Loma Prieta earthquake in 1989.

- neighboring local governments;

- regional planning commissions (the federal Economic Development Administration has funded regional planning commissions to hire a long-term recovery coordinator in the post-disaster period, especially when there is a clear relationship between recovery and a community's economic viability);

- higher-level jurisdictions, such as the county, state, or federal government; and

- nonprofit and private-sector entities that may aid relief and recovery efforts.

Coordination with nonprofit relief services. The first step in detailing this section of the plan is to establish an effective inventory of those nonprofit entities that are likely to respond to or be involved with the community in the event of a disaster. For the most part, planners will not deal directly with such services unless they are involved with long-term reconstruction. It is nonetheless valuable to be aware of their role and the external resources they may bring to the community.

FEMA maintains coordination with major national organizations, such as the American Red Cross, Mennonite Disaster Services, and many others through National Voluntary Organizations Active in Disasters (NVOAD). NVOAD thus is an effective source of information on the strengths of the various organizations and the types of tasks they typically perform. Most communities also have local and regional organizations, often including national and local businesses, that are willing and able to assist in emergencies or to donate goods and services to disaster-stricken areas. Examples include Anheuser-Busch Company's provision of drinking water during the 1993 Midwest floods, and donations by farm organizations in the past of food or livestock feed to aid other regions stricken by drought or flood. Some resources of this type may come to light during the public participation segment of the preparation of a post-disaster plan and can then be incorporated into the element of the plan providing for oversight and coordination with nonprofit disaster services.

As noted in the introduction to this section, it is necessary to have some coordination concerning incoming donations and their appropriateness for use in the local community. The American Red Cross is usually given this responsibility, with the local emergency management office taking responsibility for advertising through the news media and other channels information on the types of individual and corporate donations that would be most helpful in view of the situation. (A plainly stated delineation of these responsibilities appears in Annex L, "Volunteer Services," of the Tampa Bay regional hurricane plan (TBRPC 1992).) However, it should also be assumed that there may well be a need to coordinate the distribution of such supplies with neighboring jurisdictions and some policies to guarantee fairness and efficiency.

It should not be assumed that such aid is limited strictly to the emergency period. As noted in the example from Boone, North Carolina, concerning the effective use of disaster assistance, organizations like Habitat for Humanity may well be prepared to play a role in more long-term reconstruction, for example, by helping to restore the low-income housing stock in a community. Christmas in April is another group, similar to Habitat for Humanity, that works on repairs to homes for the elderly. Consulting local representatives of such organizations beforehand, including community development corporations, may open new avenues for effective long-term reconstruction with private resources coordinated with official local government objectives.

Coordination of temporary housing services. This is an ideal area of cooperation between emergency managers and planners. Housing is often in short supply in a disaster-stricken community because so much of it may have been devastated. Relief agencies, working with emergency management officials, are already busy providing temporary shelter for disaster victims in quickly assembled manufactured home parks, schools, or whatever other arrangements will meet people's needs in a crisis. Where then does a community put the disaster volunteers as they arrive?

An additional area of focus for some local governments, particularly in coastal areas, is the provision of emergency shelter for evacuees away from the worst-hit communities, such as those located on barrier islands. Small mountain communities vulnerable to wildfires may also fall into this category. In this instance, self-reliance is self-defeating, and what is needed is an agreement with a host community that is capable of handling some or all of the victims from the evacuated area. Planners can use the planning process in this instance to find suitable locations outside hazardous areas. Their study should first examine existing shelter locations relative to locations within hazardous areas, including the accessibility of roads that will move people out of hazard-prone locations to safe shelter.

Transportation. Disaster victims suffer disconnection with the outside world almost entirely in one of two ways: loss of communications and loss of transportation. Disruption of the latter can take a wide variety of forms, as all modes are vulnerable depending on the circumstances. A thorough plan for regional coordination of the restoration of transportation access needs to consider air, water, rail, and street and highway issues. Almost nowhere else is the need for regional cooperation so apparent because transportation routes are the ties that bind communities. In the case of state and interstate highways, railroads, and navigable rivers, they also invariably involve management by entities other than local government. Although airports are often managed by large central municipal governments, entire metropolitan areas, if not larger regions, have some stake in their restoration to normal service. Thus, even the local post-disaster plan element addressing transportation should at a minimum establish responsibility for effective liaison between local transportation officials and those in metropolitan, regional, special district, state, or federal agencies who are managing recovery in these areas.

One clear example of the stake that an individual community has in a major transportation artery involves the fate of the Embarcadero Freeway in San Francisco following the Loma Prieta Earthquake. The overhead freeway was long seen as critical in delivering a steady flow of tourists to Chinatown, but in the end its reconstruction was abandoned in favor of a sunken freeway that has reunited the community with its nearby waterfront. In that instance, San Francisco officials were able to control the outcome after a vigorous debate.

A different type of example emerged from the massive flooding of midwestern states in 1993, when thousands of miles of railroad track were rendered unusable. Railroad officials worked long hours rerouting shipments along those tracks that remained viable, adding long hours and miles to freight shipments through the Midwest. For communities along those routes that relied on the railroads to deliver farm products and other supplies, restoration of the flooded trackage to service was essential to their own economic recovery, even though they themselves could exercise no direct control over the progress of the effort. Both situations emphasize the need for local input and coordination with nonlocal officials concerning transportation issues.

The potential fragility of regional transportation corridors is an issue that especially affects the viability of emergency evacuation plans for communities, particularly in coastal or riverfront locations, with a need to remove large numbers of residents from harm's way. The discussion above about Hilton Head Island's reservations about pursuing an evacuation-based growth cap and the potential futility of doing so in light of a lack of regional coordination of emergency transportation routes illustrates the potency of this element of interjurisdictional coordination. Most major transportation routes run through numerous local jurisdictions, and traffic coordination in an emergency can be a mess. While that particular function can be handled largely through cooperative agreements among local public safety officials, it is important to know that such agreements are in place.

Beyond that, however, lies the possibility of permanent damage to transportation infrastructure, as has occurred in many earthquakes and is not uncommon in other types of disasters. Flooded or wind-damaged bridges, underpasses, and other potentially long-term obstructions to traffic require some prior consideration of intermunicipal agreements concerning the temporary rerouting of traffic and mitigation plans for the restoration of damaged transportation facilities. Very often, these considerations require cooperative efforts with county, state, regional, and federal transportation officials to effect a solution.

Emergency legislation at state and federal levels. Often, in the process of preparing a plan for post-disaster reconstruction, community officials identify needed programmatic changes at the state or federal level that would require new legislation. In such instances, the plan should include discussions of the types of legislation that would produce the needed improvements. While the local community cannot control the disposition of its proposals to state or federal legislators, a well-documented case illustrating why a certain type of enabling statute or some other measure would help often does result in new legislation. Florida and California plans, in particular, contain a number of examples of such issues. The Los Angeles plan (1994), for example, included lobbying for and supporting legislation to create disaster-loss reserve funds at the state and federal levels to implement a seismic retrofit program for state facilities.

Coordinated media contact for accuracy and consistency. Natural disasters offer wonderful opportunities for officials at all levels to garner media attention. The cacophony that is sure to result when everyone is allowed to do so is best avoided with a clear plan of action for directing media questions to a single designated source through whom information from other participants can be channeled. Not only is this a wise option within specific communities, but where questions do not pertain to a particular jurisdiction, it is also preferable, through prior agreement, to channel them to a more regional source of information, such as a county public information office or even the governor's press office. Officials drafting post-disaster plans should anticipate different levels of emergencies and consider what might be appropriate based on the geographic extent and magnitude of the disaster. In disaster field offices, both federal and state media representatives are often co-located to facilitate such coordination.

Mutual aid agreements. Especially within a diverse metropolitan area, there are going to be significant variations in the capabilities of neighboring communities to respond to the challenges of a natural disaster. No single relatively unscathed community in a disaster-stricken area can expect to remain an island of tranquility if its neighbors are struggling. Everyone benefits from quickly implementing previously developed agreements to provide assistance where it is needed. These agreements can cover virtually any of the functions previously discussed in this chapter, including the use of police and fire personnel, emergency housing, the restoration of damaged transportation routes and utilities, communications, social services, building inspectors, and, yes, even planners.

The Division of Emergency Management of the Florida Department of Community Affairs (1994) has a statewide mutual aid agreement to which local jurisdictions may become parties that covers many of these points. The Building Officials Association of Florida covers one major specific need following disasters with its own memorandum of understanding with the state to supply the inspectors needed after a disaster for habitability inspections (Florida DCA 1995b). These agreements spell out procedures for identifying needed assistance and dispatching the appropriate personnel to the requesting communities.

Floods often involve the need for additional building officials, many of whom are needed in extreme flood events to make the required substantial damage determinations under the NFIP. This is also true in nonflood events that occur wholly or partially in floodplains, as in the case of the Plainfield, Illinois, tornado. (See Chapter 9.)

The post-disaster plan offers an opportunity for community self-assessment to determine where potential deficiencies in resources and personnel might surface following a disaster. No community can reasonably ratchet up the size of its staff or its stockpile of equipment to meet all the contingencies that might occur in a disaster. The sensible approach is to identify these potential shortcomings and remedy them through interjurisdictional mutual aid agreements that allow the community to call upon outside resources when they are needed, much as communities have long done with such public safety emergencies as fires or civil disturbances.

Reevaluating and Updating the Post-disaster Plan

One final issue must be considered in completing the inventory of post-disaster plan elements—that of keeping it current. Plans that age without periodic revision become largely irrelevant, but it is not hard to build into a plan provisions for revisiting the issues addressed and updating the elements in light of new experience. Certainly, two events ought to trigger an automatic update of the plan: the actual occurrence of a disaster, which allows the plan to be tested and revised on the basis of its actual successes and failures, and changes in the comprehensive plan requirements that affect the workings of the post-disaster plan. Beyond that, the plan should include some routine periodic schedule according to which the planning department can reexamine the validity of the assumptions underlying its work plan, or simply alter some provisions to reflect changes in the community over time. The update probably ought to occur somewhere between every one and five years, depending on the frequency and severity of the natural hazards events affecting the community.

FEMA already requires post-disaster revisions of state hazard mitigation plans, but individual communities have the opportunity to monitor their own plans in far more detail. Including a program for periodic review and revision also allows a community to measure its progress and ensure implementation of those actions it decided to address in the pre-disaster period. With the widespread and growing use of various types of community and sustainable development indicators, planners have the opportunity to use this process in the post-disaster plan to incorporate into those indicators measurements of the community's progress toward a more disaster-resistant future.

Including a program for periodic review and revision also allows a community to measure its progress and ensure implementation of those actions it decided to address in the pre-disaster period.

Chapter 5

A Planner's Tool Kit

Most communities never need to avail themselves of the full arsenal of planning tools that exists to address hazard mitigation and post-disaster reconstruction issues. It is worthwhile, however, to establish a full inventory of those tools and to understand how they might be used effectively to tackle specific challenges. Most planners dealing with natural hazards issues have learned on the job and not in planning school. This chapter is designed as a primer for those new to the task and as a quick reference source for veterans.

Whole books have been written about many of the specific techniques outlined here. This chapter, therefore, will not seek to discuss any of them in depth but will provide an overview of the range of tools planners can use and references to other sources that can provide whatever depth is needed. For that reason, the text of this chapter will consist simply of brief commentaries on the most valuable features of each tool, supplemented by a pull-out chart (Figure 5-1 on page 117) comparing the circumstances under which the tools might be used.

The planning tools described in this chapter have been divided into emergency measures and the larger roster of tools appropriate to long-term hazard planning. Emergency measures may be under the direct authority of other departments. If so, the planner's role is discussed. The long-term measures have been divided into several categories. The descriptions note whether the tool is especially adaptable, or unsuitable, for particular types of post-disaster scenarios.

This chapter concludes with a model recovery and reconstruction ordinance prepared by Kenneth C. Topping specifically for inclusion in this report. The model ordinance integrates the use of many of the most essential planning and emergency management tools to facilitate post-disaster recovery and reconstruction and should be read closely in connection with the details of the tool kit itself.

EMERGENCY MEASURES
Damage Assessments

Damage assessments are a focal point of the post-disaster environment. The building department is usually in charge of this process, but planners should participate on the assessment team in order to obtain data specific to planning issues. The sidebar on the following page lists the data types that are most useful in a planning context. The challenge for planners is to help design the assessment process to glean as much useful information for local planning purposes as possible while also meeting the needs of state and federal disaster agencies considering a disaster declaration or seeking to identify specific causes of damage. Combining damage assessments with modern data management tools, such as a Global Positioning System (GPS) or a Geographic Information System (GIS), described below under "Long-Term Measures," is increasingly the sign of a department sophisticated in disaster planning operations. (For more information on this topic, see FEMA 1994, Unit 3.)

Development Moratorium

The building department is responsible for administering any moratorium on development after a disaster, but planners should coordinate with building officials so that they are aware of the time planners may need to revisit the pre-disaster plan. A moratorium can buy valuable time for planners to reassess the wisdom of rebuilding in a stricken area before the permits are issued. Planning departments must use the tool selectively, however, by applying it to areas where a strong justification emerges from damage assessments. (For more details on this topic, see the model ordinance at the end of this chapter.)

The building department is responsible for administering any moratorium on development after a disaster, but planners should coordinate with building officials so that they are aware of the time planners may need to revisit the pre-disaster plan. A moratorium can buy valuable time for planners to reassess the wisdom of rebuilding in a stricken area before the permits are issued.

Temporary Repair Permits

Because the building department is responsible for issuing repair permits, planners will not be making decisions about allowing permits for repairs. They can, however, help set policy that allows city officials to distinguish between those temporary repairs that get part of the community back on its feet and those that may compromise important opportunities for hazard mitigation. (See the model ordinance below.)

Demolition Regulations

The building department is in charge of issuing demolition permits, but planners should provide input where they feel existing regulations or practices may impede long-term planning goals, particularly in the area of historic preservation. Chapter 4 discussed the opportunities here for using emergency demolition to remove the most damaged buildings quickly, to allow neighborhoods to remove dangers and eyesores that may threaten or stymie redevelopment, and to involve special interests, such as the historic preservation community, in decisions on landmarks in order to avoid unnecessary controversy over disaster policies. (See the model ordinance below.)

Temporary housing sites can become permanent unless recovery and reconstruction are managed effectively. . . . Preparing effectively for this problem in a plan for post-disaster recovery can minimize problems by ensuring that temporary housing is provided in areas conducive to residential uses.

Zoning for Temporary Housing

Temporary housing sites can become permanent unless recovery and reconstruction are managed effectively. The administration and development of temporary housing for disaster victims is largely the domain of social services and emergency services departments. Preparing effectively for this problem in a plan for post-disaster recovery can minimize problems by ensuring that temporary housing is provided in areas conducive to residential uses. It can also allow planners to collaborate with other city officials, such as those involved in housing and human services, in identifying locations that will facilitate the effective delivery of emergency services to displaced residents following a disaster and to avoid potential social conflicts that can arise in already tense surroundings. Periodic updating will be required as land-use patterns change within the community, especially if areas suitable for temporary housing become built out. (For more information, see the model ordinance below and Governor's Office of Emergency Services (1993, Ch. 22).)

Setting Priorities for Infrastructure Repairs

Setting priorities for repairs to infrastructure is predominantly the responsibility of the public works or engineering department. Ideally, a community will

Gathering Planning Data Through Damage Assessments

The table below is an attempt to categorize for planners the types of damage assessment data most valuable for purposes of planning post-disaster recovery and reconstruction. It illustrates some of the reasons planners should involve themselves in the damage assessment process, at least to the extent of shaping the agenda for the types of information collected.

DATA NEEDED FOR POST-DISASTER RECOVERY AND RECONSTRUCTION	FLOODS	EARTHQUAKES	HURRICANES	TORNADOES	WILDFIRES
Areal extent of damage	●	●	●	●	●
Number and location of destroyed structures[a]	●	●	●	●	●
Number and location of red, yellow, green tagged buildings or unsafe buildings if tagging is not used[b]	●	●	●	●	●
Use and occupancy of each damaged structure, number of residential units by tag[c]	●	●	●	●	●
Historic status or approximate age[d]	●	●	●	O	●
Type of construction[e]	●	●	●	O	●
Condition of infrastructure—bridges, streets, sewers, water lines, etc.[f]	●	●	●	O	●
Dollar value of damage[g]	O	O	O	O	O

Key:

● = very important

O = less important

Notes:

a. Locational information is critical and unlikely to come in the form that planners would like for combining with other planning data. Usually, damage data are collected by address; planning data are often assembled by parcel number. Planners may need to devise a system for incorporating damage data into existing databases, such as a Geographic Information System (GIS) or a Geographic Positioning System (GPS).

b. Most areas subject to earthquakes are prepared to use the ATC-20 system for damage assessment with red, yellow, and green tags. With earthquakes, it is important to remember that aftershocks mean that damage assessment is done over and over again.

c. Planners need to know the uses of damaged structures. If they have a database system into which they can enter the tagging data, they will not have to rely on field inspection for this information. This is an area for preplanning. Quickly identifying the number of housing units that cannot be occupied is essential for planning shelters, temporary housing, and permanent replacement housing. Similarly, quickly identifying damaged commercial and industrial buildings can help you anticipate needs for temporary business sites and facilities.

d. Historic status is important because FEMA procedures for demolition and repairs are different for these buildings.

e. Type of construction is important because it may indicate the need for a mitigation program based on construction type (URMs or tilt-ups in earthquakes, unelevated buildings in floods, houses with certain kinds of roofs in hurricanes and wildfires, etc.). However, this can be much more problematic in the case of tornadoes.

f. Decisions about rebuilding depend on knowing the status of infrastructure.

g. Value of damage is a part of the assessment because the state and FEMA need it to determine the need for a disaster declaration and the level of aid needed.

have used its post-disaster plan to identify the most essential infrastructure and set priorities for repairs, replacement, or movement out of hazardous areas. It can then move quickly to implement a pre-existing priority list after the disaster, based on its inventory of damaged structures and roadways. Such a list must remain somewhat flexible, be updated regularly, and be revised based on emergency circumstances. This tool has some implications for planning priorities and must be coordinated with current budgetary realities, ongoing pre-disaster mitigation efforts for public facilities, and effective plans for accessing federal disaster assistance. (For more information, see BSSC (1987a); Hanley (n.d.); and David Plummer & Associates (1995).)

LONG-TERM MEASURES

In addition to rebuilding the community and restoring normal economic and social activity, all the tools below should be used to reduce vulnerability to natural hazards and enhance public safety. Many of these tools will be used outside the disaster recovery context and should be part of an ongoing program of hazard mitigation. However, to the extent possible, we attempt to discuss in precise terms the triggers that activate the use of these tools specifically in the post-disaster period. It is important also to keep in mind that the tools can be used to address hazards other than those that are mentioned specifically. Figure 5-1 may serve as a more comprehensive guide in this respect.

While the tools described below are listed in six categories related to the authority that enables planners to use them, some tools may be used in other contexts. The division of categories is not clear-cut because, in real life, communities employ a variety of methods to organize their local development codes. Many design tools separated here into the section on design controls, for instance, appear in local zoning ordinances, as do some subdivision tools. While building codes might not always be seen in that context, they do affect design and provide a form of quality control in the context of mitigating natural hazards. To avoid redundancy, however, we have listed each tool just once in the category where it best belongs.

General Planning Tools

Fee simple acquisition. The most effective but probably most costly way of moving development out of harm's way is to acquire the land and retain it in public ownership for open space. The most common use of this approach is in floodplains, perhaps secondarily in coastal zones. But it has also been used in mountainous areas including such Southern California communities as Claremont, where wildfire and landslide hazards are prevalent. Occasionally, the two objectives combine, as in Bellevue, Washington, which developed an open space program for managing riparian open space in an area with steep riparian slopes (Sherrard 1996). Boulder's plan for Boulder Creek, also a hilly riverine environment, merits attention as well (Havlick 1995). Arnold, Missouri, the subject of the case study in Chapter 8, provides a highly successful example of a community combining an ongoing greenway acquisition program with post-disaster dollars to accelerate the achievement of its objectives (Brower, Beatley, and Blatt 1987, Ch. 5; Wetmore 1996a and 1996b).

Property acquisition has a special context in the flood program because of specific National Flood Insurance Program (NFIP) provisions and funds for this purpose. The best approach remains one of targeted priorities established through a long-range plan that includes multiple objectives and funding sources to help underwrite the cost of acquisition.

The merits of property acquisition are not limited to floodplains, however. Salt Lake City, faced with resident concern about the construction of a

The most effective but probably most costly way of moving development out of harm's way is to acquire the land and retain it in public ownership for open space. The most common use of this approach is in floodplains, perhaps secondarily in coastal zones. But it has also been used in mountainous areas including such Southern California communities as Claremont, where wildfire and landslide hazards are prevalent.

Figure 5-1. Planning Tools and Their Post-Disaster Applications

TOOLS BY CATEGORY	FLOOD	HURRICANE	EARTHQUAKE	WILDFIRE	TORNADO	LANDSLIDE
EMERGENCY						
Damage assessment	X	X	X	X	X	X
Development. moratorium	X	X	X	X	X	X
Temporary repair permits	X	X	X	X	X	X
Zoning for temporary housing	X	X	X	X	–	–
Prioritize infrastructure repairs	X	X	X	X	X	–
PLANNING TOOLS						
Acquisition	X	X	X	X	X	X
Easements	X	X	–	X	–	X
Infrastructure policy	X	X	X	X	–	X
Floodplain management plan	X	X	–	–	–	–
Environmental review	X	X	X	X	X	X
Annexation plans	X	X	X	X	–	X
Stormwater management plan	X	–	–	–	–	–
ZONING TOOLS						
Nonconforming uses	X	X	X	X	X	X
Performance standards	X	X	X	X	X	X
Special use permits	X	X	X	X	–	X
Historic preservation	X	X	X	X	X	–
Density controls	X	X	X	X	–	X
Floating zones	X	X	–	X	–	X
Overlay zones	X	X	X	X	X	X
Coastal Zone Management regulations	X	X	–	–	–	–
Floodplain zoning	X	X	–	–	–	–
Setbacks	X	X	X	X	–	X
Site plan reviews	X	X	X	X	–	X
Height and bulk regulations	X	X	–	X	–	X
Wetlands development regulations	X	X	–	–	–	–
SUBDIVISION CONTROLS						
Subdivision regulations	X	X	X	X	–	X
Road width/access	X	X	X	X	–	X
Water supply	–	–	X	–	–	–
Hillside development regulations	–	–	–	X	–	X
Open space requirements	X	X	X	X	–	X
DESIGN CONTROLS						
Trees and vegetation	X	X	–	X	–	X
Design review	X	X	X	X	X	–
Building codes	X	X	X	X	X	X
FINANCIAL TOOLS						
Targeting grant funds	X	X	X	X	X	X
Relocation aid	X	X	X	X	–	X
Special districts	X	X	X	X	X	X
Redevelopment projects	X	X	X	X	X	X
Lending policies	X	X	X	X	X	X
Transfer of Development Rights	X	X	–	X	–	X
MANAGEMENT TOOLS						
Interjurisdictional coordination	X	X	X	X	X	X
Geographic Information System	X	X	X	X	X	X
Geologic investigation	–	–	X	–	–	X
Soil stability ratings	X	X	X	–	–	X
Public education	X	X	X	X	X	X

residential apartment building astride a known fault line on the Wasatch Front, acquired the parcel immediately to the north, including some old apartments it then refurbished, and established Faultline Park as permanent urban open space that serves in part as a public education tool on seismic hazards (Tyler 1995). However a community chooses to proceed, it is clear that additional money for land acquisition is often available after a disaster for those communities ready to take advantage of it. Collaboration with local officials in this area can yield significant dividends.

Easements. Easements can be a very cost-effective means of controlling development without having to accept the responsibilities of being a public landlord. One means of securing easements is to work closely with nonprofit land trusts who generally share the community's mitigation goals and are willing to move quickly to acquire conservation easements or to accept donated easements. The Nature Conservancy is a national organization that has teamed up often with local and state governments to preserve land through donations, easements, and other means. The Land Trust Alliance has produced some excellent guidebooks on this subject. (For more information, see Lind (1991); Land Trust Alliance (1993); and Trust for Public Land (1995).)

Infrastructure development policies. The placement of infrastructure in hazard-prone areas is a significant step in facilitating the development of those areas. The post-disaster period offers a time for reassessing the desirability of replacing damaged infrastructure in such locations, and of considering mitigation options (e.g., elevating roadways, widening culverts) making use of Federal Emergency Management Agency (FEMA) Public Assistance or Hazard Mitigation Grant Program (HMGP) funds to accomplish such objectives (Design Center for American Urban Landscape 1994, pp. 31-36).

Infrastructure considerations are often particularly critical when they involve facility extensions beyond the city limits. Philipsborn (1997), in the example of Boone, North Carolina, discussed in Chapter 3, notes that the city planned to "waive current policy by agreeing to extend sewer and water services to the proposed new site" of a nursing home in order to facilitate its relocation out of the city's floodplain to a new location outside the city limits. What might normally have been seen as a sprawl generator instead served a purpose for flood mitigation.

Infrastructure in the urban/wildland interface is uniquely vulnerable because of the high temperatures wildfires can generate and the speed with which they often move through an area. Where a city chooses to extend sewer and water lines and other utility services is a powerful influence on development patterns and can help orient construction away from the most hazardous areas. Where a city does choose to extend these facilities, however, it can also take precautionary measures to protect that investment. One common measure applied to both publicly and privately owned utilities is to require that power, telephone, cable, and other lines be placed underground (Slaughter 1996, Ch. 5).

While engineering measures can address many of the serious seismic safety concerns that attend the development of infrastructure and utility lifelines, it is also reasonable for planners to argue that these measures will be even more effective if siting avoids the areas where the hazards are greatest. Moreover, many public facilities influence the siting of other development that follows. The siting of these facilities and the extension of infrastructure not only can set a worthwhile public example, but also can facilitate or discourage other types of private investment. Maximizing the safety of public and utility infrastructure also increases the community's ability to recover and to restore essential services following an earthquake.

Easements can be a very cost-effective means of controlling development without having to accept the responsibilities of being a public landlord. One means of securing easements is to work closely with nonprofit land trusts who generally share the community's mitigation goals and are willing to move quickly to acquire conservation easements or to accept donated easements.

FEMA has produced a series of useful manuals addressing seismic hazard abatement for lifeline utility services. (See also BSSC (1987a) and BSSC (1987b).)

In the end, there is no substitute for incorporating natural hazard mitigation considerations into infrastructure policy as a matter of routine in all project reviews. Sometimes, this is as much a matter of influencing the timing of development as of actually preventing it, depending on the other public policy objectives involved. Adequate public facilities ordinances (APFOs) have become a means of staging growth by clarifying where and when a community intends to provide the infrastructure to support it (White 1996).

Designed primarily to steer development away from areas where local governments want to slow growth, these ordinances force developers to pay for the necessary expansion of infrastructure if they wish to build in areas where the infrastructure does not already exist. This can include impact fees for schools, the costs of adding new water and sewer lines, and a host of other particulars that facilitate the presence of new housing or commercial development. While these measures do not prevent development in hazardous areas, they can be used to raise its costs and thus provide a market mechanism for redirecting development to areas where infrastructure already exists. Much of the original objective of APFOs was to conserve public infrastructure expenditures, but communities can recraft their ordinance language to use this tool to limit development in hazard-prone areas. Obviously, APFOs are a companion measure to infrastructure development policies and help to make them more effective in their intent. They have been widely used in Florida and Maryland. (For more information, see Morris and Schwab (1991); Maryland Office of Planning (1996); and White (1996).)

Floodplain management plan (and flood insurance regulations). The regulations associated with NFIP can be viewed in either of two ways: as a set of restrictions that dictate how a community may build in a floodplain, or as a starting point for creative local efforts to mitigate flood hazards. Many communities are ambivalent when choosing between these perspectives because of development pressures, but repetitive losses and the emotional shock of a major flood have induced in others a change of heart, even to the point of relocating entire communities (Becker 1994a and 1994b). While NFIP requires only the adoption and enforcement of a floodplain management ordinance, the desire to provide a first-rate rationale for the ordinance can be the motive force behind a floodplain management plan that can examine the full range of issues facing the community. (See also Wetmore (1996a and 1996b); Schwab (1996a); Tulsa (1994); and FIFMTF (1995).)

FEMA's Community Rating System (CRS) is an attempt to provide communities with incentives through rate reductions to take those extra steps in developing and implementing an effective floodplain management plan. It uses a scoring system for a variety of activities, including public information, mapping and regulatory activities, flood damage reduction, and flood preparedness. (See sidebar). The higher the score, the more rate reductions a community earns, in 5 percent increments from the standard insurance rates. FEMA (1995e through 1995f) has produced various publications connected with CRS to delineate the point system, provide examples of quality plans, and encourage local initiative in responding to flood problems. Communities developing floodplain management plans should also take note of the Flood Mitigation Assistance (FMA) program created by Congress under the National Flood Insurance Reform Act of 1994 (P.L. 103-325) to provide grants through FEMA to communities for cost-effective mitigation projects. FMA requires a community to develop a flood mitigation plan as a prerequisite for obtaining funds for projects.

In the end, there is no substitute for incorporating natural hazard mitigation considerations into infrastructure policy as a matter of routine in all project reviews. Sometimes, this is as much a matter of influencing the timing of development as of actually preventing it, depending on the other public policy objectives involved.

CRS Credited Activities

PUBLIC INFORMATION ACTIVITIES

Elevation Certificates

Map Determinations

Outreach Projects

Hazard Disclosure

Flood Protection Library

Flood Protection Assistance

MAPPING AND REGULATORY ACTIVITIES

Additional Flood Data

Open Space Preservation

Higher Regulatory Standards

Flood Data Maintenance

Stormwater Management

FLOOD DAMAGE REDUCTION ACTIVITIES

Repetitive Loss Projects

Floodplain Management
    Planning

Acquisition and Relocation

Retrofitting

Drainage System Maintenance

FLOOD PREPAREDNESS ACTIVITIES

Flood Warning Program

Levee Safety

Dam Safety

Environmental reviews. Although they are hardly synonymous, it should not be surprising that many of the most hazardous areas are also among the most environmentally sensitive. Floodways, coastal zones, hillsides, and forested areas all provide essential habitat for countless varieties of flora and fauna, yet their scenic and other amenities are likewise immensely attractive for human development. The purpose of environmental reviews is to construct a clear picture of what resources are affected, and in what ways, by proposed development. Although the National Environmental Policy Act (NEPA) brought this mechanism to prominence on the national scene, many state laws establish environmental review mechanisms beyond those of federally mandated environmental impact assessments.

Mandelker (1997), among others, has noted that state environmental policy acts (SEPAs) responded in most cases to the failure of local planning to address environmental concerns, yet differ from local comprehensive planning in largely adopting a case-by-case approach to environmental problems by focusing on reviewing the environmental impacts of individual proposed development projects. This can lead to some duplication of SEPA reviews in local planning and development approval processes. APA's *Growing Smart*[SM] *Legislative Guidebook* has sought to integrate environmental reviews with planning and development regulations in its model state planning legislation. It also uses natural hazards as a trigger for environmentally sensitive areas ordinance reviews. The state of Washington includes geologically hazardous areas and 100-year floodplains in its sensitive areas legislation.

Annexation plans. The problem of controlling development just beyond the city limits is a classic one in American urban planning. State laws governing extraterritorial zoning controls by municipalities vary widely, so there is no good way here to discuss the issue briefly. Likewise, planners must consult state laws to determine what annexation policies will be legitimate for their own community. The essential principle for natural disasters, however, is that mitigation should be included as a routine consideration in proposed annexations, particularly in the aftermath of a natural disaster, where there may be some reason to annex a devastated area to facilitate redevelopment and where it may be in the municipality's best interests to gain greater control over the quality of that redevelopment. Healdsburg, California, for instance, requires a specific plan prior to annexation that includes an evaluation of geologic hazards. Specific plans and development agreements are potent tools for incorporating such concerns into the annexation process (Tyler 1995).

Stormwater management plans. As it is evident that storms can produce floods, it stands to reason that poorly managed stormwater flows can accelerate and exacerbate them, almost invariably adding a load of nonpoint pollutants in the bargain. In recent years, as Miller (1994) notes, stormwater management has become more holistic in many communities as they have begun to grapple with the larger impacts of past watershed management practices. Although the U.S. Environmental Protection Agency (EPA) has pushed municipalities to develop adequate stormwater management plans for environmental reasons, using the regulatory device of requiring applications for municipal stormwater permits, these have the impact of also pushing the same local governments to control flooding by better managing stormwater runoff. Local planners should seize this process as an opportunity for better water quality and nonstructural flood control rather than allowing their communities to regard these as just another set of onerous federal mandates (Schwab 1992).

The purpose of stormwater management plans, often developed by special watershed management districts, is to develop water policy for an entire

Floodplain Management Plan Elements

In formulating community development goals and in adopting floodplain management regulations, each community shall consider at least the following factors—

(1) *Human safety;*

(2) *Diversion of development* to areas safe from flooding in light of the need to reduce flood damages and in light of the need to prevent environmentally incompatible floodplain use;

(3) *Full disclosure* to all prospective and interested parties (including but not limited to purchasers and renters) that (i) certain structures are located within flood-prone areas, (ii) variances have been granted for certain structures located within flood-prone areas, and (iii) premium rates applied to new structures built at elevations below the base flood substantially increase as the elevation decreases;

(4) *Adverse effects of floodplain development* on existing development;

(5) *Encouragement of floodproofing* to reduce flood damage;

(6) *Flood warning and emergency preparedness plans;*

(7) *Provision for alternative vehicular access and escape routes* when normal routes are blocked or destroyed by flooding;

(8) *Establishment of minimum floodproofing and access requirements* for schools, hospitals, nursing homes, orphanages, penal institutions, fire stations, police stations, communications centers, water and sewage pumping stations, and other public or quasi-public facilities already located in the flood-prone area, to enable them to withstand flood damage, and to facilitate emergency operations;

(9) *Improvement of local drainage* to control increased runoff that might increase the danger of flooding to other properties;

(10) *Coordination of plans* with neighboring communities' floodplain management programs;

(11) The requirement that *all new construction* and substantial improvements in areas subject to subsidence be *elevated above the base flood level* equal to expected subsidence for at least a 10-year period;

(12) For riverine areas, requiring *subdividers to furnish delineations for floodways* before approving a subdivision;

(13) *Prohibition of any alteration or relocation of a watercourse,* except as part of an overall drainage basin plan. In the event of an overall drainage basin plan, provide that the flood-carrying capacity within the altered or relocated portion of the watercourse is maintained;

(14) Requirement of *setbacks for new construction* within Zones V1-30, VE, and V on a community's FIRM;

(15) Requirement of an *additional elevation above the base flood level for all new construction* and substantial improvements within Zones A1-30, AE, V1-30, and VE on the community's FIRM to protect against such occurrences as wave wash and floating debris, to provide an added margin of safety against floods having a magnitude greater than the base flood, or to compensate for future urban development;

(16) Requirement of *consistency between state, regional, and local comprehensive plans* and floodplain management programs;

(17) *Requirement of pilings or columns* rather than fill, for the elevation of structures within flood-prone areas, in order to maintain the storage capacity of the floodplain and to minimize the potential for negative impacts to sensitive ecological areas;

(18) *Prohibition,* within any floodway or coastal high hazard area, of plants or facilities in which *hazardous substances* are manufactured;

(19) Requirement that a *plan for evacuating residents* of all manufactured home parks or subdivisions located within flood-prone areas be developed and filed with and approved by appropriate community emergency management authorities.

Source: 44 CFR 60.22(c) (part of the National Flood Insurance Program (NFIP) Regulations for Floodplain Management). Emphasis has been added.

The Community Rating System

THE FLOODPLAIN MANAGEMENT PLANNING PROCESS

Communities in the National Flood Insurance Program (NFIP) that use the Community Rating System (CRS) receive a reduction of floodplain insurance premiums for actions they have taken to reduce flood losses. As of October 1, 1998, 894 communities, representing 66 percent of the NFIP policy base, are now participating in CRS. CRS communities are given credit points for 18 activities in four categories: Public Information, Mapping and Regulations, Flood Damage Reduction, and Flood Preparedness. The greater the number of creditable actions taken, a larger the reduction in floodplain insurance premiums for residents. Credit points are based upon how well an activity implements the goals of the CRS. Communities may receive credit points for floodplain management planning, open space dedication, and acquisition and relocation of floodprone properties.

CRS guidance materials stress that the floodplain management planning process is far more valuable than the plan document that results from it. Planning is viewed as a crucial means for overcoming the problem of conflicting goals and actions by various local government departments and by the public that may hinder flood loss reduction. There are seven recommended steps in the CRS planning process.

Problem Identification. The local government should obtain data describing water sources, depth of flooding, repetitive loss areas, special hazards, and other information from FEMA regional offices and other federal and state agencies.

Flood Hazard Area Inventory. CRS credits are given for an inventory that addresses floodprone buildings, damage projections, development trends, development constraints (including zoning and subdivision regulations), critical community facilities (i.e., hospitals, water treatment plants), and floodprone areas that provide natural and beneficial floodplain functions (e.g., flood storage areas and wildlife habitats).

Review of Possible Activities. The local government needs to review all existing and proposed activities that can prevent or reduce flood losses. It must also review activities that can protect the natural functions of the floodplain, including stormwater quality management, wetlands protection, and open space conservation.

Coordination with Other Agencies. There needs to be a review of government agencies whose activities may affect floodplain management efforts or that could support such efforts. The state NFIP coordinator, FEMA regional hazard mitigation officer, and regional planning agencies staff will be helpful in this regard.

Action Plan. This plan must include a schedule and budget for all activities that will be taken to reduce flood losses. CRS materials recommend that each community develop its own criteria for selecting which activities are appropriate to its needs and that are fiscally reasonable.

Public Input. The participating local government must document how residents, affected businesses and organizations, and local officials will be involved in the floodplain management planning process. CRS recommends a task force of community representatives.

Adoption and Implementation. The plan must be officially adopted by the local legislative body to receive CRS credit. A planning department staff person should be assigned responsibility for coordinating the implementation of actions listed in the plan.

Source: Morris (1997). CRS figures were updated in 1998.

watershed, including the full range of issues like aquatic habitat preservation, water supply, water quality (through pollution prevention and runoff controls, among other devices), scenic preservation, and the development of greenways. These plans generally rely on a good deal of interjurisdictional cooperation for their success because most of the truly effective controls on the nonpoint-source runoff that affects stormwater quantity and quality rely on local zoning and subdivision regulations (Herson-Jones 1995; Jeer et al. 1998).

Some of these local controls may be outside the planning department, perhaps in the building department, such as regulations concerning construction practices. One possibly underestimated factor in helping to minimize flooding risks due to excess runoff and water channel clogging is the application of best management practices to soil erosion and runoff from construction sites. Construction regulations adopted in the form of erosion control ordinances can require builders to undertake measures to stem erosion during the periods when bare soil is subject to the forces of wind and precipitation. These efforts can include straw bales, detention ponds, and other devices to arrest the movement of soil downhill and into waterways, where sediment can clog the flow of flood waters in an emergency. (For more information, see Kennedy (1992); NIPC (1991); Wisconsin DNR (1989).)

A related but more difficult challenge is that of controlling nonpoint runoff from agricultural operations, usually a subject tackled through state or federal environmental regulations and through programs of the U.S. Department of Agriculture's Natural Resources Conservation Service. The swampbuster provisions of the federal Food Security Act of 1986 have also gone some distance in reining in this problem. Among other notable efforts in this area are those of the states in the Chesapeake Bay region.

Capital improvements plans. Capital improvements programming is the multiyear scheduling of public physical improvements. Local governments, to be run soundly and efficiently, must have a means of projecting both their needs for physical improvements and their means over time of paying for them. The capital improvements plan (CIP) is the way to accomplish this. These improvements can include everything from street widening to sidewalk and curb repair to lighting renovations, among dozens, if not hundreds, of other possibilities. The plan deals with the means of financing these activities, such as general obligation bonds, special assessments, the use of state and federal grants, and various taxing devices. Many of these are discussed below under financial tools, but their inclusion in a CIP is critical for ensuring the priority of such projects on the local public agenda.

> The relevance for disaster planning is clear. CIPs can call for public expenditures to reduce hazards through a variety of locally appropriate hazard mitigation and disaster protection measures, including raising bridge heights in flood-prone areas, widening culverts, seismic strengthening of buildings, and the development of emergency public shelters.

The relevance for disaster planning is clear. CIPs can call for public expenditures to reduce hazards through a variety of locally appropriate hazard mitigation and disaster protection measures, including raising bridge heights in flood-prone areas, widening culverts, seismic strengthening of buildings, and the development of emergency public shelters. (For more information, see Bowyer (1993) and So and Getzels (1988).)

Zoning Tools

Zoning is a versatile tool in dealing with almost all natural hazards. It can be used:

- to prevent new development in hazardous areas;

- to allow new development in hazardous areas while minimizing densities;

- to influence the level of site plan review that a proposed development project must undergo;

- as an incentive to retrofit an existing building to resist forces associated with natural hazards (as when density bonuses are offered in exchange for retrofitting buildings);

- to control changes in existing building occupancy in hazardous areas; and

- to facilitate the post-disaster rebuilding process in severely damaged areas (Schwab 1998).

Floodplain management is the most frequent hazard-related objective of zoning because not only is flooding the most common hazard, but also because mapping of flood hazards most easily lends itself to such purposes. Most communities rely on the use of Flood Insurance Rate Maps (FIRMs) to determine the boundaries of floodplain zones in local ordinances. The mapping process itself is described in greater detail in Chapter 7. In concert with floodplain management regulations based on NFIP minimum requirements, zoning remains one of local government's most powerful tools for controlling development in special flood hazard areas, especially if it is tied to a well-prepared floodplain management plan. Nonconforming use regulations are reinforced by provisions in NFIP regarding the reconstruction of substantially damaged buildings. Setbacks can be used to provide waterfront buffers and minimize flood exposure of buildings. Density restrictions can orient development away from the most hazardous areas. All of these devices are described elsewhere in this section, but a floodplain district in the zoning ordinance is the land-use umbrella under which flood mitigation objectives can be pursued.

In a post-disaster period, a community is likely to see more requests to rebuild nonconforming uses than it would under any other circumstances. For that reason, the model ordinance presented later in this chapter offers some practical alternatives in the post-disaster setting to the strict application of normal rules concerning nonconforming uses.

Focusing strictly on hazard mitigation, however, is a major mistake. Floodplain zoning is an ideal regulatory tool for achieving multiple community planning objectives, including resource conservation, open space, water-quality protection, and recreation goals. (See also Wetmore (1996a and 1996b); Schwab (1996a and 1997); FIFMTF (1995); and Maryland Office of Planning (1993).)

Nonconforming use regulations. In zoning law, nonconforming uses are those that predate the passage or amendment of a zoning ordinance that disallows them in the district where they are found. Because they existed prior to passage of the ordinance, they are allowed to continue but are restricted by judicial and statutory rules from expanding, changing, or being rebuilt. In a post-disaster period, a community is likely to see more requests to rebuild nonconforming uses than it would under any other circumstances. For that reason, the model ordinance presented later in this chapter offers some practical alternatives in the post-disaster setting to the strict application of normal rules concerning nonconforming uses. One obvious means of preparing for such possibilities, however, is to use the pre-disaster plan to identify zoning districts with high incidences of nonconforming uses.

The ability to rebuild is the privilege most directly affected by planning for the post-disaster period and hazards legislation, most particularly NFIP. As discussed above, local ordinances adopted in conformance with NFIP allow rebuilding but require elevation to the base flood elevation if the building is substantially damaged. Local ordinances may be stricter than the federal requirements. Furthermore, the CRS offers credit in the form of reduced insurance rates for property owners in a community that requires a building to be raised to the base flood level when the cumulative cost of construction actions needed to improve or repair damage to it equals 50 percent of its market value. In such a case, the community is responsible for tracking the cumulative cost of substantial improvements or the amount of substantial damage. CRS also gives points if the community sets its substantial damage standard at less than 50 percent of market value. Normally, these requirements apply only when any single flood causes that extent of damage. Finally, note that the Increased Cost of Compliance (ICC) provision in NFIP policies issued or renewed after June 1, 1997, provides for up to $15,000 to property owners to bring substantially damaged or repetitively flooded properties into compliance with local floodplain management requirements (FEMA 1997d).

Beyond those provisions, local governments can use zoning to effect a good deal of hazard mitigation in the area of nonconforming uses. Having established restrictions pertaining to wildfire hazards, floodplain areas, earthquake liquefaction zones, landslide hazard zones, or other problem areas, local zoning can then allow planners to enforce limitations on the ability to rebuild in place once a structure has been substantially damaged from any source or for any reason. Those limitations may require options other than relocation, such as elevation, seismic retrofitting, or fire-resistant construction. Obviously, the boundaries for the defined districts must be justified through sound hazard identification techniques in order to withstand legal challenges. This is primarily a gradual remedy when planners recognize the existence of an undesirable situation and wish to use the postdisaster reconstruction process in part to force any rebuilding to comply with new standards or to eliminate uses that no longer are deemed acceptable in their current location. (See also Williams (1986, Vol. 4A, Ch. 114) and the model ordinance below.)

Environmental or hazard-related performance standards. Increasingly, detention ponds and swales are common mitigating features of new developments complying with standards for stormwater management. Even outside delineated hazard zones, development activity and planning for wider areas like watersheds can significantly affect disaster vulnerability. The case study of Arnold, Missouri, in Chapter 8 provides an illustration of how upstream development in a metropolitan area can have serious detrimental impacts on downstream communities. Such problems have been cited for years in a number of Chicago suburbs and often involve serious issues of interjurisdictional cooperation, addressed in the sections on general planning tools (above) and management tools below.

Landscaping, site plan reviews, and other tools described in this chapter all intersect at a variety of points, but may also be used individually by communities that do not adopt all of the other related devices. The postdisaster period may be an ideal time to press the political agenda for establishing new performance standards, particularly with regard to the design or rebuilding of planned unit developments.

A good example of the effective use of hazard-related performance standards in the context of floodplains is the zoning Wake County, North Carolina, employs for flood hazard areas that include not only FIRM-specified floodplains, but a list of soil types specified in the county soil survey and referred to in the ordinance as flood hazard soils, mostly consisting of silt and sand. The burden is on the property owner in those locations to prove that such soils are not part of the floodplain. The regulations vary according to the size of the drainage area, with the strictest applying in areas of 100 acres or more, where the applicant must show that any rise in water level resulting from building on the property can be contained on the property. The only alternative is to secure easements from neighboring property owners to allow for that rise. (See also Maryland Office of Planning (1995c) and Schwab (1997).)

Special use permits. Zoning ordinances often designate zones within which specified uses are permitted only if they meet certain conditions or established criteria. It is then up to local officials to grant or deny a permit application based on the compliance of the proposed use with those conditions or criteria, which must be clearly stated in the ordinance. In the post-disaster context, these criteria presumably would relate to the reduction of adverse environmental impacts or the minimization of vulnerability to natural hazards. For example, in hurricane- or tsunami-prone coastal zones or in mountainous terrain with landslide or wildfire potential, the feasibility of evacuation might be the basis for some criteria governing special use permits.

Floodplains are prime candidates for the application of this tool. For instance, in a model ordinance that Livingston County, Michigan, prepared

Landscaping, site plan reviews, and other tools described in this chapter all intersect at a variety of points, but may also be used individually by communities that do not adopt all of the other related devices. The post-disaster period may be an ideal time to press the political agenda for establishing new performance standards, particularly with regard to the design or rebuilding of planned unit developments.

for one of its townships, the only permitted principal uses in floodplain, wetland, and steep land areas are public and private nature reserves and wildlife areas, and public forest preserves, game preserves, hunting areas, fishing sites, and boat-launching sites. All other principal uses allowed in the coexisting zoning district require a special use permit. (See also Schwab (1997).)

Regulations dealing with damaged historic properties. The issue of regulation of damaged historical property was addressed in Chapter 4 under "Elements of the Post-Disaster Plan." It bears repeating that having some regulations already in place as part of a post-disaster plan makes matters easier when the problem arises. Even more important is identifying as precisely as possible all historic properties in hazard-prone areas, as well as the proposed mitigation techniques most appropriate in each case. Planners undertaking such an inventory should include not just listed properties, but any structures more than 50 years old that potentially could be listed properties, and be aware that state historic preservation officers (SHPOs) use this broader definition of their area of concern. The National Trust for Historic Preservation and SHPOs have a number of good information booklets available concerning restoration techniques for various types of historic buildings and categories of disaster damage. (See also Nelson (1991); NTHP (1993); Utah Division of State History (n.d.); and FEMA Region I (n.d.).)

Downzoning/density controls. At a minimum, planners should be able to articulate concerns about the limitations of building codes in mitigating hazards in areas where reduced density or outright prohibition of building would be a more effective solution. Better structural engineering solves many problems but not all, and it often is not the most cost-effective solution to a problem. Engineering solutions face practical limits in terms of both technology and economics. Planners should move aggressively to examine the land-use planning lessons from each disaster to identify areas where downzoning might be an effective approach in minimizing future hazard vulnerability. The key benefit of downzoning is simply that it minimizes the risk to future development.

> Downzoning is potentially one of the most politically controversial approaches to many natural hazards problems precisely because it involves at least a perceived, and often a real, diminution in the value of land for development purposes. Whether a proposal for downzoning a severely damaged area in the aftermath of a disaster will be politically palatable may depend on the degree to which planning and consensus building in the pre-disaster period have prepared people to understand its logic.

That said, downzoning is potentially one of the most politically controversial approaches to many natural hazards problems precisely because it involves at least a perceived, and often a real, diminution in the value of land for development purposes. Whether a proposal for downzoning a severely damaged area in the aftermath of a disaster will be politically palatable may depend on the degree to which planning and consensus building in the pre-disaster period have prepared people to understand its logic.

As a more general proposition, density controls established prior to an area's development are somewhat easier to sell if clearly tied to serious hazard-related concerns. In the urban/wildland interface, for example, minimum-lot-size regulations, provisions for clustered development, and other density restrictions are all zoning tools that may serve to reduce hazard vulnerability by allowing homes to be sited safe distances away from fuel sources. Performance controls can relate levels of density to slope factors and other objective hazard measures as local policy makers deem appropriate. Slope/density ratios work off the simple concept that density should decrease as slopes increase on the assumption that steeper slopes require more grading and other slope-disturbance activities. Portola Valley and Rancho Cucamonga, California, both have used slope/density regulations in order to minimize steep slope hazard problems (Olshansky 1996).

Because some seismic mitigation measures can be quite expensive, it is worth remembering that there is a converse truth: pre-existing high density may make it easier in some situations to finance the cost of stringent mitigation measures. This became apparent, for instance, in the redevelopment of San Francisco's Mission Bay area, which is largely built on relatively unstable infill. The area plan's life-safety section requires detailed soil-engineering and geologic investigations for each new building site, with especially stringent construction standards for critical facilities. Larger projects may be able to bear these costs more easily, making it logical to put higher-intensity uses on poorer soils. (See also Tyler (1995).)

Floating zones. In the zoning ordinance, a floating zone is one that has no specific geographic designation but carries instead a descriptive designation that attaches to an appropriate parcel of land when ordinance conditions are met. In the recovery period following a disaster, this tool can be used effectively to control redevelopment in a severely damaged area, as the special conditions attaching to the zone can then be put into effect. An important caveat is that not all states permit the use of this device.

The South Florida Regional Planning Council's model plans suggest the use of floating zones as one element of a post-disaster plan in which the community could decide in advance to activate predetermined density reductions according to the extent of overall property damage occurring in particular locations.

The Nags Head, North Carolina, plan offers a particularly apt example in connection with incipient inlets, areas where coastal erosion is carving out a water pathway through a barrier island. A severe coastal storm or hurricane can often sever an island in two by vastly accelerating that intrusion. North Carolina's Coastal Area Management Act addresses the problem of inlet hazard zones by allowing structures of no more than 5,000 square feet at a density of no more than one unit per 15,000 square feet of developable land. (For more information, see Williams (1986, Vol. 1, Ch. 28); South Florida RPC (1990); and Beatley, Brower, and Schwab (1994).)

Overlay districts. Overlay districts are used to solve problems in zoning codes that are not adequately addressed in conventional use districts. Generally, they aim to address specific needs that cut across other district designations and whose inclusion would result in a level of delineation in normal districts that would serve to confound zoning enforcement efforts. They also allow a degree of flexibility that is often needed in dealing with environmental constraints, with floodplains being a common example. They are called overlays because they add a separate layer of regulations to the area to which they apply that are distinct from the underlying traditional zoning. Overlay districts can be used in almost any hazard context to establish special conditions for various uses, including many of the disaster-specific tools below. Examples would include an urban/wildland interface district, a hillside protection district, a riverfront or shoreline district, or an earthquake high-hazard zone (as in areas with high soil liquefaction or along fault lines).

Arkadelphia, Arkansas, following the March 1, 1997, tornado that struck that community, established as part of its rebuilding process a design overlay district for the tornado-damaged parts of town. This enabled planners to introduce a number of measures that facilitated the development of quality affordable housing, including clustered development and parking, zero lot line zoning, and shared facilities. Pieter de Jong, project manager for the Arkadelphia Recovery Plan, pointed out that the value of the disaster overlay district for Arkadelphia is that it encourages innovative redevelopment strategies as compared to what would be allowable under the existing commercial and residential zoning district requirements (Woodward-Clyde 1997a). This approach is especially relevant for the smaller rural communities, which may be burdened with outdated (often Euclidean) zoning regulations, and are then confronted with a major disaster

Overlay districts can be used in almost any hazard context to establish special conditions for various uses, including many of the disaster-specific tools below. Examples would include an urban/wildland interface district, a hillside protection district, a riverfront or shoreline district, or an earthquake high-hazard zone (as in areas with high soil liquefaction or along fault lines).

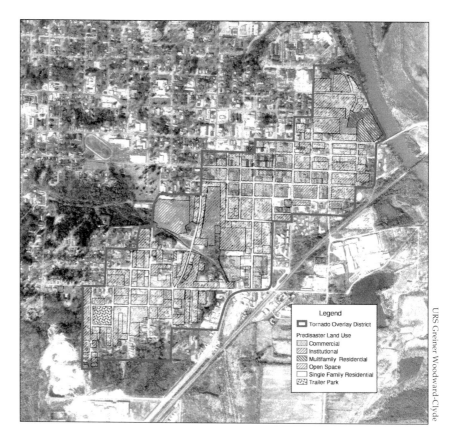

This aerial photo of Arkadelphia, Arkansas, shows the tornado overlay district the city created to facilitate reconstruction after disaster struck in March 1997, and the underlying zoning districts that pre-existed the tornado. Woodward-Clyde Consultants, FEMA's prime contractor for such planning, helped the city prepare its redevelopment plan.

Barrier islands, dune systems, tidal wetlands, estuaries, and coral reefs all pose special planning problems and opportunities not encountered elsewhere. Various federal and coastal state statutes impose specific mandates and constraints on local communities and provide particular federal mechanisms for addressing many of these challenges. In some cases, the community may be able to identify a need or opportunity to work with the state or federal government to preserve parts or all of the local coastal zone in wildlife reserves, marine sanctuaries, or even national parks.

recovery effort. It serves as an example of how this device can be used to take advantage of opportunities to reshape development in heavily damaged neighborhoods in the aftermath of a disaster. (See also Kennedy (1991); Maryland Office of Planning (1995b); and Schwab (1998).)

Coastal zone management regulations. Barrier islands, dune systems, tidal wetlands, estuaries, and coral reefs all pose special planning problems and opportunities not encountered elsewhere. Various federal and coastal state statutes impose specific mandates and constraints on local communities and provide particular federal mechanisms for addressing many of these challenges. In some cases, the community may be able to identify a need or opportunity to work with the state or federal government to preserve parts or all of the local coastal zone in wildlife reserves, marine sanctuaries, or even national parks. While many of these initiatives may be undertaken as much for environmental protection as for hazard mitigation, they often serve both purposes simultaneously, as is the case with the Coastal Barrier Resources Act.

State laws and policies can deal directly with the problem of restricting development in designated storm damage zones. For instance, Rhode Island Coastal Resource Management Council regulations prohibit reconstruction on dunes after 50 percent property destruction.

Clearly, the primary body of legislation addressing this issue is the federal Coastal Zone Management Act and its related state statutes and regulations. In addition, however, many communities enact their own special protective measures for coastal areas. The specific techniques employed in local coastal management include many of the zoning and subdivision tools detailed in this chapter, often for reasons other than hazard mitigation, such as preserving the historic or architectural character of the community. It may be noted here, though, that the replanning of badly damaged coastal planned unit developments and the use of coastal construction control lines (discussed in more detail in the Florida context in Chapter 10), which amount to setbacks based on coastal erosion, represent opportunities in the post-disaster period for planners to reduce future vulnerability. (See also Beatley, Brower, and Schwab (1994); R.I. Division of Planning (1989); and FAU/FIU (1995).)

Setbacks. Removing housing and other buildings from wildland interface hazards can be partly accomplished through required setbacks that establish minimum distances from trees, cliffs, highly flammable vegetation (e.g., shrubs and chaparral), and other landscape features that may enhance the volatility, speed, and temperature of a wildland fire. Fire officials generally recommend a 30-foot buffer between homes and wildland vegetation to reduce vulnerability. As with much else in this area, adequate hazard identification efforts can help to clarify specific local needs and thus justify effective adaptations to local circumstances.

As noted in the subsection above on coastal zone management regulations, states like Florida and Rhode Island have been using statutorily mandated setbacks to control construction near the seacoast. North Carolina's Coastal Area Management Act requires a setback of at least 30 times the average annual rate of erosion in the local area, measured from the first line of vegetation. Myrtle Beach, South Carolina, has prescribed a 50-year erosion line that allows only such uses as sundecks and gazebos seaward of that line.

Riparian corridors also deserve attention with regard to setbacks because they serve an extra function of conveying stormwater, and proper maintenance can help to reduce flooding. Experience in Bellevue, Washington, demonstrates, however, that the issue along riparian corridors, especially those with steep banks, may not always be as simple as just establishing setbacks. Retaining and replanting native vegetation may also be needed to preserve a river's viability as an effective natural channel for flood waters, reducing damage to property. These issues play a role in landscaping requirements, discussed below in the section on design review (Sherrard 1996).

California law strongly encourages the use of setbacks relative to earthquake faults in the Alquist-Priolo Act, which requires geologic investigations within one-eighth of a mile of a fault line. The regulations established by the California Mining and Geology Board require a minimum setback of 50 feet from any active fault for habitable buildings. Determining accurately the location of all such faults may require geologic investigations, a tool discussed below. (For more information, see Beatley, Brower, and Schwab (1994); Olshansky (1996); Tyler (1995).)

Site plan reviews. Site plan review almost invariably applies to new projects and only rarely to the reconstruction of existing sites. Such reviews, however, provide an opportunity for planners to assess patterns of damage in hazard-prone areas and to apply those lessons to new development. For instance, planners can consider the design and location of structures, parking lots, and other improvements with an eye to drainage, soil integrity, vegetative landscaping, and other issues that may affect the disaster-resistant qualities of a proposed development. Schwab (1993) has also suggested using site plans with proposed industrial and commercial developments to evaluate conformance with performance standards where hazardous materials are involved. This could easily be adapted to ensure the disaster-resistant storage of such materials. (See also Thurow, Toner, and Erley (1975) and Maryland Office of Planning (1995c).)

Height and bulk regulations. Height and bulk have special significance in a coastal zone, particularly in the coastal high-hazard area. A major issue that has driven some legislation and lawsuits in this area is visibility and the public's right to an ocean view. That issue clearly originated with concerns

Removing housing and other buildings from wildland interface hazards can be partly accomplished through required setbacks that establish minimum distances from trees, cliffs, highly flammable vegetation (e.g., shrubs and chaparral), and other landscape features that may enhance the volatility, speed, and temperature of a wildland fire. Fire officials generally recommend a 30-foot buffer between homes and wildland vegetation to reduce vulnerability.

Site plan review almost invariably applies to new projects and only rarely to the reconstruction of existing sites. Such reviews, however, provide an opportunity for planners to assess patterns of damage in hazard-prone areas and to apply those lessons to new development. For instance, planners can consider the design and location of structures, parking lots, and other improvements with an eye to drainage, soil integrity, vegetative landscaping, and other issues that may affect the disaster-resistant qualities of a proposed development.

about public access and aesthetics, but, in some areas, there are valid safety considerations relating to the distortion of wind patterns and flying debris that may also favor the establishment of height and bulk restrictions. Strong building code enforcement is an essential accompaniment to such regulations in any event. Nags Head, North Carolina, has combined a number of concerns with its desire to maintain a family beach atmosphere in enacting zoning changes that include strict setback, height, and open space requirements for oceanfront motels and condominiums (Bortz 1990).

Wetlands development regulations. Floodplains and wetlands are far from synonymous, particularly after two or more centuries of human activity in draining wetland areas for agriculture and development. Nonetheless, protection of remaining wetlands areas plays an important secondary role in reducing flood hazards, and while these regulations clearly serve their own environmental purposes, they also form part of an overall strategy for flood hazard mitigation. The environmental elements of a comprehensive plan should account for these benefits as a selling point for winning public acceptance and understanding of community objectives in this area. (See also Burke et al. (1988).)

Subdivision Controls

Subdivision regulations. The rules that govern the subdivision of land clearly provide some of the best opportunities planners have to create sites that are both buildable and safe. Once a lot is created, it is enormously difficult to prevent building. The roots of effective subdivision regulations in this regard stem inexorably from thorough and accurate hazard identification at the beginning of the planning process. This may include requirements for hazard assessments to accompany subdivision applications in known hazard zones. Lots can be configured to keep structures out of the floodplain, to reduce fire and landslide hazards in forested and mountainous wildlands, or to reduce the exposure of buildings to fault slippage, among other possibilities. Clustering is increasingly popular as a means of preserving open space in new subdivisions, and Arendt (1996) has addressed the merits and methods of this technique at considerable length. Various Planning Advisory Service (PAS) Reports have addressed issues concerning subdivision design for earthquake, landslide, and floodplain hazards respectively. (See also Maryland Office of Planning (1994).)

In hillside areas, the need is to pursue such subdivision design features as clustering with an eye to resource conservation and the use of those areas requiring a minimum of grading and soil-disturbing activities during construction. Special attention should also be paid to road access and minimizing the amount of linear roadway needed for access to the number of homes that will be built in comparison to conventional subdivision design (Olshansky 1996).

The mapping of special flood hazard areas offers excellent opportunities for planners to apply this practical information as they review the design and lot layout of subdivisions, consider street access and layout, the positioning of utilities and detention basins, open space dedications, tree preservation, landscaping requirements, and a host of other floodplain management issues that come into play with each new subdivision proposal. Planners can also draft subdivision ordinances that prescribe standards for these items with respect to the documented hazards. This is obviously a proactive rather than post-disaster measure, as are many of the tools discussed here, but the implications are enormous.

The Nags Head, North Carolina, subdivision ordinance requires lots on the ocean side of the major north-south road parallel to the coast to be

---

The rules that govern the subdivision of land clearly provide some of the best opportunities planners have to create sites that are both buildable and safe. Lots can be configured to keep structures out of the floodplain, to reduce fire and landslide hazards in forested and mountainous wildlands, or to reduce the exposure of buildings to fault slippage, among other possibilities.

In hillside areas, the need is to pursue such subdivision design features as clustering with an eye to resource conservation and the use of those areas requiring a minimum of grading and soil-disturbing activities during construction. Special attention should also be paid to road access and minimizing the amount of linear roadway needed for access to the number of homes that will be built in comparison to conventional subdivision design.

configured perpendicular to the ocean and road. (See Figure 5-2). If coastal erosion subsequently threatens the structures built on those lots, this configuration allows the houses to be moved landward, and the ordinance then provides for a reduction of required setbacks from 30 to 15 feet to accommodate those circumstances (Morris 1997).

Nags Head has provided for some post-disaster planning intervention to mitigate flood hazards in existing subdivisions by allowing the possibility, prior to rebuilding, of requiring that adjoining lots in common ownership be combined into one large lot (Bortz 1990).

Figure 5-2. Nags Head, North Carolina, Oceanfront Lot Requirements

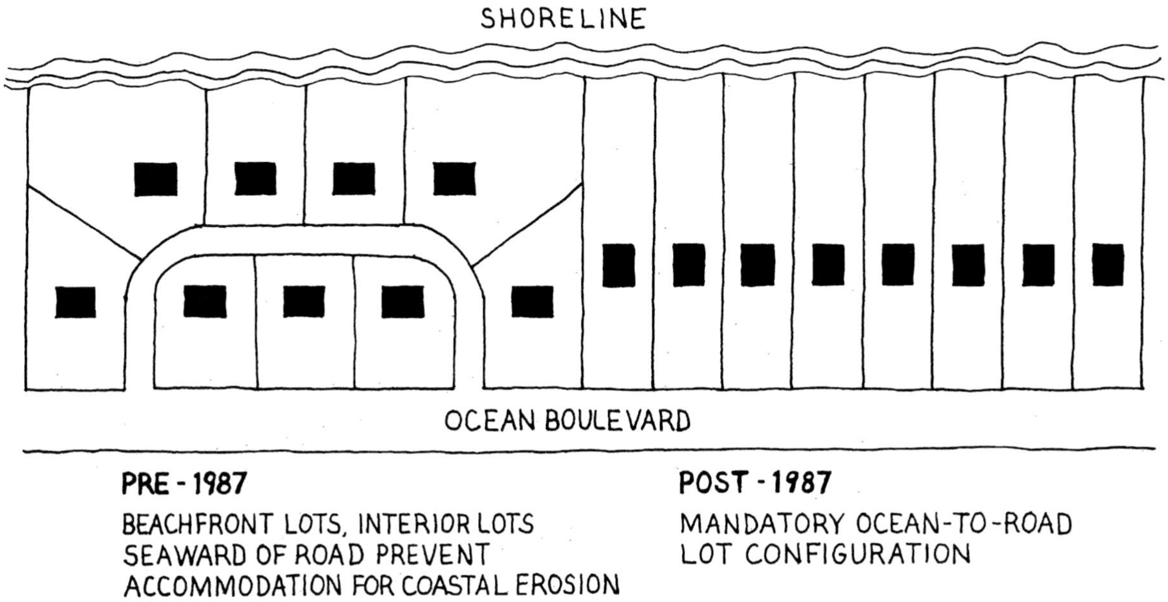

SHORELINE

OCEAN BOULEVARD

PRE - 1987
BEACHFRONT LOTS, INTERIOR LOTS
SEAWARD OF ROAD PREVENT
ACCOMMODATION FOR COASTAL EROSION

POST - 1987
MANDATORY OCEAN-TO-ROAD
LOT CONFIGURATION

As noted above concerning setbacks, California's Alquist-Priolo Act already restricts development near earthquake faults. The concept of avoiding visible or known fault lines is merely a starting point, however, for the seismic considerations that ought to enter into lot configurations and subdivision design because direct fault rupture accounts for only a tiny fraction of overall earthquake damage. Extensive local mapping of earthquake fault traces, liquefaction zones, and other natural seismic hazards is an essential prelude to effective review of lot shape, building placement and design, and overall subdivision layout in order to minimize problems. In most cases, where the hazards are known to be moderate or severe, requiring geologic investigations of the site (see the section below on management tools) will give planners better data with which to review subdivision plans and minimize exposure to seismic hazards. The use of clustering and the preservation of more geologically hazardous areas of a site for open space or parkland represent the adaptation of well-known conservation planning devices to a seismically hazardous setting. Portola Valley, California, has used this device in allowing a developer in an area crossed by the San Andreas Fault and flanked by unstable hillsides to create smaller, clustered lots and keep vulnerable areas in permanent open space. (See also Jaffe, Butler, and Thurow (1981); William Spangle and Associates (1988); Tyler (1995).)

Road width and access regulations. Another byproduct that planners can derive from thorough seismic hazard identification is the ability to identify

Extensive local mapping of earthquake fault traces, liquefaction zones, and other natural seismic hazards is an essential prelude to effective review of lot shape, building placement and design, and overall subdivision layout in order to minimize problems.

In planning new development in an area potentially subject to wildfire hazards, planners can work to ensure that local traffic will not exceed the carrying capacity of the roads for evacuation and fire access purposes. Many roads in wildfire hazard areas, particularly those with steep slopes, are notoriously narrow relative to the need for fire equipment to reach threatened areas in an emergency.

potential limitations on access to damaged areas following an earthquake. Where are the major arteries that may fail for which there are no satisfactory alternative routes? Particularly vulnerable areas may include those where access requires traversing a mountain pass or crossing a bridge over a major waterway. This is largely a transportation and capital improvements problem, but one with major consequences for recovery and reconstruction policy in the event of failure. It is also a significant consideration in identifying land-use lessons in the aftermath of a disaster and influencing post-disaster road and bridge rebuilding priorities to remedy known deficiencies (BSSC 1987a).

The same concerns can be brought to bear on post-flood transportation repairs, to say nothing of pre-flood design of subdivisions in flood hazard areas. If some roads needed for access and evacuation are washed out, are there residents who will be stranded for lack of a secondary evacuation route? The solution almost always is to locate driveways and streets in those areas of the subdivision least likely to be flooded and approaching buildings from the direction opposite the floodplain, preferably not disrupting natural drainage patterns so as to minimize erosion and runoff problems. While remedying a subdivision road design that is deficient in this regard may be more difficult, in the aftermath of a major flood it may be possible to reorient some access routes if the local government is able to acquire the appropriate properties for this purpose (Morris 1997).

In planning new development in an area potentially subject to wildfire hazards, planners can work to ensure that local traffic will not exceed the carrying capacity of the roads for evacuation and fire access purposes. Many roads in wildfire hazard areas, particularly those with steep slopes, are notoriously narrow relative to the need for fire equipment to reach threatened areas in an emergency. Planners considering road width should also consider their value as fire-breaks. In the aftermath of a disaster, as discussed elsewhere in this report, planners also have the opportunity to reassess the adequacy of local roads in terms of experience and to advocate for rebuilding them in a safer fashion (Slaughter 1996, Ch. 5).

Water supply. More detail is provided on the subject of water supply in Chapter 7. What bears noting here is that, where a city or county has no plans to extend water lines to meet development, it can insist that homes not near a natural source of accessible water for fire protection, such as a pond or stream, must include some other water supply mechanism that can assist firefighters, such as a cistern, swimming pool, or dry hydrant (NFPA n.d.).

Hillside development regulations. Wildfires have some known behavioral patterns as they sweep through canyons, down hills, and across other natural features. Many of these patterns depend on updrafts and downdrafts to feed the fire with bursts of oxygen, and flammable structures or vegetation lying in the path are extremely vulnerable. High winds are accelerated by natural wind tunnels and serve to exacerbate these patterns. Hillside development ordinances can take advantage of this knowledge to regulate the placement of structures relative to vegetation, cliffs, and other natural or landscaped features.

Regulations should serve double duty in simultaneously addressing landslide hazards. One sure way to accelerate erosion is to reduce or strip the vegetative cover that holds soil in place, so construction practices, grading, landscaping, lot orientation, and architectural design should all be reviewed with regard to the primary objective of protecting the site against such deterioration. Vegetation issues, which extend beyond considerations in subdivision review alone, are discussed separately below in a section on design controls. In addition, engineering reports on slope stability provide essential information to help planners ensure that building sites are chosen to maximize public safety. (For more information, see Olshansky (1996) and Erley and Kockelman (1981).)

Open space requirements. Hillside development virtually demands some open space concessions in order to preserve the integrity of the sensitive area involved. A community simply cannot afford to pepper the hillside environment with homes in the same way that urban flatland is developed, where grid designs and high density are often appropriate. All the risk factors already discussed—slope instability, soil erosion, loss of vegetative cover, and wildfire fuel factors—plus other community values, such as aesthetics and habitat and view protection, require a second look at the way in which steep slopes are carved into lots. Requiring the dedication of open space and parkland in such areas is a valid regulatory measure to protect all these values and to ensure public safety. In many cases, however, a community may wish to look at the use of easements or actual acquisition (perhaps through a land trust or some public/private partnership) of hillside land to get this job done (Olshansky 1996).

Flood mitigation poses another opportunity for the use of open space requirements. Preserving a linear park along riparian corridors can be part of the strategy in a planned unit development, preserving wetlands, woodlands, and other natural features that minimize flooding by controlling streambank erosion while enhancing the visual and recreational qualities of a site. The trees filter and absorb runoff, and the community gains a combination of other open space and parkland benefits. (See also Brooks and Deines (1995 and 1996.)

Design Controls

Good design of the built environment is an essential element of effective mitigation. What makes one building less susceptible to wind or fire damage than its neighbors? Why do flood waters swirl past one building, inflicting minimal damage, while another suffers the brunt of nature's blow? The answer to these questions often lies in a combination of considerations involving both the design and choice of materials in the structure itself and the design and contours of the immediate surroundings, such as the slope of the land, the vegetation, and building placement within the lot. The two previous sections dealt with the larger contexts of zoning and overall subdivision design. This section addresses issues specific to individual buildings and the parcels of land on which they sit.

Tree conservation and vegetation requirements. Landscaping and vegetation make a difference in mitigating the impacts of natural hazards. Trees break the force of the wind and stabilize the soil. Wetlands absorb much of the overflow from stream channels. Fire-resistant vegetation can retard the spread of wildfires toward vulnerable buildings. Planners can use landscaping requirements to preserve or enhance the protection such natural features afford. These requirements may be part of site plan reviews or a separate set of zoning regulations and environmental performance standards.

Landscaping requirements for shoreline properties can be tailored to meet the special needs of dune system preservation and barrier island stability. (See Figure 5-3.) While this is typically handled through required setbacks measured in relation to an established reference point in a coastal setting, it is also important in connection with not permitting other disturbances of the natural dune system. Also, requiring the use of only native vegetation in coastal areas minimizes the possibility that high winds or flooding will uproot trees, causing damage from debris (Pilkey et al. 1980; Morris 1997).

Landscaping acquires special significance in relation to wildfire hazards because vegetation becomes a fuel that feeds the hazard that is threatening people and property. The Oakland case study in Chapter 11

> Landscaping acquires special significance in relation to wildfire hazards because vegetation becomes a fuel that feeds the hazard that is threatening people and property.

Figure 5-3. Typical Dune Cross Section

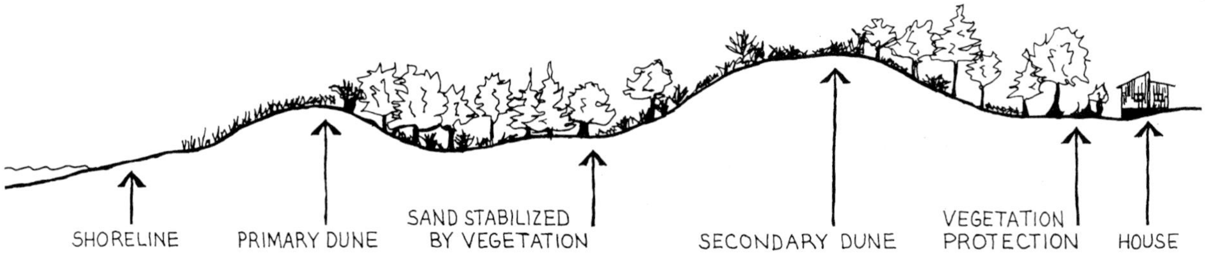

SHORELINE   PRIMARY DUNE   SAND STABILIZED BY VEGETATION   SECONDARY DUNE   VEGETATION PROTECTION   HOUSE

helps to highlight some of the practical issues of vegetation and landscaping connected with wildfire hazards, which are also addressed in Chapter 7. They are among the most essential elements of any plan to address wildfire hazard mitigation. In this case, the most salient point concerns not so much the preservation of natural vegetation, although that is often important for other reasons, but maintaining some distance between buildings and the most flammable types of local vegetation, as well as trying to use more fire-resistant vegetation wherever possible (Olshansky 1996; Slaughter 1996, Ch. 16).

Nothing holds soil in place better than living plants, so it is little surprise that tree conservation, landscaping, and vegetation all play a major role in mitigating landslide hazards on steep slopes. Clearing and grading activities disturb this natural stability and accelerate erosion, leading to potentially catastrophic landslides under extreme circumstances, such as heavy rainfalls, seismic vibrations, or rapid snowmelt. In addition to the obvious landslide and mudslide problems, there is the potential for this runoff to cause or exacerbate flooding problems, particularly where steep bluffs rise above stream corridors.

Sherrard (1996) offers an overview of an approach to the management of riparian open space in Bellevue, Washington, which combines stream corridors, forested riparian hillsides, and residential subdivisions. The approach combines tree preservation and open space dedication requirements with municipal oversight of management plans for areas of common ownership through homeowners associations. The city adopted its sensitive areas ordinance in 1987 and updated it in 1996.

Tree conservation ordinances can address development problems in forested hillsides but may be less useful in other situations, where requirements for natural landscaping and protection of grassy vegetation may apply. As with so much else in this area, specific ordinance requirements must be built on a solid base of hazard identification and environmental research (Maryland Office of Planning 1993; Duerksen 1993).

Design review. The Oakland case study in Chapter 11 offers a prime example of the importance of design review with regard to wildfire hazards, particularly in a post-disaster context. The process of design review can be used to establish conformity with important criteria both for safety and aesthetic purposes. These commonly include building size, height and bulk, view protection, avoidance of fire-enhancing features such as overhangs and the use of wood shake or shingle roofs, attached downhill-side decks, and parking and loading facilities, among others. Boulder, Colorado, for instance, has outlawed the use of wood shake shingles. Local fire safety officials often can serve as good on-staff consultants concerning design details that enhance or detract from fire safety (Olshansky 1996).

For mitigation purposes, the focus of design review obviously varies with the nature of the hazard. Overhangs are undesirable, for instance, in coastal areas, though not for the same reasons as in wildfire zones. Rather, high

> Nothing holds soil in place better than living plants, so it is little surprise that tree conservation, landscaping, and vegetation all play a major role in mitigating landslide hazards on steep slopes. Clearing and grading activities disturb this natural stability and accelerate erosion, leading to potentially catastrophic landslides under extreme circumstances, such as heavy rainfalls, seismic vibrations, or rapid snowmelt.

winds in hurricanes (and tornadoes, sometimes spawned by tropical cyclones) gain extra potency in tearing roofs off buildings because of the powerful leverage that overhangs afford. In fact, any insecurely fastened appendages, including porches, chimneys, exterior signs, lights, or doors, railings, and other adornments, may break loose and become airborne projectiles. In addition, buildings should be oriented to minimize the impact of the likely prevailing wind pattern and water flow in such storms, which for the most part is a known quantity. Although many of the best mitigation measures are related to building codes, design review plays a part in minimizing damage and danger, and there is, fortunately, a fair amount of research both already performed and underway to improve our understanding of wind-related impacts on the built environment (National Research Council 1993; FIA 1992; FIA/Hawaii 1993).

As a general matter, planners undoubtedly will be aware that, while important, hazard mitigation may not be the only, or even the primary, focus of design review following a disaster. As always, the process of post-disaster reconstruction offers an opportunity to reshape or to rationalize design compatibility in neighborhoods and commercial districts, and design review can be used to achieve aesthetic improvements that might take much longer under other circumstances. Arkadelphia, Arkansas, is a recent example of the use of design review within the context of a tornado overlay district, with the goal of developing a unified historical period appeal in the reconstruction of the central business district (Woodward-Clyde Associates 1997a).

Building codes. Planners generally have little direct influence over building codes, which for the most part are adopted at the state level and enforced by local building departments. Burby, May, and Paterson (1998) surveyed code enforcement practices and found inadequate compliance to be a major obstacle to the effective implementation of planning and development programs. They also found what they called a facilitative model of compliance, which concentrates on working cooperatively with regulated firms and individuals, to be more effective in producing results than a systematic model that concentrates on the deterrent effect of strict enforcement. Of course, the two approaches are not totally incompatible, but largely depend on emphasis, and a facilitative strategy can be just aggressive as one of throwing the book at violators. The authors attribute their findings in part to the fact that compliance is often a matter of interpretation rather than one of obeying clear-cut rules. At the same time, Burby and French (1998) examined property losses in suburban jurisdictions from the Northridge Earthquake and found lower losses where communities had expended more effort on enforcing the seismic provisions of the Uniform Building Code.

Planners are not directly responsible for building codes, but they do have varying degrees of influence over the quality of enforcement, with more likelihood of successful interaction with building officials in jurisdictions where planning and building functions are consolidated in a single department. That consolidation means that a single agency administrator is overseeing both functions and can help to coordinate policy. In smaller jurisdictions, even without such consolidation, the more informal collegiality of a small municipal staff may also facilitate communication and coordination about areas of concern to planners.

In any event, it is important to see planning controls and building codes as complementary and compatible mitigation and reconstruction tools and not as tools that are in any way competing with each other as priorities in the disaster planning context. A comprehensive approach to hazard mitigation and sound post-disaster planning will emphasize each set of controls in its

As always, the process of post-disaster reconstruction offers an opportunity to reshape or to rationalize design compatibility in neighborhoods and commercial districts, and design review can be used to achieve aesthetic improvements that might take much longer under other circumstances.

In any event, it is important to see planning controls and building codes as complementary and compatible mitigation and reconstruction tools and not as tools that are in any way competing with each other as priorities in the disaster planning context. A comprehensive approach to hazard mitigation and sound post-disaster planning will emphasize each set of controls in its own place and seek to achieve useful synergies wherever each can strengthen the gains that the other produces.

own place and seek to achieve useful synergies wherever each can strengthen the gains that the other produces. For example, making a building both structurally wind-resistant and siting it so as to minimize exterior wind impacts (for example, by putting it behind dunes and tree cover that will brake wind speeds) enhances the efficacy of both structural and locational approaches to mitigation. Using stricter building codes in more hazardous areas is another way of integrating planning and building code concerns. Planners can be effective advocates for the enactment of building codes that exceed model codes and NFIP.

Although questions were raised about enforcement following the devastation of Hurricane Andrew, where one-fourth of the $16 billion in insured losses were attributed to code violations (Burby, May, and Paterson 1998), the South Florida building code is especially geared to building wind resistance into the design of buildings in order to sustain hurricane wind damage. Ongoing wind research is expanding our knowledge of wind-resistant building qualities and is worth investigation. Planners at least would benefit from an understanding of the role and effectiveness of those codes in an overall strategy for wind hazard mitigation. (For more information, see National Research Council (1993) and Structural Engineers Association of Hawaii (1992).)

Construction techniques also can minimize obstructions to the flow of high-velocity waves in coastal high-hazard areas through construction on pilings and limiting the use of below-deck areas for carports and patios (FIA 1993c). This is congruent with NFIP regulations.

> Building with fire-resistant materials, especially avoiding wood-shake roofs and broad overhangs, is the essential change needed for adaptation to the wildland/urban interface. One approach is to specify the performance criteria for such buildings while leaving the choice of building materials to builders to demonstrate their own creativity and the viability of alternative materials if they wish to work in the interface environment.

Building with fire-resistant materials, especially avoiding wood-shake roofs and broad overhangs, is the essential change needed for adaptation to the wildland/urban interface. One approach is to specify the performance criteria for such buildings while leaving the choice of building materials to builders to demonstrate their own creativity and the viability of alternative materials if they wish to work in the interface environment. One factor making this approach advisable is the variation in local climatic and topographical factors that may require fine-tuning such performance standards from one part of the country to another (Slaughter 1996, Part II).

Seismic safety is an important premise for building code requirements in seismically active locations. While building codes, based on models developed by the three national model code organizations, are generally adopted at the state level and consigned to local enforcement, states do not always require local adoption of seismic safety provisions. One major issue in such codes is the feasibility of retroactively requiring retrofitting in existing buildings because of the potential cost implications. The balance between cost and safety considerations is one that must be decided locally based on the age and quality of the existing building stock and the public's willingness to adopt measures to ameliorate undesirable impacts on housing affordability. However, the National Earthquake Hazards Reduction Program (NEHRP) has developed useful documentation on this point. Based on studies performed on behalf of FEMA, the cost to rehabilitate existing buildings to meet the NEHRP recommended provisions is approximately $20 per square foot. The cost to incorporate seismic strengthening in constructing new buildings to meet NEHRP-recommended provisions is approximately 5 percent of the structural cost of the building, equating to 1 to 2 percent of the total cost (FEMA 1993b, 1995g).

The whole issue of building codes takes on special significance because, to date, they have played a much larger role in earthquake hazard mitigation than have land-use regulations. The job of the building code with regard to seismic hazards is to reduce the likelihood of foundation failure and to heighten structural stability against lateral acceleration forces (BSSC 1990).

Special floodproofing techniques and materials can more easily be mandated for new construction in flood hazard areas, and FEMA has already published a series of technical bulletins as guides for compliance with such construction requirements (FIA 1993a-c). The requirements in the technical guides are those of NFIP; more stringent local codes would take precedence. FEMA has also sought the inclusion of flood-resistant construction standards into the three model building codes as well as the standards of the American Society of Civil Engineers (ASCE), which has incorporated provisions for the determination of flood loads and flood load combinations into ASCE 7-95, "Minimum Design Loads for Buildings and Other Structures," and a newer "Flood Resistant Design and Construction Standard," which can be incorporated into the building codes directly or by reference. FEMA partially funded this effort by ASCE to ensure the standard would meet or exceed NFIP minimum requirements.

Financial Tools

The growing costs of natural disasters was highlighted in Chapter 1 in explaining taxpayers' concerns that governmental responses to disasters become smarter and not simply more generous. Fixing what becomes broken in a disaster often requires substantial and, sometimes, huge financial resources. A host of federal programs now exist in whole or in part to respond to those needs, and identifying priorities for targeting those resources is a major task not only for federal grant makers but also for local and state governments, which both apply for and expend the funds available. This section is designed to identify specific uses for disaster funds and the issues planners must address in order to use them as wisely and efficiently as possible.

Florida, through its Resource Identification Strategy (RIS), is helping local governments obtain vital planning and technical assistance to strengthen their communities against the impacts of natural disasters. The Florida Department of Community Affairs has partnered with the Florida Public Affairs Center at Florida State University to develop RIS, which includes an online database (www.state.fl.us/comaff/hcd/fccr/ris) with information on historical and potential funding sources for disaster mitigation, disaster recovery, and long-term redevelopment projects. For readers of this document, Appendix C provides a directory of federal disaster assistance sources.

Targeting of Community Development Block Grant (CDBG) and other grant funds. Where should the grant money go for rebuilding the community? Planners can help advance the effectiveness of local hazard mitigation policy by redirecting portions of their community's CDBG funds as the nonfederal match for federal HMGP money and doing so in a way that enhances strategic objectives in the local post-disaster plan. This strategy has continued to be pursued very effectively in facilitating many of the buyouts in Midwest communities in the aftermath of the 1993 floods. Among them were Rhineland and Arnold, Missouri.

CDBG, Small Business Administration (SBA), and Economic Development Administration (EDA) programs and funds may be applied toward rebuilding communities' economies after disasters. All three agencies incorporate and promote mitigation strategies into resources being applied to disaster-stricken areas. It is important to note, however, that these agencies do not have specific post-disaster funds available as FEMA and other agencies do under Stafford Act authorization. Communities must therefore either tap into their pre-existing block grant funds or seek agency program funds appropriated by Congress annually.

In limited cases, however, Congress may grant supplemental funding to the U.S. Department of Housing and Urban Development (HUD) or EDA

Where should the grant money go for rebuilding the community? Planners can help advance the effectiveness of local hazard mitigation policy by redirecting portions of their community's CDBG funds as the nonfederal match for federal HMGP money and doing so in a way that enhances strategic objectives in the local post-disaster plan.

after a major disaster for specific recovery needs. Such funding to HUD augments the CDBG and Home Investment Partnerships (HOME) programs, and comes from Disaster Recovery Initiative (DRI) grants. HUD's formula "considers disaster recovery needs not met by other Federal disaster programs." Communities, in addition to having significant unmet recovery needs, must also be able to carry out a disaster recovery program. Most such communities, according to HUD, are already receiving allocations of CDBG or HOME funds. The communities receiving DRI funds also must award at least half the money for "activities that benefit low- and moderate-income persons." They may use the funds for recovery efforts involving housing, economic development, infrastructure, and prevention of further damage, so long as this does not duplicate funding already available from FEMA, SBA, and the U.S. Army Corps of Engineers. Before they can receive DRI funds, however, eligible local governments must develop and submit an Action Plan for Disaster Recovery describing the intended uses of the funds. (See the HUD web site at www.hud.gov/progdesc/disaster.html.)

Relocation assistance. One major fear of homeowners considering relocation from a floodplain or other hazard zone is that they may not find adequate or equivalent housing elsewhere. Particularly for low-income families, including those living in manufactured housing, these concerns are legitimate. Special issues affecting minorities may also be a factor in some communities (see Perry, Greene, and Mushcatel 1983). These issues often include the treatment of rental housing and the relocation of tenants, and may introduce serious questions of environmental justice into the post-disaster recovery agenda. Effective acquisition and carefully targeted use of relocation assistance can persuade many of these people that the move is in their own long-term best interest and may be less painful than they thought. A planning department that gains a reputation for easing this aspect of a wrenching decision can garner valuable public acceptance of long-term hazard mitigation goals.

> One major fear of homeowners considering relocation from a floodplain or other hazard zone is that they may not find adequate or equivalent housing elsewhere. Particularly for low-income families, including those living in manufactured housing, these concerns are legitimate.

Special taxing or assessment districts. One way to send a market signal to developers and home buyers alike is to establish the principle that special services, such as those most likely to be used in an emergency by people living in hazard-prone areas, must be supported through special fees, taxes, or assessments in the area affected. The concept is akin to that commonly applied in other districts receiving special services or benefits and allows the community to establish the differential costs for those choosing to live or buy property in such areas. One example is the Lee County, Florida, All Hazards Protection District and its associated fund (Brower, Beatley, and Blatt 1987, Ch. 5).

California, in Division 17 of its Public Resources Code, enacted enabling legislation for a similar device called Geologic Hazard Abatement Districts (GHADs). Local governments may establish special assessment districts in the area of known geologic hazards and collect fees from property owners to finance repairs from landslides and implement geologic hazard mitigation measures. The local legislative body creating a GHAD may serve as its board of directors. While their use has not yet become widespread, these districts exist in some jurisdictions, such as Contra Costa County. The first two Contra Costa County GHADs were formed by the county and a subdivider prior to lot sale and development (Tyler 1995).

Tax increment financing (TIF). The underlying concept of a TIF district is somewhat opposite of a benefit assessment district, where additional taxes are levied to support additional services. A TIF district establishes a current base level of taxation determined by existing property values and assigns additional increments resulting from increases in future valuations to a special fund used to pay for infrastructure improvements within the district. In other words, the planned improvements are expected to increase property values, and those increased values, when they materialize, produce additional property tax revenues that underwrite the cost of the improvements. In a neighborhood or business district badly devastated by a natural disaster, a TIF district can be an effective mechanism for financing the reconstruction of essential infrastructure ranging from new street lights to aesthetic changes in street and sidewalk design intended to draw new business to an area undergoing substantial redevelopment. TIFs invariably have some time limit applied to their existence, so that eventually the improvements return greater tax revenues to the larger community once the mission of redevelopment has been accomplished.

Many states have statutes authorizing the use of this differential taxing device. One interesting wrinkle regarding the use of TIF districts for post-disaster redevelopment, however, is that Alaska's TIF legislation specifically limits its use to earthquake recovery purposes.

Impact fees. Impact fees are a broader application of the concept behind benefit assessment districts. The idea is to make new development pay the costs of infrastructure expansion within the local jurisdiction. Typically, these fees have been used to underwrite the expansion of or addition to schools, libraries, fire and police stations, sewer and water services, and any number of other necessary public facilities. Their legality varies widely depending on state enabling legislation and the degree of freedom local governments have to craft their own revenue enhancement schemes. Consequently, planning departments considering impact fees as a growth control measure must check the applicable state legislation, if there is any. One difference from benefit assessments is that impact fees are not tied to the value enhancement of individual properties but, instead, are tied to the impact that those properties have on the overall level of need for particular facilities or services.

In a post-disaster context, one interesting example of the use of impact fees again comes from Lee County, Florida, where, in 1993, the county's department of public services proposed the creation of an emergency public shelter impact fee. The idea was to use the impact fee on new development to fund the development of adequate shelters to house those likely to be fleeing from highly hazardous areas during a hurricane. The study documenting the proposal details evacuation lead times, the numbers of people likely to need shelter services, and other relevant details in calculating the size of the fee needed to support the necessary services. Although the proposal was never enacted in Lee County, this innovative idea could well have applicability in highly flood-prone riverine areas as well as in coastal zones.

Differential taxation. Differential taxation does not enhance the local government's revenue stream directly or for clear post-disaster purposes. It is a long-term measure aimed at discouraging development in areas that the local government would prefer to see remain as some type of open space. It has been used extensively by states as a technique for lowering the effective cost of retaining forest or farmland by taxing such lands at their current use value, rather than the value at which the market might appraise them for other purposes, such as residential development. Where a local government seeks to retain undeveloped land in that state in a hazardous area, this may be an appropriate tool, although its use is likely to be heavily dependent on state legislation. One problem that is sometimes identified in literature on this type of taxing is that owners often are induced to retain the land only while there is a marginal benefit that outweighs the profits of selling or developing. For that reason, local governments may wish to enhance the effectiveness of such taxing with the use of a device called "existing use zoning" by Humbach

In a neighborhood or business district badly devastated by a natural disaster, a TIF district can be an effective mechanism for financing the reconstruction of essential infrastructure ranging from new street lights to aesthetic changes in street and sidewalk design intended to draw new business to an area undergoing substantial redevelopment.

(1992). This device avoids the problem of takings in relation to a landowner's development expectations simply by creating a category of existing use that is applied to land that is still currently used for forestry or agricultural purposes, thus allowing the owner to retain the value that he or she currently enjoys from the use to which the property is already put. Coupling this zoning device with differential taxation would remove most of the incentives for entertaining development proposals by making clear that a developer would have to seek to rezone the property before the land could acquire any anticipated additional value. If most surrounding land were in the same category, rezoning would become particularly difficult.

Urban renewal or redevelopment funds. Planning redevelopment projects can be every bit as complex and idiosyncratic as the individual communities that undertake them, each of which has its own special distribution of manufacturing and service businesses, employment base, business district infrastructure and character, and business retention prospects. Moreover, redevelopment projects are generally not under the direct control of planning departments but are administered by separately established redevelopment agencies upon which state legislation has bestowed powers of eminent domain for purposes of land assembly and redevelopment. It is essential that such entities understand and participate in mitigation plans and plans for post-disaster recovery and reconstruction, so that redevelopment goals and projects will not conflict with local government mitigation and recovery objectives, especially if the redevelopment districts are pre-identified as being in hazard-prone areas.

> Planners need to take the initiative before a disaster strikes to collaborate with local redevelopment officials to determine what authority they may have to use the redevelopment agency as a funding source for post-disaster reconstruction purposes.

Because redevelopment funds represent an excellent potential source of money for rebuilding damaged areas, particularly in central business districts or pre-existing blighted areas, planners need to take the initiative before a disaster strikes to collaborate with local redevelopment officials to determine what authority they may have to use the redevelopment agency as a funding source for post-disaster reconstruction purposes.

Florida and California have both produced and commissioned guides and model plans to address the special problems involved in post-disaster redevelopment efforts (TBRPC 1994; Governor's Office of Emergency Services 1993, Chs. 29-30). While it is impossible here to detail the variations among 50 states in their redevelopment enabling legislation, it is interesting to consider California law because of the special attention that state has paid to post-earthquake recovery as an aspect of local redevelopment authority. As California's Seismic Safety Commission (1994a) notes, "Redevelopment agencies throughout the state have used their authority extensively to subsidize seismic retrofitting of unsafe structures and to assist with post-earthquake recovery." One interesting early example is that of Santa Rosa, which suffered a mild earthquake in 1969, in which no buildings collapsed, but many in the downtown were damaged. Santa Rosa expanded its existing redevelopment district to include the central business district and used its federal contribution of $5 million to acquire and clear some properties for a major regional shopping center. More importantly, the city over the next two years developed and adopted a resolution requiring a preliminary inspection (at city expense) of all buildings built before 1958 and setting up a program for upgrading such buildings to meet newer seismic retrofit standards (William Spangle and Associates 1980).

The passage in 1994 of California Assembly Bill 1290, which changed the definition of blighted areas, facilitated the inclusion of disaster-stricken properties so that redevelopment authorities could use their funds for mitigation. At the time, 375 redevelopment agencies in the state were overseeing 665 redevelopment project areas, many involving older down-

FEMA

Department of Housing and Redevelopment, City of Santa Rosa

towns whose buildings are more vulnerable because they were built prior to the adoption of modern seismic building code standards. The seismic commission's Compendium of Background Reports for the Northridge Earthquake cites several examples of both:

- the use of tax-increment financing to subsidize seismic hazard mitigation, largely to retrofit unreinforced masonry buildings (Culver City; Fullerton; City of Orange); and

- assistance in post-earthquake recovery, such as subsidizing repair of damaged structures, alleviating hazardous conditions (including through demolition), and providing relocation and temporary housing assistance to property owners and residents (Coalinga, Whittier, and Santa Cruz, the last being detailed in the case study in Chapter 12).

One interesting feature of California redevelopment legislation, adopted in 1964 to address tsunami damage in Crescent City after the Alaska earthquake, is the Community Redevelopment Financial Assistance and Disaster Project Law (California Health and Safety Code, Section 34000 et seq.), known popularly as the "disaster law." Its importance lies in its provisions for expedited plan adoption if the proposed redevelopment area is certified by the governor as in need of assistance and the president has declared it a disaster area. The three cities cited above have all used this measure to speed the process of adopting plans and implementing post-disaster redevelopment projects (William Spangle and Associates 1991).

Following an earthquake in 1969, Santa Rosa, California, undertook redevelopment of downtown buildings. The inset photo shows retrofit buildings and the cleared site for a new mall in 1979; the photo below shows the completed mall in 1986.

An interesting local plan for redevelopment emerged out of the devastated town of Homestead, Florida, after Hurricane Andrew. The local redevelopment agency, Homestead Economic and Rebuilding Organization (HERO), was created in the aftermath of the disaster to help rebuild a community that lost 8,000 jobs when the Homestead Air Force Base was virtually destroyed. The business community devastation was nearly as massive. Nevertheless, despite losing the presence of major league baseball for spring training, Homestead built a Grand Prix auto racing track, new housing, and a park.

Because Homestead is a smaller city (population 26,000) with a spotty planning history prior to Andrew, this attempt constitutes a potentially interesting example for other communities of similar size (Enterprise/Homestead Planning/Action Team and City of Homestead 1993; City of Homestead-Enterprise/Homestead and HERO 1993). Local or regional planners may also wish to consider the desirability of at least having in place contingency plans for the efficient post-disaster formation of such a redevelopment authority where none already exists.

Public mortgage lending subsidies and policies. Many cities and states have programs to subsidize interest rates or provide other breaks for low-income and first-time home buyers or to encourage redevelopment in blighted areas. Examples of the latter group include sweat equity and homesteading programs that allow willing buyers to acquire and rehabilitate blighted properties at little or no cost in order to put them back on the tax rolls and revitalize the community. Reexamining the policies that guide these programs with an eye to achieving hazard mitigation in the bargain is a way to leverage these public subsidies to prevent future disaster damage.

Transfer of development rights. One way of reducing density in hazardous areas is to allow property owners to sell or transfer their development rights to developers of property in other, nonhazardous areas of the community. This technique is applicable across all hazard categories if properly framed to define the boundaries of the transferring and receiving areas and the circumstances under which rights may be transferred. The technique has been used in several locations around the U.S., including Montgomery County, Maryland, where it is part of a program for protecting farmland. Using it in a natural hazards context is simply a change of purpose, but a valid one. This technique might be especially useful in the aftermath of a natural disaster as a means of persuading some landowners to redevelop outside the most heavily stricken areas. Fortunately, planners considering such options have several good resources in the planning literature to guide their thinking and steer them past any legal pitfalls (Maryland Office of Planning 1995a; Roddewig and Inghram 1987; Bredin 1998).

Scottsdale, Arizona, uses density transfers tied specifically to hazardous conditions as well as the protection of natural resources in its Environmentally Sensitive Lands Ordinance, adopted in 1991. The provisions allow transfers from areas with slopes that are unstable or exceed 25 percent, or areas appearing on the city's special features map (Olshansky 1996, Appendix C).

TDR programs require some land-use sophistication on the part of the jurisdiction managing the program. The administration of the program can take several forms. One extreme is simply to designate the sending and receiving areas and the allowable density rights in each and otherwise let the market operate within those parameters. The other end of the spectrum occurs when the jurisdiction itself serves as the broker, buying and selling land development rights. This allows greater control over prices and procedures but requires more direct oversight and staff expense. Variations on these themes involve more limited interventions based on particular policy considerations of the local government and its comprehensive plan. In any case, the local planning department must develop a substantial knowledge base concerning local market conditions and trends in order to operate an effective program that achieves comprehensive plan objectives. (See also Brower, Beatley, and Blatt (1987, pp. 133-36) and Roddewig and Inghram (1987).)

Management Tools

Coordination with neighboring jurisdictions. Beyond mutual aid agreements, discussed in Chapter 3, lie a host of potential devices for cooperation on natural hazards problems, many of which get far less attention than they deserve. Floodplain management is one area that is overly ripe for regional cooperation between neighboring municipalities, and one that can yield substantial dividends even in smaller watersheds. Despite the frequent competition between neighboring communities in large metropolitan areas, Glassford (1993) offers an intriguing contrary example of a successful cooperative agreement among seven southern Chicago suburbs in the case of Butterfield Creek. Formed in 1983, the Butterfield Creek Steering Committee (BCSC) first engaged the U.S. Soil Conservation Service (now the Natural Resources Conservation Service) and the Illinois Department of Transportation's Division of Water Resources to study flooding problems and learned that 100-year flood levels in some locations were as much as 2.5 feet higher than existing FIRMs indicated, and that the problem could get worse with further development upstream in natural storage areas.

By November 1990, BCSC had reviewed local ordinances and published its own Butterfield Creek Model Floodplain and Stormwater Management Code. The model code strengthens detention requirements, requires effective soil erosion and sediment control, encourages natural drainage practices like swales and vegetative filters, and limits many uses in the floodway. One example of implementing the last point is a sunken baseball diamond in Flossmoor, which doubles as a catch basin to retain and dissipate flood waters without damaging nearby properties. What the BCSC model demonstrates above all is the value of local leadership in establishing the basis for cooperation on natural hazards that cross municipal boundaries in a metropolitan area.

Training programs. Because the whole arena of emergency management and planning for post-disaster recovery and reconstruction involves so much technical and procedural knowledge, FEMA and state emergency management agencies have made available a number of training tools for use by local government officials. These include technical assistance available from FEMA regional offices (see Appendix D), FEMA manuals and guides for mitigation and disaster planning, and the programs of FEMA's Emergency Management Institute (EMI) in Emmitsburg, Maryland. Specifically relevant to training for post-disaster recovery are three tabletop mitigation and recovery exercises, which provide earthquake, flood, and hurricane recovery scenarios. The facilitator's guide for these exercises is available on the Internet at www.fema.gov/priv/g398.htm. This allows local officials to decide whether to stage the exercise themselves or engage their state hazard mitigation officer to do so.

Geographic Information Systems (GISs) and the Global Positioning System (GPS). Few planning concerns lend themselves better to the use of modern computer technology than natural hazards. GIS combines mapping and database features to perform data storage and computation functions that were measurably more complex prior to the advent of this technology, which continues to improve constantly, like virtually all software innovations. Properly maintained, GIS can enable planners to access more information more quickly and make better informed, more sophisticated land-use decisions than would have seemed possible just a generation ago.

Beyond mutual aid agreements lie a host of potential devices for cooperation on natural hazards problems, many of which get far less attention than they deserve. Floodplain management is one area that is overly ripe for regional cooperation between neighboring municipalities, and one that can yield substantial dividends even in smaller watersheds.

Few planning concerns lend themselves better to the use of modern computer technology than natural hazards. GIS combines mapping and database features to perform data storage and computation functions that were measurably more complex prior to the advent of this technology, which continues to improve constantly, like virtually all software innovations.

GPS technology is increasingly being used to complement GIS in post-disaster damage assessments. In rural areas, for example, it is particularly valuable in establishing the location of damaged properties for disaster assistance and mitigation planning purposes.

GIS has come increasingly into its own as an essential post-disaster tool with some of the more recent disasters, including the Northridge earthquake (Topping 1994). Topping has developed a useful list of data layers relevant to disaster needs. (See sidebar.) However, for cost reasons among others, GIS will seldom if ever be used only for disaster planning purposes, and generally has served more than planning purposes when purchased, installed, and maintained by local governments. GIS systems are complex multipurpose tools that can help local officials coordinate and integrate data concerning a wide variety of land-use concerns, including infrastructure, housing, natural resources and hazards, zoning, and commercial and industrial activities. In short, the versatility of GIS mirrors the complexity of the issues planners will face in managing post-disaster recovery and reconstruction. In making the leap into the use of GIS, however, a local government should understand the commitment it must make in terms of time and personnel to maintain the database that will allow planners and other decision makers to realize the system's potential utility (Monmonier 1997).

GPS technology is increasingly being used to complement GIS in post-disaster damage assessments. In rural areas, for example, it is particularly valuable in establishing the location of damaged properties for disaster assistance and mitigation planning purposes.

Soil stability ratings. Accessing good soil data is a necessary prelude to the development of the regulatory tools in a hillside development ordinance. Local government planners can turn to the U.S. Geological Survey (USGS) for information, much of which is increasingly available through the USGS World Wide Web site on the Internet (www.usgs.gov), and to the Natural Resources Conservation Service. Preparatory to a site plan or subdivision review, however, it would be wise to require a geologic site investigation (see below) to develop adequate data for decision making (Olshansky 1996).

Soil and water conservation districts also provide soil reports on rezonings and subdivision proposals. Communities should take these sources of information seriously, although many currently do not.

Geologic studies. The standard method for ensuring the geologic suitability of a site for development is to require the completion of a geologic, or geotechnical, site investigation prior to review. In most cases, the applicant is required to hire the engineering geologist who prepares the study. The study may then be reviewed, depending on the circumstances and the requirements of local ordinances, by the local planning agency, an outside geologist hired by the jurisdiction, and/or by a staff geologist working either in the planning department or in some other division of local government (for example, public works). The local regulations should specify the level of detail and the specific types of supporting information desired in the study, including maps. Figure 5-4 illustrates the differentiation spelled out in the regulations for Santa Clara County, California (Tyler 1995).

This tool can be linked to zoning inasmuch as those areas required to have this review would have to lie within certain zoning categories where the hazard identification process outlined in Chapters 3 and 4 has shown that there are special problems.

Salt Lake County, Utah, which faces serious seismic safety problems along the Wasatch Front as well as slope stability problems in the nearby mountains, enacted its Natural Hazards Ordinance (Salt Lake County Zoning Ordinance Chapter 19.75) in 1989. Any applicant "requesting development on a parcel of land within a natural hazards study area" must submit a natural hazards report by an engineering geologist, or in the case of snow avalanche hazard, by a experienced avalanche expert. The report

Initial GIS Data Layers Useful to Response and Recovery

PREDEVELOPED DATA LAYERS

- congressional district boundaries
- state assembly and senate district boundaries
- metropolitan planning area boundaries
- county boundaries
- city boundaries
- local community and council district boundaries and areas
- special district boundaries
- school district boundaries
- ZIP code and postal place name boundaries and areas
- redevelopment area boundaries
- Census block group characteristics, including household size, owner-renter occupancy, income, age, ethnicity, and language data
- type of unit: single-family detached, multifamily attached, *number of floors**
- type of structure: wood-frame, URM, reinforced concrete, etc.
- manufactured housing parks
- freeways, interchanges, and ramps
- arterial and local streets with address ranges and street names
- dirt roads and four-wheel drive trails
- railroads, surface rail transit lines, and stations

- international, regional, and general aviation airports
- flood hazard areas and stream beds
- areas subject to liquefaction, strong ground motion, and seismically induced landslides
- Alquist-Priolo Study Zones areas (California)
- potential dam and tsunami inundation areas
- fire hazard areas
- areas subject to slumping, ground failure, and debris flows
- existing land-use polygons and areas
- unreinforced masonry (URM) buildings
- historical buildings
- public and private schools and areas
- hospitals, including type, number of beds
- emergency medical centers
- parks, including buildings and areas
- community centers
- police and fire stations
- nuclear and conventional power plant locations
- major oil and gas pipeline and storage tank locations
- powerline, waterline, and dam locations
- digital elevation models (DEMs), topography, slope, aspect
- hazardous materials, chemical, and ordinance storage sites

INCIDENT-SPECIFIC DATABASE ITEMS

- road closures and rerouting
- building damage by address and assessor's parcel number
- infrastructure damage location and extent by facility type
- shaking intensities
- ground motion, including horizontal and vertical displacement
- areas of ground rupture, liquefaction, landsliding

- areas flooded at crest
- tsunami high water line and areas
- burned areas
- *location of shelters**
- *location of temporary housing**
- Disaster Assistance Center and service center locations
- individual assistance applicants
- public assistance applicants
- hazard mitigation analytic maps

---

* Items in italics were added to the original source list for purposes of this PAS Report.

Source: Kenneth C. Topping, *OES GIS Strategic Plan*, Circulation Draft, prepared for Office of Emergency Services, State of California.

Figure 5-4. Hazard Zones and Investigation Requirements
Summarized from Santa Clara County, California, Relative Seismic Stability Map

	HAZARDS	INVESTIGATION REQUIREMENTS
RED	Areas of high potential for liquefaction, lateral spreading, differential settlement, fault rupture, earthquake-induced landslides, tsunamis, and flooding.	Site investigations mandatory unless detailed information permits waiver.
YELLOW	Area of moderate potential for liquefaction, lateral spreading, and earthquake-induced landslides.	Site investigations required unless waived by county.
GREEN	Area with low potential for liquefaction, lateral spreading, and earthquake-induced landslides.	Site investigation not automatically required; may be required by county on the basis of detailed information.

Source: Tyler (1995)

must include a detailed site map (i.e., one inch equal to 200 feet), with delineation of recommended setback distances and locations for structures. (See Figure 5-5.) While many jurisdictions contract with an independent geotechnical expert for review of the adequacy of such studies, Salt Lake County is the only county in Utah to retain its own staff geologist within the planning department. One significant advantage of this arrangement, where the workload is sufficient to make it cost-effective, is that a staff geologist can over time develop a much stronger working knowledge of the local environment than can an outside expert.

Public education. Planners and planning departments are perennially faced with the need to improve public understanding of the goals of the planning process and the means of achieving them. Natural hazards are among the more complex issues requiring elucidation in this regard, but the stakes are high, and as has been discussed with regard to multiobjective management, other actors on the local political scene are likely both to be informed about some of the issues and to have a stake in advancing the cause of hazard mitigation and sustainable post-disaster recovery and reconstruction. However, the best time to initiate the public education is unquestionably during the pre-disaster period. Even though it may be easier and vitally necessary to get people's attention after a disaster, the message will be more effective if the groundwork for disseminating it has been laid beforehand.

Examples of good pre-disaster public education campaigns by local government, especially those involving planning departments, abound in each hazard category. While these may be developed locally and independently, sometimes they are coordinated with other entities, including the American Red Cross, which produces its own public education resources. One of the most common subjects is floodproofing, often including the use of technical open houses and other hands-on means of conveying information to homeowners (U.S. Army Corps of Engineers 1994; FEMA 1986). Glassford (1993) notes that this technique was particularly effective in reaching homeowners after flooding incidents along Butterfield Creek in the south Chicago suburbs. In addition, Florida's Department of Community Affairs (n.d.) has supported education efforts about hurricanes and other coastal hazards. USGS (n.d.) has produced public education materials concerning

> Planners and planning departments are perennially faced with the need to improve public understanding of the goals of the planning process and the means of achieving them. Natural hazards are among the more complex issues requiring elucidation in this regard, but the stakes are high, and as has been discussed with regard to multiobjective management, other actors on the local political scene are likely both to be informed about some of the issues and to have a stake in advancing the cause of hazard mitigation and sustainable post-disaster recovery and reconstruction.

earthquakes customized to individual regions of the country, such as the Bay Area and southern Alaska. FEMA (1993a) has also produced some general purpose booklets for public consumption that local officials can use, as well as providing a good deal of public education material on its World Wide Web site (www.fema.gov).

The value of public education in helping to build informed consensus behind an effective plan for post-disaster recovery and reconstruction, or an effective long-term plan for hazard mitigation, should be obvious from the foregoing discussion in Chapter 4. An informed public is a potential ally planners can ill afford to forego if they wish to address disaster issues in a serious manner.

A MODEL RECOVERY AND RECONSTRUCTION ORDINANCE

The model recovery and reconstruction ordinance that follows these introductory paragraphs is based on the principles established elsewhere in this PAS Report. It provides basic elements of a comprehensive ordinance establishing a recovery organization and authorizing a variety of pre- and post-event planning and regulatory powers and procedures related to disaster recovery and reconstruction. Designed to be adopted in advance of

Figure 5-5. Special Study Area Report Requirements, Salt Lake County, Utah

IS A SITE-SPECIFIC NATURAL HAZARDS REPORT REQUIRED PRIOR TO APPROVAL?

Land Use (Type of Facility)	Liquefaction Potential High and Moderate	Very Low and Low	Surface Fault Rupture Special Study Area	Avalanche Path Special Study Area
Critical facilities (essential and hazardous facilities, and special occupancy structures)	Yes	Yes	Yes	Yes
Industrial and commercial buildings (more than 2 stories or less than 5,000 square feet)	Yes	No	Yes	Yes
Multifamily residential structures (4 or more units per acre, and all other industrial and commercial)	Yes	No	Yes	Yes
Residential subdivisions	Yes	No	Yes	Yes
Residential single lots and multifamily dwellings (less than 4 units per acre)	No	No	Yes	Yes

Source: Salt Lake County, Utah, Zoning Ordinance, Chapter 19.75

a major disaster, it can also be quickly adapted to post-disaster conditions if it has not been adopted before the disaster.

Unlike ordinary planning ordinances, this ordinance requires involvement by many other departments within the city or county government organization under the guidance and leadership of the city manager, county administrative officer, or equivalent position. Some of the actions called for by this ordinance require direct involvement of the planning department, although frequently it will be acting in concert with other departments. Having an inherently interdepartmental focus, this ordinance structures a model process that has generic value. Due to widely ranging circumstances, however, the content may vary considerably.

The essential concepts of this ordinance include: the establishment of a recovery organization before a major disaster to prepare a pre-event plan; the adoption of that plan and this ordinance by the governing body before a major disaster occurs; and the use of the recovery plan and organization to efficiently and wisely guide post-disaster recovery and reconstruction activity. The recovery organization may be constructed differently from place to place, but the idea is to create an ongoing organization integrated with, but extending beyond, any existing emergency operations organization.

Although an existing emergency operations organization may serve as a useful base from which to fashion a recovery organization, there are certain fundamental differences in function that make it preferable to establish a recovery organization that operates parallel to the emergency response organization. Continuity of the recovery organization and expediting the rebuilding processes for which it is responsible become very important.

> Although an existing emergency operations organization may serve as a useful base from which to fashion a recovery organization, there are certain fundamental differences in function that make it preferable to establish a recovery organization that operates parallel to the emergency response organization. Continuity of the recovery organization and expediting the rebuilding processes for which it is responsible become very important.

1. Local government emergency response organizations tend to focus on emergency preparedness and response operations. Strongly oriented toward police and fire functions, during "peace-time" they characteristically handle routine local emergencies and undertake training and preparedness for disaster response operations. Typically, recovery and reconstruction functions do not fall within their purview, although this is beginning to change in some jurisdictions.

2. Some powers reflected by this ordinance are activated by the declaration of a local emergency. However, these powers are characteristically broader than emergency response powers because the latter do not include property, building, land-use, and development regulations, or the public hearing process.

3. Certain regulatory powers authorized by this ordinance are identified for initial implementation during the time in which a declaration of local emergency is in effect. However, such powers tend to be extended for much longer periods of time. Although a declared emergency may not be terminated for months after the end of emergency response operations, complete implementation of rebuilding processes often takes years.

In short, this is an emerging area of disaster management practice that crosses over into city planning, redevelopment, and building. Much of the thinking and implementation for the processes identified in this ordinance have only emerged within professional literature or practice within the past decade. Although some form of ad hoc recovery organization is created with every major disaster, such arrangements tend to exist for the peak rebuilding period and then are disbanded. As yet, very few local jurisdictions have formally created recovery organizations in advance of a disaster or maintained them continuously afterwards.

This ordinance structures many processes that tend to take place anyway after a major disaster without forethought or knowledge of available options. It provides organizational and procedural dimensions that can accelerate thinking and planning needed in advance of a disaster to recover and rebuild more wisely and efficiently than would happen were such preparation not to occur. It captures the broadest possible range of pre-event and post-disaster activities that interact with urban planning and development, recognizing that not all provisions may be germane to circumstances within individual communities.

There is little established practice of record to use as a point of departure. Few ordinances in use by local jurisdictions deal with such a broad scope of recovery functions. Those which have been adopted tend to cover a more limited range of elements, such as rebuilding, permitting, and nonconforming use procedures. With the upswing in major disasters in the last several years, however, substantial experimentation is taking place, and more communication is occurring regarding outcomes of various recovery strategies.

These processes will inevitably lead to revisions of the ideas reflected here. Therefore, this ordinance should be considered a framework for flexible application of pre-event and post-event procedures that can be modified to fit emerging ideas as well as local conditions. Although a separate ordinance is not essential to the performance of many functions, the value of adopting a recovery ordinance is in providing clear policy guidance in advance for dealing with contingencies as well as an overall rationale in case of legal challenge.

The following ordinance language is interspersed with italicized commentaries that provide alternatives or amplification. Commentaries sometimes identify areas for possible modification or explain reasons why certain provisions are included. Commentary has been omitted for sections that are self-explanatory or unlikely to require change.

Certain conventions have been included throughout the model that will require change by some local governments. Specifically, terms that are bracketed are generic and need to be replaced with specific local titles. These terms include name of jurisdiction, the name of the appropriate local legislative body (e.g., the city council), and equivalents for state emergency management agency, recovery task force, and other committees, agencies, legislation, and plans. The numbering system is designed to reflect the structure of the ordinance content and may require adaptation to the numbering of local ordinances.

A MODEL RECOVERY AND RECONSTRUCTION ORDINANCE
by Kenneth C. Topping, AICP

About the Author

Kenneth C. Topping, former consultant and City of Los Angeles planning director, is general manager for the Cambria Commuity Services District near the Hearst Castle on the Central Coast of California. He is also the author of Chapter 11 of this PAS Report, which documents the Oakland, California, wildfires of 1991.

3.17   Public Assistance Program
3.18   Reconstruction
3.19   Recovery
3.20   Recovery Organization
3.21   Recovery Plan
3.22   Recovery Strategy
3.23   Safety Element
3.24   Stafford Act

Section 4.   Recovery Organization
4.1   Powers and Duties
4.2   Recovery Task Force
4.3   Operations and Meetings
4.4   Succession
4.5   Organization
4.6   Relation to Emergency Management Organization

Section 5.   Recovery Plan
5.1   Recovery Plan Content
5.2   Coordination of Recovery Plan with FEMA and Other Agencies
5.3   Recovery Plan Adoption
5.4   Recovery Plan Implementation
5.5   Recovery Plan Training and Exercises
5.6   Recovery Plan Consultation with Citizens
5.7   Recovery Plan Amendments
5.8   Recovery Plan Coordination with Related (City, County) Plans

Section 6.   General Provisions
6.1   Powers and Procedures
6.2   Post-Disaster Operations
6.3   Coordination with FEMA and Other Agencies
6.4   Consultation with Citizens

Section 7.   Temporary Regulations
7.1   Duration
7.2   Damage Assessment
7.3   Development Moratorium
7.4   Debris Clearance
7.5   One-Stop Center for Permit Expediting
7.6   Temporary Use Permits
7.7   Temporary Repair Permits
7.8   Deferral of Fees for Reconstruction Permits
7.9   Nonconforming Buildings and Uses

Section 8.   Demolition of Damaged Historic Buildings
8.1   Condemnation and Demolition
8.2   Notice of Condemnation
8.3   Request to FEMA to Demolish
8.4   Historic Building Demolitions Review

Section 9.   Temporary and Permanent Housing

Section 10.   Hazard Mitigation Program
10.1   Safety Element
10.2   Short-Term Action Program
10.3   Post-Disaster Actions
10.4   New Information

Section 11.   Recovery and Reconstruction Strategy
11.1   Functions
11.2   Review

Section 12.   Severability

WHEREAS, [jurisdiction name] is vulnerable to various natural hazards such as earthquakes, flooding, wildfires, and wind, resulting in major disasters causing substantial loss of life and property;

WHEREAS, [jurisdiction name] is authorized under state law to declare a state of local emergency and take actions necessary to ensure the public safety and well-being of its residents, visitors, business community, and property during and after such major disasters;

WHEREAS, it is essential to the well being of [jurisdiction name] to expedite recovery and reconstruction, mitigate hazardous conditions, and improve the community after such major disasters;

WHEREAS, disaster recovery and reconstruction can be facilitated by establishment of a recovery organization within [jurisdiction name] to plan, coordinate, and expedite recovery and long-term reconstruction activities;

WHEREAS, preparation of a pre-event plan for disaster recovery and reconstruction can help [jurisdiction name] organize to expedite recovery in advance of a major disaster and to identify and mitigate hazardous conditions, both before and after such a disaster;

WHEREAS, recovery can be expedited by pre-event adoption of an ordinance authorizing certain extraordinary governmental actions to be taken during the declared local emergency to expedite implementation of recovery and reconstruction measures identified in a pre-event plan;

WHEREAS, it is mutually beneficial to cooperatively plan relationships needed between [jurisdiction name] and other state and federal governmental authorities;

WHEREAS, it is informative and productive to consult with representatives of business, industry and citizens' organizations regarding the most suitable and helpful approaches to disaster recovery and reconstruction;

The [name of legislative body] does hereby ordain:

SECTION 1. AUTHORITY

This ordinance is adopted by the [name of legislative body] acting under authority of the [authorizing legislation], [state emergency management act *or* equivalent], and all applicable federal laws and regulations.

SECTION 2. PURPOSES

It is the intent of the [name of legislative body] under this chapter to:

- authorize creation of an organization to plan and prepare in advance of a major disaster for orderly and expeditious post-disaster recovery and to direct and coordinate recovery and reconstruction activities;

- direct the preparation of a pre-event plan for post-disaster recovery and reconstruction to be updated on a continuing basis;

- authorize in advance of a major disaster the exercise of certain planning and regulatory powers related to disaster recovery and reconstruction to be implemented upon declaration of a local emergency;

- identify means by which [jurisdiction name] will take cooperative action with other governmental entities in expediting recovery; and implement means by which [jurisdiction name] will consult with and assist citizens, businesses, and community organizations during the planning and implementation of recovery and reconstruction procedures.

SECTION 3. DEFINITIONS

As used in this ordinance, the following definitions shall apply:

3.1   damage assessment survey. A field survey to determine levels of damage for structures and identify the condition of structures.

3.2   development moratorium. A temporary hold, for a defined period of time, on the issuance of building permits, approval of land-use applications or other permits and entitlements related to the use, development, redevelopment, repair, and occupancy of private property in the interests of protection of life and property.

3.3   Director. The director of the [recovery organization] or an authorized representative.

3.4   Disaster Field Office (DFO). A center established by FEMA for coordinating disaster response and recovery operations, staffed by representatives of federal, state, and local agencies as identified in the Federal Response Plan (FRP) and determined by disaster circumstances.

3.5   **Disaster Recovery Centers (DRCs).** A multi-agency center organized by FEMA for coordinating assistance to disaster victims.

3.6   **Damage Survey Report (DSR).** A claim by a local jurisdiction for financial reimbursement for repair or replacement of a public facility damaged in a major disaster, as authorized under the Stafford Act and related federal regulations, plans, and policies.

3.7   **emergency.** A local emergency, as defined by the Municipal Code, which has been declared by the [legislative authority] for a specific disaster and has not been terminated.

3.8   **event.** Any natural occurrence that results in the declaration of a state of emergency and shall include earthquakes, fires, floods, wind storms, hurricanes, etc.

3.9   **Federal Response Plan (FRP).** A plan to coordinate efforts of the government in providing response to natural disasters, technological emergencies, and other incidents requiring federal assistance under the Stafford Act in an expeditious manner.

3.10   **Flood Insurance Rate Map (FIRM).** An official map of the community, on which the Federal Insurance Administrator has delineated both the special hazard areas and the risk premium zones applicable to the community.

3.11   **Hazard Mitigation Grant Program.** A federal program that assists states and local communities in implementing long-term hazard mitigation measures following a major disaster declaration.

3.12   **historic building or structure.** Any building or structure listed or eligible for listing on the National Register of Historic Places, as specified by federal regulation, the state register of historic places or points of interest, or a local register of historic places, and any buildings and structures having historic significance within a recognized historic district.

3.13   **in-kind.** The same as the prior building or structure in size, height and shape, type of construction, number of units, general location, and appearance.

3.14   **Interagency Hazard Mitigation Team.** A team of representatives from FEMA, other federal agencies, state emergency management agencies, and related state and federal agencies, formed to identify, evaluate, and report on post-disaster mitigation needs. [Note: Not all states employ the use of this team.]

3.15   **major disaster.** Any natural catastrophe (including any [hurricane, tornado, storm, high water, wind-driven water, tidal wave, tsunami, earthquake, volcanic eruption, landslide, mudslide, snowstorm, or drought]), or, regardless of cause, any fire, flood, or explosion, which in the determination of the President of the United States causes damage of sufficient severity and magnitude to warrant major disaster assistance under the Stafford Act to supplement the efforts and available resources of states, jurisdictions, and disaster relief organizations in alleviating the damage, loss, hardship, or suffering caused thereby.

3.16   **reconstruction.** The rebuilding of permanent replacement housing, construction of large-scale public or private facilities badly damaged or destroyed in a major disaster, addition of major community improvements, and full restoration of a healthy economy.

3.17   **recovery.** The process by which most of private and public buildings and structures not severely damaged or destroyed in a major disaster are repaired and most public and commercial services are restored to normal.

3.18   **recovery organization.** An interdepartmental organization that coordinates [jurisdiction name] staff actions in planning and implementing disaster recovery and reconstruction functions. [Note: "Recovery organization" is a generic term. Other locally chosen names (e.g., The Municipal Disaster Recovery Commission) can, of course, be substituted.]

3.19   **recovery plan.** A pre-event plan for post-disaster recovery and reconstruction, composed of policies, plans, implementation actions, and designated responsibilities related to expeditious and orderly post-disaster recovery and rebuilding, with an emphasis on mitigation.

3.20   **recovery strategy.** A post-disaster strategic program identifying and prioritizing major actions contemplated or under way regarding such essential
recovery functions as business resumption, economic reinvestment, industrial recovery, housing replacement, infrastructure restoration, and potential sources of financing to support these functions.

3.21   **safety element.** An element of the comprehensive, long-term general plan
for the physical development of a community that addresses protection of
the community from unreasonable risks associated with the effects of
earthquakes, landslides, flooding, wildland and urban fires, wind, coastal
erosion, and other natural and technological disasters.

3.22   **Stafford Act.** The Robert T. Stafford Disaster Relief and Emergency Assistance Act (Public Law 93-288, as amended).

SECTION 4. [RECOVERY ORGANIZATION]

There is hereby created the [recovery organization] for the purpose of coordinating
[jurisdiction name] actions in planning and implementing disaster recovery and
reconstruction activities.

4.1   **Powers and duties.** The [recovery organization] shall have such powers as
enable it to carry out the purposes, provisions, and procedures of this
chapter, as identified in this chapter.

4.2   **[Recovery Task Force].** The [recovery organization] shall include a [recov-
ery task force *or* locally chosen term] comprised of the following officers and
members:

a. The [title of the chief executive officer (e.g., the mayor)] who shall be
Chair;

b. The [title of deputy chief executive officer (e.g., city manager or county
or town equivalent)] who shall be Director and Vice-Chair;

c. The [title of the next ranking executive officer (e.g., assistant city manager)] who shall be Deputy Director, and who shall act as Vice-Chair in
the absence of the Vice-Chair;

d. The [title of the jurisdiction's legal adviser] who shall be Legal Adviser;

e. Other members, including the [list the titles of other interested
jurisdiction officials, which might include the chief building official,
chief engineer, the director of community development or planning,
the fire chief, the emergency management coordinator, the general
services director, the historic preservation commission director, the
police chief, the director of public works, and the director of utilities],
together with representatives from such other departments and offices as may be deemed necessary by the Chair or Director for
effective operation.

*Commentary. The formal structure of a recovery organization will vary from community
to community. The important thing is to include representatives from agencies and
organizations so that the broadest array of functions that may have a direct or indirect role
in recovery and reconstruction can be addressed. Also, formal leadership may vary by size
and structure of local governmental organization. In a big-city environment, presence and
availability of the mayor or a deputy mayor may be important from a leadership standpoint,
even though recovery in many instances is largely a staff-driven process. On the other hand,
in a typical council-manager form of government, inclusion of the mayor may not be very
useful. The intent here is to provide a communications connection with the appropriate
legislative body as well as a ceremonial function.*

4.3   **Operations and Meetings.** The Director shall have responsibility for [re-
covery organization] operations. When an emergency declaration is not in
force, the [recovery task force] shall meet monthly or more frequently, upon
call of the Chair or Director. After a declaration of an emergency, and for the
duration of that declared emergency period, the [recovery task force] shall
meet daily or as frequently as determined by the Director.

*Commentary. The overall concept here is for the city manager to run the recovery task force
operations on behalf of the city council, reserving the presence of the mayor for those times when
policy matters are being discussed or at critical junctures following a major disaster. In
actuality, the city manager inevitably becomes the pivotal party for informing and advising the
city council on recovery matters, interpreting council policy and coordinating staff functions.*

4.4   Succession. In the absence of the Director, the Assistant Director shall serve as Acting Director and shall be empowered to carry out the duties and responsibilities of the Director. The Director shall name a succession of department managers to carry on the duties of the Director and Assistant Director, and to serve as Acting Director in the event of the unavailability of the Director and Assistant Director.

4.5   Organization. The Recovery Task Force may create such standing or ad hoc committees as determined necessary by the Director.

4.6   Relation to [emergency management organization]. The [recovery organization] shall work in concert with the [emergency management organization] that has interrelated functions and similar membership.

Commentary. As noted in the introductory paragraphs, there are certain fundamental differences in function that make it preferable to establish a recovery organization that can operate parallel to the emergency response organization. However, because of the inherent linkage of emergency preparedness and response with recovery, reconstruction, and hazard mitigation functions, a close relationship must be continuously maintained. For many purposes, these overlapping organizations can meet and work jointly. The value of having a separate recovery organization is best recognized when hard-core building, planning, redevelopment, and economic recovery issues require extended attention during the pre-event planning phase or during the long months and years it is likely to take to fully rebuild.

SECTION 5. RECOVERY PLAN

Before a major disaster, the [recovery task force] shall prepare a pre-event plan for post-disaster recovery and reconstruction, referred to as the recovery plan, which shall be comprised of pre-event and post-disaster policies, plans, implementation actions, and designated responsibilities related to expeditious and orderly post-disaster recovery and rebuilding, and will incorporate hazard mitigation in all elements of the plan.

5.1   Recovery Plan Content. The recovery plan shall address policies, implementation actions and designated responsibilities for such subjects as business resumption, damage assessment, demolitions, debris removal and storage, expedited repair permitting, fiscal reserves, hazards evaluation, hazard mitigation, historical buildings, illegal buildings and uses, moratorium procedures, nonconforming buildings and uses, rebuilding plans, redevelopment procedures, relation to emergency response plan and comprehensive general plan, restoration of infrastructure, restoration of standard operating procedures, temporary and replacement housing, and such other subjects as may be appropriate to expeditious and wise recovery.

5.2   Coordination of Recovery Plan with County and Regional Plans, FEMA, and Other Agencies. The recovery plan shall identify relationships of planned recovery actions with those of adjacent communities and state, federal, or mutual aid agencies involved in disaster recovery and reconstruction, including but not limited to the Federal Emergency Management Agency (FEMA), the American Red Cross, the Department of Housing and Urban Development (HUD), the Small Business Administration (SBA), the Environmental Protection Administration (EPA), the Department of Transportation (DOT), the [state emergency management agency *or* equivalent], and other entities that may provide assistance in the event of a major disaster. The Director shall distribute a draft copy of the plan to the [state emergency management agency *or* equivalent] for review in sufficient time for comment prior to action on the recovery plan by the [local legislative body].

Commentary. In contrast to most local emergency management organizations, FEMA and the state emergency management agency have substantial recovery and reconstruction responsibilities. FEMA is a significant source of funds made available by Congress under the Stafford Act for rebuilding public facilities. Because the state emergency management agency is an important point of coordination between localities and FEMA, it is important to solicit from that agency as much advance information as can be obtained regarding post-disaster procedures essential to recovery and reconstruction. For example, cities and counties should become fully informed through communication with their state emergency management agency about Damage Survey Report (DSR) and Hazard Mitigation Grant Program (HMGP) procedures before disaster strikes. Because recovery issues often affect jurisdictions outside the immedi-ate disaster area, the recovery plan should be coordinated with recovery planning activities of adjacent communities and regional entities.

5.3 **Recovery Plan Adoption.** Following formulation, the recovery plan shall be transmitted to the [local legislative body] for review and approval. The [local legislative body] shall hold one or more public hearings to receive comments from the public on the recovery plan. Following one or more public hearings, the [local legislative body] may adopt the recovery plan by resolution, including any modifications deemed appropriate, or transmit the plan back to the [recovery task force] for further modification prior to final action.

Commentary. Governing board adoption of this ordinance together with the pre-event plan is extremely important to its successful post-disaster implementation. The city council needs to become comfortable with the concept of pre-event plan and ordinance adoption in order to be supportive of greater than normal delegation of decisions to staff, which may be necessary during post-disaster recovery operations. If council adoption is not possible immediately because of the press of other business, look for opportunities to bring the plan and ordinance forward, such as when a catastrophic disaster has struck in another jurisdiction.

5.4 **Recovery Plan Implementation.** The Director and [recovery task force] shall be responsible for implementation of the plan both before and after a major disaster, as applicable. Before a declaration of emergency, the Direc-tor shall prepare and submit reports annually, or more frequently as necessary, to fully advise the [local legislative body] on the progress of preparation or implementation of the recovery plan. After a declaration of emergency in a major disaster, the Director shall report to the [local legislative body] as often as necessary on implementation actions taken in the post-disaster setting, identify policy and procedural issues, and receive direction and authorization to proceed with plan modifications necessi-tated by specific circumstances.

5.5 **Recovery Plan Training and Exercises.** The [recovery task force] shall organize and conduct periodic training and exercises annually, or more often as necessary, in order to develop, convey, and update the contents of the recovery plan. Such training and exercises will be conducted in coordi-nation with similar training and exercises related to the emergency opera-tions plan.

Commentary. Clearly, training and exercises are functions which should happen on a joint, ongoing basis with the city's emergency management organization. For greatest value, training and exercises should include careful attention to critical relationships between early post-disaster emergency response and recovery actions that affect long-term reconstruction, such as street closings and reopenings, demolitions, debris removal, damage assessment, and hazards evaluation. FEMA has developed tabletop exercises for use by communities about early recovery for earthquakes, flood, and hurricane scenarios. See Appendix C for point of contact.

5.6 **Recovery Plan Consultation with Citizens.** The [recovery task force] shall schedule and conduct community meetings, periodically convene advisory committees comprised of representatives of homeowner, business, and community organizations, or implement such other means as to provide information and receive input from members of the public regarding preparation, adoption, or amendment of the recovery plan.

5.7 **Recovery Plan Amendments.** During implementation of the recovery plan, the Director and the [recovery task force] shall address key issues, strategies and information bearing on the orderly maintenance and peri-odic revision of the plan. In preparing modifications to the plan, the [recovery task force] shall consult with City departments, business, and community organizations and other government entities to obtain informa-tion pertinent to possible recovery plan amendments.

5.8 **Recovery Plan Coordination with Related Plans.** The recovery plan shall be prepared in coordination with related elements of the [comprehensive general plan] and [emergency operations plan], or such other plans as may be pertinent. Such related plan elements shall be periodically amended by the [local legislative body] to be consistent with key provisions of the recovery plan, and vice versa.

SECTION 6. GENERAL PROVISIONS

The following general provisions shall be applicable to implementation of this chapter following a major disaster:

6.1 **Powers and Procedures.** Following a declaration of local emergency in a major disaster and while such declaration is in force, the Director and the [recovery task force] shall have authority to exercise powers and procedures authorized by this chapter, subject to extension, modification, or replacement of all or portions of these provisions by separate ordinances adopted by the [local legislative body].

6.2 **Post-Disaster Operations.** The Director shall direct and control post-disaster recovery and reconstruction operations, including but not limited to the following:

a. Activate and deploy damage assessment teams to identify damaged structures and to determine further actions that should be taken regarding such structures;

b. Activate and deploy hazards evaluation teams to locate and determine the severity of natural or technological hazards that may influence the location, timing, and procedures for repair and rebuilding processes;

c. Maintain liaison with the [jursidiction name] [emergency operations organization] and other public and private entities, such as FEMA, the American Red Cross, and the [state emergency management agency *or* equivalent] in providing necessary information on damaged and destroyed buildings or infrastructure, natural and technological hazards, street and utility restoration priorities, temporary housing needs and similar recovery concerns;

d. Establish "one-stop" field offices located in or near impacted areas where appropriate, staffed by trained personnel from appropriate departments, to provide information about repair and rebuilding procedures, issue repair and reconstruction permits, and provide information and support services on such matters as business resumption, industrial recovery, and temporary and permanent housing;

e. Activate streamlined procedures to expedite repair and rebuilding of properties damaged or destroyed in the disaster;

f. Establish a moratorium subject to [local legislative body] ratification, as provided under Section 7.3;

g. Recommend to the [local legislative body] and other appropriate entities necessary actions for reconstruction of damaged infrastructure;

h. Prepare plans and proposals for action by the [local legislative body] for redevelopment projects, redesign of previously established projects or other appropriate special measures addressing reconstruction of heavily damaged areas;

i. Formulate proposals for action by the [local legislative body] to amend the [comprehensive general plan *or* equivalent], [emergency operations plan], and other relevant plans, programs, and regulations in response to new needs generated by the disaster;

j. Such other recovery and reconstruction activities identified in the recovery plan or by this chapter, or as deemed by the Director as necessary to public health, safety, and well-being.

6.3 **Coordination with FEMA and Other Agencies.** The Director and the [recovery task force] shall coordinate recovery and reconstruction actions with those of state, federal, or mutual aid agencies involved in disaster response and recovery, including but not limited to the Federal Emergency Management Agency (FEMA), the American Red Cross, the Department of Housing and Urban Development (HUD), the Small Business Administration (SBA), the [state emergency management agency *or* equivalent] and other entities that provide assistance in the event of a major disaster. Intergovernmental coordination tasks including but not limited to the following:

a. Assign trained personnel to provide information and logistical support to the FEMA Disaster Field Office;

b. Supply personnel to provide information support for FEMA Disaster Recovery Centers (DRCs);

c. Participate in damage assessment surveys conducted in cooperation with FEMA and other entities;

d. Participate in the development of hazard mitigation strategies with the Interagency Hazard Mitigation Team (when activated) with FEMA and other entities;

e. Cooperate in the joint establishment with other agencies of one-stop service centers for issuance of repair and reconstruction options and permits, business resumption support, counseling regarding temporary and permanent housing, and other information regarding support services available from various governmental and private entities;

f. Coordinate within city government the preparation and submission of supporting documentation for Damage Survey Reports (DSRs) to FEMA;

g. Determine whether damaged structures and units are within floodplains identified on Flood Insurance Rate Maps (FIRMs) and whether substantial damage has occurred;

h. Implement such other coordination tasks as may be required under the specific circumstances of the disaster.

Commentary. To provide direction for handling of emergency response and recovery in relation to major disasters, Congress has enacted the Robert T. Stafford Disaster Relief and Emergency Assistance Act (Public Law 93-288, as amended). A substantial portion of the Stafford Act is devoted to the means by which federal funds are distributed to persons, businesses, local governments, and state governments for disaster response and recovery. For most communities, this is an important means by which disaster losses can be compensated, at least in part. Although insurance can be instrumental in personal or business loss recovery for major hurricane, flood, and fire disaster damage, it has little value for compensation from losses incurred from disasters for which insurance is too costly or difficult to obtain, such as for earthquake damage, and no value for circumstances for which there is no insurance. Some of the federal assistance is in the form of grants and loans, involving not only FEMA but also other agencies, such as HUD and SBA. The federal government has become increasingly interested in promoting more effective means of coordinating post-disaster victim services as well as mitigating hazards having to do with land use and building construction. Consequently, federal assistance to localities in many instances is contingent upon coordination of local, state, and federal recovery and hazard mitigation policies and practices. In other words, as with many other forms of more traditional assistance, the community may find it necessary to adjust its policies in order to receive federal post-disaster assistance.

6.4 **Consultation with Citizens.** The Director and the [recovery task force] shall schedule and conduct community meetings, convene ad hoc advisory committees comprised of representatives of business and community organizations, or implement such other means as to provide information and receive input from members of the public regarding measures undertaken under the authority of this chapter.

Commentary. One of the critical components in establishing a relatively successful relationship between local government and disaster victim organizations after the Oakland, California, firestorm was the series of weekly meetings held in the affected area by the assistant city manager. Direct outreach to the community should be established in advance of a major disaster through neighborhood safety or similar programs conducted by fire and law enforcement officials, ideally in conjunction with preparation of a pre-event plan. Following a major disaster, proactive outreach is critical to establishing a two-way flow of information, without which controversy inherent in post-disaster settings can become severe.

SECTION 7. TEMPORARY REGULATIONS

The Director shall have the authority to administer the provisions of this section temporarily modifying provisions of the [municipal code *or* equivalent] dealing with building and occupancy permits, demolition permits, and restrictions on the use, development or occupancy of private property, provided that such action, in the opinion of the Director, is reasonably justifiable for protection of life and property, mitigation of hazardous conditions, avoidance of undue displacement of households or businesses, or prompt restoration of public infrastructure.

Commentary. The following temporary regulations are at the heart of the recovery process. Although existing state law or city ordinances may already authorize some of these functions, it is preferable to have a single source for locally adopted ordinances that, among other things, identifies regulatory functions related to post-disaster recovery, clearly places responsibility for implementation, and provides a coordinated rationale for city intervention in case of challenge. Among the components of these temporary regulations are provisions dealing with duration, damage assessment, development moratoria, debris clearance, permit expediting, temporary uses and repairs, deferral of fees, nonconforming buildings and uses, condemnation and demolition, and temporary and permanent housing. Each of these components needs careful examination and, as appropriate, adjustment based on local policies and conditions. Pre-event adoption of this ordinance (adjusted to take into account local circumstances) provides a solid basis for initial post-disaster action and legitimizes the policies established as part of the planning process. It is not possible to anticipate the exact character, magnitude, and distribution of damage from a major disaster. Pre-adopted regulations, however, provide a basis for more efficient action that is substantially less subject to policy reversals and other uncertainties typically found in cities that have not prepared in this manner.

7.1   **Duration.** The provisions of this section shall be in effect for a period of six months from the date of a local emergency declaration following a major disaster or until termination of a state of local emergency, whichever occurs later, or until these provisions are extended, modified, replaced by new provisions, or terminated, in whole or in part, by action of the [local legislative body] through separate ordinances.

Commentary. This provision allows for flexibility in the duration of application of the temporary regulations, so that any portion can be terminated, modified, or extended depending upon local circumstances. It also reflects a recognition that temporary regulations may be in effect for an extended period of time beyond either termination of the local emergency or passage of the six-month period. Depending on the nature and scale of the disaster, such as an earthquake, temporary provisions may be in effect for several years after the disaster.

7.2   **Damage Assessment.** The Director of the [recovery team] or an authorized representative shall direct damage assessment teams having authority to conduct field surveys of damaged structures and post placards designating the condition of such structures as follows:

a. A placard indicating "Inspected—Lawful Occupancy Permitted" is to be posted on any building in which no apparent structural hazard has been found. This does not mean there are not other forms of damage that may temporarily affect occupancy.

Commentary. This is commonly known as the "green tag" placard.

b. A placard indicating "Restricted Use" is to be posted on any building in which damage has resulted in some form of restriction to continued occupancy. The individual posting this placard shall note in general terms the type of damage encountered and shall clearly and concisely note the restrictions on continued occupancy.

Commentary. This is commonly known as the "yellow tag" placard.

c. A placard indicating "Unsafe - Do Not Enter or Occupy" is to be posted on any building that has been damaged to the extent that continued occupancy poses a threat to life safety. Buildings posted with this placard shall not be entered under any circumstances except as authorized in writing by the department that posted the building or by authorized members of damage assessment teams. The individual posting this placard shall note in general terms the type of damage encountered. This placard is not to be considered a demolition order.

Commentary. This is commonly known as the "red tag" placard.

d. This chapter and section number, the name of the department, its address, and phone number shall be permanently affixed to each placard.

e. Once a placard has been attached to a building, it shall not be removed, altered or covered until done so by an authorized representative of [jurisdiction name] or upon written notification from [jurisdiction name]. Failure to comply with this prohibition will be considered a misdemeanor punishable by a $300 fine.

Commentary. *Damage assessment and the placement of placards identifying whether buildings are safe or unsafe to occupy are two functions having perhaps the most profound effects on life, property, and community recovery than any other within the post-disaster decision and action sequence towards which the provisions of these temporary regulations are directed. Damage assessment is undertaken by various entities following a major disaster, usually the city, state, and FEMA.*

There is at least a twofold purpose for these inspections. One is to determine the degree of structural damage of each building and notify the public about the relative safety of entry and occupancy. This has been a longstanding duty under local government public health and safety responsibilities with which building departments are usually very familiar. The other is to quickly estimate the approximate replacement costs of damaged buildings and other property in order to inform the state and federal governments of whether a federal declaration is warranted. Another concurrent purpose of placarding is to identify potential substantially damaged buildings. This is essential in floodplains to ensure that the home is built according to NFIP requirements (elevated); nonresidential buildings can be floodproofed or elevated if substantially damaged.

The most important element of all these concerns is the establishment of standard identification of structural damage both in gross general terms reflected in the red-, yellow-, and green-tag placard systems, as well as in the details recorded on the placards for each building. This ordinance reflects only the standard placard system, leaving to the building professionals the means by which such determinations are made and recorded in detail. The source of the language for the placard system in this model ordinance is a publication by the California Governor's Office of Emergency Services, Model Ordinances for Post-Disaster Recovery and Reconstruction. *The procedures used to make these basic safety distinctions in the California model ordinance are based on detailed post-disaster inspection methods described by the Applied Technology Council in ATC-20,* Procedures for Postearthquake Safety Evaluation of Buildings, *and in the State of California's publication,* Post-Disaster Safety Assessment Plan. *While somewhat oriented toward structural damage from earthquakes due to California's known seismicity, the placard system is adaptable to other disasters. For additional references regarding damage assessment safety notifications, the reader is referred to the International Conference of Building Officials, Southern Building Code Congress International, and Building Officials and Code Administrators International.*

7.3 **Development Moratorium.** The Director shall have the authority to establish a moratorium on the issuance of building permits, approval of land-use applications or other permits and entitlements related to the use, development, and occupancy of private property authorized under other chapters and sections of the [pertinent legislation] and related ordinances, provided that, in the opinion of the Director, such action is reasonably justifiable for protection of life and property and subject to the following:

   a. *Posting.* Notice of the moratorium shall be posted in a public place and shall clearly identify the boundaries of the area in which a moratorium is in effect as well as the exact nature of the development permits or entitlements that are temporarily held in abeyance.
   a. *Duration.* The moratorium shall be in effect subject to review by the [local legislative body] at the earliest possible time, but no later than 90 days, at which time the [local legislative body] shall take action to extend, modify, or terminate such moratorium by separate ordinance.

Commentary. *After disasters around the world, the prevailing sentiment often is to act quickly to replicate pre-disaster building patterns. In many instances, this sentiment prevails as policy despite the presence of a severe natural hazard condition, thus reinforcing the chances of repeating the disaster. The most notable example has been the rebuilding of homes in the Turnagain Heights area on land severely deformed by a landslide in the 9+ Magnitude 1964 Anchorage earthquake.*

To prevent or lessen the chances of repetition of the disaster, it may be necessary for a city to interrupt and forestall repair and rebuilding long enough to assess rebuilding options and/or to determine effective means of mitigation. The city may wish to establish an emergency moratorium on issuance of repair and rebuilding permits or on land-use approvals in areas where severely hazardous conditions are identified. The hazard may be newly detected, as in a post-earthquake circumstance where the pattern of damage or ground deformation may indicate the need for geologic studies to clearly identify such hazards as landslides, liquefaction, or fault rupture. On the other hand, the hazardous condition may be a well-known cause of prior damaging disasters, as in the Oakland Hills firestorm area, which had a long history of previous fires, or communities affected by the 1993 Midwestern floods where prior flood control and floodproofing efforts were proven ineffective.

A moratorium on development may be important for a city to undertake from the standpoint of enlightened public policy. However, since such action may be extremely controversial and unpopular, it is important to lay the groundwork with the community in advance, if possible. This subsection provides prior authorization through adoption of this ordinance before a major disaster, whereby city staff can act expeditiously in a post-disaster setting to forestall premature issuance of permits in areas shown to be hazardous. Such action is necessarily subject to local legislative review, ratification, modification, or termination.

7.4   **Debris Clearance.** The Director shall have the authority to remove from public rights-of-way debris and rubble, trees, damaged or destroyed cars, trailers, equipment, and other private property, without notice to owners, provided that in the opinion of the Director such action is reasonably justifiable for protection of life and property, provision of emergency evacuation, assurance of firefighting or ambulance access, mitigation of otherwise hazardous conditions, or restoration of public infrastructure. The Director shall also have the authority to secure emergency waivers of environmental regulations from state and federal authorities and to call upon outside support from such agencies for debris clearance, hazardous materials spills, and restoration of ground access.

Commentary. *Although clearance of privately owned debris is routinely considered a function of local government, it can become very controversial where owners take the position that such property is salvageable and has value (e.g., used brick after an earthquake). Pre-event adoption of such a provision reinforces the expectation that debris clearance functions will be carried out decisively, thus minimizing a problem otherwise compounded by city hesitation or ambiguity of intention. The U.S. Army Corps of Engineers has the lead under the Federal Response Plan for ensuring resources for local emergency and long-term debris clearance. FEMA and the state emergency management agency determine priorities for the entire disaster area.*

7.5   **One-Stop Center for Permit Expediting.** The Director shall establish a one-stop center, staffed by representatives of pertinent departments, for the purpose of establishing and implementing streamlined permit processing to expedite repair and reconstruction of buildings, and to provide information support for provision of temporary housing and encouragement of business resumption and industrial recovery. The Director shall establish such center and procedures in coordination with other governmental entities that may provide services and support, such as FEMA, SBA, HUD, or the [state emergency management agency *or* equivalent].

Commentary. *One-stop permit centers have become more common with recent major disasters, often combining the presence of multiple agencies to provide better coordination of information that disaster victims may need in order to rebuild. A prime example was the Community Restoration and Development Center established by Oakland, California, shortly after the 1991 firestorm and operated until mid-1994 with financial support from FEMA. Benefits to be gained for establishing a special one-stop center include not only accelerated review but also integration of information and permitting functions. Setting up a team of specialists working exclusively on repair and rebuilding permit issues has the added advantage of insulating normal development review from disruption by the recovery process and vice versa.*

7.6   **Temporary Use Permits.** The Director shall have the authority to issue permits in any residential, commercial, industrial, or other zone for the temporary use of property that will aid in the immediate restoration of an area adversely impacted by a major disaster, subject to the following provisions:

a. *Critical response facilities.* Any police, fire, emergency medical, or emergency communications facility that will aid in the immediate restoration of the area may be permitted in any zone for the duration of the declared emergency;

b. *Other temporary uses.* Temporary use permits may be issued in any zone, with conditions, as necessary, provided written findings are made establishing a factual basis that the proposed temporary use:

1. will not be detrimental to the immediate neighborhood;

2. will not adversely affect the [comprehensive general plan or any applicable specific plan]; and

3. will contribute in a positive fashion to the reconstruction and recovery of areas adversely impacted by the disaster.

Temporary use permits may be issued for a period of one year following the declaration of local emergency and may be extended for an additional year, to a maximum of two years from the declaration of emergency, provided such findings are determined to be still applicable by the end of the first year. If, during the first or the second year, substantial evidence contradicting one or more of the required findings comes to the attention of the Director, the temporary use permit shall be revoked.

Commentary. Most zoning ordinances have no provisions for temporary use of property following a disaster. A few allow temporary placement of mobile units or manufactured housing on residentially zoned sites pending reconstruction of a residence. Time limits vary, but are usually for a two-year period. After a major disaster, special latitude may be needed, however, to support various recovery needs. Care must be taken not to set precedents that will erode or destroy a pre-existing pattern of zoning that the city may wish to protect.

The language within this section is modeled after provisions of the Los Angeles recovery ordinance adopted after the Northridge earthquake, Temporary Regulations Relating to Land Use Approvals for Properties Damaged in a Local Emergency. *That ordinance is geared toward the needs of a large and diverse city. Smaller communities may wish to restrict temporary uses to those already allowed by the zone in which they are located, limiting the provision to temporary structures, such as tents, domes, or mobile units.*

7.7   **Temporary Repair Permits.** Following a disaster, temporary emergency repairs to secure structures and property damaged in the disaster against further damage or to protect adjoining structures or property may be made without fee or permit where such repairs are not already exempt under other chapters of the [pertinent legislation]. The building official must be notified of such repairs within 10 working days, and regular permits with fees may then be required.

Commentary. This provision is specifically written for repairs that may not be exempt under standard building code permit exemptions but which are justifiable from a public health and safety standpoint to avoid further damage to property after a disaster. It is modeled after a provision of a post-disaster rebuilding ordinance adopted in 1992 by the County of San Bernardino shortly after the Landers-Big Bear earthquake. Written before the earthquake, the ordinance was based on a pre-event study, Post-Disaster Rebuilding Ordinance and Procedures, *which included a survey of top managers and elected officials regarding various post-disaster rebuilding provisions, such as for nonconforming buildings and uses. Because of the pre-event involvement of top managers and elected officials, it was adopted after the earthquake with no controversy.*

7.8   **Deferral of Fees for Reconstruction Permits.** Except for temporary repairs issued under provisions of this chapter, all other repairs, restoration, and reconstruction of buildings damaged or destroyed in the disaster shall be approved through permit under the provisions of other chapters of this code. Fees for such repair and reconstruction permits may be deferred until issuance of certificates of occupancy.

Commentary. Pressure to waive or defer processing fees frequently arises after a disaster when victims are unsure of their sources of financing for rebuilding. It is inadvisable to succumb to pressures to waive fees entirely due to the need for cost recovery for disaster-related services at a time when there may be substantial uncertainties in revenue flows. Also, it is helpful to buy time to determine the degree to which sources other than the victims may help offset fee costs. For example, sometimes insurance will cover the cost of processing fees. Also, such costs have been covered by FEMA. Deferral of fees until occupancy permit issuance provides time in which such alternate sources can be worked out, without sacrificing the basic revenue flow to the city treasury. This provision is modeled after similar language in the Los Angeles temporary regulations.

7.9   **Nonconforming Buildings and Uses.** Buildings damaged or destroyed in the disaster that are legally nonconforming as to use, yards, height, number of stories, lot area, floor area, residential density, parking, or other provisions of the [pertinent local legislation] may be repaired and reconstructed in-kind, provided that:

a.   the building is damaged in such a manner that the structural strength or stability of the building is appreciably lessened by the disaster and is less than the minimum requirements of the [pertinent local legislation] for a new building;

b. the cost of repair is greater than 50 percent of the replacement cost of the building;

c. all structural, plumbing, electrical, and related requirements of the [pertinent local legislation] are met at current standards;

d. all natural hazard mitigation requirements of the [pertinent local legislation] are met;

e. reestablishment of the use or building is in conformance with the National Flood Insurance Program requirements and procedures;

f. the building is reconstructed to the same configuration, floor area, height, and occupancy as the original building or structure, except where this conflicts with National Flood Insurance Program (NFIP) provisions;

g. no portion of the building or structure encroaches into an area planned for widening or extension of existing or future streets as determined by the comprehensive general plan or applicable specific plan; and

h. repair or reconstruction shall commence within two years of the date of the declaration of local emergency in a major disaster and shall be completed within two years of the date on which permits are issued.

Nothing herein shall be interpreted as authorizing the continuation of a nonconforming use beyond the time limits set forth under other sections of the [pertinent local legislation] that were applicable to the site prior to the disaster.

Commentary. No issue can be more vexing to planners than whether to encourage reestablishment of nonconforming uses and buildings after a major disaster. Planners have sought for decades to write strict provisions in zoning ordinances designed to gradually eliminate nonconforming uses or buildings as they were abandoned, changed owners, or were damaged by fire, wind, or water. The latter provisions normally prohibit reestablishment of nonconforming uses and buildings where damage exceeds a certain percentage of replacement cost, most often 50 percent. This approach is logical, orderly, and normally equitable when weighing community interests balanced with those of the property owner. However, the thinking behind such provisions has been geared to incremental adjustments or termination of such uses over time, not to sudden catastrophic circumstances forcing attention to disposition of such uses as a class at a single point in time.

In theory, disasters represent an opportunity to upgrade conditions, such as parking deficiencies attributable to the nonconforming status of a building or use. More fundamentally, disasters are seen as an opportunity to eliminate uses that conflict with the prevailing pattern in a neighborhood but which remain because of legal nonconforming status (e.g., scattered industrial uses in a residentially zoned neighborhood). In reality, however, after a major disaster, local governments are normally beset by severe pressures from property owners and other community interests to reestablish the previous development pattern exactly as it previously existed, including nonconforming buildings and uses. Moreover, such pressures extend beyond the demand to reestablish nonconforming buildings or uses to include waiver of current building, plumbing, and electrical code provisions to the standards in place at the time of construction. From a risk management, liability exposure, or public safety standpoint, acquiescence to the reduction of standards in the face of a known hazard can be seen as clearly unacceptable by the local legislative body. However, zoning provisions hindering reestablishment of nonconforming buildings and uses tend to be more arguable and are more likely to be modified by the local legislative body under extreme pressures of the moment to restore the prior status quo.

In recognition of such pressures, this model ordinance language offers a straightforward trade-off that allows reestablishment of a nonconforming use or building in turn for strict adherence to structural, plumbing, electrical code, and related hazard mitigation requirements. The language assumes the existence of a commonly found provision in the pertinent local legislation (e.g., the municipal code) authorizing repair or reestablishment of a nonconforming use or building where damage is less than 50 percent of the replacement cost. It also assumes that the building was substantially weakened by the disaster and is below present code requirements.

This compromise approach recognizes that its application may require the unwelcome decision to accept continuation of disorderly land-use patterns, unless a solution can be found through redevelopment or rezoning. Instead, it places a high value on life safety.

It is important to note that the language of these provisions includes important limitations that tend to limit the economic incentive to reestablish the nonconforming use or building.

1) It does not extend any previously stipulated life of the nonconforming use—an important disincentive if the costs of replacement cannot be offset by insurance, FEMA assistance, SBA loans, or other sources of financial support.

2) It does not allow the extent of nonconformance to be increased over what existed prior to the disaster, thwarting another common pressure.

3) It requires strict adherence to existing structural, plumbing, electrical, and other requirements of the local code as well as any street setbacks stipulated within the comprehensive plan circulation element and related ordinances. This may be especially costly from a structural standpoint, for example, when replacing previously unreinforced masonry buildings after a devastating earthquake.

4) It recognizes that compliance with existing local hazard mitigation requirements may be needed, especially in cases involving increased on-site hazards because of fault rupture, landsliding, coastal erosion, or severe flooding where upgrading to current structural, plumbing, and electrical code requirements isn't enough. Compliance with the latter provision may also be sufficiently costly to discourage reestablishment of the use or other nonconforming feature.

The relative importance of post-disaster reestablishment of nonconforming uses and buildings may vary greatly from jurisdiction to jurisdiction. Therefore, the most useful time to assess this aspect of post-disaster recovery is before a major disaster, in the course of pre-event planning. Education of the local legislative body in advance can help lessen post-disaster tendencies to compromise critical hazard mitigation and public safety requirements, notwithstanding the outcome on nonconforming use and building requirements.

SECTION 8. DEMOLITION OF DAMAGED HISTORIC BUILDINGS

The Director shall have authority to order the condemnation and demolition of buildings and structures damaged in the disaster under the standard provisions of the [pertinent local legislation], except as otherwise indicated below:

8.1 **Condemnation and Demolition.** Within [a number determined by the local government] days after the disaster, the building official shall notify the State Historic Preservation Officer that one of the following actions will be taken with respect to any building or structure determined by the building official to represent an imminent hazard to public health and safety or to pose an imminent threat to the public right of way:

a. Where possible, within reasonable limits as determined by the building official, the building or structure shall be braced or shored in such a manner as to mitigate the hazard to public health and safety or the hazard to the public right of way;

b. Whenever bracing or shoring is determined not to be reasonable, the building official shall cause the building or structure to be condemned and immediately demolished. Such condemnation and demolition shall be performed in the interest of public health and safety without a condemnation hearing as otherwise required by the [pertinent local legislation]. Prior to commencing demolition, the building official shall photographically record the entire building or structure.

8.2 **Notice of Condemnation.** If, after the specified time frame noted in Subsection 8.1 of this chapter and less than 30 days after the disaster, a historic building or structure is determined by the building official to represent a hazard to the health and safety of the public or to pose a threat to the public right-of-way, the building official shall duly notify the building owner of the intent to proceed with a condemnation hearing within [a number determined by the local government] business days of the notice in accordance with [pertinent provisions of the local legislation]; the building official shall also notify FEMA, in accordance with the National Historic Preservation Act of 1966, as amended, of the intent to hold a condemnation hearing.

8.3 **Request to FEMA for Approval to Demolish.** Within 30 days after the disaster, for any historic building or structure which the building official and the owner have agreed to demolish, the building official shall submit to FEMA, in accordance with the National Historic Preservation Act of 1966, as amended, a request for approval to demolish. Such request shall include all substantiating data.

8.4   Historic Building Demolition Review. If, after 30 days from the event, the building official and the owner of a historic building or structure agree that the building or structure should be demolished, such action will be subject to the review process established by the National Historic Preservation Act of 1966, as amended.

Commentary. One of the more difficult aspects of post-disaster response and recovery in older communities is the existence of damaged historically significant structures. Since these can be very old, measures needed to make them structurally sound may be more difficult and costly and complicated than normal. Because of the emotion frequently attached to this issue and the often widely conflicting views, community controversy can erupt when a badly damaged historical structure is subject to demolition. Therefore, it is wise to have language already in place to guide the planning and building officials involved.

Because of problems with seemingly premature or unjustifiable demolition of historic structures in previous disasters, the National Historic Preservation Act of 1966, as amended, identifies steps that must be taken by a jurisdiction or owner to mitigate public health and safety hazards resulting from disaster-caused damage when using federal funding. The intent is to establish predictable rules by which proposed demolitions, except in extreme cases of danger to the public, can be reviewed by state and federal officials in order to provide time to identify options for preservation of a damaged historic building or structure. The review process is also intended to discourage hasty demolition action by local officials when such action may not be justified.

The preceding language is adapted from California's Model Ordinances for Post-Disaster Recovery and Reconstruction. *This language supplements provisions of the* Uniform Code for the Abatement of Dangerous Buildings *by providing specific time frames and actions for abatement of hazards created by damage to historic buildings. The important element of local judgment here is the establishment of a specific time frame for declaring a structure an imminent hazard to public health and safety justifying immediate demolition without a condemnation hearing. Such time frames are generally from three to five days, though sometimes stretched to ten days. After the established time frame, the threat may no longer be justified as imminent and, therefore, the remaining procedures kick in.*

SECTION 9. TEMPORARY AND PERMANENT HOUSING

The Director shall assign staff to work with FEMA, SBA, HUD, the [state emergency management agency *or* equivalent], and other appropriate governmental and private entities to identify special programs by which provisions can be made for temporary or permanent replacement housing that will help avoid undue displacement of people and businesses. Such programs may include deployment of manufactured housing and manufactured housing developments under the temporary use permit procedures provided in Section 7 of this chapter, use of SBA loans, and available Section 8 and Community Development Block Grant funds to offset repair and replacement housing costs, and other initiatives appropriate to the conditions found after a major disaster.

Commentary. The issue of post-disaster temporary and permanent replacement housing has grown to one of critical dimensions in the San Francisco area since the Loma Prieta earthquake. After that earthquake, many displaced low-income occupants of damaged or destroyed housing simply disappeared—a common pattern following many disasters. Relatively little real progress has been made since then in finding effective ways by which to handle this issue on a broad scale. For example, after the Northridge earthquake, HUD became active immediately in attempting to assist localities in dealing with housing issues. Available resources were insufficient to cover the cost of much of the replacement housing needed. Housing issues were extremely complex. Low- and moderate-income rental housing replacement problems were somewhat alleviated by the existence of a high rate of apartment vacancies. However, recession-generated housing devaluation combined with substantial damage costs altered loan-to-value ratios to uneconomical levels. Repairs of single-family and multifamily buildings dragged out for many months due to lending, engineering, and permitting problems. As a consequence, some middle-income households simply walked away from mortgages. The most visible evidence of earthquake-induced housing impacts were the large condominium and apartment complexes that remained in a fenced-off, unrepaired state until financing and repairs began to catch up two years later.

For these reasons, this section is essentially a placeholder for language that should be made more specific on the basis of a pre-event plan for post-disaster recovery and reconstruction that takes into account the level of local housing vulnerability. For example, a community with a long history of flooding may have developed temporary shelter arrangements, such as in school gymnasiums, sufficient for short-term displacement. If there are no other hazards present, that community may not need to consider replacement housing. Whereas a community in an earthquake hazard area with a large portion of its housing inventory in unreinforced masonry (URM) construction should consider both temporary shelters and interim housing, such as some form of manufactured housing, with the expectation that several years will be needed for replacement housing to be built.

A great deal more research is needed to find satisfactory solutions for prompt, efficient provision of both interim and replacement housing. Clearly, the magnitude of the Northridge housing problems caught public- and private-sector institutions off-guard. Little is yet understood regarding issues like the most effective means for dealing with damaged condominiums or the effect of the secondary mortgage market on housing repair and replacement. With downsizing of federal budgets in future years, this issue will become more critical since levels of support could be diminished.

SECTION 10. HAZARD MITIGATION PROGRAM

Prior to a major disaster, the Director shall establish a comprehensive hazard mitigation program that includes both long-term and short-term components.

10.1 Safety Element. The long-term component shall be prepared and adopted by resolution of the [local legislative body] as the safety or natural hazards element of the [comprehensive general plan] for the purpose of enhancing long-term safety against future disasters. The safety element shall identify and map the presence, location, extent, and severity of natural hazards, such as:

   a. severe flooding;

   b. wildland and urban fires;

   c. seismic hazards such as ground shaking and deformation, fault rupture, liquefaction, tsunamis, and dam failure;

   d. slope instability, mudslides, landslides, and subsidence;

   e. coastal erosion;

   f. hurricanes and other high winds;

   g. technological hazards, such as oil spills, natural gas leakage and fires, hazardous and toxic materials contamination, and nuclear power plant and radiological accidents.

The safety element shall determine and assess the community's vulnerability to such known hazards and shall propose measures to be taken both before and after a major disaster to mitigate such hazards. It shall contain linkages between its own provisions and those of other [comprehensive plan elements *or* equivalent] including, but not limited to, [land use, transportation, housing, economic development, and historic preservation, and any other pertinent element] so that development and infrastructure decisions will incorporate considerations of natural hazards.

Commentary. Although California may be viewed by some citizens in other parts of the country as perhaps atypical when considering lifestyles, ideas, the arts, or politics, it nevertheless has been the source of much forward-looking planning legislation and has recently become the site of a series of major natural disasters from which important post-disaster response and recovery lessons are being learned. One of the far-seeing components of planning legislation in California is the mandatory general plan safety element, which became a requirement after the 1971 Sylmar earthquake. Now, more than 20 years after the passage of that legislation, virtually all California cities have adopted safety elements as part of their comprehensive general plans, and many have implemented them in one specific way or another, which has helped mitigate recognized hazards.

The safety element concept can be adapted for use in many other states to help localities deal more directly with significant local hazards. Its great value is the establishment of safety considerations at the policy level and the development of hazard mapping that can serve as an undergirding for specific regulations. The discussion in Chapter 3 of natural hazards element requirements in state planning enabling legislation provides background data on the application of this concept across the country, including its use for coastal hazards in Florida, North Carolina, and Georgia. These elements can be helpful in providing greater legal defensibility of regulations establishing substantial restrictions on the use of portions of properties subject to a natural hazard, such as landslides, flooding, or beach erosion. Such considerations are important in taking into account issues related to the taking of private property in light of recent Supreme Court decisions.

There is a growing body of knowledge about the nature of many of the hazards identified in this language, yet there remains a need for further research on how to integrate this knowledge in planning practice. A need exists for more definitive guidelines on how to mitigate many of these hazards through community design and site layout. For instance, with respect to wind, it was found on the Island of Kauai following Hurricane Iniki that homes placed along the windward edge of bluffs suffered greater damage than homes that were set back. It was also found that directional placement of roof overhangs in relation to prevailing direction of storm winds was important to the degree of damage. Such practical community design knowledge on wind effects should be extended and integrated with research on other hazards. Much needed is research material providing guidance on mitigation through community design for all natural hazards.

10.2   Short-Term Action Program. A short-term hazard mitigation program shall be included in the [recovery plan]. It shall be comprised of hazard mitigation program elements of highest priority for action, including preparation and adoption of separate ordinances dealing with specific hazard mitigation and abatement measures, as necessary. Such ordinances may require special site planning, land-use, and development restrictions or structural measures in areas affected by flooding, urban/wildland fire, wind, seismic, or other natural hazards, or remediation of known technological hazards, such as toxic contamination.

Commentary. This provision extends the safety element concept into the pre-event planning for post-disaster recovery and reconstruction process, identifying key measures that would have the most value for short-term implementation. Some of these measures, such as special ordinances related to floodplain management, may already be in place. The concept here is to look beyond measures that are in place to determine which others are critically needed and to move forward toward their implementation.

10.3   Post-Disaster Actions. Following a major disaster, the Director shall participate in developing a mitigation strategy as part of the [Interagency Hazard Mitigation Team *or* equivalent] with FEMA and other entities, as called for in Section 409 of the Stafford Act and related federal regulations. As appropriate, the Director may recommend to the [local legislative body] that the [jurisdiction] participate in the state's Hazard Mitigation Grant Program, authorized in Section 404 of the Stafford Act, in order to partially offset costs of recommended hazard mitigation measures.

Commentary. This provision acknowledges FEMA mitigation programs presently operating under the Stafford Act and corresponding federal regulations. FEMA has published guidelines relative to state implementation of these regulations.

10.4   New Information. As new information is obtained regarding the presence, location, extent, and severity of natural or technological hazards, or regarding new mitigation techniques, such information shall be made available to the public, and shall be incorporated as soon as practicably possible within the [comprehensive general plan safety element *or* equivalent] and the [recovery plan] through amendment.

SECTION 11. RECOVERY AND RECONSTRUCTION STRATEGY

At the earliest practicable time following the declaration of local emergency in a major disaster, the Director and the [recovery task force] shall prepare a strategic program for recovery and reconstruction based on the pre-disaster plan and its policies.

11.1   Functions. To be known as the recovery strategy, the proposed strategic program shall identify and prioritize major actions contemplated or under way regarding such essential functions as business resumption, economic reinvestment, industrial recovery, housing replacement, infrastructure restoration, and potential sources of financing to support these functions.

11.2   Review. The recovery strategy shall be forwarded to the [local legislative body] for review and approval following consultation with other governmental agencies and business and citizen representatives. The recovery strategy shall provide detailed information regarding proposed and ongoing implementation of initiatives necessary to the expeditious fulfillment of critical priorities and will identify amendment of any other plans, codes, or ordinances that might otherwise contradict or block strategic action. The Director shall periodically report to the [local legislative body] regarding progress toward implementation of the recovery strategy, together with any adjustments that may be called for by changing circumstances and conditions.

Commentary. *The concept behind this provision is to structure the flow of local post-disaster recovery and reconstruction actions around a short-term strategy that extends the pre-event plan into greater detail at the earliest possible time after a major disaster. This may prove absolutely essential to the extent that damage conditions differ substantially from those anticipated as part of the pre-event plan. In any case, development of such a strategy in the early days of recovery has the special benefit of adding a proactive emphasis to the recovery process to counter the overwhelmingly reactive context. It can be updated as often as necessary as experience is gained and new issues emerge. It also has the added benefit of providing a source from which the pre-event recovery plan and related plans can later be readily updated.*

SECTION 12. SEVERABILITY

If any provision of this chapter is found to be unconstitutional or otherwise invalid by any court of competent jurisdiction, such invalidity shall not affect the remaining provisions that can be implemented without the invalid provision, and, to this end, the provisions of this ordinance are declared to be severable.

Chapter 6

Legal and Financial Issues

Consider these three scenarios:

- After a flood, a homeowner discovers that her substantially damaged home may not be rebuilt in the floodplain without being either elevated or relocated. She loves her riverfront view, and the idea of elevating the house has never appealed to her. She is angry that she cannot take her flood insurance and rebuild what she had before.

- An owner of oceanfront property learns that, following a mildly damaging hurricane, the city council has had a change of heart and proposes to reduce the allowable density of a zone within a certain distance of the mean high-tide line. Realizing that this limits his plans for developing the property, he confronts council members at a meeting where the proposal is under consideration. He threatens to sue if the zoning change is approved.

- The New Madrid fault finally shakes, rattles, and rolls. The owner of a retail shopping center in a small town in Arkansas watches in dismay as local building inspectors decide that the structure has now become an imminent danger to public safety. Unable to accept that the damage is as severe as the officials say, he promises to return with a lawyer to challenge the planned condemnation. He is even more upset when the city council enacts a six-week moratorium on new development permits.

Disasters are by their very nature disjointing experiences. Both mitigation and reconstruction require exercises of governmental power that leave many property owners feeling that some or all of their rights have been violated. On the other hand, many other citizens want local government to move as quickly as possible to restore order, to clean up the debris, and to remove the vacant and destroyed buildings so that redevelopment can proceed. Governments decree emergency measures based on special powers that some applaud and others fear. Nature has unleashed a second storm of human conflict and financial angst.

This chapter reviews the essential legal and financial issues that confront planners, city managers, mayors, elected officials, and others who must exercise the authority of government to initiate the process of post-disaster recovery and reconstruction.

LEGAL ISSUES
Constitutional Issues: Takings
Issues involving natural hazards and environmental protection have been at the vortex of many of the takings issues that have reached the U.S.

Supreme Court in recent years. *First Evangelical Lutheran Church v. County of Los Angeles*, 482 U.S. 304 (1987), dealt with the use of property in a floodplain. *Lucas v. South Carolina Coastal Commission*, 112 S. Ct. 2886 (1992), dealt with the use of oceanfront property on a barrier island, in a region only recently affected by Hurricane Hugo. *Nollan v. California Coastal Commission*, 483 U.S. 825 (1987), dealt with public access to an ocean view that did not itself entail any natural hazards. *Dolan v. City of Tigard*, though not decided on the basis of natural hazards regulations, also involved the use of floodplain property. Natural hazards are, of course, a type of environmental issue—one that more directly and immediately affects human safety and the sustainability of human development than do many other environmental questions.

Takings jurisprudence is a direct outgrowth of the Fifth Amendment to the U.S. Constitution, which prohibits the deprivation of property without just compensation. What constitutes a taking and under what circumstances, and what constitutes just compensation, are questions that have received a good deal of the courts' time and attention in recent decades as a result of a host of legislation aimed at protecting historic properties, the environment, and public health and safety. The premier case establishing the legality of zoning as a regulatory tool—*Village of Euclid v. Ambler Realty Co.*, 272 U.S. 365 (1926)—essentially held that, despite an estimated 75 percent diminution of value in Ambler's property as a result of the local zoning ordinance, the local government had the right to abate certain nuisances by separating incompatible land uses. Upon that legal rock, the frequently remodeled mansion of modern land-use law has largely been built.

It is not the object here to explore in detail a debate that has filled whole volumes in the legal literature. There are, instead, some essential points worth making about how takings law has come to affect planning for natural hazards mitigation and post-disaster recovery. The cases above will be used as the touchstone for some general observations about legally sound planning and land-use regulation in this area. Readers interested in a more lengthy discussion of these issues would do well to examine three anthologies edited by DiMento (1990), Hill (1990), and Callies (1993), as well as the ongoing series of commentaries in recent years in *Land Use Law & Zoning Digest*.

Rational nexus. It remains a central tenet of land-use law that one cannot use one's property in a way that endangers the health and safety of others or disturbs their effective use of their own property, for example, through excessive noise. Determining what constitutes such a nuisance has occupied many volumes of legal thought, for not every case is as clear as, say, the issue of blasting high-powered stereo speakers in one's urban backyard all night long. The whole issue of nuisance is sensitive to context. Blasting the same high-powered stereos from the deck porch of an isolated cabin high in the Teton Mountains might very well not be a nuisance because no one nearby would be disturbed. Understanding the issue of context is central to grasping the importance of hazard identification in defining nuisance related to development in hazardous areas. Certain kinds of land uses become nuisances in a hazard zone that might be perfectly acceptable and safe somewhere else. Regulations based on this principle thus depend on the context of both the natural and built environment.

Modern technology adds many layers of subtlety to the definition of nuisance in hazard zones. The very definition of danger evolves with our technical and analytical capabilities. Flying debris from poorly constructed homes in a coastal high-hazard area surely constitutes a nuisance of some type during a hurricane, but that alone would not necessarily justify a total prohibition of development anywhere near the coast if developers could prove they were able to build a hurricane-resistant home. On the other hand,

> Certain kinds of land uses become nuisances in a hazard zone that might be perfectly acceptable and safe somewhere else. Regulations based on this principle thus depend on the context of both the natural and built environment.

other nuisance issues might still be relevant, for development might disrupt the dune system, accelerating erosion elsewhere and endangering other property or public beachfront infrastructure. Moreover, there are practical economic limitations on many engineered solutions to these problems. At some point, it is simply more logical and defensible for a community to restrict development than to insist on extremely expensive structural solutions in a highly hazardous area. A community may also decide that it simply does not want the area in question to support the type of upscale development that such costs would entail, and that it does not want to create the inequities that may result with respect to affordable housing.

The traditional position of the courts has been to defer to the wisdom and common sense of lawmakers when they express a public purpose behind environmentally based land-use regulations. The practical basis for this deference is largely that legislators and regulators have had the time and opportunity to weigh these issues and reach some conclusions about the most practical way to address the problems. Limited in both time and technical expertise, the judicial system would never have the time to review the complete factual basis for many of these issues. As a practical matter, courts generally limit their scrutiny to those situations where it is not apparent that the decision makers have established adequate factual findings or, to use the phrase from the Nollan decision, a "rational nexus" between the public policy objective and their regulatory means of achieving it.

In short, to stay out of trouble, document the findings that undergird land-use regulations for hazardous areas with effective and thorough hazard identification, and then make sure that the regulations developed to address the problem can be reasonably interpreted as helping to prevent or solve that problem. Traditionally, regulations have been expected to meet three basic tests. They must:

- advance a legitimate state interest (e.g., flood control, ensuring timely evacuation, minimizing fire dangers);

- be reasonably necessary to effectuate that purpose; and

- not deprive the owner of all economically viable use of the land.

> At some point, it is simply more logical and defensible for a community to restrict development than to insist on extremely expensive structural solutions in a highly hazardous area.

Like all generalities, however, these principles are open for interpretation, which is the business of the courts in any event, and so the cases keep coming. In recent cases, the U.S. Supreme Court has been leaning toward a more generous interpretation for property owners of what constitutes a deprivation of economic use.

Robert Fulghum earned a fortune expounding on simple maxims with his best-selling book, *Everything I Need to Know I Learned in Kindergarten*. One thing all of us should have learned in kindergarten is: be reasonable. In the context of natural hazards, make sure that regulation X is logically related to the solution of problem Y. Courts will grant most legislative bodies and regulatory agencies a wide berth in adopting reasonable means of solving the problems that are identified in a statement of purpose or legislative findings. Somewhere, however, there is an invisible line that local governments occasionally cross that draws them into court on grounds of violating basic logic. For instance, it makes no sense to enact a citywide building moratorium after a flood if only 20 percent of the buildable area of a community lies in the 100-year floodplain. Thus, the question of a rational nexus between the end and the means returns us to the issue of context, which can be temporal as well as spatial. For instance, a two-year moratorium in such circumstances would almost certainly be deemed inherently unreasonable, whereas a moratorium of 30 or 60 days might not.

The *Nollan* case helped bring the issue of rational nexus to a head. There, the California Coastal Commission required the dedication of an easement, by deed, for the public to cross the Nollans' beach. The easement was part of the condition the commission established for the Nollans to gain a permit to replace their dilapidated beach bungalow with a larger house. The commission's stated rationale was that the larger house would obscure the public's view of the ocean and discourage access. The U.S. Supreme Court failed to see the connection between allowing those already on the beach to cross the property at a specified location inside the seawall and that stated objective.

In *Dolan*, however, the Court did find the necessary nexus between the legitimate interest of preventing flooding along Fanno Creek, which traversed the plaintiffs' commercial property in downtown Tigard, and limiting development in the floodplain. The Court also found a connection between the city's desire to reduce traffic congestion and the city's desire to provide a bicycle pathway. At issue, however, was whether the exactions imposed on the Dolans (dedicating a strip of land for a bicycle trail, totaling about 10 percent of the total land area of the property) were proportional to the impact of their proposed project, an expansion of the family hardware store. Here the Court adopted a "rough proportionality" test and decided that the exactions imposed went too far. With respect to the bicycle trail, for instance, the Court required that the city quantify its findings to show that the bicycle traffic along the trail really would contribute to a reduction of traffic congestion. One objection raised by some scholars (and the dissent by four Justices Stevens, Blackmun, Ginsburg, and Souter) to the decision, however, is that this requirement effectively shifted the burden of proof to the city, effectively reversing the tradition of granting such regulations a presumption of validity. (For a range of opinions and analysis on this point, see Berry; Morgan; Callies; Berger; and Kelly, all 1994).

One interesting point to note with both *Nollan* and *Dolan* is that both cases concerned an exaction that involved an easement for public use of private property, in effect, a limitation on the right to exclude. In both cases, this involved waterfront property, first for beachfront access and second for a bicycle trail along the creek, a frequent use of greenways. One issue that tends to attract judicial scrutiny faster than some other takings issues is the physical invasion of the property in question. Merely requiring the preservation of open space in a sensitive area is far less likely to trigger such scrutiny. At some point, opening land to the public is better achieved through acquisition. But as *Dolan* demonstrated again, exactly where that point lies remains a matter of context and documentation.

Ripeness. Nothing in recent U.S. Supreme Court decisions upsets the normal expectation that landowners wishing to challenge land-use regulations as takings must first test their claims through the normal administrative channels set up for this purpose. A property owner cannot normally expect the courts to accept the claim, for instance, that a new local land-use regulation constitutes a taking of property if that owner has not even applied for a permit through the established procedures that would allow that individual to present his case for a variance, special use permit, or some other exception to or application of the rule in question. The applicant must give the system a fair chance to work before crying foul.

This concept is known as the ripeness doctrine, based on the notion that the plaintiff must exhaust his or her nonjudicial remedies before the case becomes ripe for review by the courts. If a zoning ordinance or other type of land-use control establishes a means whereby an applicant can demonstrate that a regulation creates an undue hardship, or that pursuing an otherwise prohibited use of land will in a particular instance not produce the problem local government is trying to prevent, that landowner may not simply run to the courts without first testing the facts of the case before the appropriate tribunals. The longstanding common sense assumption behind the ripeness doctrine is, in part, that the case that reaches the court already will have a reasonably well-developed factual basis. It also ensures that, in addition to the landowner getting a fair day in court, the government agency under attack has had a fair chance to resolve the issue prior to litigation.

Occasionally, however, a landowner can make a reasonable claim that a regulation has taken all viable economic use of a property and allowed no avenue for appeal. In such a case, the courts are the obvious place to seek a remedy. The landowner still must prove that no such avenue existed or that pursuing a development application through the channels afforded would clearly have been an exercise in futility. This remains a difficult challenge in most instances, in spite of the decision in *Lucas*. *Lucas* was not a challenge to South Carolina's Beachfront Management Act on its face. Instead, Lucas challenged the act as a total taking of his beachfront property as applied. The case reached the U.S. Supreme Court largely because, in rejecting Lucas's claim, the South Carolina Supreme Court already had resolved the case on its merits rather than simply dismissing it for lack of ripeness.

The alternative to this scenario occurs when a landowner challenges a law on its face as an unconstitutional taking because the law affords no remedies to the total diminution of value of the owner's property, thus effecting an uncompensated taking. These cases are rare, but local officials should know how to avoid such situations. It is a fundamental principle of American land-use law that government must provide an avenue of appeal to allow adjustments in those cases where a regulation, as applied to a specific property, may unjustly effect a taking or create an undue hardship not of the owner's own making. As long as the escape hatch is there, and applicants are treated fairly and objectively, local officials can generally expect that their decisions will be legally defensible.

Temporary controls. There are times when government is overwhelmed. There are times when reasonable decisions cannot be made quickly. No one would reasonably expect a city ravaged by a serious earthquake, tornado, or hurricane to continue business as usual. Staff activities are disrupted, resources are drained, and many development policies demand to be reassessed. It makes perfect sense for a local government to call a halt to building and development permits long enough to assess the situation and assemble a rational basis for its decision making.

As a general rule, such interim development rules and moratoriums will be upheld, but planners are always well advised to check the authority for enacting a moratorium. Oregon, for instance, has a state law prohibiting local moratoriums. In most instances, moratoriums are not even challenged because most people understand the need for such measures in an emergency. Like any other regulatory constraints on development, however, they must be justifiable. For temporary moratoriums on building permits, this means that the controls should last long enough to allow the local government to resolve the new problems created by the emergency and to determine what changes in land-use policy are necessary under the post-disaster circumstances. The period of time this takes will depend on the severity of the emergency. A minor flood may not justify much of a moratorium at all. On the other hand, major disasters may justify a delay of as much as six weeks to allow the local government to muster the resources it needs to handle the load.

It is important too to distinguish here between repair and rebuilding permits and those for new development. With existing buildings, the extent of the damage will determine whether rebuilding can be justified. Getting minor repairs underway is vital to the community's economic and physical

There are times when government is overwhelmed. There are times when reasonable decisions cannot be made quickly. No one would reasonably expect a city ravaged by a serious earthquake, tornado, or hurricane to continue business as usual. Staff activities are disrupted, resources are drained, and many development policies demand to be reassessed. It makes perfect sense for a local government to call a halt to building and development permits long enough to assess the situation and assemble a rational basis for its decision making.

Courts generally understand that wise development must be tied to the availability of various public facilities, including transportation and sanitation infrastructure. Limiting growth to a level that can be accommodated through the development of such infrastructure is an entirely reasonable exercise of the police power, so long as the community makes a good faith effort to adhere to the promises of its comprehensive plan.

recovery from the disaster. New construction, on the other hand, may raise significant issues of improving hazard mitigation for future disasters, for the city has no obligation to repeat the mistakes of the past. Because minor repairs are far less likely to raise such issues and are so essential to overall recovery, they would be better addressed through mutual assistance agreements providing additional permitting personnel than through mandatory delays in permit issuance.

These issues are closely related to the legality surrounding the phased timing and growth controls involved in growth management legislation, including such approaches as adequate public facilities ordinances, discussed in Chapter 4. Courts generally understand that wise development must be tied to the availability of various public facilities, including transportation and sanitation infrastructure. Limiting growth to a level that can be accommodated through the development of such infrastructure is an entirely reasonable exercise of the police power, so long as the community makes a good faith effort to adhere to the promises of its comprehensive plan (Freilich and Garvin in Callies 1993).

Constitutional Issues: The Police Power

The police power of government is inextricably tied to the issue of takings. The police power, which includes the community's right to regulate for the benefit of public health, safety, morals, and welfare, is the bedrock of the community's justification for action. The discussion above has already dealt with the most important limitations on the government's police powers in the area of land-use controls. The objective here will be to outline a philosophy, within these limits, concerning the use of the police power as it relates to natural hazards.

Government traditionally has had wide discretion with regard to defining those health, safety, and welfare needs of the public that justify some type of regulation. For the first century of this nation's existence, government at all levels made little effort to protect the environment but did a great deal to promote its exploitation in the interest of the public welfare. This exploitation included the dispensation of millions of acres of public lands and the public subsidization of a great deal of transportation infrastructure traversing the continent, some of it including engineering measures to improve the navigability of the nation's waterways and to control flooding.

The establishment of Yellowstone National Park in 1872 signaled a dawning awareness of the importance of the natural resources and heritage this country had in many ways nearly squandered. In the growing cities, meanwhile, science and technology facilitated an improved understanding of the relationship between public sanitary infrastructure and public health. Moreover, awareness grew that many competing urban land uses were simply incompatible, particularly those that endangered human health with industrial waste and pollution. There followed movements for wilderness conservation, for public sewerage and drinking water improvements, for the regulation of housing conditions, and, by the 1920s, for zoning enabling legislation nationwide. Such public efforts reached a crescendo of innovation during the New Deal, and these efforts continued throughout the middle of the century. Renewed environmental awareness triggered new federal and state efforts by the 1960s, which continued to produce new regulatory efforts and legislation even during the 1980s.

The same dawning awareness about the consequences of our policies toward natural hazards has come more slowly, but it has come. As noted in Chapter 2, federal legislation addressing disaster recovery and natural hazards did not become comprehensive until the 1950s, and FEMA did not come into being as a unified agency until 1979, nearly a decade after the formation of the U.S. EPA. But natural hazards policy and environmental awareness cannot be divorced from each other, and our growing national commitment to environmental quality has necessarily pulled natural hazards policy along with it. The section that follows details that evolution not in the specific context of flood policy, but in the context of public policy overall. Such an evolution reflects an increased public awareness that natural hazards are a part of the environment that can never be conquered or mastered but must be mitigated intelligently through smart development practices. That need for mitigation implies an expanding role for the police power to improve human welfare and the quality of life.

For the most part, environmental and civic movements have been driven by new understandings of the relationship of human activities and development to the environment and, more importantly, to the ways in which environmental devastation has adversely affected human welfare. The change in attitudes toward our interrelationship with the environment over the past 100 years is profound. That revolution in thinking, coupled with rapid advances in environmental science and technology, has fueled a growing awareness not only of valid issues that government can address with its police power, but of increasingly effective ways of accomplishing that purpose. We know far more than we used to know, and we learn more every day.

That growing awareness leads to the primary challenge in the twenty-first century use of the police power for environmental purposes related to natural hazards. The primary issue is no longer whether the public purpose can be justified, but simply whether planning will be used effectively to document and accomplish those purposes. Public planning for natural hazards mitigation can drive the research that will undergird the documentation of the nature and scope of the problem facing each jurisdiction and of the best means of solving the problems that are identified. The basic issues we are confronting are not really growing more complex, but our abilities to confront them are, and our planning must improve accordingly.

In effect, good planning must equal good documentation of the hazards that are being mitigated, coupled with good design of regulatory and other governmental actions to address those measures. Good design of the appropriate measures, the tools discussed in Chapter 4, will involve accurate calculations of the ability of those measures to solve a proven problem within the legal parameters established under constitutional law.

In the twenty-first century, planners will no longer be able to claim that the public just does not understand the need to address a floodplain or hillside or urban/wildland interface problem. Instead, they will have to show that they have made a meaningful link in the average citizen's mind between the problem they claim to be addressing and the means they are proposing to use to solve the problem. Such an effort will involve both good documentation and effective public relations outreach to a public that may be justifiably skeptical about the quality of past efforts at floodplain or hillside management.

Planners finding themselves faced with these challenges may do well to take notice of the trends toward effective use of the local power in other areas of land-use regulation, particularly in rural areas. As Russell (1996) notes, many rural residents have in the past resisted zoning because they perceived little relationship between the results of zoning in many suburban jurisdictions and the vision they already had of an ideal rural community. But when new models for rural zoning focus on issues like natural aesthetics, the rural quality of life, a village atmosphere, and resource preservation, support materializes because residents can then see the benefits they are deriving from zoning. Likewise, Barrette (1996) also notes that many rural communi-

But natural hazards policy and environmental awareness cannot be divorced from each other, and our growing national commitment to environmental quality has necessarily pulled natural hazards policy along with it. . . . Such an evolution reflects an increased public awareness that natural hazards are a part of the environment that can never be conquered or mastered but must be mitigated intelligently through smart development practices.

Public planning for natural hazards mitigation can drive the research that will undergird the documentation of the nature and scope of the problem facing each jurisdiction and of the best means of solving the problems that are identified. The basic issues we are confronting are not really growing more complex, but our abilities to confront them are, and our planning must improve accordingly.

ties formerly averse to zoning have warmed dramatically to its use as a police power tool to regulate such unwanted, nuisance-bearing intrusions as concentrated animal feeding operations.

These examples demonstrate that, in a democratic society, the real power behind the police power is the community's willingness to police itself as a result of its own growing and sophisticated awareness of the underlying issues and how they affect the public welfare. Neighbors who are aware that more concrete along the floodway forces waters down river that could have seeped into a grassy, pervious wetland are more likely to demand an end to such land-use practices where they are not absolutely necessary. Citizens knowledgeable about the fragility of their coastal environment are more likely to insist that planning develop effective protection for the vegetation and dune systems that serve to protect them during coastal storms. In both cases, the local citizenry will be acting to some degree on its awareness that controls on development are often a far cheaper form of hazard mitigation for the community than the expensive and sometimes counterproductive structural and technological fixes that communities have relied upon too heavily in the past. They may even be aware that those allowed to perpetuate unwise development practices are, in effect, exposing their neighbors to a variety of undesirable and avoidable physical and financial costs. The bill will come due with the next disaster.

Ultimately, increasingly sophisticated voters in areas facing growth concerns tend to move toward the adoption of mechanisms for pacing and managing growth as a means of maintaining and enhancing the quality of life, the overarching goal of all the normally stated aims of the police power. The growing popularity of the use of well-designed indicators to measure the quality of life in cities, regions, and states is a sign that these voters are growing serious about establishing some performance benchmarks for the sustainability of development. The movement toward state-mandated and state-approved growth management and comprehensive plans is also a sign that many voters in those states are aware of the interdependence of their communities with others in their regions. Although only Florida has gone very far in this direction, it is even possible that many of these states eventually will ponder the merits of various sorts of mandates for the inclusion of natural hazards mitigation and post-disaster recovery in local comprehensive plans. When they do, there almost certainly will be some citizen planning movement behind the passage of the necessary legislation.

In their debates and deliberations on what should be done, all these people may well have other interests to balance against their concerns about natural hazards, but balancing competing interests has always been the mission of planning. Good planning balances these concerns intelligently, with the solid support of an enlightened citizenry.

Establishing Emergency Authorities

Chapter 3 discussed to some extent the practices already existing in numerous jurisdictions for establishing post-disaster recovery task forces. These emergency authorities are essentially interagency task forces designed to coordinate the variety of specific missions facing local government in the process of implementing the details of a post-disaster plan. They recognize the simple reality that no one local government agency can take total responsibility for performing such a wide range of functions and that the whole post-disaster effort is as holistic an exercise as may ever challenge a local government's capabilities.

They should not, however, be seen as entirely new-fangled policy instruments, but as an extension of police power functions that are

> Neighbors who are aware that more concrete along the floodway forces waters down river that could have seeped into a grassy, pervious wetland are more likely to demand an end to such land-use practices where they are not absolutely necessary.

already well established. Every state has some sort of disaster authority on the books, most of it related to the emergency period immediately following a natural disaster or to those disaster relief functions that government pursues during the short-term recovery period. Long-term recovery task forces look beyond this emergency period to the need to rebuild a community more resistant to future disasters. As such, they are an administrative and police power device that any local jurisdiction can use, and they reflect our expanding awareness that hazard mitigation and disaster recovery are not occasional twin missions spurred by aberrations in Mother Nature's behavior, but rather are an ongoing mission worthy of our prolonged attention.

Statutory Authority for Hazard Mitigation

One question that arises in some jurisdictions is Who authorized local officials to spend public money to mitigate hazards to private property? The question is, in fact, a good one because there are obvious benefits to private landowners from such expenditures, and a case can be made that they ought to spend their own money. Some states have prohibitions against the use of tax dollars for private purposes, as reflected in this opinion (92-36) from the Tulsa City Attorney:

> Under the Oklahoma Constitution. . .expenditure of tax dollars must be for a public purpose. . . .
>
> Flood proofing will increase a building's value with primary benefit to the individual property owner rather than the community and therefore does not constitute a public purpose. . . .
>
> It is our opinion that the City of Tulsa may not use sales tax funds to finance or construct flood proofing projects on private property since such expenditure would be for a private rather than a public purpose.

Still, the issue may not be that simple. Most states and cities take a different view, seeing beyond the private benefit to a larger public benefit stemming from comprehensive mitigation projects like flood protection. In any given project undertaken by a community, the public and private benefits are likely to be intermingled, with everyone benefitting marginally from everyone else's gains, at the very least by reducing the strain on the community's emergency response capabilities. This common cause view of the real facts of mitigation led to the following reasoning by Louisiana's Attorney General (Opinion 93-193) in response to a request from the Amite River Basin Commission:

> It occurs to us that most, if not all, flood protection facilities, works, and plans benefit private property and the owners thereof.
>
> The fact that the expenditure of public funds for projects in the public interest may result in the enhancement of private property does not denigrate the public nature of such projects and the public purposes served thereby.

Beyond the question of public and private benefits from mitigation expenditures, there is a larger question of statutory authority. Cities, under the U.S. Constitution, are simply creatures of the states, which are the only sovereign entities other than the federal government (and Native American tribal governments by virtue of treaty rights). This limitation of municipal powers is known as Dillon's Rule, arising out of a nineteenth-century court case outlining the principle above. Most states have addressed this problem through legislation granting certain classes

In any given project undertaken by a community, the public and private benefits are likely to be intermingled, with everyone benefitting marginally from everyone else's gains, at the very least by reducing the strain on the community's emergency response capabilities.

of municipalities home-rule powers that allow them to undertake legal and constitutional actions not otherwise prohibited by state law. A few states, such as Virginia, have retained Dillon's Rule, allowing local governments to exercise only those powers expressly granted by state law. In such cases, mitigation activities must fall under some express grant of authority from the state. While planners must know or learn their own state's statutory framework in relation to hazard mitigation authorities, even communities lacking home-rule powers often can find the authority they need under one or more state enabling acts dealing with flood relief, public safety, sanitation, or other specific concerns. There may also be legislation authorizing the expenditure of municipal funds on activities whose costs are shared by state or federal agencies, which would include most disaster-related activities (U.S. Army Corps of Engineers 1994).

Relative to the discussion that opened Chapter 3, if more states join those few that now require natural hazards elements in local comprehensive plans, the question may gradually shift from one of potentially exceeding statutory authority for mitigation activities, to one of complying with state mandates to at least plan for such needs. The issue then becomes less why? and more why not?

> While planners must know or learn their own state's statutory framework in relation to hazard mitigation authorities, even communities lacking home-rule powers often can find the authority they need under one or more state enabling acts dealing with flood relief, public safety, sanitation, or other specific concerns.

Liability for Mitigation

It is sometimes tempting for property owners to view mitigation as a guarantee against future damage from natural hazards, particularly flooding. But if a mitigation project fails to prevent damage in a future disaster, does that make government or its agents liable? In what is often seen as a highly litigious society, these are not small concerns. At the same time, there are good reasons why they should not be allowed to serve as barriers to taking action. In Chapter 10 of *Floodplain Management in the United States: An Assessment Report. Vol. 2; Full Report* (L.R. Johnston Associates 1992), prepared for the Federal Interagency Floodplain Management Task Force, land-use attorney Jon Kusler summarizes four essential points from his study of the development of the law of liability with respect to floodplain management:

1. Courts will not hold government agencies liable for flood damage if it was not caused by governmental action. In short, floods are naturally occurring phenomena, and unless government has in some way caused or increased the damages in question, it will incur no liability. However, Kusler cautions against assuming that doing nothing is the best solution since cities and states have already done a great deal to increase natural flood damages on private property through a variety of development activities in floodplains. Thus, corrective mitigation activity is more likely to be the most responsible approach.

   Solution: Ensure that staff become technically competent in dealing with natural hazards.

2. Negligence is the basis of liability, and the means to avoid negligence is to observe a standard of reasonable care. That standard of care must be exercised in relation to the seriousness of the threat posed by the natural hazard in question.

   Solution: Limit staff advice and projects to areas where they are appropriate. These areas will vary with the hazard in question but, in general, avoid overreaching in predicting and anticipating the intended results. For instance, limit floodproofing advice to lower velocities and flood depths to minimize the risk of failure. In other words, don't promise what a project may not be able to deliver.

3. Courts generally defer to legislative judgment or to the policy decisions of administrative bodies. Where nondiscretionary actions are involved, the court may find liability in cases where officials fail to carry out such duties or where there is evidence of negligence in doing so.

   Solution: Enter into contracts or agreements with property owners that exempt the local government from liability due to damage from the project's failure.

4. Government employees are generally protected from liability where they have acted in good faith, within the scope of their jobs, and without malice.

   Solution: Use nationally recognized professional guidelines wherever those are available, or the best guidance available as a substitute, and have the local governing body adopt those standards or prepare its own with the help of the planning staff (U.S. Army Corps of Engineers 1994).

FINANCIAL ISSUES

Amid the danger of disasters, there is always opportunity. Vastly improved cities can arise from the ashes or debris of a natural disaster. Part of the secret lies in local leaders' abilities to marshal the financial resources to make their community's dreams come true. It stands to reason, of course, that there must first be a dream and that it must be expressed in a plan. Moreover, good plans assign responsibilities for implementation. One of the most important responsibilities to be assigned, not only in the creation of the post-disaster recovery task force, but on a reasonably permanent basis, is that of identifying, coordinating, and seeking out the various kinds of assistance that may aid the community in rebuilding after a disaster. The individual who takes on this job ideally should have a broad and creative mind set regarding the welfare of the community and work to foster a sense of citizens as customers serviced by good planning.

Part of Chapter 3 addressed the issue of using disaster assistance effectively. A key point was that communities should look beyond disaster assistance for financial assistance in rebuilding after a disaster. By thinking holistically about the community's needs and the ways in which disaster issues affect and are interrelated with other community objectives, leaders can shape a multiobjective plan that improves more aspects of their city's life than hazard mitigation alone. We already are well trained to think of disasters as bringing suffering and misery. It is only reasonable to retrain our minds to think of the silver linings behind all that distress.

As May (1985) has noted, taxpayer dissatisfaction has grown over the years with a simplistic federal policy of simply dispensing disaster assistance to stricken communities without expecting some local effort to reduce the dangers and improve the sustainability of the community for the future. That expectation of meaningful local effort to do as much as possible to avert future disasters—and, not coincidentally, reduce the burden on the federal and state treasuries for disaster relief—will continue to grow along with the other aspects of natural hazards awareness discussed earlier in this chapter. Land-use regulation and building code enforcement are still essentially local functions in the United States. The burden is on local officials to demonstrate their own creativity and resourcefulness in marshaling financial assistance to do more than simply relieve the suffering and property damage of the moment. Increasingly, they must expect to be able to show that they have used this assistance, coupled with local resources, to make a difference.

> We already are well trained to think of disasters as bringing suffering and misery. It is only reasonable to retrain our minds to think of the silver linings behind all that distress. . . . The burden is on local officials to demonstrate their own creativity and resourcefulness in marshaling financial assistance to do more than simply relieve the suffering and property damage of the moment. Increasingly, they must expect to be able to show that they have used this assistance, coupled with local resources, to make a difference.

Insurance Claims

There is still a widespread perception, validated by a good deal of past experience, that in a real flood disaster, uninsured property owners will still have access to federal disaster aid, if for no other purpose than to facilitate the completion of relocation programs. French et al. (1996) also note in their study of the Northridge earthquake that the majority of eligible property owners in California also fail to acquire the available earthquake insurance, which is considerably more expensive than flood insurance. There is no mistaking the fact that, for many local officials and property owners alike, it is not immediately apparent why the insurance for such disasters is worth the expenditure. There is an expectation that the needed funds will find their way into town with or without the coverage.

Local budgetary officials, administrators, and planners must work to change these perceptions. Disaster assistance checks are not and will not remain interchangeable substitutes for routine insurance coverage. Local government should invest some effort and credibility in convincing its residents and property owners that insurance provides a distinct asset to facilitate community recovery and that high rates of insurance coverage in a floodplain or coastal zone serve to demonstrate the community's seriousness and commitment to effective reconstruction. This fact, in turn, will allow community leaders to better make their own case for outside assistance and to demonstrate to funders that the money and resources they provide will be used effectively. There are many ways to accomplish this, including local efforts to coordinate and distribute information about the insurance options available to residents and municipal assistance to property owners in pursuing claims.

An important policy to be aware of results from the National Flood Insurance Reform Act of 1994. Individuals in Special Flood Hazard Areas who receive disaster assistance after September 23, 1994, for flood disaster losses to real or personal property must purchase and maintain flood insurance coverage. Regulations issued by FEMA on May 1, 1996, established a Group Flood Insurance Policy (GFIP) in an effort to assist Individual and Family Grant (IFG) recipients to purchase and maintain flood insurance coverage for the first three years—the term of the GFIP coverage. At the end of the three years, individuals must purchase and maintain a standard flood insurance policy with coverage equaling the maximum IFG grant amount as a condition to receiving further assistance due to subsequent flooding.

Private Donations

People love success stories. The most frequent prelude to a success story is a valiant and sincere effort to change something, as when the citizens of Valmeyer, Illinois, finally decided to relocate from the floodplain to higher ground or when Arnold, Missouri, decided in its floodplain management plan to convert large stretches of its floodplain into greenways. It is not only public sources of disaster assistance that respond to such initiatives. Very often, private spigots open as well.

Of course, private sources of disaster assistance have long responded as well to the need to relieve the human suffering and dislocation that accompany major disasters. That is perfectly natural and reasonable, but it clearly does not represent the full scope of opportunity facing local officials after a disaster. The ability to show private funders, whether corporations, individuals, or philanthropic foundations, a plan for meaningful change is also the ability to ignite funders' imaginations at what might be and the role they may play in underwriting it. Becker (1994a) reports that Soldiers Grove, Wisconsin, in 1976 used a $13,200 community development grant from the state to hire a private consulting firm to propose a plan for implementing its

---

Local government should invest some effort and credibility in convincing its residents and property owners that insurance provides a distinct asset to facilitate community recovery and that high rates of insurance coverage in a floodplain or coastal zone serve to demonstrate the community's seriousness and commitment to effective reconstruction.

The ability to show private funders, whether corporations, individuals, or philanthropic foundations, a plan for meaningful change is also the ability to ignite funders' imaginations at what might be and the role they may play in underwriting it.

relocation from the Kickapoo River floodplain. The grant financed only 80 percent of the cost, however, so Tom Hirsch, the village's relocation coordinator, collected the remainder from floodplain business owners. That is a small sum, but Soldiers Grove is a small community that mustered far greater resources overall for its ambitious plan to redevelop in accordance with sustainable design principles that included extensive use of solar energy. Moreover, it was apparent to those businesses what they themselves had to gain or lose as the town confronted its long-term dilemma. They were

Figure 6-1. Soldiers Grove's Funding Package

STATE/LOCAL SOURCES	AMOUNT	DATE	PURPOSE
Regional Planning Commission	$4,000	May 1975	Feasibility study
State Planning Office	$2,700	May 1976	Social/environment study
Department of Local Affairs and Development	$13,200	Early 1976	Implementation study
Local businessowners	$3,300	Early 1976	Implementation study
General obligation borrowing by village	$90,000	June 1977	Site purchase
Department of Natural Resources	$42,000	Jan. 1978	Public water works
Governor's discretionary fund	$67,684	Feb. 1978	Sewer/water
	$100,000	Aug. 1978	Sewer/water
Village borrowing	$235,000	Aug. 1970	TIF startup
(Farmers Home Administration)	$240,000	Aug. 1979	Water works
	$91,000	Aug. 1979	Sewer works
	$150,000	1981	Water works
	$110,000	1981	Sewer works
	$1,072,000	1981	Community facilities
Total	**$2,220,884***		

FEDERAL SOURCES	AMOUNT	DATE	PURPOSE
Housing and Urban Development (CDBG)	$185,600	Oct. 1978	General
	$900,000	Oct. 1978	General
	$573,200	Sept. 1979	General
	$474,300	Aug. 1980	Acquisition/relocation
	$535,000	Nov. 1980	Acquisition/relocation
	$500,000	May 1981	Acquisition/relocation
	$101,000	Nov. 1982	Access road construction
Community Services Administration	$40,000	Oct. 1978	Administration
Economic Development Administration	$500,000	Aug. 1980	Acquisition/relocation
Department of Interior (LAWCON)	$500,452	July 1979	Parkland acquisition
	$145,695	Sept. 1980	Parkland acquisition
Total	**$4,455,247**		

*Total does not include funding for relocation coordinator's salary; substantial in-kind contributions of labor, office space, technical assistance, etc., from village or state agencies; funds related to relocation, but used for general community development; or private borrowing by business owners.

induced not only to contribute to support the financing of the consultants' plan, but to buy into the plan itself. They cast their lot with an innovative plan for sustainable relocation and redevelopment. (Figure 6-1 details Soldiers Grove's total funding package and the purposes to which it was devoted.)

Private donations can also take the form of land or easement donations to, through, or from private landowners and land trusts as a means of expanding the community's ability to achieve the retirement of hazardous land areas from eligibility for development without a direct outlay of cash to purchase those lands. Strategies to pursue this goal ought to be part of a community disaster assistance coordinator's repertoire of financial tools.

It is also reasonable to suppose that some nonprofit trade and professional associations might proffer help for a variety of motives. For instance, the American Institute of Architects has long maintained rural/urban design assistance teams (RUDATs), teams of professionals who make short visits to communities to assess their urban design needs, conduct local design charrettes, and collaboratively suggest solutions. This aid does not come to the community in the form of money but in the form of high-quality technical advice that ordinarily would cost money that a disaster-stricken community might not otherwise have. Some university planning and design schools often provide teams of students and professors on a similar basis for a variety of community development purposes that could very easily include post-disaster redevelopment.

Looking a Gift Horse in the Mouth

There are times when a proffered donation comes with unacceptable or undesirable strings attached or simply does not contribute to the community's existing vision for its own future. While it may be desirable, as a matter of pursuing serendipitous opportunity, to consider altering some existing plans to take advantage of such gifts, there is also great wisdom in knowing when their acceptance is merely a distraction from the community's established goals. It is important for the financial assistance coordinator to know when to say No and to turn away a gift that is less than fully helpful. This is really no different from the wisdom a community displays in distinguishing between welcome and unwelcome economic development. If a gift undermines the pursuit of goals on which the community has established a solid consensus, turn it down with a polite explanation. Who knows? The donor may even decide to offer something else more in line with your needs and wishes.

There are times when a proffered donation comes with unacceptable or undesirable strings attached or simply does not contribute to the community's existing vision for its own future. While it may be desirable, as a matter of pursuing serendipitous opportunity, to consider altering some existing plans to take advantage of such gifts, there is also great wisdom in knowing when their acceptance is merely a distraction from the community's established goals.

Chapter 7

Hazard Identification and Risk Assessment

Chapters 1 through 6 of this report addressed the central planning issues involved in preparing a community for the task of post-disaster recovery and reconstruction. Chapters 7 through 12 aim to provide some essential background for that task through a discussion of the process of documenting the problem and some case studies about specific hazards. This chapter focuses on hazard identification and risk assessment, with some discussion of mitigation opportunities for each type of hazard, as the necessary cornerstone of any plan. Chapter 6, which dealt in part with legal issues, was intended to make clear why the documentation of local natural hazards is so essential to the success of the entire effort.

The structure of this chapter is simple and is intended to focus the reader's attention on other sources of information concerning specific natural hazards, especially the local and regional variations in the manifestation and severity of those hazards. The primary outside resource for information presented throughout this chapter is a Federal Emergency Management Agency (FEMA 1997b) publication, *Multi-Hazard Identification and Risk Assessment (MIRA)*, which is a manual intended to provide planners and others involved in hazard mitigation programs with a reference detailing the essential considerations in mitigation planning for all major natural hazard categories. It is considerably more extensive than anything that can be attempted in this volume, whose primary focus is the post-disaster planning process. Moreover, because some types of natural hazards are clearly more likely to produce catastrophic disasters than others, we have included in this chapter only eight types of hazards, as compared to 23 in *MIRA*, which includes four categories of technological hazards, which are outside the scope of this report. Where other resources may also be useful to planners, we have listed them in sidebars at the heading for the type of disaster. Full citations for these sources can be found in the reference list in Appendix A.

It is worth noting here that, for a general listing of centers and institutes focusing on hazards and disasters, readers may wish to consult the Natural Hazards Research Applications and Information Center website, located at the University of Colorado in Boulder (adder.colorado.edu/~hazards/centers.html). Links to other sites can be found there. This can be a valuable resource for ferreting out detailed information both on hazard identification generally and on a variety of specific hazards. Readers may also find a general listing of mitigation information at FEMA's Web site (www.fema.gov/mit).

Following the format of *MIRA*, we also have separated our comments under each listed hazard into the categories of hazard identification, risk assessment, and mitigation opportunities in order to provide uniformity in the presentation. We have also listed the key points in each discussion to make it easy for readers to use these sections as checklists.

Figure 7-1. Map of Presidential Disaster Declarations, 1975-1995

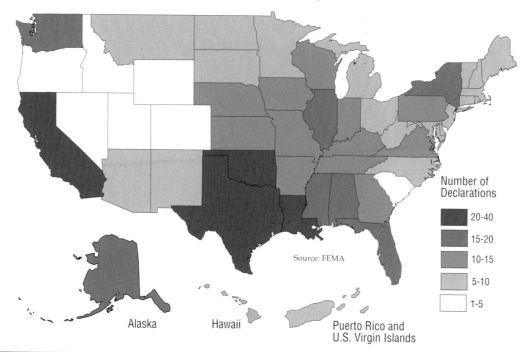

Source: FEMA

Number of
Declarations

20-40
15-20
10-15
5-10
1-5

Alaska   Hawaii   Puerto Rico and
                                U.S. Virgin Islands

ADDITIONAL RESOURCES: EARTHQUAKES

Web sites:

U.S. Geological Survey
http://www.usgs.gov/themes/
earthqk.html.

**Disaster Research Center,
University of Delaware**
http://www.udel.edu/nikidee/drc.htm.

**Earthquake Engineering Research
Center, University of California at
Berkeley**
http://nisee.ce.berkeley.edu.

**Earthquake Engineering Research
Institute**
gopher://nisee.ce.berkeley.edu/11/eeri.

**Federal Emergency Management
Agency**
http://www.fema.gov/mit/eqmit.htm.

**John A. Blume Earthquake Engineering
Center, Stanford University**
http://blume.stanford.edu.

**National Center for Earthquake
Engineering Research, State
University of New York at Buffalo**
http://nceer.eng/buffalo.edu.

**Southern California Earthquake
Center, University of Southern
California**
http://www.usc.edu/dept/earth/quake.

Regional mapping and use of GIS:

Portland Metro
600 N.E. Grand Ave.
Portland, OR 97232.

EARTHQUAKES

People tend to associate earthquake hazards primarily with California. In reality, many parts of the United States are somehow affected by seismic threats. All of the West Coast, including Alaska, faces such problems, with particularly potent threats existing in both Puget Sound, affecting metropolitan Seattle, and the southern coast of Alaska, affecting Anchorage. The latter suffered a magnitude 8.4 earthquake in 1964 that originated in Prince William Sound (see case studies in Haas, Kates, and Bowden 1977; William Spangle and Associates 1980).

In addition, faults stretch across the Southeast into Charleston, South Carolina, which suffered an estimated 7.5 magnitude earthquake in 1886, killing upwards of 100 people and doing $5 million (1886 dollars) of damage (Bollinger 1985); the Wasatch Valley of Utah; and New England. Perhaps the most worrisome of those east of the Rockies, however, is the New Madrid fault based in New Madrid, Missouri, the site of an estimated 8.0 magnitude earthquake in 1811-1812, which caused parts of the Mississippi River to run backwards, created lakes where none had existed, and even rang church bells in distant Boston. What was then a sparsely inhabited portion of the United States now contains Nashville and Memphis, Tennessee; Evansville, Indiana; and St. Louis.

Hazard Identification

Earthquakes result from the abrupt release of accumulated strain on the Earth's tectonic plates, causing trembling at the surface and for some distance below. Earthquake hazards thus arise in those areas where those plates are moving against each other, sometimes catching and arresting each other's motion until the tension is released in a sudden snapping motion. The resulting motion at the Earth's surface falls into four subcategories of seismic hazards, as detailed in *MIRA*.

Ground motion. The release of accumulated energy along an earthquake fault line sends off shock waves that travel varying distances depending on the power of the earthquake itself and the surrounding topography. These waves fall into three categories.

- Primary (P) waves, similar to sound waves, spread longitudinally at approximately 15,000 miles per hour and are the first to cause vibration.

- Secondary (S) waves cause sideways vibrations in structures and are slower. These cause more damage because they shake buildings horizontally, the main source of vulnerability for unreinforced buildings.

- Surface waves are the slowest and, as their name suggests, move along the surface, unlike P and S waves. With low-frequency vibrations, these are more likely to cause tall buildings to vibrate.

Seismic activity. While it is not worthwhile here to explore the scientific details of seismic activity, it is worth understanding the basic technical meaning of two terms that are most popularly recognized in stories about earthquakes: magnitude and intensity. According to *MIRA*, the former "characterizes the total energy released," while the latter "subjectively describes effects at a particular place." These are two very different concepts, for the first is a single number dealing with the entire event and the second varies with location, especially distance from the epicenter. Knowing both the distance of one's community from potential earthquake epicenters and the barriers to earthquake shock waves that would mitigate their impact thus has some value for estimating the degree of risk facing that community in terms of the intensity of impact. An explanation of the Modified Mercalli Intensity scale commonly used to describe intensity is shown in the accompanying sidebar. It is somewhat easy to see that earthquakes of the same magnitude produce varying intensities depending on their geographic locations.

Surface faulting. While earthquake faults occur beneath the Earth's surface, they produce effects on the surface that create obvious hazards for any structures built near or astride active faults. Planners can generally avoid the worst impacts on buildings by ensuring that structures are built away from known active fault lines, typically by using setbacks (e.g., the 50-foot buffer mandated in California's Alquist-Priolo Act). This is no pure planning solution at all, however, for ground transportation facilities, such as railroads and highways, inevitably must cross fault lines and often suffer severe damage where surface faulting occurs. In those cases, engineering solutions are more appropriate.

Ground failure. Weak or unstable soils stressed by earthquake pressures can undergo liquefaction, which can lead to ground failure. Liquefaction occurs in certain types of clay-free soils, mostly sand and silt saturated by water, which become viscous fluids under the impact of ground vibrations from shear waves. *MIRA* indicates that "the younger and looser the sediment and the higher the water table, the more susceptible a soil is to liquefaction." *MIRA* lists three types of ground failures that result.

- Lateral spreads develop on gentle slopes and involve the sideways movement of large blocks of soil.

- Flow failures, the most catastrophic, occur on slopes greater than three degrees, involve blocks of intact material riding on a layer of liquefied soil moving considerable distances.

- Loss of bearing strength entails the failure of liquefied soil that has been supporting a structure, which then settles or tilts.

Sources of earthquake hazard maps are local consultants or universities, state geological surveys, or the U.S. Geological Survey (USGS).

Earthquake Intensity

Of the two ways to measure earthquake size (magnitude based on instrumental readings, and intensity based on qualitative effects of earthquakes), only intensity can be applied to pre-instrumental earthquakes. The 1931 Modified Mercalli scale used in the United States assigns a Roman numeral in the range I—XII to each earthquake effect. The methodology is simple.

- At each location, assign a numeral to describe the earthquake effect.

- Contour the zones of similar effect.

- The earthquake is assumed to have occurred near the region of maximum intensity.

- The earthquake may be characterized by the largest Roman numeral assigned to it.

The problems with intensity are multifold. First, it is a qualitative assessment that measures different phenomena. The lower values address human response to ground motions, the intermediate values characterize the response of simple structures, and the upper values describe ground failure processes.

Another problem is that incomplete spatial coverage may lead to a mislocation of the earthquake or an underassessment of its size. This is easily visualized for offshore earthquakes or, in the case of the United States, inadequate population distribution at the time of the earthquake.

Average peak velocity (centimeters per second)	Intensity value and description	Average peak acceleration (g is gravity=9.80 meters per second squared)
	I. Not felt except by a very few under especially favorable circumstances. **(I Rossi-Forel scale)**	
	II. Felt only by a few persons at rest, especially on upper floors of buildings. Delicately suspended objects may swing. **(I to II Rossi-Forel scale)**	
	III. Felt quite noticeably indoors, especially on upper floors of buildings, but many people do not recognize it as an earthquake. Standing automobiles may rock slightly. Vibration like passing of truck. Duration estimated. **(III Rossi-Forel scale)**	
1–2	IV. During the day felt indoors by many, 0.015g-0.02g outdoors by few. At night some awakened. Dishes, windows, doors disturbed; walls make creaking sound. Sensation like heavy truck striking building. Standing automobiles rocked noticeably. **(IV to V Rossi-Forel scale)**	0.015g-0.02g
2-5	V. Felt by nearly everyone, many 0.03g-0.04g awakened. Some dishes, windows, and so on broken; cracked plaster in a few places; unstable objects overturned. Disturbances of trees, poles, and other tall objects sometimes noticed. Pendulum clocks may stop. **(V to VI Rossi-Forel scale)**	0.03g-0.04g

(continued)

Earthquake Intensity (continued)

Average peak velocity (centimeters per second)	Intensity value and description	Average peak acceleration (g is gravity=9.80 meters per second squared)
5-8	VI. Felt by all, many frightened and run outdoors. Some heavy furniture moved; a few instances of fallen plaster and damaged chimneys. Damage slight. **(VI to VII Rossi-Forel scale)**	0.06g-0.07g
8-12	VII. Everybody runs outdoors. Damage negligible in buildings of good design and construction; slight to moderate in well-built ordinary structures; considerable in poorly built or badly designed structures; some chimneys broken. Noticed by persons driving cars. **(VIII Rossi-Forel scale)**	0.10g-0.15g
20-30	VIII. Damage slight in specially designed structures; considerable in ordinary substantial buildings with partial collapse; great in poorly built structures. Panel walls thrown out of frame structures. Fall of chimneys, factory stack, columns, monuments, walls. Heavy furniture overturned. Sand and mud ejected in small amounts. Changes in well water. Persons driving cars disturbed. **(VIII + to IX Rossi-Forel scale)**	0.25g-0.30g
45-55	IX. Damage considerable in specially designed structures; well-designed frame structures thrown out of plumb; great in substantial buildings, with partial collapse. Buildings shifted off foundations. Ground cracked conspicuously. Underground pipes broken. **(IX + Rossi-Forel scale)**	0.50g-0.55g
More than 60	X. Some well-built wooden structures destroyed; most masonry and frame structures destroyed with foundations; ground badly cracked. Rails bent. Landslides considerable from river banks and steep slopes. Shifted sand and mud. Water splashed, slopped over banks. **(X Rossi-Forel scale)**	More than 0.60g
	XI. Few, if any, (masonry) structures remain standing. Bridges destroyed. Broad fissures in ground. Underground pipelines completely out of service. Earth slumps and land slips in soft ground. Rails bent greatly.	
	XII. Damage total. Waves seen on ground surface. Lines of sight and level distorted. Objects thrown into the air.	

Source: Bruce A. Bolt, *Abridged Modified Mercalli Intensity Scale, Earthquakes—Newly Revised and Expanded* (New York: W.H. Freeman and Co., 1993), Appendix C.

Risk Assessment

The USGS map, reproduced as Figure 7-2, provides some idea for planners of both the geographical distribution and level of severity of earthquake threats across the contiguous United States. Local maps, however, would need to be considerably more detailed and ought to make the best possible use of planning and development data and Geographic Information system (GIS) technologies to incorporate detailed information on building quality and infrastructure, among a variety of other data types. Portland Metro (1996) provides a good example of the use of GIS for earthquake hazard mapping in a major metropolitan region (see also Spangle Associates 1996).

Figure 7-2. Ground-Shaking Hazards from Earthquakes in the Contiguous United States

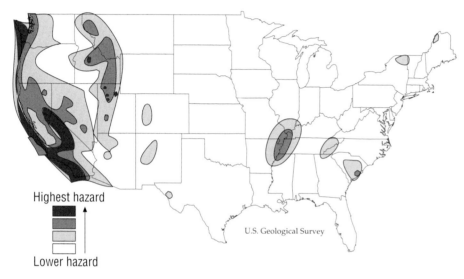

Highest hazard

Lower hazard

U.S. Geological Survey

Planners should be aware of a FEMA-developed resource, HAZUS (Hazards U.S.), that has been designed as a GIS-based system (MapInfo® and ArcView®) that can be used on a personal computer. (Chapter 24 of *MIRA* is devoted to a fuller explanation of its features.) The FEMA HAZUS loss estimation methodology is a software program that uses mathematical formulas and information about building stock, local geology, and the location and size of potential earthquakes, economic data, and other information to estimate losses from a potential earthquake. HAZUS is capable of mapping and displaying ground shaking, the pattern of building damage, and demographic information about a community. Once the location and size of a hypothetical earthquake is identified, HAZUS will estimate the violence of ground shaking, the number of buildings damaged, the number of casualties, the amount of damage to transportation systems, disruption to the electrical and water utilities, the number of people displaced from their homes, and the estimated cost of repairing projected damage and other effects.

HAZUS is being expanded into a multihazard methodology to estimate potential losses from wind (hurricanes, thunderstorms, tornadoes, extratropical cyclones, and hail) and flood (riverine and coastal) hazards.

Mitigation Opportunities

Good data on building construction are essential in effectively mapping earthquake risks at the local level. Most deaths and injuries from earthquakes result not from surface faulting or ground shaking itself, but from the damage to structures in which people may be working or residing, or from falling cornices and other debris. The structural integrity of infrastructure is also important in affecting both monetary and human losses largely because of the potential for collapse, particularly in the case of bridges, tunnels, and rail lines. Thus, loss of both life and property can be significantly reduced with seismic strengthening of buildings and infrastructure. FEMA has a variety of technical publications available, often focused on engineering issues, that detail the specifications for earthquake-resistant structural and building design. While planners are not generally involved in such design questions, it is important that they know where there are concentrations of buildings and infrastructure that require seismic upgrading.

The National Earthquake Hazards Reduction Program (NEHRP) was authorized through the National Earthquake Hazards Reduction Act of 1977, as amended (42 U.S.C. Section 7701 et. seq.). This program is charged with the development and enhancement of provisions to minimize structural damage and hazard to life due to earthquakes. FEMA is the agency responsible for managing NEHRP, whose participants also include USGS, the National Science Foundation, and the National Institute of Standards and Technology.

The *NEHRP Recommended Provisions for Seismic Regulations for New Buildings* (FEMA 222 and 223) presents minimum criteria for the design and construction of new buildings. One of its intended uses is as a source document for use in various building regulatory applications. In fact, the current editions of both the National Building Code and the Standard Building Code reflect substantially the NEHRP *Provisions* developed by FEMA. In addition, there is a great deal of compatibility between the *Provisions* and the Uniform Building Code's seismic safety criteria. The *NEHRP Guidelines for the Seismic Rehabilitation of Buildings* (FEMA 273 and 274) presents minimum criteria for rehabilitating existing buildings.

Following the creation of NEHRP, FEMA worked with the National Science Foundation, the National Institute for Building Sciences (NIBS), the American Society of Civil Engineers, the Applied Technology Council (ATC), and the National Institute for Standards and Technology to create, in 1979, the Building Seismic Safety Council (BSSC) under the auspices of NIBS. The purpose of BSSC is to address the various issues involved in developing and promulgating national regulations concerning seismic safety. Together, BSSC and FEMA provide a sizeable body of literature on the various means of mitigating earthquake risks to new and existing buildings, many of which are listed in *MIRA*. A few of the BSSC publications appear in the listings in Appendix A. FEMA's web site (www.fema.gov/mit/how2.html) also provides mitigation techniques for seismic hazards.

As was mentioned in Chapters 1 through 6 of this report, the first step in pursuing mitigation opportunities is to develop an inventory of the buildings needing seismic rehabilitation in the first place. Because the financing of seismic rehabilitation projects is often a major issue in the private sector, financial incentives tend to play a major role in facilitating the accomplishment of mitigation objectives. A good single-source document on the development of such programs is *Seismic Retrofit Incentive Programs: A Handbook for Local Governments* (California OES 1992), which grew out of a research project initiated by the California Seismic Safety Commission, and was funded by the commission, the Bay Area Regional Earthquake Preparedness Project of the California Office of Emergency Services, and FEMA. The document is also available from FEMA (FEMA-254/August 1994). It includes a series of case studies and program highlights from California communities, as well as discussions of the use of zoning as an incentive to rehabilitate, local government financing options, California seismic safety legislation, and the liability implications and considerations involved in seismic rehabilitation.

SEICHES AND TSUNAMIS

Seiches and tsunamis are both water-borne hazards that affect shoreline or coastal areas. Seiches are large waves that much resemble the rolling action of water in a bowl that is knocked off balance. They occur in inland lakes or other enclosed bodies of water when powerful waves are generated by some disturbance. The disturbance can take the form of strong winds, earthquake

Because the financing of seismic rehabilitation projects is often a major issue in the private sector, financial incentives tend to play a major role in facilitating the accomplishment of mitigation objectives.

ADDITIONAL RESOURCES: SEICHES AND TSUNAMIS

World Wide Web sites:

U.S. Geological Survey
http://www.usgs.gov/themes/
coast.html.

University of Washington
http://www.geophys.washington.edu/
tsunami.

Pacific Marine Environmental Laboratory
http://www.pmel.noaa.gov.

Also:

International Tsunami Information Center
Box 50027
Honolulu, HI 96850-4993
Telephone: 808-541-1657
Fax: 808-541-1678
E-mail: itci@ptwc.noaa.gov

tremors, or landslides from a steep shoreline slope. As these causes are diverse, the important factor for hazard identification is to be aware of their potential occurrence and to map the shoreline zones that could be affected by wave runup. Obviously, near-shore and low-lying property will be most vulnerable. Shoreline mapping is virtually a necessity in pre-disaster planning for any seismically active region that contains inland lakes or even a large bay or inlet.

Tsunamis are by nature a far more potent hazard, potentially gathering force across hundreds or even thousands of miles of ocean, where they may often be unnoticeable, to pile up walls of water towering up to 100 feet when they crash into narrow harbors and bays along the coast. Even in recent years (1992-1994), according to the USGS Web site, tsunamis have killed hundreds of people in Japan, Indonesia, and Russia. Their common English name, tidal waves, belies their origin, for they have no relationship to normal tides but result from seismic or volcanic disturbances on the ocean floor. Another less likely but possible generator is a mid-oceanic meteor strike. It is often noted that the Japanese name, tsunami ("harbor wave"), more accurately describes the phenomenon because of the way in which the long oceanic wavelength concentrates its power in a confined body of water such as a harbor. Hilo, Hawaii, has suffered significantly from tsunamis because of its location at the head of a large bay open to Alaskan earthquake-generated tsunamis from the northeast. However, the West Coast is also vulnerable. Crescent City, California, was struck by 12-foot waves following the Alaskan earthquake in 1964 (Griggs and Gilchrist 1983).

Hazard Identification

Tsunami hazards basically fall into two categories: remote-source and locally generated. Remote-source tsunamis travel long distances at high speeds for potentially an hour or more before hitting shore. Their great danger is that the high wave speed at sea slows down in shallow coastal waters, the wavelength shortens, and wave energy increases, magnifying waves to heights exceeding 50 feet during coastal runup. This process of wave transformation at the shoreline is called reflection, and its impact largely depends on the nature of the shoreline.

Locally generated tsunamis result from tectonic plate subduction, landslides, and volcanic activity. They involve events much closer to the affected shoreline and result in a much faster impact following the geologic event than is the case with remote-source tsunamis. The most significant subduction zone in the U.S. is the Cascadia, offshore from Washington and Oregon, along the Juan de Fuca tectonic plate. Oregon's Department of Geology and Mineral Industries has undertaken a tsunami hazard mapping effort because of this threat, which serves as the basis for regulations regarding construction of certain facilities in the identified tsunami inundation zones. (See Figure 7-3.) Other areas with potential tsunami threats include Puerto Rico, American Samoa, Alaska, Hawaii, and the Virgin Islands; the Pacific islands largely face remote-source hazards.

Risk Assessment

MIRA indicates that since 1770, "more than 46 remote-source generated tsunamis and 18 local tsunamis have been observed along the West Coast of the United States," but that only the 1964 Alaskan earthquake caused significant damage, largely in its impact on Crescent City, California, costing more than $7 million and 10 lives. Relative to other potential hazards, then, tsunamis constitute a smaller risk, but in the most affected areas, still require attention. Most at risk are shallow inland bays that tend to magnify wave energy to dangerous levels, accompanied by developed, low-lying coastal

Figure 7-3. State of Oregon, Department of Geology and Mineral Industries (DOGAMI), Requirements for New Construction in Tsunami Inundation Zone

TYPE OF CONSTRUCTION: ESSENTIAL AND SPECIAL OCCUPANCY STRUCTURES AS TREATED IN ORS 455.477(1) (specific applications of definitions to specific structures under consideration is determined locally)	IN STATE BILL 379	LOCAL EXEMPTIONS	PROHIBITED WITH PROVISIONS FOR DOGAMI EXCEPTIONS	MUST CONSULT WITH DOGAMI
aA Hospitals and other medical facilities with surgery and emergency treatment areas	X		X	
aB Fire and police stations	X	X	X	
aC Tanks and other structures containing housing or supporting water or fire suppression materials or equipment required for the protection of essential or hazardous facilities or special occupancy structures				
aD Emergency vehicle shelters and garages				
aE Structures and equipment in emergency-preparedness centers	X			X
aF Standby power generating equipment for essential facilities				
aG Structures and equipment in government communication centers and other facilities required for emergency response	X		X	
b Hazardous facility means structures, housing supporting, or containing sufficient quanitities of toxic or explosive substances to be of danger to the safety of the public if released	X			X
c Major structure means a building over six stories in height with aggregate floor area of 60,000 square feet or more, every building over 10 stories in height and parking structures as determined by Department of Consumer and Business Services	X			X
eA Covered structures whose primary occupancy is public assembly with a capacity of greater than 300 persons	X			X
eB Buildings with a capacity greater than 50 individuals for every public, private, or parochial school through secondary level or child care centers	X	X	X	
eC Buildings for colleges or adult education schools with a capacity greater than 500 persons	X		X	
eD Medical facilities with 50 or more residents, incapacitated patients not included in subparagraphs A to C above	X			X
eE Jails and detention facilities	X		X	
eF All structures and ocupancies with a capacity greater than 5,000 persons	X			X

Note: Provisions do not apply to water-dependent and water-related facilities, including but not limited to docks, wharves, piers, and marinas.

*Facilities marked with an X in this column were not subject to the requirements of ORS 455.477(1) prior to the passage of State Bill 379 in 1995.

regions where wave runup can do substantial damage and endanger life. On the other hand, areas with high coastal escarpments pose little if any risk. Tsunami hazard mapping is advisable for coastal communities that fit the high-hazard profile. Tsunamis have been the object of new attention from federal, state, and local planners, with FEMA and the National Oceanic and Atmospheric Administration's (NOAA) Pacific Marine Environmental Laboratory (PMEL) in the lead. The first local tsunami hazard mapping project was completed in early 1995 in Eureka, California, and serves as the prototype for similar efforts elsewhere (NOAA 1995).

Mitigation Opportunities

In some areas, shore-protection structures may limit damage from wave runup, but the most important steps in affected coastal zones are elevating buildings above flood levels, keeping the area below the building free from obstruction.

PMEL has conducted tsunami hazard mitigation workshops in West Coast communities. Warning systems can help local officials to evacuate threatened shoreline areas to prevent loss of life and are most effective when coupled over time with public education efforts. In some areas, shore-protection structures may limit damage from wave runup, but the most important steps in affected coastal zones are elevating buildings above flood levels, keeping the area below the building free from obstruction. This allows for the passage of waves and water and reduces the amount of debris that can become projectiles during serious floods. Avoiding the hazard by relocating buildings out of the hazard zone and using land-use regulations to limit new development is also an effective way to reduce potential damage. *MIRA* also suggests "landscaping with vegetation capable of resisting and reflecting wave energy" and locating streets and homes perpendicular to wave paths to allow penetration along a path of least resistance. Oregon statutes (ORS 455.446 and 455.447) and implementing regulations (OAR Chapter 632, Division 5) establish a tsunami inundation zone and regulate construction of essential facilities (hospitals, fire and police stations, emergency preparedness and communications centers); hazardous facilities (housing toxic substances or explosives); major structures (over six stories and 60,000 square feet or over 10 stories); and special occupancy structures (public assembly for more than 300 persons, schools with more than 50 students, colleges or adult education with more than 500 people, medical facilities with 50 or more incapacitated patients, jails, or any structure with occupancy exceeding 500). (See Figure 7–3.)

VOLCANOES

ADDITIONAL RESOURCES: VOLCANOES

Web sites:

U.S. Geological Survey
http://www.usgs.gov/themes/volcano.html.

Michigan Technological University Volcanoes Page
http://www.geo.mtu.edu/volcanoes/other.html

Smithsonian Institution—Global Volcanism Program
http://www.nmnh.si.edu/gvp

Alaska Volcano Observatory
http://giseis.alaska.edu

Cascades Volcano Observatory
http://vulcan.wer.usgs.gov/home.html

Hawaiian Volcano Observatory
http://www.soest.hawaii.edu/hvo

Volcanoes seldom make any secret of their presence, with few notable exceptions. Paricutin simply exploded out of flat Mexican farmland in 1943 to produce a cone more than 1,000 feet high after two years of eruptions (Griggs and Gilchrist 1983).

Hazard Identification

Volcanoes are kissing cousins of earthquake faults. They result from the same stresses along the edges of the earth's crustal plates, which allow magma to rise from the mantle below. Geologists identify three basic locations for volcanoes. One occurs where plates are being spread apart, as in the Mid-Atlantic Ridge, with Iceland being a prime example. A second occurs in what is called a subduction zone, where pressure is forcing part of the lithosphere at the edge of colliding plates downward. The most significant of these in the United States, as noted above in the discussion of tsunamis, is the Cascadia Subduction Zone, which runs along the Pacific Coast of Washington and Oregon and into British Columbia. This forms part of the well-known Ring of Fire that circles the Pacific Rim and constitutes 80 percent of the world's volcanoes, including those along the West Coast of the

U.S., including Alaska. (See Figure 7-4.) Most of these occur landward of the plate boundaries. The third occurs in hot spots in the midst of plates where magma forces its way to the surface, as in the Hawaiian islands. The geysers at Yellowstone National Park fall in the same category. The Hawaiian islands, however, are an example of suboceanic volcanic eruptions that rose above the surface of the ocean to create new landforms. In that sense, they are similar to Iceland and the Galapagos Islands.

The damages that result from volcanic activity depend on the nature of the activity, but *MIRA* categorizes the hazards as follows:

- Lava flows

- Pyroclastic flows

- Pyroclastic surges

- Lava domes

- Volcanic ash

- Volcanic gases

- Lateral blasts

- Debris avalanches

- Debris flows

- Floods

Figure 7-4. Volcanic Hazards in the Contiguous United States (based on activity in the last 15,000 years)

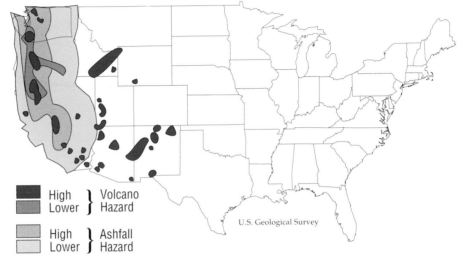

U.S. Geological Survey

Risk Assessment

Volcanoes are highly centralized hazards, and the level of risk does decrease with distance from the source. The primary danger with regard to volcanic hazards is the complacency that can result from long periods of inactivity, often extending for centuries. The infrequency of eruptions can lull communities into allowing development in highly vulnerable locations. Without accurate hazard identification and mapping, many people are unaware that their home or business lies in the path of a potential lava flow or ash fallout. Moreover, volcanic eruptions spew to the earth's surface a wide variety of mineral content that refreshes the long-term productivity of the soil. The lush valleys that grow from the rich soil provide a fatal attraction for human settlement worldwide—at least until the volcano once again explodes (Perry and Lindell 1990).

Mitigation Opportunities

MIRA describes five areas for a focus on volcano hazard mitigation:

- Use past eruptive activity to define hazard zones to guide development through land-use planning;

- Establish monitoring and detection systems to gain warning time before an eruption;

- Develop evacuation plans;

- Encourage protective measures such as the use of dust masks and goggles and changing oil and air filters;

- Couple risk assessment with land-use planning to produce strategies for reducing losses.

The primary danger with regard to volcanic hazards is the complacency that can result from long periods of inactivity, often extending for centuries. The infrequency of eruptions can lull communities into allowing development in highly vulnerable locations.

LANDSLIDES

The treatment of this hazard here will be brief in part because a good deal of planning and mitigation information concerning hillside development is already available in PAS Report No. 466 (Olshansky 1996), as well as in *MIRA* (Chapter 9).

Hazard Identification

Slope failure hazard identification begins with the recognition that any steep slope is inherently unstable, representing "an equilibrium between the geologic forces uplifting portions of the earth's crust and the forces of wind and water wearing it down." Thus, any change affecting that stability can result in landsliding or erosion if the forces generating movement overcome natural or built resistance (Olshansky 1995). Central to any good analysis, logically, is a soil stability study, which should account for the role of ground cover and anticipate the impacts of its removal. This leads to a common emphasis on the regulation of grading activities in many hillside development ordinances (Olshansky 1996).

Mapping potentially unstable slopes and detailing the natural infrastructure needed to protect them is vital to drafting effective mitigation steps to prevent landsliding or erosion. In more extreme cases, it may point to the need simply to ban any development and to acquire the land for open space. In the bargain, effective mitigation, whether it involves controlling or preventing hillside development, may also help to conserve wildlife habitat, minimize pollution from stormwater runoff, and preserve the aesthetic qualities of hillside areas.

The essential factors in landslide hazard identification are fairly simple to categorize, though dealing with them in practice can be considerably more complex. *MIRA* suggests three principal natural factors (topography, geology, and precipitation) and three principal human factors (cut-and-fill construction for highways, construction of buildings and railroads, and mining operations) that influence landslides.

Figure 7-5. Landslide Areas in the Coterminous United States

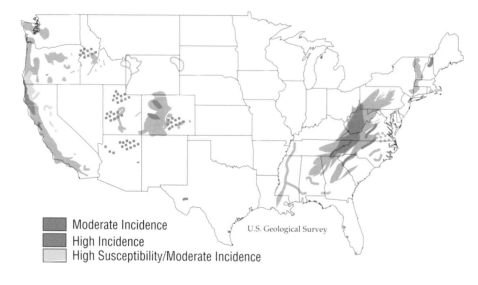

Moderate Incidence
High Incidence
High Susceptibility/Moderate Incidence

U.S. Geological Survey

Risk Assessment

Landslides are often a by-product of other natural hazards. They can also contribute to the exacerbation of other natural hazards. Heavy rainstorms, for instance, can destabilize a steep slope. If large volumes of soil flow into a waterway as the slope deteriorates, there can be downstream flooding. As noted above, volcanic activity is a severe destabilizing force on steep slopes. In the Alaskan earthquake of 1964, seismic activity triggered a massive slope failure that caused most of the resulting damage in Anchorage.

Damages from landslides are often underestimated because the damages are often attributed to the triggering event. Landslides occur in every state and U.S. territory.

Mitigation Opportunities

As noted above, Olshansky (1996) provides a substantial inventory of landslide hazard mitigation planning techniques. However, a short inventory of the primary techniques involved will suffice here.

- Use clustering to minimize the intrusion into the landscape where hillside development is necessary or unavoidable

- Use acquisitions and easements to remove as much hazardous land as possible from development

- Restrict or prohibit earth-disturbing development practices, such as grading and excavation

- Retain earth-stabilizing vegetation wherever possible (while also accounting for possible wildfire hazards where that is also relevant)

- Where possible, remove incentives to locate in hazardous settings

HURRICANES AND COASTAL STORMS

Hurricanes are the most potent and damaging subset of coastal storms. They represent the high end of a spectrum of tropical storms that begin over the oceans and usually make landfall before dissipating their energy. Tropical storms, in turn, are the major but not the only category of coastal storms. In more northerly regions, gale-force winds ride along the Atlantic coast as northeasters, bringing wet, cold weather (Eagleman 1983). In winter, such storms can produce devastating blizzards. In 1972, the town of Scituate, Massachusetts, suffered the loss of 23 homes and 360 structures with $2.5 million in damages (Rubin 1985). New Englanders, in particular, have learned to take such storms seriously.

Hazard Identification

Virtually any coastal area in the United States, including Hawaii, can be struck by a coastal storm. A violent tropical storm becomes a hurricane as winds exceed 120 kilometers (approximately 75 miles) per hour. Meteorologists view it as an intermediate-size storm, somewhere between large frontal cyclones and much smaller tornadoes, all of which share strong atmospheric vortices (i.e. whirlpools of air moving in circular patterns around a core). Unfortunately, hurricanes are the focus of a good deal of popular terminological confusion, for the same type of storm is labeled a cyclone in the Indian Ocean and a typhoon in the Pacific. They are, however, all the same. They generally do not form above 30 degrees latitude. They depend on tropical trade winds above warm ocean temperatures of at least 26 degrees Celsius (80 degrees Fahrenheit) for their formation (Eagleman 1983). They also depend on low central pressure in the "eye," or core of the hurricane, where downdrafting occurs. As they gain force over water, their wind speeds can build to nearly 200 miles per hour. Because they draw their strength from warm ocean waters, their power wanes as their path crosses land or cooler water (NRC 1993).

Because they are weather-driven phenomena, hurricanes have a clear seasonal aspect. In northerly latitudes, this season generally runs from June through November. Once they are in motion, however, they can move far beyond their tropical origins. All the Caribbean islands, plus every coastal state and province along the Atlantic Ocean and the Gulf of Mexico, including all of New England and the Canadian Maritimes, are capable of being hit by a hurricane. (See Figure 7-6.) Nonetheless, some states are visited more often than others—and typically by stronger storms. (See Figure 7-7.) Florida leads the pack, but every eastern and southern coastal jurisdiction needs to plan for coastal storms. It is only a matter of time. Hurricanes also affect the

Figure 7-6. Hurricane Landfalls in the United States, by State, 1900-1994 (hurricane categories 1-5)

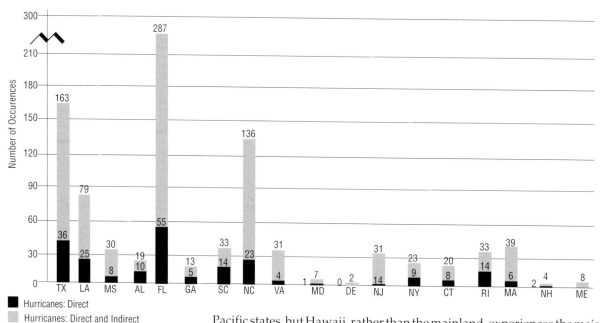

- ■ Hurricanes: Direct
- ▨ Hurricanes: Direct and Indirect

Pacific states, but Hawaii, rather than the mainland, experiences the majority of landfalls. Western states more typically experience heavy rainfalls as a byproduct of Pacific Ocean storm systems.

There are specific federal and state laws and programs that either assist or mandate planning for coastal hazards, including the Coastal Zone Management Act (CZMA), the National Flood Insurance Program (NFIP), the Coastal Barrier Resources Act, the North Carolina Coastal Area Management Act (CAMA), and Florida's Growth Management Act (Beatley, Brower, and Schwab 1994). The major coastal hazard provisions in these measures are provided in the accompanying sidebar.

Figure 7-7. Hurricane Activity in the Coterminous United States

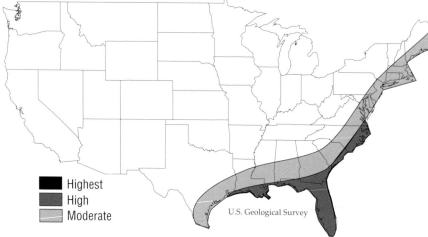

- ■ Highest
- ▨ High
- ▨ Moderate

U.S. Geological Survey

One specific area that deserves special attention in coastal storm hazard identification is the capacity of coastal areas for evacuation. Unlike some disasters, hurricanes provide predictable lead times before they make landfall. The advances of meteorological science in identifying and tracking tropical storms is the primary reason for the decline in their death toll in spite of skyrocketing coastal populations in recent decades. (See Figures 7-8 through 7-10.) Communities that were caught completely unaware just a century ago now have anywhere from several hours to several days to prepare for the event. Today, people remaining on barrier islands when a hurricane arrives may very well be there by choice. However, it is the responsibility of local emergency managers to determine how a local population could be evacuated prior to a hurricane and how long that process might take; it is the responsibility of planners to help determine what might be done to improve the situation.

Federal and State Legislation Concerning Hurricane Hazard Identification

FEDERAL

**Coastal Zone Management Act
(16 U.S.C. Section 1451 et seq.)**
The Coastal Zone Management Act (CZMA), first passed in 1972, is the single overarching federal law dealing with planning for the nation's coastal regions. Its basic aim is to encourage federal/state collaboration through the use of federal incentives in the form of matching grants. Sections 305 and 306 provide funds for the preparation and implementation of state coastal zone management plans. The act also provides for consistency between state and federal coastal plans, and federal actions must comply with approved state plans. The act is administered by the National Oceanic and Atmospheric Administration (NOAA), an agency of the U.S. Department of Commerce.

The 1980 amendments to the act (Coastal Zone Management Improvement Act) added hazards management as one of nine new elements in state coastal zone management plans. The 1990 reauthorization specified the mitigation of natural hazards including sea-level rise.

National Flood Insurance Program (NFIP)
The National Flood Insurance Program (NFIP) is not itself an act but a FEMA program based on several pieces of legislation that originated with the National Flood Insurance Act of 1968. The program deals with both riverine and coastal floodplains. NFIP is a voluntary program, but flood insurance is available only in communities with an approved floodplain management program in effect. Thus,

flood insurance is available in coastal areas, but only in those communities complying with NFIP requirements. NFIP uses Flood Insurance Rate Maps (FIRMs) that identify the boundaries of floodways and 100-year floodplains including those where flooding results from storm surges.

More specific hazard identification procedures appear in the Community Rating System (CRS), a more recent attempt within NFIP by FEMA to encourage communities to take specific steps to improve flood hazard mitigation and to exceed the minimum standards with their own regulations. CRS operates on a point system that allows reduced insurance rates for residents by following a series of hazard identification and mitigation steps through local regulation. CRS's 400-series activities deal largely with mapping and regulation of flood hazards.

**Coastal Barrier Resources Act of 1982
(16 U.S.C. Sections 3501-3510 [amended 1990])**
This act seeks to protect undeveloped coastal barrier island environments by denying federal subsidies for development in hazard-prone and ecologically significant coastal areas, designated for protection in the Coastal Barrier Resources System (CBRS). The underlying concept is that the denial of subsidies will prevent the government from financially encouraging the development of such areas, leaving the full cost of developing coastal barriers areas with the private sector. The 1990 amendments denied NFIP flood coverage to new or substantially improved structures within CBRS.

FLORIDA

Growth Management Act (Fla. Stat. Section 163.3178 (2); Fla. Adm. Code Section 9J-5.012)
Florida's Growth Management Act contains specific requirements for elements in local comprehensive plans, which must meet state approval by the Department of Community Affairs, which also promulgates the guidance and regulations for the act, as noted in the Hurricane Opal case study in Chapter 10. Communities in coastal counties must prepare plan elements for coastal high-hazard areas (also known as VE-zones) on FEMA's Flood Insurance Rate Maps (FIRMs), hazard mitigation, and post-storm redevelopment.

In these plan elements, local governments must designate a coastal high-hazard area, limit development and

public expenditures therein, and relocate infrastructure and population from such areas. They must also establish a process for identifying and ranking coastal properties for state acquisition.

**Coastal Construction Programs
(Fla. Stat. Sections 161.052-053)**
Florida has two coastal construction permitting programs operated by its Division of Beaches and Shores within the Department of Environmental Protection. The division is authorized to designate a coastal construction control line (CCCL) and to regulate structures within the CCCL, which is determined by the mean high-water line along sandy, open beaches.

NORTH CAROLINA

Coastal Area Management Act (CAMA)
The Coastal area Management Act (CAMA) mandates local coastal planning in North Carolina's ocean-

front counties. It provides for erosion-based setback requirements for coastal construction and includes three mandatory elements in local plans: storm hazard mitigation, post-disaster recovery, and evacuation.

Sources: Beatley, Brower, and Schwab (1993); Deyle and Smith (1994); Silverberg and Dennison (1993).

Figure 7-8. Deadliest Hurricanes in the United States, 1900-1994

HURRICANE	YEAR	CATEGORY	DEATHS
Texas (Galveston)	1900	4	8,000+
Florida (SE/Lake Okeechobee)	1928	4	1,836
Florida (Keys/S TX)	1919	4	600[1]
New England	1938	3	600
Florida Keys	1935	5	408
Audrey (SW LA/N TX)	1957	4	390
Northeastern U.S.	1944	3	390[2]
Louisiana (Grand Isle)	1909	4	350
Louisiana (New Orleans)	1915	4	275
Texas (Glaveston)	1915	4	275

Source: Based on Hebert and others, 1995

[1]600–900 estimated deaths, including 500 lost at sea.

[2]Including 344 lost at sea.

Figure 7-9. Costliest Hurricanes in the United States, 1900-1994

HURRICANE	YEAR	CATEGORY	DAMAGE (1990 dollars)
Andrew (Southeast Florida/ Southeast Louisiana)	1992	4	$25,000,000,000
Hugo (South Carolina)	1989	4	7,155,120,000
Betsy (Southeast Florida/ Southeast Louisiana)	1965	3	6,461,303,000
Agnes (Florida, Northeast U.S.)	1972	1	6,418,143,000
Camille (Mississippi, Southeast Louisiana, Virginia)	1969	5	5,242,380,000
Diane (Northeast U.S.)	1955	1	4,199,645,000
New England	1938	3	3,593,853,000
Frederic (Alabama, Mississippi)	1979	3	3,502,942,000
Alicia (North Texas)	1983	3	2,391,854,000
Carol (Northeast U.S.)	1954	3	2,370,215,000

Source: Based on Hebert and others, 1995

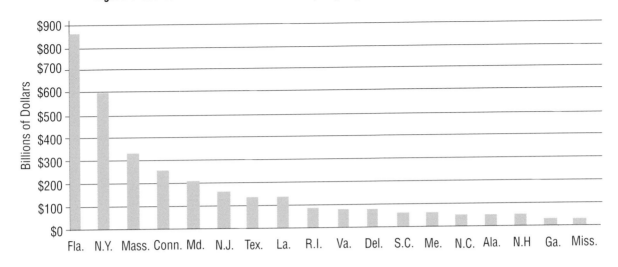

Figure 7-10. Value of Insured Coastal Property Exposures by Mainland States, 1993

The Sea Lake Overland Surge from Hurricanes (SLOSH) model is used by the U.S. Army Corps of Engineers and the National Hurricane Center to help FEMA and coastal states develop evacuation plans for populated areas. The SLOSH model differs from NFIP's coastal hazard delineations, and inundation areas shown on SLOSH maps may be more extensive than the coastal hazards shown on FIRMs.

The specific hazard issues associated with hurricanes are deceptively simple: wind and water. It is obvious enough that coastal zones can invariably expect to bear the full brunt of a hurricane's winds wherever it makes landfall. Coastal communities have little choice but to prepare for the worst and to build (or not) accordingly.

Water damage is far easier to address through land-use planning. Knowing where water is and how it will move under storm conditions is the beginning of any hazard identification effort. Areas deserving significant attention include:

- coastal high-hazard areas (V-zones in NFIP terminology);

- coastal floodplains (V-zones and A-zones in NFIP terminology);

- inland bodies of water, such as lakes, rivers, and canals;

- wetland areas, such as the Everglades and tidal marshes; and

- barrier islands and their associated inlets and sounds.

Mapping storm surge zones is basically a process of showing how far inland ocean waves can be expected to reach, and with what force. These zones are identified in local flood insurance maps, which are addressed below in the subsection on NFIP. But it is important here to understand the special characteristics of coastal areas and how they relate to water damage from coastal storms. Figure 7-11 depicts the Saffir-Simpson scale, which categorizes hurricanes based on central pressure and wind speed.

While it is valuable for coastal area planners to understand the dynamics of storm surges, it is not necessary to start from scratch in mapping surge zones. Such mapping is already a part of NFIP, which provides for mapping 100-year storm surge zones just as it does 100-year floodplains. The demarcations are based on a combination of the local topographical factors noted above plus the expected frequency of severe storms based on past experi-

While it is valuable for coastal area planners to understand the dynamics of storm surges, it is not necessary to start from scratch in mapping surge zones. Such mapping is already a part of NFIP, which provides for mapping 100-year storm surge zones just as it does 100-year floodplains.

ence. The coasts of Florida and North Carolina, for instance, have much higher probabilities of hurricane landfall than others, and this enters into the calculation. These zones are, of course, no more static than floodplains and may even be less so if predictions of sea-level rise and greater storm frequency due to climate change should happen to force a reassessment in coming years.

Even short of that, however, planners should monitor the shoreline erosion and migration of barrier islands and any development-induced changes in local vulnerability. While the problem of coastal erosion is generally limited to a fairly narrow strip of land along the ocean's edge, or at the edge of large inland bodies of water like the Great Lakes, it affects some of the most valuable and coveted real estate in the nation. Many landowners along the water's edge seem unaware of the historical mobility of the shoreline on which they depend for safety. Thunderstorms and wave action can destabilize bluffs along Great Lakes shores, causing structures

Figure 7-11. Saffir/Simpson Hurricane-Scale Ranges

SCALE NUMBER (CATEGORY)	CENTRAL (MBAR)	PRESSURE (IN)	WIND SPEED (MPH)	STORM SURGE (FT)	POTENTIAL DAMAGE
1	≥980	≥28.94	74–95	4–5	Minimal
2	965–979	28.50–28.91	96–110	6–8	Moderate
3	945–964	27.91–28.47	111–130	9–12	Extensive
4	920–944	27.17–27.88	131–155	13–18	Extreme
5	<920	<27.17	>155	>18	Catastrophic

Source: Hebert et al. (1995)

> Planners should monitor the shoreline erosion and migration of barrier islands and any development-induced changes in local vulnerability. While the problem of coastal erosion is generally limited to a fairly narrow strip of land along the ocean's edge, or at the edge of large inland bodies of water like the Great Lakes, it affects some of the most valuable and coveted real estate in the nation.

built atop them to tumble into the water. Beaches near and on barrier islands, as in the Carolinas and Louisiana, have deteriorated or shifted over time, again leaving structures exposed and destabilized. Some of these problems were discussed previously in the subsection addressing coastal storms, but coastal erosion is a much broader problem than that focus implies, for long-term erosion can have as severe an impact over time as short-run phenomena like hurricanes.

FEMA is completing a study of the economic impact of erosion and erosion mapping on communities and on NFIP, and a feasibility study of mapping riverine erosion as required under Section 577 of the National Flood Insurance Reform Act of 1994. This legislation defines an erosion hazard area as "an area where erosion or avulsion [a sudden cutting away of land] is likely to result in damage to or loss of buildings and infrastructure within a 60-year period." This definition encompasses both coastal and riverine erosion. The final report from the study will be completed by January 2000. The results and conclusions in these reports will help resolve policy debates as to whether FEMA should map erosion hazard areas and use these data in determining insurance premium rates through NFIP.

Risk Assessment

Wind. Identifying potential wind damage can be problematic for two reasons. One is that, as in the case of Hurricane Andrew, a hurricane can move across the low, flat Florida peninsula or some other strip of land with relatively unabated winds, destroying buildings, trees, and infra-structure almost at will. Hurricane-generated winds of up to 100 miles per hour have been recorded as far inland as Buffalo, New York (NRC 1993). The useful land-use planning lessons to be drawn from such widespread destruction are of necessity somewhat more limited than those for water damage. For wind damage, hurricane-resistant building codes have been the primary answer. The other problem is that hurri-canes sometimes spawn tornadoes in their wake, further exacerbating their impact. Again, wind-resistant construction is the most common solution. Risk assessment therefore consists largely in pinpointing sub-standard structures for mitigation efforts.

Rick Ibara

Difficult though the task may be, FEMA's National Hurricane Program and the National Weather Service have sought to improve our knowledge of wind patterns. FEMA's Region IV (Atlanta) released the *Inland Hurricane Wind Display Model*, designed to identify the degree of expected wind decay as a hurricane moves over land (FEMA 1995d). Such information is likely to prove most valuable in the application of new construction methods and improved building codes.

It is axiomatic, however, that hurricane winds will be most powerful as they make landfall and that coastal communities, therefore, must pay the closest attention to wind-damage issues. Analysis of hurricane wind pat-terns shows that following landfall, from one-half mile to a mile and a half inland, wind speeds decline to about 75 to 80 percent of those measured at stations with ocean exposure (TBRPC/Hillsborough County 1995). None-theless, powerful winds can be sustained well inland. Both Charlotte (Hurricane Hugo) and Raleigh, North Carolina (Hurricane Fran), experi-enced winds in excess of 100 miles per hour.

Water. Coastal geomorphology is crucial in defining storm hazards. Barrier islands have evolved as nature's way of buffering the mainland from the battering of coastal storms. These islands tend to be popular

This church on the island of Kauai in Hawaii was flattened by winds from Hurricane Iniki in the fall of 1992.

precisely because they offer the best in sand and sun to vacationers, but they are inherently unstable, consisting largely of migrating sand dunes with only modest vegetative cover. Powerful storms not only move them back and forth by scores of yards over time, but can actually destroy or sever them, eliminating landforms that once were and creating new ones that never were before. Development on such islands can be the equivalent of building castles in the sand to the extent that such coastal development collapses or implodes under hurricane pressure. Moreover, the hazards are magnified by the danger of flying debris. At the water's edge, wind and water work together to produce synergistic damage that neither might produce alone.

Offshore bathymetry (i.e., water depths to the ocean floor) also affects wave action. Deep water tends to absorb much of the wave energy below sea level. However, the steeper the shore, the closer large amounts of energy can come before dissipation occurs. In shallow water, the waves can build to heights well above normal sea level, making low-lying coastal areas highly vulnerable. In a hurricane, the low central pressure creates a bulge in the water that causes its level to rise because less air pressure is being exerted downward. The swirling counterclockwise winds surrounding the core serve to push forward the water to the right of the storm's path. The result is a wall of water that can rise as high as 25 feet as in Hurricane Camille (Pilkey et al. 1980) but more typically can be 15 to 20 feet high. How far that water reaches beyond the high-tide line depends largely on the coastal topography. Areas with high natural rock walls along the coast, which are relatively few in the southeastern United States, obviously afford better protection than most barrier islands. Even so, dunes tend to protect people and structures behind them by absorbing and breaking the force of the waves. They may not, however, survive the storm intact, so their protection is anything but permanent.

Flood potential also exists in the sound areas landward of barrier islands, as occurred with Hurricane Emily in North Carolina's Outer Banks in 1993. Counterclockwise winds can pile up water on the back side of the barrier islands, with the result that both the coastal and landward sides of such islands are vulnerable. As these landward shores are often not defined as V-zones under NFIP, however, they are not required to elevate specifically on piles and columns, but this is one more reason why local planners perhaps should pay extra attention to this aspect of the hurricane hazard. Communities may exceed the minimum NFIP requirements (and FEMA encourages this) and often do so since they have detailed knowledge of local flood hazards.

Near the shore, coastal waterways can amplify the impact of storm surges and add other dangers. Hurricane winds can move sizeable walls of water upstream along coastal tributaries, adding flooding dangers to the ordinary floodplain worries along riverbanks. Because hurricanes often generate

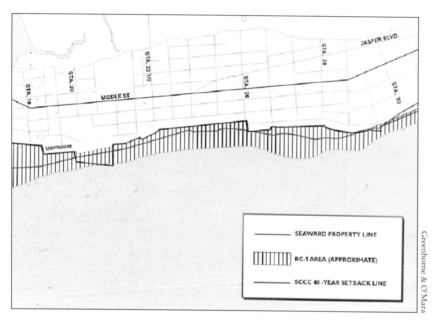

JASPER BLVD.

STA. 28
STA. 22 1/2
STA. 20
STA. 18
STA. 26
STA. 30
MIDDLE ST.
LIGHTHOUSE

——— SEAWARD PROPERTY LINE

||||||| RC-1 AREA (APPROXIMATE)

——— SCCC 40-YEAR SETBACK LINE

Greenhorne & O'Mara

The town of Sullivans Island, South Carolina, prevents the sale, subdivision, and development of the accreting dunes along the shore. In the vertical line pattern lie 80 acres of accreted beachfront land that were deeded to the Open Land Trust, which added restrictions and deeded the land back to the town. Changing these restrictions requires a vote of 75 percent of the island's registered voters.

considerable precipitation ahead of the storm front, rivers can swell with rainwater just as a storm surge moves upstream, and these combined dangers must be accounted for in riverfront hazard identification. Likewise, large inland lakes, such as are present throughout much of Florida, can flood under storm conditions and produce considerable damage.

But it is also important to focus again on the role of waterways amid barrier islands and on man-made canals. The latter were developed in some coastal areas—including barrier islands—in order to afford more property owners a waterfront location, but, in the process, they also afford more opportunities for flooding of waterfront structures. It is important also to recognize the formative nature of many inlets between or within barrier islands, for nature is forever experimenting with the shape and form of its coastal landforms, and today's tidal wetland may be tomorrow's new inlet following a major coastal storm. Wave action can scour out a new path for water where only a shallow passage had traversed the island before, and it can also relocate enough sand to fill in shallow waterways. Structures that stand in the way of this natural process are doomed even though engineering solutions may serve to delay the day of reckoning.

Mitigation Opportunities

Wind. Among the major wind hazard issues is the impact that inadequately constructed buildings and poorly secured property (trash cans, lawn furniture, or even trees) can have on neighboring properties. In the midst of the frontal impact of a hurricane, buildings and people suffer some of their worst damage not merely from the winds themselves but from the collateral impact of flying debris. The strength of buildings and infrastructure in high-hazard coastal zones thus becomes an essential focus of any worthwhile coastal storm hazard identification effort.

Construction on barrier islands and beaches tends to suffer the greatest threat from hurricane-borne winds. The combination of powerful winds and unstable soil necessitates strong countermeasures in the form of building design (such as hip roofs, avoidance of overhangs), tie-downs (especially for manufactured housing), and stabilizing measures for connections between building parts. While these are mostly building-code rather than land-use planning measures, it is worthwhile to be aware that, in assessing risks, land-use choices significantly influence the nature of the construction required to offset the threat. Building away from the shore on forested, vegetated upland, even on barrier islands, affords some greater stability and protection from wind-induced building failure. The vegetation indicates more stable soil, and the trees provide some friction and shelter to mitigate wind speed (Pilkey et al. 1980). In short, effective coastal hazard mitigation results from considering both the quality of the built environment and its location.

Water. Mitigation efforts for water damage from hurricanes are essentially those that typically apply in other types of floods. Designating special flood hazard areas in local zoning codes and then applying appropriate coastal setbacks, elevation requirements, and clustering provisions in subdivision design, preserving open space in highly sensitive areas, relocating utility lines, and buying or relocating the most vulnerable structures are all strategies that can reduce a community's vulnerability in high-risk coastal areas or along waterways subject to storm surges. Attention to erosion, scour, and sand deposition is highly important in coastal areas. Construction and site planning techniques must take into account large-area erosion patterns as well as localized scour around buildings and infrastructure. For example, many communities require septic tanks (if allowed at all) to be located landward of the building to minimize the potential of sand entering its components or of the tanks becoming exposed due to scour of overlying sand.

Construction on barrier islands and beaches tends to suffer the greatest threat from hurricane-borne winds. The combination of powerful winds and unstable soil necessitates strong countermeasures in the form of building design (such as hip roofs, avoidance of overhangs), tie-downs (especially for manufactured housing), and stabilizing measures for connections between building parts. While these are mostly building-code rather than land-use planning measures, it is worthwhile to be aware that, in assessing risks, land-use choices significantly influence the nature of the construction required to offset the threat.

ADDITIONAL RESOURCES: TORNADOES

Web sites:

Federal Emergency Management Agency (FEMA)
http://www.fema.gov/mit/hurrmit.htm.

National Severe Storms Laboratory of the National Oceanic and Atmospheric Administration (NOAA)
http://www.nssl.noaa.gov.

TORNADOES

Unquestionably the most violent storms on the planet, tornadoes also are among the most problematic hazards for planning purposes. Tornado hazards are also virtually ubiquitous within the United States. Not a single state has evaded their wrath, and they have struck in every state in nearly every month of the year (Harper 1994). Nonetheless, some states host these powerful storms far more than others, with Florida, Oklahoma, and Indiana leading the pack in terms of frequency per 10,000 square miles. (See Figure 7-12.)

Figure 7-12. Tornado Occurrence Statistics, by State, 1959-1988

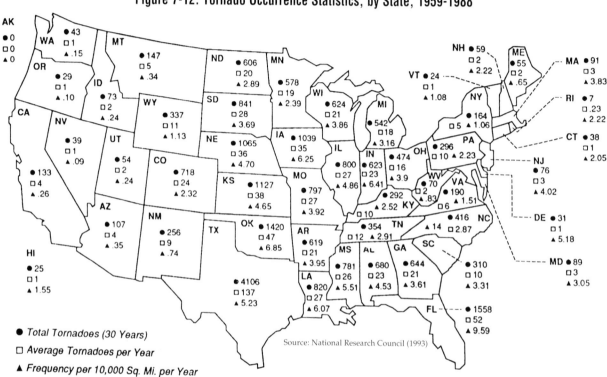

● Total Tornadoes (30 Years)

□ Average Tornadoes per Year

▲ Frequency per 10,000 Sq. Mi. per Year

Source: National Research Council (1993)

Hazard Identification

The fundamental problem for planning purposes is that tornado "alleys" can be delineated only in terms so broad as to make their application to land-use planning almost meaningless. Tornadoes materialize at the trailing edge of large frontal cyclones that result from the clash of high-pressure and low-pressure weather systems moving at continental scales across North America. The USGS map in Figure 7-13 illustrates the range and general frequency of tornadoes in the contiguous United States. The reason for the U.S. midsection's predominance in tornado statistics is the frequent collision of moist, warm air moving north from the Gulf of Mexico with colder fronts moving east from the Rocky Mountains. This also accounts for a seasonal tilt toward spring and early summer, as the northern hemisphere is heating up. Latitude makes a difference in the timing of tornado occurrences only in terms of statistical probabilities, however; there are no absolute certainties concerning time of year. Moreover, precisely because of climatic differences, southern states like Florida experience their most violent tornadoes in winter (FEMA Region IV 1993).

Local microclimates, while having no influence over large-scale thunderstorms that generally precede tornadoes, may affect the occurrence of tornadoes themselves. There is evidence, for instance, that the urban heat island effect in densely developed areas serves as a deterrent to tornado formation. Again, this is largely a matter of affecting probabilities, for tornadoes have struck in urban areas.

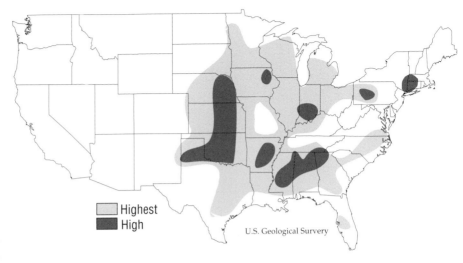

Figure 7-13. Tornado Risk Areas in the Coterminous United States

☐ Highest
■ High

U.S. Geological Survery

Risk Assessment

Perhaps the most useful point for planners is to know that most tornadoes are not the sort of extremely powerful, destructive funnel clouds that appear repeatedly in the movie *Twister*. Many, in fact, are of short duration, touch down in sparsely populated areas, and have far lower wind speeds than the Category 4 or 5 tornadoes that make national headlines. Figure 7-14 shows that severe tornadoes comprise only about 7 percent of the overall total. Another fact of considerable importance is that damages do not occur solely at the center of the tornado's path or only after touchdown. Wind damage can be severe both at the periphery and before touchdown.

Figure 7-14. Frequency of Tornadoes by Fujita Severity Scale, 1953-1989

SCALE VALUE	WIND SPEED (MPH)*	DAMAGE	AVERAGE NUMBER PER YEAR (U.S.)	PERCENTAGE
0	40-72	Light	218	29%
1	73-112	Moderate	301	40
2	113-157	Considerable	175	23
3	158-206	Severe	43	6
4	207-260	Devastating	10	1
5	261-318	Incredible	1	.0002

*Fujita defines these wind speeds as the "fastest quarter-mile wind."

Source: NRC (1993).

Mitigation Opportunities

The important point in terms of hazard identification and mitigation is that proper wind engineering can make many buildings more capable of surviving or limiting the damage from these more frequent, less violent tornadoes, whose winds are often not much worse than a serious hurricane. In other words, the same building codes that are used in hurricane-prone areas would be quite effective most of the time in highly tornado-prone areas. On the other hand, it would be financially prohibitive to upgrade most buildings to the kind of structural integrity needed to resist the most violent, but fortunately far more rare, Category 4 or 5 tornadoes. Only the most critical facilities—power stations, emergency command centers, and the like—are typically engineered to that level. For planners, making those distinctions involves critical judgments concerning the acceptability of some types of risks relative to the costs of mitigating the hazards involved, and how those judgments relate to public perceptions of risks.

Planners can take two other major steps through the process of hazard identification to deal with tornado threats in their communities. One is to work with local emergency managers to identify possible shortcomings in local tornado warning systems and then work with those managers to ensure that such systems are upgraded to meet the level of the threat in their area. While there are definite gaps in the effectiveness of tornado warning systems, meteorological research is steadily improving the predictability and warning time for tornadoes. The second step is to identify gaps in the availability of storm shelters, particularly in manufactured housing or basementless developments and areas involving elderly and disabled populations, and, again, to work with local emergency managers to improve the situation.

FLOODS

Water is the primary factor in the overwhelming majority of our natural disasters. Floods account for about 70 percent of presidentially declared disasters in the U.S. each year (Witt 1998). That percentage is almost certainly higher still for smaller, more localized disasters. Flooding is the most ubiquitous and common hazard, for every state has floodplains, and even many arid regions are at risk of damaging floods in the event of heavy rain pouring down normally dry washes and hillsides. The massive nationwide toll on lives and property from flooding drove the creation of NFIP in 1968 and continues to inspire amendments to the program. That toll had been estimated at $9 billion annually (L.R. Johnston Associates 1989) prior to the 1993 Midwest floods, whose singular $15 billion tab will push annual averages upwards for years to come.

Because NFIP plays such a special role in flood hazard identification and mitigation efforts, this section contains a number of sidebars detailing how that program, including CRS, works. To reiterate points made in earlier chapters, CRS was introduced as an incentive system to reward communities for going beyond the basic NFIP requirements in planning for and mitigating local flood hazards. The main point that needs to be made here is that NFIP is unique among federal hazards programs because it is the only program playing a direct federal regulatory role in guiding local land-use planning. With all other hazards, the federal role is one of providing either technical or financial assistance or direct disaster relief.

State involvement in mandating or overseeing floodplain management regulations is more significant than is the case with other hazards, in large part because of NFIP. Every state has some type of floodplain program with a designated manager. Ten states issue floodplain development permits directly from the state level, and others engage in a wide variety of regulatory activities or mandates for local governments (Weinstein 1996). Still, the state role is largely that of intermediary and facilitator. FEMA administers the program, and local government retains control of floodplain management planning and permitting and must choose to apply for participation in NFIP.

Appendix A, the reference list, cites a number of publications from FEMA and federal interagency sources that provide excellent resources concerning

---

ADDITIONAL RESOURCES: FLOODS

Web sites:

Federal Emergency Management Agency (FEMA)

http://www.fema.gov/mit/fldmit.htm

http://www.fema.gov/nfip/index.htm.

http://www.fema.gov/MIT/fmasst.htm

Association of State Floodplain Managers

http://www.floods.org.

NFIP Special Flood Hazard Area Designations

SYMBOL*	DESCRIPTION
A	Area of special flood hazard without water surface elevations determined
A1-30, AE	Area of special flood hazard with water surface elevations determined
A0	Area of special flood hazards having shallow water depths and/or unpredictable flow paths between one and three feet.
A99	Area of special flood hazard where enough progress has been made on a protective system, such as dikes, dams, and levees, to consider it complete for insurance rating purposes
AH	Areas of special flood hazards having shallow water depths and/or unpredictable flow paths between one and three feet, and with water surface elevations determined.
AR	Area of special flood hazard that results from the decertification of a previously accredited flood protection system that is determined to be in the process of being restored to provide a 100-year or greater level of flood protection
V	Area of special flood hazards without water surface elevations determined, and with velocity, that is inundated by tidal floods (coastal high-hazard areas)
V-1-30, VE	Area of special flood hazards, with water surface elevations determined and with velocity, that is inundated by tidal floods (coastal high-hazard areas)
V0	Area of special flood hazards having shallow water depths and/or unpredictable flow paths between one and three feet with velocity
B, X	Area of moderate flood hazards
C, X	Area of minimal hazards
D	Area of undetermined but possible flood hazards
M	Area of special mudslide (i.e., mudflow) hazards
N	Area of moderate mudslide (i.e., mudflow) hazards
P	Area of undetermined, but possible, mudslide hazards
E	Area of special flood-related erosion hazards

*Under 44 CFR 64.3 (b), insurance is mandatory in the following zones: A, A1-30, AE, A99, A0, AH, AR, V1-30, VE, V, V0, M, and E.

Source: NFIP Regulations (44 CFR 64.3), as of October 1, 1997.

Figure 7-15. General Areas of Major Flooding, January 1993 through December 1997

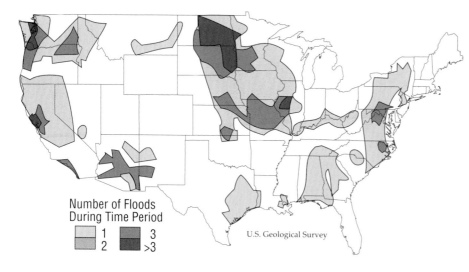

Number of Floods
During Time Period

1   3
2   >3

U.S. Geological Survey

NFIP. All these should be treated as valuable supplements to the format here, which follows that used for all other natural hazards outlined in this chapter.

Further discussion of NFIP's role in flood hazard mitigation appears below in the subsection on mitigation opportunities. In addition, planners interested in developing land-use policies to mitigate local flood hazards should consult PAS Report No. 473, *Subdivision Design in Flood Hazard Areas* (Morris 1997). Finally, because of the diverse climatic and topographical influences on local flood hazards, the discussion below will itemize special kinds of flood hazards that some jurisdictions may want to address because of their own circumstances.

Hazard Identification

Some special types of flood hazards that are typically associated with, or triggered by, other hazard types have been discussed elsewhere in this chapter (e.g., coastal storm surge zones, seiches, tsunamis, and volcanic debris flows). The focus here, then, will be on those flood hazards resulting directly from high lake and river levels due to precipitation or melting snow and ice. One other related form of flooding discussed below, constituting a special hazard in western states, involves alluvial fans. The items below basically summarize the parallel hazard identification discussion of floods in *MIRA*.

Mapping conducted according to NFIP is an overriding consideration in hazard identification. NFIP special flood hazard area designations are delineated in the sidebar. NFIP conducts the mapping of floodplains and produces and revises, as necessary, the Flood Insurance Rate Maps (FIRMs) that provide the basis for establishing flood insurance premiums and local floodplain management requirements. Local governments may, however, apply to FEMA for map revisions based on locally developed or acquired data that they feel may justify the request. Several FEMA initiatives were underway at the time this report was being prepared that will encourage communities to exert a much larger role in mapping and maintaining the accuracy of floodplains designated under NFIP. A more graphic illustration of the basic elements of the 100-year floodplain, borrowed from Morris (1997), is provided in Figure 7-16.

Riverine flooding. Typical riverine flooding involves the overflowing of the normal flood channels or rivers or streams, generally as a result of prolonged rainfall or rapid thawing of snow cover. The lateral spread of floodwater is largely a function of the terrain, becoming greater in wide, flat areas, and affecting narrower areas in steep terrain. In the latter case, riparian hillsides in combination with steep declines in riverbed elevation often force waters downstream rapidly, sometimes resulting in flash floods. (It should be noted that flash floods can also result wholly or in part from technological hazards, typically dam failures, and from natural obstructions to waterways.)

These variations in circumstances affect the duration of the inundation of the floodplain, with rapid water movement draining floodplains faster. The duration of storm patterns also affects the length of the period of inundation. Many storms unleash considerable amounts of rain within just hours, producing very short-term but damaging floods in localized areas. On the other end of the spectrum, the highly prolonged weather patterns affecting whole states in the relatively flat Midwest in 1993 left many communities inundated for weeks, and in many cases, for two or three months.

In short, the key contributing factors in identifying the scope of the local flood hazard are:

- the size of the watershed;

- development within the watershed affecting stormwater runoff;

- soil characteristics;

- topographic characteristics affecting the direction and flow of flood waters; and

- regional climate.

Ice jam floods. These merit some special consideration in more northerly communities facing cold winter climate conditions. Basically, they involve ice blocking the free flow of water downstream, causing a backup of water upstream. They often occur at particularly vulnerable locations in the river channel. Northward-flowing rivers in areas with freezing weather are especially vulnerable, as illustrated in 1997 along the Red River, which flows along the Minnesota-North Dakota border through Canada into the Hudson Bay.

Ground saturation. A significant issue in the Midwest floods of 1993 involved the fact that heavy rainfall the previous fall and spring had left the ground largely saturated and therefore unable to absorb the even more intense precipitation that occurred that summer. Under such conditions, groundwater levels are so high that the earth has lost its absorption capacity and almost all rainfall becomes floodwater, at least in the sense that farm fields and lawns temporarily become shallow ponds and marshes. This is largely a problem in flatter terrain that drains slowly and in urban areas with large percentages of impervious surface.

Fluctuating lake levels. Inland lakes are always subject to minor variations in water level simply as a function of variations in seasonal temperatures and precipitation. For the most part, small variations can be accommodated in most human waterfront activities, but prolonged wet weather patterns can induce water-level rises that threaten lakeshore areas. A few lakes, most notably Devils Lake in North Dakota and the Great Salt Lake in Utah, because of flat shoreline topography and wide variations in seasonal weather, have expanded and contracted considerably within recent years, threatening or inundating near-shore development and infrastructure.

Alluvial fans. In areas with wide valley floors beneath steep hills and mountains, particularly in regions with largely arid climates, rainfall can

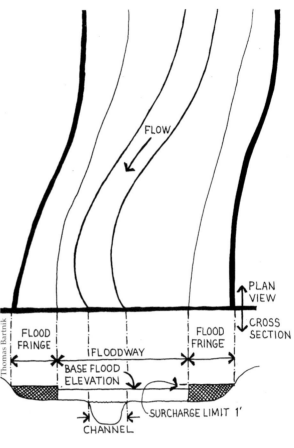

Figure 7-16. Elements of the 100-Year Floodplain

produce substantial erosion of rocks and other debris into fan-shaped deposits at the base of the incline. These formations are known as alluvial fans, and their presence, when they are obvious enough, is a signal that the area along the fan may be a dangerous location for development, particularly at the base. In a severe thunderstorm, the combination of rain and rocky debris pouring down the mountainside into the valley can produce considerable destruction, in large part because the material moves at high speeds, producing erosion and deposition at unpredictable locations.

Risk Assessment

A basic explanation of flood risk assessment terminology, a knowledge of which is a necessity for any planner involved in floodplain management, is provided in the accompanying sidebar below. Planners and public officials should also know that the use of the 100-year flood as a regulatory standard represents a compromise in the original crafting of NFIP and in no way delineates the worst possible flood that could happen, as the case study in Chapter 8 and many other historical references in this report demonstrate.

Figure 7-17 provides an example from El Paso County, Colorado, of a digitized FIRM using the rate map designations described in the sidebar on page 207. Note that the outer areas of Zone X extend the mapped floodplain

Floodplains, Storm Surge Zones, and Probabilities

Perhaps it is simply a matter of bad labeling. But many people share fundamental misconceptions about flood probabilities and frequencies. Planners cannot afford to be among them, though simple statistical literacy is an adequate antidote to misunderstanding.

Floodplain managers and others working in the field of flood hazards regularly refer to the "100-year floodplain," or the "100-year flood." Many residents of affected areas tend to assume that these terms refer to the frequency with which floods of a given size will occur in a particular area. Considerable public puzzlement, if not disillusionment with flood-control policies, can result when a 100-year flood recurs within just a few years. There is, however, nothing unusual or sinister in such an event. The 100-year designation, whether for a floodplain or a coastal high-hazard area, is a statement of probability. It means simply that the 100-year flood level, also known as the base flood level, has a 1 percent chance of being reached or exceeded in any given year. The floodway is then defined as the area along the stream channel that is designed to "carry the waters of base flood, without increasing the water surface elevation of that flood more than one foot at any point." Thus, in theory, structures elevated one foot above the level of the 100-year floodplain should avoid inundation in a base flood. This "freeboard" is recommended but not required by FEMA.

Once the 100-year flood has happened, it has the same 1 percent chance of happening the following year, and sometimes does. On the other hand, it may never recur again for hundreds of years. Long-term probabilities come and go in clusters over long periods of time, generally far longer than the period during which most U.S. floodplains have hosted modern development. After all, many American communities are still less than a century old.

Although the 100-year flood has special regulatory significance for the National Flood Insurance Program (NFIP), it has no special significance to Mother Nature. In any given year, a community may experience a 20-year flood, a 50-year flood, or even a 300-year flood. The same statistical logic applies. Those events would have, respectively, a 5 percent, 2 percent, or 0.33 percent chance of occurring in any year. And any of them could happen two years in a row. Their occurrence in any year does not change the odds for subsequent years.

What does change the odds is development in the watershed, especially in the floodplain itself. Increasing impervious surface, building obstructions to the flow of water along the riverbank, or allowing sedimentation through streambank erosion all contribute to an escalation of the probabilities of flooding, and thus change 100-year floodplains into 80-year or 50-year floodplains. Changing the landscape changes the probabilities, and that is the reason floodplain management regulations must accompany flood insurance availability.

Figure 7-17. Example of a Digital Flood Insurance Rate Map, El Paso County, Colorado

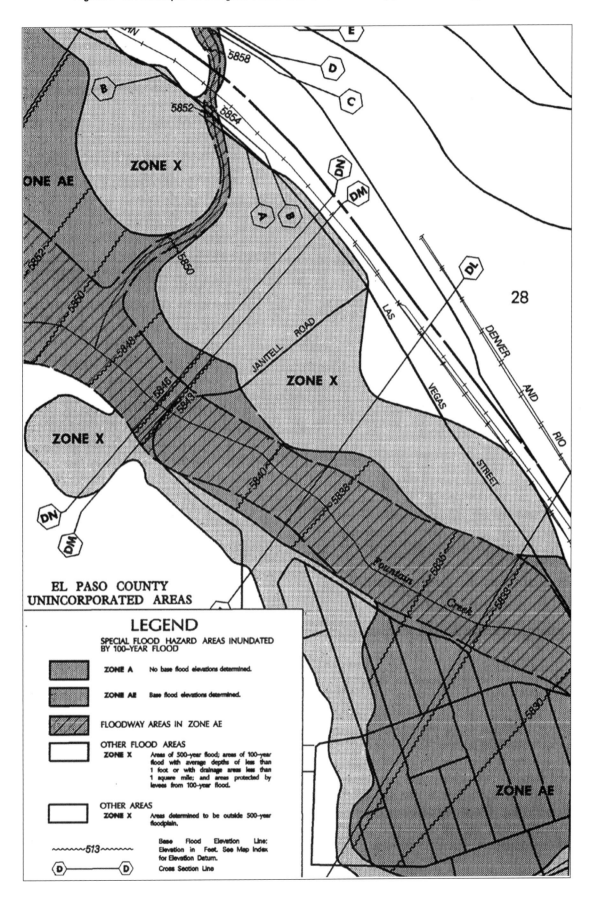

to a 500-year level, while Zone AE delineates those inundated by the flood with a 1 percent annual chance of occurring, known as the 100-year flood.

Mitigation Opportunities

Opportunities for planners to mitigate flood hazards and prevent losses of life and property are extensive, in large part because flood risks are so much more clearly definable for land-use purposes than almost any other hazard. The mapping functions of NFIP provide an effective basis for establishing flood-plain management regulations through zoning, subdivision controls, and other measures within clearly defined areas with readily quantifiable risk factors.

Because a good deal of discussion occurs elsewhere in this report, particu-larly in Chapter 5, concerning the various planning and regulatory tools that communities can use to mitigate flood hazards either before or after flood disasters occur, it is perhaps simplest here to offer a checklist originally appearing in L.R. Johnston Associates (1992), which divides mitigation strategies into four categories:

1. Modify susceptibility to flood damage and disruption

- Acquisition and demolition, and relocation of properties in flood-prone areas
- Floodplain regulations and building codes
- Development and redevelopment policies
- Floodproofing and elevation-in-place
- Disaster preparedness and response plans
- Flood forecasting and warning systems

2. Modify the impacts of flooding

- Information and education
- Flood insurance
- Tax adjustments
- Flood emergency measures
- Disaster assistance
- Post-flood recovery

3. Manage natural and cultural resources

- Preservation and restoration strategies
- Regulations to protect floodplain natural and cultural resources
- Development and redevelopment policies and programs
- Information and education
- Tax adjustments
- Administrative measures

4. Modify flooding

- Construction of dams and reservoirs
- Construction of dikes, levees, and flood walls
- Channel alterations
- High-flow diversions and spillways
- Land treatment measures

WILDFIRES

With the exception of fires triggered by lightning strikes, which are usually mitigated in their impact by the precipitation of the accompanying thunderstorm, wildfires tend to be the chancy culminations of hot, dry weather patterns that merely create the conditions for their occurrence. Once those conditions—the buildup of dry fuel to feed a fire—are in place, the occurrence of a conflagration depends simply on the right spark in the right place, and the disaster is set in motion.

But like other natural processes, such as flooding, wildfires serve a purpose in the ecosystem regardless of their inconvenience for humans. In wildlands, they have always served to clear underbrush from the forest and to allow the regeneration of certain species at the expense of others. With or without the human presence, fire is a part of nature. Moreover, it has become clear over time that, in North America, Native Americans used fire as a tool for their own management of the ecosystem, clearing hunting grounds and directing forest growth. Fire, vegetation, animals, and humans all evolved together prior to European settlement.

More modern attempts to suppress fire at all costs, coupled with the widespread deforestation and settlement of the landscape, combined to generate new and previously uncommon fire hazards affecting developed areas. The 1871 fire that destroyed Peshtigo, Wisconsin, in the heart of the nineteenth-century logging industry, gave us the term "firestorm" because of the way in which the natural and human forces together powered a frightening wildfire that surpassed area residents' worst nightmares. Numerous similar fires followed, culminating in a 1918 fire around Cloquet, Minnesota, that killed 4,000 people and remains one of the most destructive in U.S. history (Weatherford 1991). We have been forced to learn a great deal about the genesis and natural impacts of wildfires in the century that followed. While the numbers of wildfire-caused deaths have declined in this century, *MIRA* lists four major wildfires or combinations of wildfires during the 1990s alone that have taken staggering tolls in property losses and more than a few deaths and injuries. (See sidebar.) These fires now have far less to do with poor logging practices and much more to do with the intrusion of residential development into the urban/wildland interface.

Hazard Identification

What we have learned, in part, is that our efforts to eliminate wildfires from the natural environment, rather than helping matters, have served to make

ADDITIONAL RESOURCES: WILDFIRES

Web sites:

Boulder County, Colorado, Wildfire Hazards Identification and Mitigation System
http://www.boco.co.gov/gislu/whims.html.

Federal Emergency Management Agency (FEMA)
http://www.fema.gov/mit/wfmit.htm.

National Fire Protection Association
http://www.nfpa.org.

Firewise (multiple sponsors)
http://www.firewise.org.

Wildfire Losses in the 1990s

DATES	LOCATION	DEATHS	INJURIES	HOUSING UNITS LOST OR DAMAGED	PROPERTY LOSSES
10/20/91	East Bay Hills, Oakland, Calif.	25	150	3,810	$1.5 billion
10/91 (92 fires)	Spokane, Wash.	——	114	114	
10/15-11/3/93 (21 fires)	California	3	Hundreds	1,171	$1 billion
1994	Various, including Colorado	34	——	325	Not available

Source: FEMA (1997b)

such fires more severe when they occur. Vegetative fuels accumulate in the forest understory, and when fires occur, they are more severe and disastrous than might otherwise have been the case. While we are now learning how to integrate the role of wildfires into our understanding of wildland ecosystems, it is less clear that we are routinely incorporating the implications of those findings into the planning of development that is happening at the interface between our growing urban areas and these wildlands (DOI/USDA 1995). This is the area that becomes the focus of hazard identification efforts as part of the process of planning both for mitigation and for post-disaster recovery and reconstruction.

One key point of the preceding history is that, while the pattern of American urban development has shifted wildfire management attention further west, the problem is not simply a western one. The Upper Midwest, northern New England, and any other forested areas that may suffer prolonged drought, such as Long Island's Pine Barrens in this decade, are potentially at risk from wildfires. Recent case studies, such as that of the Stephan Bridge Road fire in Grayling, Michigan (NFPA 1990), continue to demonstrate that wildfire mitigation is a not a regional but a national problem. Moreover, unlike most other natural hazards, human carelessness does enter into the mix of causation. The U.S. Forest Service figures indicate that about one-fourth of reported wildfires are caused by arson, and almost another one-fourth by debris burns (FEMA 1997b).

MIRA lists three principal factors directly affecting the behavior of wildfires: topography, fuel, and weather. It also notes that other hazards contribute to wildfires and are triggered or affected by wildfires themselves, such as winds (both exacerbating wildfires and being induced by them, particularly in firestorms), mudslides, and landslides (induced by the stripping of the vegetation from hillsides, followed by rainstorms).

Risk Assessment

Nan Johnson, a planner with the Boulder County, Colorado, Land Use Department, and now working in Flagstaff, Arizona, lists the following factors, in order of importance, as items for consideration in identifying, mapping, and rating wildfire hazards in urban interface areas, based on Boulder County's experience in tapping a variety of kinds of expertise to address the problem.

1) *Site location and topography.* What types of fuels are in the area of the buildings in question? Fuels include all vegetation in the surrounding area. What fuel model classes do they fall into? Is there forest? If the area is mountainous, how stable is the slope?

2) *Building construction and design.* What materials have been used for existing buildings? How are the eaves built, and what are the overhang features? These features can produce significant updrafts that feed fires into houses and add to the severity of fire damage. Are there porches? Wooden decks add to the fuel base to prolong the fire. What materials were used for the roof and siding? Wood shake roofs, for example, are notorious fuel extenders. How flammable are the materials overall? Figure 7-18 provides a pilot area example of Boulder County's use of GIS to identify the location of various roofing materials for wildfire hazard mapping purposes.

3) *Defensible space and landscaping.* What sort of vegetation or other fuel exists in the immediate area around the structure? Tall pine trees and shrubs may be beautiful but deadly within a few feet of the house. Moreover, the composition of the transition zones away from the house

Figure 7-18. Wildfire Hazard Identification and Mitigation System, Pine Brook Hills Area, Boulder County, Colorado

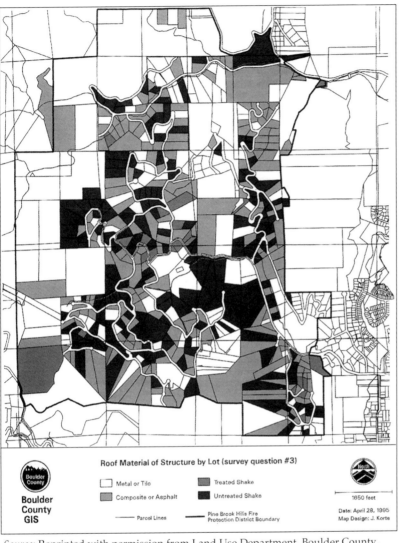

Source: Reprinted with permission from Land Use Department, Boulder County, Colorado

leading into the wildlands also makes a difference, as far away as 200 feet from the structure. What is the nature of the landscaping that surrounds the house, and is it irrigated? Various types of vegetation are more or less fire resistant than others. Find out what works locally.

4) *Access.* How are the lot structures set up? Are there power lines overhanging the property? Are there overhanging trees? Steep or tight curves leading to the property? How will fire and rescue vehicles reach the area? The case study in Chapter 6 of Oakland's East Bay Hills wildfire covers a number of typical and essential planning questions concerning access.

5) *Water.* Where is it accessible? Streams, ponds, and springs may provide natural sources of water but also have inherent limitations during a drought or when frozen. Some rural communities build cisterns to overcome these limitations, thus storing rainwater for future fire needs. Wells, swimming pools, and other devices are limited only by local planning ingenuity. Are there hydrants, and who maintains them? Dry hydrants, which consist of nonpressurized piping connected to a natural

Occupancy Hazard Classification Numbers: Fire Hazards

Because these ratings depend on a variety of factors that may vary within similar structures, this list does not provide examples. Ratings depend on individual inspections. Such ratings are used to determine minimum needed water supplies. Buildings with automatic sprinkler systems are not assigned a classification.

Class 3: Severe. High quantity and combustibility of contents; fire would tend to develop very rapidly and have high rates of heat release.

Class 4: High. High quantity and combustibility of contents; fire would tend to develop very rapidly and have high rates of heat release. Only somewhat less flammable than Class 3 fires, which often contain explosives, petrochemicals, and the like.

Class 5: Moderate. Moderate quantity and combustibility of contents; fire would tend to develop quickly with moderate rates of heat release.

Class 6: Low. Moderate quantity and combustibility of contents; fire would develop moderately with moderate rates of heat release.

Class 7: Light. Low quantity and combustibility of contents; fire would develop slowly with low rates of heat release. Most homes, hospitals, schools, and offices would fall into this category.

Source: National Fire Protection Association (n.d.).

water source such as a pond, are an option in many areas. The National Fire Protection Association (n.d.) has a manual on planning for water supplies in the wildland/urban interface that provides many of the basic details pertaining to such questions.

6) *Fire protection.* What is the nature of the fire protection that is available? What fire protection exists on site?

Because weather is such a critical factor in determining immediate risks of wildfire, monitoring of the conditions that can increase wildfire hazards in the short term is critical, even if not entirely relevant to long-term land-use planning decisions. At the very least, an awareness of the potential for wildfire incidents puts planners on the alert for the potential need to implement all or part of a post-disaster plan and to allocate resources accordingly. The U.S. Forest Service tracks moisture patterns nationwide to spot areas that are potential tinderboxes.

Mitigation Opportunities

It may seem curious that Johnson and her Boulder County colleagues list fire protection last among these six factors. But consider the probabilities of quick and efficient access by a local, often volunteer fire department in outlying suburbs or small towns to remote home sites located on steep, winding hills in the midst of a raging inferno. While firefighters in large cities may often be the first on the scene in dealing with urban fires, access to rural wildfires is often problematic. The problems created in connection with the first five issues make fire protection at best a secondary factor in the level of actual danger posed by wildfire hazards and puts mitigation at a premium.

The focus on individual properties in identifying the level of hazard is also interesting. Boulder County is requiring site plan review for each house or any expansion in excess of 1,000 square feet, although its regulations were not originally related to wildfire hazards, and it has outlawed woodshake shingles and plastic-type screening materials. The urban/wildland interface is an area where development is coming to the hazard, and thus the natural and built context is important on a case-by-case basis in determining the level of hazard to which buildings are exposed. (See sidebar.) But hazard identification can become a vital first step in designing plans to engage property owners in a proactive program to mitigate hazards prior to a disaster and to seize vital opportunities to reduce future vulnerability afterwards.

Fortunately, planners and fire officials in affected areas, plus academic and state and federal experts in forestry and fire management, have in recent years been developing computerized mapping and hazard identification models for wildfire hazards. The Western Governors Association has released its own *Hazard Assessment Methodology.* Boulder County has been using its own Wildfire Hazard Identification and Mitigation System (WHIMS), a GIS program that is allowing county planners to apply what they have learned as they review development proposals and seek mitigation before construction begins.

Chapter 8

Flood Case Study: Arnold, Missouri

JIM SCHWAB, AICP

Jim Schwab is a senior research associate with the American Planning Association. He is the principal author of this report, the editor of Zoning News, *and the author of* Planning Advisory Service Report No. 482, Planning and Zoning for Concentrated Animal Feeding Operations *(December 1998).*

Most disasters strike a single community or a relatively small region. They seldom afford opportunities for comparing the quality of communities' pre-disaster mitigation efforts or of their responses to the challenge of rebuilding afterwards. The 1993 Midwest floods, however, lasted so long and affected such a large area that they became a laboratory for comparative study by disaster experts. This case study is about one city that, because of planning beforehand, seized its opportunities in the flood's aftermath to avert future problems through aggressive mitigation and acquisition. Arnold, Missouri, may yet experience more floods like those in 1993, but it will not experience the same threat to life or damage to property. The reason is simple. The city has succeeded in removing much of its built environment from the path of danger.

Arnold is at the southern fringe of the multistate region that was affected by the 1993 floods. The city lies about 20 miles southwest of St. Louis, in Jefferson County, Missouri, at the confluence of the Meramec and Mississippi rivers. Most of Arnold lies west of a bend in the Meramec River, which rises in the Ozarks and flows north, turning gradually northeast toward St. Louis, then arcing back southward to the Mississippi River. When the Mississippi overflows, Arnold gets the backwater, which forces its way up the tributary. When that tributary overflows, it can likewise force a much smaller backwater up the narrower channels of several local creeks. All of those floodplains have seen extensive development in the last half-century. In the hilly terrain of Jefferson County, all of those low-lying floodplains were extremely vulnerable.

THE 1993 FLOODS

The series of floods that drenched nine Midwest states in the spring and summer of 1993 set records repeatedly. They saturated the soils of southern Minnesota, western Illinois, the southwestern corner of Wisconsin, most of Missouri, the eastern parts of Nebraska, Kansas, and South Dakota, and virtually all of Iowa. The most costly floods in U.S. history left a trail of $12 billion in damages plus 47 deaths, displacing more than 30,000 people from their homes. The product of an anomalous weather pattern, they differed from typical floods largely in their longevity. While most floods last at most a few days before receding, the 1993 floods persisted for months, often leaving homes and other buildings so hopelessly waterlogged that they were beyond repair. Many areas were under water for as long as two and a half months, as thunderstorms saturated the region week after week. Moreover, high water levels from a wet fall the previous year had reduced the soil's absorption capacity before the spring and summer storms ever arrived.

Photographs and news stories shared the drama with the world. When the Coralville Dam could no longer contain the Iowa River, which at 23,000 cubic feet per second (cfs) was flowing at 10 times its normal volume, the water crashing over the spillway looked like Niagara Falls. At 10,000 cfs, that excess alone was so powerful that it crushed the causeway below, sending thousands of tons of asphalt hurtling downstream. Nearby Iowa City had to close Dubuque Street, a main thoroughfare from Interstate 80 into the city's central business district, from July until late September, when the Iowa River finally receded far enough to allow street crews to clear the mud that it left behind. Des Moines suffered the loss of a water treatment plant serving a metropolitan area of 250,000 people when the raging Raccoon River crested at 27 feet and overtopped the levee and sandbags that protected it. It took two weeks to restore service. In its downtown riverfront district, Davenport, Iowa, lost the use of a minor league baseball stadium that came to resemble a huge but filthy swimming pool.

Up and down the Mississippi itself, whole small towns were being overwhelmed and at least temporarily displaced. In the end, three communities in the region—Valmeyer, Illinois, and Pattonsburg and Wakenda, Missouri—decided not to rebuild in their existing locations. With help from various agencies, including FEMA and the U.S. Department of Energy's Office of Energy Efficiency and Renewable Energy, both decided to rebuild in completely new, more sustainable, and less vulnerable upland locations (Becker 1994a and b). Dozens of other communities tackled less dramatic but equally important tasks of partial relocation and extensive mitigation of existing floodplain development. The total bill for assistance from the federal government mounted to nearly $6 billion.

THE EMERGENCY IN ARNOLD

Amid such high drama, Arnold, a city of 18,000 people, received relatively little attention. Nonetheless, city officials in Arnold were busy both in learning important lessons about disaster preparedness and in preparing plans for preventing a recurrence of the problems they were confronting. For city administrator Eric Knoll, the experience of the 1993 floods, which the city's civil engineer later determined reached the 166-year level, underlined some important themes pertaining both to short-term preparations for future flood disasters and to long-term themes of disaster avoidance (Knoll 1995).

Arnold was already growing accustomed to floods before 1993, having undergone periodic inundation since the 1970s. Nonetheless, Knoll noted, no one had kept records from the earlier floods about the nature or extent of the emergency measures used to combat flooding during those episodes. "Lack of documentation was a problem when I came here," he said. As an example, he noted, "There was no documentation from the last 20 years on how many sandbags you needed." Given the extensive development, including mobile home parks, that had occurred in the floodplain since the 1950s, sandbagging was increasingly necessary to protect many of the flood-prone residential properties in Arnold.

When the floods began in April, Knoll began to call around in search of sandbags and bought about 6,000 to secure the most vulnerable properties from flood damage. To his dismay, he soon found that this quantity, based on raw guesswork because of the lack of documentation from prior years, was grossly inadequate. The city's initial idea was to dispatch 2,000 bags each to Starling Estates and Arnold Ranch Estates, two hazard-prone subdivisions, while holding 2,000 in reserve. As the floods grew and the waters rose, however, Knoll found himself on the telephone searching desperately for supplies, especially after the U.S. Army Corps of Engineers had depleted its own supplies. The Corps's shortage forced Arnold and other cities to order sandbags from an increasingly scarce open market where, as Knoll recalled, "some companies were charging outrageous prices." Arnold, forced to pay whatever price was necessary, eventually used up to 50,000 sandbags per day in an all-out fight against the floods, ordering about 18,000 of those on the open market. Even the normal rate was 20,000 per day. Before the crisis was over, the city had used approximately 800,000 sandbags to fend off the rivers.

The hardship produced by lacking some clue to the quantities of supplies that were necessary made a lasting impression on Knoll, who recalled "vast shortages and catastrophes on supply lines." The problems were not limited to sandbags, but included such critical items as fuel. On a Sunday afternoon in the midst of the crisis, Knoll recalled, the city ran out of gasoline and had to procure an emergency supply just to keep its trucks and pumps operating.

The issue was not merely the availability of supplies but the ability to bring them into the city at points where they were needed. Arnold learned important lessons about the vulnerability of its internal transportation network, with major streets awash in flood waters. With one exception, all bridges crossing the Meramec River, which separates Arnold from the southerly approaches to St. Louis, were out of operation for months. When the flood overtook the bridges on both Tenbrook Road and Arnold Tenbrook Road, Missouri Route 231 was forced to bear the burden of all traffic from and to the St. Louis area. This created significant traffic delays and congestion from early April until late October, when all three bridges were finally back in operation.

In the midst of this evolving flood crisis, Knoll did what virtually every other mayor, city manager, and planning director (where such existed) did in small towns throughout the flood-ravaged Midwest. At the same time that he was thinking about longer-term issues that had to be addressed in the aftermath of the emergency, he had to attend to the emergency itself. In cities the size of Arnold or even smaller, there is no choice for such leaders other than to manage a multitude of tasks throughout the crisis, coordinating sandbagging efforts, communicating with homeowners, and ensuring the availability of supplies and personnel where they are most needed (Knoll 1995).

In Arnold, Knoll went out into the community a couple of times to survey the floodplains, in large part to determine where flood-fighting efforts were needed the most. Before the floods were over, the city developed between 60 and 70 sandbag sites (SEMA 1995). Knoll also procured flyers from the Army Corps telling people what to expect from the flood and how to react. He distributed a Corps document informing people on how to install sandbags where they were needed. In spite of the "tremendous help" he feels the city received from the Corps, Knoll also noted that many residents tended to want to "beat up the Corps," perhaps because of supply shortages, a reaction that Knoll regarded as unwarranted. But the sheer magnitude of the 1993 floods eroded more than the Army Corps's reputation. It helped to defeat the commitment to life on the riverfront that had previously attracted many residents, who found the event emotionally and physically overwhelming. Many, Knoll noted, "walked away and said they weren't even going to try because they had seen too many floods before."

If there is anything the city has learned very well from the experience, it is the singular importance of well-coordinated municipal operations in an emergency. Arnold's city hall is designed, Knoll said, with a disaster in mind. It is at least three feet above the 100-year floodplain. Because Arnold lies along a seismic fault line, it was built to be earthquake-resistant. The dispatch center is windowless. The police squad room, where city leaders met to plan their response to the disaster, is also windowless. A battery-powered backup generator that powers the dispatch center has reserve

In the midst of this evolving flood crisis, Knoll did what virtually every other mayor, city manager, and planning director (where such existed) did in small towns throughout the flood-ravaged Midwest. At the same time that he was thinking about longer-term issues that had to be addressed in the aftermath of the emergency, he had to attend to the emergency itself. In cities the size of Arnold or even smaller, there is no choice for such leaders other than to manage a multitude of tasks throughout the crisis, coordinating sandbagging efforts, communicating with homeowners, and ensuring the availability of supplies and personnel where they are most needed.

power that can get the system up and running just 30 seconds after a power outage. The system includes a base station and a remote base station. The city's disaster response plan calls for department heads to meet in the squad room when a disaster is imminent in order to set up operations and facilitate communications (Knoll 1995).

Several lessons were clear:

1) In smaller riverfront communities, it is seldom possible to separate short-term flood response duties from the task of developing a long-term plan for rebuilding a more disaster-resistant community. Due to small staffs and the tendency of staff members to wear many hats, the same people are usually involved in both tasks simultaneously. Training should be extensive enough to allow managers to handle the range of tasks that may befall them.

2) Documentation of prior experience in handling flood emergencies helps to establish parameters for better judgments as to the nature and extent of supplies necessary to ride out the emergency and to protect life and property while it lasts. Such documentation should specifically include data on adequate supplies of fuel for city equipment, such as water pumps and vehicles, and sandbags, and a careful correlation of such data with flood heights and the resultant vulnerability of specific parts of the community.

3) Officials should survey the situation in the community early and open the floodgates of communication to affected residents through distribution of flyers and the use of whatever other media are likely to prove effective in informing people about the best way to handle the crisis.

Typical of subdivision housing established in the 1960s, the area in which this house was built was flat and had public water, was served by a sewage lagoon, and lacked city or county zoning because it predated the incorporation of the city.

Eric Knoll, City of Arnold

PRELUDE TO A DISASTER

As Arnold's hazard mitigation grant application following the 1993 floods noted, a natural disaster requires not only a natural hazard, such as a flood, but a built environment in the path of the hazard in order to create the potential for property damage and loss of life (Arnold 1993). With that in mind, it is useful to examine the city's history to see how a pattern of vulnerability was created over time.

Prior to World War II, flooding along the Meramec River would have created minimal problems in what is now Arnold. The area was primarily agricultural, predominantly populated by farmers of German ethnic origin. Only after the war did this change. Throughout the 1950s, the demand for suburban housing drove growth outward from St. Louis, much like the pattern in most other metropolitan areas at the time. This part of Jefferson County was still unincorporated, but new public institutions developed in response to the growth that was occurring. Most significantly, the formation in 1958 of Public Water District No. 1 facilitated further growth. New subdivisions were developed in locations along the southern and western banks of the bend in the Meramec River just a couple of miles above its confluence with the

Mississippi River. New mobile home parks were also located in this area, and population in the floodplain grew accordingly. As the city's flood-plain management plan notes, "Club houses, trailer parks, and single-family residential homes were developed on the level and aesthetically rich ground adjoining the Meramec River."

Figure 8-1. History of Flooding in Arnold, Missouri

YEAR	FLOOD STAGE	FREQUENCY	TYPE
1973	39.8 ft.	29-year	Backwater
1979	38.9 ft.	24-year	Headwater
1982	43.9 ft.	100-year	Headwater
1983	39.8 ft.	29-year	Headwater
1986	36.6 ft.	14-year	Backwater
1993 (August)	45.3 ft.	166-year	Backwater
1993 (September)	38.5 ft.	22-year	Headwater
1994	41.8 ft.	50-year	
1995	41.0 ft.		

Source: Hazard Mitigation Project Application, City of Arnold, Missouri, December 1993.

By 1971, voters approved the incorporation of the city of Arnold, Missouri. By then, however, the accumulation of floodplain development, not only in Arnold but upriver along the Mississippi toward St. Louis, began to affect the city's vulnerability to flooding. In 1973, a 30-year flood (see Figure 8-1) along the Meramec River left parts of the city under water for 77 days. In 1979, a 10-year flood left behind a $1.5 million trail of damage when it receded. And in 1982, the city experienced a 100-year flood, this time a backwater flood from an overflow on the Mississippi. Throughout this time, the U.S. Army Corps of Engineers was trying to cope with regional flood threats by adding levees, none of which, however, were built in Arnold.

Because of watershedwide draining of wetlands, suburbanization, forest clearance, and the addition of flood control structures, Arnold became a victim not only of its own floodplain development, but of the increased speed and flow of the Meramec River. This increased speed and flow was due to the steady reduction of pervious surface upriver caused by development throughout the watershed and, more particularly, in St. Louis and its nearby suburbs. This growth throughout the metropolitan area steadily channeled increasing volumes of stormwater runoff down increasingly narrow river channels, outpacing the Corps's efforts to compensate with structural barriers to flooding. There is, however, no requirement in Jefferson County's development procedures for incorporating plans for stormwater management. Arnold could not control all the factors that might increase its vulnerability to flooding. The result was that the city's flood-control infrastructure became overburdened. The culverts for Pomme and Muddy creeks under Interstate 55 have become clogged, and streambanks have

Because of watershedwide draining of wetlands, suburbanization, forest clearance, and the addition of flood control structures, Arnold became a victim not only of its own floodplain development, but of the increased speed and flow of the Meramec River. This increased speed and flow was due to the steady reduction of pervious surface upriver caused by development throughout the watershed and, more particularly, in St. Louis and its nearby suburbs.

The city took stock of its situation by completing an inventory of its built environment within the mapped floodplain, which included both rivers and those portions of the Pomme, Muddy, and Little Muddy creeks affected by backwater flooding. This inventory identified 650 structures, with the oldest scattered throughout the floodway while newer ones tended to be concentrated near its fringe. Using this information, the city undertook an active effort to acquire and demolish such properties, creating 286 acres of open space for parks.

continued to erode due to increased water velocity, among other ongoing problems.

This growing vulnerability did not escape the notice of local officials. Driven by the need to cope with these problems, Arnold in 1980 joined the regular phase of the National Flood Insurance Program (NFIP) and enacted a floodplain management ordinance, making flood insurance available to local residents. In fairness to the city, it should be noted that most of the residential development then existing in the floodplain predated Arnold's incorporation as a city and, thus, predated the enactment of any of its municipal planning, zoning, and floodplain management regulations. The city was in the position of resolving pre-existing problems.

That same year, the city took stock of its situation by completing an inventory of its built environment within the mapped floodplain, which included both rivers and those portions of the Pomme, Muddy, and Little Muddy creeks affected by backwater flooding. This inventory identified 650 structures, with the oldest scattered throughout the floodway while newer ones tended to be concentrated near its fringe. This information was important because the floodway's hydrological purpose (see the definition of floodway in Appendix B) is to serve as the main channel for moving floodwater downstream, and any impediments serve to force such waters higher, effectively raising the base flood elevation. Using this information, the city undertook an active effort to acquire and demolish such properties, creating 286 acres of open space for parks. (See Figure 8-2.) In 1980, the city was one of six communities chosen to participate in a pilot project for FEMA's now defunct Section 1362 acquisition program. In that and two other buyouts under this program in 1983 and 1985, the city acquired 94 structures and 185 parcels of land (including the removal of 30 mobile home pads) to be preserved for open space in perpetuity (Arnold 1991). In addition, the city's 1991 floodplain management plan proposed the use of $30,000 for development of a comprehensive greenway plan and $90,000 over five years to acquire floodplain properties through a local use tax, which was the city's portion of a state sales tax on out-of-state sales. That tax, however, was subsequently rescinded as a result of litigation, so the city has never been able to use those funds for this purpose.

There can be little doubt that this proactive planning, although far from completing the job, significantly reduced the actual damage that occurred when the massive floods of 1993 arrived, despite continuing development in the interim. While the 1991 floodplain management plan showed 908 residential structures within the city's six floodplains (Mississippi, Meramec, and four local creeks), only 22 remained within the floodway.

There can be little doubt that this proactive planning, although far from completing the job, significantly reduced the actual damage that occurred when the massive floods of 1993 arrived, despite continuing development in the interim. While the 1991 floodplain management plan showed 908 residential structures within the city's six floodplains (Mississippi, Meramec, and four local creeks), only 22 remained within the floodway. Moreover, according to Eric Knoll, no construction occurred within the 100-year floodplain. Rather, the higher number indicates the city's use of 420 feet mean sea level as its yardstick, picking up additional properties in the inventory above the 417-foot level used previously. Newly built areas, according to Knoll, were strictly at the outer rim of the floodplain (Knoll 1996).

Lessons:

1) It is not uncommon, especially in newly developing areas of the metropolitan fringe, for cities to be faced with problems that pre-existed any zoning or floodplain management regulations, or with problems connected to development that occurred under measures less strict than those now in place. As a result, it may be impossible to find enough money for elevation, acquisition, demolition, or floodproofing of all structures that need attention, even within the minimum standards of current regulations. The role of planning is to prioritize such spending and target those properties that are most vulnerable and/or most likely to cause additional damage in a major flood.

Figure 8-2. Proposed Section 404 and Community Development Block Grant (CDBG) Acquisitions, Arnold, Missouri
(Including Section 12362 Properties in 1993 Hazard Mitigation Project Application)

TYPE OF STRUCTURE	NUMBER OF UNITS/PADS
Riverside Mobile Home Park (pads)	57
Portion of Starling Community Mobile Home Park (pads)	34
Portion of Ozark Mobile Home Park (pads)	19
Portion of Abram's Mobile Home Park (pads)	3
Purchase of mobile homes	23
Purchase of duplex structures	1
Purchase of single-family structures	89
Purchase of commercial structures	2
Total of acquisitions proposed	**222**

2) Merely acquiring flood-damaged properties after a disaster is not enough to preclude a recurrence of the same problem. Steps must also be taken to ensure that vulnerable riverfront land is no longer available for development. Arnold's planned greenway provides one of the best guarantees along these lines, but a variety of planning tools is actually available, including easements, cluster zoning and subdivision design, and limitations on the extension of needed infrastructure. The point is to take the most vulnerable riverfront land out of consideration for future development.

3) Communities in downstream locations, especially at the confluence of major rivers, cannot control much of the development within the watershed that affects their vulnerability to flooding. Regional and intergovernmental agreements concerning restrictions on floodplain development within a given watershed are clearly one option for addressing this problem but are not always easy to achieve. In the end, such a community may have to set its own example through aggressive acquisition and mitigation and effective floodplain development regulations.

1993 FLOODS: IMPACT AND AFTERMATH

As was the case elsewhere in the Midwest, a sizeable portion of Arnold's floodplain property was affected by the 1993 floods. No fewer than 528 households applied for disaster assistance, and these received more than $2 million in federal aid from the disaster housing assistance program, individual and family grants, and low-interest Small Business Administration loans. High waters affected 252 Arnold residences, three commercial sites, and one industrial site. Hundreds of other residents suffered flood-related displacement and inconveniences and loss of business. The combined damage to real and personal property totaled about $4 million (Arnold 1993). As noted earlier, traffic was dislocated for months, and sanitary sewer systems were overwhelmed, causing sewer backups into area basements.

Arnold, however, is a case where even a relatively recent political tradition of seriously attacking floodplain problems proved to be a significant asset in the aftermath of the disaster. For one thing, Arnold's earlier history

High waters affected 252 Arnold residences, three commercial sites, and one industrial site. Hundreds of other residents suffered flood-related displacement and inconveniences and loss of business. The combined damage to real and personal property totaled about $4 million.

Eric Knoll, City of Arnold

This residence, well over a mile from the Meramec River near Pomme Creek, is located in the upper reaches where the backwater from the flooding of the Meramec reaches.

of acquiring properties and preserving open space in its floodplains lent considerable credibility to its grant applications for federal assistance to do more in this vein. Certainly, in the aftermath of the 1993 floods, the federal government opened its coffers to make money available for this purpose in a way that it had never done before. But the mere availability of money has never guaranteed its effective use at the local level in the absence of meaningful planning. In Arnold, the city's 1991 floodplain management plan, drafted by its floodplain management committee after eight months of study and adopted by the city council in November 1991, projected a continuation and strengthening of the local program before anyone knew what sort of disaster would materialize. It is worth summarizing the committee's recommendations before reviewing the city's post-disaster mitigation projects:

- *Greenway.* The city's community development department was given six months to prepare a land-use plan for a designated greenway along the west banks of the Mississippi and Meramec rivers. It was also instructed to pursue state and federal funds to supplement a yearly $30,000 allotment to acquire vacant and unoccupied land, greenway access easements, and setback easements along both rivers.

- *Stream maintenance.* The city attorney and public works department were to work on obtaining right-of-way and developing inspection and clearance plans to clear vegetation and debris from stormwater channels, and to identify and replace undersized culverts.

- *Muddy Creek improvement.* More than 100 of the floodplain residential properties in Arnold were along the heavily developed Muddy Creek floodplain. The city engineer was to study solutions to this problem, including a stormwater detention facility.

- *Acquisition.* The report noted that 27 homes remained in the Meramec River floodway and were thus subject to major damage. While no current funds were available for their acquisition, the committee noted that such funds often become available after a flood. The building commissioner was instructed to red-tag damaged or destroyed buildings after a disaster and not allow their reconstruction until he had met with the owners to explain the regulations for doing so. It was clear in the plan that the city's ideal solution was to acquire all these properties for incorporation into its proposed greenway.

- *Protection assistance.* With 908 occupied floodplain properties and only 244 flood insurance policies in effect, the city needed to undertake a serious public education campaign.

- *Flood warning.* The National Weather Service had the capability of warning residents about oncoming flooding along the Mississippi and Meramec rivers, but not for local creeks subject to the effects of localized thunderstorms. The city's emergency manager was to seek ways to accomplish this.

- *Flood preparedness.* The emergency manager was also to work on a preparedness plan that would define operational procedures in future floods.

- *Critical facilities.* This section focused on increasing the flood resistance or floodproofing of local bridges, roads, interceptor sanitary sewer systems, and parks.

- *Floodplain regulations.* The committee report recommended amendments to local codes to prohibit new buildings in the floodway, to require the lowest floor elevation to be at least two feet above the 100-year flood level, and to reflect existing floodplain boundaries as a floodplain zoning classification. More important as an overarching policy was the statement that Arnold should not be satisfied with minimum national standards of NFIP but should "reinforce the need to keep the greenway areas open and protect new buildings from becoming bridge obstructions and other things that can make floods go higher than predicted."

  The new regulations took effect on April 20, 1995. They use an exclusionary zoning technique in which the only permitted uses primarily consist of open space uses such as farming, forestry, public parks, golf courses, and fishing. Conditional uses include sewage treatment facilities, commercial and industrial docks, rifle ranges, community centers, certain telecommunications devices, and single-family dwellings. But the single-family dwellings, among other requirements, have a two-acre minimum lot size, must be elevated with a basement at least three feet above the 100-year flood level, and must have all utility connections floodproofed, in addition to having a floodproofed roadway at or above the 100-year flood elevation. In short, they will have to "jump through a number of hoops," says Knoll, before being permitted.

- *Watershed management.* The community development department was to work with the federal Natural Resources Conservation Service, the local conservation district, and the county to develop a watershed management plan for two creeks and those parts of the Meramec watershed within the county, reviewing farm drainage practices, development regulations at all levels, and plans for watershed development. In effect, the city was recognizing the need to reach beyond the city limits for help in solving a problem it could not solve alone (Arnold 1991).

Although it sustained major damage during the 1993 floods and seems to have been ill prepared operationally for the scope of the disaster, the city clearly had given serious thought to the problem and was thus prepared to take steps to ensure that such a disaster did not repeat itself. Already, there were seeds of a significant plan for the future in the form of the Meramec and Mississippi greenway, accompanied by some thought about the means to implement it. The 1993 floods provided an opportunity to take advantage of such preparation by selling federal officials on the value of funding an aggressive program of acquisition. Moreover, by January 1994, the city had also developed a new flood emergency plan outlining the responsibilities of all major city officials and departments and identifying the city's most vulnerable locations and properties (Arnold 1994).

By December 1993, the city had submitted federal grant applications both for Section 1362 acquisition funds and for Hazard Mitigation Grant Program (HMGP) funds from the Federal Emergency Management Agency (FEMA) that it could combine with Community Development Block Grant (CDBG) money from the U.S. Department of Housing and Urban Development (HUD) in an extensive effort to remedy the problem. The combined acquisition program totaled nearly $3.5 million for buying structures located in

> More important as an overarching policy was the statement that Arnold should not be satisfied with minimum national standards of NFIP but should "reinforce the need to keep the greenway areas open and protect new buildings from becoming bridge obstructions and other things that can make floods go higher than predicted."

the floodplain and removing or demolishing them. The effort included the complete acquisition of one mobile home park and parts of three others as well as 89 single-family residences, one duplex, and two commercial structures, for a total of 228 structures targeted for acquisition. The city was seizing the opportunity to implement the agenda it had prepared two years before the big flood arrived.

The city's application also sought money for various infrastructure repairs and the construction of small levees protecting seven subdivisions and one mobile home park. Many of these requests dovetailed neatly with the existing agenda of the 1991 floodplain management plan, such as a proposal "to acquire a former sanitary sewage lagoon and convert it into a stormwater detention facility to reduce the amount of water that flash floods residences." Other money was to be used to elevate bridges, improve culverts, and replace low-lying roadways with new ones atop the planned levees to improve access during future floods (Arnold 1993). The city has been able to use $1.9 million in flood recovery grant money from the federal Economic Development Administration and $500,000 in CDBG funds for one road construction project that, because of unexpectedly poor soils, doubled in cost to $3.2 million from the original estimates. The remainder has come from city funds, which also financed the acquisition of the sanitary facilities.

> The city was seizing the opportunity to implement the agenda it had prepared two years before the big flood arrived.

Lessons:

1) Although no community would want a major disaster to follow so closely the preparation of a floodplain management plan or any other plan for mitigation of natural hazards, the value of thoroughness in the development of such a plan clearly paid off for Arnold. The aftermath of a disaster is no time to begin taking stock of the community's vulnerability to natural hazards, and having a wish list in place allows city officials to move expeditiously to identify significant opportunities to reduce vulnerability to future disasters.

2) Know (or find out as quickly as possible) what funds are available to pursue mitigation in the aftermath of a disaster. This inventory should be part of the city's pre-disaster planning.

3) Once a disaster has occurred, don't be bashful about seizing the moment. The moment may not come again for a long time. Implement the pre-existing wish list to the fullest, using all the help that is available for the purpose.

PROOF IN THE PUDDING

As Figure 8-1 above shows, Arnold suffered two smaller floods in the two years immediately following the big disaster of 1993. In the interim, however, it used its federal, state, and local funds to expedite the buyouts of the 228 mobile home pads and manufactured and stick-built residences targeted for acquisition in its hazard mitigation grant applications.

> Missouri's State Emergency Management Agency (SEMA) also deserves some credit for backing a successful buyout program following the 1993 floods, for there were other areas in the state—St. Charles County being a notable example—where similar massive problems of floodplain development, often involving a substantial number of mobile home parks and manufactured housing, required an aggressive buyout program as a solution.

Missouri's State Emergency Management Agency (SEMA) also deserves some credit for backing a successful buyout program following the 1993 floods, for there were other areas in the state—St. Charles County being a notable example—where similar massive problems of floodplain development, often involving a substantial number of mobile home parks and manufactured housing, required an aggressive buyout program as a solution. Overall, the Missouri program used $30 million in FEMA HMGP funds, $28 million in FEMA Public Assistance funds for demolition purposes, and $42 million in CDBG funds through HUD. By July 1995, Missouri led FEMA Region VII with 2,958 properties purchased (SEMA 1995). Arnold had contributed its own fair share of this total.

One direct result was that, in 1995, Arnold did not have to fight the river nearly so hard. There were only seven sandbag sites, in part because the need for many others had been obviated. Only 26 households applied for a modest $40,000 in disaster assistance, and many structures formerly in harm's way were no longer sitting in the floodplain (SEMA 1995).

While it is always tempting to make comparisons between the two floods, Eric Knoll cautions that it is difficult to make them reasonably. The 1995 flood reached only 41 feet on the river gauge, he notes, while the 1993 flood reached 45.3 feet, well above the 100-year level of 43.79 feet. What can be said is that Arnold was devastated in 1993, and many of the structures affected were not rebuilt in 1994. The buyouts continued through 1995 and into 1996. The city applied for more funds after the 1995 flood but did not get them. However, it did receive an additional $600,000 from SEMA as an extension of its existing grant and, at the end of February 1996, was still working to complete 34 more buyouts, among which 32 property owners had accepted offers. As the city had money left that would cover only eight or nine, it worked its way down the list on the basis of elevation and location in the floodplain.

In the meantime, Arnold city officials had worked with the state to solve the longstanding problems of internal traffic flow. The state was building a replacement bridge along Arnold Tenbrook Road to raise the pavement above the 100-year flood level and was elevating the bridge on Missouri Route 231 another eight feet, taking both out of the 100-year floodplain. Access to and through the city in future floods would be considerably less tenuous (Knoll 1996).

OBSERVATIONS AND RECOMMENDATIONS

- Pre-event planning for post-disaster recovery and reconstruction is just as important with floods as with any other natural disaster. Most communities lack the necessary funds to acquire all the flood-prone properties within their jurisdiction, or even to help private property owners mitigate such damage through measures such as elevation. But establishing and maintaining an inventory of vulnerable structures and parcels and developing a system of priorities for them will allow the community to move effectively and efficiently when funds do become available in the aftermath of a major disaster.

- With the arguable exception of volcanoes, floods provide the most easily and thoroughly mapped contours of any natural hazard. There is thus almost no reason not to establish the inventory and priorities mentioned above.

- NFIP, which requires participating communities to enact and enforce a floodplain management ordinance, does not specifically require them to develop a plan. (The Community Rating Service (CRS), however, does have a point category that allows communities to earn CRS credits toward insurance premium reductions for preparing a floodplain management plan.) Arnold, however, did not settle for doing the bare minimum required. An ambitious floodplain management plan with a visionary land-use component can become the vehicle for effective post-disaster action to reshape development patterns to create a safer community. If the plan also envisions infrastructure improvements to reduce vulnerability and maintain traffic access during a flood emergency, the community will be even better off.

- In larger cities, it may be possible to separate emergency management functions from those involving planning for long-term recovery and

Chapter 9

Tornado Case Study: Plainfield, Illinois

JIM SCHWAB, AICP

Jim Schwab is a senior research associate with the American Planning Association. He is the principal author of this report, the editor of Zoning News, *and the author of Planning Advisory Service Report No. 482,* Planning and Zoning for Concentrated Animal Feeding Operations *(December 1998).*

Tornadoes are the most capricious of natural disasters. While the gathering storm clouds and a well-defined set of meteorological conditions allow weather officials to issue some warning before most funnel clouds touch down, there is absolutely no certainty about where that descent may occur. There is no state in the Union that has not seen a tornado nor any time of year when they cannot occur, given the right weather conditions.

For land-use planners, they are the ultimate conundrum in hazard mitigation because they can strike anywhere. All that is required is a clash between warm and cold air fronts, leading to a storm front with a violent pattern of swirling winds that produce the classic funnel cloud threat. About the only thing that can be said with high probability—but no absolute certainty—is that they are statistically far less likely to touch down in a dense central city because the urban heat island effect tends to deter funnel cloud formation. Nonetheless, in 1981 a tornado struck and severely damaged an urban residential neighborhood in the center of Minneapolis. There is just no telling.

Why, then, offer any kind of case study of reconstruction following a tornado? There is, of course, always the issue of reconstruction itself, even in the absence of any clear prescription for hazard mitigation. Also, however, the case of Plainfield, Illinois, highlights in a small but significant way the opportunity for planners to move proactively after a tornado to seize identifiable opportunities to mitigate future hazards that may or may not be related to tornadoes. What follows is a success story. Most of the narrative pertaining to the disaster itself is drawn from *Winds of Fury*, a booklet produced by *The Herald-News*, an area newspaper based in Joliet, Illinois (*Herald-News* 1990). Details of the aftermath are derived from both an interview with Plainfield village planner Peter Waldock and the village's comprehensive plan (Plainfield 1995).

THE WILL COUNTY, ILLINOIS, TORNADO

The whole event defied conventional expectations. In the Midwest, the tornado season lasts until early summer. The Will County tornado struck on August 28, 1990. Late-season tornadoes are usually weak; this one ranked among the most powerful recorded in Illinois history. Packing winds of 300 miles per hour, the tornado rated F-5 on the Fujita scale of 0 to 5 that is used to measure tornado severity. (See Figure 7-16 in Chapter 7 for a description of the Fujita scale.) Less than 2 percent of all tornadoes reach F-4 or above (Duncan 1992). Storm systems carrying tornado threats generally move in a northeasterly direction, driving from the southwest. The Will County tornado turned the dial by 90 degrees, moving from the northwest in a southeasterly direction. (See Figure 9-1.)

Figure 9-1. Approximate Track of Tornado and Areas of Major Damage in Will County, Illinois

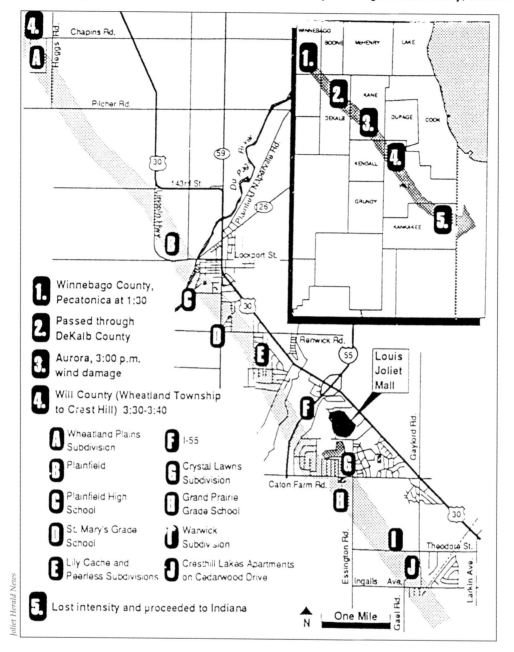

Weather officials, watching conventional tornado patterns, usually have some time in which to warn the affected populace of an oncoming or even a likely funnel cloud before it touches down. But at a crucial point, as the National Weather Service tracked the storm's progress, a second storm cell that merged with the first created microbursts, strong downdraft winds that reach the ground from the sky. The phenomenon was untrackable on radar, thus obscuring the forthcoming danger and preventing any adequate warnings to the victims in its path. The wind damage at that point of merger damaged three hangars and nearly three dozen small aircraft at the Aurora Municipal Airport. It was accompanied by hail.

The tornado, when it did materialize, was not just a single funnel cloud, but four, which had tried unsuccessfully to form earlier. These viciously spinning twisters formed after the storm cell crossed into Will County and swept down from a thunderhead cloud in a dark green sky. One official described them as the equivalent of a Norelco razor shaving the landscape. It was an awesome sight for those who saw it and managed to survive.

Many did not. The statistics alone provide some clue to the storm's impact on Plainfield and nearby communities, including parts of Joliet, which lies just five miles to the southeast. Ultimately, the tornado killed 29 people, injured more than 350, and inflicted in excess of $140 million in property damage.

Among those caught by surprise were a number of teachers and students at Plainfield High School. When the tornado struck at around 3:30 P.M., teachers were inside preparing for school, which was just a week away, and student athletes had been practicing football and volleyball on outdoor fields. No one suspected what was coming.

In a matter of minutes, the building was a shambles, three people died in the rubble, and nearly every car in the parking lot was destroyed, many overturned and lying in a pile of metal debris. The initial damage occurred as the tornado tore through the Wheatland Plains subdivision two miles north of the village. It then plowed into the high school, a Catholic grade school, and a series of subdivisions in both Plainfield and Joliet. The tornado destroyed dozens of homes in the various subdivisions. Finally, in the suburb of Crest Hill southeast of Joliet, the buzzsaw winds almost completely severed the third floor from the Cresthill Lakes apartments. Out of 371 units, the winds demolished 187, just over half.

In the end, the entire path of destruction was 700 feet wide and more than seven miles long. Illinois Governor James R. Thompson quickly requested a presidential disaster declaration and got it. Volunteers poured into the area by the next day, and the process of locating survivors, removing debris, and restoring shattered lives was underway. For most residents, it was a matter of sorting out their remaining belongings, collecting whatever insurance and federal aid was available, and rebuilding their homes. Donations poured in for those purposes, too, as when the Kodak Corporation supplied 700 cameras to allow victims to document their losses. Even the Soviet government sent help, seeking to repay Americans for the aid they had supplied to Armenian earthquake victims in 1988.

For some, in Plainfield's Lily Cache subdivision, it was the second tornado in recent memory. Another had hit that part of the village in 1984. A few people there found it all too much and sold their homes after rebuilding, as others had done after the first disaster. Although Will County ranks fourth in the state in tornado damage, there was no good statistical reason for Lily Cache to be so unfortunate. Just as a 100-year flood can strike two years in a row because the designation merely represents a 1 percent chance in any given year, so a tornado can—but will not necessarily—strike any particular location twice or more within a period of a few years, then perhaps not again for hundreds. It was dumb luck, but the despair of some Lily Cache residents is testimony to the persuasive power of experience over mere statistical probabilities. Tornado alleys exist in the mind as well as on the weather maps.

CLEARING THE FLOODWAY

Tornadoes have no special affinity for floodplains. They do show a documented preference for plains in general, as compared to hills and mountains, simply because the flat geography of the Midwest and much of the South facilitates the development of the giant storm patterns that arise out of the clash of continental-size warm and cold air fronts. Thus, it is no accident that states like Oklahoma, Kansas, and Iowa experience a disproportionate share of the nation's tornadoes. But the visitation of a tornado

In the end, the entire path of destruction was 700 feet wide and more than seven miles long. Illinois Governor James R. Thompson quickly requested a presidential disaster declaration and got it. Volunteers poured into the area by the next day, and the process of locating survivors, removing debris, and restoring shattered lives was underway. For most residents, it was a matter of sorting out their remaining belongings, collecting whatever insurance and federal aid was available, and rebuilding their homes.

After the 1990 tornado swept through Plainfield, the village acquired most of a severly damaged residential area along the DuPage River for a public park.

upon a floodplain in the midst of such geography is largely happenstance. Most of the Will County tornado's damage occurred outside the floodplains within the county, which, with the exception of the Des Plaines River, are relatively small. While an accompanying thunderstorm can aggravate wind damage with flash flooding, that was not the case in this instance. Virtually all the damage was wind-related.

But flood hazard mitigation is a serious planning issue in Will County, as it is throughout Illinois. In Plainfield, the main source of concern is the normally small DuPage River, and secondarily its tributary Lily Cache Creek, both of which flow in a south-southwesterly direction into the Des Plaines River; the latter, which cuts through downtown Joliet, empties into the Illinois River, a major tributary of the Mississippi. Plainfield also has two smaller creeks and two natural drains.

Until recently, Plainfield was a small village in the midst of northern Illinois farmland. It took its name from that landscape, whose elevation varies by only 87 feet within the municipal boundaries. In the last decade, as suburban growth spreading out from Chicago has nearly reached Joliet, some 50 miles from Chicago's Loop, homeowners from more expensive areas have eyed property in relatively cheaper Plainfield as well as in other outlying communities. Plainfield is growing fast and, in 1995, found the need to hire a second planner, according to Peter J. Waldock, then the town's chief planner. A village with fewer than 2,000 residents in 1950 had grown to 3,767 in the 1980 census and 4,557 in 1990, with projections exceeding 14,000 in 2010 (Plainfield 1995).

Plainfield has been discovered. That fact has lent a new urgency to Plainfield's floodplain management policies, which are discussed below. But it also serves as a backdrop to a part of the village's response to the opportunities for redirecting development in the aftermath of the 1990 tornado, for among the hundreds of homes destroyed were a few that sat on the banks of the DuPage River, inside the floodway.

Using $180,500 of state flood mitigation grant money it obtained from the Illinois Department of Transportation's Division of Water Resources, the village negotiated over time to acquire 10 of 11 homes in the floodway that had been damaged to an extent exceeding 50 percent of their market value, making them ineligible for reconstruction under Illinois law at the time. Those offers were based on the predamage market value (Roths 1996). One owner, as of September 1996, had refused all offers, apparently believing they were inadequate, but her rental property was denied a certificate of occupancy throughout that time, and she was not allowed to rebuild. Her lot became landlocked without road access (Waldock 1996).

In the fall of 1996, the owner was challenging the denial in court (Waldock 1996). Spurred by the requests of homeowners in Northbrook, a northern Chicago suburb, with structures along some minor floodways, the Illinois Department of Natural Resources had changed its Part 708 rules pertaining to floodplain regulations to allow the rebuilding of structures damaged by any means, but the new rules specified that the building footprint could not change, nor could there be any change in building size or location, such as turning the building (Roths 1996). Plainfield retained its more restrictive regulations. Waldock noted, however, that had the property been rebuilt, "it would have been washed away in 1996." He indicated that the village was continuing to improve its offers, but he was "not optimistic" that the village would ever be able to close on that acquisition. In the meantime, the village was grading and improving the now vacant lots with the long-term goal of reselling the land to the Plainfield Township Park District for passive recreation, most likely including such minimal features as picnic tables and grills (Waldock 1996).

Later experience has confirmed the wisdom of Plainfield's floodplain management efforts. The village exceeds National Food Insurance Program (NFIP) requirements by requiring two feet of freeboard above 100-year flood levels in its regulations. In the summer of 1996, a flood hit the entire southwest suburban region of the Chicago metropolitan area, and Plainfield was not spared. The flood along the DuPage River reached two feet above the 100-year level, into the same flood mitigation area that had concerned the village after the tornado. The acquired properties would surely have flooded, according to Waldock, but they are gone.

Four houses, all elevated, still sit there. None sustained any damage, although crawl spaces were flooded. On one house, which was earth-bermed, the two-foot freeboard was entirely used up before the waters receded. On the others, which used crawl spaces, the waters reached up four, six, and eight inches. The entire elevation scheme implemented earlier had been "very successful," in Waldock's view. "This flood experience has probably strengthened the village's resolve in enforcement of floodplain standards because we saw the base flood elevation exceeded," Waldock noted.

Citywide, 250 dwelling units "received some form of inundation," but "no known buildings that sustained FEMA's definition of substantial damage of 50 percent or greater." Of those 250, according to Waldock, "probably 100" units had more than "just a couple of inches of living space inundation," with the most severe damage approaching $60,000, still under the state threshold barring replacement. That house, Waldock noted, "complied with 1979 regulations when it was built," but the 100-year flood elevation subsequently was raised by four feet. Those circumstances serve to illustrate the effects of upper watershed development that can increase runoff and flood heights over time, which, in turn, point to the need for exceeding minimum NFIP standards. Built to current standards, Waldock said, the house in question would have sustained no damage. This contrast serves to illustrate a dilemma faced in many towns like Plainfield that have a mixture of old and new structures, some dating much earlier than NFIP. Plainfield can take steps now to keep its rapidly arriving new development out of harm's way. Its primary remedy for existing structures is to encourage floodproofing, and FEMA's Flood Mitigation Assistance Program can help communities address this problem. What Plainfield has demonstrated is a willingness to act when the opportunity arises.

One unfortunate result of the 1996 flooding is that the largest affected building was the village hall itself. More than 5,000 of its 10,000 square feet were inundated. The police department was forced out of the sewage-flooded basement, "never to return," said Waldock. The planning and building department was temporarily relocated to a shopping center by late summer after losing its original quarters, and it lost many of its records pertaining to the 1990 tornado. This flooding was entirely due to overflow from the West Norman Drain, which was designed to relieve sewage

Citywide, 250 dwelling units "received some form of inundation," but "no known buildings that sustained FEMA's definition of substantial damage of 50 percent or greater." Of those 250, according to Waldock, "probably 100" units had more than "just a couple of inches of living space inundation," with the most severe damage approaching $60,000, still under the state threshold barring replacement. That house, Waldock noted, "complied with 1979 regulations when it was built," but the 100-year flood elevation subsequently was raised by four feet. Those circumstances serve to illustrate the effects of upper watershed development that can increase runoff and flood heights over time, which, in turn, point to the need for exceeding minimum NFIP standards. Built to current standards, Waldock said, the house in question would have sustained no damage.

overflow. The village is now erecting a new building next to the old one that will be out of the floodway and elevated. According to Waldock, a deepened culvert will lower the 100-year flood elevation by four feet and mitigate much of the problem. Nonetheless, the adjustments underscore the need to be at least as careful, if not more so, about the location and protection of public buildings as the municipality is about other structures.

RECOMMENDATIONS AND OBSERVATIONS

- Communities should not be deterred from pursuing opportunities to mitigate natural hazards even when the damage was caused by a different natural hazard, such as removing or elevating or floodproofing flood-prone structures damaged by a tornado. Such structures, sooner or later, will be damaged again if they are allowed to remain and if mitigation measures, such as floodproofing or elevation, are not implemented. Regardless of the source of damage, damaged areas should always be checked against local floodplain maps in order to comply with the substantial damage provisions of NFIP.

- There are, for the most part, no effective ways to protect a community from wind damage resulting from the direct strike of a tornado as powerful as the one that struck Will County. That said, enforcement of wind-related aspects of building code standards can be effective for many catastrophic types of windstorms, including relatively low-powered tornadoes. These would essentially be the same standards that have been applied effectively in hurricane hazard zones. However, most building technologies that would be adequate to cope with an F-5 tornado are rather expensive relative to the benefits gained and can reasonably be applied only to facilities that need a high level of security, such as power plants and emergency operations centers. A community that faces the high risk of a tornado should, in any event, have an effective disaster recovery plan in place to respond to the emergency humanely and efficiently. This plan should address post-disaster hazard mitigation opportunities.

- Communities can and should make efforts to secure important and vital records in ways that protect them both from serious storm damage and from flooding. This may pose a challenge when an older public building is in a floodplain, but even minimizing the risk of damage is better than ignoring it. Among those possibilities are moving such records to safer quarters, elevating them to higher floors above probable flood elevations, and floodproofing the building. Most tornado damage to vital records can also be averted by storing them in secure, internal closets and storage rooms away from potential wind damage.

- With or without hazard mitigation opportunities like those available to Plainfield, communities experiencing widespread tornado damage should be prepared beforehand with a comprehensive plan vision of how they would like to rebuild—or not— if disaster strikes. Refinements can certainly be adopted in the post-disaster period once it is clear what needs to be rebuilt and where. But the substantial destruction wrought by powerful tornadoes provides communities with opportunities to reshape development by building more sustainably and by moving out of harm's way, creating new energy and transportation efficiencies, and even, as in the case of Arkadelphia, Arkansas (Woodward-Clyde Associates 1997a), considering new urban design opportunities that may enhance the community's attractiveness and long-term economic development potential.

Communities can and should make efforts to secure important and vital records in ways that protect them both from serious storm damage and from flooding. This may pose a challenge when an older public building is in a floodplain, but even minimizing the risk of damage is better than ignoring it.

Chapter 10

Hurricane Case Study: Opal in the Florida Panhandle

RICHARD A. SMITH AND
ROBERT E. DEYLE

Richard A. Smith is a professor of urban and regional planning at Florida State University, with primary interests in urban growth dynamics, post-storm recovery, and fair housing.

Robert E. Deyle is an associate professor of urban and regional planning at Florida State University whose research focuses on applications of planning to mitigate the impacts of natural hazards.

This case study was developed under the auspices of the Florida Sea Grant College Program, with support from the National Oceanic and Atmospheric Administration, Office of Sea Grant, U.S. Department of Commerce, Grant No. R/C-P-21B. The authors gratefully acknowledge the contributions of their colleague, Jay Baker of the Department of Geography, Florida State University, for his help in this study, as well as the invaluable contributions of three graduate students who participated in the research effort, conducted many of the interviews, and drafted the initial project report. They are Alexander Gallagher, Chris Killingsworth, and Greg Williamson.

Hurricane Opal hit the Florida Panhandle on October 4, 1995, with sustained winds of 115 mph and storm surge between 7 and 20 feet. With features of both a Category 3 and Category 4 storm, Opal was the strongest storm to hit the Florida coast since Hurricane Andrew came ashore in the Miami area in 1992. Although less powerful than Andrew, Opal is perhaps more illuminating as a case study because the number of jurisdictions experiencing the storm was greater. The principal damage from Andrew was limited to Dade County, with lesser damage to three other counties, whereas Opal significantly affected six counties in the Florida Panhandle. Furthermore, while Andrew resulted in the most costly destruction of any natural disaster in the U.S. to date, much of this damage was created by high-level winds in inland areas. In contrast, Opal was a more typical hurricane, principally affecting coastal communities and causing damage from both wind and storm surge. Most of the communities affected by Opal had also experienced other recent storms, thereby providing a context in which communities were sensitive to storm-related issues: Hurricane Erin struck the western Panhandle on August 3, 1995, while Tropical Storm Alberto caused extensive flooding in the central Panhandle in early July 1994.

Perhaps even more important for research purposes, however, is that, at the time of Opal, the first round of activities associated with the State of Florida's comprehensive planning process had been completed. As a part of this process, all coastal jurisdictions, including counties and municipalities, were required to develop a series of goals, objectives, and policies addressing storm hazard mitigation and planning for post-storm recovery. Following from this, each coastal jurisdiction was also to commit itself to a post-storm redevelopment plan.[1] These state-imposed requirements represent a unique opportunity to study the role of plans and the effectiveness of planning in dealing with natural disasters. It is this opportunity that has given rise to the following case study analysis wherein we examine the effectiveness of local planning in guiding the recovery process in communities affected by Opal.

The questions we seek to answer in this case study are: In which ways did community plans affect the communities' definition and implementation of the post-disaster recovery process?; and Given this information, how can planning and plans be made more effective instruments in this process?

THE CASE STUDY PROTOCOL

We followed the classic case-study protocol described in Yin (1984) for multiple case study research designs to identify cases, collect data, and analyze hypotheses about community recovery after Hurricane Opal. The specific cases chosen for analysis were selected from six counties and eight

Figure 10-1. Location of the Study Communities

municipalities in the Florida Panhandle that sustained severe damage from Hurricane Opal. The selection was based on surveys of the level of damage experienced in each community, as reflected in applications for federal public assistance through the Stafford Act[2], as of January 22, 1996, and in preliminary estimates of housing losses provided by the Florida Department of Community Affairs. (See Figure 10-1.) In doing so, we focused on jurisdictions with large total public assistance applications, large per-capita losses, and large housing loss estimates. In choosing the study communities, consideration was also given to those jurisdictions with existing post-storm recovery plans and policies that could be analyzed in a post-disaster context. Only Escambia County reported having an adopted post-storm recovery plan in effect at the time Hurricane Opal made landfall; Okaloosa County had a recently-completed plan that had not yet been formally adopted by the county commission.

Based on this analysis, nine jurisdictions were chosen. They are:

1) Escambia County

2) Santa Rosa County

3) Okaloosa County

4) City of Destin

5) Walton County

6) Bay County

7) Panama City Beach

8) Panama City and

9) City of Mexico Beach

Figure 10-2. Community Damage Estimates

JURISDICTION	TOTAL STAFFORD ACT APPLICATIONS AS OF 1/22/96*	PER CAPITA STAFFORD ACT APPLICATIONS AS OF 1/22/96*	PRELIMINARY HOUSING LOSS ESTIMATES** (TOTAL HOMES DESTROYED OR RECEIVING MAJOR DAMAGE)
Escambia County	$1,782,363	$8.42	432
Santa Rosa County	$5,013,278	$65.20	400
Okaloosa County	$7,811,006	$82.65	6500
City of Destin	$2,276,594	$281.76	N/A
Walton County	$4,128,124	$171.67	125
Bay County	$8,427,690	$144.91	877
Panama City Beach	$1,675,795	$48.75	N/A
Panama City	$2,221,562	$525.56	N/A
City of Mexico Beach	$397,321	$400.53	N/A

* *Source:* Florida Department of Community Affairs (1996).

** *Source:* Florida Department of Community Affairs (1995).

N/A: Not available

All of these communities had relatively high total and/or per-capita public assistance applications or housing loss estimates. (See Figure 10-2.) Despite relatively low per capita public assistance damage in Panama City Beach (where damage throughout the community was experienced), this jurisdiction was selected for consideration because of informal reports that private buildings sustained significant damage.

Information for the case studies was collected through structured interviews and analysis of newspaper articles and local, state, and federal documents. Initial telephone and field interviews were conducted during the months of January through March, 1996, with public officials responsible for post-storm recovery decision making and implementation, as well as other stakeholders and interest groups involved in community recovery issues. Draft case study summaries were prepared for each community and circulated to the interviewees for review. During the summer of 1996, field and telephone interviews were conducted with state and federal officials, and detailed analysis was performed of the local planning documents in place at the time of the hurricane. Follow-up field interviews were conducted with key local informants between August and October 1996 to clarify issues raised during review of the draft case study summaries and to pursue reflective questions about the recovery process after a longer period of time. A cross-case analysis of the nine jurisdictions was then performed to ascertain patterns in responses and outcomes that could be explained by common sets of independent factors.

> Our findings suggest that both planning, as an institution, and the plans that have been produced, played only a minor role in the recovery process following Hurricane Opal. This can be accounted for by the way in which communities viewed the recovery process—as a relatively short-term effort that followed the response phase of emergency management, the main goal of which was to reconstruct the community as it was prior to the storm, both as quickly as possible and with minimal impacts to the community's financial well-being.

SUMMARY OF KEY FINDINGS

Our findings suggest that both planning, as an institution, and the plans that have been produced, played only a minor role in the recovery process following Hurricane Opal. This can be accounted for by the way in which communities viewed the recovery process—as a relatively short-term effort that followed the response phase of emergency management, the main goal of which was to reconstruct the community as it was prior to the storm, both as quickly as possible and with minimal impacts to the community's financial well-being.

This view of the recovery process and the relative lack of a role for planners was due in part to the following factors.

- The sense of economic urgency created by the impact of the storm on the tourism base of the local economies

- The pressure from residents to restore their homes and lives as quickly as possible

- The widespread perception that state and local building codes had provided adequate protection from the storm

- The relief of local governments from much of the fiscal responsibility for recovery due to the assumption that 100 percent of the costs of disaster relief would be assumed by the federal and state government

- The failure of the existing comprehensive plan to anticipate changes in the development patterns of coastal areas

- The weakness of the storm-hazard mitigation and recovery provisions of local comprehensive plans

- The absence of post-storm recovery plans in most of the communities

- The predominant focus of the existing post-storm recovery plans on recovery operations, to the exclusion of substantive policies and implementation devices

These conditions defined planners as relatively unimportant in the recovery process because they had nothing of importance to offer. At least some part of the responsibility for these affairs lies at the feet of planners themselves. Our recommendations examine what planners can do about these circumstances.

We argue that the planning process for post-disaster recovery should be viewed in terms of three phases of activity:

a) the pre-disaster planning phase;

b) short-term recovery; and

c) long-term recovery.

Furthermore, we suggest that post-disaster recovery plans should not be called redevelopment plans because of the implications that such plans should embrace substantially different land use as the principal objective of post-disaster planning and decision making. We suggest instead that post-disaster recovery plans should be a specific application of the relevant portions of the community comprehensive plan, designed to deal with the constraints and opportunities posed by disaster conditions. When seen in this context, the post-disaster recovery plan remains a part of the community's major blueprint for managing growth, and the risks of the plan being irrelevant to community decision processes are substantially reduced. Under these conditions, the major role for planners in the recovery process is to create community plans that are relevant to the post-disaster context, and then to interpret these plans during the recovery process.

Furthermore, we suggest that post-disaster recovery plans should not be called redevelopment plans because of the implications that such plans should embrace substantially different land use as the principal objective of post-disaster planning and decision making. We suggest instead that post-disaster recovery plans should be a specific application of the relevant portions of the community comprehensive plan, designed to deal with the constraints and opportunities posed by disaster conditions.

HURRICANE OPAL AND ITS IMPACTS

Hurricane Opal struck the western Florida Panhandle between 6:00 and 7:00 P.M. EDT on Wednesday, October 4, 1995, with sustained winds of 115 mph, gusts of 143 mph, and storm surge that measured from 7 to 20 feet above sea level. Tuesday morning, before the storm, caravans of tourists and residents lined the highways and causeways trying to evacuate, and tens of thousands of coastal residents were caught in gridlock (*Sun-Sentinel* 10/6/95). Florida Governor Lawton Chiles asked President Clinton to declare a major disaster in Florida even as the storm was raging (*Miami Herald* 10/4/95). Some coastal residents who did not evacuate witnessed homes that were built slab-on-grade pushed off their foundations and destroyed in a single wave during the height of the storm (McInnis 1996). Thursday morning revealed a changed landscape with "streets and beaches littered with toilets, furniture, and air conditioners all scattered by Opal's monster tide" (*Sun-Sentinel* 10/6/95). The storm affected nearly 300 miles of the Florida coast, but the most severe damage occurred along 120 miles of coastline from Pensacola to Mexico Beach (*Sun-Sentinel* 10/6/95). According to the State Department of Environmental Protection (1995), Opal's storm surge and waves damaged or destroyed more structures than in all other coastal storms combined over the preceding 20 years in Florida.

The eye of Hurricane Opal hit the Florida coast on the Okaloosa-Santa Rosa County line. The storm wreaked some of its greatest damage to the communities on Santa Rosa Island[3] of Pensacola Beach (Escambia County), Navarre Beach (Santa Rosa County), and Okaloosa Island (Okaloosa County). Santa Rosa Island was entirely overwashed in numerous places, particularly in Navarre Beach. Dunes as high as 10 to 30 feet were flattened and scoured clean of vegetation, while beaches were severely eroded (Michael J. Baker, Inc. 1995). Many older buildings and concrete block homes, which had not been constructed in conformance with current state and local building codes, were leveled. Within the narrow area immediately adjacent to the coast, demarcated by the state's Coastal Construction Control Line (CCCL),[4]

Erosion from a storm surge during Hurrican Opal removed sand from under this hotel in Panama City, causing the deck and bottom floor to fall.

285 single-family dwellings and 652 multifamily residential units (including hotels, motels, and condominiums) were damaged beyond 50 percent of market value (Florida Department of Environmental Protection 1995). Aboveground utilities were washed away. Roads were buried under piles of sand three to four feet deep or completely washed out, while water and sewer lines were similarly inundated with sand or completely destroyed. Public beach facilities and piers were damaged or destroyed throughout the area. Flood debris was deposited on beaches and roads and, along with the sand from the beaches and dunes, was washed into Santa Rosa Sound behind the barrier island.

Robert E. Deyle

An aerial view of the overwash of Santa Rosa Island during Hurricane Opal.

The majority of the damage in the City of Destin was concentrated in the Holiday Isle area, located on a spit at the inlet to Choctawatchee Bay. In this area, approximately 24 homes were severely damaged or destroyed, and all public utilities were destroyed. In Walton County, large, bluff-like dunes provided substantial protection to developed property, despite the fact that the highest storm surge recorded from the hurricane (20.5 feet) was experienced in this area. Damage to the beach and dune system was substantial, however, with an average of 35 feet of beach recession over nearly nine miles of coastline. The majority of damage to the built environment was concentrated in the eastern end of the county where the dunes were significantly smaller. A total of 36 single-family residences and 75 multifamily residential units were damaged beyond 50 percent within the CCCL permitting zone in Walton County (Florida Department of Environmental Protection 1995).

Damage in Bay County was concentrated along the Gulf Coast in the areas of Panama City Beach and the small city of Mexico Beach. Numerous hotels, condominiums, commercial buildings, and residences were damaged or destroyed in Panama City Beach. Heavy damage to roads, infrastructure, and housing was also sustained in two unincorporated, residential beach-front areas to the east of Panama City Beach. Primary dunes were destroyed throughout the county, while beach recession averaged 34 feet. Several piers and public beach access facilities were heavily damaged along the Gulf. Mexico Beach (population 1,013) was hard hit: 50 houses were destroyed or damaged beyond repair, while streets and canals were inundated with sand and debris. Three city parks were completely destroyed. The state's figures for damages within the CCCL permitting zone in Bay County include 156 single-family dwellings and 1,042 multifamily units damaged beyond 50 percent of market value (Florida Department of Environmental Protection 1995).

Bay County also suffered damage to communities fronting on the interior bays from flooding and debris that clogged stream channels, bayous, and canals. Damage in Panama City, which fronts on St. Andrew's Bay and North Bay, was slight, however, when compared to the other communities studied. Aside from destruction of the city marina store and significant damage to seawalls and other coastal armoring, most damage was from fallen trees and other storm debris.

Public assistance claims approved by the Federal Emergency Management agency (FEMA) for reimbursement to the nine counties and cities we studied were substantial, totaling more than $29 million as of February 2, 1996. (See Figure 10-3.) As is typically the case following hurricanes, debris removal accounts for the majority of public recovery costs. Bay County and Okaloosa County had the greatest public costs from the storm, followed by Santa Rosa County and Walton County.

THE PLANNING CONTEXT OF HURRICANE OPAL

One of our main research objectives is understanding the ways in which community plans affect the post-disaster recovery process. There are many local planning instruments and policies that can affect this process. These include instruments and policies that address land development issues (e.g., zoning ordinance, subdivision regulations, future land-use map), development of individual properties (e.g., site design requirements and building codes), community development and redevelopment (e.g., economic development plans and community renewal), natural resources (e.g., beach and dune protection and restoration), and public investment (e.g., capital facilities plans), among others. Communities vary in the degree to which these instruments and policies are formulated, in the degree to which they are coordinated and amalgamated into a comprehensive plan, and in the degree to which they are made relevant to the post-disaster context. Furthermore, communities differ in the degree to which they have developed a formal post-disaster recovery plan.

In Florida, all local governments were required to prepare a comprehensive plan under the state's 1985 growth management legislation. In addition, all coastal communities were required to include a separate coastal management element in their plan and were directed to specify within this coastal element a set of goals, objectives, and policies related to storm-hazard mitigation and post-storm recovery. The mitigation requirements address impacts to beach and dune systems as well as reducing exposure of human life and property to coastal hazards through the regulation of building practices, land uses, development in floodplains, and others. Explicit post-storm recovery requirements include an objective to prepare a post-storm redevelopment plan as well as the adoption of policies that address the removal, relocation, or structural modification of damaged infrastructure and unsafe structures; limitations on redevelopment in areas of repeated damage; and the identification of areas in need of redevelopment, among

> Primary dunes were destroyed throughout the county, while beach recession averaged 34 feet.

> Explicit post-storm recovery requirements include an objective to prepare a post-storm redevelopment plan as well as the adoption of policies that address the removal, relocation, or structural modification of damaged infrastructure and unsafe structures; limitations on redevelopment in areas of repeated damage; and the identification of areas in need of redevelopment, among others.

Figure 10-3: Federal Public Assistance Approved as of February 2, 1996

COMMUNITY	DEBRIS REMOVAL	PROTECTIVE MEASURES	ROADS AND BRIDGES	WATER CONTROL	BUILDINGS AND EQUIPMENT	PUBLIC UTILITIES	PARKS AND RECREATION AND OTHER	TOTAL
Escambia County	$486,077	$448,740	$167,353	$0	$64,697	$9,949	$208,692	$1,385,508
Santa Rosa County	$672,189	$598,375	$415,327	$51,131	$32,607	$2,273,781	$179,335	$4,222,945
Okaloosa County	$4,678,681	$160,088	$59,887	$0	$33,637	$96,377	$2,201,144	$7,229,814
City of Destin	$1,971,250	$137,744	$120,594	$0	$61,031	$0	$31,297	$2,321,916
Walton County	$2,365,519	$225,111	$161,933	$0	$45,716	$0	$829,321	$3,627,600
Bay County	$5,643,748	$1,569,098	$1,851	$18,637	$4,700	$15,145	$163,484	$7,316,663
Panama City Beach	$39,616	$456,060	$0	$0	$52,582	$67,515	$200,571	$816,344
Panama City	$1,387,081	$41,444	$58,809	$64,381	$40,324	$27,367	$180,512	$1,799,918
Mexico Beach	$69,512	$129,203	$0	$6,044	$64,190	$29,713	$94,808	$393,470
Totals:	**$17,313,673**	**$3,765,863**	**$985,754**	**$140,193**	**$399,484**	**$2,519,847**	**$4,089,164**	**$29,213,978**

others. Beyond these specific mitigation and redevelopment requirements, communities were also required to identify the high-risk coastal high-hazard area and to include policies in the comprehensive plan that limit development in these areas and relocate or replace infrastructure away from them.

While all of the study communities had already adopted comprehensive plans, including the required coastal management element, by the time of the storm, we have found that most of these plans were deficient in their treatment of coastal hazards. Indeed, a content analysis of the relevant portions of the coastal management elements for the nine study jurisdictions shows that most were deficient in meeting either the requirement to include the appropriate policies or the management and regulatory devices for implementation of these policies. Thus, of 22 required objectives and policies that address storm-hazard mitigation and post-storm recovery, the average number that were included in the plans of the nine study communities was only 11. A number of jurisdictions included as few as eight items, and only one community (Okaloosa County) included as many as 19. Moreover, those items most frequently neglected were the specific hazard mitigation policies noted above, and very few of the policies included specific management or regulatory devices for implementation. These results, moreover, are not unique. In another context we have shown that coastal communities are generally deficient in the adoption of meaningful policies for dealing with storm issues and that these deficiencies can be traced to two sources:

1) the widespread lack of local interest in controlling land-use and development patterns for the purposes of hazard mitigation; and

2) the willingness of the state to ignore many coastal and storm hazard requirements in favor of other important planning issues (Deyle and Smith 1996).

These comprehensive plan deficiencies are further reflected in the near universal absence of post-storm recovery plans. Of our nine study communities, seven included in the comprehensive plan the required statement regarding the preparation of this recovery plan and, of these, only two communities had such a plan at the time of the storm. These were Escambia County, whose plan was adopted in August 1995 following Hurricane Erin, and Okaloosa County, whose plan existed only in draft form and had not yet been officially adopted. Both plans, moreover, have significant deficiencies.

The Escambia County post-storm recovery plan is composed mostly of operational procedures to be followed during the short-term recovery period. Substantive concerns consist only of lists of types of actions that may be taken for mitigation, long-term recovery, and procuring financial assistance; the plan does not obligate the county to any particular policy or course of action. Similarly, the plan fails to provide specific guidance for decision making about recovery, and it does nothing to ease the difficulties of making choices during the stressful recovery period. The parts of the plan that are potentially most useful are the details of operational procedures to be followed. These procedures are, in fact, a reflection of what is already done by county agencies rather than defining new roles or procedures to be followed during recovery. In contrast, the post-storm recovery plan for Okaloosa County goes well beyond a recovery operations plan and articulates substantive post-storm recovery objectives and policies that reflect those contained in the county's comprehensive plan. Nevertheless, the Okaloosa County plan fails to obligate the county to many specific actions. The heart of the plan is the establishment of a disaster recovery advisory committee that is charged with the study and review of development patterns, infrastructure, storm damage, and opportunities for mitigation, and the responsibility to recommend appropriate changes to the county commission for reducing the loss of life and property. The obligation of the commission to act on these recommendations is limited, however. Furthermore, many of the specific policies in the plan governing post-storm recovery options provide sufficient exceptions and loose wording to allow decision makers to avoid taking difficult actions (e.g., the terms "shall consider," "where appropriate," or "shall be guided by" are used frequently to describe how the county commission should use the findings of the committee in making decisions.)

We find that this situation is also not unique to the Florida panhandle communities. Thus, a recent survey we conducted of all coastal communities within the state regarding their fulfillment of the state's requirements for post-storm recovery plans showed that only 65 jurisdictions (of 113 responses) believed that they were required to prepare a post-storm recovery plan. Of this latter group, only 27 stated that they had actually prepared this plan. Our inspection of these documents, however, reveals that only 13 are

These comprehensive plan deficiencies are further reflected in the near universal absence of post-storm recovery plans. Of our nine study communities, seven included in the comprehensive plan the required statement regarding the preparation of this recovery plan and, of these, only two communities had such a plan at the time of the storm.

separate recovery plans, over and above the mandated inclusion of hazard mitigation and post-storm redevelopment policies in the coastal element of the comprehensive plan.

Thus, while the state has established a comprehensive planning system in which local jurisdictions are obligated to establish policies and plans for dealing with storm related issues, few of our study communities (and, as it seems, Florida communities in general) had fulfilled the promise of this system by the time of the storm. This suggests, in turn, that many of our study communities may have been inadequately prepared to deal with issues of post-storm recovery, except to the degree that other local policies and regulations, often formulated without regard to storm issues, could be brought to bear in the difficult and stressful post-storm period.

COMMUNITY RECOVERY AFTER OPAL

In spite of the planning differences among communities, all of the nine study communities followed a remarkably similar recovery process. With minor exceptions, the process was essentially administrative: no significant policy issues were raised that required extensive deliberation by city councils or county commissions, and no major policy initiatives were taken. Recovery was principally accomplished by the line agencies doing what they had to do, one puzzle piece at a time. The few instances where policy issues arose are consistent with this approach. Thus, in a number of communities there were issues concerning waivers of local permitting procedures to reduce the time or cost of obtaining permits for reconstruction of damaged private property. Similarly, in one county the commission voted to waive local side lot and road setbacks to allow homeowners to rebuild on their lots in conformance with state rules that required rebuilding further landward. In other places nonconforming uses were allowed to be rebuilt in their pre-storm locations.

All of the communities either implicitly or explicitly defined rebuilding as quickly as possible as their main post-storm recovery goal, and each pursued this goal diligently. In doing so, most followed the path of least resistance by rebuilding in ways that restored what existed before the storm. Under these terms, the major mitigation that was accomplished consisted of requiring substantially damaged structures that did not meet current building code requirements to be rebuilt according to the current federal, local, or state standards governing the elevation of structures in coastal flood hazard areas.

In the following sections, we describe how existing plans affected the recovery process, and the major actions that characterized both the short-term and long-term recovery processes in the nine study communities. Following Spangle and Associates (1996), we separately discuss the short-term recovery processes of the private and public sectors.

The Use of Plans

Despite the fact that post-storm recovery plans had been prepared within the last year in Escambia and Okaloosa Counties, neither plan was formally used to guide the recovery after Hurricane Opal. As noted above, the Escambia County plan contained little that was new; it merely described existing functions of county agencies and existing policies with no specific application to the post-disaster recovery process. This may explain, at least in part, why local officials reported that the plan was not consulted during the recovery process.

Alternatively, Okaloosa County officials state that their post-storm recovery plan was generally adhered to in the recovery process, although it was not directly consulted. Staff of the main agencies involved in the

---

In spite of the planning differences among communities, all of the nine study communities followed a remarkably similar recovery process. With minor exceptions, the process was essentially administrative: no significant policy issues were raised that required extensive deliberation by city councils or county commissions, and no major policy initiatives were taken. Recovery was principally accomplished by the line agencies doing what they had to do, one puzzle piece at a time.

recovery process, the Department of Emergency Services and the Department of Planning and Inspections, had only recently completed the plan and, therefore, reportedly did not need to refer to it. However, this evaluation only reflects use of the plan for dealing with short-term recovery issues—defined as those needed to return residents to their homes with adequate infrastructure and public facilities. Indeed, it was principally the operational elements of the plan that were used in the post-storm recovery process. This may be due, in part, to the plan having not yet been adopted by the county commission; the disaster recovery advisory committee had not been appointed, and its functions had not been performed at the time Opal struck.

In none of our study communities did the storm-hazard mitigation or post-storm recovery aspects of the local comprehensive plan have a discernible role in the recovery process. Indeed, when asked, a number of planning directors stated that there was no role, nor did they identify any implications for the comprehensive plan arising from the storm event. In two instances (Walton County and Panama City Beach), local officials maintained that their comprehensive plans called for no changes in land-use patterns in the areas affected by the storm. Thus, no issues arose during the recovery process for which the plan was perceived to be relevant. In other instances, comprehensive plan policies that could be addressed were neglected. For example, most of our study communities have adopted policies that speak to limitations on development and the removal/relocation of damaged infrastructure from the coastal high-hazard area, but these policies were not brought into play. Similarly, Santa Rosa County has committed itself to maintaining lists of repetitively damaged structures, and Walton County has adopted a comprehensive plan policy to impose requirements for the rebuilding of repetitively damaged structures that differ from the rebuilding of other damaged buildings, but there is no evidence that these lists are seriously maintained or that exceptional rebuilding constraints and prohibitions have been effected.

Private-Sector Short-Term Recovery

The process of private-sector short-term recovery in virtually all of the nine communities we studied appears to have been influenced predominately by routine administration of development management regulatory devices. Of particular importance in all of our study communities are state-imposed set-back and construction regulations that apply within the area defined by the CCCL, as well as local building codes governing construction in flood hazard areas that reflect the FEMA's requirements under the National Flood Insurance Program (NFIP). Both the state's CCCL standards and the local building codes require the elevation of residential structures within areas subject to storm-surge flooding and wave damage. In two of the communities, the local codes exceed the minimum requirements under NFIP. The Santa Rosa Island Authority (SRIA) applies V-zone elevation standards throughout the entire A-zone of Pensacola Beach and requires first-floor elevations greater than those mandated under NFIP. Santa Rosa County uses the state's elevation requirements, which are more stringent than those required under NFIP, and applies them to both V-zones and A-zones in areas of Navarre Beach. These requirements, which historically have been criticized as unnecessarily expensive by many builders, homeowners, and some local officials, have been widely embraced following Hurricane Opal. This is because most of the damage occurred to older structures built prior to contemporary local and state construction codes, many of which were concrete-block, slab-on-grade designs (Florida Department of Environmental Protection 1995). The extensive loss of these structures, compared to the

> In none of our study communities did the storm-hazard mitigation or post-storm recovery aspects of the local comprehensive plan have a discernible role in the recovery process. Indeed, when asked, a number of planning directors stated that there was no role, nor did they identify any implications for the comprehensive plan arising from the storm event.

> Of particular importance in all of our study communities are state-imposed set-back and construction regulations that apply within the area defined by the CCCL, as well as local building codes governing construction in flood hazard areas that reflect the FEMA's requirements under the National Flood Insurance Program (NFIP).

relatively small incidence of damage to structures meeting current elevation and building requirements, is taken as testimony by local officials to the effectiveness and essential correctness of these controls.[5]

Thus, to a large degree, a substantial revolution in storm-damage mitigation has taken place over the past 20 years through building less vulnerable structures. On the other hand, the general belief in, and widespread acceptance of, construction codes is offered by local officials as a reason for not taking other mitigation initiatives, such as those involving the relocation of development from damaged areas or reductions in allowable development intensity and densities in hazard-prone areas. Local officials in Panama City Beach, which also experienced extensive damage from Hurricane Eloise in 1975, maintained that the two hurricanes made it clear that you can build on the coast so long as you build properly. Under this view, as each successive storm wipes out older and more vulnerable structures, the community will be renewed with those that are more storm-resistant. This represents a politically more attractive alternative to the more aggressive mitigation option of influencing private-sector recovery through development management devices that restrict land-use types or densities in hazardous areas.

In a very few instances, private redevelopment occurred at higher levels of intensity than existed prior to the storm, such as in Navarre Beach and Panama City Beach. Several hotels were rebuilt with more units because elevating the structure provided more parking space, thus accommodating more residents. In each instance, however, the increased development intensity was within the limits allowed by the existing zoning code. Thus, from the community's perspective, no comprehensive plan issues were raised despite the presence of broad statements in their plans that call for directing development away from the coastal high-hazard area.

Public-Sector Short-Term Recovery

The public-sector process of short-term recovery, which can be distinguished as the policies and actions concerned with the restoration and reconstruction of infrastructure and other public facilities (Spangle Associates 1996), was also minimally influenced by local post-disaster recovery plans and comprehensive plans. Public-sector recovery initiatives include efforts to restore services so as to facilitate private-sector recovery as well as changes to infrastructure and facilities to mitigate future damage or improve service quality or efficiency. Decisions about how and where to reconstruct severely damaged infrastructure also can be used in concert with land development regulations to alter the intensity or density of land use in redeveloped areas and thus influence the private-sector recovery process.

Some opportunistic redevelopment and mitigation projects were conceived during the initial recovery process, using FEMA's Section 406 Public Assistance Program.[6] However, our interviews with local officials show that many of these initiatives had no foundation in existing plans. Neither of the post-storm recovery plans in place in the communities we studied specifically identifies modifications that ought to be made to vulnerable infrastructure or public facilities in a post-disaster situation. Furthermore, the storm-hazard mitigation and post-storm recovery policies of the comprehensive plans in the nine communities we studied were not used to initiate or guide changes in public facilities or infrastructure following the storm. Partly as a result of this, only minor redevelopment initiatives were accomplished during the short-term recovery process when essential infrastructure and public facilities were being restored. In Navarre Beach (Santa Rosa County), for example, storm damage created the opportunity to retrofit damaged sewer lines and sewer lift stations to provide a more efficient system, independent of mitigation considerations. In Bay County, water and sewer lines were relocated to the landward side of Spy Glass Road, and, in Panama City, a city-owned marina store was relocated further landward. But in none of these cases was the initiative identified or planned for as a potential post-storm opportunity prior to the hurricane.

Under the political pressure for local officials to return the community to normalcy as quickly as possible, many other relatively meager opportunities to mitigate the vulnerability of public infrastructure could not be implemented during the short-term recovery period and were, therefore, lost. Often at issue was both the time needed to implement mitigation and the potential expense in doing so. Moving roads or utility lines to areas that would make them less vulnerable involves time delays in the recovery process and may incur costs that far exceed those of repair alone. Most of the study communities expressed both the unwillingness to incur these time delays and an inability to bear these costs. These funding concerns then placed mitigation at the disposal of decisions made by other public agencies (and private utility providers) who controlled financial resources.

This situation is illustrated at Navarre Beach (Santa Rosa County) where damage to both utilities and roads was severe. The electric utilities are maintained by a private-sector company that initially considered rebuilding the lines underground but was dissuaded by the high costs of doing so. A proposal by the company that the county bear these additional costs was rejected by the county commission, which also did not want to assess beach residents for these costs. The county was further dissuaded by opposition from local residents who objected to the estimated five-month delay involved. Similarly, a proposal to move Gulf Boulevard, the main thoroughfare through the community, 30 feet to the north within the existing right-of-way could not be quickly implemented. Moving the road, and the underlying water and sewer lines, would have both reduced the vulnerability of the public facilities to future storm damage and allowed beachfront property owners to rebuild their structures further landward. Gulf Boulevard is a state road, and any decision to rebuild it in a different location had to be made by the Florida Department of Transportation (FDOT). At the time of the proposal, however, FDOT had already granted an emergency contract to repair the road and was unwilling to bear the extra costs that moving would entail. The county was also told that the Federal Highway Administration would not provide the additional funds, and homeowners were reluctant to endure the extra time that it would take to rebuild the road and underlying utilities in a different location. In all, both the difficulty of putting together a new workable proposal in the short time frame that was available, and arranging for the funding, proved to be too difficult a task. As a result, only minimal structural mitigation was accomplished; the road was rebuilt at its original location but with pavement almost twice as thick in order to better withstand undermining from future storms.

Longer-Term Recovery

Under these conditions the most characteristic response of communities was to pursue mitigation through longer-term projects funded under federal disaster assistance programs: the Hazard Mitigation Grants Program administered by FEMA under Section 404 of the Stafford Act, and emergency appropriations of Community Development Block Grant (CDBG) funds through the federal Department of Housing and Urban Development (HUD). Both programs are administered within the state by the Florida Department of Community Affairs (DCA). Here too, however, opportunities for effective hazard mitigation that reflected community plans, were limited.

> Under the political pressure for local officials to return the community to normalcy as quickly as possible, many other relatively meager opportunities to mitigate the vulnerability of public infrastructure could not be implemented during the short-term recovery period and were, therefore, lost. Often at issue was both the time needed to implement mitigation and the potential expense in doing so.

In most jurisdictions, the predominant role in recovery is held by emergency management officials rather than planners, and, in some jurisdictions, planners are not part of the recovery process at all. Indeed, one county emergency management director suggested, with disdain, that the planning department had no role in recovery, and, furthermore, he had no idea what the planners in his county did. This predominant role of emergency management officials, rather than planners, in the recovery process, reinforces the orientation toward short-term recovery.

Because of the untenable nature of the opportunistic view, communities fall back on the second alternative emphasizing short-term recovery. Under this view, all plans, other than those that speak to issues concerning short-term recovery operations, are irrelevant. Indeed, as Haas et al. (1977) observe, community members see no need for a plan because they already have one in their minds—the pre-disaster community. Instead, emphasis is placed on accomplishing expeditious restoration of infrastructure and public facilities and facilitating private-sector restoration.

In our case studies, this short-term recovery view is reinforced by a number of other conditions of the communities. First, while each community has included some hazard mitigation and post-storm redevelopment policies in their comprehensive plan, in many instances these appear to represent pro forma compliance with the state planning mandates for which the local jurisdictions have little interest, and hence little concern for implementation and enforcement. Our earlier study on local compliance with these mandates showed that mean compliance rates across all goals, objectives, and policies governing coastal storm hazards was only 54 percent. This compliance rate, moreover, varied considerably across different subjects; 77 percent of the evacuation mandates were followed in comparison to only 49 percent of both the hazard mitigation and post-storm redevelopment mandates (Deyle and Smith 1996). This condition of inadequate commitment to and inclusion of state hazard mitigation and redevelopment planning mandates serves to lessen the salience of these components of the comprehensive plan as an important guide for community development and recovery.

Second, in most jurisdictions, the predominant role in recovery is held by emergency management officials rather than planners, and, in some jurisdictions, planners are not part of the recovery process at all. Indeed, one county emergency management director suggested, with disdain, that the planning department had no role in recovery, and, furthermore, he had no idea what the planners in his county did. This predominant role of emergency management officials, rather than planners, in the recovery process, reinforces the orientation toward short-term recovery. Emergency managers are, first and foremost, concerned with the response phase, and they tend to see recovery as merely an extension of that process. This rationale is reinforced by the reports of a number of planning officials who stated that they were not aware of state requests for Section 404 hazard mitigation proposals and that the process of formulating and submitting these proposals was managed by the emergency management director.

Third, in most communities, the nature of the damage inflicted by the storm has not undermined the premises upon which local plans and development management policies are based. As noted above, the majority of the damage was sustained by structures built prior to the enactment of current state and local building codes, which require elevation of structures in areas most vulnerable to storm surge. In all of the communities we studied, the comprehensive plans do not call for substantial changes in existing land-use patterns in areas susceptible to coastal storms. Thus, recovery is seen as involving rebuilding to code rather than changing the intensity or density of land uses. In several communities, such as Okaloosa and Walton counties, the majority of the damage occurred within the CCCL permitting zone regulated by the state. In those cases, local officials saw no local policy issues and no reason to question the provisions of the local comprehensive plan.

Furthermore, where older, nonconforming structures are rebuilt to current building codes and site development requirements designed to reduce vulnerability to natural hazards, local officials generally do not feel that recovery is being undertaken in contradiction to the good sense of mitigation. Mitigation is accomplished but only in ways that allow the recovery process to proceed apace and only under conditions of minimal hardship to residents and property owners. Where such hardship is found to exceed a commonly understood and accepted level, local officials appear ready to relax some of these burdens or to take other measures to minimize costs and delays. In Okaloosa County, homeowners were allowed to obtain updated appraisals from private firms in an effort to reduce the likelihood that they would be required to rebuild to current standards under the county's damage threshold of 50 percent of market value. Similarly, several jurisdictions waived building permit fees and established expedited permitting processes.

The preference for relying on the structural remedy of using building codes to make privately owned structures less vulnerable to future storms has its counterpart in other public actions. In a number of the study communities, infrastructure and public facilities were rebuilt to higher design standards, thereby making roads, sewer, water, and other public facilities less vulnerable to future storms. Similarly, where damages to coastal dunes and other storm-protection systems occurred, they were met with swift action. In a number of places, emergency sand berms were constructed to provide minimal protection to development landward of the former dunes. Longer-term dune restoration programs have also been initiated in recognition of the protective functions of these systems. In other areas where structural flood protection systems, such as revetments and breakwaters, were damaged, similar initiatives have been taken to restore their protective functions as quickly as possible. Like building codes, restoration of dunes and other hazard-protection systems is a relatively noncontroversial structural action that generally allows continuation of existing patterns of development. Also, like codes, this structural restoration can be implemented without the controversy, costs, and time delays associated with the development and implementation of plans for redevelopment.

In spite of being able to meet existing recovery issues by focusing on armoring, the strengthening of buildings through construction codes, and site development regulations, communities bear a continuing cost in not engaging in a broader and more effective mitigation approach. The overwhelming reliance on building codes to protect structures is limited by design standards that will be effective only so long as the community is not challenged by a more powerful storm. Furthermore, as has been shown, the rush to recovery limits the community's ability to institute any major mitigation or other redevelopment initiatives during the short-term recovery process. Given this, communities are left to consider mitigation and redevelopment only over the longer term. We have already commented, however, on how concerns for costs, the reliance on higher levels of government for funding, and the administration of the funding cycles for the major mitigation grant programs conspire against using these funds effectively. Thus, opportunities for significant redevelopment, through changes in the location of infrastructure and in land-use density and intensity, are foreclosed by the limited initiatives taken during the short-term recovery process. Furthermore, where long-term mitigation projects are not derived from an existing plan, there is no guarantee that these initiatives will be consistent with other community planning priorities.

In addition to structuring the recovery process to proceed without adequate plans and planning, this short-term recovery orientation both derives from and then promotes the view that the local comprehensive plan is largely irrelevant to the recovery process. This view, however, is seriously shortsighted; it represents a self-fulfilling prophesy in which the belief in

Like building codes, restoration of dunes and other hazard-protection systems is a relatively noncontroversial structural action that generally allows continuation of existing patterns of development. Also, like codes, this structural restoration can be implemented without the controversy, costs, and time delays associated with the development and implementation of plans for redevelopment.

Opportunities for significant redevelopment, through changes in the location of infrastructure and in land-use density and intensity, are foreclosed by the limited initiatives taken during the short-term recovery process. Furthermore, where long-term mitigation projects are not derived from an existing plan, there is no guarantee that these initiatives will be consistent with other community planning priorities.

While the comprehensive plan may not have played a central role in the actual recovery process, as implemented, we can discern a variety of ways in which the plan has guided each community's storm-related postures and actions. These then define opportunities for enhancing the role of the comprehensive plan in disaster recovery and mitigation.

The comprehensive plan is generally used to derive associated land development regulations, including the zoning ordinance. Zoning and land development regulations appear to have been among the most important mechanisms for guiding reconstruction within each community and for providing a linkage between the comprehensive plan and the recovery process. Development regulation also provided for one of the main roles of planners in this process.

irrelevancy causes the community to act in this way, and so establish the fact. But while the comprehensive plan may not have played a central role in the actual recovery process, as implemented, we can discern a variety of ways in which the plan has guided each community's storm-related postures and actions. These then define opportunities for enhancing the role of the comprehensive plan in disaster recovery and mitigation.

First, as a general guide to the development of the community, the plan has had an impact on the intensity and distribution of development, including development in hazardous coastal areas. Thus, in a number of places, development on barrier islands and other coastal high-hazard areas has been influenced by the comprehensive plan over the longer term in ways that make these areas less vulnerable to storm hazards. If this is not always done energetically by the local community, it may be prompted by the state's plan review and approval process. In Santa Rosa County, for example, DCA had insisted on modifications to the county comprehensive plan prior to Opal that reduced both the amount and density of new development in Navarre Beach.

Second, the comprehensive plan is generally used to derive associated land development regulations, including the zoning ordinance. Zoning and land development regulations appear to have been among the most important mechanisms for guiding reconstruction within each community and for providing a linkage between the comprehensive plan and the recovery process. Development regulation also provided for one of the main roles of planners in this process. Where building permits were issued by staff within the local planning agency, which was predominately the case in the communities we studied, planners were in a position to evaluate applications for rebuilding and to advise local elected officials on the need for, or wisdom of, modifications to the community's permitting procedures or policies. Even though local regulations were sometimes waived, as in the case of rebuilding to side and front setbacks or the rebuilding of nonconforming uses, these development regulations did play a significant part in recovery

Often the interests of a community in limiting coastal development are tied to the comprehensive plan through the issue of hurricane evacuation. Our previous review of local compliance with the state's planning mandate on evacuation (Deyle and Smith 1996) showed that DCA has, for the most part, required that development densities be controlled so as to maintain hurricane evacuation clearance times and that communities were generally responsive in meeting this mandate. Similarly, our interviews with planning officials frequently raised the evacuation issue in response to questions about the implications of the storm for the comprehensive plan. In one community (Perdido Key in Escambia County), evacuation clearance times were raised as an issue in the preparation of a community master plan — not because the community necessarily had an evacuation problem, but because it was viewed as an effective argument for limiting development of high-rise condominiums that were regarded as contrary to residents' desires for the character and aesthetics of the area. In Destin, the city planning director, who joined the city more than six months after Opal, indicated she anticipated a discussion with the planning commission concerning growth limits tied to the capacity of the city's evacuation routes.

Thus, if comprehensive plans have had an effect on a community's exposure to coastal disasters, it is reasonable to believe that they also can be relevant in the post-disaster context. Ultimately, the failure of local communities to consider seriously long-term redevelopment and mitigation alternatives may reflect the failure of the community to plan for long-term, post-disaster recovery, rather than any inherent failure of plans themselves. Without a recovery plan, communities are both uncertain of what to do, cannot act quickly, and cannot take advantage of whatever opportunities are presented for redevelopment and hazard mitigation. In this regard, the contrast between Okaloosa County, which had already included the relocation of water and sewer lines from bridges in its capital improvements plan, and the other study communities is enlightening. It is to this issue of how to make the comprehensive plan relevant in the post-storm context to which we now turn.

OBSERVATIONS AND RECOMMENDATIONS

Our interest in the series of case studies has been to study the role and effectiveness of plans and planning in the post-disaster recovery process. What we have found is that, to a large degree, both planning as an institution and the plans that have been produced have played only a minor role in the recovery process. This situation may be accounted for by the way in which communities viewed the recovery process—as a relatively short-term effort that followed the response phase of emergency management, the main goal of which was to reconstruct the community as it was prior to the storm event, both as quickly as possible and with minimal impacts to the community's financial well-being.

Under these conditions, local decision makers in each community did not engage in a formal process of identifying issues, defining goals, or evaluating alternative recovery strategies. For most, what needed to be done was clear, and local officials acted responsibly in moving quickly to carry out their duties. Citizens and citizen groups, to the extent that they were involved in recovery, failed to engage decision makers in an examination of community goals and development options and, by their insistence on rapid response, reinforced the imperative of returning the community to normalcy as quickly as possible.

Many circumstances and conditions conspired to promote this view of the recovery process and the relative lack of a role for planners. Most of the recovery process appears to have been managed by a combination of emergency management, engineering, and public works personnel, to the relative exclusion of planners. The impact of the storm on the tourism base of the local economies clearly contributed to the sense of urgency that characterized the post-disaster climate. The widespread perception that state and local building codes had provided adequate protection from the storm further reduced the motivation of local officials to question the adequacy of existing planning goals, objectives, and policies, and may have contributed to the lack of long-range mitigation initiatives directed at the effects of this particular disaster.

Even external units of government reinforced this disposition. Both the state and the federal government, in bearing the entire costs of disaster relief (the State of Florida has contributed all of the nonfederal share of public assistance costs), lessened the incentives for communities to be concerned with reducing their vulnerability to future storm events through serious planning, redevelopment, and mitigation initiatives.

A major contribution to the relative unimportance of planning in the aftermath of Hurricane Opal has undoubtedly been the weakness of existing plans. While all communities had an adopted comprehensive plan that also contained policies regarding hazard mitigation and post-storm recovery, most of what was contained in these plans did not provide useful guidance to the recovery process. Generally, adopted policies ignored many of the state planning requirements and only minimally mirrored others, failing to include implementation devices to put these policies into effect. Where implementation devices were specified, they usually only repeated operational procedures and regulations already in place within the community and often failed to contain language that obligated local decision makers to

Most of the recovery process appears to have been managed by a combination of emergency management, engineering, and public works personnel, to the relative exclusion of planners. The impact of the storm on the tourism base of the local economies clearly contributed to the sense of urgency that characterized the post-disaster climate. The widespread perception that state and local building codes had provided adequate protection from the storm further reduced the motivation of local officials to question the adequacy of existing planning goals, objectives, and policies, and may have contributed to the lack of long-range mitigation initiatives directed at the effects of this particular disaster.

particular courses of action. We have already noted that, even in the instance of the two post-storm recovery plans that did exist (one officially adopted and one in draft form), the plans worked best as operational guides to short-term recovery rather than thoughtfully derived substantive policies and implementation devices. In effect, then, planners were unimportant in the recovery process because they had nothing of importance to offer. At least some of the responsibility for these affairs lies at the feet of planners themselves. The issue at hand is what can planners do about this.

Post-Disaster Recovery Planning as Blue-Sky Planning

If planners have a unique and important role to play in the recovery process, this role must correspond to their abilities to analyze problems, define alternative solutions, and fashion these solutions into plans. However, the need for rapid action and decision making in much of the post-disaster environment militates against careful data collection, analysis, and consideration. Since the opportunities to do these tasks exist almost exclusively in the blue-sky, pre-disaster environment, the major role for planners exists prior to disasters. The post-disaster, morning-after role of planners is to interpret these pre-disaster plans and make them applicable to the recovery process.

> If planners have a unique and important role to play in the recovery process, this role must correspond to their abilities to analyze problems, define alternative solutions, and fashion these solutions into plans. However, the need for rapid action and decision making in much of the post-disaster environment militates against careful data collection, analysis, and consideration. Since the opportunities to do these tasks exist almost exclusively in the blue-sky, pre-disaster environment, the major role for planners exists prior to disasters.

Thus, we believe that the post-disaster recovery planning process should be viewed in terms of three related phases of activity:

a) the pre-disaster planning phase;

b) short-term recovery; and

c) long-term recovery.

The pre-disaster phase is the period in which plans are prepared. The phase of short-term recovery follows the emergency response period in which community actions are focused on the immediate issues of protecting life and property. This response period is generally governed by an emergency response plan, is characterized by tactical actions and decision making, and provides little, if any, role for planners. The ensuing short-term recovery phase involves repair and restoration of damaged infrastructure, housing, and community facilities. Those initiatives taken with a view toward longer-term redevelopment constitute the activities of the third phase (i.e., the redevelopment of parts of the community in major and significant ways over a longer time period so as to reduce community vulnerability to future disasters or achieve other community goals such as enhanced economic vitality). Planning for this phase is similar to that done for redevelopment in other nondisaster contexts.

> Pre-disaster plans are often seen as irrelevant to post-disaster recovery, adequate distinctions are not made between response and recovery, and recovery itself is not defined in terms of short- and long-term actions and the decisions that are appropriate in each phase. We believe that this has contributed to the relatively unimportant role that planners and plans have played in recovery.

The critical role for planners during these activities is to evaluate options for repair and reconstruction against the goals, objectives, and policies in the community's plan and to advise local officials on the critical distinctions that should be made between what may be best restored to the pre-disaster state; what may be best reconstructed to a new and different state; and what may be repaired temporarily in favor of longer-term redevelopment. While this three-phase distinction is relatively straightforward,[8] we find that many planners do not have this time-ordered perspective and cannot clearly define their responsibilities in each phase of this process. Hence, pre-disaster plans are often seen as irrelevant to post-disaster recovery, adequate distinctions are not made between response and recovery, and recovery itself is not defined in terms of short- and long-term actions and the decisions that are appropriate in each phase. We believe that this has contributed to the relatively unimportant role that planners and plans have played in recovery.

Preparing Blue-Sky Plans

We believe there is merit in the preparation of a separate and distinct post-disaster recovery plan. Such plans have, in other contexts such as Florida, been called post-disaster redevelopment plans. We suggest that this latter title is ill chosen and that it has also biased community attitudes in dealing with post-disaster issues. This is because the post-disaster redevelopment plan suggests, by its title, that disasters are an opportunity for community redevelopment; that is, a rebuilding of the community or parts of it in ways that are substantially different from pre-disaster patterns. Redevelopment, however, is often neither possible nor desirable from the perspective of the community for a variety of reasons. These reasons include the often spotty and intermittent nature of disaster damage, the substantial amount of time and investment necessary for accomplishing redevelopment, the political issues and problems associated with redevelopment, and the potential desirability, from the perspective of the community, of current development patterns. Indeed, planners told us in several communities that planning boards or boards of commissioners were opposed to mitigation initiatives that were perceived to interfere with people's property rights or their ability to rebuild promptly. We do not reject the notion that redevelopment may be a useful post-disaster strategy, and we have included redevelopment as the focus of our third phase of recovery planning. What we do suggest is that redevelopment not be considered as the principal objective of post-disaster recovery planning and decision making. Recognizing that other post-disaster actions may be appropriate responses to damage from natural disasters may serve to reduce the reluctance of communities to prepare these plans.

Our ideas for the post-disaster recovery plan center this plan on the community comprehensive plan. The comprehensive plan is the product of a thoughtful process that leads to a vision of community character and the construction of an integrated set of policies necessary to achieve and maintain this character. Clearly, the community's definition of itself is applicable in both pre- and post-disaster contexts. In this sense the post-disaster recovery plan should be an extension of the comprehensive plan in which the policies and programs needed to achieve and maintain the desired community image within the post-disaster recovery context are articulated. Often this will involve many of the same policies appropriate in the pre-disaster context. However, the unique conditions and problems of the post-disaster context are also likely to involve other, unique policies for dealing with disaster-related damages, as well as unique operational procedures for dealing with the process of community recovery. This relationship between the post-disaster recovery plan and the comprehensive plan also places obligations on the comprehensive plan to be cognizant of and to address disaster-related issues. Thus, the comprehensive plan must speak to issues of natural hazards and community vulnerability.

The recovery plan should address how community goals that have already been developed and agreed upon may be met in the post-disaster context. Ordinarily the community comprehensive plan deals with future land-use patterns, and related to these future patterns, defines opportunities for redevelopment, the location of community infrastructure and facilities, the programming of capital expenditures. These activities are likely to be programmed over an extended period of time. Under certain conditions, however, this time frame may be accelerated by disaster-induced damage; that is, the necessity to repair and rebuild provides the opportunity for a more rapid realization of community redevelopment objectives. Post-disaster redevelopment, therefore, is viewed not as a new idea or as a purely opportunistic outcome of disaster damage, but

> Planners told us in several communities that planning boards or boards of commissioners were opposed to mitigation initiatives that were perceived to interfere with people's property rights or their ability to rebuild promptly. We do not reject the notion that redevelopment may be a useful post-disaster strategy, and we have included redevelopment as the focus of our third phase of recovery planning. What we do suggest is that redevelopment not be considered as the principal objective of post-disaster recovery planning and decision making.

as a specific instance of the more general redevelopment patterns articulated under pre-disaster conditions. What does differ between pre-disaster and post-disaster redevelopment, however, is the time pressure of the latter and the more difficult conditions that characterize community action in the post-disaster environment.

As this case study and many others have shown (see, for example, Haas et al. 1977; Rubin et al. 1985; Rubin and Popkin 1990; Beatley et al. 1992), the pursuit of redevelopment objectives during the recovery process is made difficult by the need to attend to shorter-term concerns. While long-term initiatives may offer more permanent ways of dealing with redevelopment issues, short-term actions are often necessitated by the personal and business disruptions caused by disaster damage. One example is the need to restore roads and utilities to residential areas so as to make them accessible and habitable as soon after a disaster as possible, as opposed to the more time-consuming actions of relocation and structural mitigation that may make these facilities less vulnerable in the long term but unusable in the short term. Another salient example is the pressure to return tourism-based businesses, such as retail shops, hotels and motels, and amusements, as well as the associated public infrastructure, to functioning as soon as possible in order to protect the community's economic and fiscal well-being. Doing so, however, often jeopardizes any significant changes in community development patterns or the ability to seriously mitigate the potential for similar destruction from future storms. This conflict is central to our distinction between the short-term and long-term phases of recovery planning articulated above.

We contend that resolution of the tension between the need to satisfy the short-term demand for community restoration against the desirability of longer-term redevelopment can only be done effectively through planning which reconciles both short- and long-term needs rather than leaving them as competing alternatives. The reconciliation of these two opposing needs will require thoughtful planning that considers each of the important components of a post-disaster recovery plan. We define these components according to the three-part distinction of:

> We contend that resolution of the tension between the need to satisfy the short-term demand for community restoration against the desirability of longer-term redevelopment can only be done effectively through planning which reconciles both short- and long-term needs rather than leaving them as competing alternatives. The reconciliation of these two opposing needs will require thoughtful planning that considers each of the important components of a post-disaster recovery plan.

a) policy and project identification;

b) policy and project implementation and decision processes; and

c) operational procedures.

Policy and project identification. The policy and project identification component of the recovery plan refers to the specification of two components: goals, objectives, and policies; and projects. This is the specification of content; that is, what is to be accomplished in recovery.

We do not argue for substantive content that is newly created in the aftermath of disasters and have argued above that the post-disaster setting makes this particularly difficult. Rather, the content of the recovery plan should be grounded in the content of its parent, the local comprehensive plan. This makes the comprehensive plan relevant to the post-disaster context as well as providing the opportunity to achieve previously articulated community goals and objects during the recovery process. Thus, for example, the focus on hazard mitigation that is central to the construction of the recovery plan should not be unique to this plan. Mitigation should be an important part of the community's comprehensive plan, and all new development and public facilities should be required to give adequate attention to mitigation possibilities. Similar mitigation policies should be applied in the post-disaster context to the reconstruction of private property, public facilities, and infrastructure.

The policy component of the recovery plan should be designed to guide public decision making in the most general way. In contrast, the definition of projects in the recovery plan should be a reflection of specific tasks that may be accomplished during recovery. Thus, for example, a community may anticipate the removal and relocation of public infrastructure out of harm's way. Again, however, the specification of projects should not be in the absence of the appropriate comprehensive plan discussion and analysis. We have already commented above on the difficulties in specifying recovery projects in the abstract and as an opportunistic response to storm damage. By grounding recovery projects in the local comprehensive plan, however, these projects become part of the overall design for the community and are related to community goals, objectives, and priorities. Indeed, these projects may be pursued in the absence of a future storm, but their inclusion in the recovery plan helps to promote them as legitimate uses for post-disaster recovery and hazard mitigation funds.

Policy and project implementation and decision processes. Policy and project implementation and decision processes include the implementation devices that are designed to put policies and projects into operation and the decision criteria under which different implementation devices are used. While implementation devices may be considered along with policy and project content in the comprehensive plan, it is likely that greater levels of detail and application to the post-disaster context are necessary. It is in this specification of implementation devices and the criteria for their use that most existing recovery plans fail. In essence, we see the processes articulated in the post-disaster plan to be those that are necessary for meeting both short-term and long-term recovery objectives under both difficult and vastly shortened time frames and decision processes.

Examples of appropriate content include:

- evaluation criteria and decision processes for distinguishing between restoration to original conditions, reconstruction with mitigation, or temporary repair with longer-term redevelopment;

- criteria for the use of various growth management devices that lower the intensity of development or remove it from particular locations (e.g., the use of eminent domain, buyouts, or transfers of development rights);

- policies for compensating property owners for constraints that may constitute takings;

- criteria for the removal of public facilities and infrastructure from hazardous areas and the procedures that are necessary for a transition between immediate service and longer-term redevelopment;

- criteria for defining priorities for long-term mitigation and the use of external funds;

- criteria and procedures for generating and using community-based disaster funds; and

- policies and procedures that govern the long-term recovery phase (e.g., financing of other capital improvements, revisions to other community projects and timetables).

Operational procedures. The third plan component, operational procedures, refers to the agency procedures appropriate for applying the implementation devices and executing the decisions made during the recovery process. These procedures go well beyond the level of detail articulated in the comprehensive plan because of the special circumstances of the post-disaster context. Thus, issues, such as the roles of different agencies in the

The policy component of the recovery plan should be designed to guide public decision making in the most general way. In contrast, the definition of projects in the recovery plan should be a reflection of specific tasks that may be accomplished during recovery.

In essence, we see the processes articulated in the post-disaster plan to be those that are necessary for meeting both short-term and long-term recovery objectives under both difficult and vastly shortened time frames and decision processes.

short-term recovery phase and the procedures for implementing building moratoriums, inspections and permitting, the licensing of contractors, and articulation with higher levels of government, are appropriate procedural content. It is these recovery operations that communities have generally addressed well in the post-disaster recovery plans we have reviewed. Recovery operations also were most frequently identified as requiring better planning by the local officials we interviewed in the communities that did not have post-disaster recovery plans. Major difficulties mentioned included contracting for debris removal, devising systems for regulating access to damaged areas, writing damage survey reports for submission to FEMA, and coordinating local permitting. While necessary, the overwhelming focus of local officials on this operational content, as opposed to the policy/project identification and policy/project implementation issues, further highlights the relatively low level of consideration and development that these post-disaster recovery plans have received.

In addition to serving as a guide to the pursuit and accomplishment of general community objectives, the post-disaster recovery plan can be useful as both a training and education device. Each of these functions also contributes to the role of planning in post-disaster recovery. These training and education functions exist in terms of each of the three plan components. As a statement of what is to be accomplished in the post-disaster context, the plan serves as a guide for public actions for both public officials and the general public. By grounding this substance in the community's comprehensive plan, and by identifying appropriate implementation devices and the criteria for their use, post-disaster decision making is removed from the burden of idiosyncratic expectations and decision-making outcomes. As a statement of operational processes, the plan also allows community agencies to know and practice the linkages and extraordinary procedures that are necessary in the post-disaster context. The marriage of all three components helps to ensure that these plans address important community development and recovery issues, as opposed to only the tactical recovery operations that emerge from the view of recovery as returning the community to the way it was as quickly as possible.

Notes

1. In this case study, we use the term "recovery" to encompass all of the actions taken to restore and redevelop a community after a disaster. Recovery is distinct from the immediate response actions taken to protect life and property. We also distinguish the separate processes of restoration and redevelopment that occur during recovery. Restoration involves repairing and reconstructing damaged infrastructure, public facilities, and private property to pre-disaster conditions. Redevelopment, on the other hand, involves reconstruction that alters the design of structures and facilities or the types or patterns of land uses so as to enhance the community in one or more ways.

The State of Florida requires communities to prepare a post-storm redevelopment plan. We think that this terminology is too restrictive since redevelopment is only one part of the recovery process. Accordingly, we use the term post-disaster recovery plan when referring to plans that are intended to guide the recovery process.

2. Public assistance is that part of federal disaster relief authorized under Section 406 the Stafford Act through which the federal government supplements the efforts of state and local governments to return to pre-disaster conditions following a presidential disaster. These efforts primarily involve repair and restoration of public facilities, infrastructure, and services. Some mitigation may be authorized as part of the reconstruction of damaged public facilities and infrastructure. Public assistance also covers debris removal and emergency protective measures such as evacuation and provision of extraordinary police and fire protection designed to save lives, protect property, and maintain operation of essential facilities in the immediate aftermath of the disaster.

3. Santa Rosa Island extends across three counties: Escambia, Santa Rosa, and Okaloosa.

4. The Coastal Construction Control Line (CCCL) demarcates an area within which permits are required from Florida's Department of Environmental Protection (DEP) for excavation or construction. The CCCL defines that portion of the beach and dune system subject to the erosion effects of a 100-year storm surge. Permit conditions include construction and elevation standards for wind, wave, hydrostatic and hydrodynamic loads, and erosion conditions designed to resist the predicted forces associated with a 100-year storm event. The proposed structure or excavation also must be located sufficiently landward of the beach and dune system to permit natural shoreline fluctuations and to preserve the dune stability and natural recovery following storm induced erosion. Any new habitable structures also must be located landward of a 30-year erosion projection line. Existing major habitable structures can be remodeled or repaired after a storm without complying with the CCCL permit conditions or the 30-year setback so long as the modified or repaired structure remains within the confines of the existing foundation and no modification of the foundation is involved. However, most local building codes apply the 50 percent damage threshold required under the National Flood Insurance Program as the threshold for requiring rebuilt structures to meet applicable building code standards. This threshold also holds for structures within the CCCL; that is, a structure within the CCCL damaged beyond the local code damage threholds is required to be rebuilt to DEP standards even where the original foundation is not significantly damaged.

5. An assessment by the State Department of Environmental Protection (1995) reports that 56 percent of the residential structures in the Florida Panhandle built prior to the implementation of the state's CCCL permitting program were damaged 50 percent or more, versus less than 1 percent (2 out of 576) of the structures built under the permitting program.

6. The only major funding source for mitigation initiatives during the short-term recovery process is FEMA's Section 406 Public Assistance Program. (See endnote 2 above.) The principal purpose of Section 406 funds is to assist in returning damaged public facilities to their pre-storm condition. However, under certain conditions, Section 406 funds can be used to reconstruct damaged facilities so as to reduce their vulnerability to future damage. As a general rule, Section 406 mitigation for a facility must be linked to the damage for which a damage survey report is written and cannot exceed the cost of the damage to the facility caused by the disaster (Andrews 1996; Loomis 1996). Such proposals must be accompanied by a cost-effectiveness analysis comparable to that required for long-term mitigation projects funded under Section 404 of the Stafford Act.

7. DCA initiated the Section 404 application process within 30 days of the storm and required that applications be submitted within 90 days (March 1, 1996). Officials in several communities told us that this gave them insufficient time to develop project proposals. FEMA regulations give the state 240 days to submit Section 404 projects, and the FEMA regional director can grant an extension of an additional 90 days. Thus, the application window could have been wider. DCA, however, requires 60 days to review proposals from the communities to make certain that they meed federal criteria and have adequate documentation. DCA consciously reduced the application time from 180 days after Hurricane Erin to 90 days after Opal in order to reduce the delay in actually receiving the federal funds after the disaster. DCA staff also felt that the longer application period after Erin had caused some communities to lose interest in the program (Smith 1996).

The state decided to allocate Section 404 funds among the counties based on total federal disaster assistance claims (public assistance as well as assistance to individuals and businesses) and required the multiple applicants within each county to rank their projects where the total exceeded their allocation. This approach was adopted to counter problems that had arisen after Tropical Storm Alberto at which time priorities for Section 404 projects were established solely by DCA.

8. We are not the first to suggest a phasing of the recovery process. Haas et al. (1977) also define a three-phase process of restoration, reconstruction period I, and reconstruction period II. This parallels our distinctions. However, Haas et al. attempt to fit very explicit types of actions into each phase and propose actual time intervals, in weeks, over which each phase occurs. Rubin, Saperstein, and Barbee (1985) found that the time intervals and sequence of reconstruction issues specified by Haas et al. were not apparent in the disaster cases they studied. Our phases also differ by extending into the pre-disaster time period and by recognizing that there may be substantial overlap between short- and long-term recovery.

Chapter 11

Wildfire Case Study: Oakland, California

KENNETH C. TOPPING, AICP

Ken Topping, former consultant and City of Los Angeles planning director, is general manager for the Cambria Community Services District near the Hearst Castle on the Central Coast of California. He is also the author of the model recovery and reconstruction ordinance in Chapter 5 of this PAS Report.

Natural hazard mitigation should help shape development as an integral part of urban planning and design. But, in cities throughout our nation, a variety of natural hazards coexist with the built environment, and safety policy issues are often postponed until a disaster occurs. At that point, however, hazard mitigation options often are restricted by the existing pattern of development, and it may be too costly or too late to appreciably modify hazardous conditions that have accrued over decades.

After disasters, critical policy choices emerge almost immediately that may force an unwelcome choice between rebuilding quickly versus more safely. Policy choices range theoretically from public acquisition of hazardous sites at one extreme to implementation of relatively minor construction code changes at the other. Viewed practically, real choices may be severely limited by economics and extreme pressures to restore normalcy.

Oakland, California, is a classic example of a community struggling with risk reduction and community improvement issues after major disasters. The Oakland Hills firestorm occurred in October 1991 just two years after the Loma Prieta earthquake. The community had not recovered from the Loma Prieta earthquake when it was hit by a much more devastating fire disaster, raising recovery issues for which the community was not prepared.

Oakland's experience highlights a variety of post-disaster planning issues and reflects a fundamental nationwide dilemma: how can communities reduce existing risks from large-scale urban/wildland interface or intermix fires in built-out urban and suburban environments? (The term "urban/wildland fire interface" generally refers to areas in which urban, suburban, or resort development closely borders or encroaches upon hilly or forested areas naturally subject to periodic wildfires. The term "urban/wildland fire intermix" generally refers to areas in which development has heavily penetrated hilly or forested areas.) The Oakland case study offers potentially valuable insights into recovery and reconstruction policy pressures and pitfalls that can help planners anticipate and prepare to mitigate such problems before disaster strikes.

While planners are often limited by political or economic factors in attempting to promote and implement wise development in urban/wildland fire interface or intermix areas, if armed with accurate information, they can influence policy and work cooperatively with others to help educate their communities toward better hazard mitigation and reconstruction practices.

THE 1991 FIRESTORM

The firestorm occurred on October 20, 1991 within a larger high fire hazard zone that is part of an approximately 60-mile stretch of hills running from the Carquinez Strait to San Jose in the east San Francisco Bay area. The fire

The fire area was part of a much larger swath of urban/wildland fire interface neighborhoods running much of the length of the East Bay Hills, from Crockett to Fremont. In the Oakland fire area, there was the additional element of extensive stands of mature nonindigenous trees, originally planted to sell land, which combined with dense private landscaping to form a charming, artificially forested, and very hazardous environment.

A variety of other features increased the hazard, including steep terrain, small lots, narrow streets, outdated water systems, and houses with wood roofs and siding and extensive eaves and balconies. Though characterized by high property values due to its excellent bay views and its woodsy atmosphere, the area was a disaster waiting to happen.

occurred in portions of the cities of Oakland and Berkeley situated near the juncture of the State Route 24 and 13 freeways. In Oakland, 2,777 units were destroyed or badly damaged. An additional 69 units were destroyed within Berkeley.

The fire happened in an economically well-off, largely built-out residential area that has a longstanding fire history linked to hot, dry fall winds and the presence of dense, flammable vegetation. Unusually strong, dry winds drove flames furiously and rapidly across an approximately two-and-one-half-square-mile area of densely developed hillside neighborhoods.

The fire area was part of a much larger swath of urban/wildland fire interface neighborhoods running much of the length of the East Bay Hills, from Crockett to Fremont. In the Oakland fire area, there was the additional element of extensive stands of mature nonindigenous trees, originally planted to sell land, which combined with dense private landscaping to form a charming, artificially forested, and very hazardous environment.

A variety of other features increased the hazard, including steep terrain, small lots, narrow streets, outdated water systems, and houses with wood roofs and siding and extensive eaves and balconies. Though characterized by high property values due to its excellent bay views and its woodsy atmosphere, the area was a disaster waiting to happen.

What lessons can be learned from this experience? The Oakland Hills fire is significant for several reasons.

1. *This was by far the worst of all the urban/wildland interface or intermix fire disasters in U.S. history.* Without proper precautions, it could easily happen again on an even larger scale in the same community or in other communities having similar conditions. Urban/wildland fire interface hazard conditions are not unique to the Oakland Hills. Rather, they are found in many older portions of hillside and mountain communities in West Coast and Rocky Mountain states, as well as flatter, heavily forested portions of Midwest and Southeastern states.

2. *The event clearly underscores the need for hazard mitigation early in the community planning and development process.* Given longstanding knowledge of the area's high fire hazard conditions, early implementation of more appropriate landscaping and development standards might have blunted the fire's devastating effects, at least to some extent. This raises fundamental challenges of how to create safer communities through effective hazard mitigation during initial phases of development as well as how to effectively address safety issues after a disaster strikes.

3. *The Oakland Hills fire recovery can be useful in better understanding the need for pre-event planning for post-disaster reconstruction.* Recent expressions by various professional staff members reflect a feeling that, in retrospect, Oakland was essentially unprepared for the scope and severity of issues faced following the 1991 firestorm. Additionally, there is the feeling that had pre-event planning occurred, the intense pressures of the post-disaster situation might have been to some extent anticipated and dealt with systematically, rather than on an ad hoc, piecemeal basis that yielded less effective results.

4. *The Oakland Hills fire recovery highlights a commonly experienced tension between the needs of residents to reestablish normal lives quickly and pressing safety post-disaster issues.* Needs of fire victims for quick action were in direct opposition to the time needed to address such important fire safety and community improvement measured as: street widening; requiring class-A roofs, nonwood siding, sprinklers, and restricting balconies and eaves; adoption of new design review requirements;

imposing safety retrofit measures on existing development; managing vegetation to minimize fire hazards yet maintain visual amenities; financing long-term costs of needed water, sewer, and street infrastructure improvements; and addressing safety issues regarding future development on remaining unbuilt private lands. As a result, certain of these post-disaster fire safety objectives were compromised or not met.

5. *The Oakland Hills fire informs us of commonly experienced post-disaster political processes that restrict opportunities for community betterment during recovery and reconstruction.* The sequence of events following the fire illustrates the high level of public sympathy for victims, substantial antagonism toward government, and an overwhelming pressure to restore normalcy that are characteristic of many reconstruction situations. In this atmosphere, safety provisions or community improvements that would impose a delay or an additional cost burden on victims are viewed as inhumane and/or confiscatory. Such situations place intense pressures upon staff to minimize development restrictions and community improvements in order to speed rebuilding, often to the detriment of future public safety.

6. *The fire illustrates the tendency in such situations to modify preferred solutions to accommodate perceived practical constraints in order to restore normalcy quickly.* Although there were generally adequate rights-of-way, many hillside streets had insufficient paved width to accommodate simultaneous inbound firefighting and outbound mass evacuation vehicular movements. This resulted in deaths on a portion of Charing Cross Road. Yet after the fire, street widening was seen as a too costly and time-consuming impediment to a quick return to normalcy. Instead, the city substituted on-street parking restrictions as the principal measure by which to facilitate future movements, both normal and emergency. Although such parking restrictions are now being implemented as the area is being rebuilt, it remains to be seen whether they work well in the long run.

> Although there were generally adequate rights-of-way, many hillside streets had insufficient paved width to accommodate simultaneous inbound firefighting and outbound mass evacuation vehicular movements. This resulted in deaths on a portion of Charing Cross Road. Yet after the fire, street widening was seen as a too costly and timeconsuming impediment to a quick return to normalcy.

7. *The Oakland hills fire has provided some positive precedents, notwithstanding the frustrations experienced during the rebuilding process.* For purposes of meeting fire victims needs, the most notable accomplishment was the successful establishment and operation, with funding from the Federal Emergency Management Agency (FEMA), of a Community Restoration and Development Center (CRDC) that provided one-stop federal and state disaster assistance, city permitting assistance, psychological and financial counseling, and other victim support services. Likewise, a positive precedent toward obtaining informed community and professional input was the Task Force on Emergency Preparedness and Community Restoration, co-chaired by the mayors of Oakland and Berkeley. The task force put forward many specific recommendations later implemented, such as:

- passage by Oakland's voters in mid-1992 of a $50 million bond election for safety improvements;

- formation in early 1993 of a benefit assessment district for a long-term vegetation management program established for the entire high fire hazard area in the Oakland Hills; and

- city leadership in formation of a vegetation management consortium, comprised of representatives from public agencies and utilities in the East Bay Hills.

CHRONOLOGY

The Oakland Hills fire area is part of the East Bay Hills, an extensive urban/ wildland fire interface area that runs approximately 60 miles along the east side of San Francisco Bay from the Carquinez Strait to San Jose. It was initially developed for residential living during the early 1900s, partly as a refuge for victims of the 1906 San Francisco earthquake.

As a result of early twentieth century land development, a variety of nonindigenous species of shrubs and trees, such as French broom, eucalyptus, and Monterey pine, were introduced and proliferated over the years to form an artificially forested environment contrasting markedly with the original natural environment of grassy, oak-studded hills.

Kenneth C. Topping

Despite the attractiveness of balconies in this hilly, wooded area of Oakland, these features represent a real danger because of their potential to catch flaming updrafts of wildfire debris.

As development accelerated before and after World War II, dense new urban forests mixed with private landscaping and development features, such as steep view lots, narrow streets, wood siding and shake shingles, extensive decks, and roof overhangs, to create a woodsy residential setting having extraordinary charm, prestige, and economic value to the community. However, with the presence of the annual dry fall winds, it also represented a deadly mix of hazardous wildland/urban interface conditions.

Over the previous 70 years, destructive fires had recurred in the East Bay Hills during the fall season, when dry offshore winds predominate. In 1923, a major fire destroyed 584 structures in Berkeley. Since the 1930s, 14 large-scale fires occurred in the Oakland Hills, including seven that originated essentially within the same canyon area where the 1991 firestorm began. In 1970, for example, a 204-acre fire destroyed 37 homes in the Buckingham Road area. Subsequently rebuilt, these homes were again destroyed in the 1991 firestorm.

Although some East Bay communities acknowledged the presence of fire risks, public sentiment and building industry opposition appeared to work against fire hazard mitigation. Water systems installed early in the area's development had not been upgraded to meet modern fire flow standards. Little emphasis was placed on upgrading lot size, paved street width, dual access, and building setback standards, except in certain new subdivisions on vacant land.

A notable exception was the *Report of the Blue Ribbon Fire Prevention Committee for the East Bay Hills Area, Urban-Wildland Interface Zone*, published in 1982 by the East Bay Regional Park District. Representing the best thinking of a variety of prominent fire, planning, parks, and forestry professionals, including then California Resources Agency Director William Penn Mott, the report recommended a series of specific hazard mitigation measures, such as the clearing of fire breaks. However, relatively few of the report's recommendations were implemented, and development continued to favor intensification of quaint, woodsy but dangerous neighborhood settings in the Oakland Hills.

The Fire and Its Aftermath

The fire started on October 19, 1991, on a hillside in an Oakland residential neighborhood near the juncture of the State Route 24 and the Route 13 freeways in the vicinity of the Oakland Tunnel. Initially contained and controlled, fire crews left the scene thinking it was fully extinguished.

The fire erupted the next day from remaining embers whipped by strong, dry northeasterly winds that quickly drove rapidly spreading flames across both freeways and through a series of residential neighborhoods, largely within Oakland. Densely built houses, readily combustible roofing and building materials, and heavy, flammable vegetation added to the intensity of a firestorm that destroyed virtually everything in its path. Narrow, winding streets in steep terrain hampered evacuation and fire truck access. Water pressure was insufficient for firefighting. Oakland hydrant connections were larger than the hose couplings of fire trucks from neighboring communities. The fire moved so quickly and intensely that firefighters were virtually helpless to contain it until the winds began to die down.

In all, the Oakland Hills firestorm of October 19-20, 1991, burned more than 1,600 acres, destroying or badly damaging 2,021 homes and 756 apartment and condominium units, killing 25 people and injuring 150 others. Approximately 10,000 fire victims were displaced by this event.

The impact of the fire on the community was staggering. Almost overnight, a huge hole had been torn in the fabric of one of its most prestigious areas, an area that represented an important source of income and leadership. There was widespread concern that fire victims would simply sell or abandon their property and choose to move elsewhere, thus threatening the future economic well-being of the community. This event drew an immediate response from elected officials, with Mayor Elihu Harris declaring the day after the disaster that "Oakland will rebuild!"

Immediate Post-Disaster Phase

The 1991 Oakland Hills firestorm challenged Oakland to address many problems of the urban/wildland interface environment that had previously received insufficient policy attention. In the context of post-disaster evaluations conducted by the media and by federal, state, and other groups, Oakland acknowledged an urgent need to develop effective near-term actions on hazard mitigation and emergency management tied to the recovery and reconstruction process. A report, *Hazard Mitigation Report for the East Bay Fire in the Oakland-Berkeley Hills*, which was issued by FEMA's Interagency Hazard Mitigation Survey Team, identified numerous emergency management and hazard mitigation improvements needed.

As in other disasters, victims needed a rapid return to normalcy. Multiple frustrations were experienced by disaster victims seeking to obtain information regarding rebuilding policy during the time it was still being formulated by staff committees. Over 50 separate neighborhood groups became involved with rebuilding issues. Many identifying themselves as "Phoenix" associations were comprised primarily of fire victims.

During this immediate post-disaster phase, a high level of public sympathy was expressed for fire victims who had lost everything and knew little about the extent to which insurance might cover their losses. Intense anger was directed toward city staff by citizens who blamed the fire department for the disaster. Many longstanding safety problems came into public view for the first time (e.g., highly flammable roofs and vegetation, substandard streets, and outdated water systems). Fire victims were annoyed by the seeming slowness with which city reconstruction policies emerged. As such rebuilding policies gradually began to take shape, anger was then redirected at city staff members promoting safety measures seen by fire victims and builders as unnecessarily restrictive or obstructive.

Within this tense situation, strong pressures were exerted by various interest groups urging the city to expedite rebuilding. The most prominent advocates

> In all, the Oakland Hills firestorm of October 19-20, 1991, burned more than 1,600 acres, destroying or badly damaging 2,021 homes and 756 apartment and condominium units, killing 25 people and injuring 150 others. Approximately 10,000 fire victims were displaced by this event. The impact of the fire on the community was staggering. Almost overnight, a huge hole had been torn in the fabric of one of its most prestigious areas, an area that represented an important source of income and leadership.

Kenneth C. Topping

Partially rebuilt houses dot the burnt-over landscape of the Oakland Hills in the aftermath of the 1991 fire.

were the fire victims themselves. Other groups sharing a similar interest were members of the building industry, some of whom came from outside the city looking for opportunity, others who represented well-established local builders, contractors, and architects. Particularly influential was an industry organization known as the Oakland Development Council. Interest groups with a different orientation included professional firefighting, planning, scientific, and forestry organizations advocating adoption of stricter hazard mitigation measures related to rebuilding. For example, concerns were expressed by representatives of the East Bay Regional Park District and Regional Water Quality Control Board, along with geologists from University of California at Berkeley, regarding potential erosion, siltation, and pollution resulting from the fire aftermath and post-fire rebuilding activities.

KEY PLANNING ISSUES
Theoretical vs. Pragmatic Policy Options

After major wildland fires and similar disasters, critical policy issues emerge regarding whether to relocate or replan the community or neighborhood to gain greater safety. In such situations, theoretical reconstruction policy options may cover a wide spectrum, ranging from land acquisition and relocation of the neighborhood or community at one end to imposition of relatively minor construction changes at the other. Choices made tend to honor victims' needs to rebuild quickly without sufficient thought to options which may be available. Yet decisions made during the early days following a disaster such as the Oakland fire may have significant long-term consequences for future public safety. Often, in the rush to restore normalcy, development is permitted under some of the same unsafe conditions that contributed to the intensity of the disaster.

The Oakland experience highlighted post-disaster pressures that work against serious consideration of relocation or redesign of a neighborhood or community on a large scale. The immediate post-disaster phase in Oakland represented theoretical as well as pragmatic policy options that inherently exist following any catastrophic disaster, whether or not acknowledged by the affected community.

1) Should the neighborhood or community be rebuilt or relocated?

2) If rebuilt, should it first be replanned?

3) To what extent should new restrictions be imposed to achieve greater safety as the area is rebuilt?

4) What retrofit requirements should be placed on damaged buildings as they are repaired?

5) What new restrictions should be placed on new development on vacant land in similar nearby areas?

Most planning issues, however, were shaped by a prevailing policy context that overwhelmingly emphasized the goal of rebuilding as quickly as possible in order to maintain the Oakland Hills as a source of revenue and community leadership. Moreover, there was no political support for imposing additional financial burdens or delays on a population who had lost all their homes and belongings.

One of the important theoretical post-disaster policy issues that might otherwise have been addressed was the question of whether to relocate rebuilding out of harm's way. This issue of whether to relocate communities or neighborhoods has emerged nationally in recent years due to excessive past costs of providing disaster assistance to areas struck repeatedly by disaster. Following the Midwestern floods of 1993, FEMA initiated a buy-out program that permanently removes development from certain areas subject to recurring flooding. This solution seldom has been used in the past except in rare cases, such as relocation of the town of Valdez following the 1964 Anchorage, Alaska, earthquake, public acquisition of the waterfront area of Hilo on the island of Hawaii after their second devastating tidal wave, and relocation of a portion of Rapid City after the 1972 flood.

In Oakland, however, relocation was not a viable option because the decision had already been made politically, in response to victims' suffering, to rebuild as quickly as possible. Moreover, at the time there was no identifiable source of funding for acquisition of property in the fire area or for rebuilding elsewhere, nor was there readily identifiable a place to relocate nearly 3,000 homes and apartments. Even had there been such financing and a place for relocation practically available, the time necessary to acquire land and rebuild elsewhere would have delayed restoration of victims' homes for too many years.

A second policy question would have been whether to replan and redesign the fire-ravaged neighborhoods for maximum safety prior to rebuilding. In Oakland, this would have meant substantial transformation of the area through extensive widening and opening of streets, clustering development densities, transferring development rights, and reorganizing open spaces in order to minimize historic fire hazards. This was not considered a viable option, however, since the funding needed to accomplish this was not available and more importantly, it would have taken too long to meet victims' needs. Therefore, few voices were raised in the public discussions on behalf of major redesign to achieve greater safety. Ideal safety-based solutions, such as resubdividing, were suggested by a few design professionals, but such recommendations were ignored due to perceived costs and practical difficulties.

A second policy question would have been whether to replan and redesign the fire-ravaged neighborhoods for maximum safety prior to rebuilding. In Oakland, this would have meant substantial transformation of the area through extensive widening and opening of streets, clustering development densities, transferring development rights, and reorganizing open spaces in order to minimize historic fire hazards. This was not considered a viable option, however, since the funding needed to accomplish this was not available and more importantly, it would have taken too long to meet victims' needs.

The local design community, under the leadership of the Bay Area Chapter and California Council of the American Institute of Architects (AIA) gave no support to replanning. In a series of charrettes conducted in different neighborhoods in early December 1991 to assist residents with suggestions regarding the rebuilding process, a great deal of attention was given to reestablishment of the architectural diversity that previously characterized various burned out neighborhoods. Very little emphasis was placed on street widening or other safety issues. Moreover, according to some planning staff members, aside from *Community Voices: A Resource Guide for Rebuilding*, a booklet published as a product of the charrettes, there was little continuing organized involvement of AIA during the rebuilding process, although a few members stayed involved personally through adoption of the new design review ordinance.

A third policy option might have been to more aggressively address the street-width issue, delaying the rebuilding process long enough to identify major emergency access and evacuation routes, determine means to fund required improvements along such routes, and conduct the preliminary engineering to establish pavement widths and grades by which to determine retaining-wall setbacks and driveway connection elevations. This would have taken additional time but would not have slowed the reconstruction process nearly as long as if the community were to have been relocated or replanned. Many other time-consuming processes needed to be undertaken, such as restoration of personal records, filing of insurance claims, and determination of home-rebuilding plan details. In actuality, many months went by before the largest flow of permit requests began. This might have allowed time to find additional funding (e.g., from FEMA or through Measure I, a bond issue that focused on safety improvements) and conduct preliminary engineering to enable selective widening. As it turned out later, the only widening funded by FEMA was for Charing Cross Road.

Highly visible in the public discussion of policy options was an inter-jurisdictional Mayors' Task Force on Emergency Preparedness and Community Restoration, established jointly by the cities of Oakland and Berkeley. Cochaired by the mayors of the two cities, this ad hoc task force included residents, professionals, professors, officials, and private-sector representatives. The Final Report of the Task Force on Emergency Preparedness and Community Restoration contained dozens of recommendations relating to post-disaster safety improvements and community betterment, many of which were later implemented.

In providing a framework for determining planning issues to be considered in its deliberations, however, the Planning, Zoning and Design Committee of the Mayors' Task Force focused on more limited and potentially conflicting goals:

- through the rebuilding process, encourage diversity in architectural design and site planning;

- allow rebuilding to occur quickly by developing an expedited process for permit review;

- encourage innovative parking solutions to help limit the number of cars along narrow roadways that need to be used as evacuation routes and primary access routes for emergency vehicles;

- seek methods for incorporating some level of neighborhood input into the design review process;

- develop mechanisms to limit the size and bulk of structures on small lots; and

- underground utilities.

A third policy option might have been to more aggressively address the street-width issue, delaying the rebuilding process long enough to identify major emergency access and evacuation routes, determine means to fund required improvements along such routes, and conduct the preliminary engineering to establish pavement widths and grades by which to determine retaining-wall setbacks and driveway connection elevations. This would have taken additional time but would not have slowed the reconstruction process nearly as long as if the community were to have been relocated or replanned.

The latter recommendation to place utilities underground was based on a safety as well as aesthetic concern. A fire department battalion chief had been killed by a falling power line during the firestorm. Also, loss of power during the firestorm had significantly interfered with operation of the East Bay Municipal Utilities District (East Bay MUD) water pumping stations, seriously interrupting water flows for firefighting.

Staff Team

During this immediate post-disaster period, planners found themselves in a support function as members of a citywide staff team coordinated by the city manager's office on behalf of the mayor and city council. Serving as advisers to various citizen and staff committees, Oakland's planners were part of a citywide effort to fashion workable policies and procedures that would expedite rebuilding of the burned area while establishing certain community safety and improvement measures. In this manner, planners were drawn into a variety of recovery policy proposals, many having to do with building, fire safety, street access and permitting issues.

A deputy city manager was assigned to establish a center for community restoration and development, CRDC, which was funded by FEMA and was a multiagency one-stop assistance and permitting operation. Another was assigned to work directly and continuously with citizens group representatives through weekly meetings held at the CRDC. Successful establishment and operation of the CRDC was a notable accomplishment during this immediate post-disaster period. Funded by FEMA through June 1994, the center has provided one-stop federal and state disaster assistance, city permitting assistance, and other victim support services in a converted grocery store near the fire area. This move toward humanizing the bureaucracy and speeding post-disaster permitting and disaster assistance services has been emulated in subsequent recovery situations, most recently after the Northridge earthquake in California.

The Emergency Order

One of the first staff products was an *Emergency Order for Fire Reconstruction and Information Regarding Emergency Preparedness*, adopted by the city council on November 26, 1991. Among other things, it required class-A or essentially non-wood roofs within an identified fire hazard area comprising all of the Oakland Hills northeast of the state Route 13 freeway. While this was an extension of prior policy for certain hillside areas, it represented a significant step from a safety planning and policy perspective. Wood shingle roofs had been demonstrated in recent decades to add significantly to fire hazards in urban/wildland interface areas. This action was even more significant in the face of intense opposition to this requirement generated by the wood shingle industry in various cities.

The emergency order also placed certain restrictions on siding, projections, eaves, decks, and balconies within that area. Some of these provisions were later softened or eliminated in response to industry and community backlash. Significantly, the emergency order did not include a staff proposal that would have required internal sprinkler systems within the high fire hazard area. This proposal was opposed by fire victims and the building industry even though average costs for such a safety measure were estimated within a relatively modest range of $3,000 to $5,000 per dwelling unit.

The emergency order also included standards for increasing street widths for evacuation and emergency vehicle response access for selected routes. For other local streets, as a substitute for widening, it recommended parking restrictions on one or both sides, depending on pavement width, to be implemented by subsequent ordinances.

The recommendation to place utilities underground was based on a safety as well as aesthetic concern. A fire department battalion chief had been killed by a falling power line during the firestorm. Also, loss of power during the firestorm had significantly interfered with operation of the East Bay Municipal Utilities District (East Bay MUD) water pumping stations, seriously interrupting water flows for firefighting.

The emergency order also placed certain restrictions on siding, projections, eaves, decks, and balconies within that area. Some of these provisions were later softened or eliminated in response to industry and community backlash. Significantly, the emergency order did not include a staff proposal that would have required internal sprinkler systems within the high fire hazard area. This proposal was opposed by fire victims and the building industry even though average costs for such a safety measure were estimated within a relatively modest range of $3,000 to $5,000 per dwelling unit.

The Street-Widening Issue

In many ways, street widening was more difficult to deal with than other issues. Many hillside streets throughout the fire area and the rest of the Oakland Hills could be seen to have insufficient paved width for normal two-way traffic, much less for firefighting response and mass evacuations. Paved widths on even arterials such as Broadway Terrace northeast of the State Route 13 freeway were barely adequate to accommodate one moving lane in each direction. Additionally there were many dead-end culs-de-sac with less than two lanes of pavement and insufficient turnarounds for firefighting apparatus.

The problem generally did not involve the need for additional dedications because in most cases rights-of-way were sufficient. The real problem was in the cost of cutting and filling on the upslope and downslope sides, respectively, to provide additional space for pavement widening and shoulders, as well as to build retaining walls on both sides. Also involved was the practical question of how long it would take to prepare widening plans from which elevations and gradients for driveway connections could be identified. Initial estimates for construction of retaining walls for upslope properties was $6,000 and for downslope properties was $10,000. Not calculated were the considerable costs for rebuilding on sites with houses that survived the fire to accommodate new locations for pavement or grades.

In addition to these costs and expected delays, proposals for street widening at the expense of fire victims were also seen as inequitable since the problem of inadequate street pavement widths was prevalent throughout the Oakland Hills. Street-widening projects had long been inherently unpopular throughout the Oakland Hills, as evidenced by the many parcels owned by the city from a widening project along Grizzly Peak Boulevard effectively halted by citizen opposition many years before.

Thus costs and practical difficulties associated with street widening, along with its essential unpopularity, persuaded the city council to minimize street widening as a solution. Instead, it chose to limit proposed widenings to very few routes and opted to honor expressed citizen preferences for on-street parking restrictions as a substitute measure to facilitate future movement. Parking restrictions are now being implemented; however, in light of recent citizen resistance, the jury is still out on how well this particular solution will actually work.

Numerous people died along Charing Cross Road, whose single lane made quick evacuation difficult.

Kenneth C. Topping

The Design Review Ordinance

One important outgrowth from the Mayor's Task Force process was the S-14 Community Restoration Development Combining Zone initially proposed by staff and prepared at the city's request by a consulting firm in mid-1992 as filing of rebuilding permits was accelerating. According to ordinance language, the zone was intended to promote the following goals:

Kenneth C. Topping

1) reconstruction that will replicate, to the extent possible, the pre-fire conditions that contributed to the distinctive character and desirability of the fire area neighborhoods;

2) design and construction that is responsive to the substantial variations in topography, access, and parcelization both within and among the respective neighborhoods;

3) facilitation and expediting of reconstruction to minimize economic and emotional hardships for fire victims; and

4) prevention of conditions that pose threats to life and property.

Many of the new homes built after the fire had considerably more floor space than those in existence prior to the fire.

The purpose of the ordinance was to place greater restrictions on new home development than were reflected in existing zoning. First established in 1935, then comprehensively revised in 1965, zoning generally allowed minimum lot sizes of 5,000 square feet on very steep terrain, with very limited setbacks, and essentially no floor area ratio (FAR) or design review requirements.

Exceptions to these generally permissive zoning provisions were found in areas of the fire area that were covered by the existing S-10 and S-11 combining zones. The S-10 zone had been mapped along ridgeline streets and protected public views from these corridors. The S-11 zone required architectural review and certain safety provisions.

The proposed ordinance dealt with site development and design review requirements, floor area ratios, height, yard setbacks, projections, parking and loading, landscaping, secondary units, and minimum lot area. The principal concern of its advocates was to reconcile three key goals; namely, recreate an atmosphere of charm through architectural diversity, expedite the permit process, and improve public safety.

Taking advantage of the relatively unrestrictive zoning still in place, property owners found it possible to replace homes previously valued in the $300,000 to $500,000 range with much larger homes in the $600,000 to $800,000 range. Fire victims were caught between their preferences for replacing the previously delightful architectural character of their neighborhoods and the economic opportunity to significantly gain added value and floor space.

Public discussion had reflected an aversion to an immediately evident trend toward building boxy, bulky homes that maximized use of the small lots using stock designs put forward by local builders. The concern was that the area would lose its essential architectural charm and the magnificent views of San Francisco Bay that had initially drawn residents and created value.

Meanwhile, fire victims were finding it possible through generous fire insurance payments to increase substantially the floor space of rebuilt homes. While there had been a fear that insurance payments would not be adequate to cover the rebuilding costs for replacement of relatively modest but architecturally interesting homes built in the 1920s through 1950s, it was soon found that, by careful photographic and other detailed documentation of previous homes and their contents, higher payments than expected could be obtained.

Taking advantage of the relatively unrestrictive zoning still in place, property owners found it possible to replace homes previously valued in the $300,000 to $500,000 range with much larger homes in the $600,000 to $800,000 range. Fire victims were caught between their preferences for replacing the previously delightful architectural character of their neighborhoods and the economic opportunity to significantly gain added value and floor space. Consequently, the proposed ordinance ran into substantial opposition from homeowners seeking to better their position as well as the building industry seeking to avoid restrictions. As the months of public review wore on, support for the ordinance waned.

According to one of the key staff members involved, the initial work done on the S-14 zone by the consulting firm of Sedway Cooke Associates was later adjusted by city staff as consensus developed over time between neighborhood representatives, the local construction industry, and design professionals. Ultimately, an ordinance was passed. However, to the frustration of many homeowners who had not yet rebuilt, it contained fewer restrictions than previously proposed. Homeowners who had waited to see what would happen with the new ordinance were dismayed because precious San Francisco Bay views that might have been protected under the more stringent proposal were no longer protected under the adopted ordinance. They were already unhappy because of the length of time it had taken to adopt the modified ordinance, during which period many homes were built to the maximum allowable height, bulk, and setback envelopes permitted under existing zoning. Also escaping the modified ordinance restrictions under grandfather provisions were many similar homes that had previously received permits but which were as yet unbuilt.

The net result was achievement of the key goal of rapid rebuilding, at the expense of another key goal of recreating a sense of architectural diversity. A staff member close to the situation recently estimated that perhaps 50 to 60 percent of the rebuilt homes were boxy standard design/build homes, rather than houses reflecting site-sensitive, diverse architectural design.

Considering the fact that permits have been issued on approximately 80 percent of the single-family home sites affected by the fire, the net effect has been to create greater intensity of development with far less architectural diversity and protection of far fewer bay views than had been envisioned. While architectural diversity and view protection may have seemed frivolous to some victims who simply wished to reestablish their lives, such elements were also known to have given this area its original value. For some staff members involved in seeing the ordinance through to adoption, there is a feeling that the ordinance may have longer-term value as the effects of its provisions are seen in areas remaining to be rebuilt and elsewhere in the Oakland Hills should the ordinance be applied there in the future.

Perhaps most critical, however, is the ultimate effect of creating greater building intensity in an area that remains seriously deficient in street widths and access. The long-term safety ramifications of this reality are yet to become clear.

Planners' Roles and Perceptions

Due to the relatively fresh experience of the Loma Prieta earthquake, Oakland's planners were able to address the initial post-disaster fire recovery situation with a certain amount of background on disaster management issues. However, the Oakland Hills experience was far more intense. Although some new thinking had been given to emergency preparedness prior to the fire, it wasn't enough.

Moreover, under immediate post-disaster circumstances, many normal planning procedures applicable to planning new development did not apply. As in many other planning situations, multiple and potentially conflicting objectives were being simultaneously sought. However, decisions were greatly sped up, and extraordinary teamwork was required. Planners were seen by administrators as having a hard time shifting gears from a rule-oriented, procedural perspective to one that was more flexible, free wheeling, and team-oriented. In this politically charged atmosphere, planners were faced with a serious dilemma regarding how strongly to promote consideration of relevant but unpopular safety measures at the risk of inviting administrative or political opprobrium.

Consequently, planners appear to have emerged with a different perception of their role as team players, heightened awareness of the complexities of the applications of various safety measures, and greater acceptance of team-oriented permit processing. Recent statements by various professional staff members reflect a feeling that, in retrospect, the city as a whole was essentially unprepared for the scope and severity of issues faced following the 1991 firestorm. Their feeling was that a pre-disaster plan might have helped city staff to anticipate and be better prepared for the types of pressures and policy issues encountered. In particular, they felt that such a plan might have reduced the time needed to sort through the various policy issues and options that had to be addressed essentially from scratch.

New Opportunities

Many new safety and community improvement opportunities emerged from the crisis. In addition to the flow of professional and community group advocacy influencing outcomes, another critical factor determinant of success in capturing such opportunities was simple proximity in time to the event.

Freshness of memories during the immediate post-disaster period was a critical determinant of which fire safety actions were ultimately successfully implemented. The window of opportunity for implementing substantial changes lasted roughly from 8 to 12 months. In retrospect, the window of opportunity for significant safety and community improvements began closing rapidly after successful passage of Measure I, a general obligation bond for selected safety improvements. Subsequently, other major measures, such as formation of the Fire Prevention and Protection District, were much harder to accomplish.

Measure I was passed by a substantial majority of Oakland voters in June 1992, raising approximately $50 million at an average annual cost to property owners of $15 per $100,000 assessed valuation over 30 years. Proceeds have subsequently funded additional safety-related capital improvements and equipment for water supply, seismic reinforcement of fire stations, access for emergency vehicles, construction of an adequate emergency operations center, development of an emergency-response-oriented citywide Geographic Information System (GIS), and communications upgrades.

Planners appear to have emerged with a different perception of their role as team players, heightened awareness of the complexities of the applications of various safety measures, and greater acceptance of team-oriented permit processing. . . . Their feeling was that a pre-disaster plan might have helped city staff to anticipate and be better prepared for the types of pressures and policy issues encountered. In particular, they felt that such a plan might have reduced the time needed to sort through the various policy issues and options that had to be addressed essentially from scratch.

Vegetation management is a serious issue in wildland/urban interface areas. Here, Monterey pine and eucalyptus plantings are encroaching on natural vegetation.

Vegetation Management

During the immediate post-disaster period, the groundwork was laid for later formation of a fire prevention and suppression benefit assessment district. Formed in March 1993, its overall goal is to reduce the number and intensity of large, destructive wildland/urban interface fires in the Oakland Hills and avoid future losses of life and property. At an annual rate of $75 per single-family unit, the district is raising nearly $2 million each year to provide a variety of fire safety services on both public and private property, including vegetation management, code compliance, training and education, additional fire suppression personnel, and public information.

Oakland's vegetation management effort has since led to formation of an intergovernmental, public-private vegetation management consortium, including the cities of Oakland and Berkeley, the East Bay Regional Park District, the East Bay Municipal Utilities District, the Pacific Gas and Electric Company (PG and E), and the University of California at Berkeley, all of which have considerable holdings in the East Bay Hills. The consortium is developing a pioneering interagency vegetation management plan having potentially far-reaching benefits.

GIS System Development

Notable among the Measure I initiatives was authorization of a portion of the funds to create a citywide GIS. This initiative was inspired in part by early efforts associated with the emergency response and recovery.

During and immediately after the firestorm, fire and GIS management professionals from the California Department of Forestry, the University of California at Berkeley, and the California Governor's Office of Emergency Management collaborated in relatively simple GIS applications that mapped fire perimeter boundaries and damage locations in relation to street center lines. One of the frustrations of field personnel in pursuing damage assessment mapping during this early period was the absence of visible addresses, since all such evidence had been destroyed by fire.

This effort was supplemented during recovery and reconstruction with a more ambitious, definitive GIS database development for the fire area, funded by FEMA. The fire area GIS included mapped features and tabular attributes, such as street right-of-way lines, parcel boundaries, addresses, and status of permits and reconstruction. It was a valuable tool in clarifying the status of permits and monitoring reconstruction progress.

Recognizing the potential benefits of such early GIS applications to future emergency management planning, response, and recovery, city staff included within Measure I an approximate $3 million amount dedicated to the development of a citywide GIS that would support a variety of emergency management and other general government functions. Formally authorized by the city council in 1994, the initial phase of this system development is underway. Parallel to this has been work undertaken by the University of California at Berkeley for the vegetation management consortium to map vegetation and other wildland fire factors throughout the portions of the East Bay Hills covered by the participating jurisdictions and institutions.

Infrastructure Improvements

A more recently completed safety initiative from the early post-disaster period was the successful formation of the Rockridge Water Assessment District, covering an area of 750 homes in the area adjacent to the south of the state Route 24 freeway and to the west of Temescal Park. Initiated by fire victims concerned about the possibility of recurrence of fire spread in the future due to inadequate water storage and line capacity, the district has been formed with the cooperation of the city and East Bay MUD, the area's water provider. Residents will pay $134.40 per year for the upgraded water system, with additional contributions to be made by the city and East Bay MUD. This accomplishment was largely due to the Citizen Water Committee, comprised of neighborhood residents whose images of helpless firemen with waterless hoses still remain fresh.

Additional opportunities successfully used following the Oakland Hills fire have included selected street improvements, such as the FEMA-funded widening of Charing Cross Road where people died trying to evacuate during the fire, formation of a sewer assessment district for 36 homes, and implementation of a major utility undergrounding effort led by PG and E.

20:20 Hindsight

Oakland is an excellent example of a built-out community struggling with hazard reduction and community improvement issues following a major disaster. As with many other built-out communities across the nation facing realities of hazard mitigation after a disaster, known hazards issues had essentially not been addressed during early development. Consequently, the community was confronted with a range of safety issues following the fire at a stage when hazard mitigation options were far more limited.

During the Oakland Hills fire reconstruction, many urban planning and design issues related to hazard mitigation and community improvement arose within a typical post-disaster reconstruction scenario reflecting commonly found tensions between humane victim response and potentially conflicting public safety responsibilities. Because the disaster affected older neighborhoods in a largely built-out environment having substandard streets, lots, and infrastructure, public controversy centered on street widening, onstreet and offstreet parking regulations, building height and bulk, setbacks, vegetation management, and water supply.

To restore normalcy as soon as possible, critical decisions were driven by practical constraints such as perceived short-term costs and inconveniences of mitigation and the extreme urgency to act expeditiously on the victims' behalf. Intense pressures were faced by staff officials responsible for reconstruction in the fire area. Safety and community improvements sought by planning and building staff through the emergency order and design review ordinance were modified during city council action, resulting in less safety value and amenities for reconstructed neighborhoods.

Nevertheless, a number of positive public-safety-related outcomes were evident. Oakland staff succeeded in using opportunities arising during the immediate post-disaster period to lay the groundwork for certain key safety

To restore normalcy as soon as possible, critical decisions were driven by practical constraints such as perceived short-term costs and inconveniences of mitigation and the extreme urgency to act expeditiously on the victims' behalf. Intense pressures were faced by staff officials responsible for reconstruction in the fire area. Safety and community improvements sought by planning and building staff through the emergency order and design review ordinance were modified during city council action, resulting in less safety value and amenities for reconstructed neighborhoods.

and community improvements. Extension of the class-A roof requirement and similar standard construction safety measures to most of the Oakland Hills was a substantial achievement. Working with other entities, the city was able to initiate a variety of other safety improvements such as retrofitting fire stations for earthquake safety, modifying the fire hose couplings to accommodate use by other jurisdictions in future fire emergencies, improving water systems, undergrounding utility lines, developing plans for a new emergency operations center, initiating the emergency management GIS, and forming the Fire Prevention and Protection Benefit Assessment District.

Seismicity Factor

While this case study concentrates on the aftermath of a fire disaster, equally relevant is the risk of a catastrophic earthquake within this area. California is a seismically active state, and the San Francisco Bay region has a repeated history of disastrous earthquakes.

Although the Loma Prieta Earthquake did substantial damage in the Bay Area, it has been portrayed by scientists as a relatively mild forerunner of a much more devastating event expected on the Hayward Fault, which cuts across many East Bay communities from San Pablo on the north to Warm Springs south of Fremont. Scientists have determined a substantial probability of a magnitude 7.0 or greater earthquake occurring on the Hayward Fault within the next several decades. Ironically, some early Oakland Hills subdivisions that were promoted as a refuge for 1906 San Francisco earthquake victims sit directly astride the Hayward Fault.

Recent studies coordinated through the Earthquake Engineering Research Institute have demonstrated that a magnitude 7.0-plus event on the Hayward Fault could produce substantially greater destruction than either the Loma Prieta earthquake or the Oakland Hills fire. In such an event, landslides and fault rupture could sever gas and oil lines that cross the East Bay Hills, causing multiple fire outbreaks. Impassable streets and broken water lines could make firefighting difficult. Depending upon weather conditions, conflagration conditions could occur on a large scale.

Significance of Narrow Streets

Thus, the issue of insufficient street widths could emerge again as a significant piece of unfinished business. As the effects of the city council decision to rely on parking restrictions instead of street widening plays out, inadequate pavement widths for firefighting and evacuation purposes could again emerge as a major problem, especially in view of the area's seismicity. In a magnitude 7.0-plus earthquake scenario, street pavement widths may become a critical factor in moving fire and emergency equipment into and people out of hilly areas.

Among Oakland staff, there remains serious concern that lack of funds to finance long-term major capital improvements to widen streets and upgrade major water delivery systems may aggravate a major hazard in the event of a catastrophic earthquake on the Hayward Fault. Current insufficiencies of water lines and storage capacities for wildland firefighting, together with possible severing of primary water lines might leave the city without water for days or weeks. Depending upon wind conditions, or without water for firefighting, large areas might be devastated by earthquake-induced fires.

Unanswered Questions

From this experience, a critically important question is, To what extent did post-disaster actions result in a net gain in public safety in which remaining hazards and risks were reduced overall? It remains to be seen whether the safety measures introduced following the most recent Oakland fire will combine effectively to lower the overall risk in the fire area as time goes on. Complete answers to this question may not be known until a more thorough assessment of recovery and reconstruction experience is conducted, or, alternatively, until the next wildland/urban fire is encountered

An unanswered strategic and tactical question important to many other communities is, What might it have taken to achieve a more ambitious street- widening effort while meeting other immediate post-disaster social, economic, and political needs? It is perhaps both inappropriate as well as unnecessary to pass judgment on the Oakland Hills situation from the outside without real knowledge of the full range of circumstances affecting actual decisions. Yet systematic, objective inquiry into this question is needed because of the potential importance of its answer to creation of greater safety in other communities affected by the threat of repetitive urban/wildland fire disasters.

Given the area's inherent seismicity, the Oakland Hills fire may be a prelude to a much larger catastrophic event. But, together with the Loma Prieta earthquake, the fire will serve as a cumulative resource for information regarding the value and effectiveness of various post-disaster strategies, actions, and outcomes. If nurtured through an ongoing preparedness and pre-event planning process, this could build up the institutional memory from which to launch the next round of advances when the next major disaster strikes.

OBSERVATIONS AND RECOMMENDATIONS

From the Oakland experience, several key observations and recommendations emerge regarding hazard mitigation and disaster recovery and reconstruction related to disasters occurring within wildland/urban interface and intermix areas. These reflect the learning cycle recently taking place within the fields of urban planning, fire protection, and emergency management as severe disasters increasingly affect populated urban, suburban, and resort areas throughout the nation and world.

1. *Planning for Safety from Wildfires.* Urban/wildland interface and intermix fire hazards are not unique to the East Bay Hills. Planners can learn to be more influential in helping communities throughout the nation reduce risks associated with urban/wildland interface and intermix areas. Expansion in recent decades of urban, suburban, rural, and resort development into forested, hilly, and mountainous areas in many regions and states has led to increasing losses of life and property in urban/wildland interface and intermix areas. Wildfire hazard mitigation is an evolving specialty that integrates insights of planners, building and fire officials, engineers, architects, landscape architects, and natural resource managers. Planning for safety from wildfires in urban/wildland interface and intermix areas is an interdisciplinary specialty that involves knowledge of the relationships between a variety of factors, including topography, layout and design of neighborhoods, population density, building intensity, intermixture of development with forested environments, flammability of vegetation, access and street widths, and sufficiency of water systems. Through preparation and implementation of land-use plans and development review processes, planners are in a position to contribute directly to improved wildland fire safety either before or, if necessary, after major fire disasters.

   Recommendation: *Planners in communities affected by urban/wildland interface or intermix hazards should seek available specialized knowledge on*

Planning for safety from wildfires in urban/wildland interface and intermix areas is an interdisciplinary specialty that involves knowledge of the relationships between a variety of factors, including topography, layout and design of neighborhoods, population density, building intensity, intermixture of development with forested environments, flammability of vegetation, access and street widths, and sufficiency of water systems.

wildfire hazard reduction in order to more effectively support local vulnerability assessment and promote hazard mitigation. APA members should seek materials by which to educate themselves and should work with emergency management officials and members of other professional associations in advocating more consistent local fire protection planning. By developing and disseminating educational materials informing elected decision makers, citizens, and educators on the most effective means of mitigating urban/wildland interface fires, planners can help their communities become more conscious of the positive values of effective fire hazard mitigation.

2. *Pre-event Planning for Wildland Fire Recovery and Reconstruction.* Pre-event planning for post-disaster recovery and reconstruction provides a comprehensive framework within which to systematically address wildfire hazard mitigation issues as well as to prepare for possible post-disaster mitigation opportunities. Pre-event planning can help address the level of risk of wildfires and the specific types of hazard mitigation that should be undertaken to improve public safety. Additionally, it can organize processes for more timely and efficient post-disaster action and help anticipate the character and intensity of policy issues about rebuilding that officials may have to face. Most importantly, it can help communities think on their feet strategically and adapt their post-disaster actions to the specific conditions faced after a major urban/wildland fire disaster. Although pre-event planning has been undertaken in relatively few communities to date, it represents an approach that could be usefully applied on a much broader basis, given its application by the planning profession and collaboration with fire safety professionals.

Recommendation: *Pre-event planning for disaster recovery and reconstruction should be specifically tailored for application in communities affected by urban/wildland interface and intermix fire hazards, applying lessons learned from the Oakland Hills fire.* The strategies, methods, techniques, and procedures put forward by this report for pre-event planning for post-disaster recovery and reconstruction should be further adapted for application to the specific problems and issues encountered in urban/wildland interface and intermix communities. This should be pursued through collaboration with such organizations as the National Fire Protection Association, the International City/County Management Association, state emergency management departments, and FEMA. Such organizations have substantial experience with wildland fire hazard mitigation and can inform the planning process of lessons learned elsewhere that can be incorporated into local pre-event plans and strategies. Much rich case study material can be derived not only from Oakland, but also from such other recent wildland fire disasters as the Black Tiger fire near Boulder, Colorado in 1989 and the fall 1993 fires in Altadena, Laguna Beach, and Malibu, California. The lessons from these experiences should be incorporated into pre-event planning that specifically addresses mitigation challenges and post-disaster recovery policy issues dealt with previously by other communities.

3. *The Need for Tailored Mitigation Solutions.* Underlying reconstruction policy choices in fire-devastated hillside neighborhoods is the fundamental challenge of how to rebuild wisely within constraints imposed by topography and existing layout. Severe constraints are imposed on reconstruction design options when hilly or mountainous terrain is mixed with antiquated subdivision patterns. In Oakland, the combina-

> Much rich case study material can be derived not only from Oakland, but also from such other recent wildland fire disasters as the Black Tiger fire near Boulder, Colorado in 1989 and the fall 1993 fires in Altadena, Laguna Beach, and Malibu, California. The lessons from these experiences should be incorporated into pre-event planning that specifically addresses mitigation challenges and post-disaster recovery policy issues dealt with previously by other communities.

tion of steep, narrow streets, small lots, dense development, flammable roofing and vegetation, insufficient water systems, and competition for prized viewsheds all figured into a political, economic, and technical mix that was very difficult to address rationally and comprehensively under the extreme pressures for immediate rebuilding. Standard wildfire mitigation measures prescribed by forestry and fire protection literature for new development in urban/wildland interface areas, such as large lots, dual access, and setbacks from slopes, simply may not be available as options in retrofitting or rebuilding areas where the basic street and lot patterns are substandard. In such instances, tailored mitigation solutions that provide an upgrade in safety and lowered overall level of risk are needed. Although their long-term effectiveness is yet to be determined, the fire protection and fire prevention districts formed both in Oakland and Berkeley together are an example of situation-specific solutions. An innovative feature of these programs is the self-imposed benefit assessment district financing by neighborhoods throughout the Oakland Hills that addresses the cost issue of post-disaster hazard mitigation.

Recommendation: *A coordinated effort by planning, forestry, fire protection, and emergency management professionals is needed at the national level to develop guidance literature describing alternate solutions for hazard mitigation, retrofitting of existing development and post-disaster rebuilding in existing hillside neighborhoods in urban/wildfire interface and intermix areas.* Such an effort could possibly include a separate PAS Report devoted specifically to problems of upgrading wildfire safety under varying conditions, including both new and existing development in areas subject to wildland fires. This would provide an opportunity to present ideal, best practice approaches to planning for new development together with alternatives to such safety solutions for retrofitting and/or rebuilding existing neighborhoods and communities. Such materials should provide locally usable material dealing with costs and benefits of wildfire hazard mitigation, including its loss prevention value, and should also address potential means for financing safety programs, such as formation of benefit assessment districts.

4. *The Tough Challenge of Street Widening.* A major conclusion from the Oakland experience is that adequate vehicular access in fire-prone hillside and mountainous areas is essential to adequate fire vehicle and evacuation movement, public safety, and loss reduction. Experience with post-disaster reconstruction around the world suggests that street widening is often one of the most needed yet most difficult to implement post-disaster safety improvements. The recent earthquake in Kobe, Japan, illustrates the difficulties to firefighters and evacuees alike posed by exceedingly narrow streets. Future widening there will be physically less difficult in essentially flat terrain than had the earthquake affected an essentially mountainous region. Yet street widening is almost universally unpopular in that it represents a direct infringement on victims' personal space as well as a source of time delay when victims wish to have the community rebuilt quickly. In hillside communities, street widening is doubly unpopular in that it is viewed as an attack on nature as trees are removed, curves straightened and retaining walls built. Yet although street widening was not seen as a generally applicable option in Oakland, it might be more feasible in other settings given sufficient advance attention by APA and other professional associations dedicated to safety in design.

Although their long-term effectiveness is yet to be determined, the fire protection and fire prevention districts formed both in Oakland and Berkeley together are an example of situation-specific solutions. An innovative feature of these programs is the self-imposed benefit assessment district financing by neighborhoods throughout the Oakland Hills that addresses the cost issue of post-disaster hazard mitigation.

Experience with post-disaster reconstruction around the world suggests that street widening is often one of the most needed yet most difficult to implement post-disaster safety improvements. The recent earthquake in Kobe, Japan, illustrates the difficulties to firefighters and evacuees alike posed by exceedingly narrow streets.

GIS is now being broadly
applied to emergency
management functions that
were previously very time-
consuming, painstaking, and
inefficient. . . . Following the
Northridge earthquake, GIS was
used to support a variety of
response and recovery
functions, such as identifying
demographic characteristics,
siting disaster service centers,
cataloging disaster survey
reports, and for hazard
mitigation planning. A model
for advance estimation of
damage patterns was
successfully used to determine
probable levels and distribution
of damage prior to field
inspections. Simulation
modeling has also been used
recently to determine fire
spread in wildland and urban
areas, and to identify alternate
traffic routing in response to
multiple road closures.

Recommendation: Future materials prepared by APA and related professional and governmental entities concerned with wildland fire hazard reduction should give special attention to techniques by which adequate paved widths can be obtained. These techniques should be seen as essential both in newly developing, existing, and post-disaster reconstruction areas. Additional circulation considerations in such situations include improved dual access to subdivisions, shoulder parking space, intermittent parking bays, single-loaded corridors with access taken only from one street, retaining walls within public rights-of-way to maximize curve radii, and grade limitations to ease movement of heavy equipment. If the physical, financial, and political solutions can be fostered for disseminating and promoting such circulation techniques more widely both to newly developing and redeveloping urban/wildland fire interface and intermix communities, long-term losses similar to those experienced in Oakland together with the difficulties associated with post-disaster street widening can be reduced to the benefit of many other communities throughout the nation.

5. *The Potential Value of GIS.* Following Oakland's lead, GIS development can be used to help communities better mitigate urban/wildland fire hazards and recover from wildfire and other disasters. Major software improvements and expanding availability of personal computers in recent years has accelerated GIS applications in a variety of planning and emergency management organizations. GIS is now being broadly applied to emergency management functions that were previously very time-consuming, painstaking, and inefficient. Starting primarily with the Oakland fire, use of GIS has expanded with each major national disaster, including Hurricane Andrew in 1992, the Midwestern floods in 1993, the fall fires of Southern California in 1993, the January 17, 1994, Northridge earthquake, and the January 1995 California floods. Following the Northridge earthquake, GIS was used to support a variety of response and recovery functions, such as identifying demographic characteristics, siting disaster service centers, cataloging disaster survey reports, and for hazard mitigation planning. A model for advance estimation of damage patterns was successfully used to determine probable levels and distribution of damage prior to field inspections. Simulation modeling has also been used recently to determine fire spread in wildland and urban areas, and to identify alternate traffic routing in response to multiple road closures. GIS is now sufficiently portable to use in field operations to assist with evacuation routing, deployment of personnel, and other emergency response functions.

Recommendation: Attention is needed to accelerate the use of information technology applications in both emergency management and planning for development in communities affected by urban/wildland fire interface and intermix conditions. Working with FEMA, state emergency management agencies, fire protection and forestry associations, and members of the planning profession should become active in organizing, promoting, and implementing GIS applications that have value both for emergency management functions, and for other day-to-day local government functions, such as comprehensive planning, current planning, and public works administration. Pre-event planning for post-disaster recovery and reconstruction should be strengthened by GIS modeling graphically and statistically portraying what-if scenarios reflecting probable effects of various wildfire and disaster circumstances. In short, GIS, should be used to empower planners with compelling information that persuades leaders to move more decisively toward needed pre-event hazard mitigation and wiser rebuilding. (See, for example, the WHIMS model described in Chapter 7 of this report in the secton on "Wildfiles.")

Chapter 12

Earthquake Case Study: Loma Prieta in Santa Cruz and Watsonville, California

CHARLES C. EADIE

Charles C. Eadie is a city planner in Watsonville, California, and served as project manager for the Santa Cruz, California, downtown recovery plan before coming to Watsonville, where he focused on integrating long-term recovery into the general plan.

This case study discusses the effect of the 1989 Loma Prieta Earthquake on the cities of Santa Cruz and Watsonville, California. Although much of the publicity associated with the earthquake focused on the San Francisco Bay area, these two Santa Cruz County communities, closest to the epicenter, sustained the major brunt of the damage. Watsonville (population 35,000) and Santa Cruz (population 50,000) are typical of small towns around the country established in the nineteenth century located adjacent to rivers, with downtown residential and commercial districts characterized by a mix of old and new structures that face the twin vulnerabilities to flood and earthquake.

Pre-event planning in Watsonville and Santa Cruz consisted of seismic safety and safety elements in the general plans that identified hazard vulnerability and established policies to incrementally improve building safety. Both communities had emergency management plans that were primarily the province of the public safety (police, fire) departments. Pre-event planning for recovery was not a part of either the general plan elements or the emergency management planning.

Both communities were overwhelmed by the breadth and suddenness of the earthquake. The limits of emergency planning became apparent as both communities rearranged their emergency operations to deal with unanticipated problems associated with business resumption, housing, and initiating recovery. In both Watsonville and Santa Cruz, the solutions involved establishing collaborative efforts with community organizations and client groups, sharing both purpose and authority. Watsonville has since adopted a community-based disaster response plan incorporating the lessons learned from Loma Prieta and linking the city's emergency response with the important resources in the community. One section of the Watsonville plan is devoted entirely to recovery.

In both communities, recovery has been a slow and uneven process. Each community sought to redefine its downtown commercial districts consistent with emerging trends. As of 1994, both downtowns were punctuated by beautiful new buildings and still-vacant lots as commercial recovery has been hampered by the California recession as well as local market factors.[1] By 1998, the two situations diverged. In Santa Cruz, the presence of a theater project, discussed below, has brought unprecedented numbers of people downtown, further catalyzing economic recovery. Three of the major vacant sites are now under construction, and some smaller sites already have seen projects completed. Overall, recovery in Santa Cruz has accelerated since 1995.

In Watsonville, on the other hand, the economy has been rather static since 1995 due to lingering problems in the local economy with high unemployment. While the downtown is not falling apart, recovery has been far slower than in Santa Cruz. In early 1998, the rehabilitation of the Jefson Hotel, which had been damaged by the earthquake and went bankrupt later, was finally completed after it had sat untouched until 1997. The city was involved in this redevelopment having produced part of the financial commitment in creating residential units.

Housing recovery has proceeded more quickly due to the availability of relief although long-term housing needs are still significant and transcend earthquake recovery.[2] The case study discusses seven issue areas:

1. Administration/Emergency Response

2. Economic Recovery

3. Housing

4. Historic Preservation

5. Seismic Safety Planning and Building Codes

6. Urban Design

7. Politics and Recovery

Long-term recovery is primarily a function of economics. All other objectives (political, social, urban design) must recognize and incorporate economic understanding into recovery planning because an earthquake is largely an uninsured disaster. Pre-event planning for recovery should be oriented to facilitate understanding of post-quake economics.

The discussion of each issue summarizes the challenges presented by the earthquake and the communities' planning responses. Each section concludes with a list of lessons that can be drawn from the Watsonville and Santa Cruz experience, including specific recommendations that other communities can incorporate into their pre-event planning.

Overall, the key findings can be distilled into the following:

1. Flexibility must be built into emergency response planning because of the high potential for unanticipated problems and challenges.

2. Success in both emergency response and early recovery depends on creatively linking community resources with government response. Pre-event planning should identify roles and relationships not only within the governmental organizations but also among the community-based organizations that will, in fact, become emergency responders. (The Watsonville Community Based Disaster Response Plan is exemplary.)

3. Long-term recovery is primarily a function of economics. All other objectives (political, social, urban design) must recognize and incorporate economic understanding into recovery planning because an earthquake is largely an uninsured disaster. Pre-event planning for recovery should be oriented to facilitate understanding of post-quake economics.

4. Although the substance of recovery is primarily economic, politics drives the process of recovery planning. There is potential for significant variation in recovery planning approaches as the experiences in Watsonville and Santa Cruz illustrate. Pre-quake planning for recovery should be based on the jurisdiction's political predisposition but recognize also that the disaster will change politics. Flexibility and responsiveness must be built into pre-event recovery planning.

5. The issues that will dominate recovery will be the issues that already are problematic for a community. An earthquake will accelerate and intensify concerns over economic health, housing, safety, and so forth.

6. Recovery involves the conflict between the community's desire to recover quickly and the need to move deliberately, pursue new opportunities, and make well-considered long-term decisions. Recovery involves transformation.

7. Over time, recovery planning merges with community planning in general. The transition raises issues of how to maintain the priority of

recovery issues amid a receding of urgency and reemergence of competing political priorities.

8. Mitigation works. Seismic strengthening will save lives, limit damage, and can facilitate quicker recovery.

CHRONOLOGY

The Loma Prieta Earthquake struck at 5:04 P.M. on Tuesday, October 17, 1989. The magnitude 7.1 quake resulted from a slip along a 25-mile segment of the San Andreas Fault located in the Santa Cruz mountains approximately 60 miles south of San Francisco and Oakland and 11 and 12 miles from Santa Cruz and Watsonville, respectively. The 15-second tremor was followed by more than 7,500 aftershocks over two years' time ranging from 1.0 to 5.4 in magnitude. Sixty-three earthquake-related deaths were recorded, including five in Santa Cruz County. The injury toll was 3,757. Although the death toll was greater elsewhere (43 died in Alameda County where the Cypress Freeway structure collapsed), by all other measures, Santa Cruz County (including Watsonville and Santa Cruz) was the hardest hit area. Other key statistics:

Pacific Avenue in Santa Cruz was the site of serious devastation after the October 1989 Loma Prieta earthquake.

- Homes destroyed: 774 in Santa Cruz County; 244 in other counties

- Homes damaged: 13,329 in Santa Cruz County; 10,079 elsewhere

- Businesses destroyed: 310 in Santa Cruz County; 56 elsewhere

- Businesses damaged: 1,615 in Santa Cruz County; 1,880 elsewhere

The disruption was particularly acute for Santa Cruz and Watsonville because the damage was concentrated in the downtown areas vital to the commercial, residential, and social/cultural identity of the communities. Each community sustained $50 million to $75 million in public and private damage, as well as sales tax losses estimated at $200,000 to $250,000 per year. The Federal Emergency Management Agency (FEMA) and California State Office of Emergency Services (OES) reimbursable expenses totaled $10.5 million for the City of Watsonville and $12.3 million for the City of Santa Cruz. Countywide, FEMA committed $12 million for temporary housing and $18.1 million in individual and family grants; Red Cross relief totaled $13.6 million; and the Small Business Administration (SBA) loaned $182.8 million. Additionally, relief monies donated directly to the cities and disburse by them totaled $1.25 million in Watsonville and $685,000 in Santa Cruz.

The response by the local governments was multifaceted and involved nearly every department at some level. The frantic pace of the emergency response and recovery planning of the first years gradually receded; five years after the disaster, both communities continue to be involved in a wide variety of programmatic efforts to support and implement recovery plans over the long haul. Both organizations changed in response to recovery

A distinguishing characteristic of an earthquake is that it strikes without warning, leaving no time to organize the planning department (or any department) to respond. Key people might be out of town or unable to function because they themselves could be victims. Therefore, pre-event planning should build in flexibility to deal with uncertainty. All personnel should understand the city's emergency response plan, even if they do not have pre-designated roles in the emergency operations center (EOC).

needs, expanding redevelopment functions, pursuing new state and federal programs and resources, investing in public works to support commercial and residential rebuilding, and reassigning and hiring new personnel. Recovery has proven to be the largest single challenge ever posed to Santa Cruz and Watsonville. These efforts are summarized in the discussion of key planning issues to follow.

Due to the breadth of planning issues encompassed in recovery, the discussion of these issues is divided into seven topic areas. The planning issues are illustrated by recounting some of the particular experiences in Watsonville and Santa Cruz. Those sections are followed by a list of lessons learned and practical tips for incorporating those lessons in pre-event planning.

ADMINISTRATION/EMERGENCY RESPONSE

This section touches on some of the operational issues facing a planning department following an earthquake by answering the question, What can planners expect to do in the wake of such an emergency? Pre-event planning should understand the possible roles and relationships that may emerge for planners.

A distinguishing characteristic of an earthquake is that it strikes without warning, leaving no time to organize the planning department (or any department) to respond. Key people might be out of town or unable to function because they themselves could be victims. Therefore, pre-event planning should build in flexibility to deal with uncertainty. All personnel should understand the city's emergency response plan, even if they do not have pre-designated roles in the emergency operations center (EOC).

In both Watsonville and Santa Cruz, damage was focused in downtown areas while widespread areas of the towns survived with minimal disruption. Loss of power and water, fires, and general confusion made people uncertain as to how serious the earthquake was.

Because neither department had an emergency operating plan, people responded in different ways. Both planning directors reported to the EOC, although in Santa Cruz the planning function in the incident command system was assigned to the water director. In Santa Cruz a few planners reported that evening to the EOC to see if there was any way they could be deployed,[3] another planner assisted other assigned staff in setting up the city's emergency shelter at the Civic Auditorium, some stayed at City Hall to help pick up the mess. One planner was designated as the city's public information officer (PIO) and worked entirely out of the EOC for more than six weeks.

All staff reported to work the next morning and self-sorted into a variety of tasks. Initially, the Santa Cruz planning director suggested that the department attend to business as usual, a concept that quickly faded. In Watsonville, the planning director began inspecting buildings along with a building official and architect whom they picked up standing at a corner. She stayed in the EOC virtually around the clock for the first 72 hours, and reported hourly to the department staff who were swamped with information requests. Early on two planners from the City of Monterey came and helped out the Watsonville planning department.[4]

Generally planning functions in the first days primarily involved information gathering, reconnaissance, responding to public information requests, and generally finding needs and filling in (troubleshooting).

Eventually planners were used to accompany out-of-town building officials for several weeks of inspections, issue expedited permits for damage repair, seek out grant and assistance funding, escort VIPs and out-of-town emergency personnel, put together damage maps and data, take photographs, and perform any number of tasks. In Santa Cruz a, staff planner who had worked closely with the downtown business association prior to the earthquake was installed as the incident commander of the downtown emergency center one week after the earthquake when the emphasis switched from life safety to planning for business recovery needs.[5] In the County of Santa Cruz, a staff planner was assigned to set up and direct a separate earthquake unit to process rebuild permits. County environmental planners worked with geologists to analyze the ongoing hazard in heavily damaged areas near the summit of the Santa Cruz mountains.[6]

Ultimately, both planning departments found themselves awash in the dual roles of assessing long-term recovery needs and expediting permit processing for the many who suffered only minor damage and were eager to commence with repairs. Procedures and policies had to be formulated to handle the extra demands and address a variety of concerns.[7] Staff assignments had to be adjusted to meet the needs.

A common experience of planners involved in major roles after the earthquake was a recognition of the importance of planning skills, which incorporate the ability to bring people together in stressful settings to sort out complex situations and create plans to address critical needs. Planning had to be done quickly, without reference material, and was complicated by limited information and highly frazzled emotions. Normal hierarchical structures were disrupted and supplemented or replaced with ad hoc working associations combining city staff and community volunteers. Changes were rapid as conditions changed hourly or daily. Information needs were enormous and communication channels overloaded. Instead of relying on procedures and rules, much of what was done was invented based on the needs of the situation.

For the Watsonville planners and some Santa Cruz planners, the workload was extraordinary;[8] for others, it was less or about as usual. The variation depended on assigned tasks, personal circumstances, and the inclination for functioning well in chaotic situations.[9] Stress levels also varied, and typically were enormous for those who had significant roles. Aftershocks were especially disconcerting,[10] occurring unexpectedly and bringing on the possibility of additional damage. Unlike other disasters, where safe places or high ground can be found, an earthquake represents fundamental instability as terra firma loses its firmness. Eventually, mental health care was made available for responders as part of the emergency assistance countywide.

For the Watsonville planners and some Santa Cruz planners, the workload was extraordinary; for others, it was less or about as usual. The variation depended on assigned tasks, personal circumstances, and the inclination for functioning well in chaotic situations. Stress levels also varied, and typically were enormous for those who had significant roles. Aftershocks were especially disconcerting, occurring unexpectedly and bringing on the possibility of additional damage. Unlike other disasters, where safe places or high ground can be found, an earthquake represents fundamental instability as terra firma loses its firmness. Eventually, mental health care was made available for responders as part of the emergency assistance countywide.

Lessons

1. Pre-event planning should be cognizant of the variety of tasks that planners may be assigned to undertake and specify where volunteers and outside assistance can be plugged in.

2. Pre-event planning should include community-based organizations and vulnerable subpopulations and client groups. They will assume key roles or present unanticipated challenges following an earthquake.

3. Personnel shifts are inevitable, so any pre-event staffing structures must be loosely formatted to allow for adjusting to the major surprises that eventually to emerge.

4. Client groups outside city government will seek to work with staff with whom they are most familiar, and the organization should be prepared to adjust accordingly.

5. Planning skills will be needed, as ad hoc working groups will form around the need to solve unanticipated problems.

6. Administrative hierarchies will change following a disaster; new working relationships need to be formed.

7. Pre-event planning should systematically identify an array of resource opportunities to begin pursuing during recovery; the personal knowledge of staff people should be drawn out and catalogued pre-quake.

8. Planners and other staff will have to assume tasks for which others are responsible in the early hours before the assigned responders are on the scene.

9. New specialized personnel may be needed (e.g., translators to help bridge language and cultural gaps).

10. Mental health assistance is critical. Despite admonitions, people will inevitably make extraordinary commitments, which eventually take their toll in stress.

11. The responsiveness, judgment, creativity, and initiative of individuals and organizations is tested because much of disaster response does not go by the book.

12. Record keeping is difficult because so much moves so quickly, but it will be extremely important later, especially for justifying reimbursement requests. Pre-event planning should anticipate this need, perhaps even designating on the spot historians.

ECONOMIC RECOVERY

The economic damage from the earthquake in both Watsonville and Santa Cruz was concentrated in the downtown central business districts, a result of the combination of alluvial soils and old unreinforced masonry buildings (URMs).

Prior to the earthquake, both downtowns were economically viable but also fundamentally vulnerable, experiencing the frailties common to downtowns nationwide due to changing demographics and competition from regional shopping centers. Downtown Watsonville's redevelopment project was struggling to put together a development for the 200 block of Main Street where older buildings had been razed in the 1980s. Downtown Santa Cruz featured the Pacific Garden Mall, a 1969 pedestrian-oriented makeover of Pacific Avenue into a serpentine one lane of traffic with parking and extensive brick and wood landscaping planters and seating. The community in 1989 was engaged in acrimonious debate about whether street people, overgrown and dated landscaping, and perceived anti-business and change-resistant politics were threatening the long-term viability of the 20-year-old Mall.

The earthquake completely disrupted both downtowns. In Watsonville, 22 buildings were demolished with a loss of nearly 700,000 square feet of retail space, including 48 percent of the square footage in the 300 and 400 blocks of Main Street and the backbone of downtown, Ford's department store.

Santa Cruz lost one-third of its 1 million square feet of downtown commercial square footage, and another third was heavily damaged. Losses included the Cooperhouse, the historic heart and anchor of downtown, as well as two department stores that never returned.

In the short term, the challenge for both communities was to minimize business disruption by recovering inventory and relocating businesses.[11]

In the long term, recovery has involved transformation of the downtowns based on an acceleration of pre-quake trends: downtown Watsonville evolving toward a Latino-based ethnic market; Santa Cruz moving away

---

The earthquake completely disrupted both downtowns. In Watsonville, 22 buildings were demolished with a loss of nearly 700,000 square feet of retail space, including 48 percent of the square footage in the 300 and 400 blocks of Main Street and the backbone of downtown, Ford's department store. Santa Cruz lost one-third of its 1 million square feet of downtown commercial square footage, and another third was heavily damaged. Losses included the Cooperhouse, the historic heart and anchor of downtown, as well as two department stores that never returned.

from general retail to a specialty retail, services, and entertainment center serving a student-based clientele. The recovery of both downtowns has been hampered by fundamental market weaknesses, earthquake-related losses of general retail, and the recession/restructuring of the state and national economy. Watsonville, with an agricultural economic base, suffered from restructuring in the food processing industry, while Santa Cruz, with a university- and tourism-based economy, was aided by increasing enrollment at the University of California at Santa Cruz (12,000 students).

A major factor in the economic recovery equation is that, unlike floods, fires, or hurricanes, an earthquake disaster is largely uninsured. Private-sector recovery thus depends on the ability to find capital to finance reconstruction. In Watsonville and Santa Cruz, commercial recovery has proven more problematic than residential. Funding sources are more limited, investment risk is greater and more sensitive to recessionary forces, and residential property owners typically have more equity and other financial potential.

Short-Term Economic Recovery

Short-term economic survival for most merchants depended upon their ability to access and recover inventory from heavily damaged buildings. This was a major issue in Santa Cruz. Public safety officials almost immediately following the earthquake had cordoned off the nine square blocks around the Pacific Garden Mall because of the continuing threat to life safety posed by aftershocks and tottering buildings. No pre-event planning had been done about what to do next, however, and, by the end of the first week

These temporary pavilions began to house Santa Cruz businesses the day after Thansgiving in 1989 in order to salvage the Christmas buying season for merchants. Intended to last for six months, they in fact remained for several years.

following the quake, the downtown merchants were completely frustrated and angry over the city's inability to deal with the access issues. The life safety value that dominated emergency response decisions eventually had to be compromised by the merchants' need for economic survival, and the contentious situation was diffused through a collaborative planning process involving merchants and city staff setting priorities and creating procedures that dealt with a range of problems related to access to property, including coordination and sequencing of demolitions.[12] The city's emergency operations center was moved downtown.[13] The merchants provided volunteers to help staff the downtown center.[14]

Charles C. Eadie

As the access issues were being resolved, relocation questions were being addressed, also involving intense cooperative efforts of numerous people including city staff, merchants, and others. Seven temporary pavilions were erected on parking lots adjacent to Pacific Avenue.[15] Although some merchants relocated out of the downtown, space was found for everyone who wanted to stay, which maintained shopping patterns and the economic integrity of the downtown.

For the community and the hundreds of volunteers and staff who worked cooperatively under intensely stressful conditions, the successful reopening of downtown Santa Cruz by Thanksgiving was an exhilarating accomplishment and a testimony to the ability of people to come together in times of disaster. Paradoxically, the euphoria of the early recovery resulted in some unrealistic expectations regarding long-term recovery, as there was talk of rebuilding Pacific Avenue within a year and a setting aside of longstanding political animosities. The reality has been a checkered[16] and difficult re-building including a boisterous community planning process that saw old political habits reemerge.

In Watsonville, the access concerns did not become as problematic as in Santa Cruz.[17] Attention was primarily focused on the housing issue, where the bulk of the controversy resided. Many merchants were able to relocate in two recently completed shopping centers outside of the downtown; consequently, merchant relocation was largely a private sector issue. A few merchants relocated in trailers set up in parking lots behind the 300 block.

Both communities lost significant sales tax revenue as a result of the damage downtown; these revenues were estimated at $200,000 in Watsonville and $250,000 annually in Santa Cruz. This was offset, in part, by the passage of a local countywide sales tax measure in 1990 which generated funds for the jurisdictions to use for earthquake recovery.[18] This funding proved instrumental in facilitating recovery because the cities had funds that could be applied creatively in a variety of projects as needed, based entirely on local considerations (unlike outside grants).

Long-Term Economic Recovery

As part of Santa Cruz's Downtown Recovery Plan, Pacific Avenue was completely rebuilt in 1993, three years after the earthquake.

For Watsonville, long-term economic recovery was linked to the rebuilding of Ford's department store, which was the longest continuously operating department store in California. Prior to the 1989 quake, the Ford's chain had expanded to 12 stores in several other central coast cities. Ford's was more than a shopping stop for Watsonville; it was a major employer and the symbolic heart of its town.[19]

With Ford's as the number one economic priority, city leaders and Ford's officials convinced the Small Business Administration (SBA) to grant the largest single SBA loan in history, $24 million. Plans were drawn and processed, and construction was underway within one year. The grand reopening of Ford's occurred on October 17, 1991, exactly two years following the earthquake and townspeople were ecstatic over the quick recovery.

Unfortunately, circumstances conspired to sabotage the store's rebuilding. The earthquake also closed Ford's stores in Santa Cruz and Hollister, and the recession hit the other remaining stores hard. Ford's hired a new marketing manager who miscalculated its market, attempting to replace a moderately priced merchandise line with a high-end Nordstrom's look. As a result the beautiful new Watsonville store lost money from day one, and the entire Ford's chain filed for bankruptcy in 1992.

Like Santa Cruz, the rebuilding of downtown Watsonville proved to be a long-term proposition. Several commercial projects have been completed in the 300 block by 1994, as well as a number of rehabilitation and repair projects on Main Street. The Resetar Hotel was converted to residential housing in 1992. A business incubator proposed by a nonprofit economic development corporation in 1990 was finally completed in 1996 after a long struggle. Another project, involving repair and rehabilitation of the Jefson hotel, was suspended when the property owners became financially insolvent in 1991 and was still unable to proceed as of December 1996.

The City of Watsonville undertook a range of actions in an effort to bolster private-sector efforts. In the spring of 1990, the Urban Land Institute (ULI) was invited to prepare a plan for downtown.[20] The redevelopment district was revamped and the time frame extended. The city created a housing and economic development department, and established an economic development committee. A grant-funded, 208-space parking garage was completed in 1992.[21] Watsonville applied for and received designation by California as a Main Street Demonstration City in 1992.[22] The city purchased the old post office building on the plaza and attracted the local community college to the site. A youth center was completed in 1994, and a new downtown community center opened in 1990. A streetscape plan was adopted in 1992 and has been implemented incrementally in conjunction with new development projects.

Santa Cruz also supported recovery with significant public investment. Following approval of the Downtown Recovery Plan in 1991, Pacific Avenue was completely rebuilt in 1993 with $5 million in new streetscapes, and $5 million[23] in utility and infrastructure reconstruction. Like Watsonville, Santa Cruz constructed a new parking structure and revitalized redevelopment by creating a merged redevelopment district, including the downtown area and other commercial areas of the city.[24] In the first five years of recovery, downtown Santa Cruz saw the completion of several repair and rehabilitation projects and the construction of several smaller new infill buildings.

The sixth year of recovery, 1995, proved to be a major positive turning point for the downtown commercial areas in both Santa Cruz and Watsonville. In May, a nine-screen cinema complex opened in Santa Cruz on the site formerly occupied by the town's major department store. The project was an immediate success and has exceeded all expectations, bringing upwards of 750,000 people a year into the downtown and filling the new multilevel parking structure on most weekend nights. The evening foot traffic generated on Pacific Avenue by the theaters has allowed other retailers to extend their hours and has created a lively and youthful atmosphere in the downtown. This is a far contrast from the pre-earthquake situation where evening business was limited and the downtown was not a comfortable place at night for many people.

Ironically, the cinema complex, which was conceived within the first year following the earthquake and had been a cornerstone of the Santa Cruz Downtown Recovery Plan, was delayed approximately one year and almost was not built when the city council opted to financially support a competing theater project. That project, in a less strategically important downtown location, had not yet broken ground by the end of 1996.

The developers of the successful cinema project, after failing in their effort to win city council support, reevaluated their project, restructured their financing, cut out some amenities, and, after some financial soul searching, decided to go forward anyway. The city eventually added limited redevelopment funds to support some of the off-site improvements.

The success of the Santa Cruz theaters was not unnoticed by others. Several smaller infill retail projects followed the cinema complex in 1995 and 1996, aided also by the improving California economy. These well-crafted buildings clearly captured the quality look and image envisioned by the design standards of the Santa Cruz Downtown Recovery Plan. The city redevelopment agency also invested in physical enhancements downtown, for example, by rebuilding some of the connecting pedestrian alleyways.

Charles C. Eadie

Although some critics saw it as unneeded, this parking structure in Watsonville, financed in part by the Federal Economic Development Administration, won an award and became a crucial factor in downtown recovery.

With the exception of the St. George Hotel and the nine-screen cinema complex, the large vacant sites in downtown Santa Cruz have proved more difficult to rebuild. On the site of the former Cooperhouse, a five-story retail and office project was approved in the early 1990s, but as of 1996 construction had yet to begin, plagued by difficulties in securing tenants and financing. Four other larger key sites also were still vacant in late 1996 and faced similar obstacles. In response, the city in late 1996 began discussing the possibility of becoming more active in facilitating larger-site projects.

The recovery in Watsonville was boosted in 1995 by the opening of a major department store, Gottschalk's, in the 80,000-square-foot building rebuilt by the former Ford's department store in 1992. The city played a major role in brokering the deal and securing the tenant, and participated financially with a $500,000 low-interest-rate loan of Measure E money. The city also commissioned a market study in 1994 as part of the recruitment effort to demonstrate the potential buying power of the regional Latino market. After a slow start, Gottschalk's was succeeding financially in 1996, tuning its products and services to the burgeoning Hispanic market, while simultaneously regaining the more traditional pre-quake Ford's clientele.

Downtown Watsonville was also boosted by the immediate success of the location of a community college satellite campus on the downtown plaza, in the building formerly occupied by the post office. The city spent $1.7 million of redevelopment funds to purchase and rehabilitate the building and then arranged to lease it to Cabrillo College. In 1996, the city and Cabrillo joined forces again to successfully win a $3.2 million federal grant (Economic Development Administration) to finance a new expansion of the campus. The city committed another $1.4 million in redevelopment funds, with another $200,000 coming from the Cabrillo foundation.

In 1995, Watsonville began work on a Regional Latino Marketplace Plan for its downtown area, in conjunction with Main Street Watsonville. The plan will combine physical improvements with marketing and retail strategies aimed at strengthening the downtown as a specialty destination area attractive not only to the majority Latino population, but also to tourists in the Monterey Bay region.

For Watsonville, the economic context of recovery continued to be challenging into 1997. Unemployment hovered in the 18 to 20 percent range, the lingering result of restructuring in the food processing industry and the lack of available industrial land to diversify the agriculturally based economy.

The city has responded with a variety of efforts. It successfully competed to be designated as one of 30 Rural Enterprise Communities in the country (one of two in California) by the federal government in 1995, a 10-year program that brings more than $200,000 annually for youth programs and job training. The city also qualified for a state enterprise zone designation in 1996. The *Watsonville 2005: General Plan* calls for a 200-acre industrial annexation, for which the city was seeking approval in 1996. Over the long term, city officials are hoping that industrial annexation will generate new employment that ultimately will provide economic support for the long-term recovery of the downtown and the community as a whole.

Lessons

1. Short-term survival of damaged business districts is critical to long-term economic recovery. Pre-event planning should include inventory recovery and businesses strategies. Community-based disaster response planning should clarify to businesses how the government operations will shift after a disaster (e.g., incident command system); the relationship between government and businesses (and representative associations) should be clearly established and understood.

2. The post-earthquake economy can be radically altered by the loss of retail viability in vulnerable areas such as downtowns. Pre-quake trends will be accelerated, and problems or weaknesses will be intensified. Recovery planning must account for changed conditions.

3. The financial wherewithal of businesses and property owners is a major variable affecting economic recovery. Large corporate owners will have a different ability to sustain the economic hit and rebuild than small local businesses. There also will be different capacities from among different large corporations or various small businesses. Pre-event planning should take into account ownership patterns and work with businesses in vulnerable areas to anticipate needs.

4. Unlike other forms of disaster, earthquake losses are largely uninsured, making the economics of private recovery more difficult and fundamentally more central to the recovery process.

5. Retrofit greatly improves the recovery potential for an individual property owner. It will not guarantee survival of the building in all cases, but it did make rebuilding feasible in many instances in Santa Cruz and Watsonville.

6. For private owners of real property, retrofit does not improve short-term cash flow and therefore is a difficult cost to justify pre-quake, especially since the risk is uncertain.

7. The costs of rebuilding and rehabilitating damaged commercial areas are difficult to bear. In Santa Cruz, an economic study done following the earthquake estimated that the downtown would have to increase business by 35 percent above pre-quake levels just to replace and repair the lost square footage. This explains the incremental nature of rebuilding.

The financial wherewithal of businesses and property owners is a major variable affecting economic recovery. Large corporate owners will have a different ability to sustain the economic hit and rebuild than small local businesses. There also will be different capacities from among different large corporations or various small businesses. Pre-event planning should take into account ownership patterns and work with businesses in vulnerable areas to anticipate needs.

8. Significant economic assistance in all forms is needed. In pre-planning for recovery, communities should identify possible resources of all kinds and move quickly to secure them.

9. There is a window of opportunity during the first six months following a disaster when a community is most likely to receive economic assistance. The paradox is that recovery needs are not altogether clear while the assistance window is widest. Grants applications may need to be written and rewritten or renegotiated later to fit what actually is needed when the funding becomes available.

10. Local funding sources are best and are critically important. Watsonville was able to use both Measure E and donated relief funds to leverage long- and short-term recovery.

11. External variables can significantly affect the economics of recovery (e.g., the health of the national or regional economy including business cycle, borrowing costs and requirements).

12. The private and public sector must work together for recovery to succeed. The creation and adoption of the Santa Cruz Downtown Recovery Plan by Vision Santa Cruz was a successful example of bringing diverse interests together on recovery issues.

13. Pre-existing plans and ordinances may be inadequate to deal with changed post-earthquake economic realties. To the extent that the context has changed, so must the content and purposes of relevant general area or specific plans.

14. Long-term recovery issues will involve issues that already are important in the community but in more stark or difficult forms.

15. Economic recovery planning needs to involve all the tools available to a community, including redevelopment and application of relevant assistance programs, such as a Main Street designation.

16. Pre-event planning should identify assistance programs applicable to older areas where damage is likely to be concentrated. These areas typically are the most economically vulnerable. Assistance programs such as for housing or economic revitalization, can be refocused or expanded to assist in recovery.

HOUSING

Housing was the preeminent recovery issue in Watsonville. The earthquake engendered an almost startling recognition about how bad housing shortages and conditions had become. Damage was concentrated in the primarily Latino residential areas near downtown where 550 residences were yellow tagged (damage-limited entry) and 406 red tagged (major damage).[25] Initially 1,500 people were homeless. Some stayed in their yards. Others set up makeshift camps in the parks. Many of the displaced refused to go into any building (including officially designated shelters) because of knowledge of the Mexico City earthquake and the significant casualties caused by aftershocks. Relief efforts were complicated by language barriers (English-speaking responders trying to assist Spanish-speaking victims). Pre-quake overcrowding was revealed as typically more than one family would give the same address to relief agencies such as FEMA. The 1990 census confirmed the conditions: 25 percent of all households and nearly 40 percent of rental housing in Watsonville was classified as overcrowded.[26]

One short-term issue was finding sites for FEMA trailers. An interagency task force including city, county, and housing authority representatives met for

There is a window of opportunity during the first six months following a disaster when a community is most likely to receive economic assistance. The paradox is that recovery needs are not altogether clear while the assistance window is widest. Grants applications may need to be written and rewritten or renegotiated later to fit what actually is needed when the funding becomes available.

this purpose. At issue was land use. The county, with strict growth control and agricultural land preservation policies,[27] was concerned that short-term housing could be converted to long-term and thereby become growth inducing. The city did not want to use vacant commercial sites for housing and did not have large tracts of residential land that could accommodate trailers. The task force decided to limit housing sites to public properties only and eventually found suitable locations for 85 trailers at the County Fairgrounds,[28] behind the Watsonville branch of the County Courthouse, and at a Catholic middle school just outside town that had utility services. For many of the displaced families, the FEMA trailer was their first experience in living in a unit that they did not have to share with another family.

Faced with the overwhelming need for housing, Watsonville planners drafted an earthquake rebuild ordinance within the first four days after the quake that suspended the limits on rebuilding nonconforming uses and established a permit streamlining procedure.[29] The goal was to get as many people back to normal as soon as possible in order to focus limited resources on the bigger questions.

In addition, people were encouraged to add new units as part of their rebuilding. With the downtown neighborhoods zoned for multiple densities, many lots were capable of adding one or more cottage units. The city further facilitated the creation of new housing by granting variances on setbacks and allowing dwellings with nonconforming setbacks to expand.

The city also participated financially in rebuilding many private housing projects. More than $800,000 of the $1.25 million donated to the city's earthquake relief fund was directed to 79 residential repair projects where the money was critical to making the rebuilding feasible.[30] The city also used Measure E[31] and Red Cross[32] money to fill funding gaps of several major new low-income housing projects.[33]

In the short term, these efforts were successful in restoring and in some cases expanding the damaged housing stock following the earthquake. There was no net loss of permanent housing in Watsonville.

In the long term, city officials, realizing the enormous unmet need for housing, adopted a revised housing element in 1992 and new general plan in 1994 that called for adding 5,300 dwelling units through new construction, annexation, and increasing urban densities.[34] A new Housing and Economic Development Department was established by Watsonville following the earthquake. The city's ability to expand its housing stock, however, is under the aegis of the Local Agency Formation Commission (LAFCO), which rules on annexations and which may have different priorities that could limit the city's ability to achieve its housing goals.[35]

Santa Cruz also responded to housing needs by loosening the zoning ordinance provisions regarding nonconforming uses, although not taking as liberal an approach regarding variances and increasing densities. Housing displacement was far less severe in Santa Cruz, and the priority for recovery was on the downtown business district. The Santa Cruz Downtown Recovery Plan does call for increased housing development adjacent to the commercial core, such as through the eventual redevelopment of sites along the dry side of the San Lorenzo River levee and on the upper floors of commercial buildings. (That housing as yet is only a proposal and would necessarily have to follow levee improvements scheduled for completion in 2002.) Santa Cruz also directed Red Cross money to housing projects, one example being the new St. George Hotel, which includes single-room-occupancy units above the commercial ground floor.[36] Both Santa Cruz and Watsonville have provided funds, technical assistance, and other forms of support that were instrumental in the successful construction of new projects done by local nonprofit housing development corporations.

Faced with the overwhelming need for housing, Watsonville planners drafted an earthquake rebuild ordinance within the first four days after the quake that suspended the limits on rebuilding nonconforming uses and established a permit streamlining procedure. The goal was to get as many people back to normal as soon as possible in order to focus limited resources on the bigger questions.

Lessons

1. Pre-event planning should identify strategies to provide immediate and short-term housing, taking into account cultural and social concerns as well as locational issues.

2. Housing recovery may proceed faster than commercial recovery because of the existence of many federal and state programs for low- and moderate-income housing that can be focused on a community recovering from an earthquake. New projects and rehab projects with housing subsidies were among the first projects to get rebuilt.

3. Local resources directed toward private housing projects can be critically important in recovering housing stock. Pre-event planning should address the question of how and whether to direct relief money to housing.

4. Low-income populations and their housing stock are likely to be the hardest hit by an earthquake because low-income rental stock is likely to include old housing in vulnerable areas. Short- and long-term housing responses should be tailored to meet the needs of special or highly vulnerable populations.

5. If housing is a priority for the community, there are various ways to facilitate its construction through zoning/rezoning and policies regarding variances and densities. Pre-event planning should address the question of how to handle non-conforming uses.

6. Pre-event planning can anticipate housing displacement based on risk/vulnerability assessments. Retrofit/strengthening programs can help minimize housing displacement.

7. Resource and assistance programs should be identified in advance and pursued actively following the disaster. Existing city programs, such as those for housing rehabilitation, can be redirected with a recovery focus.

8. The creation or expansion of redevelopment districts for economic recovery can also support housing (e.g., through set-aside provisions or other funding mechanisms).

9. Pre-event planning for housing recovery should involve a wide range of community housing resources, such as nonprofit housing development agencies, churches, and legal aid.

10. Long-term housing needs will need to be reevaluated in light of post-quake conditions and incorporated into other long-range planning documents, such as the general plan.

11. Short- and long-term planning for housing recovery must address policy obstacles. Procuring adequate temporary housing sites may involve extensions of infrastructure and also raise land-use issues. Efforts to address long-range housing needs may face obstacles such as lack of land in built-out communities or limits based on zoning, environmental constraints, or growth limitation policies.

Short- and long-term planning for housing recovery must address policy obstacles. Procuring adequate temporary housing sites may involve extensions of infrastructure and also raise land-use issues. Efforts to address long-range housing needs may face obstacles such as lack of land in built-out communities or limits based on zoning, environmental constraints, or growth limitation policies.

HISTORIC PRESERVATION

The experience of both Watsonville and Santa Cruz illustrates the difficulties of dealing with historic buildings following an earthquake. Each city lost important historic buildings, particularly the Cooperhouse in Santa Cruz (the former county courthouse) and the Oddfellows building in Watsonville. Downtown Santa Cruz was a registered historic district that included both registered landmarks such as the numerous other distinctive buildings dating from the nineteenth and early twentieth century that were integral to the historic district. The majority of the 37 commercial district demolitions in downtown Santa Cruz and 22 in downtown Watsonville involved URM historic buildings. In 1992, the State Office of Historic Preservation decertified the downtown Santa Cruz historic district.

The earthquake illustrated without question the vulnerability of historic buildings, even where retrofitting has taken place. The buildings were severely damaged and reports by emergency inspection teams[37] were virtually unanimous in support of demolition.

For public officials, there were intense pressures weighing in favor of demolition. The damaged buildings posed a continuing threat to life safety, especially with progressive weakening due to aftershocks. The presence of unabated hazards posed a liability threat to the cities, and boarded-up buildings could become a long-term attractive nuisance. Recovery of the business districts depended on timely completion of demolitions to reopen the streets to autos and pedestrians and to remove the threats to adjacent structures that were posed by damaged buildings. In addition, the FEMA requirement that demolitions be completed within 30 days to qualify for reimbursement, combined with the logistics of preparing for and carrying out massive demolition work, placed an added pressure to act quickly.[38]

St. Patrick's Church in Watsonville was rebuilt replicating its pre-earthquake architecture and using surviving elements of the original building such as its stained glass windows.

For property owners, the economics did not generally favor trying to save a severely damaged building. Retrofits do not achieve the same level of safety as a newly constructed building, yet the costs per square foot for repairing and then retrofitting a heavily damaged building in many instances proved to meet or exceed the cost of a new building.[39] Older buildings, while often possessing fine design or other characteristics had numerous negatives: inefficient or outdated floor plans; lack of handicapped accessibility; poor energy efficiency; lack of floodproofing; outdated plumbing, heating, and electrical systems; high maintenance costs.

Charles C. Eadie

In short, a property owner could spend the same millions of dollars on a repair/retrofit as a new building and have a less marketable and outdated facility that would still be vulnerable to sustaining heavy damage in a subsequent earthquake.[40]

Historic preservation advocates faced the twin dilemmas of not having resources to offer that could offset the economics,[41] and being unprepared for the exigencies of the emergency response processes that suspended normal channels of political deliberation amid circumstances that weighed heavily in favor of demolition.

From the losses, a residue of bitterness remains. Some local preservationists felt they were left out of the loop and should have had a stronger voice (e.g.,members of the Santa Cruz City Historic Preservation Commission). City officials in both communities resented the critical attitude taken by some of the statewide historic preservation advocates who they saw as blinded by their single-purpose advocacy and, therefore, unwilling or unable to understand the circumstances driving the decisions. Some also thought them to be unrealistic in assessing the economics of trying to save the damaged buildings.[42]

With nearly all the downtown demolitions completed by November 1989, the historic preservation battle in Santa Cruz eventually was waged in 1990 over the St. George Hotel, which initially was yellow tagged (not condemned). When the owner subsequently applied for a demolition permit, the city council sought detailed cost estimates to restore the building. Not surprisingly, the experts differed: the owner's engineering estimates were higher than an estimate prepared at the behest of preservation advocates. Eventually, both sides agreed to bring in a third estimator (an engineering firm acceptable to both sides) whose figures supported the building owners' engineer. The city council issued a demolition permit, but FEMA had to withhold approval because the State Historic Preservation Officer (SHPO) did not concur.[43] A court case ensued, but the drama concluded on site as the hotel caught fire one Sunday afternoon and burned beyond repair.[44]

Ultimately, the historic preservation responsibility falls to the property owner. The government could not force someone to fix a building when it is economically infeasible to do so. The concurrence process offers no positive incentives; the sanction (no reimbursement of demolition cost) does not alter the economic equation and, in the aftermath, seems unduly punitive.

Despite the losses, both downtowns have retained elements of their historic character. Efforts were made to address historic concerns, albeit with mixed results. On the positive side:

- Both communities adopted modified building codes that have more flexible standards to facilitate repair and retrofit (see discussion of building codes).

- A few of the URM historic buildings were repaired and reopened where the combination of less severe damage and an owner's personal commitment (bolstered by deep pockets) made that decision feasible.

- A number of other historic buildings survived (non-URM; that is, reinforced concrete or wood frame structures) and were retrofitted and remain as key placemakers (Watsonville's Resetar Hotel; Lettinich Building; Mansion House; Palomar Hotel; ID Building in Santa Cruz).

- Some elements from the Cooperhouse and other historic buildings in Santa Cruz, such as ornate exterior trim pieces, were saved during the demolition process and turned over to the city museum.

- The St. George Hotel in Santa Cruz and St. Patrick's Church in Watsonville were rebuilt with design features that replicate the demolished buildings.

- Post-earthquake design guidelines and some of the new buildings in both Watsonville and Santa Cruz include design features that reflect the historic character of the downtowns.

- New streetscapes in both downtowns were designed to enhance the historic image.

- The exterior facade of a nineteenth century bank building in Santa Cruz was saved with city redevelopment funds. After standing like a movie prop for several years, the old walls were reattached to an entirely new structure.

> Despite the losses, both downtowns have retained elements of their historic character. Efforts were made to address historic concerns, albeit with mixed results.

On the negative side:

- The Trust Building in Santa Cruz, after standing for more than two years, burned down from a fire attributed to transients camping inside just as the owner was prepared to begin a repair and retrofit project.[45]

- The Jefson Building in Watsonville sits boarded up nine years after the earthquake. The building's owner staved off the wrecking ball, only to see the building fall victim to economic failure as retrofit costs approached $100 per square foot.

Lessons

1. Pre-event planning is critical to successful resolution of historic preservation issues. Community historic plans and programs need to fully consider the earthquake threat, including how decisions will be structured in the city's emergency response format.

2. The federal review process[46] leaves all parties dissatisfied and should be reconsidered. The concurrence process creates an unintended incentive to early demolition as owners fear being hamstrung and made financially vulnerable through delays.[47]

3. Historic preservation planning should make retrofit a higher priority, even if the work itself has to compromise historical integrity.

4. Although retrofit does not ensure that a building will survive, it can reduce the likelihood of demolition in many cases if damage is limited so as to make repair economically feasible. (It also reduces the life-safety risks; the Cooperhouse retrofit saved lives.)

5. The engineering profession should increase training and education regarding the evaluation and strengthening of historic buildings so that more engineers are qualified to conduct and review engineering analyses of historic buildings.

6. Pre-event planning should understand the historic documentation requirements (Historic American Building Survey and Historic American Engineering Report) of the National Park Service prior to demolition. Following those procedures improves the chances of reimbursement in contested demolition decisions.[48] FEMA would require documentation to the appropriate level in accordance with those standards.

7. Losses of historic image and character can be mitigated during recovery through sensitive design of new buildings and, in some cases, exact or approximate replications.

8. Publicly owned historic buildings have a much better chance for survival than privately held buildings because of eligibility for FEMA reimbursement.[49] One strategy for historic preservation could involve joint public/private ownership to allow for reconstruction reimbursement.

9. The preservation cause could be advanced by establishing one or two high priority buildings that officials could work around or delay demolition decisions while resources are sought.

10. Preservation will not be a viable option in most cases of severe damage unless funding sources are developed and made available for property owners.

> Although retrofit does not ensure that a building will survive, it can reduce the likelihood of demolition in many cases if damage is limited so as to make repair economically feasible.

SEISMIC SAFETY PLANNING AND BUILDING CODES

In California, all jurisdictions are required to adopt safety elements as part of their General Plans. Both Santa Cruz and Watsonville had adopted these general plan elements in the 1970s, which included mapping of high seismic risk areas subject to liquefaction and landslide potential. These maps accurately anticipated the concentration of damage in the downtown areas.[50]

Both cities adopted policies intended to minimize risks. For example, the Santa Cruz plan established new policies requiring site-specific geologic investigations for new development in liquefaction areas and required the adoption of the revised California Uniform Building Code every three years or as often as a new edition was available. Policy for existing buildings called for the city "to continue to initiate . . . abatement of buildings susceptible to severe earthquake . . . damage." That policy, however, was qualified by the following statement:

> This policy should reflect a long-range approach in order to avoid economic hardship and/or dislocation problems. Structures should be allowed to remain as is, whenever possible, if their occupancy is significantly reduced or their use is made less critical. In addition, special attention should be given to the preservation of buildings of historic or aesthetic value; they should be strengthened rather than eliminated, whenever possible.[51]

In practice, this meant that occupancy of many of the upper floors of the downtown URM buildings was prohibited unless seismic abatement was done. Retrofits were encouraged with remodel permits.

The policy helped minimize the loss of life and injury that occurred during the Loma Prieta Earthquake because the most dangerous upper-floor space was unoccupied, although less effectively than a full retrofit of the majority of the buildings would have provided.[52] Overall, some buildings that received seismic retrofits were resilient enough to be repaired, and other buildings had partial retrofits that saved the building from collapse but did not prevent the need to demolish. The damage to newer buildings was limited, even in the liquefaction areas, a testimony to the effectiveness of the building codes.

With successive building code editions, the seismic provisions became incrementally more demanding. While these new demands were largely workable with regard to new projects, they became increasingly difficult to apply to retrofit projects. Thus was born the Uniform Code for Building Conservation (UCBC) and the State Historic Building Code, California's attempt to apply different standards for URMs that would improve their safety, albeit not guaranteeing their survivability.[53]

While the UCBC provided a good starting point for URMs, Santa Cruz ran into the problem of how to deal with an older reinforced concrete structure, specifically the Palomar Hotel. This seven-story building, constructed in the 1930s, sustained major but repairable damage. Both the owner and city officials sought to avoid demolition inasmuch as the hotel represented an important commercial and housing anchor downtown. Repairing to current codes would have been economically infeasible, however, thereby resulting in demolition. The dilemma was solved by the city adopting a policy that applied the 1970 UBC standards to any building that was built prior to 1970 but which did not fall under the provisions of the UCBC.[54] In essence, the city made a decision about acceptable risk in order to advance the recovery process.

Compromises such as this illustrate the importance of applying codes based on a negotiated process involving the facts at hand. It would be

Both cities adopted policies intended to minimize risks. For example, the Santa Cruz plan established new policies requiring site-specific geologic investigations for new development in liquefaction areas and required the adoption of the revised California Uniform Building Code every three years or as often as a new edition was available. Policy for existing buildings called for the city "to continue to initiate . . . abatement of buildings susceptible to severe earthquake . . . damage."

difficult to reach the decision to apply the 1970 code in advance, without knowing the specific costs and engineering challenges that were revealed after the earthquake. Decisions about what constitutes acceptable risk are difficult to make in the abstract, absent a specific understanding of benefit and risk. The rehabilitation of the Palomar Hotel in Santa Cruz was vitally important to recovery in downtown Santa Cruz and now has far improved the building's resiliency, although it does not meet current code standards. The city's flexibility regarding code standards made possible an operational definition of acceptable risk.

As a result of the earthquake, both Santa Cruz and Watsonville are far safer places than before. The URM hazards are abated, and new buildings are substantially safer not only with regard to seismic hazards, but also for fire and flood resistance. Both downtowns are in a 100-year floodplain and, since they participate in the National Flood Insurance Program (NFIP), the buildings are required to meet local floodplain management requirements. New and retrofitted buildings are either elevated one foot above the base flood elevation, or they are designed to be watertight to the floodproofed design elevation with walls impermeable to water and structural components that are capable of resisting flood forces.[55]

Lessons

1. Hazard mapping can accurately identify areas of high vulnerability, but the resiliency of vulnerable areas will be a function of the commitment (political and financial) to pre-event mitigation in those areas.

2. To be effective in engendering mitigation, hazard mapping should be accompanied by pre-event planning that considers earthquake scenarios in order to dramatize the risk and to sensitize the community and stakeholders to the potential losses.

3. Pre-event planning should acknowledge the potential need to apply different standards to different buildings following the earthquake. The choice of standards for repair or rebuilding has major economic implications; therefore jurisdictions should anticipate a process of reaching decisions regarding acceptable risk through code requirement decisions.

4. Pre-quake retrofit is exceptionally difficult economically,[56] and is unlikely to occur without assistance programs and modified building codes that facilitate economically feasible, incremental improvements in building safety.

5. Minimal amounts of seismic strengthening can be surprisingly effective, to the point of saving both lives and buildings.[57] Conversely, a full retrofit does not guarantee structural survivability. This creates a challenge for pre-event mitigation planning, which must temper the desire for uniformity in requirements with realism about feasibility.

6. Incorporating multihazard mitigation in rebuilding communities greatly increases resiliency and reduces risk, and can accomplish other goals, such as energy efficiency.

URBAN DESIGN

Invariably, a disaster such as an earthquake raises a fundamental question: If this area sustained such damage, should rebuilding take place in this location? Rarely, however, is relocation a viable option; settlement patterns generally are not subject to radical change. Watsonville and Santa Cruz are typical of small older towns throughout the nation established in the 1800s

Pre-event planning should acknowledge the potential need to apply different standards to different buildings following the earthquake. The choice of standards for repair or rebuilding has major economic implications; therefore jurisdictions should anticipate a process of reaching decisions regarding acceptable risk through code requirement decisions.

Charles C. Eadie

The new streetscape and rebuilt structures in the 300 block of Watsonville helped improve pedestrian quality and reestablish the downtown's historic flavor.

in floodplains of small rivers where urban form makes only limited accommodation of the locational risks.[58]

Communities like Santa Cruz and Watsonville are characterized by a rich tapestry of building types representing a wide variety of architectural forms, historic eras, and styles. An earthquake presents an urban design challenge in this type of community by disrupting the normal incremental evolution of the urban pattern and inserting a revolutionary event. Reconstruction of a devastated downtown district results in an unusual concentration of construction at one time in the historical continuum, amid a context that has been irreparably altered through the loss of buildings that may have served as key placemakers, important historical background buildings, or which provided examples of desired architectural characteristics.

Both communities sought to retain the historic image and character of their downtowns despite the staggering losses. A priority for Santa Cruz was to create urban design "first principles," which dealt with building height and scale, architectural features, and the interrelationship between buildings and streetscape.[59] The challenge in Santa Cruz was to redesign the Pacific Garden Mall, a much beloved semi-pedestrian landscaped mall, and overcome the loss of historic buildings such as the Cooperhouse. The task was to find a balance that recognized that aesthetic charm was a necessary prerequisite for economic viability while ensuring that certain retail needs (e.g., adequate parking, circulation, lighting, and building space characteristics) were not compromised.

The Santa Cruz Downtown Recovery Plan contains many elements that illustrate the economic/urban design compromise. A full pedestrian mall was rejected by the merchants; instead, one lane of traffic, limited amounts of parallel (not diagonal) street parking, wide sidewalks for outdoor cafes, and landscaping amenities were incorporated to serve the pedestrian orientation. Buildings are required to be a minimum of two and a maximum of five stories,[60] with step-backs above the second floors to maximize sunshine, and are subject to detailed design guidelines regarding signage, facades, awnings, fenestration, and more. The detail in the design guidelines reflects the tremendous amount of community interest in the form and image of the rebuilt downtown.

Watsonville's downtown is built around its historic town square, and Main Street also serves as State Highway 152, two factors that both resolved and limited some of the urban design options that were debated extensively in Santa Cruz. Urban design was a major aspect of the ULI study done in March 1990 to address recovery issues in Watsonville, and ULI-recommended design elements have been incorporated into many new building projects.

Some of the new architecture in both communities is distinctive; some less so. The willingness of the property owner to spend money and the talent of the architect are variables that can delimit the effectiveness of design guidelines.

Public building projects provided opportunities to advance urban design goals. The parking structures built in both communities were designed to look like commercial buildings and incorporated retail space along the street frontages. Watsonville purchased and refurbished/retrofit the old post office building on the plaza, which now serves as a community college classroom building, and invested $800,000 to upgrade the rebuilding of the high school auditorium to include an 800-seat performing arts theater, completed in 1994, and operated jointly with the Pajaro Valley Unified School District. Watsonville also built a new Youth Center, adopted a new downtown streetscape plan, and has established a facade improvement program as part of the Main Street program. Santa Cruz used redevelopment funds to save the facade of a historic bank building and completed the rebuilding of Pacific Avenue at a cost of $10 million (including utilities and streetscape).[61]

Public investments can set the tone for urban design. Opportunities can be found for creating new placemakers through the reconstruction of public buildings.

Lessons

1. Decisions made at the early stages of the emergency response, such as demolition, will profoundly affect urban design.

2. Key placemakers, such as important buildings or urban use patterns may be destroyed by the earthquake. Post-quake planning must compensate for those losses.

3. Public investments can set the tone for urban design. Opportunities can be found for creating new placemakers through the reconstruction of public buildings.

4. Economics and urban design are interwoven. Policies/development standards addressing scale, height, use intensity, parking, and other requirements need to be reevaluated and possibly rewritten based on new post-quake conditions.

5. Planning approvals for new buildings may need to be done in advance of the adoption of recovery plans or design guidelines. Efforts should be made to support expected standards through informal review processes.[62]

6. A rebuilding challenge is to retain the essential desired place characteristics while transforming and modernizing. Incorporating contemporary building characteristics, while respecting preexisting scale and character, can be a major political, economic, and aesthetic challenge.

7. The severity of the loss and the enormity of the post-quake rebuilding opportunity/challenge combine to heighten and intensify citizen interest in rebuilding. Urban design issues are typically where citizen concerns get articulated; a downtown is often considered the community's living room by the local populace.

8. Rebuilding provides an opportunity to incorporate multiple-hazards mitigation. Various requirements (e.g., floodway limits on building footprints) may create constraints to recovery that need to be overcome.

POLITICS AND RECOVERY

The Loma Prieta Earthquake left political changes in its wake, an understandable consequence given the economic, social, and physical upheaval caused by the disaster. While pre-event planning cannot predict political consequences, it should be sensitive to the fact that politics will change. Any pre-event planning structures will have to be flexible to accommodate those changes. Pre-event planning should understand that the hardest hit areas or populations will demand political attention that will alter pre-quake politics.

In Santa Cruz, post-quake politics evolved to include a greater recognition of the importance of economic planning. Prior to 1989, the progressive-dominated political paradigm was largely anti-growth. The community feared that development would compromise community character, and, as a result community planning began with a philosophy of preservation and keeping the lid on growth. The combination of the growth control orientation and the personalities of some of the key politicians had resulted in land-use review and planning processes that were considered exceptionally complex, complicated by a plethora of advisory groups and commissions. Consequently, development interests and investors perceived Santa Cruz to be a risky place to do business.

The earthquake, in the words of one city official, opened up Pandora's box because antidevelopment and change-resistant politics were antithetical to the new need to plan for a transformation of downtown and attract investment capital (developers!).[63] The longstanding feuding between the business interests and the progressive politicians had to give way in order for recovery to occur.[64]

The ensuing recovery planning process responded to the political context. It began with a series of community planning lectures featuring nationally known theorists.[65] The talks helped the town set aside the losses and think about the planning opportunities that recovery could afford. A 36-member advisory body, Vision Santa Cruz,[66] was established in January 1990 that included wide representation of neighborhood and community groups, business, finance, labor, and nonprofit organizations. Vision Santa Cruz incorporated as a nonprofit with 501c(3) tax status in order to accept and solicit contributions for recovery planning.[67] Recovery planning efforts and staff support for Vision Santa Cruz were centered in a newly created Redevelopment Department in response to the emerging economic priority and the perception that the pre-quake planning processes would not work.

Vision Santa Cruz embarked on a frenzy of planning activity, including two major studies, several issue papers, and a number of community workshops that resulted in principles to guide recovery planning, which were presented to the city council in May 1990. This was followed with the preparation of the Downtown Recovery Plan, adopted unanimously by Vision Santa Cruz on May 31, 1991. Altogether, the process involved more than 251 meetings and events, including six public hearings, one weekend charrette, five workshops, six block meetings, 11 consultants, seven task forces, four VSC chairs, and 50-plus board members.

The ensuing recovery planning process responded to the political context. It began with a series of community planning lectures featuring nationally known theorists. The talks helped the town set aside the losses and think about the planning opportunities that recovery could afford. A 36-member advisory body, Vision Santa Cruz, was established in January 1990 that included wide representation of neighborhood and community groups, business, finance, labor, and nonprofit organizations.

Although faced with the enormous challenge of uniting long-feuding political factions, Vision Santa Cruz succeeded in bringing the community together and forging a compromise middle ground that previously had not existed in Santa Cruz.

Watsonville at the time of the earthquake was in the throws of political upheaval. A lawsuit by the Mexican American Legal Defense Fund (MALDEF) had succeeded in forcing the city to convert from citywide to district elections on the argument that the Latino population had been underrepresented in the past. The first district elections were scheduled for November amid some political rancor and bitterness over the MALDEF lawsuit, which had been fought by the previous city council.

The earthquake forced a postponement of the elections until December and initially provided fuel for the political fires as some people used the confusion and difficulty of the emergency response period as a platform to criticize the old city council.

Ironically, while there was some initial distrust of the new city council by the old guard, the earthquake recovery had the effect of pulling the community together, as acrimonies of the emergency response period subsided. A Downtown Recovery Committee was established and business interests, such as Ford's, were reassured that the city council was going to be supportive of their efforts. Community leaders old and new worked diligently to address the housing and economic problems,[68] and the city embarked on an ambitious and eventually successful process of critically evaluating the emergency response and creating a community-based disaster response plan that organized the relationships among all the groups who had been flung together ad hoc to address the needs. The Downtown Recovery Committee eventually was reconstituted as an Economic Development Council that continues to pursue a variety of economic opportunities five years after the earthquake.

> Recovery planning refocuses attention on longstanding problems and issues that may have been politically intractable in the past. Examples include: appropriate levels of growth or economic development; infrastructure capacities; acrimonious political environment; distribution of political power.

Lessons

1. The status quo is not an option following a significant disaster; planning takes on added urgency. Pre-quake political patterns, habits, and processes may operate too slowly or otherwise prove obsolete, thus creating short-term political turmoil.

2. Recovery planning refocuses attention on longstanding problems and issues that may have been politically intractable in the past. Examples include: appropriate levels of growth or economic development; infrastructure capacities; acrimonious political environment; distribution of political power.

3. Recovery may require community political objectives to change in order to come into confluence with the interests of key stakeholders in rebuilding (e.g., property owners, certain interest groups).

4. Any systematic assessment of recovery issues will uncover philosophical differences about the proper roles of the private and public sectors in rebuilding. Common understanding must be found to move forward. Once again, the lack of private earthquake insurance tends to force recovery toward more public-sector involvement.

5. Pursuing new opportunities through redevelopment or major change is more politically difficult and time consuming than simply rebuilding or repairing what existed before because agreement must be reached on a redefined community vision or plan.

6. Economic necessity may engender political and policy shifts where conditions require more than simply rebuilding (e.g., where costs rise due to new requirements for safety in retrofit and new construction). Retail trade may need to increase, infrastructure may need to be upgraded.

7. Fast-track politics of recovery limit time available for decisions or issues to ripen politically and thus add stress and complication.

8. New political interests may coalesce and need time to organize (e.g., a property owners association or an ethnic coalition may become a necessity where none existed prior to the earthquake).

9. Should hazardous areas be rebuilt? In large part, settlement patterns are fixed and not amenable to major changes. For example, initial efforts by Santa Cruz County planners[69] to limit rebuilding in certain rural areas (facing newly revealed hazards that were difficult to assess) were rebuffed after major political controversy.

11. Political imperatives may be at odds with what is needed from an economic procedural, or administrative perspective. This can make the decision-making process complicated and time consuming. For example, a community nonprofit agency may win support for a politically attractive rebuilding project but prove unable to perform due to lack of development experience.

The appropriate planning tools format (area plan, specific plan, redevelopment plan, etc.) will be determined only as other political and economic variables play out. In Santa Cruz, it took nine months to reach agreement on whether to have a Downtown Recovery Plan and what it should contain. Completing the planning process took another year.

12. Unexpected and/or time-consuming political battles can command the time and attention of the community and thus hold up other decisions. For example, a historic preservation battle over demolition can delay decisions about adjacent properties and affect political discussion on other issues.

13. Planning may proceed in fits and starts because the perception (and hence political definition) of what recovery requires changes over time.

14. Citizen involvement is critical, albeit time consuming and politically challenging. New avenues for participation are needed during the recovery process. Community volunteers/participants can make significant positive contributions.

15. The appropriate planning tools format (area plan, specific plan, redevelopment plan, etc.) will be determined only as other political and economic variables play out. In Santa Cruz, it took nine months to reach agreement on whether to have a Downtown Recovery Plan and what it should contain. Completing the planning process took another year.

OBSERVATIONS AND RECOMMENDATIONS

Because most of the specific observations and recommendations regarding the lessons learned and how they could be incorporated into pre-event planning are contained in the preceding discussion of specific issues, these final comments focus on how communities might effectively proceed with pre-event planning.

Above all, it is important to have a strategic approach because it is difficult to muster enthusiasm and administrative energy for pre-event disaster planning. Although vitally important, emergency managers and planners always face the problem of pursuing a hypothetical situation that tends to be overshadowed by the immediate crises and activities of the day. Therefore, the following strategies are suggested:

1. *Integrate pre-event disaster and recovery planning into the other planning and program efforts.* For example, work on economic development planning in a downtown area could be expanded to include analysis of disaster vulnerability and an implementation program to address those vulnerabilities. A housing element could include a program to protect low-income housing through seismic retrofit and strengthening; a historic preservation program could make seismic concerns a top priority; a neighborhood improvement program could include foundation bolting or other earthquake protection measures.

2. *Cultivate advocates.* Generally it is possible to find community members, politicians, or interest groups that have or potentially could have a strong interest in seismic safety issues. Candidates include those with high vulnerabilities (e.g., historic preservationists), community activists seeking a broader portfolio, or people with an intellectual or altruistic concern. Without advocates, it is virtually impossible for a planner to sustain the interest. As education is expanded, more people will recognize their own vulnerabilities and become more interested in pursuing mitigation.

3. *Be practical; avoid a doomsday mentality.* If the threat is perceived to be too substantial, there is a tendency for people to become fatalistic and unwilling to act. Recognize that small steps can be effective and that risk reduction is always an achievable goal; any improvement counts.

4. *Use scenarios and involve the community in risk assessment.* The limitation evident from the Loma Prieta experience is that hazard identification in a planning document does not dramatize the risk sufficiently to set in motion pre-event emergency and mitigation planning. Combining the characteristics of the built environment with the underlying soil types allows for fairly specific scenario development. Work with the vulnerable populations (building owners and tenants) on imagining the disaster so that their own preparedness takes into account their interaction with the government's emergency response. Use risk scenarios as a springboard for generating action.

5. *Develop a community outreach strategy that sets priorities according to risk and which has a definite time frame and benchmarks.*

6. *Keep up with evolving technology.* New soils analyses from the United States Geological Survey (USGS), geographic information system (GIS) formats, and changes in building engineering are examples of fast-evolving technologies that can support pre-event disaster planning.

7. *Use outside resources.* Earthquake-prone states and regions are beginning to follow the California example of having a seismic safety commission or other entity that can provide technical support to local jurisdictions in their attempts to prepare and mitigate for earthquakes. The private sector is increasingly sensitive to earthquake risks and could bring resources to the table that could advance local efforts.

8. *Prepare a community-based disaster response plan.* Again, using scenarios and examples such as Watsonville, it is possible for a community to assess the resources in the community and devise ways of linking the community organizations with the government to establish in advance the relationships that invariably will congeal following the earthquake.

Earthquake-prone states and regions are beginning to follow the California example of having a seismic safety commission or other entity that can provide technical support to local jurisdictions in their attempts to prepare and mitigate for earthquakes. The private sector is increasingly sensitive to earthquake risks and could bring resources to the table that could advance local efforts.

Notes

1. Watsonville has been staggered by unemployment upwards of 20 percent in the 1990s; an economic study done for Santa Cruz estimated that retail trade would have to increase 35 percent to support the costs of rebuilding lost commercial space downtown.

2. By 1991, 90 percent of the residential damage in Watsonville had been repaired or rebuilt; by 1994, the combination of new and repaired housing projects resulted in no net loss of housing due to the earthquake, although Watsonville, with an agriculturally based low-wage economy still faces acute housing needs.

3. The answer was no; the EOC people were too preoccupied sorting out their own roles to be able to work in any others.

4. A good indication about how frantic the times were is the fact that the Watsonville planning director to this day does not know their names.

5. See discussion under Economic Recovery section (below).

6. The earthquake did not behave as expected in that area, calling into question all the previous assumptions that were guiding hazard avoidance mapping and regulations. Geologists could not agree either, and summit area residents became extremely angry about having their rebuilding delayed. Eventually the county agreed to issue permits despite continuing uncertainty about the risk potential.

7. See, for example, the discussion of nonconforming uses in Chapter 5 of this report.

8. The workload will also be a function of personnel status of the department. Santa Cruz was fully staffed with 12 planners, plus clerical and a housing/rehab division of five staff. Watsonville was shorthanded by three unfilled vacancies, leaving just three planners, plus three rehab staff. One planner and one secretary had been on the job only two weeks.

9. Likewise, staff roles varied at the County of Santa Cruz where some planners did not come to work at all due to disruption in their personal lives.

10. In the county, some key staff members typically left the government center following any major aftershock, often not returning for several days.

11. The urgency was heightened by the need to complete clean-up, demolitions, and relocation in time for the Christmas shopping season, beginning the day after Thanksgiving. The month of frenzied activity in Santa Cruz culminated with city crews working into the night before Thanksgiving completing temporary paving and sidewalk repair on Pacific Avenue.

12. The author of this chapter conducted the access planning and was put in charge of the downtown operations center at the request of the downtown merchants.

13. Because of the downtown's location in a floodplain, the emergency center had been located in a fire station on high ground more than one mile away. This situation resulted in a number of communication problems involving the EOC, City Hall, and the downtown operations center. These problems were alleviated when all emergency personnel were shifted to the downtown location.

14. From October 24 through December, more than 5,000 access requests were handled without injury or incident.

15. The pavilions were operated by the Phoenix Partnership, which consisted of the Chamber of Commerce, the Downtown Association, and the Cultural Council of Santa Cruz County. The partnership jointly secured a line of credit to acquire and construct the pavilions. Volunteer real estate professionals and attorneys arranged the leasing, and labor unions helped with donated construction.

16. Five years after the earthquake, 11 Pacific Avenue demolition sites have been rebuilt, two are under construction, and 16 sites are vacant. Five of the 10 major sites are rebuilt or under construction. Rehabilitation has been completed on the five major rehabilitation sites.

17. There are a number of reasons for this, including fewer merchants, less problematic safety issues because of a wide Main Street, and different patterns of damage. City

officials early on decided to allow access to every building, and a process was set up that addressed merchant needs within the first week.

18. Measure E established a six-year, one-half cent override, which generated approximately $12 million to $15 million each for Santa Cruz and Watsonville, and lesser amounts for Capitola, Scotts Valley and the County of Santa Cruz. It was the only tax measure ever supported by the local chambers of commerce.

19. Watsonville residents typically expected to meet friends and acquaintances at Ford's; a trip to Ford's was a social event as well.

20. The Urban Land Institute donated the services of its panel; the city paid expenses.

21. The grant was cofunded by the Federal Economic Development Administration and the California Department of Commerce.

22. The Main Street program provides the city with technical assistance for downtown marketing and physical improvements, and involves the creation of a nonprofit organization to manage and implement the program.

23. FEMA funding covered most of the cost because of the replacement of damaged streets and utilities.

24. Special state legislation was passed in 1990 at the city's behest that allowed for an expedited process for creating a redevelopment district.

25. Eventually, only 52 of the damaged residences were demolished because even major damage proved to be repairable (e.g., picking up a house and rebolting it to a rebuilt foundation).

26. The census definition of overcrowding is more than 1.01 persons per room. Common conditions brought on by a regional shortage of housing included several families sharing a house, unmarried farm workers packed into a few rooms, and conversion of nonhabitable space for residential use.

27. Although many considered the preservation of agricultural land to be a growth control tool, the policy in fact promoted population growth due to the conversion of crops in the 1980s from orchards to more labor-intensive crops like strawberries. Agricultural employment nearly doubled without a concomitant increase in available housing for farm workers.

28. A new sewer line was run to the fairgrounds, an action that overcame previous resistance based on the concern for growth inducement.

29. Minor damage permits could be issued over the counter or even on site by inspectors (e.g., for chimney repairs). People could rebuild what they had before and could use photographs, tax records, or any available documentation to establish previous use.

30. The city council established a staff committee in 1989 with clear direction to disburse funds quickly in accordance with specified criteria.

31. A six-year, one-half cent, countywide sales tax override for earthquake relief was approved by voters in 1990.

32. In September 1990, the Red Cross granted $8 million to Santa Cruz County jurisdictions, including $1.7 million to the City of Watsonville. The money was from funds that were donated to the Red Cross nationwide after the earthquake but that had not been directed to the area. A major lobbying and political effort on the part of Watsonville and the other communities hard hit by Loma Prieta resulted in a change of Red Cross policy and receipt of the grant funds.

33. For example, the city committed $795,000 of Red Cross money and $250,000 of redevelopment funds to a 42-unit housing project downtown built by a nonprofit and valued at more than $7.5 million.

34. The California Department of Housing and Community Development designated the city for special recognition (a blue ribbon housing award) on the basis of its housing element and demonstrated commitment to housing.

35. The county's general plan policies oppose development in most of the areas under consideration for annexation by the city, and LAFCO policy is to favor the county's plan in areas outside the sphere of influence, which needs to be amended to include these areas sought by the city for housing.

36. The commitment totaled $406,000 of the $11.25 million project.

37. Engineering teams were brought in by the state OES through the ATC-20 process (Applied Technology Council).

38. The 30-day time limit was later extended. Demolition reimbursement was critically important for recovery. Demolition reimbursement requests totaled $3.43 million in Santa Cruz.

39. St. Patrick's church in Watsonville decided to repair rather than demolish based on initial cost estimates, but as the cost calculations and engineering became more precise, the costs rose to the point where it no longer made sense to repair. The church was demolished and rebuilt instead, incorporating stained glass and the design elements from the old church.

40. The Cooperhouse was a total economic loss despite a retrofit that was nearly completed at the time of the earthquake. The building did not collapse, and lives were saved, illustrating both the value and the limits to retrofitting.

41. The only hard dollars available involved a state preservation program for temporary shoring, and the amounts were minimal (e.g., $50,000 compared to project costs in the millions).

42. After touring the St. George Hotel, a contractor brought in by state historic advocates stated that the work should cost no more than $8 to $10 per square foot, a simple tie-and-anchor job. The construction manager for the St. George owner, whose own estimates were several fold higher, responded with a challenge: "If you can do it for $15 a foot, I'll sign a contract with you right now!" The contractor hemmed and hawed, left town, and never was heard from again.

43. FEMA, California OES, and SHPO have a memorandum of understanding that requires SHPO concurrence for any FEMA-funded demolition of historic buildings taking place beyond 30 days after the disaster.

44. Investigators attributed the fire to transients living inside.

45. Both the Trust Building and St. George Hotel fires confirmed city officials' worst fears about the potential for unresolved building decisions to create an attractive nuisance of boarded-up buildings.

46. Section 106 of the National Historic Preservation Act of 1966 establishes a review requirement for buildings 50 years or older involving the federal granting agency and the SHPO. In Loma Prieta, the review was suspended if demolitions occurred within 30 days of the disaster. Subsequently, California law has been changed to cut the deadline to three to six days after the disaster. FEMA reimbursement for demolition was contingent on SHPO concurrence on structures torn down beyond the 30-day emergency window, although the SHPO never concurred, and FEMA approvals came on appeal by the City of Santa Cruz.

47. In the case of the Trust Building, an argument could be made that the length of time for concurrence contributed to the loss of the building, which burned two years after the earthquake. The owner was awaiting demolition concurrence on the adjacent Elks Building so he could start work to repair the Trust.

48. FEMA finally approved reimbursement in 1994 for the Trust and Elks building demolitions. City officials credited careful historic documentation as a factor.

49. The Porter Building, a URM on land owned by the City of Watsonville, was repaired in part with $800,000 in FEMA money through a complicated arrangement involving the partnership that was leasing the building prior to the earthquake and who previously had invested money in remodeling.

50. The Santa Cruz Seismic Safety and Safety Element also mapped historic areas with high potential for liquefaction including the Pacific Garden Mall.

51. See page 54 of the *Seismic Safety and Safety Element*, City of Santa Cruz, July 1976.

52. An attempt by the city's building inspector in the mid-1980s to pursue a mandatory retrofit failed, illustrating the economic problems (viz., retrofit is a cost without a commensurate increase in rent—economically weak downtowns or older areas cannot sustain new costs or regulations); the political problems (viz., a city council will not voluntarily impose costs in a situation where a future risk can be discounted); and acceptable risk challenges (viz., the building official's estimates of cost were based on a standard that was economically infeasible resulting in political opposition that killed the program, truncating any consideration of options that could have compromised safety to achieve practicality).

53. Another state program required jurisdictions to inventory their URM building stock as a first step toward assessing and initiating planning that would encourage seismic retrofitting. Paradoxically, the inventory files that were in the process of being compiled by Santa Cruz planning staff became the basis for the demolition files after the earthquake.

54. The 1970 code was chosen specifically because the steel content requirement was raised from one to one and a half in the 1973 code. Application of that requirement would have rendered the project infeasible.

55. Parts of downtown Santa Cruz also are located within the more restrictive floodway, and, therefore, the downtown rebuilding requirements include provisions to ensure that there is no net increase in flood water impediments in these areas. The pre-quake building footprints were either maintained or increases were offset by other reductions (e.g., the demolition of one building for a parking lot was used as credit for the expansion of another building's footprint).

56. The viability of retrofit will be a function of the economic strength of the district, as well as the financial wherewithal of the property owners. Typically, the most vulnerable buildings tend to be located in older and economically less viable areas, such as aging downtowns, compounding the dilemma.

57. Some major damage was averted and buildings were salvageable in instances were minimal retrofits were done in conjunction with other repair or maintenance (e.g., improving the roof to wall connections in conjunction with re-roofing).

58. The woodframe buildings built in downtown Santa Cruz in the nineteenth century were replaced with brick URMs after devastating fires in the early twentieth century. Rebuilding for one hazard (fire) overlooked the threat of another (earthquake).

59. Vision Santa Cruz commissioned an urban design study that adopted first principles and was completed in spring 1990. See the discussion of Vision Santa Cruz in the Political Issues section of this chapter.

60. The prohibition of one-story buildings creates a short-term economic impediment. Multistory buildings are more expensive and the market for upper-floor office space is limited. The requirement, however, is important in the long term for recreating the pre-quake scale and form of the downtown and maximizing the intensity of development downtown to obtain a viable critical mass.

61. Most of the Pacific Avenue construction will be reimbursed by FEMA.

62. For example, the consultants preparing the Downtown Recovery Plan in Santa Cruz were hired by the city to provide informal design review for projects coming up in advance of the plan adoption. Communication between the consultant and property owners and their architects was encouraged.

63. In speeches after the earthquake, the mayor acknowledged her personal need to change by noting that her well-practiced negative body language previously aimed at developers during city council meetings would have to go.

64. While the ULI panel in Watsonville focused on downtown land-use and design issues, the primary ULI recommendation for Santa Cruz was for the feuding interests to work at getting along better.

65. The series was put together by an environmental studies professor at the University of California at Santa Cruz, with university sponsorship. The lectures were well attended and televised on local cable television.

66. Even the name was controversial. Growth control interests preferred "Restore Santa Cruz"; "Partnership Santa Cruz" represented a pro-business perspective. It took a month of debate before the so-called "Gang of 36" finally settled on the moniker, Vision Santa Cruz.

67. Vision Santa Cruz collected a total of $161,700 in cash contributions and 55 in-kind contributions valued at $150,000. These contributions paid for economic and urban studies prepared in early 1990 and also supported the creation of a downtown storefront information center opened later that year, which provided meeting space and featured a scale model of the downtown built by volunteers, planning displays, and exhibits.

68. One observer suggested that the small-town intimacy of Watsonville was a key factor in supporting recovery, stating "The fact that people knew each other by their first names made it easier for people to be concerned with more than their own interests."

69. While not the subject of this case study, the Santa Cruz County experience is relevant to illustrate a political issue.

BY MICHAEL J. ARMSTRONG

*Associate Director for Mitigation,
Federal Emergency Management
Agency*

Thank you for taking the time and showing the interest to read and review this Planning Advisory Service Report. I hope that you find it to be a valuable resource for years to come. It is also my hope that, at some time in the future, we can all point to it as having made a significant contribution toward making our communities and the nation as a whole disaster resistant.

In summary, the PAS Report you have just finished reading describes the importance of planning for post-disaster recovery and reconstruction. It describes the unique architecture of disaster response and recovery, and outlines the goals, considerations, and processes that provide the underpinnings of this type of planning. It presents suggestions for plan content and provides a model recovery ordinance. It chronicles case study examples of communities that have learned the hard way the value of hazard mitigation and planning for recovery in the pre-disaster time frame.

Most importantly, this document also illustrates how hazard mitigation can be incorporated into everyday planning before the next disaster strikes, to reduce the need to deal with post-disaster reconstruction issues. Incorporating hazard mitigation considerations into the thought processes and decision making that comprise local planning reinforces community sustainability and strengthens community planning programs. It ensures that the community survives natural disasters so that it can grow and develop as it was envisioned.

The series of severe natural disasters that has plagued this country over the last several years has taught us that successful recovery begins with the forging of relationships between local, state, and federal governments as well as local private and nonprofit organizations. Unfortunately, too often these relationships are formed after a disaster has struck. Recognizing the value of establishing strong relationships both within the community and between local, state, and federal governments, FEMA launched its Project Impact/ Building a Disaster Resistant Community initiative in 1997. Through Project Impact, FEMA provides funding and technical assistance to encourage communities and states to initiate and implement pre-disaster mitigation activities based upon the framework of mitigation planning. Mitigation planning embraces the two-pronged approach of incorporating mitigation activities into day-to-day community operations, as well as focusing on what the local government can do to plan for post-disaster recovery and reconstruction. The implementation of mitigation planning and cost-effective mitigation projects through Project Impact will lead towards our national goal of safer, disaster-resistant, and more livable communities.

In conclusion, it is my sincere hope that the ideas and concepts included within this PAS Report motivate you to go forward in your respective disciplines, be it local elected official, academician, planner, emergency manager, or business leader, and initiate actions that, in whole or in part, will contribute to making your community more disaster resistant. Because in the end, your most important role is that of citizen—working as a neighbor as well as a worker, a family member as well as an employee, and a taxpayer as well as a professional. Together we can forge a new, planned approach to living with the hazards facing our built environment. This report provides the concepts and processes, but it is up to each of you to make it happen.

All Federal Emergency Management Agency documents in this reference list are available at no cost from the FEMA Distribution Center, P.O. Box 2012, Jessup, MD 20794-2012, 1-800-480-2520. The center can also be reached by fax at 301-362-5335.

Alinsky, Saul. 1972. *Rules for Radicals.* New York: Random House.

Altshuler, Alan. 1965. *The City Planning Process: A Political Analysis.* Ithaca, N.Y.: Cornell University Press.

American Institute of Architects (AIA), Bay Area Chapter and California Council. *Community Voices: A Resource Guide for Rebuilding.* 1992.

Andrews, James. 1996. Bureau of Recovery and Mitigation, Florida Department of Community Affairs, Tallahassee. Telephone interview, 15 July.

Arendt, Randall. 1996. *Conservation Design for Subdivisions: A Practical Guide to Creating Open Space Networks.* Washington, D.C.: Island Press.

Armstrong, Michael. 1998. Presentation to "Communities in Harm's Way" conference, Wingspread Conference Center, Racine, Wisconsin. January 14.

Arnold, City of, Missouri. 1991. *City of Arnold Floodplain Management Plan.* Adopted November 27.

———. 1993. *Hazard Mitigation Project Application.* Revised December 20.

———. 1994. *Flood Emergency Plan for the Meramec and Mississippi Rivers.* January.

Barrette, Michael. 1996. "Hog-Tied by Feedlots." *Zoning News* (October): 1-4.

Barton, Allen H. 1969. *Communities in Disaster.* New York: Doubleday Anchor.

Beatley, Timothy, David J. Brower, and Anna K. Schwab. 1994. *An Introduction to Coastal Zone Management.* Washington, D.C.: Island Press.

Beatley, Timothy, Sandra Manter, and Rutherford H. Platt. 1992. "Erosion as a Political Hazard: Folly Beach After Hugo." In *Coastal Erosion: Has Retreat Sounded?*, edited by Rutherford H. Platt et al. Boulder, Colo.: Natural Hazards Research and Applications Information Center.

Becker, William S. 1994a. *Rebuilding for the Future. . . A Guide to Sustainable Redevelopment for Disaster-Affected Communities.* Washington, D.C.: U.S. Department of Energy. September.

———. 1994b. "The Case for Sustainable Redevelopment." *Environment & Development* (November): 1-4.

Berke, Philip R., Jack Kartez, and Dennis Wenger. 1994. "Recovery After Disasters: Achieving Sustainable Development, Mitigation, and Equity." College Station: Texas A&M University, Hazard Reduction and Recovery Center.

Berger, Michael M. 1994. "Not Always Right to Try to Get As Much As You Can." *Land Use Law & Zoning Digest* 46, no. 7: 4-6.

Berry, James F. 1994. "The *Dolan* Case: Grabbing Tigard by the Tail?" *Environment & Development* (August): 1-3.

Blakely, Edward J., Ph.D., former Policy Advisor to the Mayor, City of Oakland. Verbal communications with Ken Topping, various dates.

Bollinger, G.A. 1985. "The Earthquake at Charleston in 1886." In *Societal Implications: Selected Readings.* Earthquake Hazards Reduction Series 14. Washington, D.C.: Federal Emergency Management Agency.

Bortz, Bruce. 1990. "Pre-Storm Mitigation and Post-Storm Reconstruction—A Plan for Nags Head." Presented at South Carolina Sea Grant Consortium, Eighth Annual Winter Conference, Columbia, South Carolina. January 16.

Reference List

———. 1998. Planner, Town of Nags Head, North Carolina. Telephone interview with Jim Schwab, 21 January.

Bowyer, Robert A. 1993. *Capital Improvements Programs: Linking Budgeting and Planning.* Planning Advisory Service Report No. 442. Chicago: APA.

Bradford, Janet K., Chris Hatcher, Raymond A. Zilinskas, Stanley Wiener, M.D., Clinton R. VanZandt, Peter F. Bahnsen, and William M. Medigovich. 1992. *Biological Hazards and Emergency Management.* Working Paper No. 82. Boulder, Colo.: Natural Hazards Research and Applications Information Center.

Bredin, John. 1998. "Transfer of Development Rights: Cases, Statutes, Examples." *PAS Memo.* November.

Brooks, Kenneth R., and Vernon P. Deines. 1995. *Local Planning Guide to Wetlands and Riparian Areas in Kansas.* Topeka: Kansas Water Office and Kansas Department of Wildlife and Parks.

———. 1996. "Wetland and Riparian Areas Planning." *Environment & Development* (March/April): 6-7.

Brower, David J., Timothy Beatley, and David J.L. Blatt. 1987. *Reducing Hurricane and Coastal Storm Hazards Through Growth Management: A Guidebook for North Carolina Coastal Localities.* Chapel Hill: University of North Carolina, Center for Urban and Regional Studies. July.

Brown, Phil, and Edwin J. Mikkelsen. 1990. *No Safe Place: Toxic Waste, Leukemia, and Community Action.* Berkeley: University of California Press.

Building Official and Code Administrator (BOCA). 1994. "Emergency Response and Damage Assessment of the Northridge, California, Earthquake." *BOCA* 28, no. 2: 20-27.

Building Officials Association of Florida (BOAF). 1994. *Building Department Guide to: After a Disaster!* Pinellas Park, Fla.: BOAF.

Building Seismic Safety Council (BSSC). 1987a. *Abatement of Seismic Hazards to Lifelines: An Action Plan.* Earthquake Hazards Reduction Series 31. Washington, D.C.: FEMA.

———. 1987b. *Abatement of Seismic Hazards to Lifelines: Proceedings of a Workshop on Development of an Action Plan, Volume 6: Papers on Political, Economic, Social, Legal, and Regulatory Issues and General Workshop Presentations.* Earthquake Hazards Reduction Series 31. Washington, D.C.: FEMA.

———. 1990. *Seismic Consideration for Communities at Risk.* Earthquake Hazards Reduction Series 13. Washington, D.C.: FEMA.

Burby, Raymond J., and Linda C. Dalton. 1993. *The Role of Land Use Plans and State Planning Mandates in Limiting the Development of Hazardous Areas.* New Orleans, La.: University of New Orleans, College of Urban Affairs.

Burby, Raymond J., and Steven P. French. 1998. "Seismic Safety in Suburbia: Code Enforcement, Planning and Damages in the Northridge Earthquake." *Earthquake Spectra* 14, no. 1. February.

Burby, Raymond J., and Steven P. French with Beverly A. Cigler, Edward J. Kaiser, David H. Moreau, and Bruce Stiftel. 1985. *Floodplain Land Use Management: A National Assessment.* Boulder, Colo.: Westview Press.

Burby, Raymond J., Peter J. May, and Robert C. Paterson. 1998. "Improving Compliance with Regulations: Choices and Outcomes for Local Government." *Journal of the American Planning Association* 64, no. 3. Summer.

Burke, David G., Erik J. Meyers, Ralph W. Tiner, Jr., and Hazel Groman. 1988. *Protecting Nontidal Wetlands.* Planning Advisory Service Report No. 412/413. Chicago: APA.

Burton, Ian, Robert W. Kates, and Gilbert F. White. 1993. *The Environment as Hazard.* second edition. New York: Guilford Press.

Byrne, Jim. 1998. Project manager, Town of Boone, N.C. Telephone interview with Jim Schwab, 7 December.

California Office of Emergency Services (OES). 1992. *Seismic Retrofit Incentive Programs: A Handbook for Local Governments.* Sacramento: OES.

California, State of, Seismic Safety Commission (CSSC). 1994a. *A Compendium of Background Reports on the Northridge Earthquake (January 17, 1994) for Executive Order W-78-94.* Sacramento: CSSC. November 9.

———. 1994b. *Northridge Earthquake: Turning Loss to Gain.* Report to the Governor, Governor's Executive Order W-78-94. Sacramento: CSSC.

———. 1988. *California at Risk: Steps to Earthquake Safety for Local Governments.* Sacramento: CSSC. June.

Callies, David L. 1994. "Nexus Redux on Required Land Dedications." *Land Use Law & Zoning Digest* 46, no. 7: 3-4.

———, ed. 1993. *After* Lucas*: Land Use Regulation and the Taking of Property Without Compensation.* Chicago: American Bar Association.

Cannon, Lou. 1997. "Five Years After Hurricane Iniki, Trouble Still Plagues Paradise Known as Kauai." *Washington Post.* December 21.

Central United States Earthquake Consortium (CUSEC). 1993. "Pre-disaster Planning for Recovery: A Multi-state Challenge—and Opportunity." *The CUSEC Journal* 1, no. 2: 1-11. Summer.

———. 1996. *Earthquake Vulnerability of Transportation Systems in the Central United States.* Memphis, Tenn.: CUSEC.

Charlestown, Rhode Island, Town of, in cooperation with University of Rhode Island's Coastal Resources Center, Rhode Island Sea Grant, and Rhode Island Emergency Management Agency. 1997. *Strategy for Reducing Risks from Natural Hazards in Charlestown, Rhode Island.* Final Draft. Charlestown, R.I.: Town of Charlestown. September.

Coleman, Ronny J. 1996. "A Historical Perspective." In *California's I-Zone: Urban/ Wildland Fire Prevention and Mitigation,* edited by Rodney J. Slaughter. Sacramento: California Fire Marshal's Office.

David Plummer & Associates, Inc. 1995. *Collier County Post-Disaster Transportation Infrastructure Analysis.* Final Report. June 30.

Dennison, Mark S. 1996. "Zoning and the Comprehensive Plan." *Zoning News* (August): 1-4.

De Sario, Jack, and Stuart Langton, eds. 1987. *Citizen Participation in Public Decision Making.* Westport, Conn.: Greenwood Press.

Des Moines, City of. 1993a. *City of Des Moines Residential Recovery Flood Recovery Program: Hazard Mitigation Grant Application.* September.

Des Moines, City of, Office of the City Manager. 1993b. "City Council Communication 93-355: September 7, 1993, Agenda."

Design Center for American Urban Landscape, College of Architecture and Landscape Architecture, University of Minnesota. 1994. *Recovery and Resettlement: A First Look at Post-Flood Recovery Planning Issues in the Upper Mississippi River Valley.* Minneapolis: University of Minnesota. December.

Deyle, Robert E., and Richard A. Smith. 1994. *Storm Hazard Mitigation and Post-storm Redevelopment Policies.* A Report of a Project to the Coastal Zone Management Program, Florida Department of Community Affairs (Contract No. 930S-07-13-00-15-012). Tallahassee: Florida Planning Laboratory, Department of Urban and Regional Planning, The Florida State University.

———. 1996. "State Planning Mandates: State Implementation and Local Government Response." Tallahassee: The Florida Planning Laboratory, Department of Urban and Regional Planning, Florida State University.

DiMento, Joseph, ed. 1990. *Wipeouts and Their Mitigation: The Changing Context for Land Use and Environmental Law.* Cambridge, Mass.: Lincoln Institute of Land Policy.

Doctor, Thomas H., former Manager, Community Restoration and Development Center, City of Oakland. Letter communication dated October 9, 1994.

Drabek, Thomas E., and Gerard J. Hoetmer, eds. 1991. *Emergency Management: Principles and Practice of Local Government.* Washington, D.C.: International City Management Association.

Duerksen, Christopher J., with Suzanne Richman. 1993. *Tree Conservation Ordinances: Land-Use Regulations Go Green.* Planning Advisory Service Report No. 446. Chicago: APA.

Duncan, Randall C. 1992. "Tornadoes in Kansas: When Theory Becomes Reality." *Natural Hazards Observer* 16, no. 5: 1-3. May.

Eagleman, Joe R. 1983. *Severe and Unusual Weather.* New York: Van Nostrand Reinhold Company.

East Bay Regional Park District. 1982. *Report of the Blue Ribbon Fire Prevention Committee for the East Bay Hill Area, Urban-Wildland Interface Zone.* Oakland, California. February.

Enterprise/Homestead Planning/Action Team and the City of Homestead. 1993. *The Plan for the Community Redevelopment Area.* Prepared for HERO (The Homestead Economic and Rebuilding Organization). Homestead, Fla.: City of Homestead. July.

Erley, Duncan, and William J. Kockelman. 1981. *Reducing Landslide Hazards: A Guide for Planners.* Planning Advisory Service Report No. 359. Chicago: APA.

Escambia County, Department of Growth Management, Planning and Zoning Division. 1995. *Post-Disaster Redevelopment Plan.* Adopted August 4, 1995, by the Escambia County Board of County Commissioners. Pensacola, Fla.: Escambia County.

Federal Emergency Management Agency (FEMA). 1986. *Flood Emergency and Residential Repair Handbook.* Washington, D.C.: Federal Emergency Management Agency.

——. 1987. *Reducing Losses in High Risk Flood Hazard Areas: A Guidebook for Local Officials.* Washington, D.C.: FEMA.

——. 1990. *Post-Disaster Hazard Mitigation Planning Guidance for State and Local Governments.* Washington, D.C.: FEMA.

——. 1993a. *Are You Ready? Your Guide to Disaster Preparedness.* revised edition. Washington, D.C.: FEMA.

——. 1993b. *Seismic Considerations for Communities at Risk.* Washington, D.C.: FEMA.

——. 1994. *A Citizen's Guide to Disaster Assistance.* Washington, D.C.: FEMA.

——. 1995a. *Disaster Assistance: A Guide to Recovery Programs.* Washington, D.C.: FEMA.

——. 1995c. *National Mitigation Strategy: Partnerships for Building Safer Communities.* Washington, D.C.: FEMA.

——. Mitigation Directorate. 1995d. *Mitigation: Cornerstone for Building Safer Communities.* Washington, D.C.: FEMA.

——. 1995e. *National Flood Insurance Program/Community Rating System: Example Plans.* July 1994, with July 1995 Revised Pages. Washington, D.C.: FEMA.

——. 1995f. *CRS Coordinator's Manual.* Washington, D.C.: FEMA.

——. 1995g. *Typical Costs for Seismic Rehabilitation of Existing Buildings, Second Edition, Vol. 1–Summary.* Washington, D.C.: FEMA.

——. 1996. *Guide for All-Hazard Emergency Operations Planning.* Washington, D.C. FEMA.

——. 1997a. *A Guide to Federal Aid in Disasters.* Washington, D.C.: FEMA.

——. 1997b. *Multi-Hazard Identification and Risk Assessment: A Cornerstone of the National Mitigation Strategy.* Washington, D.C.: FEMA.

——. 1997c. *Report on Costs and Benefits of Natural Hazard Mitigation.* Washington, D.C.: FEMA.

——. Federal Insurance Administration and Mitigation Directorate. 1997d. *Interim Guidance for State and Local Officials: Increased Cost of Compliance Coverage.* Washington, D.C.: FEMA.

——. 1998a. *The President's Long-Term Recovery Action Plan, 1997-1998 Winter Storms, Florida.* Washington, D.C.: FEMA.

——. 1998b. *The President's Long-Term Recovery Action Plan for the March 1998 Georgia Floods.* Washington, D.C.: FEMA.

——. 1998c. *The President's Long-Term Recovery Action Plan for the March 1998 Alabama Floods.* Washington, D.C.: FEMA.

——. 1998d. *The Federal Response Plan (for Public Law 93-288, as Amended).* Final Draft. Washington, D.C.: FEMA. December. (Updates FEMA 229, April 1992)

Federal Emergency Management Agency (FEMA), Region I. Undated. *Safeguarding Your Historic Site: Basic Preparedness and Recovery Measures for Natural Disasters.* Boston: FEMA, Region I.

Federal Emergency Management Agency (FEMA), Region IV. 1993. *Winter Storm, March, 1993: Interagency Hazard Mitigation Team Report.* In Response to the March 13, 1993 Disaster Declaration for the State of Florida (FEMA 982-DR-FL). Atlanta: FEMA, Region IV.

Federal Emergency Management Agency (FEMA), Region V. 1996. *National Flood Insurance Program: Post-Flood Standard Operating Procedures and Program Guidance.* Chicago: FEMA, Region V.

Federal Insurance Administration (FIA). 1992. *Building Performance: Hurricane Andrew in Florida: Observations, Recommendations, and Technical Guidance.* Washington, D.C.: FEMA.

——. 1993a. *Flood-Resistant Materials Requirements for Buildings Located in Special Flood Hazard Areas in Accordance with the National Flood Insurance Program.* Technical Bulletin 2-93. Washington, D.C.: FEMA.

——. 1993b. *Non-Residential Floodproofing—Requirements and Certification for Buildings Located in Special Flood Hazard Areas in Accordance with the National Flood Insurance Program.* Technical Bulletin 3-93. Washington, D.C.: FEMA.

——. 1993c. *Free-of-Obstruction Requirements for Buildings Located in Coastal High Hazard Areas in Accordance with the National Flood Insurance Program.* Technical Bulletin 5-93. Washington, D.C.: FEMA.

Federal Insurance Administration, in cooperation with the State of Hawaii Office of Civil Defense and Kauai County. 1993. *Building Performance: Hurricane Iniki in Hawaii, Observations, Recommendations, and Technical Guidance.* Washington, D.C.: FEMA.

Federal Insurance Administration, Office of Loss Reduction. 1990. *Design Manual for Retrofitting Flood-prone Residential Structures.* Washington, D.C.: Federal Emergency Management Agency.

Federal Interagency Floodplain Management Task Force (FIFMTF). 1995. *Protecting Floodplain Resources: A Guidebook for Communities.* Washington, D.C.: U.S. Government Printing Office.

Florida International University/Florida Atlantic University (FAU/FIU) Joint Center for Environmental and Urban Problems. 1995. *Pre-Storm Planning for Post-Storm Redevelopment: Policies and Options for Florida's Beachfront Areas, Final Report (Phase III).* Ft. Lauderdale, Fla.: FAU/FIU Joint Center for Environmental and Urban Problems.

Florida Department of Community Affairs (DCA), Division of Emergency Management. 1994. *Statewide Mutual Aid Agreement.* Tallahassee: Florida DCA. April 27.

——. 1995a. *Summary of Initial Damage Assessment—Housing Losses.* Tallahassee: Florida DCA.

——. 1995b. *Memorandum of Understanding Regarding Mutual Aid for Disaster Response and Recovery.* Tallahassee: Florida DCA.

——. 1996. *Damage Survey Report Summary.* February 5. Tallahassee: Florida DCA.

——. 1997a. *The Local Mitigation Strategy: A Guidebook for Florida Cities and Counties.* Tallahassee: Florida DCA. June.

——. 1997b. *Workbook in Local Mitigation Strategy Development.* Tallahassee: Florida DCA. June.

——. undated. *Breaking the Cycle: How Starting Now on Long-Term Redevelopment Can Help Florida Avoid Economic Disaster.* Tallahassee: Florida DCA.

Florida Department of Environmental Protection (DEP), Bureau of Beaches and Coastal Systems. 1995. *Hurricane Opal—Executive Summary of a Report on Structural Damage and Dune Erosion Along the Panhandle Coast of Florida.* Tallahassee: Florida DEP.

Foster, Jill. 1997. Long-range planner, Town of Hilton Head Island, S.C. Telephone interview with Jim Schwab, 13 February.

——. 1998. Telephone interview with Jim Schwab, 23 January.

French, Steven P., Arthur C. Nelson, S. Muthukumar, and Maureen M. Holland. 1996. *The Northridge Earthquake: Land Use Planning for Hazard Mitigation.* Final Report to the National Science Foundation (CMS-9416458). Atlanta: Georgia Institute of Technology, College of Architecture, City Planning Program. December.

French & Associates, Ltd. 1995. *Flood Hazard Mitigation in Northeastern Illinois: A Guidebook for Local Officials.* Chicago: Northeastern Illinois Planning Commission. Prepared with a grant (06-06-61015) from the Economic Development Administration, U.S. Department of Commerce. July.

Friesema, H. Paul, et al. 1979. *Aftermath: Communities After Natural Disasters.* Beverly Hills, Calif.: Sage Publications.

Geipel, Robert. 1982. *Disaster and Reconstruction.* London: George Allen & Unwin Ltd.

Glassford, Peggy. 1993. "Teaming Up to Save a Stream." *Environment & Development* (August): 1-4.

Glassheim, Eliot. 1997. "Fear and Loathing in North Dakota." *Natural Hazards Observer* 21, no. 6: 1-4. July.

Godschalk, David R., David J. Brower, and Timothy Beatley. 1989. *Catastrophic Coastal Storms.* Durham, N.C.: Duke University Press.

Goering, Laurie. 1993. "'A Bad Dream That Never Ends': Soggy Des Moines Gets Help in Tackling Flood Cleanup." *Chicago Tribune.* 25 July.

Governor's Office of Emergency Services, State of California. 1993. *Earthquake Recovery: A Survival Manual for Local Government.* Sacramento: Governor's Office of Emergency Services, State of California.

Grant, James. 1993. Planning Department, City of Des Moines, Iowa. Telephone conversation with Jim Schwab, 15 July.

Griggs, Gary B., and John A. Gilchrist. 1983. *Geologic Hazards, Resources, and Environmental Planning.* Second Edition. Belmont, Calif.: Wadsworth Publishing Company.

Growing Smart™ Legislative Guidebook: Model Statutes for Planning and the Management of Change. 1996. Phase I Interim Edition. Chicago: American Planning Association.

Haas, J. Eugene, Robert W. Kates, and Martyn J. Bowden, eds. 1977. *Reconstruction Following Disaster.* Cambridge, Mass.: MIT Press.

Hanley, Paul. *Reducing Earthquake Hazards in the Central United States: Critical Facilities.* Undated. Urbana: Department of Urban and Regional Planning, University of Illinois.

Harper, Charles. Harper Perkins Architects, Wichita Falls, TX. 1994. Telephone conversation with Jim Schwab, 11 March.

Harris, Elihu and Loni Hancock, Mayors, Cities of Oakland and Berkeley. *Final Report, Task Force on Emergency Preparedness and Community Restoration.* February 3, 1992.

Havlick, Spenser W. 1995. "Paradise in the Rockies." *Environment & Development* (January): 1-3.

Herald-News, The. 1990. *"Winds of Fury": The Will County Tornado of 1990.* Sun City West, Ariz.: C.F. Boone Publishing Co.

Herson-Jones, Lorraine M. 1995. *Riparian Buffer Strategies for Urban Watersheds.* Washington, D.C.: Metropolitan Washington Council of Governments.

Hill, G. Richard, ed. 1993. *Regulatory Taking: The Limits of Land Use Controls.* Revised Edition. Chicago: American Bar Association.

Hilton Head Island, South Carolina, Town of. 1993. *Post-Disaster Recovery and Mitigation Plan—Town of Hilton Head Island, Beaufort County, South Carolina.* Hilton Head Island, S.C.: Town of Hilton Head Island. Revised in June from June 1, 1991, edition.

Holway, James M., and Raymond J. Burby. 1993. "Reducing Flood Losses: Local Planning and Land Use Controls." *Journal of the American Planning Association* 59, no. 2: 205-16. Spring.

Homestead, City of-Enterprise/Homestead and Homestead Economic & Rebuilding Organization. 1993. *A Plan for The Homestead Pioneer Center.* Homestead, Fla.: City of Homestead. September.

Humbach, John A. 1992. "Existing-Use Zoning." *Zoning News* (December): 1-4.

Innes, Judith E. 1996. "Planning Through Consensus Building: A New View of the Comprehensive Planning Ideal." *Journal of the American Planning Association* 62, no. 4: 460-72. Autumn.

Interagency Floodplain Management Review Committee. 1994. *Sharing the Challenge: Floodplain Management into the 21st Century.* Washington, D.C.: Executive Office of the President.

Jaffe, Martin, JoAnn Butler, and Charles Thurow. 1981. *Reducing Earthquake Risks: A Planner's Guide.* Planning Advisory Service Report No. 364. Chicago: American Planning Association.

Jager, S., and G.F. Wieczorek. 1994. *Landslide Susceptibility in the Tully Valley Area, Finger Lakes Region, New York.* U.S. Geological Survey Open-File Report 94-615.

James, Alvin, former Director of Planning, City of Oakland. Verbal communications with Ken Topping, various dates.

Jeer, Sanjay, Megan Lewis, Stuart Meck, Jon Witten, and Michelle Zimet. 1998. *Nonpoint-Source Pollution: A Handbook for Local Governments.* Planning Advisory Service Report No. 476. Chicago: American Planning Association.

Johnson, Nan. 1996. Department of Land Use, Boulder County, Colo. Telephone interview with Jim Schwab, 4 December.

Kartez, Jack D., and Charles E. Faupel. 1994. "Comprehensive Hazard Management and the Role of Cooperation Between Local Planning Departments and Emergency Management Offices." Unpublished paper.

Kelly, Eric Damian. 1994. "Supreme Court Strikes Middle Ground on Exactions Test." *Land Use Law & Zoning Digest* 46, no. 7: 6-9.

Kennedy, Carolyn. 1991. "Standards for Overlay Districts." *Zoning News* (August): 1-3.

———. 1992. "Minimizing Environmental Damage on Construction Sites." *Environment & Development* (April).

Knoll, Eric. 1995. City Administrator, Arnold, Mo. Interview with Jim Schwab, 6 February.

———. 1996. Telephone conversation with Jim Schwab, 29 February.

Krakauer, Jon. 1996. "Geologists Worry About Dangers of Living 'Under the Volcano'." *Smithsonian* 27, no. 4: 32-41. July.

Land Trust Alliance. 1993. *Conservation Options: A Landowner's Guide*. Washington, D.C.: Land Trust Alliance.

Lee County, Florida. Resolution No. 90-12-19. Adopted December 5, 1990.

Lind, Brenda. 1991. *The Conservation Easement Stewardship Guide*. Washington, D.C.: Land Trust Alliance.

Long Island Regional Planning Board. 1984. *Hurricane Damage Mitigation Plan for the South Shore—Nassau and Suffolk Counties, N.Y.* Hauppauge, N.Y.: Long Island Regional Planning Board.

Loomis, James. 1996. Bureau of Recovery and Mitigation, Florida Department of Community Affairs, Tallahassee. Telephone interview, 15 July.

Los Angeles, City of, Emergency Operations Organization. 1994. *Draft Recovery and Reconstruction Plan*. January.

Lozano, Gary. 1993. Planning Department, City of Des Moines, Iowa. Interview by author, 25 September.

L.R. Johnston Associates. 1989. *A Status Report on the Nation's Floodplain Management Activity: An Interim Report*. Prepared for Interagency Task Force on Floodplain Management. Washington, D.C.: FEMA. April.

———. 1992. *Floodplain Management in the United States: An Assessment Report. Vol. 2; Full Report*. Washington, D.C.: Federal Interagency Floodplain Management Task Force.

Mader, George G., William E. Spangle, and Martha L. Blair. 1980. *Land Use Planning After Earthquakes*. Portola Valley, Calif.: William Spangle and Associates, Inc.

Mandelker, Daniel R. 1997. "Melding State Environmental Policy Acts with Land-Use Planning and Regulations." *Land Use Law & Zoning Digest* 49, no. 3: 3-11. March.

Maryland Office of Planning. 1993. *Preparing a Sensitive Areas Element for the Comprehensive Plan*. Baltimore: Maryland Office of Planning. May.

———. 1994. *Clustering for Resource Protection*. Baltimore: Maryland Office of Planning. October.

———. 1995a. *Transferable Development Rights*. Baltimore: Maryland Office of Planning. January.

———. 1995b. *Overlay Zones*. Baltimore: Maryland Office of Planning. March.

———. 1995c. *Achieving Environmentally Sensitive Design in Growth Areas through Flexible and Innovative Regulations*. Baltimore: Maryland Office of Planning. April.

———. 1996. *Adequate Public Facilities.* Baltimore: Maryland Office of Planning. June.

Massachusetts Department of Environmental Management (DEM), Flood Hazard Mitigation Program. 1996. *Flood Hazard Mitigation Planning: A Community Guide.* Boston: Massachusetts DEM. October.

May, Peter J. 1985. *Recovering from Catastrophes: Federal Disaster Relief Policy and Politics.* Westport, Conn.: Greenwood Press.

McElyea, William O., David J. Brower, and David R. Godschalk. 1982. *Before the Storm: Managing Development to Reduce Hurricane Damage.* Chapel Hill: Center for Urban and Regional Studies, University of North Carolina. April.

McInnis, John. 1996. City Administrator, Mexico Beach, Fla. Telephone interview. 28 February.

McSweeney, Kevin. 1997. "Planning for the Mornings After." Session presented at the APA National Planning Conference, April 7.

Michael J. Baker, Inc. 1995. *Hurricane Opal —Florida Panhandle Wind and Water Line Survey.* Alexandria, Va: Michael J. Baker, Inc.

Miller, Ward S. 1994. "Developing a Proactive Watershed Program." *Environment & Development* (October): 1-4.

Monmonier, Mark. 1997. *Cartographies of Danger: Mapping Hazards in America.* Chicago: University of Chicago Press.

Moore, C. Nicholas. 1995. *Participation Tools for Better Land-Use Planning.* Sacramento, Calif.: Center for Livable Communities.

Moore, Marilyn A. 1992. "After the Big One." *South Florida* 45, no. 12: 32-37. October.

Morgan, Terry. 1994. "Exactions as Takings Tactics for Dealing with *Dolan.*" *Land Use Law & Zoning Digest* 46, no. 7: 3-9.

Morris, Marya. 1997. *Subdivision Design for Flood Hazard Areas.* Planning Advisory Service Report No. 473. Chicago: APA.

Morris, Marya, and Jim Schwab. 1991. "Adequate Public Facilities Ordinances." *Zoning News* (May): 1-3.

Nags Head, North Carolina, Town of. 1988. *Hurricane and Storm Mitigation and Reconstruction Plan.* Adopted by Nags Head Board of Commissioners, October 10.

National Academy of Sciences, National Research Council. 1982. Committee on Methodologies for Predicting Mudflow Areas. *Selecting a Methodology for Delineating Mudslide Hazard Areas for the National Flood Insurance Program.* Washington, D.C.: National Academy Press.

National Earthquake Hazards Reduction Program (NEHRP). 1994. *Preserving Resources Through Earthquake Mitigation.* NEHRP Biennial Report to Congress, Fiscal Years 1993-1994. Washington, D.C.: NEHRP.

National Fire Protection Association (NFPA). undated. *Planning for Water Supply and Distribution in the Wildland/Urban Interface.* Quincy, Mass.: National Fire Protection Association.

———. 1990. *Stephan Bridge Road Fire: Case Study.* Quincy, Mass.: National Fire Protection Association.

———. 1991. *The Loma Prieta (San Francisco/Monterey Bay) Earthquake: Emergency Response and Stabilization Study.* Prepared for FEMA, U.S. Fire Administration. Grant EMW-90-G-3440. Washington, D.C.: U.S. Government Printing Office.

National Oceanic and Atmospheric Administration (NOAA), Pacific Marine Environmental Laboratory. 1995. *Tsunami Hazard Mitigation: A Report to the Senate Appropriations Committee.* March 31.

National Research Council (Panel on the Assessment of Wind Engineering Issues in the United States). 1993. *Wind and the Built Environment: U.S. Needs in Wind Engineering and Hazard Mitigation.* Washington, D.C.: National Academy Press.

National Trust for Historic Preservation (NTHP). 1993. *Treatment of Flood-Damaged Older and Historic Buildings.* Information Booklet No. 82. Washington, D.C.: NTHP.

Nelson, Carl L. 1991. *Protecting the Past from Natural Disasters.* Washington, D.C.: The Preservation Press, National Trust for Historic Preservation.

New Hanover County Board of Commissioners and Wilmington City Council. 1993. *Policies for Growth and Development: Wilmington-New Hanover County Land Use Update.* Wilmington, N.C.: New Hanover County and City of Wilmington.

Northeastern Illinois Planning Commission (NIPC). 1991. *Model Soil Erosion and Sediment Control Ordinance.* Chicago: NIPC. September.

Oakland, California, City of. *Emergency Order for Fire Reconstruction and Information Regarding Emergency Preparedness,* adopted November 26, 1991.

Ohlsen, Christine, and Claire B. Rubin. 1993. "Planning for Disaster Recovery." *MIS Report* 25, no. 7. Washington, D.C.: International City Management Association. July.

Olshansky, Robert B. 1989. "Landslide Hazard Reduction: A Need for Greater Government Involvement." *Zoning and Planning Law Report* 12, no. 3: 105-12.

———. 1995. "Planning for Hillside Development." *Environment & Development* (September/October): 1-4.

———. 1996. *Planning for Hillside Development.* Planning Advisory Service Report No. 466. Chicago: American Planning Association.

Operation Urban Wildfire Task Force. 1992. *Report of the Operation Urban Wildfire Task Force.* Washington, D.C.: Federal Emergency Management Agency, U.S. Fire Administration.

Ozawa, Connie P. 1991. *Recasting Science: Consensual Procedures in Public Policy Making.* Boulder, Colo.: Westview Press.

Palm, Risa I. 1990. *Natural Hazards: An Integrative Framework for Research and Planning.* Baltimore, Md.: Johns Hopkins University Press.

Palm Beach County Board of County Commissioners. Undated. *Palm Beach County Post-Disaster Redevelopment Plan: A Guide to Restoring the Economic and Social Viability of Palm Beach County.* Two volumes. Palm Beach, Fla.: Palm Beach County. (Issued in 1996.)

Perry, Ronald W., Marjorie Greene, and Alvin Mushcatel. 1983. *American Minority Citizens in Disaster.* Final Report. National Science Foundation Grant No. PFR-80-19297. Seattle: Battelle Human Affairs Research Centers.

Perry, Ronald W., and Michael K. Lindell. 1990. *Living with Mt. Helens: Human Adjustment to Volcano Hazards.* Pullman: Washington State University Press.

Petak, William J., and Arthur A. Atkisson. 1982. *Natural Hazard Risk Assessment and Public Policy: Anticipating the Unexpected.* New York: Springer-Verlag.

Philipsborn, Clancy. 1997. Mitigation Assistance Corporation, Denver. Telephone interview with Jim Schwab, 10 February.

Pilkey, Orrin H., Jr., William J. Neal, Orrin H. Pilkey, Sr., and Stanley R. Riggs. 1980. *From Currituck to Calabash: Living with North Carolina's Barrier Islands.* Second Edition. Durham, N.C.: Duke University Press.

Pinellas County Department of Civil Emergency Services and Pinellas County Planning Department. 1994. *Post-Disaster Redevelopment Guide for Pinellas County.* Clearwater, Fla.: Pinellas County Board of County Commissioners. March.

Plainfield, Village of. 1995. *Village of Plainfield Comprehensive Plan.* Plainfield, Ill.: Village of Plainfield. December 18.

Portland Metro. 1996. *MAD GIS: Metro Area Disaster Geographic Information System.* Portland, Ore.: Portland Metro.

Rapport, Ezra, Deputy City Manager, City of Oakland. Verbal communications with Ken Topping, various dates.

Rhode Island Department of Administration, Division of Planning. 1989. *Hazard Mitigation Plan: Status of Recommendations.* Providence: Rhode Island Division of Planning.

Rice, Benjamin. 1996. Portland Metro, Portland, Ore. Telephone conversation with Jim Schwab, 18 November.

Roddewig, Richard J., and Cheryl A. Inghram. 1987. *Transferable Development Rights Programs: TDRs and the Real Estate Marketplace.* Planning Advisory Service Report No. 401. Chicago: APA.

Roths, Richard (FEMA Region V). 1996. Telephone conversation with Jim Schwab, 27 September.

Rubin, Claire B., with Martin D. Saperstein and Daniel G. Barbee. 1985. *Community Recovery from a Major Natural Disaster.* Monograph #41. Boulder: University of Colorado, Institute of Behavioral Science.

Rubin, Claire B., and Roy Popkin. 1990. *Disaster Recovery After Hurricane Hugo in South Carolina.* Working paper #69. Boulder, CO: Institute of Behavioral Science.

Russell, Joel. 1996. "The Need for New Models of Rural Zoning." *Zoning News* (June): 1-4.

Saniter, David J. 1998. Emergency programs manager, Lee County, Florida Telephone interview with Jim Schwab, 22 January.

Schwab, Jim. 1993. *Industrial Performance Standards for a New Century.* Planning Advisory Service Report No. 444. Chicago: APA.

———. 1994. *Deeper Shades of Green: The Rise of Blue-Collar and Minority Environmentalism in America.* San Francisco: Sierra Club Books.

———. 1996a. "'Nature Bats Last': The Politics of Floodplain Management." *Environment & Development* (January/February): 1-4.

———. 1996b. "An Interview with: J. Gary Lawrence." *Environment & Development* (May/June): 8-9.

———. 1997. "Zoning for Flood Hazards." *Zoning News* (October): 1-4.

———. 1998. "Post-Disaster Zoning Opportunities." *Zoning News* (August): 1-4.

Schwab, Jim, with Amy Van Doren. 1992. "Ready or Not, Stormwater Deadlines Loom." *Environment & Development* (May): 1-3.

Sherrard, David. 1996. "Managing Riparian Open Space." *Environment & Development* (January/February): 6-7.

Silverberg, Steven M., and Mark S. Dennison. 1993. *Wetlands and Coastal Zone Regulation and Compliance.* Somerset, N.J.: John Wiley & Sons, Inc.

Skinner, Nancy, and Bill Becker. 1995. *Pattonsburg, Missouri: On Higher Ground.* Washington, D.C.: President's Council on Sustainable Development.

Slaughter, Rodney, ed. 1996. *California's I-Zone: Urban/Wildland Fire Prevention & Mitigation.* Sacramento: California Fire Marshal's Office.

Smith, Dennis. 1996. Bureau of Recovery and Mitigation, Florida Department of Community Affairs, Tallahassee. Telephone interview, 4 December.

———. 1997. Telephone interview, 16 December.

Smith, Herbert H. 1979. *The Citizen's Guide to Planning.* Chicago: APA Planners Press.

Smith, Maura, Recovery Project Manager, City of Oakland. Verbal communications with Ken Topping, various dates.

So, Frank S., and Judith Getzels. 1988. *The Practice of Local Government Planning.* Washington, D.C.: International City Management Association, Municipal Government Series.

Solyst, Jim. 1990. *A Governor's Guide to Emergency Management.* Washington, D.C.: National Governors' Association.

South Florida Regional Planning Council (RPC). 1990. *Post-Disaster Redevelopment Planning: Model Plans for Three Florida Scenarios.* Tampa: South Florida Regional Planning Council.

Spangle Associates. 1996. *Using Earthquake Hazard Maps for Land Use Planning and Building Permit Administration.* Report of the Metro Advisory Committee for Mitigating Earthquake Damage. Portland, Ore.: Portland Metro.

Spangle Associates and Robert Olson Associates. 1997. *The Recovery and Reconstruction Plan of the City of Los Angeles: Evaluation of Its Use after the Northridge Earthquake.* Portola Valley, Cal: Spangle Associates. August.

State Emergency Management Agency (SEMA), State of Missouri. 1995. *Out of Harm's Way: The Missouri Buyout Program.* Jefferson City, Mo.: SEMA.

Structural Engineers Association of Hawaii (SEAOH). 1992. *Tips on Improving Wind Resistance for One Story Single Family Dwelling Repairs on Kauai.* Hawaii: SEAOH. October.

Sun-Sentinel. Fort Lauderdale, Fla. October 6, 1995, Page 1A.

Tackett, Michael. 1993. "Rivers, Danger on the Rise in Des Moines." *Chicago Tribune,* 14 July.

Tampa Bay Regional Planning Council (TBRPC). 1992. *Tampa Bay Region Hurricane Recovery Planning Project, Volume I-Phases I and II Regional Recovery Planning Guide.* St. Petersburg, Fla.: TBRPC. January.

——. 1994. *Model Community Post-Disaster Economic Redevelopment Plan.*

Tampa Bay Regional Planning Council and Hillsborough County Planning and Development Management Department. 1995. *Model Local Government Disaster Mitigation and Redevelopment Plan and Model Local Redevelopment Regulations.* September. Prepared under Subgrant No. 95-CZ-10-13-00-21-021. Tallahassee: Florida Department of Community Affairs.

Thurow, Charles, William Toner, and Duncan Erley. 1975. *Performance Controls for Sensitive Lands: A Practical Guide for Local Administrators.* Planning Advisory Service Report No. 307/308. Chicago: APA.

Topping, Kenneth C. 1991a. *Key Laws, Codes and Authorities Affecting Recovery and Reconstruction.* Los Angeles: Consultant Report No. 1.

——. 1991b. *Feasibility of Existing Organization and Procedures for Recovery and Reconstruction.* Los Angeles: Consultant Report No. 2.

——. 1991c. *Land Use Issues in Recovery and Reconstruction.* Los Angeles: Consultant Report No. 3.

——. 1991d. *Recommended Changes to Draft Recovery and Reconstruction Plan.* Los Angeles: Consultant Report No. 4.

——. 1991e. *Land Use/Reuse Issues Recovery and Reconstruction Plan.* Los Angeles: Consultant Report No. 5.

——. 1992a. *Report on Recovery and Reconstruction Plan Revisions: City of Los Angeles.* Los Angeles: Consultant Report No. 6.

——. 1992b. *Oakland Hills Fire Prevention and Suppression Benefit Assessment District Report.* Consultant report prepared for City of Oakland. October 15.

——. 1994. *OES GIS Strategic Plan.* Circulation Draft. Prepared for Office of Emergency Services, Sacramento, Calif.

Topping, Ken, and Mark Sorensen. 1996. "Building Disaster-Resistant Communities." *Environment & Development* (May/June), p. 11.

Trust for Public Land. 1995. *Doing Deals: A Guide to Buying Land for Conservation.* Washington, D.C.: Land Trust Alliance.

Tsunami Hazard Mitigation Federal/State Working Group. 1996. *Tsunami Hazard Mitigation Implementation Plan: A Report to the Senate Appropriations Committee.* April.

Tulsa, City of. 1994. *From Rooftop to River: Tulsa's Approach to Floodplain and Stormwater Management.* Tulsa, Okla.: City of Tulsa.

Turner, Steven. Undated. *Reducing Earthquake Hazards in the United States: Historic Resources.* Urbana: Department of Urban and Regional Planning, University of Illinois.

Tyler, Martha Blair. 1994. William Spangle & Associates, Portola Valley, Calif. Telephone interview with Jim Schwab, 27 May.

——. 1995. *Look Before You Build: Geologic Studies for Safer Land Development in the San Francisco Bay Area.* U.S. Geological Survey Circular 1130. Washington, D.C.: U.S. Government Printing Office.

Underhill, Ruth M. 1956. *The Navajos.* Norman: University of Oklahoma Press.

U.S. Army Corps of Engineers. 1994. *Local Flood Proofing Programs.* June.

U.S. Department of the Interior (DOI) and U.S. Department of Agriculture (USDA). 1995. *Federal Wildland Fire Management Policy and Program Review.* Draft report. Washington, D.C.: U.S. Department of the Interior. June 9.

U.S. Environmental Protection Agency (EPA), Office of Solid Waste and Emergency Response. 1995. *Planning for Disaster Debris.* Washington, D.C.: U.S. EPA. December.

U.S. Fire Administration (USFA). 1990. *Public Fire Education Today: Fire Service Programs Across America (1990 Edition).* Emmitsburg, Md.: U.S. Fire Administration.

——. 1993. *Directory of National Community Volunteer Fire Prevention Program: Community-based Fire Prevention Education Initiatives.* Emmitsburg, Md.: U.S. Fire Administration.

U.S. Geological Survey. undated. *The Next Big Earthquake in (name of area) May Come Sooner Than You Think: Are You Prepared?* Various regional offices. (Each brochure has the same generic title but for the location and is customized to the area for which it is produced.)

U.S. Government. *Hazard Mitigation Report for the East Bay Fire in the Oakland-Berkeley Hills.* FEMA Hazard Mitigation Survey Team Report. San Francisco: U.S. Government Printing Office, 1992.

U.S. Public Law 448. 90th Cong., 2nd sess. 1968. *National Flood Insurance Act of 1968.*

U.S. Public Law 152. 91st Cong., 1st sess. 1969. *Housing and Urban Development Act of 1969.*

U.S. Public Law 234. 93rd Cong., 1st sess. 1973. *Flood Disaster and Protection Act of 1973.*

U.S. Public Law 288. 93rd Cong., 2nd sess. 1974. *Disaster Relief Act of 1974.*

U.S. Public Law 707. 100th Cong., 2nd sess. 1988. *Robert T. Stafford Disaster Relief and Emergency Assistance Act.*

U.S. Public Law 325. 103rd Cong., 2nd sess. 1994. *National Flood Insurance Reform Act of 1994.*

Utah Division of State History, Office of Historic Preservation. undated. *Bracing for the Big One: Seismic Retrofit of Historic Houses.* Salt Lake City: Utah Division of State History.

Venice, City of. Planning Department. 1994. *Creating a Hurricane Tolerant Community.* Venice, Fla.: City of Venice.

Waldock, Peter J. 1996. Planning Department, Village of Plainfield, Ill. Interview with Jim Schwab, 6 September.

Walsh, Edward, and Judith Berck. 1993. "When Only Running Water Is in Streets, a City Improvises." *Washington Post*, 15 July.

Weatherford, Jack. 1991. *Native Roots: How the Indians Enriched America.* New York: Fawcett Columbine.

Weinstein, Alan C. 1996. "Revisiting the National Flood Insurance Program." *Land Use Law & Zoning Digest* 48 (10): 3-8.

Wetmore, French. 1996a. *Reducing Flood Losses Through Multi-Objective Management.* Madison, Wis.: Association of State Floodplain Managers.

——. 1996b. "Flooding and Planners." *Environment & Development* (July/August). White, S. Mark. 1996. *Adequate Public Facilities Ordinances and Transportation Management.* Planning Advisory Service Report No. 465. Chicago: APA.

William Spangle and Associates, Inc. 1988. *Geology and Planning: The Portola Valley Experience.* Portola Valley, Calif.: William Spangle and Associates, Inc.

——. 1991. *Rebuilding After Earthquakes: Lessons from Planners.* International Symposium on Rebuilding After Earthquakes, Stanford University, August 12-15, 1990. National Science Foundation Grant No. CES-8901101. Portola Valley, Calif.: William Spangle and Associates, Inc.

William Spangle and Associates, Inc., with H.J. Degenkolb & Associates and Earth Science Associates. 1980. *Land Use Planning After Earthquakes.* Portola Valley, Calif.: William Spangle and Associates, Inc.

Williams, Norman. 1986. *American Planning Law: Land Use and the Police Power.* Wilmette, Ill.: Callaghan and Company.

Wisconsin Department of Natural Resources (DNR). 1989. *Wisconsin Construction Site Best Management Practice Handbook.* Madison: Wisconsin DNR.

Witt, James Lee. 1998. *Director's Weekly Update.* September 8.

Wolensky, Robert P. 1993. *Better Than Ever! The Flood Recovery Task Force and the 1972 Agnes Disaster.* Stevens Point, Wis.: University of Wisconsin-Stevens Point Foundation Press.

Woodward-Clyde Associates. 1997a. *Arkadelphia Recovery Plan.* Gaithersburg, Md.: Woodward-Clyde Federal Services.

——. 1997b. *College Station Recovery Plan.* Gaithersburg, Md.: Woodward-Clyde Federal Services.

Wright, James D., Peter H. Rossi, Sonia R. Wright, and Eleanor Weber-Burdin. 1979. *After the Clean-up: Long-Range Effects of Natural Disasters.* Beverly Hills, Calif.: Sage Publications.

Yin, Robert K. 1984. *Case Study Research: Design and Methods.* Beverly Hills, Calif.: Sage Publications.

Ziegler, Edward H., Jr. 1997. *Rathkopf's The Law of Planning and Zoning.* Second volume. Deerfield, Ill.: Clark Boardman Callaghan.

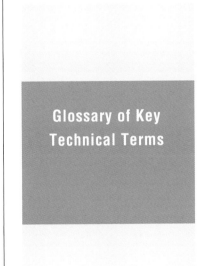

alluvial fan   A gently sloping, fan-shaped landform created over time by the deposition of eroded sediment and debris. These areas are common at the base of mountain ranges in arid and semiarid regions, such as the American West, and are subject to intense flash flooding, deposition, erosion, and debris flow.

base flood   As defined under the National Flood Insurance Program (NFIP), the flood having a 1 percent chance of being equaled or exceeded in any given year. (See also **one hundred-year flood**).

coastal construction control line (CCCL)   In Florida, an area within which permits are required from the state Department of Environmental Protection (DEP) for excavation or construction. CCCL defines that portion of the beach and dune system subject to the erosion effects of a 100-year storm surge. Permit conditions include construction and elevation standards for wind, wave, hydrostatic and hydrodynamic loads, and erosion conditions designed to resist the predicted forces associated with a 100-year storm event. The proposed structure or excavation also must be located sufficiently landward of the beach and dune system to permit natural shoreline fluctuations and to preserve the dune stability and natural recovery following storm-induced erosion. Any new habitable structures also must be located landward of a 30-year "erosion projection" line. Existing major habitable structures can be remodeled or repaired after a storm without complying with the CCCL permit conditions or the 30-year setback, so long as the modified or repaired structure remains within the confines of the existing foundation and no modification of the foundation is involved. However, most local building codes apply the 50 percent damage threshold required under the NFIP as the threshold for requiring rebuilt structures to meet applicable building code standards.

coastal high-hazard area   As defined under the National Flood Insurance Program (NFIP), an area of special flood hazard extending from offshore to the inland limit of a primary frontal dune along an open coast and any other area subject to high-velocity wave action from storms or seismic sources.

community   As defined for the purposes of the National Flood Insurance Program (NFIP), any state, area, or political jurisdiction or any Native American tribe, authorized tribal organization, Alaska native village, or authorized native organization that has the authority to adopt and enforce floodplain management ordinances for the area under its jurisdiction. In most cases, a community is an incorporated city, town, township, borough, or village or an unincorporated area of a county or parish. However, some states have statutory authority that varies from this description.

Community Rating System (CRS)   A voluntary system under the National Flood Insurance Program (NFIP) in which communities undertake planning and regulatory activities beyond NFIP minimum requirements in order to obtain credits that earn premium reductions for flood insurance for their residents and property owners. These activities are delineated in the CRS guidelines but include four general categories: public information; mapping and regulatory activities; flood damage reduction; and flood preparedness. The premium reductions come in a series of 5 percent steps based on points earned under the system.

disaster A major detrimental impact of a hazard upon the population and economic, social, and built environment of an affected area. Logically, a natural disaster results from the impact of a natural (as opposed to human-caused or technological) hazard upon the built environment of an affected area. (See also **declared disaster** and **major disaster**.)

emergency As defined in the Stafford Act, "any occasion or instance for which, in the determination of the president, federal assistance is needed to supplement state and local efforts and capabilities to save lives and to protect property and public health and safety, or to lessen or avert the threat of a catastrophe in any part of the United States." Almost all states have related or similar definitions in their own disaster legislation.

emergency operations plan See **emergency response plan**.

emergency period The period commencing immediately with the onset of a natural disaster during which a community's normal operations, such as communications, transportation, and commerce, are disrupted or halted, and ending when danger from the hazard itself has ceased and initial response activities, such as search and rescue and debris clearance and removal, have commenced, at which point the community can begin to restore normal services and functions.

emergency response plan A document that contains information on the actions that may be taken by a governmental jurisdiction to protect people and property before, during, and after a disaster.

exposure The number, types, qualities, and monetary values of various types of property or infrastructure and life that may be subject to an undesirable or injurious hazard event.

federal coordinating officer The person appointed by the Federal Emergency Management Agency (FEMA) director (by delegation of authority from the president) to coordinate assistance in a federally declared disaster.

Federal Emergency Management Agency (FEMA)-state agreement A formal legal document between FEMA and the affected state that describes the understandings, commitments, and binding conditions for assistance applicable as a result of a declaration by the president. It is signed by the FEMA regional director and the governor.

Flood Insurance Rate Map (FIRM) As defined under the National Flood Insurance Program (NFIP), an official map of the community on which the administrator of the Flood Insurance Administration has delineated both the special flood hazard areas and the risk premium zones applicable to the community.

floodplain (or flood-prone area) As defined under the National Flood Insurance Program (NFIP), any land area susceptible to being inundated by water from any source.

floodplain management As defined under the National Flood Insurance Program (NFIP), the operation of an overall program of corrective and preventive measures for reducing flood damage, including, but not limited to, emergency preparedness plans, flood control works, and floodplain management regulations.

floodplain management regulations As defined under the National Flood Insurance Program (NFIP), zoning ordinances, subdivision regulations, building codes, health regulations, special purpose ordinances (such as a floodplain ordinance, grading ordinance, and erosion control ordinance), and other applications of the police power. The term describes such state or local regulations, in any combination thereof, which provides standards for the purpose of flood damage prevention and reduction.

floodway See **regulatory floodway**.

fuel Combustible plant material, both living and dead, that is capable of burning in a wildland situation; any other flammable material in the built environment that feeds a wildfire.

Fujita scale   A scale devised to describe the intensity of tornadoes based on estimated wind speed.

ground failure   Permanent deformation of the soil, including faulting, consolidation, liquefaction, or landslides. Ground failure can cause extensive damage to buildings and lifelines, and development in areas prone to ground failure should be avoided.

ground motion   Movement of the ground resulting from earthquake-generated waves in the earth. Ground motion normally includes horizontal and vertical components, although the horizontal movement is more severe and causes the greatest damage. Building codes normally address horizontal motion, as vertical motion usually does not exceed gravity design.

hazard   An event or physical condition that has the potential to cause fatalities, injuries, property damage, infrastructure damage, agricultural loss, damage to the environment, interruption of business, or other types of harm or loss.

hazard identification   The process of defining and describing a hazard, including its physical characteristics, magnitude and severity, probability and frequency, causative factors, and locations or areas affected.

Individual Assistance programs   Supplemental federal assistance available under the Stafford Act to individuals and families; includes disaster housing assistance, Individual and Family Grants, unemployment assistance, grants, loans, legal services, crisis counseling, tax relief, and other services or relief programs.

Interagency Hazard Mitigation Team   In the aftermath of a presidentially declared disaster, the team appointed through the Federal Coordinating Officer to examine the impact of the disaster in a timely fashion and to identify specific opportunities for hazard mitigation uncovered by their investigation.

lifeline systems   Public works and utilities, such as electrical power, gas and liquid fuels, telecommunications, transportation, and water and sewer systems.

liquefaction   The temporary loss of shear strength in a water-saturated, cohesionless soil deposit, or temporary transformation of unconsolidated materials into a fluid mass.

long-term recovery   See **reconstruction**

major disaster   As defined in the Stafford Act, "any natural catastrophe (including any hurricane, tornado, storm, high water, wind-driven water, tidal wave, tsunami, earthquake, volcanic eruption, landslide, mudslide, snowstorm, or drought), or, regardless of cause, any fire, flood, or explosion in any part of the United States, which in the determination of the president causes damage of sufficient severity and magnitude to warrant major disaster assistance under this act to supplement the efforts and available resources of states, local governments, and disaster relief organizations in alleviating the damage, loss, hardship, or suffering caused thereby."

mitigation   Sustained action taken to reduce or eliminate the long-term risk to human life and property from natural hazards and their effects. Note that this emphasis on long-term risk distinguishes mitigation from actions geared primarily to emergency preparedness and short-term recovery.

modified Mercalli scale   A system for the qualitative assessment of earthquake intensity based on surveying the visible damage caused by the earthquake. Its use predates the development of the Richter scale (see below) and is therefore often used to estimate the severity of earthquakes that occurred prior to the availability of modern scientific instrumentation.

multiple-objective management A holistic approach to floodplain management (or the management of other hazards) that emphasizes the involvement of multiple distinct interests in solving land-use problems related to the hazardous area. For instance, parks and recreation interests might advocate for a greenbelt along a river corridor, while tourism interests may see the same idea as a new business opportunity, and fiscal conservatives see savings to be gained in local expenditures for infrastructure in a vulnerable area.

mutual aid agreements Agreements between local, state, regional, and/or national agencies to reduce duplication and increase the effectiveness of emergency response and other post-disaster activities. Such agreements are often used to provide supplemental staff assistance in the post-disaster environment.

natural hazard Hurricanes, tornados, storms, floods, tidal wave, tsunamis, high or wind-driven waters, volcanic eruptions, earthquakes, snowstorms, wildfires, droughts, landslides, and mudslides.

new construction As defined under the National Flood Insurance Program (NFIP), structures for which the "start of construction" commenced on or after the effective date of a floodplain management regulation adopted by a community. It includes any subsequent improvements to such structures. The same concept could be used in connection with local land-use regulations applying to other types of defined hazardous areas.

one-hundred-year flood The flooding event that has a 1 percent chance of being equaled or exceeded in a particular location in any given year (see **base flood**). While this is the most common reference point statistically because it is used for regulatory purposes in the National Flood Insurance Program (NFIP), the same language applies in referring to other actual or hypothetical events in terms of their statistical probabilities, such as a 50-year flood, a 350-year flood, etc., referring respectively to a 2 percent chance or a 0.285 percent chance of being equaled or exceeded in any given year.

planning for post-disaster reconstruction The process of planning (preferably prior to an actual disaster) those steps the community will take to implement long-term reconstruction with one of the primary goals being to reduce or minimize its vulnerability to future disasters. These measures can include a wide variety of land-use planning tools, such as acquisition, design review, zoning, and subdivision review procedures. It can also involve coordination with other types of plans and agencies but is distinct from planning for emergency operations, such as the restoration of utility service and basic infrastructure.

preliminary damage assessment (PDA) The joint local, state, and federal analysis of damage that has occurred during a disaster and which may result in a presidential declaration. The PDA is documented through surveys, photographs, and other written information.

Public Assistance programs Supplemental federal assistance available under the Stafford Act to state and local governments or eligible private, nonprofit organizations. Such assistance can include: cost-share funding of debris clearance, emergency protective measures for preservation of life and property, repair and replacement of roads, streets, bridges, water control facilities, public buildings, and public utilities; community disaster loans; use of federal equipment, supplies, and personnel facilities; repairs to federal aid system roads when authorized by the U.S. Department of Transportation; and other assistance.

reconstruction The long-term process of rebuilding the community's destroyed or damaged housing stock, commercial and industrial buildings, public facilities, and other structures. As used here, it is the last phase of the community's reaction to the natural disaster. This process is also sometimes referred to as "long-term recovery."

recovery   The process of restoring normal public or utility services following a disaster, perhaps starting during but extending beyond the emergency period to that point when the vast majority of such services, including electricity, water, communications, and public transportation, have resumed normal operations. Short-term recovery does not include the reconstruction of the built environment, although reconstruction may commence during this period. Long-term recovery (see **reconstruction**) is the process of returning the community, to the extent possible, to the conditions that existed prior to the event, preferably while taking advantage of opportunities to mitigate against future disasters.

redevelopment   This concept is similar in the post-disaster concept to reconstruction but deals with rebuilding the community's economic activity. It is different from economic recovery in that it goes beyond the process of merely restoring disrupted economic activity to the creation of new economic opportunities and enterprises in the aftermath of the recovery period, particularly including those that arise as by-products or direct outcomes of the disaster itself. A famous historic example of this last phenomenon would be the way in which the city of Chicago reshaped much of its economy and urban design in the aftermath of the Great Chicago Fire of 1871.

regulatory floodway   As defined under the National Flood Insurance Program (NFIP), the channel of a river or other watercourse and the adjacent land areas that must be reserved in order to discharge the base flood without cumulatively increasing the water surface elevation more than a designated height.

repetitive loss   A property that has had two or more claims of at least $1,000 paid by the National Flood Insurance Program (NFIP) within any 10-year period since 1978.

response   Actions and activities that support state and local government efforts to save lives and to protect public health, safety, and property.

Richter scale   A logarithmic scale for measuring the magnitude of an earthquake through the measurement of seismic waves recorded by seismographs at a point 60 miles from the epicenter. This measurement is very different from the severity of an earthquake's effects, measured on the Modified Mercalli Scale (defined above). Magnitude is related to wave amplitude and is recorded on a logarithmic scale. Each single-unit jump in magnitude reflects a 32-fold increase in seismic energy generated by the event.

risk   The potential losses associated with a hazard, defined in terms of expected probability and frequency, exposure, and consequences.

risk assessment   A process or method for evaluating risk associated with a specific hazard and defined in terms of probability and frequency of occurrence, magnitude and severity, exposure, and consequences.

Saffir/Simpson scale   A system for evaluating the intensity and magnitude of hurricanes, based on wind speed, storm surge, and central pressure and ranging from the weakest (Category 1) to the most powerful (Category 5).

[seismic] safety element   The element of a local comprehensive plan that describes local [seismic] hazards and addresses special considerations within a seismically active area for mitigating earthquake hazards. "Safety" elements are required for local governments in California and Nevada; although they often focus on seismic hazards, they include other local hazards as appropriate.

seismic zone   A generally large area within which seismic design requirements for structures are uniform.

short-term recovery   See **recovery**

Special Flood Hazard Area As defined under the National Flood Insurance Program (NFIP), land in the floodplain within a community subject to 1 percent or greater chance of flooding in any given year.

Stafford Act The Robert T. Stafford Disaster Relief and Emergency Assistance Act (P.L. 93-288, as amended by P.L. 100-707), which provides the greatest single source of federal disaster assistance.

state coordinating officer The individual appointed by the governor to act in cooperation with the federal coordinating officer (see above) to facilitate disaster response and recovery efforts.

structure As defined under the National Flood Insurance Program (NFIP), a walled and roofed building, including a storage tank for gas or liquid, that is principally above ground, as well as a manufactured home.

substantial improvement As defined under the National Flood Insurance Program (NFIP), any reconstruction, rehabilitation, addition, or other improvement of a structure, the cost of which equals or exceeds 50 percent of the market value of the structure before the "start of construction" of the improvement.

urban wildfire A fire moving from a wildland environment, consuming vegetation as fuel, to an environment where the fuel consists primarily of buildings and other structures.

urban/wildland interface A developed area occupying the boundary between an urban or settled area and a wildland characterized by vegetation that can serve as fuel for a forest fire.

vulnerability The level of exposure of human life and property to damage from natural hazards.

watershed management The implementation of a plan or plans for managing the quality and flow of water within a watershed, the naturally defined area within which water flows into a particular lake or river or its tributary. The aims of watershed management are holistic and concern the maintenance of water quality, the minimization of stormwater runoff, the preservation of natural flood controls, such as wetlands and pervious surface, and the preservation of natural drainage patterns. Watershed management is, in many ways, an enlargement of most of the concerns that underlie floodplain management.

wildland An area in which development has not occurred with the exception of some minimal transportation infrastructure, such as highways and railroads, and any structures are widely spaced and serve largely recreational purposes.

Disaster Recovery Programs, Federal Response Plan

Program	Agency	Assistance Provided	Activating Mechanism	Eligibility
Emergency Haying and Grazing	Agriculture, Dept. of (USDA), Farm Service Agency (FSA)	Emergency authority to harvest hay or to graze land devoted to conservation and environmental uses under the Conservation Reserve Program.	AWD	I/B
Emergency Loans	USDA, FSA	Low-interest loans to family farmers and ranchers for production losses and physical damage.	PD; designated by Secretary of Agriculture or Administrator, FSA (physical losses only).	I/B
Noninsured Crop Disaster Assistance Program	USDA, FSA	Direct payments to reduce financial losses resulting from a natural disaster that causes production loss or prevents planting of crops grown commercially for food or fiber, for which federal crop insurance is not available.	AWD	I
Emergency Conservation Program	USDA, FSA	Cost-share payments to rehabilitate farmlands damaged by natural disasters and to carry out emergency water conservation or water-enhancing measures during times of severe drought, in cases when the damage or drought is so severe that federal assistance is necessary.	AWD	I/B
Agricultural Marketing Transition Act (AMTA) Program	USDA, FSA	Direct payments to eligible producers of program crops that comply with AMTA requirements.	AWD	I/B
Conservation Reserve Program (CRP)	USDA, FSA	Voluntary program that offers annual rental payments, incentive payments for certain activities, and cost-share assistance to establish approved cover on eligible cropland.	AWD	I/B
Farm Operation Loans	USDA, FSA	Loans and loan guarantees to be used for farm operating costs.	N/P	I
Farm Ownership Loans	USDA, FSA	Direct loans, guaranteed loans, and technical assistance for farmers in acquiring or enlarging farms or ranches; making capital improvements; promoting soil and water conservation; and paying closing costs.	AWD	I

The following abbreviations are used throughout this appendix in the columns "Activating Mechanism" and "Eligibility": presidential declaration (PD); available without declaration (AWD); federal agency (F); state agency (S); locality (L); individual/family (I); nonprofit organization (N); Native-American tribe (T); business (B); and not provided (N/P).

Program	Agency	Assistance Provided	Activating Mechanism	Eligibility
Emergency Food Assistance (Emergency Food Stamp and Food Commodity Program)	USDA, Food and Nutrition Service (FNS)	Direct payments to states for specified uses.	PD; declaration by the Secretary of Agriculture.	S/I
Food Distribution	USDA, FNS	Donations of USDA-purchased foods.	PD; declaration by Secretary of Agriculture and compliance with eligibility criteria.	F/S/L/N
Emergency Watershed Protection (EWP)	USDA, Natural Resources Conservation Service (NRCS)	Direct payments and technical assistance to install structural and nonstructural measures to relieve imminent threats to life and/or property, and to purchase floodplain easements. Technical assistance, such as site evaluations, design work, and installation inspections, also are provided through the program.	AWD; triggered by state NRCS Conservationist.	S/L/N/B/I
Water Resources	USDA, NRCS	Project grants for the installation of preventive measures such as dams, channels, flood warning systems, purchasing easements, floodplain delineation, and land treatment. Advisory and counseling services are also available.	N/P	S/L/N
Resource Conservation and Development (RC&D)	USDA, NRCS	Technical assistance and loans to finance local project costs. Projects may include: land and water conservation; resource improvements; recreational development; and waste disposal projects.	AWD	L/N
River Basin Project	USDA, NRCS	Technical assistance. Special priority is given to projects designed to solve problems of upstream rural community flooding; water-quality improvement that comes from agricultural nonpoint sources; wetland preservation; and drought management for agricultural and rural communities. Special emphasis is placed on helping state agencies develop strategic water resource plans.	AWD; triggered by NRCS State Conservationist	F/S/L
Soil Survey	USDA, NRCS	Technical assistance. Objective is to maintain up-to-date, published surveys (and soil survey data in other formats) of counties or other areas of comparable size for use by interested agencies, organizations, and individuals; and to assist in the use of this information.	N/P	S/L/N/B/I

The following abbreviations are used throughout this appendix in the columns "Activating Mechanism" and "Eligibility": presidential declaration (PD); available without declaration (AWD); federal agency (F); state agency (S); locality (L); individual/family (I); nonprofit organization (N); Native-American tribe (T); business (B); and not provided (N/P).

Program	Agency	Assistance Provided	Activating Mechanism	Eligibility
Federal Crop Insurance Program	USDA, Risk Management Agency (RMA)	Direct payment of insurance claims. Insurance against unavoidable causes of loss, such as adverse weather conditions, fire, insects, or other natural disasters beyond the producer's control.	No activating mechanism is needed; but availability is based on crop-specific sales, closing dates, and the availability of crops in particular counties.	I
Business and Industrial Loan Program (B&I)	USDA, Rural Business Service	Guaranteed and direct loans up to $10 million. Possible disaster uses include drilling wells, purchasing water, or tying into other water programs.	AWD	B/N/T and public bodies
Farm Labor Housing and Grants	USDA, Rural Housing Service (RHS)	Loans and grants to provide housing and related facilities for domestic farmers.	No deadlines.	I/B
Rural Housing Site Loans	USDA, RHS	Loans on the purchase and development of housing and necessary equipment that becomes a permanent part of the development (e.g., water and sewer lines).	AWD	N
Rural Rental Housing Loans	USDA, RHS	Loans for the purchase, building, or repair of rental housing. Funds can also be used to provide water and waste disposal systems.	AWD	I/S/LB
Water Assistance Grants, Emergency Community (ECWAG)	USDA, Rural Utilities Service (RUS)	Project grants to help rural residents obtain adequate water supplies.	PD	S/L/N
Water and Waste Disposal Loans and Grants	USDA, RUS	Project grants, direct and guaranteed loans to develop, replace, or repair water and waste disposal systems in rural areas and towns having populations of 10,000 or less.	AWD	L/N/T
Voluntary Organizations Recovery Assistance	American Red Cross, Mennonite Disaster Service, the Salvation Army, and member organizations of the National Voluntary Organizations Active in Disaster	Mass care (shelter and feeding), welfare inquiries, health and mental health services, child care, home repairs (labor and funding), emergency communications; debris removal, burn services, cleaning supplies, personal property, distribution of supplies, transportation, loan personnel, and other specialized programs and services.	Disaster event.	I
Economic Adjustment Program—Disaster Economic Recovery Assistance	Commerce, Department of (DOC), Economic Development Administration (EDA)	Planning and technical assistance grants to state and local governments for strategic recovery planning and implementation to focus on job retention/creation to help offset the economic impacts of a major disaster.	PD; requires supplemental appropriation (SA)	S/L/N/T

The following abbreviations are used throughout this appendix in the columns "Activating Mechanism" and "Eligibility": presidential declaration (PD); available without declaration (AWD); federal agency (F); state agency (S); locality (L); individual/family (I); nonprofit organization (N); Native-American tribe (T); business (B); and not provided (N/P).

Program	Agency	Assistance Provided	Activating Mechanism	Eligibility
Economic Adjustment Program — Disaster Economic Recovery Assistance	DOC, EDA	Revolving loan fund grants to state and local governments to provide a source of local financing to support business and economic recovery after a major disaster where other financing is insufficient or unavailable.	PD; SA	S/L/N/T
Economic Adjustment Program — Disaster Economic Recovery Assistance	DOC, EDA	Infrastructure construction grants to address local recovery implementation needs for new or improved publicly owned infrastructure after a major disaster, support job creation and retention, leverage private investment, and help accelerate and safeguard the overall economic recovery of the disaster-impacted area.	PD; SA	S/L/N/T
Disaster Relief, Corporation for National Service (CNS) Grantees	CNS	Program grants designed to provide long-term disaster relief services and alleviate community needs arising from a disaster.	PD	S/N
Beach Erosion Control Projects	Defense, Dept. of (DOD), Army Corps of Engineers (USACE)	Specialized services. USACE designs and constructs the project.	Decision of the Chief of Engineers	S/L
Emergency Rehabilitation of Flood Control Works or Federally Authorized Coastal Protection Works	DOD, USACE	Specialized services to assist in the repair and restoration of public works damaged by flood, extraordinary wind, wave, or water action.	Approval by HQ-USACE.	S/L/N/I
Emergency Water Supply and Drought Assistance Programs	DOD, USACE	Emergency supplies of clean drinking water for human consumption and construction of wells.	Assistant Secretary of the Army for Civil Works designates the area as "drought distressed."	L
Flood and Post-Flood Response, Emergency Operations	DOD, USACE	Specialized services, such as flood fighting and rescue, protection of federally constructed shore or hurricane projects, and post-flood response assistance.	Designation by USACE district commander.	S/L
Watercourse Navigation: Protecting, Clearing, and Straightening Channels	DOD, USACE	Specialized services, such as clearing or removing unreasonable obstructions to navigation in rivers, harbors, and other waterways or tributaries.	Decision of the Chief of Engineers.	S/L

The following abbreviations are used throughout this appendix in the columns "Activating Mechanism" and "Eligibility": presidential declaration (PD); available without declaration (AWD); federal agency (F); state agency (S); locality (L); individual/family (I); nonprofit organization (N); Native-American tribe (T); business (B); and not provided (N/P).

Program	Agency	Assistance Provided	Activating Mechanism	Eligibility
Community Disaster Loan Program	Federal Emergency Management Agency (FEMA)	Program provides loans not greater than 25% of the local government's annual operating budget.	PD	L
Cora C. Brown Fund	FEMA	Grants to disaster victims for unmet disaster-related needs.	PD, designation for individual assistance.	I
Crisis Counseling Assistance and Training Program (CCP)	FEMA; Dept. of Health and Human Services (HHS)	Grants to states providing for short-term counseling services to disaster victims.	Governor's request	I, via S
Fire Suppression Assistance Program	FEMA	Project grants. FEMA approves a grant to a state on the condition that the state takes measures to mitigate natural hazards, including consideration of nonstructural alternatives.	Decision by FEMA	S
Hazard Mitigation Grant Program (HMGP)	FEMA	Project grants to implement hazard mitigation plans and prevent future loss of lives and property.	PD	L/N, via S
Individual and Family Grant (IFG) Program	FEMA	Grants to individuals administered by the State. Objective is to provide funds for the expenses of disaster victims that cannot be met through insurance or other assistance programs.	PD, designation for individual assistance. Requires specific request by state governor.	I, via S
Legal Services	FEMA	Free legal advice and referrals. Assistance includes: help with insurance claims; counseling on landlord-tenant and mortgage problems; assistance with home repair contracts and consumer protection matters; replacement of legal documents; estate administration; preparation of guardianships and conservatorships; and referrals.	PD, designation for individual assistance.	I
National Flood Insurance Program (NFIP)	FEMA	Insurance benefits against losses from floods, mudflow, or flood-related erosion.	AWD	I/B/S
NFIP, Community Assistance Program	FEMA	Grants to States for technical assistance to resolve floodplain management issues.	AWD	S/L
Public Assistance Program	FEMA	Project grants. Funds can be used for clearing debris; emergency measures, and repairing or replacing damaged structures, roads, utilities, and public buildings and infrastructure.	PD, designated for public assistance.	L/N, via S

The following abbreviations are used throughout this appendix in the columns "Activating Mechanism" and "Eligibility": presidential declaration (PD); available without declaration (AWD); federal agency (F); state agency (S); locality (L); individual/family (I); nonprofit organization (N); Native-American tribe (T); business (B); and not provided (N/P).

Program	Agency	Assistance Provided	Activating Mechanism	Eligibility
Temporary Housing Program	FEMA	Direct-payment grants and services. Grants include transient accommodation reimbursement, and home repair, rental, and mortgage assistance. Services may include a mobile home.	PD, designation for individual assistance.	I
Financial Institutions, Regulatory Relief for Federally Insured	Federal Deposit Insurance Corporation (FDIC) and other Federal Regulatory Agencies	Specialized services. Supervisory agencies can grant regulatory relief to insured institutions. Regulatory relief includes: lending assistance; extensions of reporting and publishing requirements; waivers from appraisal regulations; and implementation of consumer protection laws.	PD; other disaster that affects the ability of a federally insured financial institution to provide normal services.	N/B
Donation of Federal Surplus Personal Property	General Services Administration (GSA)	Donations of surplus personal property to eligible recipients.	N/P	S/L/N/public airports
Disposal of Federal Surplus Real Property	GSA	Sale, exchange, or donations of property and goods.	N/P	S/L/N
Disaster Assistance for Older Americans	HHS, Administration on Aging	Direct payments to state agencies focused on aging-related services.	PD	I, via S
Mental Health Disaster Assistance	HHS, Public Health Service	Project grants to provide emergency mental health and substance abuse counseling to individuals affected by a major disaster.	Supplemental appropriation by Congress relating to PD.	I, via S
Community Development Block Grant (CDBG) Program— Entitlement Grants	Housing and Urban Development, Dept. of (HUD), Community Planning and Development (CPD)	Formula grants to entitlement communities. Preferred use of funding is for long-term needs, but funding may also be used for emergency response activities.	PD	L
CDBG — State's Program	HUD, CPD	Formula grants to states for non-entitlement communities. Preferred use of funding is for long-term needs, but funding may also be used for emergency response activities. States establish methods of fund distribution.	PD	L, via S
Mortgage Insurance for Disaster Victims Program (Section 203 (h))	HUD	Provides mortgage insurance to protect lenders against the risk of default on loans to qualified disaster victims whose homes are located in a presidentially designated disaster area and were destroyed requiring reconstruction/replacement. Insured loans may be used to finance the purchase or reconstruction of a one-family home that will be the principal residence of the homeowner.	PD	I

The following abbreviations are used throughout this appendix in the columns "Activating Mechanism" and "Eligibility": presidential declaration (PD); available without declaration (AWD); federal agency (F); state agency (S); locality (L); individual/family (I); nonprofit organization (N); Native-American tribe (T); business (B); and not provided (N/P).

Program	Agency	Assistance Provided	Activating Mechanism	Eligibility
Reclamation States Emergency Drought Relief Act of 1991	Interior, Department of the (DOI), Bureau of Reclamation	Loans; grants; use of facilities; construction; management and conservation activities; and purchase of water for resale or for fish and wildlife services. Temporary drought assistance may include the drilling of wells, installation of equipment, improved reporting of conditions.	Request for drought assistance and approval by Commissioner of Reclamation.	F/S/N/I
Disaster Unemployment Assistance (DUA)	Labor, Dept. of (DOL), FEMA	Direct payments of DUA benefits and reemployment assistance services. Objective is to provide assistance to individuals who are ineligible for regular unemployment compensation programs and who are left jobless after a major disaster.	PD, designated for individual assistance. PD may be limited to DUA only.	I, via S
Employment: Job Training Partnership Act (JTPA), National Reserve Emergency Dislocation Grants	DOL, Employment and Training Administration	Program provides states with grant money to provide individuals with temporary jobs and/or employment assistance.	PD	I, via S
Price-Anderson Act	American Nuclear Insurers and Nuclear Regulatory Commission (NRC) (for commercial nuclear power plants) Department of Energy (for DOE facilities)	Payment of liability claims that arise from a nuclear power reactor accident. Insurance-provided assistance may compensate victims for: increased living expenses after an evacuation; unemployment; business losses; environmental cleanup; reduced property values; and costs associated from bodily injury.	AWD	I
Price-Anderson Act	NRC	Insurance reimburses states and municipalities for costs necessarily incurred in providing emergency food, shelter, transportation, or police services in evacuating the public after a nuclear power reactor accident.	AWD	S/L
Economic Injury Disaster Loans (EIDL)	Small Business Administration (SBA)	Direct loans to small businesses and agricultural cooperatives. Loans are only available to applicants with no credit available elsewhere and the maximum amount of an EIDL loan is $1,500,000.	PD; declaration of a disaster by the Secretary of Agriculture and/or SBA declared disaster.	B
Physical Disaster Loans (Business)	SBA	Direct loans to businesses and nonprofit organizations. Loans provided to repair or replace uninsured property damages caused by disasters. Loans limited to $1,500,000.	PD or SBA declaration	N/B

The following abbreviations are used throughout this appendix in the columns "Activating Mechanism" and "Eligibility": presidential declaration (PD); available without declaration (AWD); federal agency (F); state agency (S); locality (L); individual/family (I); nonprofit organization (N); Native-American tribe (T); business (B); and not provided (N/P).

Program	Agency	Assistance Provided	Activating Mechanism	Eligibility
Physical Disaster Loans (Individual)	SBA	Direct loans. Loans to homeowners and renters to repair or replace uninsured damages to real and personal property caused by disasters. Loan amounts limited to $200,000 to repair or replace real estate, and to $40,000 to repair or replace personal property.	PD or SBA declaration	I
Social Security Assistance	Social Security Administration (SSA)	Advisory and counseling services to: (1) process SSA survivor claims; (2) assist in obtaining necessary evidence for claim processing; (3) resolve problems involving lost or destroyed SSA checks; and (4) reprocess lost or destroyed pending claims.	PD and AWD	I
Donations, International	State, Department of.	Donations including items of need and cash.	Request for international coordination assistance from FEMA's Donations Coordinator.	I
Transportation: Emergency Relief Program	Transportation, Department of (DOT), Federal Highway Administration (FHWA)	Formula and project grants to repair roads. FHWA can provide: (1) up to $100 million in funding to a State for each natural disaster or catastrophic failure; and (2) up to $20 million in funding per year for each U.S. territory. Special legislation may increase the $100 million per state limit.	PD, AWD	F/S
Tax Refund, Alcohol and Tobacco	Treasury, Department of the, Bureau of Alcohol, Tobacco, and Firearms	Specialized services to provide federal alcohol and tobacco excise tax refunds to businesses that lost assets in a disaster.	PD	B
Savings Bonds Replacement or Redemption	Treasury, Bureau of Public Debt	Specialized services. Bureau of Public Debt expedites replacement of U.S. Savings Bonds lost or destroyed as a result of a disaster.	PD	I
Taxes: Disaster Assistance Program	Treasury, Department of the, Internal Revenue Service (IRS)	Advisory and counseling services. IRS provides information about casualty loss deductions, claim procedures, and reconstruction of lost financial records.	PD	I/B
Forbearance on VA Home Loans	Veterans Affairs, Department of (VA)	Encourage lenders to extend forbearance to any borrowers who have VA home loans and who are in distress due to disaster; provide incentives to such lenders.	PD	I

The following abbreviations are used throughout this appendix in the columns "Activating Mechanism" and "Eligibility": presidential declaration (PD); available without declaration (AWD); federal agency (F); state agency (S); locality (L); individual/family (I); nonprofit organization (N); Native-American tribe (T); business (B); and not provided (N/P).

Support/Service	Agency	Assistance Provided	Activating Mechanism	Eligibility
Coastal Zone Management; Hazards, Environmental Recovery, and Mitigation	DOC, National Oceanic and Atmosphieric Administration (NOAA)	Assistance to state and local governments in mitigation and recovery/restoration planning; post-event permitting assistance; compilation of coastal photogrammetry and digital multispectral data for precise shoreline and vegetation change; water-level data for storm-surge and flooding prediction and mitigation.	PD for post-event; AWD from coastal state(s) for pre-event planning	S
Reestablishing Local Survey Networks	DOC, NOAA	Provision of survey mark data to local and State agencies for reestablishing their geodetic control networks; reestablishment of national network if warranted.	PD; AWD depending on funding availability	S/L
Coastal Zone Management Administration Awards	DOC, NOAA	Grants to states for the management of coastal development to protect life and property from coastal hazards.	AWD requires supplemental appropriation by Congress relating to PD for post-storm coastal hazard mitigation and recovery activities.	S/L/T via S
Coastal Zone Management Fund	DOC, NOAA	Emergency grants to state coastal zone management agencies to address unforeseen or disaster-related circumstances.	AWD subject to amounts provided in appropriation acts. No funds currently appropriated.	S/L/T via S
Technical Support	DOC, National Institute of Standards and Technology	Disaster damage surveys, assistance in procurement of consulting services, evaluation of structural and fire performance of buildings and lifelines.	Federally declared disasters to buildings and lifelines, on cost-reimbursable basis.	F/S/L

The following abbreviations are used throughout this appendix in the columns "Activating Mechanism" and "Eligibility": presidential declaration (PD); available without declaration (AWD); federal agency (F); state agency (S); locality (L); individual/family (I); nonprofit organization (N); Native-American tribe (T); business (B); and not provided (N/P).

Directory of Federal Emergency Management Agency (FEMA) Regional Offices

REGION I (Boston)
J.W. McCormack Post Office
    and Court House, Room 442
Boston, MA 02109-4595
Telephone: 617-223-9540

States:
Connecticut; Maine; Massachusetts;
New Hampshire; Rhode Island;
Vermont

REGION II (New York)
26 Federal Plaza, Room 1337
New York, NY 10278-0002
Telephone: 212-225-7209

States:
New Jersey; New York; Puerto Rico;
Virgin Islands

REGION III (Philadelphia)
Liberty Square Building
    (Second Floor)
105 South Seventh St.
Philadelphia, PA 19106-3316
Telephone: 215-931-5608

States:
Delaware; District of Columbia;
Maryland; Pennsylvania; Virginia
West Virginia

REGION IV (Atlanta)
3003 Chamblee-Tucker Road
Atlanta, GA 30341
Telephone: 770-220-5200

States:
Alabama; Florida; Georgia; Kentucky;
Mississippi; North Carolina; South
Carolina; Tennessee

REGION V (Chicago)
175 W. Jackson Blvd. (Fourth Floor)
Chicago, IL 60604-2698
Telephone: 312-408-5501/5503

States: Illinois; Indiana; Michigan;
Minnesota; Ohio; Wisconsin

REGION VI (Denton)
Federal Regional Center
800 N. Loop 288
Denton, TX 76201-3698
Telephone: 940-898-5104

States: Arkansas; Louisiana; New
Mexico; Oklahoma; Texas

REGION VII (Kansas City)
2323 Grand Blvd., Suite 900
Kansas City, MO 64108-2670
Telephone: 816-283-7061

States: Iowa; Kansas; Missouri;
Nebraska

REGION VIII (Denver)
Denver Federal Center
Building 710, Box 25267
Denver, CO 80225-0267
Telephone: 303-235-4812

States: Colorado; Montana; North
Dakota; South Dakota; Utah;
Wyoming

REGION IX (San Francisco)
Building 105
Presidio of San Francisco
San Francisco, CA 94129
Telephone: 415-923-7100

States:
American Samoa; Arizona; California;
Guam; Hawaii; Nevada; Common-
wealth of the Northern Mariana
Islands; Federated States of Micronesia;
Republic of the Marshall Islands;
Republic of Palau

REGION X (Seattle)
Federal Regional Center
130 228th St., S.W.
Bothell, WA 98021-9796
Telephone: 425-487-4604

States: Alaska; Idaho; Oregon;
Washington

THE NATURAL HAZARDS ELEMENT

Planning for the reduction of losses from natural hazards has been largely driven by concerns for public safety. California, for example, uses the term "safety element" to describe a required local comprehensive plan element that involves the assessment of a variety of natural hazards.[1] Other issues that justify such planning—including fiscal and economic instability—are derived mostly from the consequences of failing to adequately exercise the police power to ensure public safety in the face of natural disasters. This remains true even with planning for long-term recovery and post-disaster reconstruction: the aftermath of one natural disaster is simply the prelude to the next one.

States and communities across the country are slowly, but increasingly, realizing that simply responding to natural disasters, without addressing ways to minimize their potential effect, is no longer an adequate role for government. Striving to prevent unnecessary damage from natural disasters through proactive planning that characterizes the hazard, assesses the community's vulnerability, and designs appropriate land-use policies and building code requirements is a more effective and fiscally sound approach to achieving public safety goals related to natural hazards.[2] Attending to natural hazard mitigation can also provide benefits in other local policy areas. Minimizing or eliminating development in floodplain corridors, for example, provides environmental benefits as well as potential new recreational opportunities. Communities can often profit from undertaking post-disaster reconstruction actions that at other times might be too controversial or cumbersome—the notion of striking while the iron is hot. Where a disaster has destroyed a marginal business district, for example, planners can seize the opportunity to use redevelopment to effect a rebirth that might not otherwise be possible.

Building public consensus behind even the most solid plans can be a challenging task, especially in jurisdictions exposed to multiple hazards. It is recommended that the development of a natural hazards element, including plans for post-disaster recovery and reconstruction, come from an interdisciplinary, interagency team with broadly based citizen participation to ensure both a range of input and effective public support. Community experience in dealing with natural hazards plans, whether for mitigation or post-disaster recovery, or both, has consistently demonstrated that this topic demands a wide range of input and expertise.

The following model incorporates the best practices found in state statutes[3] plus other best practices drawn from exemplary local planning for natural hazards and long-term post-disaster recovery. These best practices from local planning are identified in the commentaries to sections within the model.

The Natural Hazards Element in the *Growing Smart*[SM] *Legislative Guidebook* (Chapter 7. Local Comprehensive Plans)

MODEL NATURAL HAZARDS ELEMENT

7-210 Natural Hazards Element [Opt-Out Provision Applies]

(1) A natural hazards element shall be included in the local comprehensive plan, except as provided in Section [7-202(5)] above.

(2) The purposes of the natural hazards element are to:

   (a) document the physical characteristics, magnitude, severity, frequency, causative factors, and geographic extent of all natural hazards within or potentially affecting the community, including, but not limited to, flooding, [seismicity, wildfires, wind-related hazards such as tornadoes, coastal storms, winter storms, and hurricanes, and landslides or subsidence resulting from the instability of geological features];

Commentary. Obviously, the presence and prevalence of specific natural hazards varies widely not only among states, but even within states at both regional and local levels. This section lists all major categories while allowing states to use only those that apply, although it is clearly better to list in the statute any hazards that may apply somewhere in the state. Flooding, however, is a universally applicable concern.

  (b)   identify those elements of the built environment and, as a result, human lives, that are at risk from the identified natural hazards, as well as the extent of existing and future vulnerability that may result from current zoning and development policies;

  (c)   determine the adequacy of existing transportation facilities and public buildings to accommodate disaster response and early recovery needs such as evacuation and emergency shelter;

  (d)   develop technically feasible and cost-effective measures for mitigation of the identified hazards based on the public determination of the level of acceptable risk;

  (e)   identify approaches and tools for post-disaster recovery and reconstruction that incorporate future risk reduction; and

  (f)   identify the resources needed for effective ongoing hazard mitigation and for implementing the plan for post-disaster recovery and reconstruction.

(3)   The natural hazards element shall be in both map and textual form. Maps shall be at a suitable scale consistent with the existing land-use map or map series described in Section 7-204 (6)(a) above.

(4)   In preparing the natural hazards element, the local planning agency shall undertake supporting studies that are relevant to the topical areas included in the element. In undertaking these studies, the local planning agency may use studies conducted by others. The supporting studies may concern, but shall not be limited to, the following:

  (a)   maps of all natural hazard areas, accompanied by an account of past disaster events, including descriptions of the events, damage estimates, probabilities of occurrence, causes of damage, and subsequent rebuilding efforts;

Commentary. *With regard to flooding and coastal storm surge zones, the local jurisdiction may simply incorporate the existing National Flood Insurance Program (NFIP) maps and U.S. Army Corps of Engineers/National Weather Service storm surge maps. State and U.S. Geological Survey maps should provide at least a starting point for areas with seismic hazards. Portland Metro, in cooperation with the Oregon Department of Geology and Mineral Industries (DOGAMI), has undertaken an effort funded by Federal Emergency Management Agency (FEMA) to complete seismic hazard mapping of the entire Portland region using geographic information systems (GIS).[4] The department is also mapping tsunami hazard areas along the Oregon coast as a FEMA-funded sequel to the first such project, completed in early 1995 in Eureka, California.[5] In states with volcanoes, the mapping should include lava, pyroclastic, and debris flows and projected patterns of ash fallout in the surrounding region, including the potential for flooding from the blockage of rivers. Other sources for potential problems include the National Weather Service for storm and wind patterns and some innovative new GIS techniques in Colorado for mapping wildfire hazards.[6]*

  (b)   an assessment of those elements of the built environment (including buildings and infrastructure) that are at risk within the natural hazard areas identified in subparagraph (a) above as well as the extent of future vulnerability that may result from current land development regulations and practices within the local government's jurisdiction;

Commentary. *The study in subparagraph (4)(b) is also known among disaster officials and experts as a "vulnerability assessment" and serves two purposes: (1) to identify vulnerable structures; and (2) to determine the cause and extent of their vulnerability. For example, the California Governor's Office of Emergency Services has outlined procedures used by various communities for inventorying seismic hazards.[7] The subparagraph emphasizes the importance of including the impact of natural hazards in a buildout analysis in order to assess the potential consequences of current laws and policies, including those pertaining to the extension of public infrastructure in hazard-prone areas.*

This requirement can be tailored to the actual hazards a state may be dealing with, as

California and Nevada have done with seismic safety. One striking example is a 1979 Los Angeles ordinance that mandated both an inventory and a retrofitting program that over time has upgraded the seismic stability of the city's housing stock. The format for this with regard to flood hazard areas is already reasonably clear as a result of NFIP regulations, which include requirements for elevating substantially damaged or improved buildings above the base flood elevation. Analysis of wind-related problems is more likely to result in building code changes to strengthen wind resistance, as in southern Florida.

    (c)   state or other local mitigation strategies that identify activities to reduce the effects of natural hazards;

    (d)   an inventory of emergency public shelters, an assessment of their functional and locational adequacy, and an identification of the remedial action needed to overcome any deficiencies in the functions and locations of the shelters;

    (e)   an identification of all evacuation routes and systems for the populations of hazard-prone areas that might reasonably be expected to be evacuated in the event of an emergency and an analysis of their traffic capacity and accessibility;

Commentary. *This study is a good place to marry the expertise of planners (including transportation planners) and emergency managers. While the latter can identify the resources and the needs in this area, the former can help integrate that knowledge into routine planning for hazard-prone areas. Lee County, Florida, has used such studies to evaluate its shelter availability for disaster purposes. Because of limited access to its offshore location, Sanibel, Florida, has gone even further in using evacuation and shelter capacity as the basis for growth caps.*

        An interesting example of a natural hazards element component dealing with these issues appears in Florida Stats. Section 163.3178 (2)(d), which requires a "component which outlines principles for hazard mitigation and protection of human life against the effects of natural disaster, including population evacuation, which take into consideration the capability to safely evacuate the density of coastal population proposed in the future land use plan element in the event of an impending natural disaster."

    (e)   analyses of the location of special populations that need assistance in evacuation and in obtaining shelter;

    (f)   an inventory of the technical, administrative, legal, and financial resources available or potentially available to assist both ongoing mitigation efforts as well as post-disaster recovery and reconstruction;[8] and

Commentary. *Jurisdictions across the country have experimented with a number of means of facilitating and empowering efforts to reduce their vulnerability to natural hazards. Some of these involve the use of performance and design standards that give planners and planning commissions greater authority to insist that new development meet strict standards of hazard mitigation. For example, Wake County, North Carolina, requires that, in drainage areas of 100 acres or more, the applicant must show that any rise in water level resulting from building on the property can be contained on that property, with the applicant's only alternative being to secure easements from neighboring property owners to allow for that rise. Portola Valley, California, is a good example of seismic and hillside hazard mitigation in its use of cluster zoning for new subdivisions in certain areas.[9] Jurisdictions also have experimented with means of financing such efforts. A clear starting point is to center somewhere in local government a periodically updated repository of information about outside funding sources both from government and the private sector, including voluntary resources from nonprofit organizations. The advantage is that the community can then, in the event of a disaster, tap these resources expeditiously, preferably with the added advantage of an already developed plan for reconstruction. In addition, this study will serve to highlight funding mechanisms through local government, such as the All Hazards Protection District and Fund created by Lee County, Florida, in 1990 to support local hazard mitigation programs.[10] That fund depends on a property tax levy; in 1993, Lee County also considered, but did not pass, a proposal for an impact fee targeted at hazard-prone areas to fund emergency public shelters.*

(h) a study of the most feasible and effective alternatives for organizing, in advance of potential natural disasters, the management of the process of post-disaster long-term recovery and reconstruction.

Commentary. Numerous studies have examined at some length the potentials and pitfalls of various structural arrangements for organizing interagency, interdisciplinary task forces to oversee the process of long-term recovery and reconstruction following a disaster. Such plans have also been developed in Los Angeles;[11] Nags Head, North Carolina, and Hilton Head Island, South Carolina, among other jurisdictions, and are mandated for coastal communities in Florida and North Carolina. Two overriding principles seem to emerge from such efforts to date: (1) that successful implementation depends heavily on support from top local officials, whether that be the mayor or city manager; and (2) that a recovery task force should include representatives of all major agencies potentially involved in the reconstruction effort, specifically including but not limited to safety and emergency management forces, planning, building inspectors, public works, and transportation. It is vitally important in the aftermath of a disaster that all these agencies know not only what the others are doing, but who should report to whom for what purposes.

(5) The natural hazards element shall consist of:

(a) a statement, with supporting analysis, of the goals, policies, and guidelines of the local government to address natural hazards and to take action to mitigate their effects. The statement shall describe the physical characteristics, magnitude, severity, probability, frequency, causative factors, and geographic extent of all natural hazards affecting the local government as well as the elements of the built environment within the local government's jurisdiction that are at risk;

(b) a determination of linkages between any natural hazards areas identified pursuant to subparagraph (a) above and any other elements of the local comprehensive plan;

(c) a determination of any conflicts between any natural hazards areas and any future land-use pattern or public improvement or capital project proposed in any element of the local comprehensive plan;

(d) priorities of actions for eliminating or minimizing inappropriate and unsafe development in identified natural hazard zones when opportunities arise, including the identification and prioritization of properties deemed appropriate for acquisition, or structures and buildings deemed suitable for elevation, retrofitting, or relocation;

Commentary. This language is drawn from Florida Stats. Section 163.3178 (2), which outlines the components of the coastal management element required of all communities within coastal counties, and (8), Subdivision (2)(f), which states that a redevelopment component "shall be used to eliminate inappropriate and unsafe development in the coastal areas when opportunities arise" (emphasis added). Paragraph (8) requires that each county "establish a county-based process for identifying and prioritizing coastal properties so they may be acquired as part of the state's land acquisition programs." The language has been combined and adapted here in part because it is also possible for the community itself to use state and federal funds to acquire, for example, substantially damaged floodplain properties and to relocate their residents. Tulsa, Oklahoma, and Arnold, Missouri, provide excellent examples of this strategy, in large part because they developed ongoing acquisition programs that were already in place before in the predisaster period. This is, in effect, an "issues and opportunities" component of the natural hazards element.

(e) multiyear financing plan for implementing identified mitigation measures to reduce the vulnerability of buildings, infrastructure, and people to natural hazards that may be incorporated into the local government's operating or capital budget and capital improvement program;

(f) a plan for managing post-disaster recovery and reconstruction. Such a plan shall provide descriptions that include, but are not limited to, lines of authority, interagency and intergovernmental coordination measures, processes for expedited review, permitting, and inspection of repair and reconstruction of buildings and structures damaged by natural disasters. Reconstruction policies in this plan shall be congruent with mitigation policies in this element and in other elements of the local comprehensive plan as well as the legal, procedural, administrative, and operational components of post-disaster recovery and reconstruction.

(6) The natural hazards element shall contain actions to be incorporated into the long-range program of implementation as required by [name of appropriate section]. These actions may include but shall not be limited to:

(a) amendments or modifications to building codes and land development regulations and floodplain management and/or other special hazard ordinances, and development of incentives, in order to reduce or eliminate vulnerability of new and existing buildings, structures, and uses to natural hazards;

(b) implementation of any related mitigation policies and actions that are identified in other elements of the local comprehensive plan;

(c) other capital projects that are intended to reduce or eliminate the risk to the public of natural hazards;

(d) implementation of provisions to carry out policies affecting post-disaster recovery and reconstruction as described in subparagraph (5)(f) above, such as procedures for the inspection of buildings and structures damaged by a natural disaster to determine their habitability as well as procedures for the demolition of buildings and structures posing an imminent danger to public health and safety; and

(e) implementation of provisions to ensure that policies contained in other portions of the local comprehensive plan do not compromise the ability to provide essential emergency response and recovery facilities as described in the local emergency operations program, such as:

1. adequate evacuation transportation facilities;

2. emergency shelter facilities; and

3. provisions for continued operations of public utilities and telecommunications services.

Notes

1. Calif. Govt. Code Section 65302 (g) requires a safety element "for the protection of the community from any unreasonable risks associated with the effects of seismically induced surface rupture, ground shaking, ground failure, tsunami, seiche, and dam failure; slope instability leading to mudslides and landslides; subsidence, liquefaction, and other seismic hazards identified pursuant to Chapter 7.8 (commencing with Section 2690) of the Public Resources Code, and other geologic hazards known to the legislative body; flooding; and wild land and urban fires." In addition to the mapping of seismic and geologic hazards, the element is to address "evacuation routes, peakload water supply requirements, and minimum road widths and clearances around structures, as those items relate to identified fire and geologic hazards."

2. See generally Roger A. Nazwadzky, "Lawyering Your Municipality Through a Natural Disaster or Emergency," *Urban Lawyer* 27, No. 1 (Winter 1995): 9-27.

3. The following state statutes provide for natural hazards planning: Arizona (Ariz.Rev.Stat. Section 11-806B), California (Cal.Gov't.Code Section 65302(e)(7) & (g)), Colorado (Colo.Rev. Stat. Sections 30-28-106, 31-23-206), Florida (Fla.Stat.Ann. Sections 163.3177(6)(g), 7(h), 163.3178), Georgia (Ga. Code Ann. Section 12-2-8), Idaho (Idaho Code Section 67-6508(g)), Indiana (Ind.Code Section 36-7-4-503), Iowa (Iowa Code Section 281.4), Kentucky (Ky.Rev.Stat.Ann. Section 100.187(5)), Louisiana (La.Rev.Stat.Ann. Section 33:107), Maine (Me.Rev.Stat.Ann. tit. 30A Section 4326A(1)(d)), Maryland (Md. Code Ann. tit. 66B Section 3.05(a)(1)(viii)), Michigan

..Code Ann. Section 76-1-601(2)(h)), & (l)), North Carolina (N.C.Gen.Stat. ...at. Section197.175), Pennsylvania (53 ...island (R.I.Gen.Laws Section 45-22.2-6(E)), South Carolina (S.C. Code Ann. Section 6-7-510), Utah (Utah Code Ann. Section 10-9-302(2)(c)), Vermont (Vt.Stat.Ann. tit. 24, Section 4382(a)(2)), Virginia (Va. Code Ann. Section 15.1-446.1.1), Washington (Wash.Rev. Code Section36.70.330(1)), West Virginia (W.Va. Code Section 8-24-17(a)(9)).

4. See *Using Earthquake Hazard Maps for Land Use Planning and Building Permit Administration*, Report of the Metro Advisory Committee for Mitigating Earthquake Damage (Portland, Ore.: Portland Metro, May 1996) and *Metro Area Disaster Geographic Information System: Volume One* (Portland, Ore.: Portland Metro, June 1996).

5. National Oceanic and Atmospheric Administration (NOAA), Pacific Marine Environmental Laboratory. *Tsunami Hazard Mitigation: A Report to the Senate Appropriations Committee* (Seattle, Wash.: NOAA, The Laboratory, March 31, 1995).

6. Colorado has been increasing its attention to both the wildfire issue and hazards generally. See *Land Use Guidelines for Natural and Technological Hazards Planning* (Denver: Colorado Department of Local Affairs, Office of Emergency Management, March 1994). An interesting source on the mapping of wildfire hazards is Boulder County's site at http://boco.co.gov/gislu/whims.html.

7. *Earthquake Recovery: A Survival Manual for Local Government* (Sacramento: California Governor's Office of Emergency Services, September 1993), Chs. 9-10.

8. For a discussion of approaches to drafting floodplain management ordinances, see Jim Schwab, "Zoning for Flood Hazards," *Zoning News* (Chicago: American Planning Association, October 1997). See also Marya Morris, *Subdivision Design in Flood Hazard Areas*, Planning Advisory Service Report No. 473 (Chicago: American Planning Association, September 1997).

9. William Spangle and Associates, Inc., *Geology and Planning: The Portola Valley Experience* (Portola Valley, Cal.: William Spangle and Associates, 1988).

10. Lee County, Fla., Resolution No. 90-12-19.

11. The Northridge earthquake in February 1994, which occurred shortly after the adoption of the Los Angeles plan, afforded the rare opportunity for the National Science Foundation to underwrite two independent analyses of the plan's utility and effectiveness in the aftermath of that disaster. Spangle Associates with Robert Olson Associates, Inc., prepared *The Recovery and Reconstruction Plan of the City of Los Angeles: Evaluation of its Use after the Northridge Earthquake* (NSF Grant No. CMS-9416416), August 1997. The other study is *The Northridge Earthquake: Land Use Planning for Hazard Mitigation* (CMS-9416458), December 1996, by Steven P. French, Arthur C. Nelson, S. Muthukumar, and Maureen M. Holland, all of the City Planning Program at the Georgia Institute of Technology.